W9-BMG-910

Date Due		
Mar 12'41		
Mar 24'41		
Apr 9'41		
May 2'41		
Jun 20'41		
May 28'42		
JUN 11 '53		
MAY 24 '56		
JAN 1 6 '62		
APR 3 - '62		
SEP 14 1995		
0 9 SEP 1996		
OCT 10 1997		

Editor in Politics

MRS. ADELAIDE WORTH BAGLEY DANIELS

wife of Josephus Daniels

Editor in Politics

BY JOSEPHUS DANIELS

"These things I saw and part of them I was."
—VIRGIL

CHAPEL HILL: *The University of North Carolina Press*

1941

LEE COUNTY LIBRARY
SANFORD, N. C.

COPYRIGHT, 1941, BY

THE UNIVERSITY OF NORTH CAROLINA PRESS

PRINTED IN THE UNITED STATES OF AMERICA

Van Rees Press—New York

PJ

LEE COUNTY LIBRARY
SANFORD, N. C.

TO

MY WIFE, MY BEST COUNSELLOR

ADDIE WORTH BAGLEY DANIELS

"The truest and tenderest and purest wife ever man was blessed with. To have such a love is the one blessing, in comparison of which all earthly joy is of no value; and to think of her is to praise God."

FOREWORD

THE PERIOD between 1893 and 1912 embraced the second Cleveland administration and the rise and fall of Fusion government in North Carolina. It witnessed the meteor-like emergence of William Jennings Bryan to leadership in the national Democratic Party in a battle royal with the forces of Grover Cleveland. It saw the exclusion of the Democratic Party from power for nearly a score of years. In all that period, as editor and official in the Cleveland administration and as member of the Democratic National Committee and sometime author of its campaign textbooks and director of publicity, I had intimate touch with party affairs.

They were stirring years in the life of the United States and in North Carolina. Internecine party conflicts in the Republic and the State created divisions and bitterness and not a little tragedy. They lasted almost a generation—in fact, until the Democrats elected Aycock Governor of North Carolina in 1900, and in 1912 elected Wilson as President of the United States.

In the national domain I have sought to give revealing glimpses, gathered from an inside seat in the Cleveland administration, as seen in the important measures which Cleveland proposed, some of which he saw shipwrecked by the split in the party; to draw pen-pictures of the men who were in the public eye, with incidents illustrative of the period.

I have endeavored to recreate the atmosphere of the strenuous political battles and racial conflicts in North Carolina during the Fusion rule (1895-1899) and the history-making policies when the Democratic Party regained power (1899-1912). This volume (Volume II) is thus a story of my active participation in political life, with brief office-holding, along with my devotion to journalism, embracing the campaign that put Woodrow Wilson in the White House and events in State and national life while the Democratic Party was in the minority.

Volume III will deal with the Wilson administration—The Story of The New Freedom—by a member of Wilson's Cabinet for eight years, with a survey of political and administrative policies, naval activities, the World War, the League of Nations combat in which Schoolmaster Wilson and Scholar-in-Politics Lodge fought without gloves, the aftermath of war, and an appraisement of the commanding figures of the Wilson era, with incidents in Europe during and after the Peace Conference in Paris. It will deal at some length with national and state policies and will seek to portray the leaders up to Franklin Roosevelt's rise to power as Governor of New York and his election to the presidency of the United States.

Volume III will be followed by Volume IV, covering the New Deal, particularly the working out of the Good Neighbor Policy in the Western Hemisphere, with special reference to Mexico, where I served as Ambassador of the United States, part of the time as Dean of the Diplomatic Corps.

I attempt no comprehensive history of my times, but have related what I was privileged to observe and have portrayed events in which I participated, sometimes as official but most of the time as reporter and editor. In my appraisement of men to whom I have assessed praise and of those whom I have blamed, I have not consciously been influenced by my personal regard or the contrary. To quote Woodrow Wilson's preface to *Division and Reunion,* I can truly say: "I cannot claim to have judged rightly in all cases as between parties. I can claim, however, impartiality of judgment; for impartiality is a matter of the heart, and I know with what disposition I have written."

Josephus Daniels

CONTENTS

PART THREE

The Fight for Free Silver

PART FOUR

Fusion Rule in North Carolina

PART FIVE

War at Home and Abroad, 1898

PART SIX

The Turn of the Century in State and Nation

PART SEVEN

State Democracy in Power

ILLUSTRATIONS

Editor in Politics

I GO TO WASHINGTON, D. C.

O N TO WASHINGTON!"—
That was the cry of dynamic Jubal Anderson Early when
in 1864 the threatened invasion of the Federal capital by Confederate
cavalrymen made Washingtonians shake in their boots and gave uncomfortable hours to Abraham Lincoln on a sleepless pillow in the
White House. Early's horses champed their bits in the hearing of the
war strategists and in sight of the towering dome, but the invitation
to enter was lacking and, in fact, superior force denied Early the
coveted prize of capturing the Federal capital. Almost three decades
later, with no warlike aims, a young Tar Heel editor, born in Washington, N. C., reached the national capital to witness the inauguration of Cleveland. His ambition then was limited to securing a small
salary so that he could make a living from Uncle Sam and carry on
his newspaper in Raleigh while seeing the wheels of Federal government turn over, perhaps pushing a small wheel himself.

I little suspected that my arrival in Washington on March 4, 1893,
to occupy a government job, would be an introduction to national
politics in which I was to be absorbed for some years, or that later it
would lead to a return trip to Washington for the eight years of the
Wilson administration, or that it would afterward find me for more
than seven years Ambassador from my country to Mexico in Franklin
Roosevelt's administration. In 1893 I felt the urge of national interests
but was moved, mainly, to seek the position because it meant financial
ease and enabled me to carry on my editorial work at long distance.

My youthful enthusiasm for Cleveland made me happy to serve
even in a subordinate position in the administration of the man
whose victory in 1884 had been to me the promise of a united America
and of better government. As I left Raleigh for Washington, I recalled
how I had been thrilled some years before by an incident related to
me by Walter H. Page, who as secretary of the Tariff Reform Club of
New York had hailed Cleveland's election as the dawn of a better
day. According to Page the incident ran like this:

LEE COUNTY LIBRARY
SANFORD, N. C.

"You know that Henry Ward Beecher, whose family was among the leading founders of the Republican Party, supported Mr. Cleveland, and many believe that he influenced enough votes to elect Cleveland. In the early fall of 1885, when Mr. Beecher returned to Brooklyn from his summer vacation, the Democrats staged a reception in his honor and to rejoice in the early achievements of the Cleveland administration. I was there, full of admiration and enthusiasm for the great preacher and for Cleveland. The club house was jammed before Mr. Beecher arrived and he had to be lifted over the crowd to a place on the stairway. When the cheering subsided, Mr. Beecher raised his hand and made the shortest and most eloquent speech I ever heard. It was in these words: *We were not mistaken in our man.* The applause and shouting continued for many minutes, so long, in fact, that Mr. Beecher could not have been heard if he had tried to say more; and, like his hearers, he saw that to say more would have been an anticlimax."

I doubt if any voter in America looked forward with more enthusiasm than I did to the reforms that would follow Cleveland's second inauguration. On the day after his defeat in 1888 my paper had predicted that he would be called back. On March 5, 1889, I felt exactly as did the lovely mistress of the White House. Mrs. Cleveland fully intended to come back. In bidding good-bye to an old colored servant of the White House, Jerry Smith, a fine North Carolina Negro, she said, "Now, Jerry, I want you to take good care of all the furniture and ornaments in the White House, for I want to find everything just as it is now when we come back again just four years from today." The President talked in a different vein: "You cannot imagine the relief which has come to me with the termination of my official term." But Mrs. Cleveland won, and Cleveland had an attack of *animus revertendi*.

The convention that nominated Mr. Cleveland in 1892 was one of the most spectacular in the party's history, because of the position of the New York delegates, who favored Hill, and the brilliant speech of Bourke Cockran, who threatened the party with defeat if Cleveland were nominated. The speech of the Federal soldier, General Bragg (afterward Minister to Mexico), culminating with the famous sentence, "We love Grover Cleveland for the enemies he has made," destroyed the effectiveness of Cochran's eloquence. It became a campaign slogan. The Tammany threat against Cleveland failed, as like threats of that organization were impotent to defeat Tilden, Wilson, and Roosevelt, the only Democrats elected president since the war of the sixties. (Tilden was elected but was denied the office.) In all these years Tammany has not picked a winner, though its loyalty to the party on election day has insured Democratic victory in the Empire State.

With the close of the 1892 campaign the circulation of my paper, *The North Carolinian,* partly paid for by the Democratic Committee, was greatly reduced. I had fewer than two thousand paying subscribers and little advertising. The paper was not paying expenses. The future looked dark. Early in 1893 I learned that Hoke Smith was to be Secretary of the Interior in Cleveland's Cabinet. I wrote that I would be glad if he could give me a position with him. He telegraphed me to meet him in Washington when Cleveland was inaugurated.

I was glad to witness the inauguration. Grover Cleveland was no orator and I was not stirred as I listened to his inaugural address. However, I felt a sense of satisfaction when this minister's son closed with his confession of faith: "After all, I know there is a Supreme Being who rules the affairs of men and whose goodness and mercy have always followed the American people, and I know He will not turn from us now if we humbly and reverently seek his powerful aid." As I witnessed the inauguration my mind went back to 1884 when, as president of the "Cleveland and Hendricks Club" in Wilson, I had organized a torchlight procession with regular tar barrels and an old-fashioned "rousification," the biggest Wilson had known.

Many had attributed Cleveland's defeat in 1888 to his famous low tariff speech containing the sentence that will live: "It is a condition which confronts us—not a theory." I listened as in his inaugural address he repeated consecration to the cause that had defeated him in 1888, hearing what I had expected. As he faced the sea of upturned faces, his clear voice rang out: "The verdict of our voters, which condemns the injustice of maintaining protection for protection's sake, enjoins upon the people's servants the duty of exposing and destroying the brood of kindred evils which are the unwholesome progeny of paternalism."

At dinner at the old Arlington, with my friend James Norfleet, we rejoiced to have lived to see inaugurated a real Democrat defeating the "robber barons." It seemed almost too good to be true. The next morning I reported for duty at the Interior Department and was

assigned to temporary work at a salary of $1,600 until I was shortly
made chief of the Appointment Division with a salary of $2,000. In
an era of six-cent cotton and with Coxey's army in the offing, that
was "a whale of a lot of money" to a country editor whose paper was
in the red. As head of personnel and recognized as an intimate friend
of Secretary Hoke Smith, I came in close contact with Democratic
senators and representatives, and that acquaintanceship stood me in
good stead in the years to come. The Secretary told me he would refer
to me applicants for positions. I was later promoted to the position
of chief clerk at a salary of $2,750, a position that made my office the
clearing house of the Department. Every afternoon I brought to the
attention of the Secretary all matters of importance, thus keeping
him in touch with the work of the various bureaus.

My wife, baby, and I, and a colored nurse lived in Washington on
a little over $100 a month, sending the balance to Raleigh to keep
my paper going. Of course we economized almost to the bone. In
all the two years my wife and I could not afford to go to a theater
more than twice. Comparatively, living was cheap in Washington at
that time. Shortly after I entered upon my duties, I began to look for
a boarding place at a moderate price in a good neighborhood for myself, our baby Adelaide, my wife, and a colored nurse. I found several
places I liked, but at each of them the landlady would ask about my
family. When I answered that I had a young daughter fourteen months
old, the invariable answer was, "We do not take babies." That was
final, and I was bowed out as if I were asking something that would
bring ruin on the house. Finally, after weary afternoons of searching
and being regarded as an undesirable citizen because I was the father
of a baby, I found a place on K Street, near Franklin Square, where
my wife and Adelaide and I spent many happy hours, most of them
in Franklin Park, where the baby dearly loved to see the birds and
watch the ducks swimming in the pond. They were halcyon days.
My wife and I often recall them and our delightful association with
Senator Turpie, of Indiana. We ate at the same table and he, along
with all in the boarding house, became fond of the baby, and on Sun-
days we would sit together in the park and watch her ecstasy over
the flowers and birds. He was *the* scholar of the Senate, a cultivated
gentleman of the old school. With the approach of summer, my wife
took the baby to Raleigh to let her have the run of the big and shady
yard during the hot season. Our rooms in Washington were on the

third floor and quite hot. Early in July she wrote that Adelaide was sick. And then I was summoned to stand helplessly and broken-heartedly to watch her waning strength and quiet passing into the better land. Until then I had not known what sorrow was, for death had never entered our home after the death of my father, who died away from home when I was too young to understand the loss. This first child, only eighteen months old, was the joy of our lives and to this day my wife and I recall her prattling as she found life joyous and made it a song for us.

While I was appointment chief an incident occurred which gave me many a good dinner and brought me into association with some of the brightest minds in public life in Washington. One day I was summoned to the Secretary's office and introduced to Mr. John Chamberlain, the famous proprietor of the finest and most expensive hostelry—very much like a club—in Washington. Mr. Smith handed me a letter written in the clear and small handwriting that characterized Mr. Cleveland's letters and signed by Grover Cleveland. It was the first of Mr. Cleveland's handwriting I had seen in Washington, with reference to any appointment. The letter stated that he was presenting his "very old and good friend," John Chamberlain, and he would be happy if the Secretary could find it proper and convenient "to grant his request." When I had finished reading the letter, I was told that the bearer wished promotion for a close friend, a Mr. Thorne, a former actor, who held a clerkship in the Patent Office. Mr. Smith added, "I wish you would look into this and see what can be done." Of course, I knew a request from the President was an order, but I queried, "By what right, Mr. Secretary, does the gentleman who signs that letter presume to proffer any request to this Department?" It was a jocular remark, but, strange to say, Mr. Chamberlain was surprised, if not amused, that an official in a small place should make such a remark about the great President of the United States. At any rate, somehow it caught his fancy—I never knew why—but after I had arranged the promotion for his friend I learned that he said to his guests (he always called his paying patrons "guests") many complimentary things about me. Shortly I received an invitation to dine and meet some of his friends at one of his periodical formal dinners in his private dining room. I was too poor to sport a dress suit and was on the point of declining when my boyhood friend, Dr. Sterling Ruffin, afterwards a leading doctor of Washington and physician of

Woodrow Wilson and other famous men, offered to lend me his suit. Between the doctor and my wife, I was properly attired and I attended my first dinner with senators and diplomats and Cabinet ministers in Washington. It was the beginning of many such dinners at Chamberlain's—the best Washington ever knew—where I won the friendship of the princes of story tellers, among them Senator Jo Blackburn, of Kentucky, and Private John Allen, of Mississippi. It was better than any theatrical or humorous show to sit and hear the badinage between Blackburn and Allen and others, for Chamberlain's dinners brought together the wit and wisdom of official Washington. And aside from the good stories, some of them rather broad, a youngster learned many off-the-record stories of politics and politicians and statesmen, too, for the saying of Tom Reed, "a statesman is a dead politician," had not then been accepted. There were real statesmen and great men on the stage in that era, and big issues and difficult problems tested their ability.

Upon my return from the first Chamberlain dinner, my wife was waiting for me and enjoyed my relating some of the anecdotes and witty sallies, the like of which had endeared Chamberlain to Cleveland. "I didn't feel so bad in my borrowed dress suit," I told her, "seeing that Senator Blackburn's vest did not reach his pants." I repeated Blackburn's gag that when John Allen first came to Congress he didn't have a dress suit, and when invited to dinner he would telegraph to Isidor Raynor, Baltimore congressman, to send over his dress suit. Then John Allen would wait at the old B. & O. depot till the train came in to get the suit and change clothes in the carriage en route to the dinner. Blackburn had added, "It didn't cost John anything because he has both telegraph and express franks." I related to her also the gags the guests got off at the expense of my host, whose menu was the best and whose charges were regarded as exorbitant. One was that of a young man who came in with a friend to dinner and ordered steak smothered in onions. He called the waiter back and said, "No, leave off the onions. I am calling on a lady tonight." A gentleman at the next table remonstrated, "Don't change your order for onions, for when the waiter brings you your bill, it will take your breath away." Another like story: A diner, wishing to economize, ordered nothing but a glass of buttermilk. When the bill was presented it was $1.35. "It's robbery," he said, "to charge $1.35 for a glass of buttermilk. I demand to see the proprietor." Mr. Chamberlain heard his protest, refused to revise the bill, and said, "You must realize, sir, that the price is high because buttermilk is out of season."

Mr. Chamberlain told me many stories of what had occurred in that room, where the men who made history had been accustomed to gather. I found myself wishing the walls could talk. One of his stories interested me very much, particularly because it concerned the cause of my first political grief as a small boy, when Tilden was denied the presidency in 1876. As nearly as I can recall it, Mr. Chamberlain related:

"I have always kept this chair [placing his hand on the back of the chair on which I was sitting], for it was while occupying this chair that William E. Chandler, chairman of the Republican Committee, made the decision that cost Tilden the office of the presidency, to which he had been elected. On the November night of the election, 1876, William E. Chandler, Zack Chandler, and other Republican leaders gathered here to dine and receive the election returns. After they had finished my terrapin and champagne, the *pièce de résistance* of the Chamberlain house, the telegrams began to pour in. By eleven o'clock that was the bluest and most dejected gathering I have ever seen, notwithstanding the champagne. New York, New Jersey, Indiana, Connecticut had all cast their electoral votes for Tilden. The Southern States, like North Carolina, which had voted for Grant in 1872, and other Southern States were in the Tilden column. All the early New York papers, except the *Times* had conceded Tilden's election. There was little news from South Carolina, Florida, and Louisiana, but they also seemed to have gone Democratic. Some of the leaders conceded defeat. Not so William E. Chandler. He sat and pored over the returns, pencil in hand, adding up electoral votes and combinations. A short time before midnight, the newspaper correspondents who had been clamoring for a statement for an hour from Chairman Chandler, were admitted. They asked question after question, to which Senator Chandler made no direct answer. Shortly before midnight, Chandler rose from his seat and read a telegram he was giving out for publication. It was in these words:

'HAYES HAS CARRIED 185 electoral votes and has been elected President.'   William E. Chandler, Chairman

When the reporters plied him with questions as to what states he claimed that Hayes had carried Chandler refused to answer.

'The telegram contains all I have to say,' he remarked, and the newspaper men rushed out to send the claim. Some of them felt it was a bluff. Not so Chandler. He ordered the room cleared and was closeted with his associates nearly all night, sending telegrams. I knew only that something important was brewing, but later it became public property that Chandler had resolved to have the returning boards in Florida, South Carolina, and Louisiana, controlled by his party, certify the election of Hayes electors in order to make good his claim that Hayes had won. As you know, that is what happened. The plot was conceived in this room and, as you know, carried out, although the Democrats threatened force to prevent what they called 'stealing the presidency.' I had nothing to do with 'the Crime of '76,' as Henry Watterson called it, but it was in this very place that the conspiracy was hatched."

As I went home after hearing even greater details than I have recorded, my mind went back to the home of my youth in Wilson in 1884, when for a long time the electoral vote hung in the balance and Sheriff Jack Simms was saying in loud, indignant tones, "The Radical thieves stole the Presidency in 1876. They are preparing to do it again."

OUR FIRST WHITE HOUSE RECEPTION

I shall never forget the first reception my wife and I attended at the White House in the early part of 1894. She was thrilled when the invitation came, bearing the White House seal. It wasn't usual for chief clerks to be included. "What shall I wear?" was my wife's first thought. She was no Flora McFlimsey, but she said, "I have nothing to wear that would do for a White House reception," and she and her mother set out to obtain a white silk dress in the style of the day. She looked her best—as beautiful as Mrs. Cleveland (I thought more so), who had a loveliness of a quality all her own. I went in a borrowed dress suit. We had never been caught in such a jam. But it thrilled us to watch the grand procession as the President and Mrs. Cleveland and the members of the Cabinet and their wives descended the wide steps to the music of the Marine Band. We both had an acquaintance with the President and with Mrs. Cleveland, who pleased my wife by recalling welcoming her to the White House when she visited it as a bride. I had time for only a word, but thanked the President for the tentative tender of the position of Public Printer, which did not materialize. "I did not think Mr. Benedict would accept when I sent you word that you were next on the list," he said as we passed on down the line to exchange hasty greetings with the Cabinet group and afterwards with the members of Congress and others we knew, and on to the dining room where the jam was greater than in the East Room. Many a new dress was crushed in the shoving and pushing. But it wasn't half as much of a crush as in Jefferson's and Jackson's day. In after years we attended many White House receptions, and in the Wilson administration and also in the Franklin Roosevelt days were in the receiving party. But that first reception was a thrill far greater even than when we helped to receive in the White House Balfour and Joffre and others of the special delegations from the allied countries who came during the World War to confer and to obtain loans of honest-to-goodness Uncle Sam money, which, with armed Americans, saved their countries.

THE CLEVELANDS

The best pen-picture of Mrs. Cleveland was contained in the Washington correspondence of *The News and Observer* about that time. It read:

"Mrs. Cleveland has been criticised for wearing beautiful clothes. She has earned the reputation of being the most elaborate dresser 'since the days of Queen Elizabeth,' and when she appears in public the paragraphers are bound by every right and admiration to rave over her dress creations. They are wonderful, beautiful, bewildering and so dainty that she might well have stepped from a pictured canvas in the Louvre or borrowed herself from an ancestral gallery. Nothing so remarkable as her Washington and Gray Gables costuming has ever been seen.

"The secret of all this is all the more wonderful to fathom when one finds out that Mrs. Cleveland's dress allowance is small. She sets apart a certain sum for necessary gowns; as she told a young lady friend visiting the White House, 'I allow myself not a dollar over that sum, and I can spend it all in a season or make it last throughout the year.'

" 'How much is it?' asked the girl friend, overcome by curiosity.

" 'It is less than $1,000 a year, and from that I must buy my diplomatic reception gowns, my regular house reception dresses, and my gloves and everything of the toilet.'

" 'H-how in the world do you do it?' gasped the friend, 'when you are actually obliged to have twelve public evening dresses that must be cabled all over the world to sustain the reputation of the country?'

"Mrs. Cleveland smiled her sweetest smile, but would say no more.

"That night at her own dinner table there sat the diplomats, resplendent in silks and jewels. At the head of the table sat the hostess, wearing a rose pink satin dress. It was walking length, blouse effect, not a ruffle or particle of trimming anywhere. But from the rim of the low corsage to the tip of the skirt there was not an inch unspangled with gold. A bit of old lace at the corsage brim relieved the rose from the skin.

" 'Her maid has been putting spangles on rose silk for days,' soliloquized the young guest, 'and, ah, I see my lady has taste!' "

It could not be said that Grover Cleveland was loved by the people so much as he was respected by them. He had none of the graces of the popular orator, or the ability to remember names and make every acquaintance feel that he held him in his affection. He had not won his way on the hustings, and had none of the tricks of the man of the glad-hand. He obtained popular favor by a conscientious practice of the sound doctrine he originated: "Public office is a public trust." His speeches had sincerity, information, and punch—with little attempt at rhetorical adornment. In the popular mind sentiment was not attributed to Grover Cleveland. He opened his heart to few, and it was not until after his death that the letters revealing his tenderness to those admitted to the sacred precincts of his friendship enabled the people to realize that beneath what many thought a reserved and phlegmatic exterior he was in fact a man who loved and could phrase his affection in tender terms.

Mr. Cleveland showed he was the true son of a Presbyterian preacher, not only by regular attendance at Dr. Sunderland's church, but also in other ways. In March, 1896, writing to Dr. Merle Smith of the selection of chaplains for the Army and Navy, he said: "If we could get such a man as Mr. Smith, Dr. Van Dyke, or Mr. Wood we'd have it about right.... The Episcopalians have secured more than their share, and we poor Presbyterians have been rather badly left." Exactly twenty-one years later, when I was Secretary of the Navy, I appointed Dr. Van Dyke as chaplain in the Navy, thus carrying out a cherished purpose of Mr. Cleveland. In doing so I was not influenced either by Presbyterian Elder Woodrow Wilson or my Presbyterian wife.

THE INTERIOR DEPARTMENT A LIBERAL EDUCATION

I N MY POSITION in the Interior Department, I obtained inside views, sometimes in advance, of what was going on. Secretary Smith talked with me freely about departmental policies and politics and would often send for me after Cabinet meetings and talk over what had occurred in these sessions, the discussions of which were not divulged to the public. Like Woodrow Wilson, he wished a sympathetic hearer upon whose loyalty and sympathetic coöperation he could depend. As a young man deeply interested in all public matters, I looked forward eagerly to Mr. Smith's recital of Cabinet talk and was better informed in what was going on in the Cabinet circles than men in Washington who held higher positions.

Hoke Smith and I had many things in common. He was a native of North Carolina, and so was I. His father, born in Maine, had taught in Catawba County as a young man and had later been a professor in the University of North Carolina. His mother was a member of the prominent Hoke family of North Carolina, a sister of General Robert F. Hoke, the most distinguished Confederate general from North Carolina, who in ability, character, and looks resembled Robert E. Lee. Secretary Smith treated me as a younger brother and made me his confidant, not only on matters relating to his Department, but also on matters concerning administration discussions and secrets and political and executive policies. As his executive officer, charged also with matters of appointments, and liaison officer with legislators and other officials, I was privileged to have an inside seat behind the scenes in most important matters that went on in Washington in the first years of the Cleveland administration. I found that the Interior Department touched every part of the country. In the early days it was mainly concerned with public lands and acted as the guardian of the Indian. As time passed it acquired other duties—the paying of pensions to soldiers and sailors, the granting of patents, the work of the Geological Survey, the direction of Federal assistance in education, the taking of the census, the government of Alaska and all territorial possessions, the government of St. Elizabeth Hospital and Howard University, and almost everything else that was not the function of the other departments, together with hundreds of appointments of agents and other officials. It was a liberal education in all matters touching those government functions that passed through my hands. I interested myself in all, and in so doing came in contact with people in all parts of the country, particularly in the West.

It was during my service in the Interior Department that I learned at first hand of the exploitation of the natural resources of the West to the enrichment of political favorites. I became a believer in conservation and rejoiced in Cleveland's vigorous efforts to protect the Indians and in Hoke Smith's deep interest in saving the lands and natural resources that had not been already gobbled up. The graft was so entrenched that all the wrongs could not be corrected; many Westerners were not ready to welcome any plan that postponed development in the national interest. If all the truth about the oil and land grabbing could be gathered and published, it would make a damning record of exploitation of the natural resources which should have been reserved for all the people. Later I stood with Theodore Roosevelt and Pinchot in their policy of conservation, and, in the Wilson administration, prevented the exploitation by profiteers of Teapot Dome and naval oil reserves in California.

"There is not enough space between the top of his ears and the top of his head," was the queer reason that my good friend, Judge Lamereaux, Commissioner General of the Land Office, gave when I recommended my college friend, A. C. Shaw, son of Colonel John D. Shaw, of North Carolina, for appointment in the Legal Department in 1893. Judge Lamereaux seemed in earnest. However, I was able to convince him of Shaw's ability, and he served until the Ballinger scandal stirred the country. Shaw knew Pinchot was right in the charges he made and had the evidence. Taft stood by Ballinger, while those like Shaw walked the plank voluntarily. Nobody knew better than Shaw how Uncle Sam had been robbed of his land and natural resources in the West. He stopped some of the exploitation when it was attempted by wholesale in the Taft administration. When the Ballinger scandal broke, Shaw had the honesty and courage to surrender his job rather than be silent when it behooved an honest official to tell the truth.

When the Cherokee strip was opened, preliminary to the admission

Above, Mr. and Mrs. Grover Cleveland. *Below*, The wedding of Grover Cleveland and Miss Frances Folsom in the White House in 1886 (*Handy Studios*).

President Cleveland shooting ducks on Currituck Sound in North Carolina. His companions are, *left,* Pierce Hampton, North Carolina legislator, and, *right,* Joseph Jefferson, carrying a jug. From a drawing by Norman E. Jennett.

of Oklahoma to statehood, Hoke Smith offered me an important land-office position at Guthrie at an increased salary over the one I was receiving. He said that Oklahoma would soon be a State and that I could come back to Washington as a United States Senator in a few years. It appealed to me, but my heart was set upon going back to Raleigh as editor, as soon as financial conditions permitted. However, I had a part in all that related to the set-up in Oklahoma and in the appointment of officials. I made lasting friends with many Oklahomans, particularly with Robert L. Owen, afterwards United States Senator when Oklahoma was admitted as a State, and also member of the National Democratic Committee who directed most of the patronage in the Cleveland administration. He was part Indian and looked it. The friendship then formed was lasting, and we coöperated in the Wilson administration when he was a leader in the Senate.

The most difficult selection was that of a governor for the territory. Such bitterness between factions I had never seen or such charges of unfitness. Finally Hoke Smith decided to ignore recommendations of all factions and appointed Governor Renfrow. This pleased me because he was a native of Johnson County, North Carolina, and had relatives back home who were my friends.

In my position I came in contact with men who either were intertested in the protection of the Indians or who desired to exploit them. In the former class, I became friendly with Mr. Stanley, who told me much about the Indian life of which I was ignorant. I then regarded the Indians as inferior to Anglo-Saxons. Mr. Stanley said that one of the chief problems arose out of the marriages between Indian women and white men. I asked in my ignorance, "Is it possible that any self-respecting Anglo-Saxon contracts such a marriage?" He paused a moment before he replied, "I married one!" In order to help me over my embarrassment, or to add to it, he added, "My wife is a college graduate and graduated also at the Boston Conservatory of Music, plays and sings beautifully, and speaks three languages; I doubt if your wife is so accomplished." I was duly and properly rebuked.

I came in very close touch early with a rare spirit in the Cleveland administration, Judge Lochren, Commissioner of Pensions. He had been a soldier in the Federal Army and was an able lawyer. Afterwards he was appointed by Mr. Cleveland on the Federal bench. He was from Minnesota. I learned then and afterwards that high-class

Democrats who lived in states like Minnesota, where there was no opportunity for political preferment, were probably more devoted to their principles than Democrats who lived in states where they belonged to a majority party. No man at that time could have been a Democrat from Minnesota unless he believed in the principles of the party or had inherited the faith. Lochren was a just and honest man but he brought down upon himself the wrath of leaders in the Grand Army of the Republic because he put a stop to the wholesale granting of pensions to people who did not deserve them. That was Cleveland's policy. He had been denounced by the G.A.R. in his first term because he had vetoed many special pension bills. Hoke Smith was in entire sympathy with that policy and so was Judge Lochren. Under the Cleveland administration no pension was granted unless it clearly came within the law. Examiners were instructed to put a stop to the wholesale pensioning of people not entitled to it. That was sound but it brought to Hoke Smith undeserved denunciation. Judge Lochren, zealous to grant a pension to deserving men, was adamant against letting down the bars, as had been done in the Harrison administration.

Republican papers, because Smith was from Georgia, said that the South was in the saddle, and that Smith was from a strong Confederate family and his course was actuated by sectional feeling. It was most unjust. Smith's position was the same as that of other courageous officials, all of them Northerners with honorable records in the Federal army. The recollection of the denunciation of a Southern man as head of the Interior Department caused Wilson in 1913 to decline to consider a Southern man for that portfolio.

Before I had been in office long an old schoolmate of mine, who was then what was called "a sundown doctor," Dr. Sterling Ruffin, later one of the most eminent physicians in Washington, confided to me that he desired to resign his clerkship in the Treasury Department, where he was on duty from nine until four, so that he could devote his whole time to the practice of medicine. He could hardy afford to do this unless he could secure some temporary income. He told me if he could be named on the board of medical pension examiners it would give him enough income to justify him in resigning and practicing medicine. At my request Judge Lochren readily assented to appoint him. However, when he found he was a "sundown doctor"— that is, practicing only after office hours—he said he did not see how he could do it. This was a disappointment to me and to my friend. That night we called on Judge Lochren at his home. Ruffin always had a manner that won friends. He made such a fine impression that after talking a few minutes Judge Lochren said that no mere regulation should stand between Ruffin and the opportunity he coveted. He was appointed secretary of the board, which enabled him to begin practicing at the time of a Democratic administration, when many Southern men were coming to Washington.

PALMETTO'S CHIVALRIC HAMPTON

I early was admitted to delightful intimacy with General Wade Hampton, the distinguished Confederate cavalryman. Hoke Smith, who had married the daughter of another distinguished Confederate general, Thomas R. R. Cobb, admired Wade Hampton. When the new regime under Tillman defeated the old aristocratic party in the Palmetto State, General Hampton was retired from the Senate. Beyond his plantations and a home at High Hampton, in the mountains of North Carolina, General Hampton had little. His family had been large slaveholders and very rich before the war of the sixties. It wasn't easy for him to adjust himself to the New Day. He was loyal to the restored Union, but the days of his prime had been in the Confederacy and afterwards in the overthrow of carpet-bag and Negro misrule in proud South Carolina. Hoke Smith asked Cleveland to appoint him director of railroads, a semi-sinecure position in the Interior Department, and the President was glad to do it. The appointment carried a good salary and was a godsend to Hampton. His lameness—a legacy of the war—made getting about difficult, and he felt the need of a young arm to aid in locomotion. As chief clerk of the department in which he held a position of dignity, and as the son of a neighboring state, I was often asked by General Hampton to accompany him to some public gathering or to the theatre. I was glad of the opportunity to know him well and to be the recipient of his many interesting and stirring reminiscences. He was never fully reconstructed and spoke disdainfully of "slobbering" about the reunion of the blue and the gray. "I must go to a slobbering match between General Gordon and Corporal Tanner of the G.A.R. tomorrow night," he said to me one day, "and I'll be glad if you will go with me." I was happy to comply, both because I loved to be in his company and because I wished to hear Gordon, the most eloquent Confederate, and

Tanner the most eloquent G.A.R. orator. He had lost both arms in the war. We arrived early. General Hampton declined a seat on the rostrum, saying his lameness made it difficult. "The truth is," he whispered to me, "I don't wish to be observed when I will be expected to applaud the slosh about the uniting of brothers the old Confederates and Yankees will indulge in." It was an enthusiastic meeting, with the Stars and Stripes and the Stars and Bars intertwined, and soldiers of North and South fraternizing and women crying in patriotic fervor. I liked it all, but the old cavalry officer *sub rosa* sniffed his disapproval of the gush. "Let's go," he said. "I am a good citizen of the United States, I love the Stars and Stripes, and I would fight for them, but I cannot join in this sob-stuff." He loved Gordon but thought he was overdoing the hands-across-the-Potomac oratory and somewhat apologizing for the Confederates, and he wouldn't stand for it.

The two most militant leaders of South Carolina in the late eighties and late nineties were General Hampton and Benjamin R. Tillman, who ousted Hampton and the old order from political control. As in 1893-94 I was admitted to friendship with General Hampton, later in 1913-17, when I was Secretary of the Navy and Tillman was Chairman of the Naval Affairs Committee of the Senate, my best friend in the Senate was Senator Tillman, who like Hampton in his last days needed a young man to lean upon. I have always been happy that I enjoyed the friendship of Palmetto's two strongest men who, differing widely in many things, were alike in sterling honesty and sincerity. That I should have been privileged to enjoy such close association with the political duellists of South Carolina was as strange as it was delightful. Nobody could know General Hampton without admiration for his courage and his readiness to sacrifice all for his convictions, and I loved Tillman for his like courage and patriotism. Hampton was the personification of the chivalry of the Old South. Tillman personified the New South, and I was in hearty sympathy with his more practical progressive views suited to the New Day.

Years afterwards, when General Hampton and his niece, wife of the distinguished Dr. William S. Halsted of Johns Hopkins, were dead and High Hampton had passed into the hands of Mr. E. L. McKee, my wife and I spent a week in the cottage General Hampton had built, and heard many stories about him and his niece and her husband.

The first Toddy Well I ever saw was constructed on the piazza in the Hampton cottage. It was round and extended deep into the ground so that the whiskeys were kept cold and the glasses frosted. No manufactured ice in those days! There was a windlass turned by hand which would bring up a circular set of shelves. The bottom shelf held tall, well-filled whiskey bottles; the next shelf held glasses for the juleps. Abundant mint grew in the garden adjoining the cottage. All was ready to make the cool and delicious toddies for which High Hampton was famous. Not many years ago when the cottage was burned, one of the Hampton andirons, brought up from South Carolina before the Civil War, escaped destruction. A mould of it was made by the McKees, and my wife was given a set for our cottage at Lake Junaluska. The andiron framework represents little near-naked pickanninies. It would be easy to imagine that the wood burning on the fire had been brought in on their backs. My wife and I love the andirons—but we have no Toddy Well!

FANCY LADIES OUT OF LUCK

When Hoke Smith became Secretary of the Interior in 1893, taking the census had been completed and the number of employees had to be reduced. It was hard every week to discharge fifty or more clerks. Practically everyone dropped needed the job. The acting director in the Census Bureau who was in charge of the work until Carroll D. Wright was appointed, was a "high-flyer." It was common report that the young women who received the highest pay were those who found favor in his eyes, and it was believed that some of them were not as good as they ought to have been. It was soon learned that in making up the list of discharges he had marked women of high character and efficiency for dismissal while good-looking and frivolous girls, not very efficient, were retained. Secretary Smith asked me to find a reliable man who could be trusted and to authorize him to make up the list of discharges and pay no attention to the acting director. As a result, John S. Donnell, of Mississippi, as straight a man as ever lived, was named. He had been employed in the Census Bureau from 1890 and knew the history of every clerk. It was a heartbreaking job, but he did it conscientiously. As soon as each clerk was dropped, she would make a bee-line for the United States Senate, and the next morning the office of the Secretary and my office would be pretty well filled with people who had been notified of their discharge, accompanied by one or more senators. Those who had been appointed by Republican endorsement now came up with Democratic senators, some very insistent. I observed that the Spoils System practiced in the Census Bureau had grown into a real evil. When it became known that one young woman of doubtful character and very beautiful was on the list for dismissal, a colored messenger said, "Shore thing, there ain't no chance for high-flying ladies and gemmuns in this administration." I received calls and thanks after office hours from a dozen of the ladies who had resented the airs and reputation of the flirtatious clerks, and had remained in the Department only because of their poverty. One young woman on the discharge list appeared, demanding reinstatement. She was backed by three senators. When I declined, one of the senators, reputed to be very fond of her, said he would appeal to the Secretary, and if he did not reinstate her, he would go to the President. He did both without success. I later learned he found a position for her in some other department of the government. As a rule, the senators who came with these young women did so in response to telegrams from home, and when they learned the truth, they did not press the matter further. When one senator was very insistent I intimated that the clerk whose retention he demanded did not enjoy a very savory reputation. He desisted. I did not tell him that it was her association with him that had injured her reputation.

A MODERN BLEEDING KANSAS

I will never forget the strange mission of a woman with a strong, weatherbeaten face but with eager eyes betokening intelligence, who came several times in 1894 to see me. She had a letter from a member of Congress, commending her highly. She wanted me to put her in touch with President Cleveland, Senator Gorman, Mr. Whitney, and other leaders of the Democratic Party. She told me the story of her life and her mission somewhat as follows:

"I was born in Louisiana and was married a few weeks before the beginning of the Civil War. I loved my young husband— O how I loved him! He was enthusiastic for the Southern cause. So was I. He was among the first to enlist. I could not bear the separation. So I put on the clothes of a man and enlisted the same day. It was not difficult. In the first days of war, there were no physical examinations. I, with my young husband, could handle a gun as well as any man, and I was the best cook in the company. We had many adventures and hardships. I did not mind. I had my husband, and he had me always, and we were very happy. He fell sick the day the news of Appomattox reached our place. I nursed him tenderly, but he died. I was mustered out as I had enlisted, as Pierre ——. I have never had a happy day since."

That was her story but I could not see why she had come to me with it many years after the war. She then related that she had spent some time in the Southwest. "I have come to Washington," she said, "because I know the Democrats will have a hard time in the coming election. The only way we can win is to colonize Democrats from the South in Nevada, New Mexico, Arizona, and other thinly-populated States, admit new States to the Union, control those States, and by that means and by dividing Texas into five States with ten senators, make the Senate safely Democratic for all time." I was amazed at her far-reaching plan of colonizing Democrats from the South to insure national Democratic control. She had it all figured out—knew where the men could come from, what it would cost to get them settled in the West—and as the population of those States was small, it would have required the emigration of only a few thousand young Southerners to insure Democratic supremacy. She wanted Senator Gorman to back the enterprise, saying that she wished to do in the Southwestern states what the Abolitionists had done in Kansas and Nebraska in the fifties. It seemed to the party leaders with whom I discussed the idea chimerical to induce enough Southern Democrats to emigrate for political purposes. She believed it practical, economical, and necessary if the Democratic Party was to remain in power. A woman who had served as a soldier four years in the war and endured hardships was the type who might have carried out her plan if properly sponsored and financed. I was interested in her if not in her political colonization method of carrying elections. One day she dropped in, discouraged because the party leaders had lacked vision, to say good-bye. I never heard of her again. I thought often of the business-like way in which she talked when planning political colonization and how tender and sweet her voice was when she spoke of her young husband. Is it too great a strain on credulity or faith to believe that together they are bivouacking in the tents of the Eternal City?

III

T. R. AND CIVIL SERVICE

I HAD NOT been long in Washington when I met Theodore Roosevelt for the first time and under circumstances rather embarrassing to me. Before that meeting he had sent one of his trusted clerks, a native of my home town of Wilson, N. C., Paul V. Bunn, to ask me to assign efficient clerks to the Civil Service Commission. The Congress, not very favorable then to the Commission, made no provision for a sufficient office staff, and each Department assigned a certain number of clerks to the Commission. Roosevelt complained that the poorest clerks were assigned to him and asked for better ones. I complied with the request. I was impressed by Bunn's admiration for Roosevelt. It was his ability to attract young men that constituted one of Theodore's finest qualities. If Roosevelt had told Bunn to jump into the Potomac, his confidence in his chief was so great that he would have done so, certain that Roosevelt would have rescued him.

Under the Civil Service law when a Department needed a clerk in the Census, requisition was made to the Civil Service Commission. It sent over three names together with data about each, and the law required that one of the three be appointed. Beyond that, having never read the law, I supposed a Department had the right to make investigations of the three eligibles with freedom to select any one of them. I had not been long in discovering that almost every position was held by a Republican and I felt, as did Jefferson, that when there were vacancies, if Democrats had shown their fitness, they should be appointed. One day when Mr. Donnell, of Mississippi, an official in the Census, brought in three names with their papers, I observed that one lived in Mississippi. Donnell, a Mississippian, said that he was rather surprised and added that, believing only Republicans had a chance to be appointed, few in his State stood the Civil Service examinations. "Look into the Mississippi man," I said, "and if he is all right we will give him the vacancy." He went to see the Congressman who represented the district in which the applicant lived and asked about him. As no appointment was made at once, the Congressman, thinking Donnell had come from the Civil Service Commission, called to see Mr. Roosevelt and asked him to expedite the appointment. Neither the Congressman nor I knew that what we had done was illegal and the Congressman frankly told Mr. Roosevelt that Mr. Donnell had made the inquiry. Teddy went up in the air, rushed to the Interior Department, and reported the incident to Secretary Smith, who had known nothing about the matter. Mr. Smith sent for me, introduced Mr. Roosevelt, who, with his teeth showing, asked about it. I related what had been done as stated above.

"Did you not know it was against the law for information of this character to be given to any person?" I told him I did not. Then he showed me the statute. He said that what had been done would destroy the merit system and restore the spoils system and that he was not certain he should not make an example of me, the Congressman, and Mr. Donnell. I replied that if we had known the law and were trying to evade it, the Congressman would not have gone to see him and disclose what was being undertaken.

"Yes, that's so," said Roosevelt, "and I see there was no intention to violate the law because you did not know it, but don't let it happen again!"

When I next saw him, he looked fierce and then held out his hand in greeting, saying with a friendly twinkle that he wasn't quite sure he had done right; that in fact "all three of you ought to have been sent to jail."

I kept a copy of the Civil Service law on my desk after that and followed it to the letter. As to the vacancy, the first name on the list was selected, and in that case the Mississippi man was not appointed. Hoke Smith saw the possibility of Roosevelt's making a big fuss out of the affair and was glad when frankness caused Mr. Roosevelt to understand and to accept the statements. I did not know what the penalty was for violating the Civil Service law, but I was very careful to inform myself and not to violate it either in spirit or in letter while I was in office. I had a dread of Teddy's teeth and a fear of seeing such headlines in the newspapers as:

ROOSEVELT INDICTS
DANIELS FOR VIOLATING
THE CIVIL SERVICE LAW

And it might have happened!

My chief duty was with reference to appointments. Civil Service rules did not then apply to promotions or demotions. One administration promoted clerks of its party and often demoted clerks of the other party. The Pension Department had most employees. Two new assistant commissioners of pensions had been promoted from long service, Dominic I. Murphy, of Washington, who afterwards became pension commissioner, and Henry C. Bell, of Illinois. The Harrison administration had reduced efficient Democrats to provide promotions for Republican clerks for purely political reasons. Murphy and Bell recommended that every person who had been promoted because he was a Republican should be reduced and every Democrat who had been demoted by the Republicans should be promoted. That seemed to me sound justice. I coöperated. In so far as this was done to right wrongs, I deemed it justifiable, but some good Republicans were demoted solely because they had been originally promoted by political friends.

I remember one case in particular. An attractive young man, John Langley, was pension examiner with a salary of $2,750, purely by political endorsement. He had read law and gave promise of the prominence which he afterwards obtained by being elected to Congress. He heard that the axe was about to fall on his head and he was to be reduced to his old salary of $1,400. He came over to the Department to talk with me about the matter. He unbosomed himself and told me of what he stated was his great ambition. He said he had been raised a Republican in Kentucky, had followed his father's politics without examination of the questions that had divided the two parties, and had secured this position in Washington to go to law school. He told me that he had reached the conclusion that the Republican Party was wrong on the tariff. He added he had given the tariff profound study and now believed that protective tariff was the mother of injustice and political corruption; he said that he wanted to stay in Washington only a couple of years to get out of debt and a little ahead, and then he intended to go back to Kentucky and enter politics as a Democrat. That sounded very good to me. I believed he was sincere. He told Judge Lindsay, Senator from Kentucky, the same thing and Lindsay fell for it. He urged that Langley be retained at the same salary. When I communicated what he had said to Deputy Commissioners Bell and Murphy, they went up in the air. Bell said Langley was "a damned hypocrite." They said Langley was the smooothest little partisan in Washington and was pretending virtue only to prevent a reduction in his salary. They added that he had been the most active partisan in the whole pension office and had not only gotten himself promoted by politics but had used his pull to demote many Democrats. He had secured the reduction of a wounded Federal soldier who was a Democrat from the West, although he knew that this veteran had two children, one in college, and that the reduction in salary would compel him to take his daughter out of college. Langley was unmarried. With this information I convinced Hoke Smith that Langley should swap places with the soldier who had been so cruelly and unjustly treated. The Federal soldiers in the Pension Office—and it had been the custom to give them the best positions—were up in arms against Langley for his bad treatment of one of their comrades. They rejoiced when Langley got a dose of his own medicine and the old soldier was put back at his old salary and was enabled to return his daughter to college. After his reduction of salary, I saw Langley now and then. I never heard anything more about his having been converted to the Democratic attitude on the tariff. The next I heard about him was contained in a letter from the Chairman of the Democratic Committee of Kentucky, who stated that Langley was a candidate for Congress and that he understood I knew something about him which was to his discredit. I related the incident of his treatment of the Federal soldier, but it had no effect on the campaign in a Republican district and he was elected to Congress. I have seen very few more attractive young men. It was a tragedy that he should have been so wanting in integrity. In later years he was found guilty of conspiring to get rich by violating the prohibition laws. He was caught red-handed and had to serve a term in the penitentiary.

There have been many crimes committed in the name of Civil Service reform and many incompetents have been given life employment by being covered into Civil Service without examination. As far back as 1885 in the *State Chronicle* I had advocated that reform and supported General W. R. Cox (pioneer Civil Service reformer in North Carolina and distinguished member of Congress from the Raleigh district who led the last charge by the Confederates at Appomattox), when he was chairman of the Civil Service Committee of the House of Representatives. But I never believed it should be used to give life tenure to political appointees or should embrace any officials holding positions having direction of policies.

I saw a side of Grover Cleveland and Theodore Roosevelt which lessened my admiration for both. Mr. Cleveland and Mr. Roosevelt both advocated Civil Service reform and yet they were guilty of a piece of injustice that was to me inexplicable. Among the new friends I made in Washington was General George D. Johnston, a member of the Civil Service Commission, of which Mr. Roosevelt was chairman. Roosevelt was appointed by Harrison and was continued in office by Cleveland. General Johnston, while serving as professor in the University of Alabama, was appointed on the Commission in the first Cleveland administration on the recommendation of Senator White, afterward Chief Justice, and other Southern leaders. He was born in Hillsboro, N. C., and his father moved to Alabama when he was a small boy. In the war of the sixties he was promoted from lieutenant to brigadier general. He won his spurs in the battle of Atlanta, given new interest by Margaret Mitchell's *Gone With The Wind*. Though wounded, he captured more men than he led, bearing off as trophies two flags and 350 stands of arms. He took part in the battle of Bentonville, N. C., but at the time of the surrender he was on his way to report to Lieutenant General Taylor.

One day early in the Cleveland administration, General Johnston came to me in distress, saying he knew my friendship was so genuine he wished to give me the facts and ask my advice. He had received a message from the President asking for his resignation. Upon inquiry he had learned that Mr. Cleveland had been led to make the request because Mr. Roosevelt had reported that Mr. Johnston was a Southern spoilsman and had stood in the way of the merit system. General Johnston gave me the situation in substantially these words:

"I was a disciple of the merit system long before Cleveland or Roosevelt. I had been appointed in the first instance because of my devotion to that principle. During the Harrison administration, just two months before his term expired and after his defeat, the President, after filling all the positions in the Post Office Department with Republicans appointed for party services, issued an order covering them into the Civil Service, thus giving them a life tenure without any examination to test their fitness. I took the ground that, before being given life positions, they

Upper left, General Wade Hampton, United States Senator from South Carolina; Director of Railroads in Cleveland's administration. *Upper right,* Hoke Smith, Secretary of the Interior in Cleveland's administration; Senator and Governor. *Below,* the old Hampton Lodge, "High Hampton," at Cashiers, North Carolina. The "Bishop's Room" extension is shown on the left.

Left, William Ruffin Cox, distinguished Confederate General, Chairman of the House Civil Service Commission, and Secretary of the United States Senate. *Right,* Robert F. Hoke, uncle of Hoke Smith; distinguished General in the Confederate Army, who resembled Lee in character and favor.

should give evidence of their qualifications by standing the examinations, as is required of all others. My position was—and it is sound—that the proposed action was undermining the merit system. Mr. Roosevelt thought the members of the Commission should support President Harrison. That was the only disagreement we ever had, but I saw he resented my insisting on the merit system under a Republican President as I had stood for it under a Democratic President.

"Of course, I felt that when the President of my party came into power I would be treated with justice. Imagine my feeling when Cleveland listened to Mr. Roosevelt's unjust charge and, without a hearing, asked for my resignation. I wrote him and asked an interview but received no answer. The Louisiana and Alabama Senators have told him of my career and have disproved the charges of Roosevelt, who is seeking to have only 'yes' men on the Commission. As a matter of fact at that time, of the 200,000 employees in the Civil Service of the United States, only 43,000 were classified according to the rules of the Civil Service reform. Of that 43,000, a large percentage were examples of how a defeated party had, in the last few hours of its power, used Civil Service laws to furnish permanent berths for its members who owed their original selection to political influence."

I advised Mr. Johnston to see Secretary Smith and I talked to the Secretary about the injustice being done a good man. He knew Johnston well as a man of high character and a supporter of the merit system. When he heard Mr. Johnston's story, Mr. Smith was indignant and volunteered to talk to Cleveland, who was, he felt sure, acting under misinformation. He did see Cleveland and assured him that the request for Johnston's resignation was an injustice to a good man. But Cleveland could not be budged. He had listened to Roosevelt, who was influential with the Civil Service Reform Association, and declined to change his action. However, the next day, Mr. Cleveland tendered the position of Consul at Madagascar to Mr. Johnston. He had given his word to Roosevelt to change the Civil Service Commission, but he showed his confidence in Johnston by offering him a position with a larger salary. Some of Johnston's friends advised him to take it. In talking to me about the situation he confided that he had no means, was dependent on his salary to send his child through college. He was as honorable and high-minded a man as I have ever known, and high-spirited. He could not have slept with himself if he had accepted office from a man who had wronged him as cruelly as Cleveland had wronged him.

I did not see Roosevelt again after I left Washington early in 1895 until he came to Raleigh in a presidential swing around the circle in 1904. It was at the time when he was roasting "the malefactors of great wealth" and opposing railroad monopoly. He greeted me cordially and we talked about the big fight he was waging against selfish interests, just before he presented the Patterson cup in the Senate Chamber to John Charles McNeill, of Scotland County, who had written the best book of the year. His speech at the Fair Grounds, in which, teeth showing, he arraigned "the malefactors of great wealth" was Bryan-like, and I led the applause. There was much surprise on the part of my Democratic friends, who had read my excoriations of T. R. when he was a candidate, that I could have become a booster of his address. "When a Republican gets on my platform," I said, "I share it with him and do not let him shove me off."

There were other times when at a distance I felt drawn to T. R., as when he favored the income tax amendment and when in 1912 he rang out for progressive policies and exposed his old party for being the agent of privilege. It was in that year that T. R. attained his highest place. On the day he dissolved the Progressive Party, which he had led in a real crusade, and returned to his old affiliations and tried to make Henry Cabot Lodge the Republican candidate for President, T. R. lost his leadership. In his hatred of Wilson and his habit of vitriolic attack on everything and everybody he did not like, he steadily lost influence. All the same, there was still a great sentiment for the Rough Rider, whose patriotism and courage were a national asset, and if he had lived until 1920 his party would almost surely have nominated him for President.

In 1914 I spoke with him on Flag Day at Boston. He expressed his warm affection for Franklin D. Roosevelt, who was Assistant Secretary of the Navy, and told me that from Franklin he had a good account of what I was doing for the Navy. He related some of his experiences when he was Assistant Secretary and of his lasting interest in the Navy. "You have the best Cabinet job and I wish you well," he said, as he was leaving to make a second speech after having spoken at that banquet.

From time to time until the World War, I heard of words of commendation from him and later of criticism. I was glad, when the war came in 1917, that he sought to lead the army rather than to command the fleet. I recall that when T. R. went to Washington to make application for an army command, Senator Swanson, chairman of the Naval Affairs Committee, urged me to see Wilson and advise him to accede to T. R.'s request. "It would be good politics," said Swanson. I thought then that he had come to see me at Franklin D.'s request, but that was only a suspicion. I was sure Franklin wished his distinguished cousin selected, though he never asked me to see anyone about it. I thought it would be a mistake equal to a blunder, and told Swanson so. I was with Pershing and against any political general, even one so brave and fine as T. R.

IV

DESERVING DEMOCRATS

W ASHINGTON WAS full of "deserving Democrats" in the years
1893-94, many of them from North Carolina. Among the
most aggressive applicants for office from that State was Walter R.
Henry, son-in-law of ex-Governor Holden. He was a tall, red-headed
man of large frame, whose stentorian voice had been heard in the
campaign in every county in North Carolina. He wished a diplomatic
mission abroad, and most people in the State favored his appointment. He literally bombarded Ransom, who became so impatient
with his insistence that he would have refused his endorsement except for Henry's supporters at home. Finally, having secured a promise from the State Department, Ransom sent for Henry, saying he
had good news for him. Henry came into the Senator's large committee room all smiles. There were a dozen people present.

"Mr. Henry," bland-like said Ransom, "I have good news for you.
At last I have secured the promise of a diplomatic appointment for
you where you will have an opportunity to distinguish yourself in the
diplomatic service."

Visions of Rome or Madrid or Rio flashed through Henry's mind
as he saw his own commanding figure presenting credentials in a
dignified Foreign Office abroad.

"Thank you, General, I am sure neither you nor Mr. Cleveland will
ever regret the confidence you have reposed in me. What is the mission to which I am to go?"

"To Curaçao, Mr. Henry," said Ransom. "A delightful post." Ransom afterwards felt it should be "Cure-a-Sore" but it did not cure
Henry's sore.

"What is the salary?" asked Henry. Ransom did not know; the
State Department would furnish all the information. It began to
dawn on Henry that he was being shunted off to an insignificant
place. He blurted out, "Where in the hell is Curaçao?" Ransom did
not know. Those present smiled; some laughed. Henry said "I never
heard of the place." Ransom expressed surprise that a man of Henry's

wide knowledge had never heard of that important post, which he said was in South America, right on the ocean, a most delightful place in Dutch Guiana. Henry rose and said, "I will see what I can learn about Curaçao."

Within a half hour he returned in rage and hate, his crimson hair aflame, his huge body looming so large he looked like a Brobdingnag, his face as red as his hair. Looking down at Senator Ransom he literally roared. Putting hate in every word, Henry thundered:

"General Ransom, I have been insulted. I looked up this Curaçao, and I don't believe you know a thing about it, or you would not have permitted me to be insulted as I have been. Curaçao is right on the Equator, the thermometer never falls below 130, there is an earthquake there every other day of the year, smallpox and yellow fever are rampant the year around, and I would just as soon go to hell. You can take Curaçao and go to hell with it. I am going home.

"I am through with the Democratic Party, now and forever. You can tell Mr. Cleveland if that is the way he rewards faithful Democrats I don't want anything more to do with him or his party!"

He strode out. Ransom was happy that he was rid of Henry's importunities. The next thing heard of Henry in a political way after his denunciation of Ransom and Cleveland to all who would listen to him, was that he had joined the Republican Party and was appointed in McKinley's administration as National Bank Examiner. I always liked him and tried to help him, and I believe he would, sans his vanity, have proved a good official.

Early in the administration Senator Ransom recommended me for Public Printer and Secretary Lamont told the Senator he believed that the appointment would soon be made. Lamont reported, however, that the President had offered the place to E. C. Benedict, who had been Public Printer in 1885-89. Cleveland said to Lamont, "I offered it to Benedict last month. He declined and I wrote him again, urging his acceptance, but I do not think he will accept. If he does not, I will appoint Mr. Josephus Daniels. Tell him so." Ransom added that Cleveland knew about me and my loyal support. Ransom said:

"Cleveland does not know many people, leaving the personal touch to Lamont. But if a name is associated with something in which he is interested, it sticks. There are two North Carolinians he never forgets—Josephus Daniels and Kope Elias. I do not regard it as complimentary to either of you, for it is your exceptional names that stick. He probably never knew any other man named Josephus. He asked me if you were related to Charles Daniels, a distinguished lawyer and congressman of Buffalo. I told him you were of the same family. I didn't know. But it could do you no harm, since the President spoke in high terms of Daniels. As to the name Kope Elias who, having heard it once, could forget it? He's likely to give you and Kope appointments, not because you are particularly qualified but because your names stick in his mind among his supporters. If you were named Smith and Kope was a Jones, you'd have no place in Cleveland's list."

Kope Elias was later appointed Collector of Internal Revenue, but Senator Vance, who broke with Cleveland on the silver question, would not permit his confirmation by the Senate. The friendship of Mr. Cleveland for Mr. Elias continued, and Elias urged Cleveland to become a candidate in 1904; but Cleveland declined, writing, "One of the most ardent hopes of my life is to see our grand party regain the confidence of people, again win victories; but my place must hereafter be in the ranks."

At that time there were no Civil Service rules governing appointments in the Public Printer's office, and Senator Ransom could have obtained many positions for his constituents if I were Public Printer. It paid a fine salary, too, and I was keen for the important place. I confided to my good friend Phil Wiley, a Raleigh man I had known as a fellow amateur editor, a master printer in the Public Printer's Department, the probability of my good luck. He asked me if I could stand an examination as a practiced printer, saying that if I were appointed some senator might make the point against me unless I could answer the questions propounded. Every night for several weeks, with a case of type and books giving instructions for making up forms, with Wiley as my preceptor, I sought to master enough knowledge to meet any test the senators might prescribe. It was hard work. However, Mr. Benedict changed his mind and the hoped-for appointment did not come. Cleveland offered me the position of Secretary of the Territory of Alaska, with a larger salary than I was receiving. My baby was young and my wife and I could not think of going into what we thought was a frozen country. The Raleigh paper also had

a pull. Years afterward when I visited Alaska I recalled the opportunity to have become a resident, but, though charmed with the country, I did not regret my 1893 decision. "You would have succeeded to
the governorship of Alaska," Hoke Smith said to me when I declined.

I learned early in Washington that Senator Ransom was not only
persona non grata at the White House, but was positively abhorred
and had been advised by friends in the Cabinet that Mr. Cleveland
would not even receive him. Why? The story was that Mrs. Cleveland
had believed Ransom was their best friend. When she had gone to
Washington as a bride, the chivalric Ransom had won her regard.
When the 1892 campaign for the nomination came on, and the Clevelands observed that under the leadership of Ransom all the delegates
from North Carolina except three had voted against Cleveland, they
felt that in spite of many assurances of friendship, Ransom had
failed them. One report was that Mrs. Cleveland was so hurt that she
cried, and when Grover saw her tears he swore a big round oath that
Ransom was one senator who should never put his foot in the White
House while the Clevelands were there. And that was the status in
the spring and early summer of Cleveland's administration when
scores of North Carolinians arrived in Washington daily to seek Federal office. Times were bad in North Carolina and many looked to
Federal jobs for bread and meat. Many of them were my friends and
I wished to help them. When Vance's recommendations were not
honored, that frank-spoken Senator told his visitors the truth, and
they all looked to Ransom to secure the positions they desired.

And Ransom could not even get his nose inside the White House!
Whitney and Lamont were his friends, and they advised that Ransom
say nothing and bide his time. These and two or three North Carolinians were the only ones who knew the true situation. Nobody suspected it from Ransom's manner. If it had gotten out he felt he would
be a ruined man. He never showed his master diplomacy so beautifully as in those days. He received the North Carolinians, listened to
their pleas, promised consideration to all and offices to some—but on
condition that they go home and be patient, assuring them that as
soon as the stress was over they would be remembered. Most of them,
seeing no hope otherwise, took the Senator's advice and returned
home, only to flood his office with letters and recommendations. His
life-long policy was rarely to answer a letter. He religiously lived up
to it. The result was that my mail was deluged with letters from

friends—"Please see Senator Ransom and tell him," or, "See him and find out when I may expect an appointment." It took much of my salary to pay my postage bills, for I wrote letters every night with my own hand. Two nights in every week I went to the old Metropolitan Hotel, where Ransom reigned as king, to tell him of my letters and to get information to appease importunate correspondents. Some of the seekers for office would not take Ransom's advice to stay at home but camped in Washington. I could not tell any of them Ransom's status at the White House and I could not understand his confidence that later on he would be reinstated in favor and would be the dispenser of fat offices.

The first thing to break the ice was Cleveland's making up his mind to appoint Kope Elias Collector of Internal Revenue in the Western District. By immemorial rule Vance had the right to name appointees in the Western District. Ransom saw his chance to win favor at the White House. He recommended Elias, and his name was sent to the Senate. The rupture between Ransom and Vance was now complete. "Cleveland may appoint Kope," said Vance, "but he will never be confirmed." He was as good as his word, for Vance had more staunch friends in the Senate than Ransom. But Ransom stood up for Kope and won Cleveland's approval. Though that made possible the *rapprochement,* it gave Ransom no offices to dispense and he was growing desperate because he could not easily hold off the men who had been promised places.

Ransom could not secure the appointment of Charles B. Aycock (afterwards Governor), who was endorsed by everybody for district attorney. It was an impasse. Aycock, sick of waiting and really needing the salary, having left his law office half a year to campaign for Cleveland, wrote me that unless he could be appointed at once he would write Ransom and Vance that he wished his name withdrawn. I communicated with Ransom, who was much disturbed. He suggested that I go to see Attorney General Olney. I did so. He examined Aycock's papers, was convinced that the incumbent's activity in politics was not becoming, and decided to remove him. In a short time (it seemed a long time to us) Aycock was appointed. It was a great relief. I was glad of the opportunity to come in touch with Olney, a truly able man, as his service as Attorney General and later as Secretary of State proved. In after years, when Woodrow Wilson urged him to go as Ambassador to Britain, I was to be confirmed in my earlier estimate of him. However, able as he was, Mr. Olney never overcame the railroad attorney attitude and most of his recommendations to judicial appointments were railroad attorneys who in the Franklin Roosevelt administration would have been excluded because they were "economic royalists."

In 1894 Judge Bond, of the Circuit Court of Appeals, died, leaving a vacancy in the district of which North Carolina was a part. The Raleigh bar endorsed the Honorable Richard H. Battle as his successor. I went to see Mr. Olney and told him of Mr. Battle's high character and ability. "But," he said, "the overwhelming endorsements for Judge Simonton would seem to indicate that he should be appointed." I asked to see the papers in the case. "Certainly," said Mr. Olney. I discovered that from nearly every State in the Union there were the strongest and most numerous endorsements and recommendations for Simonton from distinguished members of the bar. I made a copy of the names and residences of the endorsers. To my astonishment I found upon investigation that the bulk of the letters were from the chief counsel of nearly every railroad system in the United States, many of whom could not have known Judge Simonton. I learned then that there was a sort of free masonry among railroad executives by which judicial appointments were controlled by an interchange of recommendations. If I had been in Mr. Olney's position and was without knowledge of the methods in vogue to secure the letters of endorsement, I probably should have acted as he did. It was by such methods that the Federal bench was packed with railroad and monopoly lawyers whose minds ran along with the minds of the leaders of big business. And not even the Supreme Court escaped such packing.

Early during my service in Washington, I came into friendly relations with Josiah Quincy, of Massachusetts, who was Assistant Secretary of State. He was close to Mr. Cleveland and had rather a free hand in selecting ministers and consuls. At that time none of these positions came under Civil Service. Great care was taken to appoint men who could extend the commercial dealings between this country and the one to which they were assigned. Because there were some misfits and some men named who did not bring credit on their country, the impression has been created that most appointees were of that type. The contrary was true. The bulk of the men selected by Assistant Secretary Quincy were chosen because of their ability to promote trade.

At a later period all consuls were named after a competitive Civil Service examination, following the policy of having only career men in the diplomatic service as is the plan of European countries.

I had an intimate friend, Alfred D. Jones, of Raleigh, who in the Cleveland administration, asked to be appointed Consul General at Shanghai. He was endorsed by both Senators and urged by Congressman Bunn of his district. But there were no results. I went to see Mr. Quincy, told him of the ambition of my friend, and asked that he see him and then judge of his fitness. He asked me to bring Jones to call. I did so, Quincy had a penetrating eye and was not apt to misjudge a man.

"Why do you wish to go to Shanghai?" he asked Jones.

"To promote trade, particularly in textiles," replied Jones. He then proceeded to show the need of the Chinese for cotton goods and told what proportion they purchased from Britain and other countries, displaying accurate knowledge of the textile industry in our country. Coming from a textile State he had studied the situation. Mr. Quincy was also from a textile State and knew his cotton industry. He and Jones talked half an hour about how to induce the Chinese to buy more textiles. He wanted a consul general in Shanghai who would care little about social functions and protocol but who would have zeal to increase trade with China. The next day Quincy informed me that he had been pleased with my friend's conception of the large opportunity for service and would recommend him for the appointment. What got Jones the place was his ardent interest in what is the chief function of diplomats—to increase trade relations, open new markets and promote friendly relations, the last being essential to the other two.

Jones was not to live long. I received information in the summer of 1914 that he had been given leave of absence and was en route home with an attendant. I was to learn afterwards from Bishop Lambuth, missionary bishop, of the Southern Methodist church in China, that Jones had busied himself to help the missionaries as well as to promote trade—that he was attacked with fever that made him delirious. He died on the steamer en route from China, and when his body arrived in Washington I accompanied it to Cary, North Carolina, and we buried him in the ancestral lands of his family, among the earliest settlers and best citizens of Wake County. Bishop Lambuth told me Jones had won the love of a noble American lady in

China who, though far away, sorrowed with his neighbors. My wife and I felt the loss of a dear friend, made doubly dear because he had been an attendant at our wedding and because our baby had been attracted to him in Washington in the last days before he sailed to his diplomatic post.

When I went to Washington to become Secretary of the Navy, in March, 1913, one of my first visitors was John Barrett, Director General of the Pan-American Union. "It is good to meet again," he said, "and I recall my lasting gratitude to you when we were youngsters here in Cleveland's second administration." A mutual friend had told me that a distinction had been conferred on Barrett by the District of Columbia, an honor above that conferred upon any other American. Asked the distinction given, he said: "They've named a street for him." I replied that I had never heard of Barrett Street. "No," he replied, "it is I Street because of John's egotism." Maybe he did think well of himself. He may have contracted that air, but he had won high place and rendered important service as a diplomat and as a pioneer in better relations between the countries on this continent.

My mind went back to the Cleveland days in 1893 when Barrett and I became friends through William L. Wilson and Benton McMillan, leaders of the House. It seems that a short time previous to our meeting, John Barrett was a journalist in Seattle and had arranged for a tariff reform swing around the circle by eminent tariff reformers—William L. Wilson and Benton McMillan, and others. Barrett, a Vermonter, who was then a Democrat, had the faith to believe that if the doctrine of tariff reform was preached by able men in the Northwest, that section could be converted to Democracy. At any rate, he organized the expedition, and though it did not then make the Pacific slope Democratic the speakers sowed the seed which in the Woodrow Wilson and Franklin Roosevelt days was to bear a rich harvest of Democratic representatives and senators. My family had not come up from North Carolina, Barrett was not married, and we foregathered often. He confided to me that he had come to Washington in the hope of securing a position in the consular service, but as there were no Democratic senators from Vermont and Washington (the States of his birth and residence) to press his application, he was finding it hard sledding, even though he had the endorsement of Wilson and McMillan. I offered to introduce him to my friend Josiah

Quincy, Assistant Secretary of State, who was the dispenser of consulates by the State Department.

"Mr. Quincy," I said in introduction, "I wish to introduce you to a rare friend, a Vermont Democrat who believes so strongly in tariff reform that he undertook to convert the Pacific Slope to our doctrine," and I told of his crusading work. Barrett, young and attractive, favorably impressed Quincy. I didn't see Barrett after that for some days, and was gratified and astonished one morning to pick up the *Washington Post* and read the headlines: "JOHN BARRETT HAS BEEN APPOINTED MINISTER TO SIAM." Knowing that he had not aspired higher than a consulate, I asked him what rabbit foot he had used to get the place. It seems that he had made a study of Siam and its trade in connection with his newspaper work in Seattle. For some reason he spoke of that to Quincy and later Cleveland sent to the State Department for some information about Siam. Quincy recalled what Barrett had told him about Siam and told the President, "I will ask John Barrett to call and he can give you the information." As a result of the call, and because he could give Cleveland exactly what he wanted at that time, the President offered him the position of Minister to Siam. It was a godsend to the ambitious young journalist who had begun to despair of securing a government position.

I recall one story about his resourcefulness that created many laughs in Washington when he was Director of the Pan-American Union. Some sort of Pan-American gathering was being held in Washington—a scientific one, I think—at which many learned men were to present papers. After the first few days, the attendance petered out and at one session a distinguished South American found that there was only a handful of hearers when the hour came for him to speak. He said it was "an insult to invite me to come thousands of miles to speak to empty benches." Hearing that the speaker was in high dudgeon, Barrett sent him word that there had been a mistake in the hour when he was to make his address, and one hour later a distinguished body of Americans and diplomats would be present for the meeting. He then rushed down to the Willard and made arrangements whereby one hundred of the best-looking waiters in morning coats should march into the hall at the appointed hour, headed by Barrett and the Ambassador from the speaker's country. The Speaker thought he was highly honored by the presence—as he was told—of the most distinguished men in Washington. The waiters evidenced appreciation of his address, applauding liberally at a signal from Barrett. They earned their money, and the savant never knew the trick played on him. It is not surprising that a man of such resourcefulness should win appointments from Cleveland, McKinley, Roosevelt, Taft, and Wilson.

THE CLEVELAND-HILL FEUD

Cleveland had reached the White House in 1893 after defeating the presidential aspirations of Senator David Bennett Hill, who had succeeded Cleveland as Governor of the Empire State, and I witnessed the renewal of their political feud while in Washington. Cleveland had been opposed for the nomination by Tammany, and it was that opposition which brought nation-wide applause when General Bragg, placing Cleveland in nomination, declared, "We love him most for the enemies he has made." Hill had real ability but trusted to machine politics. Cleveland's appeal was to the people over the machine. In the Senate, in 1893, Hill stood with Cleveland for the gold standard and against Cleveland in the tariff fight. He was the strongest opponent of Bryan's income tax, and was the head and front of the Democratic coterie that could almost always be counted upon to be against the administration.

That opposition culminated in Hill's success in defeating Cleveland's two nominations for the Supreme Court bench in 1894. I followed that conflict with as much partisanship for the President as hostility toward Hill. In the preliminary campaign for the nomination I had been against Hill, though I had not enough influence to control a vote in the Convention or money enough to go to the Convention, which I wished to do. Undoubtedly, the Cleveland partisans believed that Hill had betrayed Cleveland in 1888, when Hill carried New York for Governor and Cleveland lost it for President. Was Hill a party to the defeat of Cleveland and was getting rid of him so that Hill could be the nominee in 1892? I was convinced this was true by friends in Washington. Years afterwards, St. Clair McKelway, editor of the *Brooklyn Eagle,* said that this belief did Hill an injustice, and that Hill was elected because German Republican brewers and those they controlled, left their party to work for Hill because he had been against any so-called "sumptuary legislation."

There was no justification for the refusal to confirm either Mr. William I. Hornblower or Mr. Wheeler H. Peckham. They were both New Yorkers and constituents of Cleveland and Hill. But the President had violated the most sacred and absurd traditions of "senatorial courtesy" in not asking Hill's advice, and neither of the men named were Hill men in New York politics. Besides, Hill wished to show the country that Cleveland had no influence with senators. When he had defeated both of Cleveland's nominees, the "Old Man" in the White House played a trump card. Senator Chandler, Republican Senator, who had a habit of making biting statements, was quoted as boasting that Cleveland "could not make any nomination that the Senate would confirm." Cleveland's answer was, "I'll name a man tomorrow whom the Senate will unanimously confirm and for whom that pestiferous wasp will himself be compelled to vote."

It was a master stroke, wholly unexpected, when he turned away from New York, leaving Hill responsible for denying the high place to a New Yorker, and went to Louisiana and named Senator Edward Douglas White. The nomination was unanimously confirmed. I had, in dealing with appointments, come into friendly relations with Senator White and rejoiced that a Southern man—one who had worn the gray—was to go on the bench. Cleveland not only drew rings around Hill but gave the country a great man who was later to win distinction as Chief Justice. Moreover, as White was a devout Catholic, the appointment was hailed by his church with pride and satisfaction. Southerners and Catholics felt that they had long been denied recognition, and together they praised Cleveland. That master stroke was the end of Hill. He was outgeneraled at the Chicago Convention, he was defeated for election as Governor in 1894, and his star steadily waned.

To me Hill had always been a sinister influence, as had been his manager, "Blue Eyed" Billy Sheehan, the lawyer-lobbyist for privilege. In the 1892 campaign, Tammany was in revolt against Cleveland and threatened his defeat. I was thrilled when I learned, while in Washington, the inside story of what happened when Whitney and Gorman persuaded Cleveland against his will to attend a harmony dinner with Tammany leaders, in which, urged by Billy Sheehan, Tammany leaders demanded a pledge of offices. Cleveland whacked his big fist on the table and said: "I will not go into the White House pledged to you or anyone else. I will make no secret promises. I'll be damned if I will." The frightened Tammany Boss Croker said, "This must stop, Mr. Sheehan; I agree with Mr. Cleveland. He cannot make any pledges and it is not right to ask for them." That ended the meeting. In the election Tammany gave Cleveland a great majority.

There is retribution in history. Years later, the organization Democrats of New York, dominated by Tammany, undertook to elect this same Sheehan to the United States Senate. A young State Senator— Franklin D. Roosevelt—organized a score of liberal Democrats who refused to enter the caucus and prevented the election of Sheehan. In one respect at least, the mantle of Cleveland descended on Franklin D. Roosevelt. As one far removed but deeply interested, I was thrilled by Cleveland's defiance. Afterwards my first knowledge of and admiration for Franklin D. Roosevelt came when he finished the job Cleveland began, by the elimination of Sheehan from leadership in the Democratic party when he compassed his defeat for United States Senator.

My position enabled me to secure positions for quite a number of North Carolinians in 1893 and 1894, when a salary of $720 or $840 looked very big in North Carolina. I appointed a number as watchmen and messengers, who lived in Washington on twenty-five or thirty dollars a month and sent the balance home. Most of them were men who in ordinary times would not have thought of accepting positions of that character, but the hard times at home made them a godsend. It was peculiarly gratifying to me when I was able to secure an important position in the Census Bureau for my friend Thomas M. Robertson, who had led the fight for me in the legislature for State Printer. He had a genius for the character of work in the Census Bureau. He soon became an expert, and Carroll D. Wright, Superintendent, promoted him to a high position, where he rendered valuable service. He was sent to investigate corporations engaged in combinations in restraint of trade. He acquainted me with the practices, illegal and some of them near brigandage, which he discovered in some monopolistic concerns. If the Department of Justice had been zealous to prosecute the wrongs that existed, the trust evil could have been crushed before it grew to control the chief industries and business organizations in the country. But the shady practices continued and grew while evidence obtained by Robertson and others of unlawful practises lay at hand to be covered with cobwebs.

Some of the men from North Carolina appointed to small positions had never before been out of the State. Congressman Woodard, of the

Second District, obtained from Logan Carlisle, Chief Clerk of the
Treasury, the appointment of Frank Rouse, a constituent, from Greene
County and deputy sheriff, as watchman in the Treasury. Rouse was
ignorant about Washington's ways. Upon receiving the letter from
his congressman that Mr. Carlisle had appointed him, the man from
Greene County took the first train for Washington, arriving there at
seven o'clock one Sunday morning. Finding that Mr. Woodard was
not in his office, he proceeded to the residence of Mr. Carlisle on K
Street, rang the doorbell long before anybody was awake (the Greene
man was accustomed to rise with the sun). Finally a servant appeared
and asked him what he wanted. "I have important business with the
Secretary of the Treasury," he replied. He would not disclose its nature to anyone but the Secretary. The servant told him to come back at
ten o'clock. The man from Greene walked into the sitting room, took
a seat, and said as composedly as if he were in his own home, "I will
wait." Pretty soon the Secretary, being awake, called to the servant
and asked who the visitor was. "Show him up," he said. Asked his
business, Rouse informed the Secretary that Mr. Woodard had written him to come at once to accept the appointment which Mr. Carlisle had given him. He showed by his papers that he was to be a
watchman in the Treasury. Mr. Carlisle, sensing that he was dealing
with a real man not acquainted with Washington ways, never let him
see that he had broken any rules. He told him that he was sure they
would get along well together and asked him to present himself to
his son, Logan, at the Treasury Department at nine o'clock the next
morning, when he could take the oath and enter upon his duties. He
bowed the man from Greene out with as much courtesy as if he had
been a new Comptroller of the Currency. When Mr. Woodard next
visited the Treasury he learned of what had happened. Mr. Carlisle
and Logan loved to tell the story with many good laughs. "But,"
Logan said to Woodard, "it was well that your man from Greene
called to see my father instead of me. I'd probably have let him know
what a hoosier I thought a man was who would wake me at that un-
earthly hour Sunday morning." Probably, it was another case of the
general who said to the green private, "It is well for you that you did
not act toward a second lieutenant as you did to me. He'd have put
you in Limbo."

There were a number of places in 1893-94 not under the Civil Service—watchmen, messengers, laborers, some clerks, and others. We

found the incumbents had been appointed upon Republican influence and many were Washingtonians. Hoke Smith decided to appoint a number of young men from Georgia who lacked the money to go to college upon condition that they would give their nights to finishing their college course or studying law or medicine. The pay was from $50 to $70 a month. Upon like conditions scores of young men were appointed upon the recommendation of congressmen from other States. A finer body of messengers never served their country, and a good proportion of them, who otherwise would have been denied such opportunity, prepared themselves for useful careers.

As to the watchmen, we found that most of them were Federal soldiers appointed because of politics, most of them drawing pensions, some enough to support them without a salary as watchman. Some of these were replaced. What a howl went up because a Southern Secretary and a Southern Chief Clerk were discharging the men who had saved the country when Rebels from Georgia and North Carolina were trying to destroy it! But investigation proved that the most capable Federal soldiers had been retained and the captain of them all had a record of which the G. A. R. was proud—Captain Halleck— a fine gentleman. Some weeks after my resignation as chief clerk I was in Washington when the watchmen and messengers in a body called to see me and presented me and my wife with a beautiful bowl and berry spoons and forks, with words of appreciation in a leather-bound book containing the autographs of the donors.

All during the spring and summer of 1894 the shadow of a Fusion movement in North Carolina rested upon Democratic leaders. The division in the Democratic Party in the nation was so deep and so bitter that its coming defeat in 1894 was foreshadowed. About that time the Charlotte *Observer* and other Southern papers, foreseeing what would happen, proposed that the Democrats of the South cut loose from any connection with the National Democratic Party and make their fights on local issues entirely. There seemed an ineradicable difference between what might be called the Cleveland wing and the Bryan wing.

V

SENATOR RANSOM'S DIPLOMACY

I LEARNED MANY inside stories of incidents and events in my frequent conversations with Senator Ransom, Senior Senator from North Carolina, in those days when I visited his room two or three times a week, usually trying to help some "deserving Democrat" obtain a position. He was accomplished in diplomacy and had rare charm. Being for the time *persona non grata* at the White House, he loved to discuss some topic of other days, particularly early events in North Carolina in which he had figured. He had rare conversational gifts and an almost perfect memory. He told me of a visit he made as a boy with his father to his distinguished kinsman Nathaniel Macon, after that "last of the Romans" had retired to private life. General Ransom, as nearly as I can recall it, related the visit as follows:

"Mr. Macon was living very simply at his home on Buck Creek. My father was wearing a new elegant suit of broadcloth, and after greetings, the first question Mr. Macon asked was: 'Cousin, how much did that suit of broadcloth cost you?' When the amount was stated, Mr. Macon said that his suit was made of wool grown on his plantation and tailored at home, the only money cost being for buttons. I wasn't impressed with his economical ideas, for my father was so much better dressed. In a friendly way he criticized my father for spending so much money for fine apparel. They fell to talking about tariffs and other public questions which did not interest me. My chief impression was of the dignity and benignity of the old man, and his friendly words as he placed his hand on my head. My father told me that I had seen the greatest living statesman, and should be proud of the opportunity and of being kin to him."

Knowing of my admiration for Macon, the General related from time to time stories of Macon's peculiarities and virtues. One I recall is that he said that at home and at the county courts he always attended, Macon wore the same kind of simple home-made clothes common to other farmers, but when he went to Washington, where

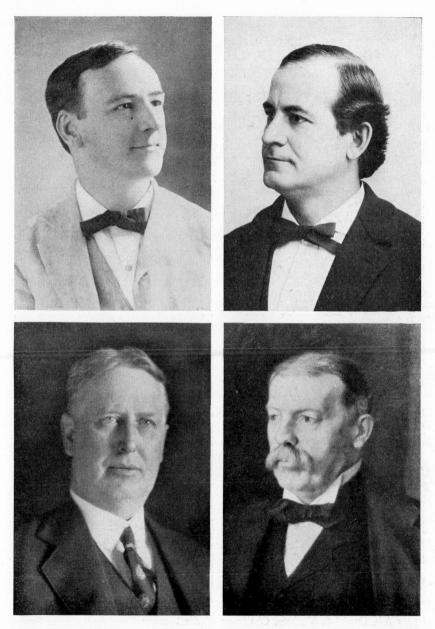

Upper left, Josephus Daniels, Chief Clerk in the Interior Department. *Upper right,* William Jennings Bryan at about the time he was a member of the House of Representatives. *Lower left,* Dr. Sterling Ruffin, prominent physician of Washington, D. C. *Lower right,* Richard Olney, Secretary of State in Cleveland's Cabinet.

Upper left, Daniel S. Vorhees, Chairman of the Finance Committee of the Senate (Brown Brothers). *Upper right,* John G. Carlisle, Secretary of the Treasury in Cleveland's Cabinet (Brown Brothers). *Lower left,* Walter Q. Gresham, Secretary of State in Cleveland's Cabinet (Wide World Photos). *Lower right,* Arthur P. Gorman, Democratic leader of the Senate (Brown Brothers).

he was a leader, having been both Speaker of the House and President of the Senate, he conformed to the fashions at the capital, having his broadcloth suits made by the most fashionable tailor, and he gave as his reason: "In dress no man should wear clothes that make him conspicuous. If I were to wear linsey-woolsey in the Senate, people would think only of how strangely I was attired. If I should wear a fine broadcloth suit made by a Washington tailor in Warren County, again my clothes would make me conspicuous."

It was while discussing the Aycock appointment as District Attorney that General Ransom told me one night, in his most graphic manner, a historical North Carolina story that thrilled me. It was the story of Ransom's most important service. He narrated with vividness his success in securing from Federal Judge Brooks a writ of habeas corpus for Josiah Turner, editor of the *Raleigh Sentinel,* who, on a charge of insurrection, had been confined at Yanceyville with a Negro under sentence of death in a loathsome cell, being later imprisoned in a room in the court house in which Stephens had been murdered. Stephens was a State Senator and one of the Governor's detectives who was killed by the Ku Klux on the allegation that he was responsible for barn-burning in Caswell County. After Turner and others had been jailed, Kirk (Holden's military officer) refusing bail, application for a writ was made to Chief Justice Pearson, who, acknowledging the right of the writ, refused to address it to any sheriff or to call out the *posse comitatus* on the ground that it would precipitate civil war in the State. Pearson was roundly denounced because he said, "The judiciary is exhausted," thus keeping Turner and other patriots in jail without a right to be heard. Ransom described the deep feeling at the impotency of lawyers to secure bail for the men imprisoned because of politics and because Turner's excoriations of Holden had infuriated Holden and the other Reconstructionists. Could anything be attempted? In a word-picture that almost made me feel I was an actor in those days, Ransom told this story of the part he played. I can hope to convey only a hint of his interesting portrayal:

"When Pearson declared, 'the Judiciary is exhausted,' our only recourse was to apply to the Federal Court for a writ of habeas corpus, but as they were politically in sympathy with the Republican Party, most lawyers thought that a forlorn hope. In the extremity I had a conference with Governor Graham, Bat Moore,

Judge Badger, one night as to the next move. It was decided to apply to Judge Brooks at Elizabeth City, but we all felt that the greatest secrecy should be preserved, fearing that if Holden knew we intended to see Brooks, he would bring pressure to bear on Brooks. I told my associates that I knew Brooks, that he was not very partisan, and that it was possible he might be persuaded to grant the writ. It was decided that I should unheralded go to see Judge Brooks and try to persuade him to grant the writ. I drove all night and upon reaching Elizabeth City called at the Judge's residence. I made up my mind that I must enlist Mrs. Brooks on my side and laid myself out to win her. [No woman could resist the charm of the General.] She invited me to go with them to church. I was outwardly as devout as she was. She invited me to supper. At the appointed time, I touched upon the distress of men who were jailed with criminals and denied even the poor privilege of making a defense of the charges against them. I drew a picture of Turner confined in a stinking cell with a Negro murderer and others whose wives were not even permitted to see them. I saw that she sympathized and I painted the picture as black as it was and perhaps a little blacker, though the true conditions were so terrible they could hardly be exaggerated. She declared, 'it is a shame,' and I saw that she was deeply moved. The Judge listened, asked a few questions, but gave no indication of his feelings. I stressed the history of habeas corpus, how the judiciary in every period had invoked it when men were incarcerated by the military and how the executive and State judiciary had surrendered to Kirk and his illegal and bloody army. I was appealing to him as the inheritor of English justice to grant the writ and give them the privilege of at least presenting their side of the case before an honorable and unbiased Federal judge. Tactfully I pointed out that he was the only man who could uphold justice, and I delicately pictured the high place in history he would win for himself and how he would uphold the great traditions by issuing the writ. I pointed out that the Fourteenth Amendment and a recent Act of Congress he had not seen until I showed it to him, gave him jurisdiction. Soon I saw I had touched the mainspring of his thought and action. I turned to other subjects, complimented Mrs. Brooks upon the excellent supper and beautiful flowers. If I do say it myself, I saw that I had won the wife first and she now became my advocate with her husband. Before leaving I had his order and drove all night with it safely pinned in my inside pocket. Nobody, outside a small circle, knew anything about my visit, its object or my success until the papers were served. It came like a thunder-clap to Holden. He wired a protest to President Johnson, expressing his determination not to recognize the action of Judge Brooks and not to yield. The Attorney General at Washington gave an opinion that the Governor must execute the writ. Andrew Johnson, sick at the persecutions under Reconstruction, was planning a better policy toward the South, for which he was narrowly to escape conviction under impeachment charges. Judge Brooks opened court in Salisbury and all Kirk's prisoners were discharged over the protest of the lawyers of the Governor. That virtually ended Holden and military rule in North Carolina. Turner was to return to his sanctum and apply the lash so vigorously that it was not long before Holden was impeached and the terror of Reconstruction measures removed from the people. We can never repay the debt we owe to Judge Brooks and the support Andrew Johnson gave in a dark hour."

Ransom's contemporaries regarded this successful diplomacy as the best contribution he made to his State in his long and distinguished career. I am sure he looked back upon the achievement with the greatest pride and satisfaction, and undoubtedly when the story of what he had done became generally known, it helped greatly to give him the toga he wore so many years. His most permanent contribution in the Senate was the laying of the foundations for redeeming the lands adjacent to the Potomac south of the White House. He had the vision of the beautiful mall as it is today and pioneered its redemption.

Senator Ransom loved to distribute Federal offices, but at times he was bitter toward men to whom he gave positions. He regarded himself as sort of a feudal lord and expected every man appointed upon his recommendation to render villein service as in a real feudal system. I recall one expression he used when a public official, who owed promotion to him, did not support him in the next campaign. He said, "Every time you give a man an office, you make one ingrate and a dozen enemies." He certainly made enemies of those who unsuccessfully applied to him, but nearly all who received appointments at his hands gave him loyal support.

It pleased me to feel that General Ransom liked me personally, though he often did not approve my views and my actions. I reciprocated with a regard heightened by his many evidences of friendship. But while we both were Democrats and I always gave him my personal support, we looked upon life from widely different points of view. He had genius as a conversationalist and I often remained late at his hotel to hear him give his views along with his interesting reminiscences. He believed that men who had won wealth and position had always ruled the world and always should. And he deliberately stood with them when he was forced to take sides. One night as I sat in his room in Washington, he gave me this advice and a leaf out of his experience:

"I have often observed that you do not give sufficient weight to the views of men of wealth. The fact that they have succeeded attests their ability and you will do well to stand with them. Unless you do, I am afraid you will not succeed as you might. I am giving you this advice out of my own experience. When I was a young man, just beginning the practice of law in Warrenton, a young teacher of parts was principal of the Warrenton Academy. The trustees were the leading men of the community, men of wealth and influence. There came serious disagreement between the young teacher and the trustees. I ardently espoused the cause of the teacher and thereby became involved in conflict with the responsible men of the community. It cost me their friendship. I lost them as clients and, for a long time, felt their all-powerful opposition. When too late, I saw my error. I have never again made a like mistake."

I felt my admiration for him diminish as he gave counsel contrary to all my instincts of what I should do and think. Years later, when I had fought powerful interests in North Carolina and aroused their opposition, Ransom reminded me of the advice he had given me and told me it was not too late to change my course. He did not sense that sincere and honest convictions would not permit me to follow any course contrary to my sense of public duty.

Some years later Ransom was in Raleigh, en route to Wake Forest where he was to deliver the Commencement address. A few days previously *The News and Observer* had copied an article from a Northern paper which compared senators to race horses. It ran something like this:

" 'How shall we enter Ransom?' the jockey asked the turfman.

" 'Don't enter him in the races at all—he can neither run nor pace nor trot. Enter him for style and proud manner and flowing mane. That's all he is good for. For looks and posture he is a winner.' "

This too severe estimate of Ransom probably arose from his habit of walking in the rear of the Senate Chamber pulling down his cuffs in full view of the visitors' gallery.

I had not personally copied the article. I thought it unjust in its satire. Because of my regard for Ransom, I would not have printed it. However, I did not disavow the act of my associate, who inserted it in the belief that it was funny. It stung Ransom and in the company of several gentlemen at the Yarborough House he took me to task severely. This offended me and when Ransom had finished I turned to the Honorable R. O. Burton, a leading lawyer who was in the company, and said, "Burton, I advise you never to become an editor. If you do, you will fill your columns every week with praise and support of a Senator and then one day, if an article not commendatory is printed in your paper, he will forget all the good things you have said of him and rebuke you for the one thing he does not like."

I was both hurt and mad, and without saying a word to Ransom turned on my heel and walked away. A short time later Ransom, accompanied by Burton, came to my office and said, "My dear boy, if I said anything that could hurt you and make a rift in our friendship, I deeply regret it and hope you will forgive me. I have loved you long and am proud of you and wish you to know of my real friendship. I spoke hastily and was rather 'ragging' you than criticizing you."

We went together, as friend—that relation always existed—to Wake Forest where I wrote an appreciative report on his eloquent address. I have often wondered how far he would have gone if he had studied as diligently in his mature years as in his youth and had married himself to some right cause that was not popular. He had the capacity to go to the top and narrowly missed it.

General Ransom was rewarded for his staunch support of Cleveland's policies by appointment as Minister to Mexico at the expiration of his senatorial term. He looked every inch a diplomat and was not long in walking into the good graces of President Diaz. Indeed, President Diaz thought so highly of him, as did his associates also, that he was arbitrator between Mexico and Guatemala. Writing of that service and of the personal life of Ransom, Archie Butt, after a visit to Mexico, gave this pen picture:

"I have seen him sit for hours without speaking; then suddenly the whole trend of his thoughts would be revealed in a question addressed to his son: 'Bob, I wonder what all the people are doing at home.' 'They are well,' Bob would say. 'God bless 'em,' the General would say, 'but it takes a mighty long time to hear from them.' ...

"I really think the General is more homesick in Mexico than physically ill. It would be a great pity if any concatenation of events should force his retirement just as this period. We need such a man as Minister Ransom. American wealth is pouring into Mexico, and it is only prosperous in proportion to the population of North American people there.

"Ransom pursues his North Carolina habits in his tropical home. He rises about 7:00 A.M. and strolls for an hour in the Park in front of the Legation. He has a simple breakfast served him about nine. Then the offices of the Legation are opened for business. He has many callers. He leaves very little to the attaches, and looks to the merits of every case himself. The time usually devoted to siestas in Mexico the General spends usually in reading Mexican history. It's an old worn-out copy which lies on his bedroom table and he reads it as religiously as Thackeray's daughter did *David Copperfield*—Ransom is a great Homeric scholar. About five in the afternoon he strolls on the Paseo, which, by the way, was planned and built by Carlota, who is now in a madhouse in Belgium. It is one of the most beautiful bits of boulevard in the world.

"General Ransom never ventures out after dark, for the air gets cold and pneumonia is almost as deadly in Mexico City as yellow fever is in Vera Cruz. It is at night mostly that the General misses his old friends at home, and usually the last thing he says before retiring is, 'Bob, my son, God bless you, Bob—Bob, I wonder what they are doing in North Carolina tonight, Son.' "

VI

TACKS IN THE DEMOCRATIC COFFIN

W HEN I WENT to Washington I expected to see tariff reduction made the first and paramount reform undertaken. I am sure that was Mr. Cleveland's and Hoke Smith's expectation. But the panic which began in Harrison's administration burst with violence on the country soon after Cleveland was inaugurated. Bland and Bryan and Vance traced the trouble to the demonetization of silver. The New York bankers attributed it to the law that required the purchase of large quantities of silver by the Treasury. I was disturbed when Hoke Smith returned from a Cabinet meeting one day in May and told me that Mr. Cleveland, instead of tackling the tariff at once, intended to call a special session of Congress to repeal the purchasing clause of the Sherman Act. "It will bring no relief," I said, "and it will split a victorious party." He debated the question, more to clarify his own thoughts, I think, than because he regarded my opinion on finance highly. I felt, and it was a strong conviction, that Cleveland should mobilize the party for the promised reduction of the tariff at once, and leave the money problem untouched until tariff reduction had been effected.

"That was Cleveland's intention when he was inaugurated," said the Secretary, "but the panic has compelled him to act to strengthen the public credit, which he believes is being undermined by the continued purchase of silver." Mr. Smith continued:

"Under the Sherman Act the Treasury has bought $147,000,000 worth of silver, paying for much of it in gold. The Treasury has been drained of $87,000,000 in the fiscal year. The gold reserve is going down steadily. It is feared that the gold reserve cannot be preserved without an issue of bonds. Mr. Cleveland says that the only way to save the Treasury and the country is to stop the purchase of silver."

Mr. Smith agreed with his chief. I told him that Cleveland's remedy, instead of curing, would aggravate the disease.

The metropolitan press and bankers thundered that conditions could be improved only by stopping the purchase. The Chambers of Commerce demanded action, pointing out that the intrinsic value of silver was only fifty-three cents while a congressional act compelled the continued coinage, predicting that the country would soon be on a silver basis. Mr. Smith quoted Carlisle's change of view, from a silver to a gold-standard advocate, as an argument in support of Cleveland's position.

The proposal for repeal precipitated a bitter fight and acrimonious debate. I went up to the House to hear the speeches of two men I had come to love—William L. Wilson, who opened the debate for repeal, and William Jennings Bryan, who spoke against repeal.

Much has been written of "scholars in politics," but William Lyne Wilson was the greatest of that era, as Woodrow Wilson was, of a later time. These two Wilsons would have been congenial spirits and it is a pity they did not occupy public station in the same decade. Bryan, younger and far more eloquent, seemed to me to have the better of the debate, but as I had been raised under the leadership of Vance, an able silver advocate, I naturally was more easily convinced that Bryan was right.

In his speech, Bryan declared: "No man will go further than I to uphold the hands of the President when he is right, but he can no more measure the wishes and necessities of the people of this country by a consideration of the sophistries emanating from Wall Street than a man can measure the depths of the briny deep by dipping his finger in the foam."

The day after Bryan had spoken, as I took the street car to go to the Capitol, a gentleman rose and greeted me with, "The speech you made yesterday was the greatest in the annals of American history." He spoke in loud tones and everybody turned to look at me. I sensed that he thought I was Bryan and decided not to disabuse his mind. So, trying to look modest, I replied, "I am gratified that you liked it for it came from my sincere conviction." All the way to the Capitol he continued in extravagant terms, in a voice that caused all eyes in the car to turn to us, to praise the speech and predict that it would land me in the White House. Just as the car was turning into the Capitol grounds, thinking I had practiced the deception long enough, I turned and asked the gentleman, "Who do you think I am?" He said "Bryan, of Nebraska." I told him I could not accept compliments that I did not deserve. We walked to the Capitol together and I told him my real name. At that time, while there was little resemblance, Bryan and I were both clean shaven, young and slender. The next Sunday as I started into church just ahead of Bryan, the Nebraskan called, "See here, young man, you must walk circumspectly or you will destroy my reputation." The gentleman who had mistaken me for Bryan had told him of the incident. It was not the first time I was so complimented. In the campaign of 1896 I accompanied Bryan on his speaking tour through New England and many nights shook hands with thousands of people who thought they were greeting the Nebraskan.

The prediction I had made to Secretary Smith that introducing the question would divide the Democratic Party came true. Cleveland won in the House by a margin of 131, but he had four fifths of the Republican vote, whereas on a free coinage amendment the Democratic vote was 104 "ayes" and 114 "nays." The big fight was in the Senate. There it was so hard-fought that Mr. Cleveland resorted to the use of patronage to carry his point. He was neither better nor worse than his predecessors, but in his extremity he did what was contrary to all his professions. It was necessary to have the support of Senator Voorhees, Chairman of the Finance Committee, "Tall Sycamore of the Wabash," as he was called in Indiana. He could not be consciously influenced by patronage, but his friends were given positions liberally. He warmed up to the President and in the crisis was a tower of strength to the administration. Like Carlisle, he had been a silver advocate, but the fact, as he said, that Cleveland's remedy for the panic was the only one that appealed to the bankers and business men, influenced him greatly.

"I will not turn the other cheek," Cleveland had said to Carlisle, and no Democrat could be appointed who did not favor repeal. "If they want a fight, I will give them one," he told Vilas.

It was during the silver debate that the term "Cuckoo Senator" was first coined. The able and usually restrained Senator Morgan, of Alabama, speaking of the union of opponents of silver, Democrats and Republicans, said, "They stick closer and more affectionately to each other than stamps stick to a love letter." He attacked Democrats who stood with Cleveland, saying, "The trumpet has sounded, the forces are marshalled, the clock has struck at the White House, and the cuckoos here all put their heads out of their boxes and respond to inform us of the time of day."

It was while offices were given only to congressmen who favored repeal that I had a memorable conversation with Bryan. Some time before, he had made recommendations for receivers and registers of land offices in Nebraska. I had made out the papers for appointment of the men he recommended and had given them to Secretary Smith. Returning from the Cabinet meeting one day, Mr. Smith called me to his office and said, "The President will appoint nobody to office in Nebraska unless he is recommended by Secretary Morton. Go over and ask Mr. Morton for his recommendations for the vacant offices and make out the papers, to go to the White House, of the men Mr. Morton recommends." I could see that this was not very pleasing to Mr. Smith, for he was not an admirer of the Secretary of Agriculture. I followed his directions, for he was only obeying his White House orders.

It was the day after that conversation that Bryan called. By this time we had become good friends, but, of course, I could not tell him of the directions Cleveland had given to Hoke Smith. However, I let him understand I was personally with him. He said:

"I wish you would say to Secretary Smith that I desire only to know whether he wishes my recommendations for office. If he does not, and will tell me, I can tell my friends in Nebraska that my recommendations are not desired, can relieve myself, and can relieve you from my letters. I have recommended, in accordance with a long practice that a Congressman is entitled to name, as officers in his district, the men who have the backing of the Democrats of that district. If they are to be turned down because I am to be denied rights granted to other Congressmen, let me know it. I am at least entitled to that consideration."

I could not tell Bryan that only Morton's word went, but when the appointments of Morton's men were sent to the Senate, I saw him one day and he said, "Tell the Secretary I will trouble him with no more recommendations since the administration is using offices to get votes for repeal." He sensed the situation as it existed.

For a time congressmen avoided Morton because when they visited the Agricultural Department he would often take out a speech and say: "Let me read you a speech I am to make next week." The helpless congressmen would sit uncomfortably as Morton read on and on and on. If he appeared interested and complimented Morton, his request would be granted. Otherwise, it was just too bad for the constituent. This speech-reading habit was talked about so generally that Berryman had a cartoon in the *Star,* picturing Morton reading to the President his annual report while Cleveland was fast asleep.

Undoubtedly most Democrats in the House who voted with Cleveland did so because of loyalty to the leader and because the panic had stampeded them. However, the distribution of offices "where it would do the most good" counted for some votes. While the fight was waging in the Senate and the issue hung in the balance, I was an unwilling participant, from loyalty to my chief, in office brokerage. Returning from the Cabinet one day Hoke Smith sent for me and said, "Go to see Senator Bate and Senator Ransom and tell them I am ready to appoint the men they recommended a short time ago." Looking back upon that circumstance I have no doubt that the question of giving offices where they might do the most good had been discussed in the Cabinet and that Hoke Smith was doing his part. I shall never forget the dignity and bearing of Senator Bate of Tennessee, when I carried the message. He sensed at once, I am sure, that the offer was an anchor to windward in the fight and also that Cleveland was ready to grant his requests for appointments in the hope of getting his vote. For some months the Senator had been asking without success the appointment of an old friend as inspector in the land or Indian service. Bate seemed surprised and I thought hesitated for a moment about accepting the appointment. Afterwards when the charge was made that Cleveland was using patronage to secure senatorial support, I understood his hesitation, but no amount of patronage could seduce the brave old Confederate Senator! Nor could strong church support at home. During the Civil War, the Federal troops had occupied and injured property in Nashville, Tennessee, that belonged to the Southern Methodist Church. The church officials asked Senator Bate to introduce a bill to have payment made. He did so, and on the eve of its passage, it was reported that a considerable part of the claim was to go to Colonel Stahlman, who had been in Washington urging the appropriation. Senator Bate telegraphed to certain church officials, who wired that there was no truth in the report. After the bill became a law, it was discovered that the early report that for lobbying for the measure Colonel Stahlman was to receive a large sum, was true. Senator Bate was outraged and spoke his mind in denouncing the church authorities who had deceived him. As a Methodist I felt, along with others, a sense of humiliation and thought the church ought to return the money. Colonel Frank Robbins, a distinguished lawyer in North Carolina and a member of a strong Methodist family, and others, withdrew from the church, in protest.

At another time, before the silver fight was over, returning from a Cabinet meeting Mr. Smith told me that Gorman and others were trying to effect a compromise. "I don't believe the President will accept anything but unconditional repeal," he said. "He believes, and sincerely, that unless the drain of gold is stopped the country will go on the rocks." "Does the President believe repeal will restore normal conditions?" I asked. "Absolutely," he said. "He has not the slightest doubt of it."

I was not surprised when a majority of the Democratic senators, thirty-seven of the forty-four, outlined a plan written by Gorman to continue the purchase of silver to July 1, 1894; that the bullion in the Treasury up to that date should be coined; and that there should be no further issue of notes of a smaller denomination than $10. It was defeated. I asked Secretary Smith what he thought of it. He was greatly disturbed and said, "I went to see Lamont and Gresham yesterday and suggested that in the absence from the city of the President the members of the Cabinet talk the matter over. They agreed, and this morning we met at Lamont's house. Gresham and I hoped for some adjustment. Herbert seemed agreeable but non-committal. Carlisle evidently would like an adjustment but will not commit himself. The rest were vigorous in opposition to the proposed compromise. The meeting was abortive. It all depends on Cleveland and I doubt if he will budge an inch."

After Cleveland's return, Hoke Smith told me of the Cabinet meeting. "Cleveland is adamant," he said. "He declared he would fight it out on the line he had started if it took all his four years. He slammed his fist on the table so hard that papers flew to the floor and I was afraid he would bruise his hand." The firmness and determination of Cleveland won. The East rejoiced. The West and South were routed. Repeal carried in the Senate by a vote of 48 to 37, nearly all 37 being cast by Democrats. It had already passed the House. Hoke Smith stood by his chief and told me that if good times were restored Cleveland would be the most beloved President since Lincoln. His love for courage had given him enthusiasm for his chief.

"But if conditions do not improve?" I suggested.

Events did not justify Mr. Cleveland's faith and Hoke Smith's optimism. Cotton went down below six cents; wheat, to thirty cents; and the farmer was nearer starvation than ever, and when Cleveland was unmercifully roasted for a private sale of $65,000,000 of 3 per cent bonds through the Morgan firm, which, it was claimed, had enabled Morgan to clear $7,000,000, I could not refrain from telling my superior that I feared the wreckage of the Democratic Party at the next election. It was a true prophecy.

The Democrats emerged from the silver battle hopelessly divided, and that division was to keep them out of office until Wilson was elected in 1912. Writing to *The Atlantic Monthly* in 1897, Woodrow Wilson said, "It was the President's victory and everybody knew it. He had forced the consideration of the question; he had told Senators plainly, almost passionately that he would accept no compromise." Cleveland won, but it was a Pyrrhic victory. His remedy for the return of prosperity failed. Bryan was to win the leadership of the party, though Cleveland's opposition aided in his defeat in 1896.

During the long debate in the Senate, North Carolinians were deeply interested. They did not need to ask where Vance stood. He stood always in principle with

> "Tall men, sun-crowned, who live above the fog
> In public duty and in private thinking."

The question asked in North Carolina was, "What will Ransom do?" If he voted with Cleveland the opposition in North Carolina threatened his defeat. If he did not vote with Cleveland, he would be outside the breastworks. Civil Service reformer that he was, Cleveland was not above using patronage "to save the country," as he regarded the repeal question. Ransom had never taken part in debates on the currency question or on the tariff, though he was regarded as sympathetic with the protection element of the party. At heart, he was in favor of the gold standard and incidental protection, but had generally followed legislative instructions and given no offense. Now he had to take sides. He decided to throw his lot with the President and, skillfully, on the side used all his influence for repeal. North Carolina did not know his position until the roll was called. Vance voted against repeal and fought it with all the earnestness of his soul, believing Cleveland was controlled by the Money Power. Ransom voted for repeal and incidentally and, most important for his present ends, voted himself the distributor of the Federal patronage in North Carolina. In his State, the people roared their condemnation of what they called "Ransom's betrayal." He maintained his equanimity as he had done when he couldn't get in sight of the White House, but whereas he had then sometimes been petulant, he now beamed on everybody as he dispensed patronage, building up an army ready to champion his reëlection.

In the meantime, Vance, whose health had been failing, died in 1894. His death demonstrated the affection of the people of the State. His body was carried to Raleigh where it lay in state in the rotunda of the Capitol, the scene of his great service as War Governor in the sixties, and in 1877-78 until he was elected to the United States Senate, in which he served with great distinction until his death. Like Niobe, North Carolina was "all tears" as men, women, and children gathered by the tens of thousands in sincere mourning as the special train bore the body of their greatest statesman for interment to his native lofty mountain home at Asheville. The people who had voted for him and trusted him from the time he was elected to Congress in the fifties, having given him every post of honor in peace and war, felt that this definition of greatness applied to their beloved Vance:

> "Greatness lies not in being strong, but in the right use of strength; and strength is not used rightly when it serves only to carry a man above his fellows for his own solitary glory. He is the greatest whose strength carries up the most hearts by the attraction of his own."

To succeed Vance, Governor Carr named ex-Governor Jarvis, and he came to Washington to carry on where Vance left off. Cleveland's plan to end the panic proved a dud—at least the times grew worse. In 1894, a coalition of Republicans and Populists carried North Carolina and Ransom was defeated, but soon, a vacancy occurring as Minister to Mexico, Ransom was given that post. Cleveland felt, and perhaps truly, that Ransom had lost his toga by standing by him. Ransom's friends created that impression. At any rate, the eloquent Senator lost nothing in standing by Cleveland except the support of his home people. Honoring him for long and distinguished service in Reconstruction days and as a brave Confederate General, most of them never forgave his vote for the gold standard. When his mission in Mexico ended, he retired to his farms and never again took part in public affairs. He never forgave those who opposed his reëlection to the Senate.

The summer of 1894, with the Tariff bill pending, witnessed the much heralded march on Washington by Coxey's army. The prosperity Cleveland thought would follow the buttressing of the gold standard did not materialize. Ex-President Harrison said that "the tumult of this wild sea would be calmed" if the people could be assured there would be no tinkering with the great god Protection. There were three million people out of employment when in March Jacob Coxey's army of unemployed started out for the nation's capital. It was to be a sort of "petition in boots"—minus the boots, for many were too poor to have shoes—in a demand that the Cleveland administration issue five hundred million dollars of paper money to relieve the distress. That was the first time I heard anybody—it was Samuel Gompers—declare that "Government must provide work for all." Coxey's army increased in the first days of the march, and many in Washington feared it portended a sort of French Revolution. The extra guard on duty near the White House was housed in temporary barracks to be ready to protect the President. After the army degenerated into a small body, the press boys dubbed the shack "Fort Thurber," after Cleveland's private secretary, who had caused its erection. By the time, footsore and weary, the army reached Washington, it had been reduced to a few hundred ill-clad men and boys. I went out to see the army and saw that it had comprised only a straggling body of the hungry who could harm nobody and whose condition excited sympathy from warm hearts and ridicule from others. The ineffective marchers presented their petitions, the leaders were arrested for carrying banners on the Capitol grounds and trampling on the grass—lame conclusion of a revolution—and generous people in Washington fed the tired members of the revolt which had petered out.

Tom Reed had predicted, "The Democratic mortality will be so great next fall that their dead will be buried in trenches and marked 'Unknown.' " When the election returns came in, Champ Clark said, "It is the greatest slaughter of the Innocents since the time of Herod."

In place of 219 Democrats and 127 Republicans in the House, the turnover gave the Republicans 244 and the Democrats 104. The opponents of Cleveland placed the blame on him, but Cleveland, who always thought he was right, had no sense of defeatism. On the contrary, he said the party had been chastened for its sins, to wit:— not following his leadership in all things.

Mr. Cleveland attributed the crushing defeat solely to the failure of the Democrats in Congress to give him solid support in silver and tariff legislation. The silver advocates put all the blame on Cleveland's determination to force the gold standard, and the protection Democrats charged that Cleveland's emphasis on what they called "near free trade" drove away manufacturers and workers.

Undoubtedly, the best policies of Cleveland, for example, tariff reduction, his refusal to approve the "taking" of Hawaii, his brave upholding of the Monroe Doctrine in the Venezuela dispute, also cost the party support in the November election.

As if these just and unjust grievances were not enough to give the Democratic party a knockout blow in the November election, the action of Cleveland in reducing the fine imposed by Secretary Herbert on the steel trust for making defective armor plate, added other tacks in the Democratic coffin. If the Navy had placed the defective armor plate on a battleship, it would have made the ship an easy prey for an enemy shell and invited the destruction of the ship and all on board. Instead of imposing a fine, Secretary Herbert should have prayed judgment, for conduct near treasonable, on the company contracting to furnish plate of the best quality. He was undoubtedly influenced by conflicting evidence as to the persons responsible for the criminal defective armor plate. There was indignation when Cleveland was persuaded by the company to reduce the fine imposed by Herbert from 15 to 10 per cent. "Another proof that Cleveland is on the side of monopolies," cried his critics. His friends answered that he was convinced by the company that it and the Government had been victimized by dishonest workmen, who indignantly denied the charge. The crime was at the door of the company that had contracted to furnish armor plate of a certain quality and had palmed off defective plate. If the workmen were also treasonable they should have been punished. If the officials knew of the skulduggery and permitted it in order to save money, they ought to have gone to prison, for they were potential murderers. If they did not know of the defects they were guilty of such negligence as to justify punishment on that score. Summing up, after exhaustive hearings, the House Naval Affairs Committee in August, 1894, told the whole story of the fraud, detail-

Upper left, James H. Blount, "Paramount Blount," whom Cleveland sent to Hawaii to study the question of annexation (Brown Brothers). *Upper right,* Franklin Delano Roosevelt, school boy, who opposed taking Hawaii and the Philippines. *Lower left,* John Barrett, Director General of the Pan American Union. *Lower right,* Alexander C. Shaw, pioneer conservationist in the Interior Department.

William Lyne Wilson, Chairman of the Ways and Means Committee in Cleveland's administration.

ing the criminal deficiency in the armor, and declared that "no fine or money compensation is an adequate atonement for such wrongs."

When in 1913 I became Secretary of the Navy, there was still indignation among ordnance officers over the danger to which the defective armor plates subjected the personnel of the Navy. The scare to the steel company put the fear of God in its heart, and though by attempting combinations to fix prices it sought to secure excessive profits, there was never any suggestion again of defective armor plate.

In the election of 1894, the Democratic rout was almost complete. New England and the Middle States had gone Republican almost solidly. In the West, about the only Democrats elected to Congress were those who favored silver and repudiated Cleveland. Seeing he could not be reëlected to the House, Bryan had become candidate for the Senate with little expectation of election, but he became the recognized leader of the defeated Democratic Party in his State.

Worst of all, as it seemed to me, my own State, North Carolina, by a singular fusion between the Populists and the Republicans, defeated every Democrat for the House of Representatives except one, and elected two United States Senators; and the Fusionists gained complete control of the State.

VII

CLEVELAND RIGHT AND CLEVELAND WRONG

I F, IN THE year 1893, I, a subordinate in Washington with no influence, was disturbed as I saw Cleveland pursuing in money legislation what I regarded as an unwise course, my whole heart rejoiced in his magnificent courage in opposing the forcible annexation of Hawaii and Britain's disregard of the Monroe Doctrine in Venezuela. Cleveland was a firm believer in the Monroe Doctrine as it was enunciated. He rejected the imperialistic interpretation put upon it by wielders of the Big Stick, who held that no European country could grab land on the Western Hemisphere but that no like prohibition to add to its domain was imposed upon the United States. And in both instances, which tested his courage, Cleveland maintained the American hostility to colonialism. He detested the use of force to compel a small country like Hawaii to yield its sovereignty by the methods employed to dethrone its queen. He showed Jacksonian grit in compelling Great Britain to respect the Monroe Doctrine.

Shortly after Cleveland was inaugurated, a revolution in Hawaii, hatched by Americans and promoted by the American Minister, had seized the government. Harrison, denying that the overthrow of the monarchy was promoted by his officials, proposed a treaty to annex Hawaii. After study Cleveland withdrew the treaty from the Senate and sent the Honorable James H. Blount to Honolulu to study the situation. The opposition papers sought to discredit him by calling him "Paramount Blount." He was an able Georgian, and when he returned from Hawaii I had the privilege of hearing him relate his experience and give the reasons for his recommendation which convinced Cleveland. His conclusion, in a long report, was that "the American Minister and the revolutionary leaders had determined on a new addition to the United States and had agreed on the part each was to act to the very end. If the votes of persons claiming allegiance to foreign countries were excluded, "annexation would be defeated five to one." The New York *Times* said it "revealed a conspiracy, which if not repudiated by this nation, would sully and blacken the fair name of the United States." When Cleveland withdrew the treaty from the Senate the storm broke. Cleveland was cartooned standing by Queen Lil (a dusky lady), who was calling him (as she did in her letter) "My great and good friend."

"Old Man Manifest Destiny" paraded and shouted that Cleveland was a traitor because he had "hauled down the American flag," and vocal America was full-throated in denunciation. The Senate bent to the storm. In the end, Cleveland failed. Years afterwards, when the annexation of Hawaii was achieved, Cleveland wrote to Olney, "Hawaii is ours. As I look back upon the first steps of this miserable business and as I contemplate the means used to complete the outrage, I am ashamed of the whole affair."

Cleveland was not opposed to the annexation if it was the will of the people of Hawaii. His indignation was against the skulduggery and hypocrisy and the overt acts of men under the American flag hatching and carrying out the conspiracy. Those islands would have come to us of their own accord in good time. But it was magnificent to see Grover stand his ground unmoved while the storm raged about him! And I felt comradeship with a man who could be so brave in an unpopular cause. Talking over this and other times when Cleveland stood almost alone, a friend said to me, "For a long time I could not understand Cleveland. Then suddenly it came to me—when Cleveland is sure he is right, he doesn't give a damn."

Even though vocal public sentiment ran strong against Cleveland, when McKinley became President and he submitted a treaty of annexation, its ratification failed to materialize immediately. That pleased Cleveland, who wrote to Olney, "All the influence of this administration appears unable to bring to a successful issue the Hawaiian monstrosity." It was not until Admiral Dewey's victory that McKinley carried out what Cleveland called "the Hawaiian monstrosity," saying to Cortelyou, "We need Hawaii just as much and a good deal more than we did California. It is Manifest Destiny." More wrongs have been committed by governments under the name of Manifest Destiny than Madame Roland said had been committed "in the name of liberty." Whenever a greedy strong nation wishes to annex or exploit a weak nation, it calls its avidity, "Manifest Destiny," or, to quote McKinley in the taking of the Philippines, "benevolent assimilation," or Gladstone's statement that what actuated Britain in a certain piece of imperialism was "philanthropy and 5 per cent"—only he should have substituted 25 to 100 per cent.

While Cleveland was battling at Washington against the beginning of imperialism, and I was stirred to the depths by my hatred of colonialism, a youth by the name of Franklin Delano Roosevelt, a Form V boy at Groton School, was taking the negative side in a debate on the query: *"Resolved,* that Hawaii shall be annexed to the United States." Could the veil of the future have been lifted, would Cleveland have been cheered to know that a future President had stood unmoved by the jingo sentiment that swept the country? Later, when the paramount issue in the Bryan campaign was the returning of the government of their country to the Filipinos, would Bryan have been glad to know that the youthful Roosevelt as a debater at Groton was standing with him against the imperialism that had the enthusiastic support of young Roosevelt's fifth cousin, Theodore?

In the historic Venezuelan episode President Cleveland and Secretary Olney won lasting fame, except with Anglophiles, by the able and courageous assertion of the power of the Monroe Doctrine and the resolve to uphold it at all hazards. Speaking of that great State paper, Cleveland said later, "In no event will the American principle [The Monroe Doctrine] ever be better defined, better defended, or more bravely asserted than was done by Mr. Olney in this dispatch." Cleveland called it a "twenty-inch gun." The Cleveland declarations upon the virility of the Monroe Doctrine will always stand as the necessary corollary of Monroe's immortal statement. Many years later, when it was suggested in Mexico that Britain might send its ships to enforce claims for expropriation of its oil properties, I was asked by a colleague of the Diplomatic Corps what course the United States should pursue. My answer was: "Send a copy of the Monroe Doctrine, Olney's first dispatch, and Cleveland's immortal message, and tell the world that Cleveland's enunciation stands." I added, "Cleveland laid down America's policy and was prepared to enforce it and no subsequent administration would dare to depart from the Cleveland declaration."

In his courageous action, Cleveland did not listen to Ambassador Bayard's desire for a milder course. The distinguished Bayard followed too often the attitude of other Ambassadors to Great Britain who were not willing to stand up to John Bull. He didn't like Cleveland's aggressiveness toward Britain. I suggested this advertisement:

Wanted: An American Ambassador to the Court of St. James who is more like Olney than Bayard, more American than British.

Whatever widely different views Americans had of domestic policies, Cleveland's wise handling of international questions set the pace for all others to follow if we wish to avoid embarking upon colonialism and imperialism. In his first term, Cleveland had been strengthened in his belief in the rights of small nations by his experiences with Germany concerning Samoa. In his second term, he acted firmly when Britain, in 1893, demanded certain territory in Venezuela and threatened to enforce its claims for 33,000 square miles. Venezuela denied the claim and requested American intervention in her behalf. Mr. Cleveland and Secretary Gresham suggested arbitration. Britain refused to arbitrate and Sir Julian Pauncefote declared it was "a controversy with which the United States have no apparent practical concern," insisting that Secretary Olney, who succeeded Gresham, had misapprehended the meaning of the Monroe Doctrine. Cleveland's answer was to ask Congress for authority to appoint a commission "to determine the true division line between the Republic of Venezuela and British Guiana." The commission was named, headed by Justice Brewer. It was only after the action by Congress and the appointment of American commissioners to ascertain the facts, that Britain came down from its high horse and agreed to arbitration, recognizing that Cleveland would uphold the Monroe Doctrine even if he had to fight the great British Empire.

CLEVELAND AND THE PULLMAN STRIKE

"If I had a position in this Administration big enough, and had the standing to make my words carry and my action affect the course of events, I would resign and express my sentiments in words that would wake up the country." That declaration I made to Secretary Hoke Smith on the day that Cleveland ordered out troops to break the railroad strike in Chicago. Hoke had, before that incident, talked to me about Debs, whom he had heard in Atlanta years before, and had told me of his admiration of Debs' courage. Hoke in Georgia and I in North Carolina had seen railroad domination and wished to end it. He was troubled but did not resign, not feeling as deeply as I did about flaunting the Governor of the State and using Federal troops to beat down the railroad workers. I was convinced that calling out the soldiers to transport the mail trains was a subterfuge, while the real reason was to use them to break the strike. I told Hoke I saw no greater reason for carrying a letter than transporting a passenger. I was somewhat radical in those days. Later, when I knew Altgeld well and heard him give the inside story, I was all the more convinced that Cleveland was not wise. Altgeld blistered Cleveland, but Grover ordered out the troops and moved the trains, though not without loss of life and crushing laborers' rights.

Secretary Gresham was one member of the Cabinet who, like Hoke Smith, did not agree, in the early days of the discussion, that troops should be sent to Chicago. Gresham knew the Middle West better than any of his associates. It was his liberalism, repudiated by the Republican Party, that caused him to support Cleveland in 1892.

Henry George voiced the sentiment of a large element when he said at a big meeting of protest at Cooper Union on July 12: "I yield to no man in my respect for the rights of property, yet I would rather see every locomotive in this land ditched, every car and every depot burned and every rail torn up, than to have them preserved by means of a Federal standing army." *Per contra* many agreed with Cleveland's statement: "If it takes the entire army and navy in the United States to deliver a postal card in Chicago, that card will be delivered." Allan Nevins truly said in his biography of Cleveland:

> "Somewhere between these two views lay the true course. If Cleveland had possessed a more sober, careful and unprejudiced Attorney-General, he would probably have found it.... In Olney's eyes, it was tortious or criminal for a worker on an interstate railroad to quit his job, or to enter a combination to quit the job, or to do *any other act* in furtherance of a strike. If this were so, just how much freedom was left to railway men?"

The railroad strike troubles actually began when the Pullman Company reduced wages 20 per cent. Contrary to promise, the Company discharged the committee which had called on its president and asked for a restoration of wages. Salaries of officers and dividends to stockholders were not reduced. Eugene Debs at first had no plans of violence, as was shown by his proclamation addressed to the strikers. "I appeal to you to be men, orderly and law-abiding. Keep away from places where large crowds congregate." Later, strikers undertook to prevent the operation of trains. The Superintendent of the Railway Mail Service notified Cleveland that mail trains were running as usual. The Federal District Attorney said, "Violent interference with transportation is imminent." Cleveland ordered out the troops, although Debs made a sworn affidavit that there was no actual violence anywhere. Federal judges enjoined Debs and others who had committed no violence. The result was somewhat like that predicted by Benjamin Franklin when informed that King George would send Red-coats to Boston to put down rebellion. Franklin replied, "if sent they will not find a rebellion, but they will create one." That's what the Federal troops did at Chicago.

The dynamic Governor Altgeld wired Cleveland that ordering the troops under General Miles was "entirely unnecessary and unjustifiable." He said the application for troops had been made by men who had from "selfish and political motives wanted to ignore the State Government." His letter was conclusive proof to me that he was ready and able to handle the situation and had called out soldiers where needed. Altgeld added that if the situation got so serious that the State forces could not control it, he would "promptly and freely ask for Federal assistance." That time, he said, had not arrived and he protested against the presence of the troops and asked for their immediate withdrawal. His letter impressed me then as one of the best presentations I had ever read. After the passage of years, a re-reading accentuates that impression. While he did not stress States' rights, he maintained that Cleveland's act was "in violation of a basic principle of our institutions." Even after troops were out, Debs was determined to prevent violence. He said, "We hold the position that we can win without even the semblance of violence, and if we cannot, I prefer to lose rather than tolerate violence." But all his followers did not listen to Debs. The Governor vigorously criticized the blanket injunction against the strikers, calling the injunction a "ukase." Debs resisted the injunction. Altgeld's second letter left Cleveland not a leg to stand on. General Miles wired Cleveland that conditions were bad and he wished a concentration of troops at Chicago. Cleveland believed Miles. He thought Altgeld was more or less of an anarchist. He and Olney were contemptuous of the Governor's reasoning. Cleveland issued a sweeping proclamation against any and all persons engaged in obstructions and directed them "to retire peaceably to their respective abodes on or before twelve o'clock noon on the 9th of July." Those who did not would be regarded as "public enemies." Debs declared the proclamation "a plot to place Chicago under martial law at the instigation of the railway companies."

The next day Cleveland issued a second proclamation ordering all good people to "retire peaceably to their respective abodes on or before three o'clock in the afternoon of the 10th day of July." Debs and his associates were arrested. They telegraphed Cleveland proposing a settlement and peace, asking nothing but that the men be returned to their former positions. They said they did not ask the recognition of their organization.

Cleveland's second mistake was in not meeting the men half way. Instead he said they were doing the martyr act. Debs became defiant from Cook County Jail. Cleveland appointed a high-grade commission to make full inquiry. They reported losses, including hire of deputy marshals, at $685,308; the heavy losses of earnings by railroads and workers; twelve shot and fatally wounded. Concluding, the Wright Commission found that "the conditions created at the Pullman City enable the management at all times to assert with great vigor its assured right to fix wages and rents absolutely and to refuse that sort of independence which leads to labor organization and their attempts at mediation, arbitration, strike, etc." Debs characterized the Pullman Company as "remorseless as a man-eating tiger." Debs was convicted of violating the injunction and was sentenced to six months in prison. When Debs carried the case to the Supreme Court, which sustained the verdict of the Circuit Court and vindicated the legality of Cleveland's course, Cleveland was highly gratified because, as he said, it established "in an absolutely authoritative manner, and for all time, the power of the national government to protect itself in the exercise of its functions."

During all those weeks I surged with indignation and expressed myself freely to Secretary Hoke Smith. I was sure that at heart he had sympathy for Debs and the strikers, but no member of a Cleveland Cabinet would buck so determined a President as Grover. From that time on I became a foe of "government by injunction." The strikers were not without blame, but the real originators of the trouble were the officers and owners of the Pullman Company. The only thing that happened to the Company was to strengthen its views in autocracy in fixing wages of their workers, increasing their own salaries, and in adding to their dividends.

VIII

CLEVELAND FIGHTS "THE GREAT GOD PROTECTION"

I F I HAD found that my early political idol had feet of clay in his severe blow to labor and States' rights in the Pullman strike and had regarded his paramounting of the silver issue as bad politics, as I did, my heart leaped with joy when Cleveland, rather belatedly, began the fight for tariff reform. If he had, immediately upon his inauguration, called a special session of Congress to enact a low tariff bill, he would have won. Instead he let himself believe that the great financiers were right and pressed first for the repeal of the purchase of silver. As I clearly foresaw and told Hoke Smith, that issue split the party in two and so injured Cleveland's prestige that he ended his term repudiated by his party which in March, 1893, was ready to follow where he led.

If Cleveland erred as to time, he erred in nothing else in his tariff program. After the silver fight was won, he turned to tariff. The platform upon which he went to victory denounced protection as a fraud and the McKinley act as "the culminating atrocity of class legislation." It had failed as a revenue producer and as a promoter of prosperity. Cleveland turned a deaf ear to those who urged longer delay. He had already lost time. The country was fortunate that as Chairman of the Ways and Means Committee it had the scholarly and gifted William L. Wilson, of West Virginia. He had gone from president of the University of West Virginia to Congress, a pioneer "brain-truster." I had known Mr. Wilson before I went to Washington. When he delivered the Commencement address at Wake Forest College in North Carolina, that institution conferred on him the degree of LL.D. It is the natural pride of Wake Forest that it was the earliest institution to recognize the greatness of William L. Wilson. It was also the first institution to confer a like degree on Woodrow Wilson.

William L. Wilson accepted my invitation to spend the next day in Raleigh as my guest. I felt highly honored, for I had predicted in my paper that he would soon succeed to national leadership. At a breakfast to which a dozen prominent citizens were invited to meet him, I recall two incidents. Dr. Richard H. Lewis told, and he was past-master as raconteur, the story of the man in Sampson County who, wishing to plow his field, found he had only apparatus for a double team and had only one bull. He devised the plan of harnessing himself in with the bull. At the word "Go," the bull set off at a rapid pace, far beyond the speed the man could maintain. As they tore through a village, the people came into the street to see the strange team. The man was almost exhausted. As nobody came to his relief, he cried, "Head us, somebody! Darn our fool souls! Stop our damn team!" With much difficulty the mad flight was checked and friends began to remove the harness from the man. "Don't mind me," he said, "get the bull out of the shafts. Unloose him, I'll stand." That story, told in inimitable style, greatly amused Mr. Wilson, who could hardly check his laughter. "Unloose him," he repeated, "I'll stand."

Two years afterwards, when I came to know him well in Washington, he often recalled his visit to Raleigh and laughed as he said, "Unloose him, I'll stand."

After that story, at the breakfast, the talk took a more serious turn and was quite instructive. I suppose it turned on North Carolina's claim to having been the mother of three presidents—Jackson, Polk, and Johnson. However, all three had to go to Tennessee to win fame. Would they have reached the White House if they had remained in the old State?

"In my opinion James Knox Polk was a very small potato, about the smallest man who ever reached the presidency," said W. J. Peele, a young lawyer and author, who prided himself, and not without cause, on his scholarship. He gave his appraisement of Polk in an *ex-cathedra* way that implied that nobody could think otherwise. I do not know whether he had heard of Theodore Roosevelt's slighting reference to Polk. I did not share the estimate of either Roosevelt or my Raleigh friend. I turned to Mr. Wilson and said, "I do not share my friend's appraisement of Polk. How does he stand in comparison with the other chief executives of the country?" Mr. Wilson laid down his knife and fork, paused a moment, and then in quiet fashion that held all of us to close attention reviewed the life of Polk and closed his remarks, which were a liberal education to those who knew little of Polk, with the statement that in his judgment Polk ranked with the five ablest statesmen who had been elevated to the presidency. He reviewed his early successes in Tennessee which under his leadership became a Democratic State, gave a graphic story of his distinguished service as a Speaker of the House, his greatness as a leader of his people in conducting the Mexican War, and his record as chief executive. He then took up his State papers and declared that they were worthy to rank with those of Jefferson and John Quincy Adams and Madison. When he had finished even the young lawyer had learned that Polk was a statesman of the first rank. I wished Theodore Roosevelt might have heard Mr. Wilson's exposition of Polk's career.

Too little is known of William Lyne Wilson by the American people. His sweetness of character and deep devotion to his ideals, and his modest courage added to his ripe knowledge, entitle him to rank among the noblest public figures in our country. It is a happy memory that I was admitted to his friendship and permitted to observe his services to his country in difficult days when he stood true to his convictions, in the knowledge that such devotion might close his political career.

After graduating at the University of Virginia, Mr. Wilson enlisted in the Confederate Army, serving under the famous J. E. B. Stuart. Though licensed to practice law, he was deterred from practicing by the Test Oath until 1871, when he began the practice at Charlestown, West Virginia. He was soon called to the presidency of the newly established University of West Virginia, leaving the collegiate walks when elected to Congress in 1882. He helped to frame the Mills bill when there was a battle royal between the real tariff reformers and the "incidental protection" element of the Democratic Party. It was in that famous contest over the speakership, when Hill stood for Crisp and Cleveland supported Mills, that Mr. Wilson became a national figure. The fight over the speakership was regarded as preliminary to the coming presidential struggle for the nomination between Grover Cleveland and David Bennett Hill. Rugged and able Roger Q. Mills, of Texas, was the militant champion of a tariff for revenue only, while suave and able Charles F. Crisp would take a little high tariff in "his'n," and had the support of Hill and the old Randall element. The Ransom element in North Carolina looked with favor on Crisp, while the Vance element stood for the Mills principles.

I recall the first time I ever saw William L. Wilson. A delegation of North Carolinians, favoring a repeal of the internal revenue tax on tobacco and home-made whiskey, was making an argument before the Ways and Means Committee for their indefensible position in 1887, when Chairman Mills interrupted to ask the North Carolina spokesman:

"If we lose the revenue from tobacco and whiskey, from what source will we derive enough revenue to meet the expenses of government?"

I was sitting near Mr. Wilson, and he whispered: "That is a question to which a Democrat can give but one answer."

We waited for the North Carolina speaker to name the sources of taxation he thought should be substituted for the taxes he wished repealed. He seemed stunned for a moment, and Mills pursued his advantage. "Will you impose a heavier tax on the food and clothing of the people?"

Finding himself after a pause, the North Carolinian answered: "It is not for us to write a revenue bill. That is your job. It is for us to tell you that this tax bears unfairly upon the tobacco State of North Carolina, and other States that grow the weed and grow corn for which there is now no market. We leave it to your wisdom to substitute some other tax."

It was a lame answer and the North Carolinians retired, most of them convinced that Roger Q. Mills and William L. Wilson had a sounder attitude toward taxation than they themselves were advocating.

MADE A GREAT TEAM

With Cleveland directing policies from the White House and William L. Wilson the lead horse in the House in 1894, I had the feeling that at last the country would have a tariff bill stripped of every schedule of selfish interest. Time had not absolutely been lost in writing the bill, for while the silver measure was being debated, Wilson and others had been framing a tariff measure. Fifty days save one after the repeal of the Sherman Act, Mr. Wilson introduced his measure in the House. The Walker tariff in the Polk administration (and Polk had a large hand in its preparation) was regarded by Blaine as the nearest perfect of all the tariff measures in the history of the country. As presented to the House the Wilson tariff bill came next to it in being free from log-rolling or special benefits to particular interests. It did not escape vigorous attack, some of the main assaults from the South being led by the growers of sugar in Louisiana, and from the North, by the powerful sugar trust which had been in the habit of writing schedules that poured millions into their coffers. These and other interests, seeing themselves separated from their subsidy, predicted that the bill if passed would "ruin the country." Republican and some protection Democratic papers joined in the cry. I have heard that cry from the beneficiaries of favors all my life. They never are concerned about their own sugar rag! They are unselfishly concerned about "the dear people" they have been exploiting.

The debate was closed by Thomas Brackett Reed in opposition and William Lyne Wilson in its support. I rarely left the Interior Department to hear the debates in Congress. But both days—January 8 and 9, 1894—I was in my seat in the House early. It was a never-to-be-forgotten debate. Tom Reed, very able, large of frame, and powerful in debate, more than pleased his party; he frightened the Democratic leaders, who knew there were scores of Democrats who were for "tariff for revenue with incidental protection," meaning they wanted some gravy for manufacturers or others in their districts. This Democratic back-firing was disturbing to Wilson. Would two-score Democrats voice their opposition in their vote to which they had given expression as they pleaded for "a little sugar in their'n"? That danger sat heavily on Democratic leaders. When the cheering over Reed's great effort ended, all eyes were turned toward the slight figure and classic face of William L. Wilson. He was pale and his long labors in drafting the bill had weakened his not robust frame. He was palpably nervous. Would he measure up to the height of the historic occasion? I felt that he would, but admired him so much that I was deeply anxious.

He began in a low voice: "Mr. Speaker," enunciating distinctly and speaking with such perfect knowledge of his subject and such evident sincerity as to hold the undivided attention of the crowd that overflowed the Chamber of the House. I do not know how long he spoke altogether, but it took part of two days. You couldn't think in terms of time as you were borne upon a flood of quiet and restrained eloquence and unanswerable logic. But I do remember he was so eloquent that it stirred my enthusiasm to its depths, as he appealed to his fellow Democrats to forget this or that schedule and register their votes for tariff reform. Foreseeing that some would break away, he said:

> "We know from all experience of the past that not all who march bravely in the parade are found in line when the musketry begins to rattle. Reform is beautiful upon the mountain top or in the clouds, but oftimes very unwelcome as it approaches our own threshold."

He answered the argument that a period of depression is no time to reduce the tariff. He said that protection, when expelled (in the Walker tariff in 1846), "never came back with the intelligent assent of the American people—it crept stealthily in through the back door, when the people were in the agony of the Civil War, and now it seeks to hold its position because the people are in the agony of a commercial crisis." Answering the pleas of selfish and rapacious beneficiaries who were opposing reduction, Mr. Wilson compared them to "the English landlords who met, when famine was filling thousands of graves in Ireland, to protest against any lessening of the tax on bread."

He compressed the true principle of taxation in: "I hope to live to see the day when no tax-payer in this country will pay a single dollar that will not go straight, untolled and undiminished, into the tax-payers' treasury." When applause had subsided, he added: "If that be revolutionary make the most of it." Confounding those who fooled many workers, Mr. Wilson showed that not until labor was organized were wages increased, and declared, "If protection improves the well-being of the American worker, I am a protectionist from this time forward." He stunned tax protectionists when he said that Hamilton, their pioneer, had frankly admitted, "It ought to be the capital object of industry to reduce the price of labor." He showed this had been done by textile manufacturers in New England by bringing in French Canadians and by steel barons and others by bringing in immigrants from Hungary, Poland, and Italy, thereby displacing steady American labor. He quoted from the report of the *Steel and Iron Association* which termed union labor as the "most serious rebellion against employers"—and Wilson said that attitude and that language were "drawn from the fealty of a subject to his King"—that is, "a rebellion of organized labor against their employers, a breach of allegiance by a citizen to his government, of the feudatory to the lord

of the manor, or of the retainer to the baron of the castle!" He added,
"The Carnegie works put down the rebellion and are running on
non-union labor." During the session, petitions galore signed by
workers against any reduction in schedules were received. Wilson
showed that "coercion methods" had been employed, and some who
had refused to sign were discharged. That brought Republicans to
their feet to disclaim coercion, and Wilson effectively put a quietus
upon them, particularly those from New England, by saying, "When
John Quincy Adams was presenting petitions here for the abolition
of slavery, there came up to the House a petition signed by slaves of
the South, praying that slavery might be continued." Republicans
sought to trap him by saying Wilson was comparing free working
men to Negro slaves, but he got the better of them saying that no one
"above the intelligence of a slave" would put such a construction
upon his words.

In view of the large taxes on incomes by a later Democratic administration, it seems strange that the levy of an income tax of 2 per cent
on the net earnings of corporations and 2 per cent on personal incomes in excess of $4,000 should have called forth such furious de-
nunciations. Elihu Root and David Bennett Hill saw in it a Pandora's
box of destructive ills. If the word "Bolshevist" had been coined then,
all advocates of the income tax would have been called by that name.
Mr. Wilson proved that a duty of 100 per cent means that a laborer
must work two days to get that which he should otherwise get by one
day's work.

Mr. Wilson told his fellow Democratic Party that if it failed to
stand for the great cause of tariff reform it "ought to go out of power,
as it will."

I recall vividly how Mr. Wilson's earnestness grew as he appealed
to his fellow-Democrats, whose desertion he feared. I dare not attempt
to recall the words and they were heightened in effectiveness by a
sincerity that lifted him to the heights of eloquence. The substance
was to recall what must have been the life-long regret and remorse of
the men who, having the opportunity to associate themselves with the
greatest patriots in the files of time, permitted some fear or objection
to some phrase in the Declaration of Independence to deny them the
glory of the immortality that became the fortune of all who signed
that chart of liberty. "This is a roll of honor," he said. "This is a roll
of freedom, and in the name of honor and in the name of freedom,

I summon every Democratic member of this House to subscribe his name upon it."

The effect of Wilson's speech was indescribable. From my seat I saw Mr. Wilson seem to totter as he finished, and saw he was almost physically exhausted. Immediately, Bryan, Benton McMillan, John Sharpe Williams and Henry St. George Tucker, their faces beaming with admiration, rushed to the place where Wilson was standing, lifted him on their shoulders, and carried him aloft over the House while the floor and the gallery rang with applause and cheers. It was a scene that stands out among the notable oratorical triumphs in congressional history. More than forty years have passed since I was thrilled by that speech, but sometimes I can almost feel that I am hearing again the rich cadence of that winning voice and the cheers which stirred all hearts. The appeal had gone home. Most of those Democrats who could not subordinate private subsidy to the public good abstained from voting. The vote was 182 to 106, with sixty-one members not voting.

The tariff bill so ably piloted through the House by Mr. Wilson went to the Senate where the Democrats had a clear but small majority. "What will the Senate do?" was everywhere asked. Mr. McElroy in his *Life of Cleveland* gives a story which was repeated from lip to lip in Washington. He says, though it was doubtless an invention, it fairly represented the opinion of Mr. Cleveland. It ran thus:

"One night Mr. Cleveland was roused from a heavy sleep by his wife, who whispered: 'Wake up, Mr. Cleveland, wake up, there are robbers in the house.' 'Oh no, my dear,' replied the President, turning heavily, 'I think you are mistaken. There are no robbers in the House, but there are lots in the Senate.' "

The Senate deliberated and deleted and added to the House bill for weary weeks. Finally, after 634 alterations in the measure, some of them cutting it until if it had been human it would have bled, the mutilated measure passed the Senate. Almost every Senator who wanted a little graft was accommodated. However, Vance and Voorhees and Vest and Vilas and others had stood firm for a real tariff reform measure. It had the bad fortune to be in the hands of Senator Gorman. He was one of the most astute men in public life, a straight party man, but he had no zeal for reform or righteousness. He compromised, saying it was essential to do so—and perhaps some compromise was necessary—until he had compromised the substance and bone and sinew out of the Wilson measure, and had compromised the pledges of his party. Cleveland wrote Wilson that those responsible for the dilution were guilty of "the abandonment of Democratic principles," as indeed they were. While the measure was being cut and slashed in the Senate, every selfish interest desiring protection had its lobby in Washington. The sugar trust was investigated and suspicion attached to several Senators who had gotten rich by trading on their advance knowledge of the sugar and other schedules, but the whitewash brush was applied.

When, finally, the Senate had emasculated the bill, and Mr. Wilson had asked the House as a choice of evils to accept the Senate's mutilated amendment, Mr. Cleveland, under date of August 13th, wrote Wilson:

"I suppose a man, depressed and disappointed, may write a word of sympathy to another in like situation. We both hoped and wrought for better things, but, now that we know our fate, I shall not let a moment pass before I acknowledge the great and unselfish work you have done in an attempt to bring about an honest and useful result."

I recall the commotion in Washington when it was believed that Cleveland would veto the emasculated bill. Most of the Democrats urged his signature because of the good things in the measure. In fact, Senator John M. Palmer, of Illinois, wrote Cleveland: "If you allow the bill to become a law without your signature, you abdicate the leadership of the Democratic party on the issue that made you President. The commander of an army, and the leader of a party must share the fortunes of their followers." Cleveland refused to sign, even if to do so he "abdicated the leadership of his party."

Cleveland stood his ground bravely in that critical conflict. In his letter to Representative Catchings (August 27), he said that he would not veto the tariff measure because that would separate him from his party and because "it will certainly lighten many tariff burdens that now rest heavily upon the people" and because "it is the only barrier against the return of mad protection" and "furnishes a vantage-ground from which must be waged further aggressive operations against protected monopoly and governmental favoritism."

It was Bryan who forced the income tax provision in the Wilson-

Gorman Tariff Act. Mr. Cleveland, Mr. Carlisle, and Mr. Wilson did not wish it incorporated in the tariff measure. Indeed, Mr. Carlisle sent word to the House leaders that the administration wished the income tax and the tariff to be separate measures. Then it was that Bryan displayed constructive leadership. His personal pleas for its inclusion in the pending measure did not avail. He therefore secured enough signatures to call a caucus of the Democratic members and that body decided that both tariff and income taxes should be embraced in one bill. The victory, however, was short-lived, for the Supreme Court by a majority of one held that the imposition of an income tax was unconstitutional. It is impossible to convey the incensed feeling at the action of the court. Neither Thomas Jefferson nor Andrew Jackson nor Abraham Lincoln nor later Franklin Roosevelt, was more severe on court decisions in their day than Bryan. Immediately upon the delivery of the decision, Bryan sounded the note that a constitutional amendment must be adopted to enable the government to tax wealth. That was in 1894. It was just nineteen years afterwards that Bryan saw the ripened fruit of his planting. There was significance and satisfaction that Bryan was then Secretary of State and officially proclaimed the ratification on February 25, 1913, just a little over a month before Woodrow Wilson's inauguration. It came at the very time that Congress was making ready to write a new tariff measure. Wilson and Bryan recommended, and Underwood and Claude Kitchin and Cordell Hull brought into being an income tax measure along the same line that Bryan had drafted ten years earlier. If amendments to the Constitution carried the name of the real author, as some treaties do, the Sixteenth Amendment would be called "The Bryan Amendment."

Not long after William L. Wilson had accepted the Senate amendments, which almost broke his heart, I had a long talk with him. He showed me a letter from Cleveland which contained the famous expression: "Our abandonment of the principles... means party perfidy and party dishonor." He was in the bluest and most depressed mood over the end of what had begun as a glorious crusade. He told me of his only consolation—the letter from President Cleveland, who had assured him that they were in the same boat. He reviewed for me the long fight, his rejoicing in the early stages and the victory in the House, only to be turned to bitter ashes by the surrender of the Senate. Turning from the long conflict and its scars, he talked of his own situation and the future that awaited him at home. He had heard from his district. He foresaw the defeat that awaited him unless the tide could be turned. He had alienated the silver people by voting to repeal the Sherman Act. He had won the active opposition of the big protected interests in West Virginia by his tariff fight. And Democratic constitutents were dissatisfied because he had placed so few of them in office. He had two letters from "the best character of men who wish appointments," but he said he did not know how to get them appointed. Here was the leader in Congress for the administration, the cleanest, straightest, and most scholarly man in Congress, who didn't know how to secure an appointment from an administration of which he was the chief spokesman in Congress. In fact, he was a baby in practical politics. While he was bemoaning his inability to get his friends placed, congressmen of little ability were getting plenty of their constituents placed. Seeing how helpless Mr. Wilson was, I told Hoke Smith of the situation. The next day at Cabinet meeting, Secretary Smith related what I had told of Mr. Wilson's situation, and Cabinet members offered to place a number of his constituents in positions, and I did likewise in the Interior Department, with the concurrence and approval of the Secretary. But it was too late. The damage had been done. I felt the defeat of Wilson as a personal and national loss. Shortly afterwards he was appointed Postmaster General when he ought to have been Ambassador to France. However, with the assistance of Newton D. Baker, also of West Virginia, as private secretary, he made an efficient Cabinet Minister. It was then that Baker got his first taste of official life in Washington, where he was later to guide the destiny of the Army (and guide it with marked success) in the greatest war in our history. Baker was young, studious, modest and retiring at that period. He developed and became very like his chief. Both were devoted to books, indifferent to the usual political practices; both were of slight build, but seemed to tower in the rare height of the eloquence they reached when upholding some great principle or noble cause.

William L. Wilson was never quite so happy as when in the House, perhaps not so happy there as when he was a professor in the University of West Virginia. It is a tragedy that constituents are not wise enough to give long terms to such gifted patriots.

When Mr. Wilson retired as Postmaster General in 1897, he entered upon his duties as president of Washington and Lee University, a worthy knight of learning succeeding the chivalric Robert E. Lee. It was a rare privilege to the students to sit at his feet, with the same sort of illumination that Princeton students received from Woodrow Wilson, as both these gifted men discoursed on political economy and social science and current public affairs.

Mr. Wilson's health being impaired, he contracted tuberculosis and was, as Cleveland sadly said, "sentenced to Arizona." Wilson had never made money, and Cleveland, feeling that his friends should relieve him from anxiety for lack of funds, conceived a plan of helping him. In a letter to E. C. Benedict, he said:

"I have thought a great deal about what you told me of our dear friend Wilson. I have hit upon a plan which I think would succeed in overcoming the difficulty arising from his delicacy and aversion to anything that looks like charitable treatment. He has often spoken of his desire and intention to write a history of the last Democratic administration. Why could not a modest sum —say $5,000 be raised among his friends to be paid him for doing such a work in Arizona or some better climate, if it can be found?"

That generous plan was carried out.

Wilson died October 17, 1900, passing away before he was able to write his contemplated book dealing with the Cleveland administration, in which he contributed so much to the advancement of its best policies. He was held in affectionate regard by Mr. Cleveland, who, attending the funeral of his valued friend and counsellor, "cried like a baby."

Under the leadership of Mr. Cleveland, $100,000 was raised for the William Lyne Wilson endowment for the Department of Economics at Washington and Lee, in memory of the foremost scholar in politics of the Cleveland era.

In our political history there was no more beautiful friendship than that between Cleveland and Wilson.

IX

WASHINGTON A GOSSIP FACTORY

I soon learned that Washington has only one industry that works overtime—the gossip factory to which is attached a scandal engine-house. It was particularly busy in the summer of 1893 and afterwards.

Mr. Cleveland was fond of duck hunting and his favorite hunting grounds were in Currituck Sound, North Carolina. He would slip away from Washington in the season and come back with the trophies of his skill. Every time he would leave Washington, gossip mongers would whisper: "Grover has gone off on another drunk." Some people in Washington actually believed his voyages to Currituck Sound were excuses for a drinking bout. But not so in North Carolina, where Pierce Hampton, the expert duck hunter of Currituck, would report after Cleveland had gone away that "Grover is the best shot of all his party. When he draws a bead the ducks know there is no escape for them." He denied the Washington gossip to inquirers, saying, "No man can bag as many ducks as Grover unless he is sober." So North Carolinians had the evidence to disprove the slander with which I was familiar. But it persisted nevertheless, in spite of the facts.

I recall that in the fall of 1894 Cleveland was expected to come to North Carolina. Writing from Gray Gables (September 25)—where he was having a good time and catching some pretty good fish—to Captain Robley Evans, he said, "It looks to me as though we might as well as not settle on giving up our North Carolina trip, I am afraid that flies and mosquitoes will continue to outnumber the birds." North Carolinians have forgiven him everything else except his giving the State the reputation for harboring mosquitoes!

Though Cleveland was not guilty, as gossip said, of heavy drinking, he loved a good dram on his fishing trips. In preparation for such a voyage, he wrote from Princeton to Captain Evans, also a connoisseur on what was good to drink: "About whiskey—I will take one of my big glass jugs containing two quarts, or perhaps another package I happen to have, containing, I think, two gallons. I'll look out for it, anyway."

Those near Cleveland in Washington knew he was not a well man, though they at first had no thought that he was suffering from a serious malady. That was kept a profound secret even when in June, 1893, an operation was performed on the yacht *Oneida,* anchored in East River. The entire upper jaw from the first bicuspid tooth to just beyond the last molar and nearly up to the middle line was removed as was also the soft palate. The doctors feared cancer, but the operation removed all growth. It was while he was thus suffering and, as he and the doctors too believed, he was facing death, that the purveyors of scandal plied their nefarious trade.

But the slanderers did not stop with spreading stories that Cleveland got drunk; they spread outrageous yarns that he beat his wife and treated her cruelly and shamefully. During the campaign of 1888, there was an organized whispering brigade that carried these falsehoods, with assertions of Cleveland's alleged excess in drinking, to all parts of the Republic. The slander came out in the open in the statement in a Worcester, Massachusetts, paper quoting a clergyman. A lady sent the clipping to Mrs. Cleveland, who wrote an answer that every decent person received with gladness and approval. Mrs. Cleveland said, "every statement is basely false," adding, "I can wish the women of our country no greater blessing than that their homes and lives may be as happy and their husbands may be as kind, attentive, considerate and affectionate as mine."

Cleveland had to run the gamut of other vile tongues of slander. In the campaign of 1884 Republicans of the baser sort broadcast a report that Cleveland was the father of an illegitimate child by Maria Halpin. The Buffalo *Evening Telegraph* in that year was responsible for the first attempt to besmear Cleveland. It printed the story that Maria Halpin was a widow with two children, who was working in a Buffalo dry goods store when she met and had an affair with the bachelor Grover Cleveland. The story alleged that their son, Oscar Folsom Cleveland, duly acknowledged, was born September 14, 1874, and was sent to an orphan asylum March 9, 1876, when a court decreed that his mother, who was drinking herself into madness, was incompetent to care for him.

Preachers and other good men were circularized in the campaign and urged "not to put an adulterer in the White House." When this attempt to destroy him became nation-wide, a friend wired Cleveland and asked what answer should be made to the scandalous propaganda. His answer was, "Tell the truth." What was the truth? The accepted explanation was that a friend of Cleveland, a married man, was the father of the child and Cleveland, then a bachelor, remained silent to shield the friend. Simultaneously with Cleveland's three-word answer, Maria Halpin was spirited away, said to be kept in hiding in Canada during the campaign, or she disappeared of her own accord to escape notoriety. Republican politicians said Democrats kidnapped her to prevent her publicly accusing Cleveland. Democrats said Republicans took her to Canada to prevent her making a statement exonerating Cleveland and thereby killing their nefarious campaign propaganda. Cleveland's "Tell the truth," satisfied most voters that he had nothing to conceal; respectable Republicans were ashamed of the attempt to besmirch an opponent; and the low-down methods received a rebuke by the American voters in November.

A story was circulated in Washington that the Buffalo Democrat who kept Maria Halpin in hiding in order to protect Cleveland, was denied admission even to speak to Cleveland after he was inaugurated, and returned home greatly aggrieved, claiming his friendly act cost him several thousand dollars and otherwise inconvenienced him. He was bitter in condemning what he called Cleveland's "ingratitude." He probably expected to be rewarded by appointment to office. This was told to me by a New York Democrat who said he would vouch for its correctness, but it came to him second hand. He did not claim that the kidnapping was done at Cleveland's request or that Cleveland even knew of it. If the woman had been kept out of the country against her will no doubt she would have made a scene after her release.

I wonder why a certain segment of the American people love to invent or circulate slanders about men in high places. As a youngster I went to Washington to witness the inauguration of President Garfield. With a friend I had a room in a boarding house near the Capitol. We were regaled by the woman who kept the boarding house with whispered gossip that the new President "wasn't all that he ought to be," and, she added, "his wife knew of his bad conduct and was on the point of securing a divorce when his nomination for the presidency caused her to suffer rather than have a public scandal." She regaled that scandal to two youths who were perfect strangers to her, and seemed to roll it as a sweet morsel under her tongue. Certainly there wasn't the slightest foundation for her defamation of a great and good man.

Afterwards the scandalmongers circulated the report in confident whispers that while Mr. Arthur was President he had questionable relations with a fine lady who afterwards became the wife of a prominent and honored gentleman. The lies about President Theodore Roosevelt's love of drink that led to drunkenness were never stopped until Mr. Roosevelt silenced the slander by court proceedings. That was a brave and manly way to pillory slanderers. Not even Woodrow Wilson escaped malicious and unfounded organized false propaganda. The higher the mark the more the attempt to besmirch. Fortunately, the muckrakers can rarely make the mud stick.

Perhaps my later skepticism and reaction against such gossip resulted from two slanderous tales invented about me. In 1914, the centennial of the naval battle on Lake Champlain, where Commodore MacDonough won a signal victory over the British, I was invited to a preliminary celebration at Vergennes, Vermont, near the waters on which MacDonough's victorious ships were fashioned, being made ready for action within eighty days after the trees of which they were constructed were standing in the forest. At night, after the day's celebration, I attended a banquet of Vermont editors and delivered an address. There was plenty to drink but few of the quill-drivers partook freely. The banquet ended at a late hour and I had to rise early the next morning and sail across Lake Champlain to take part in the historical exercises at Plattsburg. My wife did not accompany me to Vergennes, but met me at Plattsburg. Accompanied by Mr. Wadhams, the treasurer of the American Bar Association and brother of my close friend Commodore Wadhams, my wife, Mrs. Wadhams, Mrs. Martin H. Glynn, wife of the Governor, and others had seats on the grandstand, where they could hear the speeches and witness the pageant reënacting the scenes in the war between the British and the Americans of a previous century. I had been detained and arrived late. A lady sitting just behind my wife called out in loud tones, "Why don't they begin?"

"They are waiting for Secretary of the Navy Daniels, who is on his way from Vergennes," was the answer.

"There is no use waiting on him," said the first speaker. "He was drunk at a banquet in Vergennes last night."

Mr. Wadhams, fearing such comment might annoy my wife, quietly left his seat, went over to the scandalmonger masquerading as a lady, and told her that she was mistaken. "Secretary Daniels is a teetotaller and doesn't even know the taste of alcohol, and besides, Mrs. Daniels is sitting just over there and your statement would annoy her if she heard it."

"You may believe he wasn't drunk if you want to," was the reply, "but I got the information from a reliable party. However, I am sorry for his wife and hope she did not hear me."

My wife had not heard, but Mr. Wadhams told us afterwards of the incident.

About that time the band struck up "The Army and Navy Forever," followed by "The Star-Spangled Banner," and Governor Glynn and I and British and American distinguished guests were escorted to the platform by Lieutenant Governor Conway, and the speeches and pageant began. Nobody could have discovered from my speech that I had been "drunk at Vergennes last night." As a matter of fact, I did not know the taste of the brands served at Vergennes, or at any other banquet. At the formal dinner which followed at the home of Lieutenant Governor Thomas F. Conway, of Plattsburg, the story of my alleged intoxication amused the guests, who knew of my abstemiousness. "If you get the credit," said a General who liked his toddy, "it is a great pity that you did not get the pleasure of the glass."

It was about that time that my wife and I spent the week-end at Hyde Park as the guests of Assistant Secretary Franklin Roosevelt and his wife and mother. My wife related the gossip about my being "drunk at Vergennes," whereupon Mrs. James Roosevelt told of a report which had incensed her a short while before. A female relative of the rector of the Hyde Park church attended by the Roosevelts, upon her return from a visit to Washington, on a call upon Mrs. James Roosevelt communicated a salacious piece of gossip as this conversation discloses:

"Isn't it dreadful that dear Franklin is compelled to associate with that terrible man Secretary Daniels?" asked the visitor.

"What do you mean?" inquired Mrs. Roosevelt. "Secretary Daniels is a man of the highest character and Franklin admires him very much."

"But you do not know about him and his habits," said her visitor.

"I have just returned from Washington and was told by truthful people that the Secretary has affairs with all the Navy ladies."

When that wholesale indictment of the Secretary of the Navy and "all the Navy ladies" got out in Washington, it greatly amused "all the Navy ladies" who heard how they had been slandered. They would have been scandalized if they had not had been able to laugh. One fascinating "Navy lady," who had a fine sense of humor, said to me, speaking of the report that the rector's relative carried to Hyde Park, "Why was I omitted when you were having affairs with all the Navy ladies? Do I lack charm?" she asked in bright badinage.

Since then, when gossipers have whispered to me stories about alleged bad habits of men in high station, I have been inclined to think there must be many exaggerations, seeing that not even a teetotaller could escape the tongue of purveyors of lies dressed up and told in respectable circles often by evil-minded persons and oftener by morons masquerading as intelligent members of society and sometimes by just plain gossipers who love to retail whatever they hear.

X

I PURCHASE *THE NEWS AND OBSERVER*

IN JUNE, 1894, Secretary Hoke Smith delivered the commencement address at the University of North Carolina. As his father had been a professor there before 1860, Hoke had fond memories of the place. He invited me to accompany him. On that visit I had a talk with General Julian S. Carr, of Durham which had far-reaching influence on my life. He informed me that *The News and Observer* was in a bad financial condition. He said he had furnished some money to buy an engine and other machinery for it and had been asked to furnish more money to keep it going, but had declined to do so. He asked me if I was still of the opinion that I would like to edit *The News and Observer,* and recalled that a few years before I had talked with him about the matter and he had told me that if I could buy the paper he would give me financial backing. I now answered that I was very anxious to get the paper and would do anything to secure it. He said that he was quite certain it would have to be sold because neither he nor Major Tucker, who had advanced some money, were willing to put up more, and that if I wanted it, he would help me to get it.

General Carr had sold me *The State Chronicle* in 1885 and had permitted me to fix the price and terms. His friendship was manifested in affection and financial support. We were both staunch University men and active members of the Methodist Church, never missing a commencement or a conference. He was a native of Chapel Hill and left the University before he was of age to enter the Confederate Army. Returning, he became a partner of Colonel W. T. Blackwell and James R. Day, later buying them out and becoming head of Blackwell's Durham Bull Tobacco Company. He had advertising genius and was a pioneer in testimony advertising, printing pictures of Gladstone, Tennyson, and other distinguished men smoking Durham Bull tobacco. It was said that his next advertising feat would be to paint the Durham Bull on the pyramids. He made Durham Bull the biggest and widest-known smoking tobacco in the world and was reputed in the eighties to be the richest man in the State. Certainly he was the most generous, giving liberally to colleges and churches and paying the expenses of young men and women to go through college. He set the standard in giving and in promoting all good causes in the State. His devotion to his Confederate comrades knew no bounds. He was one of the first to advocate establishment of the Soldiers' Home by the State, and became a trustee of it. He was the head officer of the State and National Confederate Veterans, and his gray Confederate suit was worn at all Confederate gatherings. He cherished everything that honored his comrades in arms, but devotion to the cause that had enlisted his enthusiasm as a youth did not militate against his devotion to the reunited Republic. I recall that he stole the show in Washington when the statue to General U. S. Grant was unveiled in that city. When the stated oration had been delivered, General Carr, wearing his Confederate uniform, with an American Beauty rose on his coat (he wore a flower every day), stepped to the front. Uninvited, he made a patriotic address upon the indissoluble union of the indestructible States and Grant's generous spirit at Appomattox with his declaration, "Let us have peace." His eloquent speech stirred the hearts and won the applause of the great gathering of Grant's comrades of the sixties, met to do honor to their commander. That spontaneous act was characteristic of the golden-hearted North Carolinian.

Returning to my conversation at Chapel Hill, General Carr suggested that R. T. Gray, Esq., prominent lawyer, be retained to buy the paper when it was put up for sale at auction. I told him it would be essential, if I were to secure it, that my name should not be mentioned in connection with it at all. I knew Colonel A. B. Andrews, of the Southern Railroad, would not wish me to have the paper, and if he thought as earnest an advocate of railroad regulation as I had been would be in charge, he would either buy it or help somebody else to do so. I told General Carr I was quite sure that if the Duke interests had any intimation that I was to edit the paper, they would not be agreeable because my paper had been severe on the methods of the Tobacco Trust. We agreed, therefore, that he would see Mr. Gray and give him carte blanche to carry on the arrangements if the paper was sold. I suggested to him that Mr. Gray was known by everybody in Raleigh to be an intimate friend, and if he were prominent in the matter it would be suspected that he was acting for one or both of us.

General Carr agreed and said he would ask Mr. Gray to retain a lawyer to make the purchase who was not closely enough associated with either one of us to arouse suspicion. I went back to Washington in great suspense and anxiety. I did not dare go to Raleigh or to Durham until the matter was worked out. On June 29 *The News and Observer* announced that the property had passed into the hands of a receiver upon the application of the R. F. Morris and Son Manufacturing Company of Durham, which was controlled by Mr. Willard, father-in-law of Captain Ashe, and that William C. Holman had been appointed receiver—he was a relative of Mr. Willard—and the day of sale was set for July 16, with the terms one-third cash and the balance in six and twelve months. It was pretty clear afterwards that Mr. Willard felt that the paper could not go on without loss of money and he was unwilling to meet the continuing deficits. *The News and Observer* attributed the loss of money to the establishment of the *State Chronicle* as a daily and said that the division of insufficient patronage was the cause of its financial difficulties. Upon the leasing of the *Chronicle* in 1893 by *The News and Observer,* the receipts about equaled the expenses, Captain Ashe said, until the panic came on, when the stockholders were unwilling to provide the money necessary, and it had gone into the hands of a receiver. He added, "If I had any means, the intended sale would not be made."

On July 17 *The News and Observer* announced that *"The News and Observer* was yesterday sold to J. N. Holding for $6,810.00 and until the sale is confirmed by the court, the paper will be carried on as usual." The bidders were R. T. Gray, J. N. Holding, and S. W. Holman. Holman bid up to $6,700 and that evidently was his limit. It was then knocked down at $6,810 to Mr. Holding and it was reported generally in Raleigh that he was representing Edwards and Broughton. He denied it and said that it was the intention of the buyers to make the paper the best in the state and it went without saying, he added, that it would be true as steel to the Democratic Party.

I then went to Raleigh from Washington, and in company with Mr. R. T. Gray, who had received the transfer from Mr. J. N. Holding, I asked Mr. Holding to become a stockholder in the paper and a director. He said, "What have you got to do with it?" "Well," I said, "you bought it for me." He answered, "The dickens I did. I had no idea you were in any way connected with it. I thought you were too happy in Washington to think about coming back to Raleigh to run a newspaper." He was pleased to accept and he coöperated with Mr. Gray in drawing up the papers of incorporation. When he became financially hard-pressed in conducting the Askew paper mill, he would ask me to pay him in advance for paper so that he could buy sulphite, which I often did. This brought us close together in mutual helpfulness.

Upon the organization of the new company, *The News and Observer* was valued at ten thousand dollars. As a matter of fact, with the lawyer's fees and the money General Carr had put into the purchase of it and the paying of its debts, it had cost him that much. I put the *North Carolinian* in at two thousand dollars but that gave us no money. I travelled from Washington to Occoneechee, General Carr's farm, to discuss with him a plan that I had worked out to secure liquid capital and to buy some new printing machinery, by trying to get one hundred men in North Carolina each to take a share of one hundred dollars. I told him the paper was bound to lose money for a time and I could not call upon him to put it up and I didn't have it. He agreed to the plan. I sent a letter to a hundred picked men in North Carolina, stating that I had bought the paper, outlining what I hoped to do with it, and asking each one to send $100 for one share of stock, saying it would be in the nature of preferred stock and whether the paper paid or not each stockholder would secure the daily edition free ($7.00) each year in lieu of dividend. The letter in my own handwriting was photostated and was as follows:

DEPARTMENT OF THE INTERIOR
WASHINGTON

Personal.

July 30th, 1894.

My dear Sir and Friend:

I have an option on the News and Observer. It is my desire and my ambition to purchase it and make it the best newspaper we have ever had at the capital. I believe that you will agree with me that just at this time there is pressing need for a daily and weekly at Raleigh that will be an aggressive exponent of Democracy, free from factions and favoritism. I believe that, with the proper help, I can make such a paper—one that would be in touch with the democracy of every county in the commonwealth; one that would be open to all shades of opinion within the party; one that would be as broad as the principles of our party are lasting.

A paper that would uphold and defend the principles of the party, and would not use its power to elevate favorites or punish enemies, would certainly succeed if it had sufficient capital to make it thoroughly independent. Alone I have not the money to make the purchase. I desire—and I desire it more earnestly than I can put into words—to interest 100 Democrats in the State in the purchase. If I can do that the success of the paper will be assured from the start. This would give *ten thousand dollars* in cash and good notes which would be sufficient to pay off all obligations and to purchase new and improved material. I write to request you to take one share of stock at the par value of $100.00. The investment will yield you 7% whether the company earns a dividend or not, i.e. you will receive the daily edition free. This will form a part of the contract.

I write to you because I believe you have confidence in my ability to make a successful paper, in my fairness to deal justly by all men, in my devotion to Democracy rather than for my partisanship for men; and also because I know your interest in the political and material welfare of the State.

I shall be personally grateful if these reasons induce you to make the investment with me. Every energy of my life will be given to make the enterprise a financial success.

As time is the essence of this business I beg that you will let me hear from you this week, enclosing a check or authorizing me to draw on you for $100; or if you prefer, send $50. cash and your note for $50. payable Jan. 1, 1895. Address me care Interior Department, Washington, D. C.

With sentiments of esteem and high regard, I am,

Sincerely yours,

JOSEPHUS DANIELS.

The responses to that letter were better than I expected. Out of the hundred letters sent, over seventy drew favorable responses immediately, and others later—and this in a period when money was so tight that $100 was as big as $1,000 is now. Most of those responding wrote letters which gave me much encouragement. Some offered to take additional stock.

On August 8, the sale having been confirmed, *The News and Ob-*

server announced that from what it had heard Josephus Daniels had obtained control of *The News and Observer*.

The directors elected at the first meeting of the stockholders were J. N. Holding, N. B. Broughton, C. M. Busbee, F. B. Arendell, W. N. Jones, R. T. Gray, and John B. Kenney. I was made president, J. N. Holding vice-president, H. W. Jackson secretary and treasurer, and R. T. Gray attorney. After a brief period, J. N. Holding sold his stock, and W. N. Jones became vice-president of the company as well as director, and H. W. Jackson became director as well as secretary and treasurer. Later Carey J. Hunter succeeded John B. Kenney, who was on the board of directors only a short time.

W. N. Jones, who became vice-president and remained in that place for a long time, was a tower of strength to the paper. He was a practical printer, had worked at the case, and, when he was a very young man, had gone out on a strike with the printers of Raleigh. He was conservative by nature and had gone on strike from a sense of loyalty to his fellow craftsmen. He often said that the strike was the best thing that happened to him, for being out of a job and having a few dollars, he went to Wake Forest, where he was educated, became trustee and attorney of the institution, read law, and for many years was an honored member of the Raleigh bar. We became warm friends. He was a man of sterling character. I found his judgment was sound, his friendship could be relied upon, and on many matters our convictions were similar. This was particularly true of questions affecting the liquor traffic and clean government in the city and county, and we waged many battles together for civic improvements. When the position of labor commissioner was established at the earnest request of Governor Scales, who had confidence in his conservatism, Jones accepted, but he continued his law practice. The law establishing the position of labor commissioner was not a good one, and with the limitations imposed by demand of mill owners very little could be done.

When the saloons were driven out of Raleigh and a dispensary established, Mr. Jones, although he did it with great reluctance, became one of the dispensary commissioners, believing that, by a dispensary, the evil influences of the liquor traffic could at least be lessened.

An incident occurred at his home on one occasion during the session of the Baptist State Convention, which he often told with great mirth. As president of the Convention, he was entertaining the most

Facsimile of the letter written by Josephus Daniels "to a hundred picked men in North Carolina" concerning his purchase of *The News and Observer*.

distinguished members of that body, preachers of North Carolina and visiting members. His wife, wishing to have a little wine in one of her desserts, sent down to the dispensary to make a purchase. Their young son, knowing that the wine had been purchased, shocked the good brethren at the table by calling out in a loud voice to his mother, "The man with your liquor is here." It created much amusement, for Jones was a consistent total abstainer.

To return to *The News and Observer,* H. W. Jackson, who became secretary and treasurer of the company, held that position until he moved to Richmond to become president of the Virginia Trust Company. His chief duties as secretary and treasurer of *The News and Observer* were to put up his own private collateral at the bank so that in hard times *The News and Observer* could borrow money to run on. His wise counsel was the strong right arm on which I knew I could always lean, especially in bad years. I had first known Jackson at the University of North Carolina. He was a senior when I went there in 1885 to read law. I was attracted to him at first meeting and we became warm friends. Our friendship ripened when we came to Raleigh. I went to him in all my business dilemmas, and if the situation was dark he would always quote a homespun philosophy. He said the wisest statement he had ever heard any mortal man make was that of an old farmer in Randolph County, who, mixing all the metaphors, gave this counsel: "Ef you keeps up hopes and stick to 'em, after a while you will crawl through." Jackson also had another piece of encouraging counsel for those who were struggling. "Russell Sage had a maxim," he said, "that next to a good bank account is a stiff upper lip." I often attributed the final success of *The News and Observer* as much to a stiff upper lip and to Jackson's advice in financial matters as to anything else. In the hard years of 1894, 1895, and 1896 the paper had to borrow money every summer to carry it through, and the Commercial National Bank of Raleigh, of which Jackson was an officer, loaned me money on security that the bank examiner would not have passed. Jackson put up his own collateral to guarantee the loan and sometimes he did this without saying a word to me about it.

When I purchased *The News and Observer* and consolidated it with my weekly *North Carolinian* it was my heart's desire to call the combined papers *The North Carolinian.* My interest then in the outside world was secondary. My horizon, except for quadrennial interest in national politics, was centered in my native State. I returned home to serve in its educational, political, industrial, and religious progress. Therefore, the name *North Carolinian* fixed both the home of its publication and its spirit. Moreover there had gone into the consolidated papers the hopes, labors, and disappointments of a score of high-minded writers and patriots who had spent themselves in the endeavor to build up a prosperous and useful journal. Before my purchase *The News and Observer* had become the residuary of the unsuccessful *Sentinel, News, State Chronicle, Observer,* and *Intelligencer,* and maybe other paper ghosts. My paper really represented the forward looking spirit of the *State Chronicle* and the *Farmer and Mechanic.* It seemed to me there was no name so suitable for the paper I hoped to make as the name of my State. I argued with friends that *The News and Observer* had no significance as to its habitat— that it might as well be printed in Maine as in North Carolina, whereas the name *The North Carolinian* had tar on its heels and would represent and speak for the State whose name it bore and no other name was so fitting for a paper at North Carolina's capital. My friends and family, advertising agents, subscribers, directors, all opposed my suggestion. They said the old name had history and prestige, that to change the name would be like starting a new paper. "The people are accustomed to call their morning Raleigh paper *The News and Observer* if they like it, and 'The Nuisance Disturber' if they don't like it, and if you change the name now in the transition of editors, advertisers will think it is a new paper and advertisers steer clear of new papers." One friend, combating my desire for the change of name, said, "You might as well change your name from Josephus Daniels to Walter Raleigh." I countered by saying, "That would be an improvement, but my mother, seeing I was named for my father, would veto it." I had to yield to superior numbers, though if the paper had been paying well I would have taken the chance. But as I was buying a paper showing a monthly deficit I did not dare to make the venture, much as I wished to do so. For some years the new company printed two weekly papers—virtually a semi-weekly —one called *The North Carolinian* and the other the *Farmer and Mechanic*—the latter chiefly devoted to agriculture and labor and industry. When the time came that weeklies made up out of a daily no longer had a field in an era of free rural delivery, we stopped their publication and concentrated on the daily. I still cherish the desire to print a high-grade weekly named *The North Carolinian*. Some day I may do it.

The first thing I did with *The News and Observer* was to buy new type and change the form and drop the name *Chronicle* from the masthead in its initial issue under my management, that of August 12. New, better and bigger headlines were introduced. General Carr, my financial backer, took personal interest in the enterprise and caused a new head to be drawn, which made the title-page carry typical North Carolina symbols. A print of it appears in this volume. General Carr, who had an artistic taste, was much pleased with the new heading, and I liked it, but critics poked fun at it and said it made the paper look like a country sheet. I answered, "It is a country paper, racy of the soil. Why shouldn't it look the part?" Later when the paper was converted from four into eight narrower pages, General Carr's ornamental head had to be discarded because it was too wide. Its place was taken by the simple one now familiar to all the paper's readers.

One of the early reforms was to take all advertisements off the front page. Up to that time a part of the front page was filled with advertisements. Indeed that was the practice of many newspapers of the period. It was not until many years later that the Baltimore *Sun* and the Springfield *Republican,* among the last, denied advertisers the right to appear on the first page.

After buying the paper, but before the announcement was made, I had seen William E. Christian in Washington and had engaged him to go to Raleigh and take a position on the staff of the paper. He was a grandson of Mr. John Branch, the leading Richmond banker, and had married the daughter of Stonewall Jackson. He had done some brilliant writing on New York papers, had been editor of a paper in San Diego, and had been half owner of the Charlotte *Democrat* along with W. J. Yates, the veteran journalist of the State. He had an original style and indulged in descriptive powers which attracted much attention. He was the type of journalist who worked brilliantly when the spirit moved him but was not suited for the regular work day by day. In the 1894 and 1896 campaigns particularly he did some splendid writing. He had the knack of making fun of political opponents by describing their peculiarities and by combining half praise and half knocks, which was something new in North Carolina journalism. His writings were greatly enjoyed, and those whom he ridiculed generally took it in good part. As an example of the descriptive powers, his story of his first visit to the Democratic headquarters with his description of James H. Pou, state chairman, is illustrative. He described him as "a smooth-shaven gentleman with a face of thirty-five and a voice of seventy, with an affidavit appearance and the air of mystery about him." His interviews with Marion Butler and Spier Whitaker and Harry Skinner and other leaders of the Populist Party were out of the usual line. The high-water mark of his writings in that period told the story of his entering the office of the judge of the Superior Court of Wake County at midnight and finding closeted there Marion Butler, the head of the Populist Party and Judge Spier Whitaker former Democratic State Chairman. Shortly before that time in the Democratic primary, Judge Whitaker had been defeated for re-nomination by William R. Allen, of Wayne, and I had been active in the support of Allen's candidacy. With his other friends and many relatives we had succeeded in carrying Wake County for Allen against Whitaker, who lived in Wake. He was very sore over his defeat. In resentment he immediately resigned his seat on the bench and Allen was appointed by Governor Carr to succeed him. Not long before the primary, I printed a story about an order Whitaker gave when holding court in Johnston County which made him very unpopular with the farmers all over the district. He was presiding in Smithfield on one of the hottest days in history. In accordance with immemorial custom, the farmers who came in the court room and were selected to serve on the jury wore no coats. Sitting in their shirt sleeves, and collarless, they passed upon questions presented to the jury. Judge Whitaker announced that this was disrespect to the court, and directed that every man who served upon a jury or came into his court should show his respect by wearing his coat. Few of the farmers had brought their coats to town. It infuriated them and when they had a chance to vote for another judge, Whitaker didn't get enough votes in farm districts to know he was running. But that was not the only reason he was defeated. While an able lawyer, he put on more "lugs" than pleased North Carolina people. Allen was quite the reverse, very popular, with almost enough kinsfolk to turn the tide if the vote had been close.

The other member of the editorial staff was Fred L. Merritt, who had been editor of *The North Carolinian*. He was really the managing editor and had real ability. He had been elected to the Legislature from

Upper left, W. N. Jones, Vice-President and Director of *The News and Observer* and President of the Baptist State Convention. *Upper right,* R. T. Gray, lawyer and director and attorney of *The News and Observer. Lower left,* J. N. Holding, member of the Raleigh Bar, who purchased *The News and Observer* for Josephus Daniels. *Lower right,* Cary J. Hunter, director of the *The News and Observer* and leading Baptist.

Facsimile of *The News and Observer* of August 16, 1894, showing the new head which General Carr caused to have drawn. In the design are national and state emblems. The picture is that of Charles Mather Cooke, of Franklin County, whose nomination for Congressman from the Fourth District is announced in this issue.

Wake County immediately after his graduation from Wake Forest College, and he made quite a local reputation as a young political speaker in the campaign. He had edited *The North Carolinian* from the time I went to Washington until he transferred to *The News and Observer* when I purchased it. He and Christian both wrote editorials. I wrote a number of them and sent them down from Washington. Merritt was methodical, careful, and accurate and he and Christian made a good team. The work divided itself at first by Christian's really becoming the city editor and Merritt the managing editor and editorial writer.

F. B. Arendell, who had been with Page on the *State Chronicle* in a business capacity, came on the paper as travelling representative. He wrote articles from various parts of the State, solicited advertisements and subscriptions, and grew into a capable political correspondent in the campaigns which followed. He often accompanied the candidates to the speaking places and was so fond of the political game that it was hard to tie him down to soliciting advertisements. In the campaigns of 1896 and 1898 he was particularly effective. He could go into a crowd and sense its feeling, and while he was not a trained journalist his descriptions of political meetings were so graphic and accurate that Democratic speakers would ask that Arendell be sent to accompany them. Political speakers do not like to have what they say reported very accurately because they make practically the same speech throughout the campaign. Arendell quoted very little from their speeches but would quote from people who heard them and would give the atmosphere of the meeting. He did it so realistically that his reports were Democratic propaganda and made people in the next town anxious to hear the speaker. He did not stay with the paper very long, but became associated with the B. F. Johnson Book Publishing Company. His large acquaintance with public men of the state and his persuasiveness enabled him to secure the adoption of their school books. Up to that time he had never had any title, but going to Tennessee to represent his book house, he asked me for a letter of introduction to influential public men. He suggested that in writing, instead of calling him 'Mister' I should call him 'Colonel,' saying that it would give him more influence with people if they thought he had a title. I wrote a letter to friends and newspaper men in Tennessee introducing my good friend, "Colonel F. B. Arendell, who had long been of the staff of my paper" and commending him highly. Some of the papers printed my letter and ever thereafter my former associate in journalism was known as Colonel. He said it was worth many dollars to him. He is the only man I ever knew to be given the title of colonel who had not won it in war, who was frank enough to adopt it without any pretense of military service.

For a long time John Wilber Jenkins was on the staff of *The News and Observer,* first in charge of the Durham Bureau and afterwards coming to Raleigh and serving as city editor. In the 1895 Legislature, Christian covered the House and Jenkins the Senate. In 1896 he became editor of the Charlotte *News* and returned to Raleigh as editor of the *Times* in 1900. This was not my first association with Mr. Jenkins, for he was on the staff of the *State Chronicle* in the early nineties at the time that George P. Pell was city editor. Pell and Jenkins made a good team, starting as journalists when mere boys. Pell afterward won high position as Superior Court Judge and served for a long time on the Corporation Commision.

The two road field marshals of the paper were H. B. Hardy and Wiley M. Rogers. They travelled from county seat to county seat soliciting subscribers and renewals. Rogers had been with *The News and Observer* under Captain Ashe, and Hardy had been with me on the Wilson *Advance, State Chronicle,* and *North Carolinian.* In addition to his ability to get subscribers and collect money, Wiley Rogers could sense the political situation in any county he was visiting, better than anybody else in the state. He did it because nobody ever thought he was trying to interview him. His only business seemed to be to get subscribers. He never called the paper *The News and Observer* but always called it "The Old Reliable," and when he would come in on Saturday night with his subscriptions and money, I made it a point to find out from him the drift of sentiment. His instinct was unerring. It was from Hardy and Rogers that I first sensed the fear that the Democrats would lose the State in 1894 and communicated it to State Chairman Pou. He thought they were mere newspaper drummers and didn't know what they were talking about. I thought he knew much more about it than they did, but then and afterwards I came to rely upon Rogers in many ways.

There was no man who travelled in the State in those days—and it was a day of a host of capable and popular drummers (in fact, the commercial tourists had great influence in politics in North Carolina at that time)—who was more popular than H. B. Hardy, 'Ben Hardy,' as everybody called him. He loved people, loved to go among them. He was quite a musician and at the courts would give concerts, always using his musical gifts to further his business of soliciting subscribers. We were sworn friends from boyhood and I had an affection for him and he for me that was dear to both of us and lasting.

With these two men in the field on the subscription line, the circulation of the paper steadily increased. They never had to be told that when the paper was making a fight they ought to go to the town where they could further the interests of the paper and cash in on the paper's policy. If, for instance, a story was in the paper boosting a town or some industry, or had in any way pleased the people of the town, Hardy or Rogers was in that town the next morning and rolling up a big list of subscribers. They were hard times, too, 1894, 1895, and 1896—days when money was as scarce as hen's teeth—and their success under those conditions was a great test of their salesmanship and of devotion to the paper.

The typographical department was well organized also. J. C. Birdsong, who had been State librarian, an old-time Confederate soldier-printer, was foreman, and Samuel Bogasse was assistant foreman. When Mr. Birdsong retired, Mr. Bogasse took his place. He was an artist as well as a printer. Bad typographical appearance was to him a sin.

When the organization of the corporation was effected and I had gone to Raleigh and set the sails of the ship, I was in a dilemma as to what I should do. I was chief clerk of the Interior Department with a salary of $2,750, was living in Washington on half that amount, saving everything possible, and sending half the salary to Raleigh to keep *The North Carolinian* going. I debated whether, having secured what I regarded as a capable staff for the paper, it would be better for me to remain in Washington for a time, send the paper $125 a month, and write the editorials and Washington news from the capital, or to go home. I decided to stay on the remainder of that year and see how matters worked out. Having reached this conclusion, I made a suggestion to Captain Ashe that he accept a place on the paper to write editorials. I think this proffer pleased him, showing that I had kind feelings after our wide disagreements, but he declined—very naturally, too—because the clash between us of policies and opinions, rather than of political convictions, might have been embarrassing. Moreover he was the older man and abler and probably would not have felt that he could write on the paper without full authority when for so long a time he had laid down the law.

During the Christmas holidays of 1894 I went to Raleigh to confer with my friends as to my duty, and early in the New Year (1895) resigned my position in the Interior Department and printed the following as the leading editorial in *The News and Observer:*

ANNOUNCEMENT

I have resigned my position in Washington, D. C., and returned to Raleigh to undertake the active editorial management of The News and Observer upon its entrance on its 38th volume.

Never in the history of the State, except in the similar evil days of 1868-69, was there greater need of a fearless newspaper at the capital of the State to expose the revolutionary proceedings of the men whom chance and conspiracy have temporarily put in control of the destiny of the Commonwealth.

In this crisis that confronts the patriotic people of my State, I could not feel that I was doing my whole duty, as a son, in any other way than by becoming an active member of the army that must needs band together to redeem the State from the rule of prejudice and revolution.

The people of North Carolina are at heart patriotic, honest and conservative. They love peace, concord and justice. They want to control their own destinies and will not brook boss rule. They have fallen on evil times and have felt the burden of low prices and unjust legislation. Because in two years the Democratic party did not undo the bad legislation of a quarter of a century of Republican misrule, many good men voted against its candidates last November and many more did not vote at all. The Democratic party deserved a measure of rebuke because it had not done its full duty. But in the disappointment incident to continued depression, the Government of the State was turned over to incompetent and in some instances corrupt hands.

The people have been deceived and grievously are they repenting of the results of November's election. When the high-handed proceedings of this revolutionary body are fully known, there will be a revolutionary feeling, and those who "prefer reform to office" will repudiate the men who have betrayed their trust and sought to carry them bag and baggage into the Republican party.

I have never lost faith in what Mr. Lincoln called the plain people. I know the honesty of purpose that actuates them, and I know that they are and ever have been devoted to the fundamental doctrines of the party of Jefferson and Vance. Those who are honest Populists will shrink from the unholy alliance, falsely called marriage, which selfish men, for money or office, have procured to be celebrated between them and their ancient enemy.

"The Populist party was organized as a protest against the legislation of the Republican party," was the Populist slogan three years ago. Now, these who have been the trusted leaders of the Populists have either formally joined the Republican party, or what is worse, are acting the part of Dr. Jekyll and Mr. Hyde, and pretending to the Populists to be Populist, while at the same time promising the Republicans to stand by them in every emergency. These two-faced men may win place and position for a while but the day will come when their hypocrisy will be exposed and their sin uncovered and they will be seen in their true light and detested by all good men.

In the contest for the redemption of North Carolina, the State calls upon every son to do his full duty. Just as certain as light follows darkness, as truth crowds out error, as right succeeds over wrong, just so sure will the Democratic party be called again to administer the affairs of the State. For twenty-five years this party of the people has been in *control*. Not a breath of suspicion of *corruption* attaches to its record. This will not be forgotten. The contrast will make the record shine with increased brightness and with one accord the good people will call the Democratic party back to deliver them from "the body of this death."

As an humble worker in the ranks of Democracy I have come home to join in the fight for the redemption of the State.

JOSEPHUS DANIELS

In 1895 *The News and Observer,* with qualms and fears, purchased three Mergenthaler lintoype machines and installed them in its office. No linotype machines had at that time been brought to North Carolina. Their installation was decided upon because the cost of publishing the paper was always equal to and sometimes exceeded the receipts. Investigation showed that type could be set cheaper on the linotypes even counting the investment. Before taking the step, I had seen the working of these machines in Washington City. I therefore sent L. F. Alford, a practical and skilled printer who had learned the trade with me on the Wilson *Advance,* and who had had two years' experience in the Government Printing Office, to the factory

7/34

LEE COUNTY LIBRARY
SANFORD, N. C.

at Brooklyn to learn all about the machines. He reported favorably, and after he had learned to operate them we bought three machines and Alford came to Raleigh in charge of them. The introduction of these machines was almost as much a sensation in 1895 as the visit of an aeroplane to Raleigh in 1917. I had been thinking for a year about installing them, not only on account of the cost of hand composition but also because of its slowness, and had been deterred from it largely by the fact that their introduction would necessarily lay off some of the old-time printers who had reached a place in life when they could not be transferred from the case to the machine. I talked to them freely about it. The older ones were opposed to the innovation. The younger ones were keen for it. Strange to say, I was so doubtful about their operation in Raleigh, where there were few skilled men, that I kept the old type to be set by hand ready for any emergency. It was not until some months of operation that we felt safe in selling the old type and relying solely on the linotype. People from all over the state coming to Raleigh would make *The News and Observer* office their chief place of interest. A reception was given when the type-setting machines were installed and Raleigh people came in droves. I remember very well what the Honorable Cyrus B. Watson, leading lawyer and Democratic candidate for governor in 1896, said about them after watching them for an hour. "Why," he said, "these machines have more sense than most men. If I come back to the Legislature, I am going to introduce a bill to give them the right to vote." It took some time to teach the old-fashioned printers to run the linotypes, but in a brief time some of the youngest ones became as expert and fast operators as could be found anywhere.

About the time I resigned my position to return to Raleigh, Bill Russ, popular and witty clerk of the court, said to me, "I hear you are thinking of throwing up your paying job in Washington [$2,750 a year] and coming back to Raleigh to try to make a living running a daily newspaper." I told him I had resigned and was coming back home to run the paper. He looked at me as if I were little more than a moron and said, "You are certainly one damn fool." He had been clerk on the *News* and had written locals for the paper when it failed. That experience made him pity my folly. A few years later, when times were hard and I had to borrow money to meet the pay-roll, I dropped in the Clerk's office one day and this conversation ensued:

"Bill, do you remember what you said to me when I threw up my

job in Washington and came home to run *The News and Observer?"*
I asked.

"Yes," he replied. "I told you that you were a damn fool to try to
do what a dozen other men had tried to do and failed."

"You were right," I answered in my depression.

But we were both wrong. I never did a more daring or a wiser
thing.

Not long after my return to Raleigh (1895) I had occasion to visit
Washington, and at that time I was invited to come to the Interior
Department at a certain hour. When I arrived I found the large office
of the Chief Clerk filled with friends with whom I had served. I observed beautiful silver on a desk in the center of the room and I was
presented, for myself and my wife, in words of cordiality, with a case
of silver teaspoons, knives, and forks, given by the watchmen and
messengers and a large Louis XV berry bowl and spoon, salad fork
and spoon, and a dozen individual berry forks by other officials of
the Department.

Under the rules no money could be solicited in the Department for
a token to an official. My friends, therefore, waited, without my
knowledge, until two months after I was in private life to make the
presentation.

XI

THE OPENING GUNS IN THE WAR
ON THE UNIVERSITY

D URING THE campaign of 1894 the antagonism of denominational
colleges to appropriations for the university and other state
colleges, blazed forth. Prior to that time, representatives of the Baptist,
Methodist, and Presbyterian colleges had gone to the Legislature and
protested against appropriating money, particularly to the University,
unless it would agree to change its course so as to admit only post-
graduates. Their opposition, while not successful, had helped to keep
down the appropriation to the University. The heads of the church
colleges felt that enlargement of the University meant the impair-
ment of attendance at their colleges. Up to 1894, however, this issue
had never been prominent in politics except in a county here and
there, but the Reverend Columbus Durham, who was called Secretary of the Baptist State Convention—a position which gave him
more power than a Bishop—had organized his church so that the
bulk of its preachers and many of its laymen were antagonistic to the
University. In Wake County the Fusion candidate for the Legislature
made attacks upon the University, and in quite a number of other
counties they did likewise, and were encouraged thereto by some of
the denominational leaders. These Fusionists thought that by taking
such a course they could draw to their support the leaders of the
church colleges. Undoubtedly in some counties this helped, but in the
main the city church people voted the Democratic ticket and a number of country preachers and country laymen voted the Populist
ticket. Comparatively few were influenced in their vote by the school
question.

The Reverend Columbus Durham was a remarkable man. A native of Cleveland County, he was a brother of Plato Durham, who
had been a conspicuous leader of the Ku Klux Klan and member of
the Constitutional Convention, a man of brilliant parts, who died
early. The Reverend Columbus Durham was an intense man without
the least shadow of humor. He asked no quarter and gave none. He

Members of the editorial staff of *The News and Observer: Upper left*, John Wilber Jenkins. *Upper right*, Fred L. Merritt. *Lower left*, W. E. Christian. *Lower right*, F. B. (Falc) Arendell.

Upper left, Leroy F. Alford, mechanical superintendent of *The News and Observer* since November 1, 1895. *Upper right,* Herbert W. Jackson, treasurer of *The News and Observer* and its financial angel. Later president of the Virginia Trust Company. *Lower left,* Wiley M. Rogers, circulation manager of *The News and Observer.* *Lower right,* H. B. Hardy, who, with Rogers, was one of the "road field marshals" of the paper.

convinced himself that the prosperity of the University would work to the injury of Wake Forest College. He believed the success of Wake Forest College was essential to the Baptist Church. With this premise, he set out to destroy anything that stood in the way. He travelled over the State to Baptist associations and with ability, vigor, and viciousness attacked everybody and everything that stood against his propaganda.

At that time the Presbyterian and Methodist churches, except in small numbers, were not as zealous as Dr. Durham had induced many Baptists to be. However, Dr. Charles E. Taylor, President of Wake Forest College, one of the best scholars and one of the gentlest men that ever lived, had, under the influence of Dr. Durham, written a pamphlet against "State Aid," as it was called, for higher institutions of learning. It was temperate and able and by all odds the best argument issued during the period when the contest was bitterly fought in the State. Of course Dr. Taylor's pamphlet lost much of its significance when I and others pointed out that Wake Forest College would never have been blessed with so able a man as Dr. Taylor if he had not been educated at the University of Virginia; that his whole education was due to Jefferson's wisdom in establishing a State University. After writing this pamphlet, Dr. Taylor had very little to say. He was so sweet a spirit that he could not join in the sort of campaign which Dr. Durham and Dr. Kilgo waged. His life was bound up in books, in teaching young men, in the sweet influences that touched the lives of every young man who went to Wake Forest College and of all who knew him. The bitterness that came up in my relations with Dr. Durham, had its compensation in the delightful remembrance of the very dear friendship between Dr. Taylor and myself and our wives. He had made his argument, an argument which his church leaders felt he ought to make, and then he stood aside while the more vigorous men who loved a fight went to the front.

Dr. Taylor started in North Carolina something that his successors followed. Every commencement we looked forward to his address to the graduating class. It was always brief—a perfect piece of English —and had about it beauty and strength and the best and broadest Christian spirit. For many years I never missed going to Wake Forest College commencement and for two reasons: first, to hear Dr. Taylor deliver the address to the graduating class—it was the event of the

year in the college as long as he was President—and second, my wife
and I were always invited to dine at Dr. Taylor's (whose wife and
daughters were choice spirits), and we always had frozen raspber-
ries. Nothing quite so delightful ever tempted my appetite. I do not
know which I enjoyed more, Dr. Taylor's address or the frozen rasp-
berries, but I remember them both as a combination making most
delightful commencement occasions. He laid deep and broad the cul-
tural life of Wake Forest and drew around him half a dozen of the
best scholars in the South, of whom Laneau, Royal, Poteat, Sledd,
Sikes, and Carlyle to mention only those who were most prominent
in the public eye, were men of rare gifts. He was not a money-getter
in the sense that modern college presidents must be, but it was Dr.
Taylor who interested James A. Bostick in Wake Forest College.
Bostick was of the Standard Oil group, not so rich as the Rockefellers,
Flaglers, and others, but he had millions. He was a Baptist and Dr.
Taylor went to see him in New York and won his friendship and
admiration. In very lean years Mr. Bostick helped Dr. Taylor, and
later because of Dr. Taylor, even though he had passed away, Wake
Forest received more than a million dollars from the Bostick fund.

The issue of "State aid to higher institutions of learning," which
was the phrase employed by the opponents to State colleges, was in-
tensified by Dr. John C. Kilgo in the election of 1894. Dr. Kilgo later
became quite as vigorous and quite as vicious against State appropriations for higher institutions of learning as Dr. Durham. After Trinity
College moved to Durham, Dr. Crowell, its President, found that the
income was much less than his ambitious plans demanded. As a
speaker, he did not arouse the interest of the people and the college
did not prosper under him as its friends desired. There came friction
between the faculty and trustees and he resigned. To succeed him,
Dr. Kilgo, of South Carolina, was elected President. He was a South
Carolinian Methodist preacher who had a sort of hypnotic eloquence
at times. It was said in South Carolina that he had been an ardent
Tillmanite and had lost caste by his intense radicalism. However that
may be, if he ever had any radicalism in South Carolina, he packed
it up and threw it into the Pee Dee River before he crossed into North
Carolina, for from the time he arrived, he associated himself with
influences that could not have had any sympathy with Tillman or
with tillers of the soil.

Hardly had the Legislature been organized before the plans already matured to fight even necessary appropriations for the University and other State colleges materialized. There was a sensation every day during that Legislature, but not one of them created as much interest in educational circles as did that staged between the advocates of the University and other State institutions on the one hand, and the opponents of necessary appropriations for their growth and expansion, on the other. The debate was staged with all the settings for a great conflict. Dr. George T. Winston, President of the University, and Dr. Columbus Durham, the two leaders of the fight, were on hand. Durham, who didn't know a joke if he met it in the road, was terribly in earnest, with sledge-hammer blows hitting at all the enemies of his policy right and left; Winston was suave and witty, though feeling that the life of the institution was at stake. Each had summoned the best forces at his command. Most of the leaders of the Republicans and Populists in the Legislature were on Dr. Durham's side. He believed that the hour had come when the University could be placed in what he called its proper place; that is, at the apex of education, not teaching the regular branches, which were pursued by most of its students, but working on so advanced a level that it could not in any way draw students who might attend the church colleges.

The debate was hot and furious from beginning to end. Dr. Durham denied that he was trying to tear down the University and declared that he was fighting the sentiment that there was no place in the educational system for denominational schools. He also declared it to be his belief that the wisest policy was to separate the University in toto from the State, give it a self-perpetuating board, let its friends throughout the whole country come to its rescue, endow it, and stop forever the row before every recurring Legislature. That policy, of course, would have destroyed the University, because its life depended, as does every other State university to a large degree, upon appropriations from the public treasury. In one breath Dr. Durham said he didn't want to tear it down, and in the next, that he wanted to put it in the same place with denominational colleges, dependent upon gifts from its wealthy friends. The University had no wealthy friends and its advocates, while they would welcome endowment, would never consent to have it supported wholly in that way, for it would then cease to be a State university and would become a private institution influenced by its rich supporters. Dr.

Durham could not see that education for all, from the lowest to the highest, was a State duty, and yet he resented it deeply when *The News and Observer* said he was fighting the University. He declared that no institution had ever been made a great university while it had its hand in the treasury. *The News and Observer* had been going at him pretty hard and it had got under his skin; so he turned in his address and made an attack upon the paper and declared, "Josephus Daniels is not fit to run a newspaper." In its account of Dr. Durham's address, *The News and Observer* said, "and then the great orator and statesman and sometime minister of the gospel sat down." The next day *The News and Observer* answered Dr. Durham's attack upon it in kind, saying:

> "Because of his connections, we have admitted to this paper contributions from Dr. Durham's pen that ought never to have seen the light and which if written in his personal capacity could not have cumbered these columns, but while showing many courtesies, we respectfully decline to permit Dr. Durham to exclude all other matter from the paper in order to make place for his lengthy epistles. Our declination to vacate the tripod in his favor probably accounts for his unmannerly and ungentlemanly attack made in our absence without provocation. If Dr. Taylor would be rid of the incubus of Dr. Durham's advocacy of Wake Forest, he would have an increase of one hundred more students in the next twelve months. Wake Forest is a great institution in spite of Dr. Durham."

President Winston brought in his big guns. Charles B. Aycock, a Baptist, then district attorney and later governor, expressed the very gist of the Durham propaganda when at the climax of an eloquent address which stirred all present he said: "The gentlemen have said 'We love the University. God bless it! We therefore will take away its appropriation!'"

But Aycock was a Democrat and the Legislature was Fusion. Dr. Winston was wise enough to bring into play, or rather give way to, influential men in the other party to do the most effective firing. Daniel L. Russell, afterwards the Republican Governor, who had been educated at the University, spoke strongly in favor of its large support, and after he had finished, the most eloquent Negro politician of his day, who was then a power in the Fusion cause, the Reverend R. H. W. Leak, Methodist preacher of Raleigh, unlim-

Upper left, Rev. Columbus Durham, prominent Baptist preacher and leader of the opposition to appropriations for the University of North Carolina. *Upper right,* Rev. John C. Kilgo, president of Trinity College; Methodist Bishop; foe of the University of North Carolina. *Lower left,* Rev. John E. White, distinguished Baptist preacher, who succeeded Columbus Durham as corresponding secretary of the Baptist Convention. *Lower right,* Dr. Charles E. Taylor, president of Wake Forest College.

Upper left, Needham B. Broughton, joint owner, with Dr. C. T. Bailey and C. B. Edwards, of the *Biblical Recorder*. *Upper right,* C. B. Edwards, who refused to allow an article attacking Broughton to be printed in the *Biblical Recorder*. *Lower left,* Benjamin N. Duke, vice-president of the American Tobacco Company. *Lower right,* J. B. Duke, founder of the American Tobacco Company.

bered himself and said he never expected to see the day when a poor Negro would have to come before the Legislature of his State and beg them not to tear down an educational institution. "I couldn't go and none of my race can go," he said, "but you can always count on the Negroes. We are going to ask for a university for ourselves, and help, and the State ought not to withdraw a dollar it is paying to any institution of learning." The introduction of Leak into the discussion infuriated Dr. Durham, who charged Dr. Winston with seeking Negro support. But the great speech that defeated the fight against the University appropriation was made by Major W. A. Guthrie, of Durham, a leader of the Populist forces. He was in Danville when he heard the meeting had been called to consider the appropriation and learned that members of his party were about to, as he called it, "commit suicide by fighting the University." Major Guthrie was born in Chapel Hill, had gone out of it when he was a boy into the Confederate Army, had returned and married there the sister of General Julian S. Carr, and had a love for it almost surpassing the love of a man for his wife. After the war, Guthrie had joined the Republican Party and had been its most eloquent supporter in Fayetteville, where he lived for a time; but he had become disgusted with it and had gone with great enthusiasm into the Populist Party because he believed the two old parties had lost their virtue and vigor. He believed there was a call in the country for a new party that would get rid of all the old issues and divisions.

Somebody in Raleigh telegraphed him at Danville that the fight against University appropriations was to come up and he dropped everything, hurried to Raleigh, and said, "I have come to save my party from making a fool of itself. I didn't join the Populist Party to see it turn its back upon education." He was itching for a fight and had told most of his friends he was going to make the fur fly. And he did. When he finished, there wasn't anything left of Dr. Durham's lurid arguments, and the mild arguments of other speakers had been destroyed, and nobody afterwards could get up any real fight in that Legislature. Guthrie blew up the whole machinery and scattered its parts so that its engines couldn't toot again that year.

Major Guthrie knew that Durham was the big man, and he knew that Durham had great power and influence; so he went after him with hammer and tongs. He said he hoped "the time will come when newspaper men will edit their newspapers and preachers will fill their pulpits and let the country have peace." He showed that Dr. Durham's opposition, however he might feel, was really to destroy the University; that the University was imbedded in the State constitution; and that legislators were by oath compelled to support it. And if Dr. Durham and other advocates would come out in the open and show their real purpose, instead of fighting with the fine Italian hand, to injure it, they would demand that the clause of the constitution establishing the University be taken out. But as long as that clause was there, every man who took the oath to support the constitution was bound to support the University.

Not only did Russell, afterwards to be Governor, and Major Guthrie go before the committee, but Marion Butler, who had more influence than anybody else in the Populist Party, threw the weight of his influence to the University, of which he was a graduate, although he made no speech. At a meeting in February of the National Farmers' Alliance and Industrial Union in Raleigh, Butler declared that the University "is the best property the State owns although it costs the State very little money," adding, "The University educates many poor boys who could not acquire equal education elsewhere." He declared it was the head of the public school system of the State and cost each taxpayer less than four cents a year. In that speech, but even more so in his private conversation with the Populists in the Legislature, Butler did yeoman service for his alma mater. In all the political bitterness of that day—and no words can describe it—University men always felt that they were under obligation to Butler in that crisis although Guthrie deserved the greatest credit for his eloquent and convincing speech and for taking the laboring oar in the big debate.

It was during this session of the Legislature that Bill Bryan, of Chatham, Populist member of the House, received the name of "Little Bill Bryan," by which he went ever afterwards. He introduced a bill to take away all the appropriations from the University, and when the bill came up for consideration, he sought to convey the impression that it was a local measure of no importance. He said that it was a "little bill," and but for the vigilance of the reporters, its destructiveness might never have been discovered. They found out what it was about and called it to the attention of members of the Legislature, who demanded that it be explained before it was voted on. When it was read and found to be a "little bill" taking away all appropriation from the University, even those who would have liked to reduce the appropriation, could not stand for it and it was tabled, with great contempt for "Little Bill Bryan," who gained other notoriety as member of The Pee Dee Bee Commission.

During the long-drawn-out fight against adequate or even small appropriations for the University, a small Baptist association in the mountains and one in a Piedmont county, where *The News and Observer's* circulation was not large, passed resolutions saying *"The News and Observer* is an enemy of the Baptist church." This troubled some of my friends, but my answer was effective. I said that if the good people who voted for the resolution had read the paper they would not have voted for it. Further, I answered:

"As proof that the North Carolina Baptists regard The News and Observer as friendly to the Baptist church and its institutions, W. N. Jones, President of the Baptist State Convention and trustee of Wake Forest College, is vice-president of The News and Observer Company and a stockholder and director; N. B. Broughton, Secretary of the Baptist State Convention and trustee of Meredith, is a stockholder and director; and Cary J. Hunter, President of the Board of Trustees of Wake Forest College, is a stockholder and director—that these three leading laymen could not be induced to support the paper if it were not a champion of the moral causes which the Baptist church champions. In addition, other trustees and members of the faculty of Wake Forest and Meredith College are stockholders and staunch friends of the paper, and at various times the Managing Editors, the Associate Editors, City Editors, Sports Editors, and in fact most members of the staff of the paper are or have been graduates of Wake Forest and could not be induced to help make a paper inimical to their alma mater and their church."

That ended the charge. As a matter of fact I proved that Dr. Durham and others in their zeal for their college were departing from the fundamental principle of the Baptist Church—the complete separation of Church and State. They had felt the hard hand of a State establishment of Church; their preachers had suffered persecution in the Old World; the New England Church establishment had driven their great preacher, Roger Williams, out because he would not conform; the Virginia Episcopal Church, State controlled, had put Baptist preachers in jail "for the crime of preaching the Gospel"; and in colonial days there had been modified persecution of Baptists and Quakers by church establishment in North Carolina. I stressed that the iron of opposition to State direction of Church or Church direction of State had entered their souls. Not even their best trusted leaders could induce many of them to countenance, even if not direct, any practice that tended in the direction of dictation of State by Church or Church by State. I quoted the highest Baptist authorities throughout the long years against the trend in the dangerous direction of the course pursued by Dr. Durham. I said that I would not trust John Calvin or John Wesley or Cardinal Wolsey or the Pope of Rome to influence government, or trust Constantine or Henry VIII or Napoleon or Governor Berkeley to have voice in directing the Church.

In my paper I called on Baptists and Methodists and all others to accept the sound and essential principle that it was the first duty of the State to provide public schools for all, from primary to the postgraduate instruction, without any denominational instruction, and to require compulsory attendance of all children. I stressed the sound doctrine that it was the inherent right of parents to send their children to a church or private school if they preferred such an instruction and were willing to pay for it, but if tax-payers of any church undertook to say to the State: "Thus far shalt thou go in providing public instruction and no further," they were opening a crack in the door that would lead to uniting the functions of Church and State. I declared, and reiterated, that likewise if the State should say to the Church: "Thou shalt preach this doctrine or provide this course of study," the State would be invading the sacred and God-given powers of religious bodies. All my arguments had the sanction of Baptists from the earliest time, who had preferred persecution to accepting dictation in the relations between man and his Maker.

In this year (1895), upon the death of Dr. C. T. Bailey, his son Josiah William Bailey, who was to be active first in his church and then in politics and was later to go to the United States Senate, became editor of the *Biblical Recorder*. He began his career by the most intemperate denunciation of the right of women to preach. His father had held the same view, but, in comparison to the vigorous opposition of the son, the father was mild. The paper was owned jointly by N. B. Broughton, C. B. Edwards, and Josiah W. Bailey. Mr. Broughton was a very ardent Christian, and whenever there was a religious revival going on, all business had to take second place. One week Mr. Broughton left his business and went to Greensboro to take an active part in a revival being held by a Quaker woman evangelist. While he was there, young Bailey wrote an editorial for the *Biblical Recorder,* severely berating Broughton. "Mr. Faucette, the printer, brought the editorial to me," Mr. Edwards later told me, saying, "Of course I have no right to supervise what young Mr. Bailey writes, but I felt it my duty to show you this editorial because I could not conceive it was the proper thing for an editor to write such an article about one of his partners in his absence and without his knowledge." Mr. Edwards added, "I told Mr. Faucette to lose the article and not let it go in the *Recorder* and, if Bailey said anything to him, to tell him that he had freedom to write anything he chose on Baptist doctrine and religious subjects but he could not abuse Needham Broughton as long as I lived and had any money in the paper." There was never any love between Bailey and his partners. The father had sided with Dr. Columbus Durham against appropriations for the University, but his fight had not been as vigorous as that of Durham or Kilgo. Young Bailey, with great zeal, took up the fight begun by Dr. Durham, along with the Reverend John E. White, who succeeded Dr. Durham as corresponding secretary of the Baptist Convention.

Neither Bailey nor White (who had inherited the fight but was free from bitterness), nor any other of half a dozen Baptists, could fill the shoes of Dr. Columbus Durham but they were later to become aggressive. Dr. Durham had created an organization. He was tremendously and terribly in earnest. He believed the growth of Wake Forest College depended upon keeping the University and the State College small. And that accounted for his uncompromising fight.

XII

THE CLARK-KILGO-GATTIS BATTLE

O NE OF THE longest and most hotly contested battles in the history of North Carolina, in or out of court, grew out of the hostility of Dr. Kilgo, President of Trinity College (now Duke University) to the State University; his defense of the tobacco trust and the gold standard; and Judge Walter Clark's pillorying of Dr. Kilgo as the foe of the University for his "deification" of wealth and "wirepuller of the ward type when he lived in South Carolina." No two men in such high station have indulged in more vituperative language. Clark was a Methodist and trustee of Trinity, a Methodist College. He was a militant liberal and was a vigorous assailant of the Tobacco Trust. Kilgo was ambitious to secure large gifts for Trinity from Duke. Clark was to become Chief Justice of his State, and Kilgo was to become Bishop of his Church—both men of marked ability who upon occasion showed they were experts in fiery vituperation. The celebrated Gattis-Kilgo suit, in which the Reverend T. J. Gattis sued Kilgo and Duke for $100,000 for libel, began in 1898 over a comparatively unimportant matter and ran on in the press and in the courts for many years. Because my paper was critical of Dr. Kilgo's tirades against Jefferson and the State University, and because it had been, from its inception, a foe of Duke's Tobacco Trust and had supported Judge Clark for nomination for Supreme Court Judge, the impression prevailed that I was in league with Clark in initiating the controversy. The contrary was true. I had nothing to do with it, and if my advice had been asked I would have advised Clark against making the issue with Kilgo over the latter's proposal to elect professors of Trinity for a longer period than one year. That was the least of the differences that started the trouble. I was not a trustee and had no voice.

When Dr. Kilgo was elected I wished him well, and my paper gave him welcome and support. Judge Clark was selected by the board of trustees to express the welcome and support. I was still in Washington when Dr. Kilgo became President of Trinity College in 1894. I wrote to him urging him not to join in the fight against public appropriations for the State University, saying I did not agree with the position taken by the Reverend Columbus Durham, and declaring that, in my opinion, it was not in keeping with the best thought of nine-tenths of the American people. I went on to say:

"I cannot believe that any good would come to Trinity by joining with the opponents to State appropriations to the University and I do see much harm that might possibly come to it. I know you will be guided by your sense of what is best for the college and I have run the risk of giving advice unsought and possibly winning your disapproval by this letter, but I am so anxious for your success in the State and the growth of Trinity College and, likewise, for the prosperity of our State University, which belongs to all of us, that I run the risk of expressing my convictions of what is best for you, the Church, and the State."

Dr. Kilgo did not even show me the courtesy of acknowledgment of this friendly word of warning. I learned later that letters of similar import were written to him by Robert L. Durham (close kin of the Reverend Columbus Durham), the Reverend R. S. Webb, and others. My letter was prompted by the most friendly motives, but I soon was made to feel that my advice was not agreeable—that it was, in fact, resented.

At the inauguration of President Kilgo, Judge Walter Clark, speaking for the trustees, said, "We believe, aye we *feel* that, in the providence of God, we have found a worthy successor of our two Presidents." As time went on, Clark became the ablest antagonist of Kilgo. The long fight, which lasted for years—from 1895 to 1901—began when Kilgo proposed that the term of a professor be for four years instead of one. It was defeated and Clark said Kilgo had proposed it to keep himself in power. Kilgo wrote Clark, asking if he had made such a statement. Clark, replying, said, "Kilgo's tenure would be short," and added:

"The growing opposition to you, which has become intense with many, in the tobacco section especially; your reported speeches attacking the honesty of silver men (who constitute nine-tenths of the white men of North Carolina); the attacks you have made on the State University; the quarrels you have managed to get up and keep up with Dr. Kingsbury, Rev. Mr. Page, Mr. Webster and others, have created antagonism which must shorten your stay, unless you are protected by a four years' term or some influence not based on a public esteem. . . .

"The attempt of northern multi-millionaires to capture, by gifts and endowments, the control of the education of the children of the people, has created a sensitiveness on that subject in the public mind. The charges in the public prints however, intimating that the consideration of the gift by members of the Tobacco Trust to Trinity was that the youths were to be proselyted and taught political heresy foreign to the faith of their fathers, would have had small effect with so just a people as ours, if, by your parade of your gold-standard views (which must have an untoward effect on the minds of the young men in your care), and your reiterated and ostentatious assertion of your superiority to public opinion had not given color to their charge. If your perseverance in that line of conduct shall deepen in the public mind the suspicion into conviction (however unjust it may be in fact), wealthy syndicates may give you money, but the public will not send you boys."

The trustees passed resolutions saying that the charge of Clark was contradicted by the facts and that Clark ought to tender his resignation as a member of the board. Replying to the Chairman of the board, Clark denounced the censure upon him and declared that "if a trial had been instituted or an opportunity given, I could and would have laid before the committee evidence that should have satisfied an impartial body of men that I was justified in every word in my letter of the 14th of July, 1897." In the same letter, Clark went on to say of Kilgo:

"Recently, in an affluence of sycophancy, he led a procession to the house of Mr. Duke and, in a public speech, extolled him as the greatest man the State had ever produced and as superior to all the sacrifices of blood and treasure the State had ever made; that, in comparison with this gift of money, the primacy of Mecklenburg, the thousands who had offered up their lives at Moore's Creek, at King's Mountain and all these years down to Cardenas, were as dust in the balance. In substance he said, 'My Lord Duke, Give us Money and Your Name Shall Be Exalted Above all Names.' This deification of wealth—no matter how obtained—is not Christian education. This is not the language, these are not the thoughts, which a college president should teach his pupils. How much personal gratuity had so grateful a man received? Why did the Board not try him? Dr. Kilgo's reputation in South Carolina was that of a wirepuller, of the ward politician type. His performances in this State have justified his reputation. Length of years has not reformed him. He was a short time in Tennessee. One of the most distinguished members of your church in that State (not a layman), said to me, 'We know the fellow well. He is a scrub politician. If your committee wanted information I could have given it to them.'"

After this hot correspondence, the board called a meeting "to consider and determine all matters pertaining to charges made by Justice Clark against Dr. John C. Kilgo." As a result of the trial—Clark did not appear—the trustees unanimously declared that the charges had not been sustained, after Kilgo made an eloquent and moving address that was approved by the Board.

Judge Clark made an application to the board of trustees to permit him to speak before them but they refused, unless he would promise not to print his speech. He would not accept the terms. Therefore, the only way the trustees learned what was in the speech was by reading it in *The News and Observer* of September 4, 1898. It occupied fourteen columns. A little later Dr. Kilgo made a speech, replying to Clark, and *The News and Observer* printed it in its issue of September 11, 1898. It occupied ten columns. My paper also printed Dr. Kilgo's attack upon B. C. Beckwith, who had gone into South Carolina and had said that Dr. Kilgo's reputation in South Carolina was that he was hostile to monopoly, and showed that he had changed his whole attitude since coming in contact with the Dukes. It is a wonder that *The News and Observer* didn't burn when it printed Kilgo's attack on Beckwith and Beckwith's reply to Kilgo (September 11, 1898). Neither one of them wore any gloves and it was a battle royal.

Among other things that Judge Clark charged was that Dr. Kilgo had said, "If you are hunting for vice and immorality you would not go into the immoral sections of North Carolina, commonly called 'dark corners,' but you would go into the graded schools and other Christless institutions of learning." Judge Clark quoted the Honorable John R. Webster as his authority for this. He also charged that, because General Julian S. Carr, who had given the land upon which Trinity College was built, was a trustee of the University of North Carolina and one of its strongest supporters, Dr. Kilgo had ordered

General Carr's picture taken down from the walls of Trinity College and said it was not fit for the cellar of any institution. Dr. Kilgo denounced Clark as "a demagogue and a leveler."

Clark, in a long statement printed in *The News and Observer*, declared he had been prevented from giving evidence and from delivering his address at the trial. On September 25, 1898, my paper printed a reply by the Reverend Thomas Jefferson Gattis to Kilgo's address, and Kilgo's critics printed and distributed a pamphlet entitled *Suppressions and Omissions in the So-Called "Minutes" of the So-Called Investigation of Dr. John C. Kilgo by the Board of Trustees of Trinity College, August 30-31, 1898*. The claim was made that all damaging evidence was omitted from the printed proceedings of the trustees. It was said that the Reverend Mr. Gattis was authority for Clark's charges reflecting upon Dr. Kilgo's reputation in South Carolina. Referring to Gattis in his speech, Kilgo said that "behind a pious smile, a religious walk, and a solemn switch of the coat-tail, many men carry a spirit unworthy of them," and added, "Between the man hiding himself by the highway and making a victim of an innocent traveller and the man who, in the dark, assassinates the character which a man has tried to build for himself, send me to the woods with a revolver and let me murder every passer-by rather than malign my fellow man." The fact that Gattis had the name Thomas Jefferson aggravated Kilgo's hostility. Jefferson was anathema to him.

The trustees, in printing the proceedings, included the speech of Dr. Kilgo in which he had severely and most viciously animadverted on Gattis. Thereupon Gattis instituted a suit against Dr. Kilgo, B. N. Duke, W. H. Branson, and W. R. Odell—the latter three rich trustees—and asked for $100,000 damages. The case was tried in Granville County, and the jury gave a verdict of $20,000 in favor of Gattis. The Supreme Court granted a new trial on the ground that Kilgo's speech of defense was privileged. In the second trial, in 1901, Gattis obtained a verdict for $15,000. The Supreme Court granted a new trial and the case was removed to Wake County. About the time of the trial an illiterate juror, R. N. King, made an affidavit that he was approached by ex-Sheriff Rowan Rogers to help out the defendant. *The News and Observer* made a vigorous demand for a full investigation. After the charge by King that he had been approached to help out Kilgo, a regular juror, S. P. Markham, testified that J. P. Sorrell asked him to work for the defendant (Kilgo backed by Duke), in *Gattis* vs. *Kilgo* and had suggested that they would pay him. Judge Fred Moore, who was presiding, issued a rule to show cause why Rogers and Sorrell should not be attached for contempt and an attempt to influence jurymen for Kilgo and Duke. Both these men were put in jail and Judge Moore imposed sentences of thirty days on both of them for jury tampering. The attorneys for Dr. Kilgo and Mr. Duke made emphatic denials that they had had anything to do with tampering with jurors. *The News and Observers* said, "Go higher up. If Kilgo and Duke had nothing to do with it, the question is who was responsible." It called upon Rogers and Sorrell to speak out and tell who put up the money to induce them to tamper with the jury so that those "higher ups" could escape the punishment which they deserved. Rogers and Sorrell, the next day, were bound over to court for embracery and held for the next term of court. At the next term these men were both found guilty of embracery and Judge Allen gave a sentence of six months in jail. Never were such pleas put forth to a judge to let them pay a fine instead of sending them to jail, but the pleas were refused. Rogers asked that Sorrell be not punished and that his sentence be added to his own for he was responsible for what Sorrell had done. *The News and Observer* said, "It is a serious matter. Rogers and Sorrell must squeak or they must suffer."

In November the Gattis-Kilgo-Duke case came to the Supreme Court and was passed upon, *The News and Observer* characterizing it as a dog-fall. Two justices of the Supreme Court affirmed the lower court, which had entered a non-suit because of lack of malice, and two were for reversing it. Judge Clark did not sit on the case. Under the rule the decision of the lower court was permitted to stand unless it was reversed, which denied Mr. Gattis trial by jury and he was taxed the costs. *The News and Observer* said, "It is unfortunate from every standpoint and it decides nothing and does not vindicate any of the parties or settle the controversy."

Thus, the most sensational and hotly contested litigation in a half-century ended. *The News and Observer* reviewed the case in a long article and declared that Mr. Gattis should not have been denied the right of trial by jury. Later, in announcing the death of the Reverend T. J. Gattis in its issue of May 22 the paper said, "Mr. Gattis died with a consciousness that 99 people out of every 100 people of

North Carolina never doubted his integrity. The verdict of every jury that tried his case was approved by nine-tenths of the people."

It was generally believed that Judge Clark was the inspiration of the Gattis suit. Ex-Governor Jarvis (June 17, 1905), wrote: "The whole trouble, in my opinion, harks back to Judge Clark. But for him there never would have been a Gattis-Kilgo case. I am sorry for dear old Brother Gattis, who has allowed himself to be used by others."

The ablest lawyers in the State had been retained by both sides. The most brilliant speech was made by the Honorable Cyrus B. Watson, attorney for Gattis, who made a statement, still quoted, that "The motto of Trinity College should be changed from, '*Eruditio et Religio*' to '*Eruditio et Religio et Cherooto et Cigarretto.*'" The long duration of the trial made the phrase "Kilgo-Gattis Controversy" familiar to the whole State and it was said that a Negro boy born during the talk of the celebrated case was named by his parents "Kilgo-Gattis Controversy."

The News and Observer, beginning with commendation of Dr. Kilgo when he came to the State, grew to be a critic only when he defended monopoly, berated Jefferson, and was the spokesman of monopolists, particularly the Dukes, whose purse was open to him. Every utterance he made along these lines was printed and criticized. In his first address on Christian education, Dr. Kilgo declared the church colleges were "free from the fury of the rabble and the helplessness of the multitude." He had not then come fully to adulate, as he did later, great combinations of wealth, for he said in his inaugural address "The glory of Cambridge is Harvard and the shame of New York is Wall Street." Dr. Kilgo's eloquence captivated Mr. Duke and they were much together. The old man was fond of telling people that Dr. Kilgo was the greatest preacher and the most wonderful man who had ever come to North Carolina. Mr. Duke was a thoroughgoing Republican who believed that men who had made money were entitled to rule the country. His son, the master mind of the tobacco world, James Buchanan Duke, was also a strong Republican. In the late nineties, asked to name the two greatest Americans, Duke answered: "William McKinley and Mark Hanna." That fixed his political status and standards. Dr. Kilgo either came to have that belief or accepted the Duke opinion, for in the early years of his presidency he berated all Jeffersonians and Jefferson's principles. He declared that commerce had done more to Christianize the Orient than the missionaries. He praised the invasion of China and Japan by the tobacco interests.

As Dr. Kilgo went about the State, in sermons and speeches bitterly denouncing Jefferson and all his doctrines and calling him an infidel who wanted to destroy the foundations of society, I felt that it was my duty to dissent and to say some very plain things about the tendency of his teachings and also to say that he was more interested in pleasing the Dukes than he was in anything else. He succeeded in two ways: 1. Mr. Duke became more and more infatuated with him and gave more and more money to Trinity College. 2. He secured almost as effective an organization of the Methodist preachers and a large body of the laymen in the fight against State institutions of learning as Dr. Durham had done in the Baptist Church. As a matter of fact, when *The News and Observer* and Dr. Kilgo in the long years were at outs, he was a little more bitter against me than Dr. Durham, if possible. He undertook to lay down the principle that any Methodist who wouldn't make war on the State institutions was not a good member of the Church and had violated his pledge to "support its institutions." In fact, at one time so great was his influence and so determined was he to keep his Church as a militant organization along the policies he had laid down that when the *Morning Post* was established in Raleigh, a number of Methodist preachers quit taking *The News and Observer* and subscribed to that paper which had been established by the Southern Railroad and was also supported more or less by the Dukes.

XIII

FUSIONISTS OUTGENERAL DEMOCRATS

D URING THE CAMPAIGN in North Carolina in 1894, I kept in close
touch with the political situation and received assurances from
time to time from political leaders that although the Republicans
and Populists had fused, the Democrats would carry the State. Toward
the end of the campaign, I went home for a week or ten days and
spoke in Wake and surrounding counties and in the last days of the
campaign filled some appointments that had been made for Governor
Glenn in Cabarrus County. I shall never forget the anxious night I
spent in Concord. Not long before leaving Washington, there were
cases of smallpox which came very close to me. One of the law examiners, whose office adjoined mine with a door between, and who
came in very often to see me, was stricken with smallpox as were
several messengers in the Department who had gone in and out of
my office. The excitement in the Department was so great that business had to be suspended and I ordered everybody in the Department
to be vaccinated. I was in trepidation because, having come in such
close contact with one who had smallpox, I feared that I might
have it and might give it to my son, who was only a few months
old. After vaccination I was assured that there was no danger of my
taking the disease.

I reached Concord about dark on the evening before the day I
was to speak in the morning at Mount Pleasant and at night in Concord. When I went to my room I was suffering with headache and
pains all over my body. I could not go to sleep. I felt sure that I had
the smallpox, and I got up during the night fifty times to look in the
mirror to see if there was any evidence of it. They say a man's hair
can turn white in one night. Certainly a man can live ten years in
one night, as I did. In addition to the pain and aches, I was greatly
troubled as to my duty. I was scheduled to speak at Mount Pleasant
and to come in contact with hundreds of people who would be there.
If I had the smallpox, of course, I ought not to go; if I did not have
it, it was my duty to fill the engagement. Halting between the two

opinions, I tossed on my bed all night, promising myself that before I went into the country the next day I would get Dr. Robert Young, a physician and a good friend of mine, to examine me and tell me what to do. Toward daylight, I fell off to sleep and woke up without any pain or aches and communicated to nobody the terror of the night. Still I had some qualms. However, the drive to Mount Pleasant on a crisp October day made me feel all right and I went out and made the speech in a county in which Populism was strong and which elected to the Legislature a Populist, who afterwards became Speaker of the House. That night I spoke at Concord. Afterwards I told Dr. Young how near I came to spreading smallpox all over Cabarrus County and he agreed with me it would not have been as bad as what had been spread before by Fusion speakers.

At the Democratic State Convention in North Carolina held in 1894, the news of the strength of the fusion between the Republicans and the Populists came from most parts of the State. The terms of four members of the Supreme Court expired that year; they were all renominated and a platform was framed looking to holding the Alliance men in the Democratic Party by assuring them that the party's attitude was for free silver and legislation giving justice to the farmers.

The Populist convention that year was held on August 2. It was very largely attended and nominated for Chief Justice, W. T. Faircloth, of Wayne, who had been on the Supreme Court bench when the Republicans were in power, and D. M. Furches, of Iredell, who afterwards became Chief Justice by appointment of Russell. It accepted and lauded the plan, in operation in a number of Western States, of a non-partisan judiciary, and it endorsed for positions as Associate Justices Walter Clark, Democrat, then a member of the court, and H. G. Connor, eminent lawyer of Wilson, who had won reputation as a Judge of the Superior Court, also a Democrat.

The Populists regarded this as a fine piece of strategy. They thought thereby to strengthen themselves with dissatisfied Democrats, of whom there were a number, and with the Republicans. As they had given the other two places to the Republicans and taken none for the Populists, they thought it would satisfy the Republicans, as it did. The Democrats had renominated for places on the Superior Court bench the four men who were then on the court, of whom Judge Clark was one. There were some Democrats who said that in view of the doubt in regard to the election, it would be very much better if the Supreme Court could be assured of the presence on it of two such men as Clark and Connor. As they had not been asked to accept, and had not been consulted about the matter, it was argued there was no reason why they should not permit themselves to be voted for as Democrats. On the other hand, there was intense feeling, and most of the Democratic lawyers and Democratic leaders felt that if Clark and Connor should say nothing their silence would be virtual acceptance and their names would be used to bolster up the Fusion Party. Many Democrats took strong ground that Clark and Connor should repudiate the endorsement of what was called by the Democrats "the conspirators." The discussion grew to white heat. Clark had not a few enemies and critics in the Democratic Party. He was never very popular with the party organization. These enemies circulated the report that he had been consulted and had almost solicited the endorsement. Certainly it insured his reëlection, for he was also on the Democratic ticket. As to Connor, he was off the bench and if his name was to be used at all, it would be in opposition to the regular Democratic nominee for the position, Judge James C. McRae, who had been appointed to the bench by Governor Holt. When that fact became clear, Judge Connor issued a card stating that he had never been consulted about the use of his name and would not permit it. The Populists resented this very much and declared that the Democrats were unwilling to have a non-partisan judiciary and were determined to pack the court with men who would uphold partisan legislation regardless of its constitutionality. This issue flared up for a time, but after Connor's card it died down. I had urged Connor to refuse the support tendered. He refused to swallow the bait.

The burden of *The News and Observer's* policy was that honest Farmers' Alliance men ought to affiliate with the Democratic Party, to which they had always belonged, and not go into another party. It was very clear that the solid Negro vote and a fusion of Republicans and Populists would certainly win if their political leaders were able to induce the bulk of the Farmers' Alliance men to join the Populist Party and support the Fusion ticket. The campaign developed into one of great bitterness. In Wake County the Fusionists nominated Jim Young, Negro editor of the *Gazette,* for the Legislature, and in Eastern North Carolina a number of other Negroes were nominated. Some of the Populists gagged at this, and many of

Upper left, Zebulon Vance Walser, Republican Speaker of the House in 1895. *Upper right,* J. Frank Ray, brilliant Democratic parliamentarian in the Fusion Legislature, who outwitted the Fusionists. *Lower left,* Thomas Williams Mason, who was favored for United States Senator and Railroad Commissioner. *Lower right,* S. B. Alexander, Congressman, State Senator, and President of the Alliance.

Upper left, Judge Armistead Burwell, member of the Supreme Court of North Carolina. *Upper right,* Chief Justice Walter Clark, of the Supreme Court of North Carolina. *Lower,* Judge James C. MacRae, member of the Supreme Court of North Carolina.

them quietly did not support the candidates, but forty thousand or more North Carolinians had crossed the Rubicon. Their disappointment and hatred of Cleveland and their feeling that his gold standard policy had been responsible for their lack of prosperity, dominated them. Men who a few years before had been the most bitter in denunciation of the Republican party and its Negro cohorts, actually joined hands and defended the nomination of Negroes for office. Harry Skinner, who two years before had been denied the nomination for Governor on the Populist ticket because of his announcement of his firm belief in white supremacy, had now taken a front seat on the Fusion Band Wagon and was ready to become a Republican and to swallow his former declarations.

Butler on the Populist side and Pritchard on the Republican side were the chief leaders in Fusion, although the father of the fusion between the two parties who professed opposing principles was Major Hiram L. Grant, of Wayne County. He was a Northerner by birth, who had come down as one of the carpet-baggers and had been the Republican leader in Eastern North Carolina for many years, becoming post master at Goldsboro. Although an intense Republican, he was a successful business man and manufacturer in Goldsboro and had the confidence, in his business affairs, of the solid people of Goldsboro. However, he regarded a Negro as a black white man. In all political relations he was cheek and jowl with them and was much hated and feared by the Democrats of his section.

After the election in 1892, when it was seen that the Republicans and Populists together had more votes than the Democrats, Major Grant suggested to Marion Butler, then publishing the *Caucasian* at Goldsboro, that politics in North Carolina had become a matter of arithmetic; that if the Republican vote was added to the Populist vote, the Democrats could be defeated. And he pointed out that the Republicans were willing to give the Populists half of all the offices they could win in the State at large and most of them in Eastern North Carolina. Butler, who at that time had forgotten all his Democratic proclivities and had been the subject of so much abuse by so many Democrats that he could not affiliate with them, took his pencil in hand, and he and Grant worked out the scheme which was adopted by the Fusionists in 1904. It succeeded. Mathematics ruled the day, and when the election was held it was found that the Fusionists had elected six out of nine congressmen, had elected all their nominees for the Supreme Court, had controlled the Senate, which was composed of twelve Democrats, sixteen Republicans, and twenty-one Populists. In the House the Democrats had elected forty-one members, the Republicans thirty-two, and the Populists forty-seven. The Supreme Court Justices—W. T. Faircloth, Chief Justice, and David M. Furches, Associate Justice, were Republicans of the old order. The Populist elected was Walter A. Montgomery. The Democrats defeated were Chief Justice Shepherd and Associate Justices Burwell and McRae. It was almost a clean sweep, tremendously greater than the leaders of the parties had expected, and it stunned the Democrats. All the week before the election Chairman Pou had assured the people, and *The News and Observer* had congratulated the people, that the argument was all in favor of the Democrats and that they would win on a plurality vote.

The Democrats who had believed the flattering predictions were thunderstruck. The day after the election, *The News and Observer* headlines said *"Big Democratic Losses. The whole country turns against the Party of the People. William L. Wilson probably defeated, etc.,"* as to national returns; but its big streamer said: *"The State Safe. North Carolina Democratic By A Large Majority. Nine Democratic Congressmen. The Legislature Will be Organized By The Democrats."* The editorial, while deploring the Democratic defeat in the United States, which it attributed to the division of the party caused by Cleveland's insistence on the gold standard, said, "Home interests are of first importance to us," and rejoiced in the victory which the State Chairman proclaimed upon information obtained by telegrams from Democratic chairmen in counties which afterwards turned out to have gone Fusion. In a way this was natural, because the towns in which the votes were first counted were strongly and often solidly Democratic; but in the country the precincts were often just as solidly Fusion and overcame the town vote. The next day *The News and Observer,* still cautious and unwilling to admit what it regarded as black disaster, had headlines: *"The Legislature Is Close. Republicans and Populists Confident."* But on the second day following, *The News and Observer* admitted that the Fusion had carried six members of Congress and the Democrats elected only three: Woodard in the second, Shaw in the third, and Lockhart in the sixth. The next day it said *"The Democrats Have Lost Everything."*

Then a very disturbing thing occurred to me. When the paper admitting that the Fusionists had carried the State reached Goldsboro, Captain Nathan O'Berry, Chairman of the Democratic Party of the county, sent me a telegram saying, "Please never let *The News and Observer* darken my doors again. Any Democratic paper that will give up an election before the official count is made is not the Democratic paper I want to subscribe to." The Captain, who had never been very much in politics and never wanted office, was one of the county chairmen who had been able to hold his county in line against the greatest odds, for Grant lived in Wayne and Fusion had been born there. O'Berry's leadership had been one of the outstanding victorious leaderships of the State. He believed if he could carry Wayne against big odds, the other counties might be carried and probably had been carried. He resented my newspaper's admitting party defeat. When the official vote had been announced, Captain O'Berry was flabbergasted and withdrew his telegram, and our former warm friendship was strengthened and cemented. In his day, the State has had no citizen who, in patriotic devotion to all good things, stood superior to Nathan O'Berry.

Immediately after the election, confident that the Fusionists had come in for a long regime of power, and feeling the need of a daily newspaper at the capital, Marion Butler announced that his paper would become a daily on the first of January and he moved to Raleigh with a capital of ten thousand dollars. *The News and Observer,* noting this announcement, suggested that a good name for it in Raleigh would be *The Daily Marionette.* The *Caucasian* was moved from Goldsboro to Raleigh. It had been established by Butler at Clinton when he was a rantankerous White Supremacy Democrat, and now it was to come to Raleigh as the organ of what *The News and Observer* called "the black and tan party," with the purpose of unifying the Populists and Republicans in a compact and permanent party.

XIV

THE FUSION LEGISLATURE OF 1895

QUITE A NUMBER of the Populist members almost bolted in the opening session of the 1895 Legislature at the turning out of the Confederate soldier, Reitzel, of Catawba, who had been doorkeeper in the former Legislature. He had joined the Populist Party but was refused reëlection, and a very black Negro, Abe Middleton, from Duplin County, was put in his place. Middleton was a smart Negro. He had really been one of the triumvirate of Butler, Grant, and Middleton, who had made it possible to fuse in the counties of Sampson and Duplin. Abe Middleton was Butler's first lieutenant to keep the Negroes organized without offending Populists who had all their lives been opposed to Negro participation in politics. Middleton's election as doorkeeper was a bitter pill, but the resentment following the election of 1894 was so great that many Populist members could be whipped up to almost anything to beat the Democrats. When Fusion rule ended, Abe Middleton turned his attention to agriculture and led his race in becoming productive citizens. Abe eschewed politics and organized the first Negro Farm Coöperative in the State.

The delicate task of satisfying the Populist pie-eaters and the Republican pie-eaters was undertaken by Butler and Pritchard and their assistants. The first thing to do was to elect the Speaker of the House. The Republicans claimed this place and offered the Populists a little more patronage if they would let them have the Speaker. It was agreed that Zebulon Vance Walser, Republican, of Davidson County, should be the speaker. He was well educated, having graduated in law at the University of Michigan. When he made his first appearance in politics, Senator Vance was alive, and he sent Walser word he would either have "to cease being a Republican or change his first name; that it was an offense to see anybody going around in North Carolina bearing the name of Zebulon Vance and preaching bad doctrine." Walser was very proud of his name and always liked to hear people call him Zebulon Vance instead of Mr. Walser.

The bulk of the members of that Legislature were men without former experience. Many of them did not know what the previous question meant and had no parliamentary knowledge. The Democratic members elected were men of experience and were well organized. Moreover, they were determined to drive a wedge in between the Populists and the Republicans at every possible point. The most astute of these Democratic parliamentarians was J. Frank Ray, of Macon County, who had long been in the Legislature, who was as keen as a briar, full of wit, and who could introduce more dilatory motions and tie up legislation longer than any man I have ever seen. Frequently in the first days of the Legislature, when the Populists and Republicans had a big majority, I saw him smilingly keep everything at a standstill for a whole legislative session. Walser was no match for him, and the Republicans and the Populists had no man on the floor who could equal him.

The Legislature had not been in session long before it became apparent to the Fusion leaders that they could not carry out their legislative policies in the ordinary way; that there was too much difference of opinion among their members; and that the perfect organization of the Democrats and their superior tactics would bring confusion. Indeed, they lost some measures on the second reading because of lack of team work and organization. They therefore hit upon the policy of having a caucus every night and agreeing upon what legislation should be considered and enacted the next day. These caucuses were secret. Every member was pledged to vote for any and every motion made by the man in charge of a bill and to vote against every proposition made by the Democrats, no matter what it was. These caucuses lasted often until after midnight in order to drill their forces so that the next day they would follow like sheep. This caucus program was the real Legislature and the legislative session was a mere ratifying body. The Democrats made speeches and motions and would tie up things for a while, but with clock-work precision the Fusionists were able to put through their measures even if it took them quite a time to do it. The big job, therefore, of *The News and Observer* was how to get the news, for all the news was in the caucus. If I do say it myself the success demonstrated that the staff had capacity, versatility, and diplomacy. These caucuses were first held in the hall of the House of Representatives and were often very exciting sessions. Members would air their grievances and some of them would threaten to bolt over certain measures, and it took a great deal of tact and conciliation for leaders to agree upon the policies. *The News and Observer* forces were therefore at their wit's end to report the Fusion caucuses. They did it marvellously well considering the difficulties. Political reporting for *The News and Observer* by its staff took on new color. When Fred Merritt suspected trades for office, he used the sledge hammer. He put two and two together and said it was four. Falc Arendell sought direct information, over a glass of beer, from Fusionists who loved the "critter," and often got the news on the principle of *in vino veritas*. It was different with W. E. Christian. He was an artist in description of men and he made them like the pen pictures he drew of them. The Fusion leaders hated me; they fought Fred Merritt; they didn't know Arendell was priming the pump; but at first they liked the artistic manner that W. E. Christian employed to depict their doings. He was gifted in the artistry of words, and in the description of men and their peculiarities he was a master.

In the early days of the caucus, when the members did not know each other, sometimes Arendell would go into the caucus boldly and take a back seat, but this lasted only a brief time. Merritt made a practice of going into the gallery and getting under the benches, and in the dim light, with pencil in hand, he would take down word for word what was said. They got on to that, and one night a member arose in the caucus and said, "I believe a *News and Observer* man is in the gallery," and they appointed a committee to search the gallery. It took some time for the committee to climb the steep stairway, and when they got there Merritt had vamoosed and had gone into a room on the third floor, formerly the library, where he locked himself in and had to stay there until the caucus adjourned after midnight. Sometimes Fusionists held their caucus at the Wake County courthouse. Nobody was allowed in the caucus unless he was vouched for by the doorkeeper of the House or Senate. Members of *The News and Observer* staff at these first meetings would climb a tree outside the courthouse where they could only look in and guess what was being said or done, but they often guessed right.

These methods of getting the news soon availed little. The Fusionists became vigilant. It was necessary to resort to other means. There never was a body in the world (as the publication of the executive sessions of the Senate discloses), some members of which did not leak, either consciously or unconsciously. It was not long before we found out the men who would talk, and *The News and Observer* had on its staff a dozen or more volunteers, men who loved to hang around the Yarborough House and talk politics, who knew some of the Fusion members back home and cultivated them. They would be sitting around the hotel smoking around midnight when the members would come in—it was but a step to Denton's Bar—and some of these volunteer reporters took the keenest delight in pumping out of these members over a glass of beer everything that had happened. Of course the members never supposed these gentlemen had anything to do with the newspaper. They didn't have, except in a voluntary way. Almost every Democrat in politics regarded himself as a detective, and nothing made them so happy as to corkscrew some information about what happened at the caucus and let *The News and Observer* men have it. In that way, the news leaked out, but it was almost always long after midnight before the paper could go to press.

One night the caucus lasted until one o'clock and people passing by could hear loud speaking as members of the caucus warmed up. Every member was required to promise solemnly that he would not disclose anything done or said in the caucus. That night every source of information was dried up. Arendell, Christian, Merritt, and the volunteers came in empty-handed. The people of the State had begun to brag about *The News and Observer* and how it could get the news in spite of every difficulty, and we were very proud of it. It was our big asset. To fall down that night would have been to confess failure. All the sources having dried up, about one o'clock I went to the Yarborough House. It was almost deserted. I asked the clerk for the number of the room of a certain Populist Senator whom I had known long and well. He gave it to me. I went up the stairs to the third floor where he had a room near the rear in the wing. I first saw that the course was clear and then knocked on his door. It took some time to wake up the Senator. He came to the door in his night clothes, and when he saw me asked "What in the hell do you want?" "Quick," I said, "let me in. It is very important." As I entered, I called him by his first name as in the old times before he had turned Populist and said, "I am in great trouble and I have come to you for help." I told him I understood very important things had been done at the caucus that night and there had been hot debate, but that our usual sources of information had failed. As we had not been able to get a thing, I had come to him for help on the basis of our old friendship. He could swear upon occasion and he swore at me *à la* the army in Flanders. He wanted to know, "By God!" if I thought he was the sort of man who would betray a confidence and tell a newspaper that was fighting him every day, etc. I remained half an hour listening to his tirade and pleading with him for the news. Finally he asked, "Did anybody see you come in?" and I said, "No, there wasn't a man in sight." "Well, get your pencil quick," he said. I was provided with a pad and in the dim light he proceeded to dictate to me the outline of what had been done and something of the row in the caucus. He wouldn't let me go out of his room until he had looked out to make certain that the course was clear. I hurriedly wrote the story. I never had quite such a thrill in my newspaper life. Members of the staff had been getting scoops every night and I had been getting little. Their curiosity was piqued to know how I had managed to succeed where they had failed. They do not know until this day. The publication created the greatest sensation—one that can hardly be imagined today. All the amateur reporters were crowding around to know how it had been done.

The Fusionists were furious when *The News and Observer* carried the full account. I think if it had been found out who had betrayed them, they would have torn him to pieces, limb by limb. Butler was white with rage and threatened that "the damn scoundrel who had given the information should be expelled from the caucus and expelled from the Party." Either a resolution or a motion was made when the Legislature met to appoint a committee to investigate the leak. The galleries were crowded and the feeling was tense as the debate proceeded. Presently the Senator who had given me the information arose and in a towering rage delivered a terrible philippic against "the infernal scoundrel" who had given the information. I had a seat in the rear gallery and heard him denounce the paper in terms that would almost require asbestos for printing. Nobody ever suspected him. He went through the session completely trusted by his associates and later was a leading factor in defeating Democratic motions and measures. I didn't see him for several days, but in the Senate lobby one day he came up to me and said, "How is that damn lying sheet of yours getting along?" He always made it a point to be very vicious in denouncing the paper when he came in contact with me and I always accepted his denunciations without comment. We met very often in the years following but neither of us referred to that night.

Butler printed his newspaper, the *Caucasian* daily, so that while *The News and Observer* was daily printing the proceedings and roasting the Fusionists, the *Caucasian* was printing their side of the story and roasting the filibustering Democrats. The colored members of the Legislature had their organ, so that they could not be overlooked in the distribution. Early in January, people of Raleigh were notified by the *Gazette,* the Negro organ, that Raleigh would be gerrymandered so that the Negro would no longer be denied control of local government. The *Caucasian* warned its readers every day not to believe anything that *The News and Observer* printed. "The desire of *The News and Observer,*" it said, "is to create friction, break up coöperation, and defeat legislation which people expect. This unworthy desire shall not be gratified if it is in our power to prevent it."

There had been hope on the part of the Democrats that there would be a split between the Republicans and the Populists over the election of United States Senators. Fortunately for the Fusionists, there were two vacant seats. The death of Vance had created one, and Ransom's term had expired. Colonel Oliver Dockery, "the old war horse," as he was called, came to Raleigh and entered the race for Senator, but he had seen his best days. There was no finesse about the old man. He was an 1868 and 1869 Republican and never got over it until he joined the Populists, although most of his descendants later became Democrats after the big Democratic victory of 1898. He was of the old issue and Pritchard of the new. He was from Eastern North Carolina and the bulk of the Republican legislators were from Western North Carolina. The old man had no chance, but he lingered about, associating with the old-time Republican "has beens." Pritchard did not win so easily as had been expected.

Eugene Holton, of Winston-Salem, had been chairman of the party during the campaign and he had been in touch with the legislative candidates. He had done more to bring the Populists and the Republicans together than any other Western Republican. He was astute and capable. When the Republican caucus met to name Vance's successor, Pritchard defeated Holton by a vote of 38 to 21. Butler had no trouble with the Populists. At the joint caucus, Butler and Pritchard were selected for the Senate. The Fox from Sampson demanded the long term of six years. He was able to compel the Republicans to accept that and to take the two-year term for Pritchard.

The Democrats were in trouble about their candidate for the Senate. They could not win but they were resolved to put the best foot foremost so as to lay the foundation for a winning campaign in 1896. Vance was dead and nobody had arisen to take his place. Ransom had lost his influence with the rank and file of the party when he voted for Cleveland's repeal of the Sherman law. Jarvis was growing old and the Ransom adherents hated him. They felt that his candidacy against Ransom had hurt the party. And so, when the Democrats held their caucus, they did the unexpected. They turned down all the men who had been candidates for the Senate and cast their votes for two men who had never thrown their hat into the senatorial ring. They voted for Thomas W. Mason, of Northampton County, Ransom's county, instead of Ransom, who thought that was the unkindest cut of all. He never forgave it. To be denied a vote of confidence after his long term in the Senate and his distinguished service was gall and wormwood to him, but to give the honor to a man from his home county whom he did not like made him furious. Of course he was a diplomat and congratulated Mason. More than once afterwards he unbosomed himself to me and talked about the ingratitude of the Legislature and the absurdity of voting to send to the Senate a man who in that body, as he believed, would never have any influence. Mason was, in fact, a man of fine parts but had never been ambitious, or if ambitious had seen that whatever honor came to Northampton County or that section would go to Ransom. In that county there was another able man, afterwards Superior Court Judge, Robert Peebles, who was ambitious and felt that Ransom stood in his way. When Ransom voted with Cleveland on the silver question, Peebles made warfare on him in his own county, the first open warfare Ransom had ever met at home. For Senator from the West, the Democrats voted for Lee S. Overman, and that vote of confidence, followed later by his selection as elector at large in 1900, gave Overman a position which helped to elect him to the United States Senate when Pritchard's term expired. He was also, like Mason, a free silver man and had been private secretary to Vance when he was governor and had the confidence of the Vance people.

The legislative question that interested people of Eastern North Carolina more than any other was the county government system.

Under that system, the control of the finances of the county was in the hands of magistrates appointed by the Legislature and not elected by the people. This prevented Negro magistrates in the East and Negro power in county finances. The Democrats believed that a change in the system would bring the State back to the bad conditions that existed in the days of reconstruction. They would have sacrificed almost anything to keep the county government system. Democrats in Western North Carolina had grown restive and had assented to it only because they were ready to make sacrifices to protect the white people in the East. There were a number of Populists from Eastern North Carolina who did not wish to repeal the county government system. Some of them were outspoken. Others were trying to find some compromise which would protect the Eastern counties and still hold the Fusion Alliance men. Republicans in the Legislature would agree to nothing except the repeal of the system, so that every county, whether white or black, could control all the county affairs. It was not until late in February that Populists who hesitated to run the risk of Negroes in office in Eastern North Carolina could be whipped in line. Butler finally lined them up. Some of them warned Butler that it would result in what did happen in 1898 and it would be the undoing of the Fusion. The Republicans made repeal a condition even to Butler's election as Senator. They had promised the Negroes and the Eastern Republicans that much, and the Negroes and the Eastern Republicans were on hand to see that they got it.

When the Legislature of 1895 met, the Republicans demanded changes in the legislation so that the majority of the voters, whether white or black, could control in the cities of the East. Under the Democratic rule, New Bern, Wilmington, and all the Eastern towns were governed by special acts. White folks controlled by ward management, called gerrymandering although the Democrats called it by another name—even though the Negroes might have a majority. Following the county government repeal, bills were passed for the towns in Eastern North Carolina which would put the Republicans in control of these Eastern cities. This was inconsistent, but they said if the Democrats could do it, they could do the same thing. On February 28, *The News and Observer* said that Jim Young's bill to Negroize Raleigh would give 935 Negroes full control of the city. Young was the Negro legislator from Wake County on the Fusion ticket, and very influential—in fact, outside of Butler, Pritchard, and

Holton, hardly any man had so much influence as Jim Young. He was a very bright mulatto and was reputed to be a son of a prominent white man in Vance County. I guess that was true. His political astuteness was attributed by Democrats to his white blood.

He was as smart as he could be and generally managed to secure what he wished, although when it came to getting through his bill for Raleigh, the Wake County country Populists gagged. The Populist Senator from Wake County, Mr. A. C. Green, refused to let the bill pass in the shape Young demanded. Green returned to the Democratic Party when the issue was clear-cut. He was an honest and courageous man, of force and integrity. In 1898, he led Populists back into the Democratic Party.

Toward the close of the session one morning, in the House the Negro Representative Crews, of Granville, introduced a resolution that "the House adjourn in honor of Fred Douglass," who had just died. The resolution was adopted. *The News and Observer* called it "the climax of infamy," and pointed out that the Legislature had refused to adjourn in honor of Washington and Lee on their birthdays, but had reserved this great honor to the Negro miscegenationist. *The News and Observer* said that this act endorsed miscegenationism and declared, "Fusion is a marriage of two parties having no principle in common. The endorsement of a miscegenationism leader is the legitimate heir of that union." It said that Fred Douglass was a wonderful Negro and that as long as he was true to his race he stood as its foremost man, but when he married a white wife, he was severely criticized by self-respecting Negroes as well as white people in every part of the country. It went on to say, "The essence of Fusion is to break down all barriers and solve the Negro question by marriage between the races." The *Caucasian* squirmed and denied that the Legislature had refused to adjourn for Washington and Lee, but *The News and Observer* retorted that it had not adjourned in their honor although that had been the custom in North Carolina since the Civil War. Cartoons in *The News and Observer* pilloried the adjournment in honor of Fred Douglass. One of them showed the Fusionists scorning the ladies who begged them to honor the Confederate dead and obeying the demand of the Negroes by honoring Fred Douglass. Another cartoon showed Pritchard and Butler tied to the corpse of Fred Douglass. This incident aroused great indignation, and the Populist members, most of whom said they did not even know the resolution was introduced and had not heard it, were very sore. The Reverend R. H. Whitaker, D.D., who wielded a caustic pen, wrote a letter purporting to be from the wife of one of the Populist members to her husband, indignantly denouncing the Legislature for passing the resolution and telling him if he voted for it, never to dare come home again; she did not want him and would not own a husband who had so disgraced his family and the South. This letter, which was admirably written, was copied all over the State, and Whitaker kept up the correspondence and wrote several other letters, one from the husband trying to defend it, another apologizing for it, another saying he wasn't there that day and begging her to take him back and promising he would be a Democrat if she would do it. In the hope of palliating the widely criticized adjournment in honor of Douglass, the leaders saw something must be done. The Legislature, therefore, made an appropriation of $10,000 to complete the Confederate monument in Capitol Square. In the next campaign they preened themselves, saying: "When we reached Raleigh we found the Democrats had left the Confederate monument uncompleted. We showed our patriotism by appropriating the money to complete the erection."

In the campaign of 1894 the Fusionists had denounced the election law, saying it was framed to enable the Democrats "to steal 40,000 votes." They set about framing a new election law to keep themselves in power, making a worse law than they had condemned. The Fusionists were a unit in action: in appointing election officials it gave one to the Populist Party and one to the Republican Party, thus giving absolute control to their party under the guise of fairness. Colored ballots were permitted so that Negroes could be instructed that by voting a certain colored ballot they were voting "straight Republican." No privacy in voting was permitted.

XV

JOSIAH TURNER—STORMY PETREL

A T THE CLOSE of the Legislature of 1895, the sum total of it, as stated in *The News and Observer,* was that it had increased appropriations $125,000, had created 3,600 new offices, which had been filled by Fusionists, many of them Negroes, had passed no law against trusts, and had appropriated $4,630 to Josiah Turner on a claim on his old public printing contract, which, in spite of its doubtful legality, rejoiced most people because in the Reconstruction period Turner had done the State a great service and was now poor and down and out. In 1895 Turner was a Fusionist. He came to Raleigh berating the Democrats. He thus found favor with the Fusionists but it created no resentment on the part of the old-time Democrats because they knew that since his retirement from the *Sentinel* he had been "ferninst" everything. He spent most of the session of the Legislature talking to the members and anybody who would listen to him. The burden of his song was that he had driven out the carpet-bag and scalawag crowd that disgraced the State in 1868-9, with Littlefield and Swepson at the head, but that when the Democrats came in, part of their leaders were Swepson's lawyers and some of them had been in league with the Reconstructionists on bond matters. He was very garrulous and abusive of everybody, but it was the kind of garrulity and abusiveness which offended nobody because through it all ran the feeling that he had risked his life and made the issues which had brought the Democratic victory in the early seventies and then had been turned out to grass while men who had done little received the honors.

There never has been in the State an editor who, for a brief time, was so dynamic as Josiah Turner. He had been a Whig before the War Between the States and had served in Congress. He never had poise or wisdom, was always extreme in utterance. When the war ended, Andrew Johnson appointed Holden provisional governor, and it was largely due to Turner's audacity and leadership that Holden was defeated for election in 1866. This was before the Reconstruction measures. The vitriolic language he employed when he talked about

Holden could be printed on nothing but asbestos. As evidence of this, hearing that he was to be arrested by Governor Holden he showed his defiance by writing the following letter to the Governor:

"To Governor Holden: You say you will handle me in due time. You white-livered miscreant, do it now. You dared me to resist you. I dare you to arrest me. I am here to protect my family: the jacobins of your club, after shooting powder in the face of Mrs. Turner, threw a five-pound rock in her window, which struck near one of my children. Your ignorant jacobins are incited to this by your lying charges against me that I am the King of the Ku Klux Klan. You villain; come and arrest a man and order your secret clubs not to molest women and children.

"Yours with contempt and defiance,

"Josiah Turner, Jr."

Turner came to our house very often during the Legislature of 1895. He claimed, and I guess it was a true claim, that he had managed the campaign which elected my wife's grandfather, Jonathan Worth, Governor in 1866. Worth was State Treasurer in 1862-6, and had been a strong Unionist. However, though he stood almost alone in opposition when the Legislature passed the Secession Ordinance, after North Carolina went out of the Union, he stood with his State and held office as State Treasurer during the Confederacy. He therefore had the confidence of all the old Union and Whig element in the State, and the leaders who had carried the State out of the Union understood that the only man who had a chance of election was some man who in 1860 had been a Union man. Therefore Turner could rally to Worth's support all the influences of the State except those which afterwards formed the Republican Party. "Worth was not anxious to run," said Turner to my wife one day, adding, "I've a right to sass you and any or all the Jonathan Worth children or grandchildren because I made the old Quaker Governor of the State." My wife always welcomed him and he spent many mornings at our home telling her about her grandfather, berating Holden, Reconstructionists, and the Democrats who had ignored or repudiated him. Sometimes I would remain at home to listen to his reminiscences, some of them rambling and disconnected. I quote the substance of one phase of his story: "Worth had been through so many stormy periods he did not seem to wish to lead any new fight in the disturbed conditions. I knew he was the only man who could beat Holden." To hear Turner talk about Holden was to hear only vitriolic language. Turner continued:

"I would go in Worth's office and persuade, or almost persuade him to run, and then Kemp Battle and others who wanted everything to be smooth and easy, would persuade him not to run, and for some time he was undecided. Finally, he came to feel that it was his duty. When he announced his candidacy, I sent the message all over the State, travelled many miles and made many speeches in many counties and the organization was effected very quickly, and to the surprise of most people, he was elected. It surprised nobody more than Andrew Johnson, who had appointed Holden, and the action at that time was supposed to have caused Johnson for a moment to contemplate joining hands with the Reconstructionists. But when he found that Worth had been originally a Union man, and his administration was conservative and looking toward peace and justice, he listened to many recommendations of Worth and some of them he approved, particularly along the line of pardons."

In 1865 the Raleigh *Sentinel* had been established, to destroy Reconstruction, by the Reverend William E. Pell, a Methodist preacher who had edited the Raleigh *Christian Advocate*. He was a prominent preacher of his church and interested in public affairs. His sons won high places in their professions. Seaton Gales, on the editorial staff, was one of the most gifted of the young lawyers of Raleigh and was a descendant of the celebrated editor, Joseph Gales, who came to Raleigh under Nathaniel Macon's influence and established the Raleigh *Register* early in the century. Joseph Gales, Jr., and William W. Seaton were partners in editing the *National Intelligencer* at Washington. Gales wrote well, but he was more eloquent with the tongue than with the pen. He had something of the courage and defiance of the new order that animated Turner. It was not long before Turner secured ownership of the paper from Pell, who could not blister with the withering scorn which was necessary at that day for an editor who was fighting the Reconstruction movement.

Just as long as it was necessary to tear down, to destroy the Reconstruction leaders, to pillory them, to give them names that stuck, and to organize people in opposition to things that were wrong, Turner was the ideal leader and was the idol of the more aggressive part of the so-called Conservative Party, which was to become the

Conservative-Democratic Party and then the Democratic Party. That evolution of the name was necessary. After Appomattox, when politics began to shape themselves in the State, the old-time Whigs like Worth, Vance, Graham, and Badger, and others who had engaged in many conflicts with the Democrats before the Civil War, did not relish taking the name Democrat. In order to unite the white forces of the State it was deemed wise to use no old party name, and so Worth was elected as head of the Conservative Party. Later it was called the Conservative-Democratic Party. It was not until 1872 or later that all the prefixes were dropped and it became the Democratic Party. By that time the old Whigs and Democrats had begun to think so much alike that names didn't matter. I have heard some of the old-time Democrats say, "We had to get the old Whigs in by using a good deal of soft soap, but after we got them in, they were better Democrats than we were and got most of the offices."

Turner's ambition was to be elected to Congress and when the Democrats came into power he became a candidate. A large element of the party felt that he was too violent and that to send so vindictive and abusive a man to Congress would injure the standing of the South in the national capitol, when the right policy was for the South to obtain its place on equal terms at Washington. The program of Ransom and other leaders was to soft-pedal all things that widened the breach. Turner's defeat soured him and he turned his shafts on Vance, Merrimon, and Ransom and the other Democratic leaders, particularly the Camerons and Grahams in his own county. He abused them as severely as he had ever abused Holden, Littlefield, and Swepson, politicians and exploiters of the Reconstruction era. He was never very careful about his facts. If he decided to pillory any man, he did so as viciously for a man as honorable as Vance as he did for a man as contemptible as Littlefield. This vehemence destroyed his influence in the Democratic Party, because, while there were a few Democrats who had stood in with the gang issuing fraudulent bonds, when Turner tried to place Vance in the category of men who had not been true, people began to say he had lost his judgment, and then that he had lost his mind. And indeed he would rave against them so as to cause many of his best friends to feel he was an impossible leader. He became a sort of Ishmael in politics with his hand against every man almost, and every man's hands against him. It was pitiful. As he grew older and talked about it, his extreme language rather justified those who had denied him position. At the same time, even those who could not support him regretted that the one man who had done most to destroy Reconstruction should have received no reward for it.

After Turner's paper began to strike blindly at almost everybody, the Conservative Democrats felt the need of a paper which would not be so violent. The Raleigh *News* was established, and Turner's paper, which had never been profitable, ceased to pay. Its presses and machinery were finally absorbed by the *News*. Later Turner ran as an Independent for the Legislature from Orange County and was elected with Republican support. That made the righteous Democrats grieve that one who had been their beau ideal in the time when denunciation and destruction was the essential thing should have fallen from his high estate. In the Legislature he devoted himself largely to tirades against people he did not like. Some of his denunciations were undoubtedly deserved, but many of them were unjust. He did not distinguish between the man who had been a rascal and the man he did not like.

Turner gave to Reconstructionists names of contempt and ridicule, which stuck; as for example, "Windy Billy Henderson Who Stole Darr's Mule," "Chicken Stephens," "Greasy Sam Watts," "Ipecac Memminger." He remembered every mistake or crime, and pilloried the Reconstruction leaders. His pen was dipped in gall and he relentlessly held up to contempt Holden and all his associates. In the days of deepest gloom he gave hope to the Conservatives and put fight into them. "To him," says historian Hamilton, a master of events in that era, "more than to any other man belongs the credit for the speedy overthrow of Reconstruction in North Carolina." He was especially severe on Holden, and enumerated the many offices the Governor had given to his relatives, and in the *Sentinel* quoted this Scripture: "But if any provide not for his own, and especially those of his own house, he has denied the faith and is worse than an infidel."

It is a thousand pities that before he died, Josiah Turner did not return to normal thinking so that he could have told, without passion, the story, accurately and historically, of his participation in the stormy days between 1866 and 1870. His life was often in imminent danger. Once when he came to Raleigh from Hillsboro, the city government then under the control of the Reconstructionists, plotted his life, and William E. Pell, son of the preacher who established the *Sentinel,* told me that when he knew of the plot to kill Turner he boarded the train at the water tank before it got into Raleigh carrying with him four pistols, two of which he gave to Turner and two of which he carried himself. He said that Turner was able to defy the crowd which, intent upon his life, was overawed by Turner's audacity and courage. I have heard Pell hour after hour talk of how Turner, without money and without anything except his audacity, carried on in those days. He was often attacked and his life was in jeopardy. His office was in a constant state of siege, but neither threats nor anything else moved him. Pell said he was the only man he had ever known who did not know the meaning of fear. That was true of Pell also, for in those days he was associated with Turner on the *Sentinel* and was his self-appointed bodyguard. It was known in Raleigh that anybody who touched Turner would be got by Pell. I do not think that any man had so faithful a Boswell as Turner did in Pell. He never forgot anything that a Republican did that was wrong, and as long as he lived he had the same feeling toward them that Turner had in 1869 and 1870.

Turner's plea to the Fusionist Legislature of 1895 was that he had been paid on the wrong basis—that he had been paid $4,000 less than he was entitled to receive because he had been paid on the basis of the letter *M*, which varies in condensed or extended type, and is therefore unreliable as a standard of measure. He urged that he should have been paid by the em quad, a perfect square which is not variable. In this day printers figure their estimates on the em quad and not on the letter *M*. When the Fusionist Legislature of 1895 heeded Turner's plea and voted him the $4,000, his old and, as some said, questionable claim, no Democrat dissented. They felt that the Fusionists were going to spend all the money in sight anyway, and for a little of it to give comfort to the old war horse who had turned himself out to grass was some compensation for putting his life in jeopardy at a time when the policy of destruction was necessary as the prelude to the policy of construction.

There are men who are born to tear down wrong, and upon occasion these men are more valuable than the wisest man who builds up. Turner was this type of man. For the duty of construction in a new day, he was unsuited, and his leadership passed. If he had died at the height of his fight, or when he had won first blood, there would have been a monument erected to him in Raleigh.

XVI

CONFUSION OF FUSIONISTS—AND FISTICUFFS

O NE OF THE things which the Legislature of 1895 did that brought
it into greater ridicule and contempt than anything else, was
the creation of what *The News and Observer* called "the great tri-
angle" commission to investigate the Patty D. B. Arrington case. This
lady was a native of Nash County and belonged to an excellent family,
having married early in life a well-to-do farmer and business man,
Billy Lou Arrington. They were estranged and much litigation followed in contests for property. Mrs. Arrington felt that she had been
unjustly treated and Mr. Arrington felt the sting of her sharp tongue.
Litigation went on year after year and Mrs. Arrington lost her various
cases in several courts. She had at various times as her attorneys such
eminent men as Charles M. Cooke, Charles B. Aycock, and Judge
Spier Whitaker. Every time she would lose her case, she would denounce her lawyer as having joined a conspiracy to defraud her.

Finally, the judges and the lawyers came to regard her pleas as not
worthy of notice, and she said she could not get justice in the courts.
For years, she had beset every judge who had held court in her
district, to take up her case, and had offered to retain any lawyer
who would look into it, but said all of them were in a conspiracy
against her. When the Fusionists came into power, she thought she
saw a chance to get justice. Day after day she talked to the members
of the Legislature, and she put her story in such a light that she seemed
to be a helpless woman who had been wronged systematically and
cruelly. Not a few legislators felt sympathy for her. A bill was introduced to appoint a commission "to investigate the Patty D. B. Arrington case." Nobody thought much about it until after it had been
adopted and the committee appointed. Most people regarded it as a
great joke or a piece of silly legislation. The members who voted for
it thought it could do no harm, and might assuage the feelings of a
lady who felt she had been wronged. When the commission organized,
therefore, it was dubbed by Christian of *The News and Observer*
staff as "the Peedybee, or Pee Dee Bee, Commission," and it was

Left, the Reverend W. E. Pell, founder of the Raleigh *Sentinel. Right,* Josiah Turner, editor of the Raleigh *Sentinel* and Stormy Petrel of the Reconstruction Era.

Left, Norman E. Jennett, the "Sampson Huckleberry," gifted cartoonist who here portrays himself drawing cartoons for *The News and Observer* during the Fusion Era. Note the "Fusion" cartoon on the floor. *Right,* Cartoon by Jennett in *The News and Observer,* September 6, 1895. The head on the dasher is an excellent likeness of A. Campbell (Hoola-Boom), chairman of the Pee Dee Bee Commission.

never called anything else. This way of giving names to damn a thing had been made very popular in North Carolina by Josiah Turner and was followed by *The News and Observer* in its war on the Fusionists.

The Peedybee Commission was composed of A. Campbell, Republican, of Cherokee, said by *The News and Observer* to be a "freak of the first order who takes his anti-prohibition three times a day. Campbell is a joke with a stovepipe hat and store teeth." Christian had dubbed him "Old Hoola Boom" after a ridiculous character who had appeared in a popular play in Raleigh during the Legislature. The name stuck and even his friends called him Hoola Boom. At first he rather liked Christian's appellation and loved to see his picture in the paper with his stovepipe hat on. Later, when he became chairman of the Peedybee Commission, he resented what *The News and Observer* said about him. The second member of the Commission was the Reverend Mr. Phillips, of Pitt County, a Republican, of whom *The News and Observer* said, "He is a fine specimen of the genus fusionist. He is now said to be Seventh Day Adventist, having left the Baptist Church (of which he was a member), because of drinking to excess."

I asked John Jenkins, city editor, to write his recollection of "Hoola Boom" and of the time that Christian thought he had killed the Cherokee representative. He writes:

"When Campbell, the Representative of Cherokee County appeared in the 1895 Fusion Legislature, he was a tall, lank specimen and wore a long-tailed coat and top hat. There was a tradition that there was only one beaver hat in the county, which was worn by the man sent to the Legislature. He wore that hat. Christian seized upon it and promptly named him 'Hoola Boom,' after a character in a musical comedy then running. It fitted him like a glove, so that Campbell of Cherokee, became known all over the State as 'Old Hoola Boom.' He wore a double set of false teeth, held in his mouth by a spring. While he was speaking one day and opened his mouth wide, they fell out. He caught them before they reached the floor. When the tax bill [The Revenue Machinery Act] was being debated, one member offered an amendment: 'That double sets of false teeth held in the mouth by a spring shall be taxed ten dollars per set, *Provided* that when caught on the fly they shall be exempt from taxation.'

"Getting tired of being made the butt of Christian's cruel wit, one night, drunk as a lord, Old Hoola Boom, strode into *The News and Observer* editorial room, with a big bull-dog pistol in his hand and roared:

" 'Where is the son of a bitch that wrote that article about me? I'm going to lick a skillet of piss out of him.'

"Merritt, Managing Editor, who sat opposite editing telegraph copy, promptly dived under the table. I managed to dodge into the little room next door. Christian was at the side writing. Acting like a flash, he picked up one of the heavy splint-bottom chairs we used, and hit the drunken old intruder squarely on the head. He fell like an ox, senseless. Whether the blow knocked the sense out of him or he was too drunk to stand, we never knew. Anyway, he lay there knocked out cold. Fearing he had been killed we rushed out for Dr. Sexton, who was next door. The doctor said he had a severe concussion. He worked over him and gave him a shot in the arm. You can imagine how relieved we were when the old man opened his eyes. Of all things we didn't want a dead legislator on our hands in the office. Such things are hard to explain. When he opened his eyes, the first thing he said was, 'Where am I at? What happened?' We explained to him gently that he must have hurt his head when he fell. I don't think Hoola Boom ever knew what hit him. Anyway, we never told him. So the incident ended and the belligerent old mountaineer never shot anybody."

I cannot say that any of us blamed Hoola Boom for his hatred of the paper. Early in the session, when Christian wrote him up with good-natured humor, he liked the prominence it gave him. It was only when, as chairman of the Pee Dee Bee Commission, he and his colleagues in an impossible position made spectacles of themselves, and the darts burnt his skin, so that he sought to kill his tormentor. Mr. Jenkins thus tells of incidents relating to other members of the Pee Dee Bee Commission:

"When the Commission was supposed to meet, Phillips—called the 'Fill-up Phillips'—was found dead drunk, lying among the trunks in the Yarborough House baggage room. I wrote a one and a half column article telling this and attacking all three of the committee men.

"You were down from Washington, sitting in your editorial den with Judge Avery. I wanted you to see the article before it went in as I knew it would draw fire. You read it over and said:

'That's pretty hot.' Turning to Judge Avery, you asked, 'What do you think of it, Judge?' 'Well, if it is all true, you can print it,' the judge said, 'but if it is not true, it is highly libelous.'

"Turning to me, you said, 'Will you swear to this, John?' 'Yes,' I said. 'Will you fight for it?' 'Yes.' 'Will you die by it?' 'Yes.' 'Run it, then.' You decided. We ran it.

"Phillips was a preacher, and shortly after his debauch, he obtained permission to preach in Metropolitan Hall, and went to *The News and Observer* and asked that his preaching appointment be printed. It appeared thus on Sunday morning: 'Reverend and Legislator Phillips, of Pitt County, member of the Pee Dee Bee Commission, will preach at Metropolitan Hall this afternoon at three o'clock. That is, he will preach if he is sober.'

"When Phillips called to get revenge, the offending member of the staff could not be located, and he left breathing out slaughter. Christian dubbed the third member of the Commission, Bryan, Populist member from Chatham County, 'Little Billee' from the character in *Trilby,* most popular novel of the day, because one day he introduced what he called 'a little bill,'—an alleged local measure. When examined the bill contained a provision repealing all appropriations to the University.

"Promptly for these publications *The News and Observer* drew three libel suits for large amounts. Nothing came of them. The Pee Dee Bee Commission was laughed out of existence. It was from the start made a joke and the commissioners made it a reproach."

The paper was cruel in its flagellations. In the perspective of time, I think it was too cruel. One of the most influential Republican leaders who took an active part in political affairs was Richmond Pearson, son of the distinguished Chief Justice, for whom he was named. The son served in Congress and as Minister to Persia. *The News and Observer* did not spare him. Christian got under his skin by ridicule and sarcasm. Infuriated, Pearson used language that invited a fight or a duel. As the latter was out of date, Christian decided to put shot into Pearson's body. Mr. Jenkins, who was then city editor, at my request, writes this graphic account of what followed:

"Billy Christian did not know what fear was. He poked fun at Fusionists with no trace of malice. However, the name he gave them stuck and brought them into ridicule. Christian's most exciting adventure was when he went gunning for Richard Pearson, a Republican leader. Pearson had been bitter in a published denunciation of Christian because Christian's ridicule had punctured his skin, and Christian was determined to reply in old-fashioned Southern style of shooting. As soon as I read what Pearson had said of Christian, I hurried to *The News and Observer* office, knowing Christian would not stand for the denunciation. I learned that, armed with a gun, he had just left for the Park Hotel, where Pearson boarded. I got there too late. The lobby was seething with excitement, everyone talking at once. As Pearson was going up the stairs, Christian had fired, barely missing him because of the turn in the stairs. I saw trouble ahead for Christian—arrest and jail for an attempt to kill. The thing to do was to get Christian out of the way before the arrival of the police. Hal Ayer and I hustled him into a hack, put him on the train, and took him to a hospital at a near-by town and entered him for treatment of a nervous disorder. Returning some days later to his post he found that the excitement had blown over. Pearson did not press for his arrest and the Democratic policemen were not keen to do anything to a reporter who was pouring hot shot by ink and lead into the Republicans."

It was Fred Merritt, managing editor, who obtained the sobriquet of "Fighting Editor." He wielded "a nasty quill," and his strictures went home. Within a few years he repulsed a dozen attacks from people who had been criticized in the paper. He was thin and wiry and the best scrapper on the staff. I recall several fist fights in which he got the best of very large men, who thought they could silence criticism by resorting to fist fighting. After he had downed a two-hundred pounder, nobody wished to tackle "the little bantam writer."

In the latter part of April the directors appointed by the Fusion Legislature to take charge of the Penitentiary drove out to the State Prison and were refused admission by Superintendent Leazar, who contended that he was legally in control. The men who went to take charge, under Fusion control, held a sort of open-air meeting for thirty minutes in the rain, which was the occasion for Christian's calling W. H. Kitchin "Mr. Rain-In-the-Face," a name which stuck to him for some time. When they were denied admittance and Superintendent Leazar continued to carry on State Prison operations, the next move was for State Treasurer Worth to close the purse strings, and my paper denounced what it called the "outrageous conduct" of Treasurer Worth, saying he was prejudging the decision of the courts. The litigation was long drawn out, and the Supreme Court came in for severe criticism. In August the court rendered its first decision upholding the Fusion contentions. *The News and Observer* made this mild criticism of the Supreme Court:

"Coming into office as non-partisans, these three lawyers have rendered the most infamously partisan decision that disgraces the pages of the Supreme Court reports. The decision was rendered for no other reason than that there was no other cloak to protect the villains who framed the State bills to suit their inclination."

It added that the decision ought to be called "a decision to permit fraud and to protect scoundrels who perpetrate it." There had been during the Legislature many charges of corruption in certifying bills enacted, which had not been passed, and in altering bills to suit the desires of the Fusionists. The Democrats alleged that this course had been pursued in several cases, particularly the case upon which *The News and Observer* animadverted severely against the Supreme Court. The wonder is that I was not cited for contempt.

The litigation over Fusion legislation and over contests for offices, and the scandal and ridicule over the Peedybee Commission, kept the State in a tension during the spring and summer of 1895.

The News and Observer's partisanship was open, fierce, and sometimes vindictive, and was carried in news stories as well as in editorials.

In the so-called "off year" of 1895 and in the 1896 campaign and others until Fusion was "dead and damned," the feature in *The News and Observer* that was most popular were the cartoons drawn by Norman E. Jennett. We called him "Our Sampson Huckleberry" because he came from the county of Sampson famous for its big berries and as the home of Marion Butler, the brains of Fusionism.

Governor Elias Carr, returning from a visit to Sampson, brought with him and gave me a copy of the Sampson *Democrat* containing a picture of Marion Butler. He said it had been cut out of wood by a young boy working in the printing office and it was his first attempt at making cuts. He drew his pictures on wood and engraved them with a pocket knife. Before that time Jennett had won a ten-dollar prize from the Atlanta *Journal* for a drawing to be used to boost the

Exposition. The picture represented a farmer holding the world in his arms, the title being "Atlanta Will Own The Earth This Year." The picture of Butler made the future Senator look like Mephistopheles.

The Governor was pleased and asked me if it wouldn't be a good idea to get that young cartoonist to make some pictures for *The News and Observer*. I got in touch with Jennett and offered him a position at six dollars a week to come to Raleigh and assist as mailing clerk and make an occasional picture on the side. The income of the paper at that time did not justify employing another person. I told him we would buy chalk plate and give him a chance to draw. He jumped at the chance and his crude pictures made a strong appeal. When the campaign of 1896 opened he had attained facility. His cartoons hit the bull's eye every time, even if they lacked the skill of Davenport. He knew little about politics or the political situation but caught on rapidly. After a bit he was relieved of his work as clerk. He and I would confer daily upon the character of the cartoons. He eagerly devoured the editorial page to see what I was writing about. He would then draw a suggestion of a cartoon and bring it in to me and we would decide together what particular Republican or Populist deserved to be hit over the head that day. Then he would undertake the task. He was the finest huckleberry that ever came from Sampson. He was of Quaker stock, a lovely boy who walked into people's hearts. He was the first man who undertook cartooning in a North Carolina paper. He drew pictures at a time when people were superheated. He pilloried men the Democrats hated. From many sources he received suggestions of cartoons. He would first draw his picture with a pencil, then cut it on the chalk plate, and make the cut himself out of molten metal. Of course such cuts could not be otherwise than crude, but they told the story and they made a hit.

I do not know how we could have gotten along in the campaigns of 1896 and 1898 without Jennett's cartoons. While they were hard-hitters he never had any feeling about the persons he was caricaturing. At first some of those who wished to be regarded as leaders in the Fusion Party would come to Jennett and ask him to do them a favor by caricaturing them. Tom Bailey (brother of Senator Bailey), McKinley's post master at Raleigh, requested Jennett to put him in as often as possible. He said, "The oftener I am in *The News and*

Observer, the more influence I have with the Republicans. They think you do not make a man's caricature unless he is influential." He was frequently accommodated, even before he was appointed post master. He attributed the position as post master in part to the prominence *The News and Observer* cartoons gave him.

After a time Jennett saw that he needed a course in drawing if he was to succeed in his calling. He wished to go to New York to an art school that trained cartoonists. He had no money and I had very little more than he had. He talked to me about his ambition and I told him we would help him as much as we could but that wasn't enough to enable him to take the big step. He had never seen a town bigger than Raleigh, and the six dollars a week he was paid when he first came to Raleigh seemed to him then a big sum. While he was drawing cartoons he came in touch with General Julian S. Carr of Durham, one of the richest men in the State at that time, and the largest contributor to the Democratic Party. Carr had a real fondness for Jennett and would occasionally write him a letter and would drop into see him when he was in Raleigh. One day Jennett told me he had been talking to several gentlemen who would lend him a little money to go to an art school in New York and added, "I believe General Carr would help me if I could get in touch with him. I have written him a letter telling him of my ambition and saying, if he would help me, I would pay him back when I was able." He had drawn a perfect likeness of General Carr on an envelope and said, "I think I will send this to him without any name or address. Everybody in North Carolina knows General Carr and I think it will reach him. Don't you think that will make a hit with him?" I assured him it would and that his idea was a stroke of genius. He sent the letter, which read:

Hon. Julian S. Carr,   Raleigh, N. C.,
Durham, N. C.   Nov. 13th, 1896.

Dear Sir:

I have just received notice from the National Academy of Design in New York City, that my drawings have been adjudged and found good enough to entitle me to a year's training for the entrance fee, which is the sum of $10.00 (ten dollars).

I am naturally very anxious to accept this wonderful opportunity—but first I must have financial aid, so the object of this letter is to ask you for a loan, say fifty dollars to start with, I can only give my word of honor as security.

If you will help me, I will guarantee to return all money loaned with interest. Thanking you in advance, I am

Yours very gratefully,
Norman E. Jennett.

It was the first letter General Carr ever received without his name or town on it, but just his picture. It pleased him very much. He took the first train for Raleigh, sent for Jennett to come to the Yarborough House and have dinner with him, gave him a check for $100 and told him there was plenty more where that came from and for him to go to New York and make himself a great cartoonist.

"I had a hard time," said Jennett, "the first year I was in New York. Of course I got work on the side as soon as I could for I wanted to be self-supporting and I lived very simply. About every two or three months General Carr would come to New York and send for me to come down to the Waldorf-Astoria to take dinner with him and that would set me up."

When the ambitious young artist started for New York (he had never been away from home), I secured a return-trip ticket for him over the Old Dominion, giving one month's stay in the big city. I had no money to give him but newspaper men then could secure transportation passes. Recalling the great adventure, Jennett years afterwards said, "Mrs. Daniels stuffed my pockets with biscuits and other lunch and I set forth. I still have that return-trip ticket."

When the campaigns of 1898 and 1900 came on, Jennett, by his study in New York, had improved his drawing and I asked him to come to Raleigh and help us out. He was glad to do so and his cartoons were believed by Simmons and Aycock and other leaders to have been one of the greatest factors in winning victories. After the election he returned to New York and was, for a long time, cartoonist on the New York *Herald,* where he originated the Sunday cartoon of Marcelline, the famous clown, which ran for a long time. Afterwards he did special work. When aviation publications were established he gave himself to drawing aeroplanes and was a pioneer on the staff of an aeroplane journal.

In my paper I made it a rule to keep watch for things new and strange and racy of the soil. There was rarely an issue without a Tarheel story illustrating incidents peculiar to our people, particularly

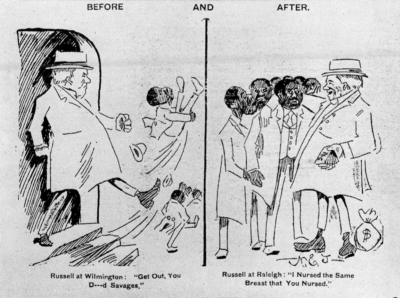

BEFORE — AND — AFTER.

Russell at Wilmington: "Get Out, You D---d Savages."

Russell at Raleigh: "I Nursed the Same Breast that You Nursed."

Upper left, Colonel J. C. L. Harris, right-hand associate and counsellor of Governor Russell; helpful visitor in *The News and Observer* office. *Upper right,* Daniel L. Russell, Governor of North Carolina, 1897-1901. *Below,* A cartoon by Jennett in *The News and Observer* of May 17, 1896, which shows the change in Governor Russell's attitude toward the Negroes when he wanted their votes.

Upper left, Colonel Harry Skinner, leading Populist, who became United States District Attorney and represented Judge Purnell in contempt proceedings. *Upper right,* Major William A. Guthrie, able and eloquent champion of the University. *Lower left,* Dr. Cyrus Thompson, Fusion candidate for Governor; chairman of the Populist State Committee in 1898; Secretary of State and opponent of Pritchard for the United States Senate. *Lower right,* Cyrus B. Watson, Democratic candidate for Governor in 1896.

those with a humorous touch. Dignified court scenes were often the setting of the best true stories. Perhaps the one most illustrative occurred in Harnett County court when Judge H. G. Connor was presiding. A well-to-do citizen of Harnett, addicted to drink, one day got full at Sanford and hired a special train to carry him to his home in Broadway village. The news gave gossips something to talk about. Later he was the hero of an incident staged in Harnett court. Malcolm Fowler is authority for a story printed in *The State* about "Mister Tom," who was summoned to serve on the jury. Hearing that Judge Connor had been detained at home by illness, the prospective juror proceeded to get so drunk that when his name was called in court he was too drunk to answer, and the prosecuting attorney issued a warrant for contempt of court. When sober, "Mister Tom" was aghast with fear. His lawyer advised him to plead guilty and throw himself upon the mercy of the court. He scorned the advice, saying, "I'll admit I was drunk but I could not be guilty of contempt of Judge Connor's court." Mr. Fowler thus gives a graphic pen-picture of the scene in court:

"The state's case was soon presented. It proved that Mr. Tom had been legally and lawfully selected and summoned as a juror and that he had accepted said summons. Further, he had arrived in town the day court opened, had promptly got drunk and certainly hadn't answered when his name was called. On this triumphant note the prosecutor rested his case.

"Judge Connor peered over his bench at Mr. Tom. 'Does the defense wish to offer any evidence?'

" 'Yes, suh, your Honor, I do,' replied Mr. Tom, rising to his feet. He leaned over to his lawyer and whispered in Colonel McLean's ear. 'Remember, Dan Hugh, just let me talk, and if it doesn't work I want to hear you do the most pitiful job of begging you ever did in your life!'

"He was sworn and took his seat in the witness chair, a pathetic looking old man with a mournfully drooping mustache.

" 'Your honor,' he began in a low vibrant voice, 'I whole-heartedly deny being in contempt of your court. I do submit to being publicly drunk but I claim extenuating circumstances.'

"A gleam of interest kindled in Judge Connor's eye. 'The Court will be pleased to listen to your extenuating circumstances, Mr. Tom.'

" 'Thank you, suh. Your Honor has long been aware of the

high esteem in which he is held by myself and the other good citizens of Harnett. It is needless for me to emphasize that point but I merely wished to mention it in passing so that my later conduct may be more clearly understood.'

" 'Go on, Mr. Tom.'

" 'Well, suh, when the news came that you were ill and would probably be unable to open court I became very despondent. And, Your Honor, I claim that it was a perfectly natural reaction for me to wander across to the bar and take a drink to revive me from my depressed mood.'

"He gazed pleadingly toward the bench and Judge Connor nodded understandingly.

" 'Shortly thereafter,' continued Mr. Tom, a note of utter sadness edging his tone, 'I heard that your Honor was seriously ill and would be unable to hold court at all. I was so grieved at hearing your illness was so severe that I had a number of drinks before I could regain my composure.'

"He paused, looked toward the crowded courtroom and received several nods of confirmation from the interested spectators.

" 'Well, suh, your Honor; when I heard still later that you were desperately ill, that death's door was about to open for you, my grief was limitless and I admit that in the extremity of my sorrow I did get drunk, but never was I in contempt of your Honor's court. That's all, Judge,' Mr. Tom concluded, an old man with slumped shoulders and mustache drooping penitently.

" 'Mr. Clerk,' said Judge Connor, clearing his throat and turning to the Clerk of the Court, 'Make this entry: Directed verdict of not guilty in contempt of Court. Admitted guilty of publicly drunk and let defendant pay costs. And collect these costs from Mr. Tom before he completes laying the blame for the whole mess on me and I have to pay them! Call the next case.'

"And Mr. Tom, shoulders erect and smiling triumphantly, proudly took his seat."

The year 1896 dawned with politics dominant. It may be said that the political discussion opened on the first day of the year when Marion Butler, who had been elected to the United States Senate, made his first set speech in the Senate, which caused *The News and Observer* to say:

"Marion Butler, who traded away whatever political principle he had when he fused with his old radical enemies, flashed his maiden sword in the Senate and it was a characteristic exhibit.

He brought a slanderous and disgraceful accusation against the Democratic Party in North Carolina and no one knew it better than this turn-coat and blatherskite. He evidently has cheek and it is a great sorrow that the great Vance were not living and in the Senate to peel the hide off this young boastful slanderer of his betters."

There developed one of the most bitter fights for the gubernatorial nomination in the Republican Party. Oliver Dockery was the candidate of the Old Guard and Daniel L. Russell was the candidate of an element of the party which was ready to and did resort to highway robbery to defeat Dockery. This skulduggery began in Wake County, where Parson Leak and the bulk of the other Negro Republicans, who were advocating Dockery, were out-generalled by Jim Young and Loge Harris, Russell leaders. Though four-fifths of the Republicans wanted Dockery, by shrewd manipulations the Russell men selected the delegates. The same sort of manipulations went on in other counties, and when the Republican State Convention met, the Russell men obtained control of the committee on credentials. Ruthlessly and with utter disregard of even common decency, it threw out the Dockery delegates and thereby nominated Russell. I attended every session of the Convention and saw the high-handed methods and printed the sordid story in my paper.

Before the Republican State Convention met in Raleigh in 1896 two mass meetings were held, one for Dockery and one for Russell. Most of the Negroes in Raleigh were for Dockery. Russell, who was always violent in language, had called the Negroes "savages" some time before. Now, in order to secure their support, he made a speech in Raleigh in which he sought, in violent abuse and slander of his own race, to embitter the Negroes against their white neighbors but, happily for the peace of the community, my paper said, the Negroes "are more peace-loving and law-abiding and friendly than to follow the counsel of selfish white demagogues." In fact, a capable Negro physician in Raleigh, Dr. L. A. Scruggs, made an address following Russell's speech in which he said he wanted to make an eternal and everlasting protest against the efforts made by Russell to array the black man against the white man. He pleaded with all to keep down such inflammatory political harangues as were delivered by Daniel L. Russell and told the Negroes to spurn such men as Russell and to condemn their vile utterances. "I despise them," said Dr.

Scruggs, "and any man or men that make such statements, and if I were a god I would forever damn the man who utters such sentiments."

Russell, in his speech, had denied that he had called the Negroes savages merely having said that there were "black savages and white savages." He declared that John Brown was one of the heroes of the world's history and that his picture should hang in every Negro's home. He promised that, if he should be elected Governor, the Negroes who put him in office should have all the oats and fodder there was to give; that every office should be held by a Republican. Fusion was offered the Populists, conditioned upon their supporting Russell for Governor. It was now up to Butler and the Populists to refuse to fuse without the governorship and silver electors or to surrender. Butler and Guthrie continued to insist on their demands for some time and Guthrie never surrendered. He knew the Republicans well, and he knew that if Russell was Governor the wrongs he predicted would occur, and the party would be brought into disgrace. Personally honest himself and sincerely believing that the Republican Party had become the annex of Wall Street, he wanted to fight and he did fight.

It did not take Butler very long to see that the Republicans had a trained army of voters and if they could capture one-third or one-half of his crowd, they could carry the State. Though having a much larger vote the Republicans offered to give the Populists half the offices. If he fought, Harry Skinner and other influential Populists would lead a bolt for fusion with the Republicans. Later, as he always did when it was to his personal advantage, Butler made a trade that was in his own interest. He agreed upon a fusion ticket on which his popular rival, Dr. Cyrus Thompson, received the nomination for Secretary of State. Thompson wanted the job, and he was smart enough to see that there was no possibility of securing it except by fusion.

Norman Jennett's first cartoon of the campaign after Russell's nomination was of his attitude toward the Negroes: Before the nomination, "Get out, you d—d savages," and after the nomination: "I nursed the same breast that you nursed." Following this cartoon *The News and Observer,* from time to time, printed extracts of what Russell had said about the Negroes when he was not in politics: among them, "All Negroes are natural born thieves. They will steal six days in the week and go to church on Sunday and shout and pray it off."

The Democrats were at sea. There was sentiment in favor of the nomination of Charles D. McIver for Governor. They couldn't have done better. McIver declared his chief interest was in the education of the people and that, having dedicated his life to that holy cause, he could not permit his name to be used for any public office. General Julian S. Carr, Walter Clark, free silver men, were suggested as the Democratic nominees for Governor. It was believed that Clark could carry a large element of the Populists as well as the Democrats. General Carr was very strong not only with the Democrats and a certain part of the Populists, but also with a few Republicans disgusted with Russell who declared they would support him if nominated.

As the time for the convention drew near, it was evident that General Carr was the favorite. He had long been looking toward the governorship and was ambitious to hold that office. He had been an unsuccessful candidate in 1892, though he would have won that year if the Alliance men had not dictated the nomination of a man of their organization. This year the nomination was virtually tendered to him and if he had been willing to accept it, he would have obtained it by acclamation. One day I received a message from Mrs. Carr asking me to come to Durham to see her. She was a woman of fine sense and character, devoted to her husband, whom she understood well. She knew he was fond of me and she and I were always the best of friends. She said:

"You know Mr. Carr and you know what politics means. He cannot say 'no' to anybody and if he runs for governor the politicians will bleed him to death. Moreover, his inability to say no is his greatest virtue and his greatest weakness. He ought not to go into politics and I know it. I want him to have anything in the world he wants but I feel that his entrance into politics would not bring him happiness but the contrary and I want you and his friends to dissuade him from accepting the nomination."

Mrs. Carr had always felt that her husband's success was along other lines than in politics, and she knew the political game well enough to know that a man esteemed to be a millionaire, in a campaign like the one of 1896, would be besieged from the beginning to the end to put up much money. General Carr did not feel this himself. In fact, if he had a dollar and his party or his church wanted it, he was generous often beyond his ability. I knew the General's heart had been set upon the governorship and I hesitated to dissuade him, but my friendship impelled me to do so. Not long before the convention he wrote a letter to some friends declining the nomination already virtually in his hands. He said that his business associates, to whom he was committed by every consideration to carry on the great business of which he was the head, strenuously objected to his entering the field of politics. I joined with his wife and business associates to urge him to decline to lead the party. The convention then drafted as its candidate the Honorable Cyrus B. Watson, of Forsyth. He came nearer being a great man, without quite reaching it, than any other man of his day in Piedmont North Carolina. He was the leader of the Winston-Salem bar. Perhaps no jury lawyer of the time was his equal. He loved a fight in a court house and never had an antagonist of whom he was afraid. He had wit and eloquence, rarely combined.

XVII

MY FIRST NATIONAL DEMOCRATIC CONVENTION

ALL OVER America in 1895 there were silver conventions in counties and states. Captain S. A. Ashe issued a book on free silver,
which was widely circulated. Butler and Pritchard both voted for
silver in the Senate. A conference was held in Memphis, called by
Senators James K. Jones, Democrat, of Arkansas, and Senator Teller,
Republican, of Colorado. It was as largely attended and as enthusiastic as any National Convention. It was at this convention that Bryan
made his first speech outside of Congress in a national gathering.
This convention outlined the plans and effected an organization
which resulted in the nomination of a silver man for President on
the Democratic ticket in 1896 and organized the silver Republican
Party, which endorsed Bryan for President. In my paper (May 26)
I had declared for the nomination of Bryan, calling him "the most
eloquent public speaker in America," and adding, "He is a sensible,
honorable, and brave man and would create an enthusiasm that would
be as surprising to the whole country as Vance's campaign of 1876
was in North Carolina."

As evidence of the sentiment in North Carolina in 1896 on the silver question, the vote for a free coinage of silver declaration was
875⅔, whereas the gold standard received 31⅓ votes in the State convention. The delegates elected to the National Convention were all
silver men but without instructions as to candidate. In a ward meeting in Raleigh to elect delegates, Fabius H. Busbee, an able lawyer,
counsel for the Southern Railway, who was going to the Chicago
Convention as proxy for the national committeeman, said he would
like to be selected as delegate to the county convention. As he was a
corporation attorney, B. C. Beckwith, a militant silver lawyer, in the
public meeting asked Busbee, "Are you in favor of free silver?"
Busbee replied, "Yes, but I am not a damn fool about it." Beckwith
appealed to the gathering not to elect Busbee, and he was defeated.
In the atmosphere of the hour a man had to be militant for 16 to 1.
It recalled to me a story told by Bill Arp, the first Southern columnist.

He said that when Georgia seceded the men were so eager to "whip the Yankees" that they volunteered in larger numbers than could be given arms. It was therefore necessary to limit enlistments until equipment arrived. How should the first selection be made? A country enthusiast suggested, "Stand 'em all up in a row, spit on 'em and don't let any man go first unless he is so hot he sizzles."

Some time before the meeting of the convention which elected delegates from the Fourth Congressional District, I made up my mind to secure election as a delegate to the National Convention, if possible. Friends gave assurance of support, but when I talked to my good friend, Sheriff Ellington, of Johnston, he told me Sheriff Mack Page of Wake had talked to him some weeks before and he had promised to support Page, not knowing that Wake might have another candidate. He felt bound by that pledge. In a contest between Page and myself, we would have divided Wake County, and it might well have resulted in both delegates being elected from some other county.

I was anxious to be elected to that convention so that I could vote for Bryan. I decided to talk with Page about the matter and see if I could induce him to withdraw. We were good friends and he was a stockholder in my paper. He was a popular and capable officer. He told me that there was one reason why he wished to be a delegate. In the previous year, his daughter being a student at the State Normal College at Greensboro, he had attended the commencement and heard Bryan speak; he was then convinced that Bryan was the man who ought to be nominated, and he wanted to go for no other purpose except to vote for Bryan. He said to me, "Josephus, you know I am an old man. I was in the Confederate Army and this is the last opportunity I will ever have to be a delegate to a National Convention. My heart is set upon it, and I wish it more than I can tell. You are a young man and you have all life before you. You let me go this time and there will be plenty more conventions for you."

I had the same feeling about Bryan that he had. I felt that Bryan was the strongest man the Democrats could nominate, and I had been greatly attracted to him personally. Nobody was talking Bryan much, and Captain Page was not publicly announcing that he wanted to go to vote for Bryan. In fact, none of the candidates for delegates that year was stressing any particular man. I thought about the matter several days and the more I thought about it, the more I wanted to

Upper left, Theodore F. Kluttz, member of Congress who seconded the nomination of Bryan. *Upper right,* Captain M. W. Page, first Bryan delegate elected in 1896. *Lower left,* Jesse W. Grainger, of Kinston, delegate to the National Democratic Convention in 1896. *Lower right,* Walter E. Moore, Bryan delegate in 1900, Judge, and Speaker of the House in 1901.

Upper left, Clement Manly, State Chairman of the Democratic Executive Committee in 1896, who was successful in fusing Democrats and Populists for Bryan. *Upper right,* Arthur Sewall, nominated for Vice-President on the Democratic ticket. *Lower left,* Judge Charles F. Warren, who led the North Carolina parade for Bryan at the National Democratic Convention in 1896. *Lower right,* William Carey Dowd, editor Charlotte *News,* Speaker of the House in 1911, and delegate to the National Democratic Conventions in 1896 and 1912.

go but the more I had a hunch that I ought not to stand in the way of an older friend whose heart was set upon the election and whose views accorded so entirely with my own. And so, after sweating blood over it for some days, I went down to the sheriff's office and told Captain Page I had asked my friends to support him. He was elected.

Looking back upon it and recalling my feelings, I might have characterized it as a real renunciation. Indeed it was, and I was quite miserable about it for a time but felt that I had done the right thing. It has been one of the outstanding lessons of my life. I found that the man who is unselfish and surrenders something which he covets very much often thereby does more to advance himself than by pressing his ambitions. When I withdrew in favor of Captain Page I had not the remotest idea of being elected national committeeman. My renunciation was entirely without any thought that I was kicking myself upstairs. Senator Ransom had been national committeeman for many years, and the position therefore seemed to be beyond the grasp of a young editor.

I went to the Chicago Convention in the capacity of reporter and travelled with most of the delegation. On the train Captain Page asked me, "Why don't you run for national committeeman? I have talked with the delegates and they are determined not to elect Ransom again. I do not think his name will be presented. Governor Jarvis, who is a Bland man, is a candidate for it, but I talked today with Mr. Grainger, of Kinston, and Captain Emory, of Halifax, and they have both agreed with me that we ought to elect you." This interested me. These three gentlemen took the matter up with other delegates and secured the pledged support of a majority of the delegation for my election before reaching Chicago. Ransom did not attend, giving his proxy to Fabius H. Busbee. This had been expected. On June 14, writing to Don Dickinson about what the gold men should do at the convention, Cleveland said, "Ransom, of course, will do as we desire. He was here a few days ago full of disgust and discouragement. He said he would be this way about convention time and he seemed indifferent whether he went or not. What do you want us to do about him?" Ransom's proxy was voted with the Cleveland group, though his State delegation was strong for Bryan.

Governor Jarvis and some of the others had gone on another train. Our delegation talked more or less about Bryan, but, outside of Captain Page, nobody was committed to him, although Ben Lacy and Captain Peebles were strongly inclined to his nomination. When we reached Chicago we were greeted by an interview in the papers, in which Governor Jarvis announced that North Carolina would cast its vote for Bland for President. As the four or five delegates on the Governor's train were all for Bland, he supposed they represented the sentiment of the delegation. As soon as we had registered at the hotel, I went over to Bryan's little hotel to call on him and made an engagement for a part of our delegation to see him that night. About a dozen of the members went with me, headed by Colonel A. M. Waddell and Theodore Kluttz. Bryan captivated them. In the course of the conversation, Colonel Waddell, after conferring with the other delegates in that group, told Bryan that the majority of the North Carolina delegates would support him for nomination and would hold a meeting next day and so declare. Bryan asked them not to do it, saying that, if they favored him, he believed they could do more to promote his nomination by not bringing him out as a candidate. It would be best, he thought, to let the older candidates measure their strength and for us to be ready to come to him at the time when it would be more valuable than to bring him out early as a candidate. His seat at the convention was contested. In fact, the Democratic National Committee had seated the J. Sterling Morton gold delegation from Nebraska, and Bryan had to make the fight for a seat in the Convention. He thought it might militate against his chances if he were contesting for a seat and the nomination at the same time. The other delegates thought Bryan's suggestion was wise, and we returned to the hotel as enthusiastic for Bryan that night as the bulk of the Convention was after they had heard his Cross of Gold speech.

Next day, when the delegation met, they elected Kluttz, a Bryan man, chairman of the delegation and elected me national committeeman by a vote of 13 to 8 over Governor Jarvis. It surprised the Governor very much and he was a little cool about it at first. Some of his friends said that the Ransom men on the delegation had wanted to defeat him because he ran against Ransom for the Senate. As a matter of fact, however, there was only one man on the delegation who could have been influenced by the Ransom-Jarvis fight and that was Captain Emory, of Halifax. The Baltimore *Sun's* story from Chicago said:

"Ex-Senator Jarvis is anxious to succeed General Ransom on the National Committee and his friends are working up a sentiment for him. His chief opponent is Josephus Daniels, editor of the Raleigh *News and Observer*. It is said that General Ransom will not attend and that his proxy as committee man is in the hands of F. H. Busbee of Raleigh and Mr. Busbee is also being urged by his friends to contest with Daniels and Jarvis. It is said that Daniels is an intense silver man and his candidacy has reached a point where he will be hard to defeat."

On the night we arrived in Chicago I met Harry L. West, the prize correspondent of the Washington *Post* and afterward Commissioner of the District of Columbia. In his telegram from Chicago next day he predicted, as did most of the correspondents, that Bland would be nominated, but said, "Josephus Daniels, of North Carolina, the newly elected National Committeeman, predicts that it will be Bryan. He is the only man here who thinks so." Frank A. Richardson, the veteran correspondent of the Baltimore *Sun,* quoted me as saying that the delegation was divided between Bryan, Bland, and Boies, probably as favoring the former, adding, "I think highly of Mr. Bryan myself," said Mr. Daniels, "and I'm doing all I can for him."

That was the first National Democratic Convention I had attended. It was an exhilaration from begining to end. Our delegation, having been the first to declare itself for Bryan, naturally gained more prominence than it would otherwise have done. First and last, I took every member of the delegation, except Governor Jarvis and one or two others, over to see Bryan. He knew, before he was seated in the convention, that not even his delegation from Nebraska was more enthusiastic for his nomination than the North Carolinians. It was a battle of giants in that convention. The Cleveland element of the party, standing for the gold standard, had the ablest leadership from the East and North. As late as the middle of June Cleveland, though discouraged, hoped that the Chicago Convention could be controlled by his supporters; and, though he never even hinted it, he hoped he would be the nominee of the party on a gold standard platform "to save the country." On the 16th of June he issued an address "to Democratic Voters," urging them to make a firm stand, saying: "A Cause worth fighting for is worth fighting for to the end." He said the country would not vote for silver coinage. In his extremity, Cleveland even warmed up to Tammany and wrote a warm letter to Sheehan, whom he had flouted in 1892, saying in a long letter: "I am confident that the voice of the Tammany Society, always potent in party council, will not fail to be heard in warning and protest on an occasion which especially inspires patriotism."

The first big battle in the convention was over the election of a temporary chairman. The silver men were determined, at all hazards, seeing that they had a large majority, to elect one of their own members as temporary chairman, who would sound the keynote. They were successful and elected Senator John W. Daniel, of Virginia. He was easily the most finished speaker in the Senate. They called him "the Lame Lion of Lynchburg." He had been a Confederate soldier, and was a lawyer of eminence and author of standard law books. He had been likened to a Roman Senator, and, clean-shaven, he looked the part. He had electrified so many audiences that the silver men expected him to make the great speech of the convention. There were no amplifiers then, and the only hope of a speaker's being heard was that he have a carrying voice. Daniel's voice was well suited for the Senate or for a small gathering but he was unable, being hoarse, to make himself heard in a buzzing audience of many thousands. The same was true of practically every other speaker during the convention, except Bryan.

Of course the great fight, except for the nomination, was in the committee on platform. The fight of the silver men was led by Senator James K. Jones, of Arkansas. He belonged to the Kimbrough Jones family, early settlers in Wake County, North Carolina, and his father had been one of the founders of Wake Forest College. He was a dominant man, able and strong without any gifts of eloquence. He always won his victories by his *fortiter in re*. He did not know the meaning of the *suaviter in modo*. He could have fought a battle on the Grant lines of massing superior troops, but he had none of the Stonewall Jackson ability by tactics, manœuvers, and surprises to win victories.

The endorsement of Cleveland's administration and the gold standard was led by Senators Hill, of New York, Vilas and Gray and Governor William E. Russell, of Massachusetts, although they had other astute men, in fact the strongest men in the convention from the Northeast. Some of their ablest men had been denied seats in the convention in the contested cases. Except for Bryan's speech, the great speech of the convention was made by William E. Russell, although more was expected of the speech of David Bennett Hill, who suffered even worse than Daniel in delivery. Daniel could be heard the first ten minutes and did arouse some enthusiasm, but Hill could scarcely be heard at all outside the small area occupied by the delegates, and his speech was disappointing in the extreme.

Russell's speech, though lacking the Bryan voice—it did not carry as far as the Nebraskan's—was a classic. He was the most gifted and the most promising Democrat in America in that day among those who stood for the Cleveland policies. His every sentence was chiselled and he spoke with a sincerity and earnestness that captivated those who heard him. He had no lute in his voice like Bryan but he had what was quite as effective, a tone of sincerity and a perfection of style that gave emphasis to all he said. He attracted me more than any man in the convention except Bryan.

It had been whispered that Senator Jones had asked Bryan to close the debate on the platform. His fame as an orator had gone before him. All the silver men were saying, "Wait until you hear Bryan," and there was a buzz of expectancy. If he had not possessed eloquence and if he had lacked the marrow of sincerity, the fact that the man on the farthest seat in the great auditorium could hear his every word would have given him a power incomparably greater than any other speaker. He did not seem to raise his voice at all. He seemed to be speaking with less effort than anyone who had preceded him, and that was always true of him. His voice was made for great gatherings. As he stood there on the platform, waiting for the enthusiasm to spend itself so that he could be heard, he was every inch an Apollo, young, lithe, with flashing eyes and a great jaw that gave him power which seemed not quite in keeping with his sweetness. He was good to look upon. Except Russell, the others who had spoken were of the older statesmen. Bryan was the new prophet of the West as Russell was of the East.

Writers of that day and later historians have said that an unknown man captured the convention by one speech. Not so. Bryan did not suddenly reach that pinnacle. Behind that memorable hour was a brilliant record of achievement in the halls of Congress and on the hustings. He had won two elections to the National House in rock-ribbed Republican districts in Nebraska. He had charmed "listening Senates" in a noble argument for tariff reform which Champ Clark declared was "the greatest and most brilliant Bryan ever delivered."

In the battle between giants in the epoch of silver discussions the pebble in the sling of the young David from Nebraska had compassed the political death of more than one political Goliath.

Bryan had not been speaking five minutes before he held the convention rapt. I had never dreamed that a mortal man could so grip and fill with enthusiasm thousands of men. He used no statistics in his speech. He got off the beaten path. Every few minutes he had to stop to give the people a chance to applaud. Sometimes the whole convention, or it seemed like the whole body of people, were standing shouting as if lifted above themselves. I say the whole convention. I must except the gold men. Hill, Russell, and the rest of them sat like stone men, seeming to look upon the frenzied throngs as if the shouters were beside themselves. They couldn't understand it. To them free silver was a heresy, and they thought there was nothing but free silver in Bryan's speech.

The truth is, free silver was the expression of the hope for legislation of a people who had been through the panic and hard times and were seeking to strike at government by privilege. There were thousands who did not know anything about free silver and did not care anything about it who were enthusiastic for Bryan. It was a conflict, rather, of man against money. Bryan made that clear, although he paramounted silver and made it the first remedy. In the North Carolina delegation we had men who were supposed to be proof against being taken off their feet by eloquence. Up to the minute Bryan touched him and gave him an enthusiasm that I never dreamed possible, Charles F. Warren, of Washington, spectacled and dignified, had sat as if he were in a court. Suddenly he was as thrilled as the most enthusiastic youngster. Hardly had Bryan finished before Warren grabbed the North Carolina banner and, followed by the entire delegation and thousands of other shouting, yelling people, paraded over the hall until there wasn't a dry thread upon him. I, there and then, made up my mind that no man is proof against eloquence. What was true of Warren was true of the other delegates. My old friend Governor Jarvis, who had been aloof because youngsters of the delegation had refused to vote for Bland, caught the contagion and shouted with the boys. I do not know how long the parading and band-playing and enthusiasm lasted. I have been in a number of national conventions and have heard the bands play and seen people march by rote, but nothing of that kind occurred in Chicago on that day when Bryan spoke. It was spontaneous. Attempts to shorten or quell it were as impossible as the attempt of Canute to drive back the waves of the ocean. The fountains in the hearts of men were stirred. They believed that Bryan was a young David with his sling, who had come to slay the giants that oppressed the people and they felt that a new day had come and, with it, a new leader. Clean of limb, clean of heart, and clean of mind, he was a vital figure. Many felt about him that day as the Israelites felt about David when he came forth as their champion. It was hard for me to write a telegram that night because, like the others, I had been swept away on the tide of hero worship.

When that speech was ended, the Bryan enthusiasts wanted a ballot at once for President, and a movement was started to compel voting while the people were under the spell of Bryan's eloquence. He showed great wisdom in advising them against that course. When his friends told him he had made a mistake in helping to prevent the convention from balloting until the next day, he said; "If the people want me nominated and that feeling could not endure overnight, it would perish before the campaign was a week old."

The resolution to endorse the Cleveland administration was defeated by a vote of 564 to 357, and the vote on adopting the platform was 624 for free silver and 301 against it. On both these votes, North Carolina voted with the majority. That night I telegraphed to *The News and Observer:*

"North Carolina was in it today. The delegation has all along favored Bryan for president. He has not been a candidate and it was urged by some that the delegates had made a mistake in choosing him but today's developments more than justify the wisdom of selecting the eloquent Nebraskan. He closed the debate for the silver forces on the platform, replying to Hill and Russell, the gold leaders. It was a crucial position. It is putting it mildly to say that Bryan captured the Convention. They simply went wild and when he had finished the delegates bore him on their shoulders down the hall amid such enthusiasm as was never witnessed before. He took a seat with the North Carolina delegation when the enthusiasm had somewhat subsided and soon it broke out afresh. Captain R. P. Peebles, J. H. Currie, Charles F. Warren, J. W. Grainger, Tom Emory, W. C. Hammer, B. R. Lacy, W. C. Dowd, and others lifted the Nebraskan on their shoulders amid deafening applause and it was moments before he could gain *terra firma*. Nothing could have prevented his nomination if a vote could have been taken then."

When Bryan was placed in nomination it was seconded by Theodore F. Kluttz of North Carolina, long a member of Congress from the Salisbury district. He had married a sister of Joseph P. Caldwell, who was to take the lead against Bryan in North Carolina.

Dr. C. M. Rosser, in his excellent life of Bryan, *The Crusading Commoner,* says that before any ballots had been taken Bryan made this statement to the Doctor and Mrs. Bryan: "So that we both may sleep well tonight, I am going to tell you something. I am the only man who can be nominated. I am what they call the logic of the situation."

The next day, when the balloting for the presidential nomination began, the advocates of the other candidates felt that Bryan's speech had spent its force and, instead of swaying the convention, its effect had been ephemeral. On the first ballot Bryan received only 103 votes out of something like a thousand cast. The thick-and-thin Cleveland men refused to participate. They started the first "sit down strike." They debated whether they would bolt the convention after the refusal to endorse Cleveland's administration, or vote for a gold standard man, or remain as non-participants. They decided on the third course. There they sat, grim and silent, refusing to vote, and were recorded as "not voting." Bryan gained on the next ballot and each succeeding one and on the fifth was nominated unanimously, the others withdrawing.

John W. Jenkins, special correspondent of *The News and Observer,* wired:

> "Immediately after the nomination of Bryan, a number of North Carolina delegates called on the future president in his modest apartments. Immense crowds were thronging the rooms as North Carolinians came into the room headed by National Committeeman Daniels. Mr. Bryan grasped him by the hand and said, 'Josephus, next to Nebraska, I owe more to the North Carolinians than to any other delegates. I owe them more than any other people.'"

With Bryan's nomination, the convention recessed, fearing to make a mistake in nominating a running mate. A sort of caucus about the vice-president was called by Senator Jones, who was the

Upper left, James K. Jones, Senator from Arkansas, who led the fight for the silver men in the National Democratic Convention. *Upper right,* John W. Daniel, Senator from Virginia, "the Lame Lion of Lynchburg." *Lower left,* William E. Russell, Governor of Massachusetts, who led the Cleveland men at the National Democratic Convention. *Lower right,* Joseph Clay Stiles Blackburn, Senator from Kentucky, who aided Jones in the 1896 fight of the silver forces.

William Jennings Bryan and Senator Stephen Mallory White, of California, taken in Kansas City, after the nomination of Mr. Bryan by Senator White, for the presidency of the United States.

acknowledged leader of the silver forces. To it was invited one representative from each State that was voting for silver in the convention. Senator Jones invited me as the new committeeman from North Carolina. The business of that meeting was to suggest a candidate for Vice-President. There were a number of names presented. Bryan arrived a little late and listened with concentrated interest to what was being said. The nomination was offered to Bland, who declined. It was either offered to Boies, or his friends said he would not take it. There was the suggestion of Daniel and others. Finally several senators, led by Senator Blackburn and Senator Money advised that John R. McLean, publisher of the Cincinnati *Enquirer,* who had received Ohio's vote for the presidency and whose Ohio paper had been a strong advocate of free silver, was the strongest man to nominate. "We are going to need money," said one of McLean's supporters in the caucus. "You cannot run a campaign or win an election without organization, and you cannot secure an organization without money. I know what I am talking about. John McLean has the money and he will let us have all that is necessary. Nominate him and we need not worry about the finances. He is very strong in Ohio and can carry it. He can bring an element to the support of the ticket that no other man can bring, etc." Some of the New England delegates proposed Arthur Sewall, who had followed his father as shipbuilder at Bath. He had been a member of the National Committee for many years, and was an upstanding Democrat in the staunchest Republican state of New England. He was one of the few strong men in that part of America who, by conviction, were for free silver. Although a friend of Cleveland, he had separated from him when Cleveland demanded the repeal of the Sherman Silver Act. He was reputed to be a very rich man, and his supporters thought he would finance the campaign if nominated.

Although the youngest member of the committee, I whispered to Chairman Jones, "Don't you think Bryan ought to be consulted?" He replied, "Certainly." Bryan listened to further discussion, including additional appeals for the nomination of John R. McLean, who would "finance the campaign." During the discussion Bryan sat with tense face. I kept my eyes upon him and observed how his face hardened when one of his supporters spoke for McLean. I knew little about McLean. Senator Blackburn told me of the great sacrifices McLean had made in his fight for free silver in Ohio and that his paper was the only one in the Middle West that could be relied upon to preach silver doctrine.

When they had all finished, Senator Jones turned to Bryan and said, "You are the nominee of the Party and you are the chosen leader. We would like to have a suggestion from you if you have any to make." I can see him now as he arose. His infectious smile, which had attracted thousands, was gone. He looked more as I imagine David looked when he was in combat with the giant, every muscle strained, taut, with his jaw set. He began very pleasantly and said that, having just been chosen leader of the Party, he had been given very little time to consider the matter and he had hoped the delegates of the convention could bring larger knowledge and more wisdom than he had to the selection of a candidate for Vice-President. He thought it a matter of supreme importance that the ticket be harmonious; it would be fatal to nominate a man for Vice-President who was, in principles and in convictions, not a true yoke-mate of the nominee for President. And then, after some more discussion, he turned to the names of the men who had been suggested and, with a sort of impressive finality, said, in substance:

"If the Convention should nominate John R. McLean, I would decline the nomination for the presidency. I would not run on a ticket with that man. He is an immoral man. He preaches free silver but all his connections and all his interests are with those who exploit the public for their private benefit. His nomination would give the lie to our professions. We would be selling the Party's birthright for his campaign money. We cannot win this election by appealing to men who stand for privilege. There are too many clean and honest men who believe in the new doctrine we shall preach in this campaign for the Party to tie to a man of McLean's standards."

You could almost see the men who had advocated McLean gasp. Joe Blackburn, who loved to play poker with McLean and loved Bryan like a sweetheart, said to me, "Josephus, this is magnificent, but it is not war. You cannot win victory by driving off everybody who isn't 100 per cent virtuous." There was no appeal. There was little discussion. Bryan had given notice that the Democratic Party, under his leadership must be dominated by men clean of life and free from any suggestion of privilege hunting. Blackburn was right; it was magnificent, but it was not war—and yet I left the room that day with a new elevation of spirit and I said to myself that a new day had dawned and a man had come into leadership who truly incarnated the principles of Jefferson with the virtues and courage of a Savonarola.

The vice-presidency was not so easily settled as the members of the committee thought it would be when the caucus was over. Bryan's remarks were heard by only two score men. The North Carolina delegation had previously decided to present the name of Judge Walter Clark, of North Carolina, and he was placed in nomination by John Henry Currie, of Cumberland, and received the entire twenty-four North Carolina votes and as many as sixty other votes. Other States had been instructed for a favorite son and they had to have a run for their money. Mr. Bryan, after looking the field over, thought it was wise to nominate a man from the East. Since there had been suggestions that this was a sectional fight the nomination of a man from Maine would make it a national fight, and Arthur Sewall was nominated.

The special *News and Observer* correspondent from Chicago referred to the fact that Mrs. Bryan had thanked me and members of the delegation for supporting Bryan, and he said, "Josephus Daniels is the youngest member of the National Committee. He attended the meeting this afternoon. Daniels was with Bryan, and they looked like boys beside the gray-headed leaders on the committee."

With reference to Mr. Bryan's statement about McLean, it should be said that when the caucus met it was agreed that whatever was said in it would be confidential. I do not know how soon the statement about McLean reached the Ohio editor. His paper supported the ticket. In later years his papers, for he had become the owner of the Washington *Post* as well as the Cincinnati *Enquirer,* were not only antagonistic to Bryan but were most critical and hostile.

I had the opportunity at Chicago to have quite a chat with William E. Russell, Governor of Massachusetts, who was the leader of the gold forces. I had been much attracted to him in his several successful candidacies for Governor of his State. If the silver question had not divided the party hopelessly in those years, he would have come to the front as the greatest Democratic leader in the East. He held sound Democratic views on the tariff and other questions that divided the parties. He had looked forward to a unified Democratic Party to follow the Cleveland administration, and there was a feeling that he was to wear Cleveland's mantle. Only a few days after the Convention adjourned he was found dead in a Canadian Fishing Camp, from heart disease. A flood of regret went all over the country, for he was the hope of the New England Democracy. For a long time the Democracy of New England had wandered in the wilderness for the lack of an inspiring leader. When he first carried Massachusetts for Governor, Russell made one of the happiest retorts to a criticism of his candidacy that is on record. I remember reading it at the time and speaking about it at Chicago. In Massachusetts the bulk of the men of wealth and college education were Republicans. Russell was of the old New England stock, a Harvard graduate and one of the young men who came out of Harvard who was looked to by all his classmates and teachers as a coming man. The bulk of the Democrats in Massachusetts were people who worked in the mills and factories and Russell's support was, therefore, confined largely to the independent highbrows and the mass of men who toiled for their support. A supercilious Republican, sneering at him, said that the only support Russell had as a candidate for Governor was "from Harvard and from the slums." In a speech that put him in the Governor's chair, Russell quoted the slurring expression and said, "It is true that the only people who are supporting me for governor are the people who think and the people who suffer." Bryan had great admiration for Russell and paid high tribute to him when he died.

The nomination of Bryan swept the country like wildfire. Even in New York City it was received, by the men who toiled, with enthusiasm. If the election could have been held in September, before the business men in the East could have raised their great campaign fund and effected their wonderful organization and before Mark Hanna could have developed, in one campaign, as the most astute national chairman of a generation, Bryan would have been President.

XVIII

"WE'LL SHOOT THE GOLD BUGS, EVERY ONE!"

H ARDLY HAD THE Democratic Convention adjourned and the committee been organized, when the big job that confronted the Bryan supporters was to secure the unified support of the silver men of the country. There was no trouble about the Silver Republicans. Their leader, Henry M. Teller, of Colorado, one of the really great men of his day, a man who had saved the South from the Force bill and had led the fight for many fine measures, was a devoted free silver man. He had reached the place where he put the cause of free silver above party. Acting with Senator Jones, of Nevada, who was the white-bearded free silver man of the Senate, they had created such a sentiment in the West for free silver that the people were determined to vote for any party that made it the chief issue. They came out at once, without reservations, for Bryan and Sewall and entered the fight enthusiastically. Their convention was in fact a ratification meeting.

The Populist National Convention met on July 21 at St. Louis. There were rumors that Mark Hanna had been getting in his work with some of the delegates. There were quite a number of middle-of-the-road Populists, who had left the two old parties and had no confidence in either. They wanted to nominate an independent ticket, but Bryan had the hearty and enthusiastic support of the Western Populists and was so highly regarded by the Silver Republicans and the most sincere Populist leaders that these middle-of-the-road fellows felt they must change their tactics.

Senator Jones, national chairman of the Democratic Committee, and Senator Stone of Missouri, vice-chairman, wired me to come without fail to St. Louis to the meeting of the Populist Convention. They wished me to find out everything I could about the attitude of the North Carolina Populists. As it turned out, and as they then believed, the action of the North Carolina Populists might determine the action of the St. Louis Convention. Colonel Polk, of North Carolina, who had been the head of the National Farmers' Alliance, had

been succeeded by Marion Butler, who was the head of the North
Carolina Populist delegation at St. Louis. I therefore left Raleigh with
the Populist delegation from our State and travelled with them from
Raleigh to St. Louis. Some of them had been old Democratic friends,
and almost all of them were, at heart, enthusiastic for Bryan and
Sewall.

I had not been in St. Louis long before I became convinced that
Butler was playing a double game. He was telling Senator Teller
and Senator Allen, the Republican and Populist leaders for Bryan
and Sewall, and other leaders of the Populists and Silver Republican
forces, that he was strong for Bryan but that he was having a very
difficult time to bring the Populist forces to the support of Sewall.
The truth is, he was fomenting under-cover opposition to Sewall.

The other big Populist leader was Tom Watson, of Georgia, more
brilliant and audacious than Butler but neither so cunning nor so
shrewd. He was out and out against Bryan. He wanted the nomination himself. He had left the Democratic Party in Georgia, and the
bitterness there was so great that he felt the Georgia Democrats would
never forgive him or permit him to have position. Therefore he was
ready to knife the Democratic Party and Bryan and disappoint the
hope of the bi-metalists. Butler let it be known that he was embarrassed by Watson's actions. Maybe he was. At any rate, there were
two opinions about him. One was that he was afraid of Watson,
afraid if he took a strong stand against Watson's idea of nominating
a Populist for Vice-President, he would lose the leadership of the
middle-of-the-road men. The other opinion was that he was in the
employ of Mark Hanna and was shaping events so as to keep his
standing with the silver men and yet make such trades and com-
promises as would keep up the fusion in North Carolina between
the Populists and Republicans and make such divisions in the Populist forces in the West as would please the Republicans.

Having travelled out in the same train with the Populists to
St. Louis, I went to their hotel and stayed with them and attended
most of their caucuses until they became secret. Also, being an unknown young man, I went into the meetings of all the State delegations of the Populists in the St. Louis hotels and, as a newspaper
reporter, got in touch with other newspaper correspondents. The
night after I arrived, at a conference with Senator Jones, Senator
Teller, and Senator Allen, I gave them the first information they had

that Butler was going to throw them down, that he and men of his type were determined to nominate a Populist for Vice-president and they were going to do it for trading purposes. Senator Allen, who had assurances to the contrary from Butler, could not believe it, and Jones, who felt that he had assurance also, doubted my information. The Texas Populists were the most insistent middle-of-the-road men, and in their conferences, which I attended, they were vicious, and their loud-lunged men would call out "Who is Arthur Sewall? We like Bryan, but we will not support a Maine Yankee." Their loud-voiced delegates went from delegation to delegation, and I discovered that many of them had called on Butler before they made these pilgrimages.

Butler did not want Watson. He disliked him. He knew Watson would take the scepter from him if he could. He wanted to hold the reins but he feared Watson. Moreover, he saw that, to hold his power, he must be the national chairman of the Populists during that campaign. He knew that his professions and leadership compelled him to be for Bryan, but to be for Bryan in such a way that silver men of the West would understand they had to make terms with him. Butler, with the cunning that always characterized him, seemed to be in the background, not to be directing the forces, letting Teller and the silver men believe he was trying to hold the unruly horses in hand and then quietly and without saying anything publicly, unleashing the wild horses.

The really sincere silver men were there in great numbers. The Populists who had felt the grind of low-priced cotton and hard times were there with a fervor such as might characterize a religious gathering. They had clubs and everybody sang. Their favorite number was "We'll Shoot the Gold Bugs, Every One," and they sang it with a spirit and a cadence that stirred the convention. That was about the only singing in that campaign. Its sentiment voiced the spirit of passion, even hate, of the campaign. The hard times were too depressing and the bitterness too deep to admit of the sort of singing campaign which had previously marked presidential years. As I heard the singing by the Populists I recalled that Cleveland had made his come-back in 1892 to the music of a campaign song that enlivened Democratic meetings from coast to coast. It was first heard in the Convention that nominated him, caught the imagination of his supporters, and was everywhere sung in tune and out of tune:

"Four more years of Grover—
Out they go, in we go,
Then we'll be in clover
Four more years of Grover."

This air lent itself to singing in the mass, and the words stimulated the enthusiasm and whetted the appetite of "deserving Democrats." The line, "out they go" and "in we go," had in it a promise that the Government from top to bottom was to be in the hands of those who would do most to restore the Democrats to power.

Of course Cleveland did not inspire that campaign song. He pitched his campaign on great measures, emphasizing the need for tariff reform. His devotion to a reform of the Civil Service would have made him prefer a more dignified and elevated campaign sentiment, unrelated to a suggestion of the distribution of offices. Office seekers, in fact, were his detestation. However, he became the beneficiary of those whose political activity was increased by the hopeful line, "In we go."

That was the last presidential campaign that marched to victory to the melody of song. It was a revival of campaigns of former years when poets tuned their lyres to commend their favorite or belittle their opponent. I recall as a boy hearing my mother, who was a Whig before 1860, repeat snatches of campaign songs that had come down to her from the famous Clay-Polk contest. Two lines, as I recall, ran like this:

"Ha, ha, ha, what a nominee
Is James K. Polk of Tennessee."

That was the song, derogatory in character, most in vogue. She recalled one verse of another loved by supporters of Clay in the same campaign, of a somewhat different ring:

"The moon was shining silver bright,
The stars with glory crowned the night;
High on a limb the 'same old coon'
Was singing to himself this tune:
Get out of the way, you're all unlucky,
Clear the track for old Kentucky."

After the Cleveland campaign the old-fashioned campaign singing went into "innocuous desuetude," to quote a Cleveland expression.

It wasn't the only old-time political custom that went into the discard. The processions, carrying torchlights by night and banners by day, to the music of bands, was also marked for slaughter. I recall having my arms blackened with tar, as a youth in Wilson, carrying real light-wood torches in Cleveland parades. Each marcher furnished his own torch-light and the members of the band volunteered, so that no money was required to stage a procession. The marchers were enthusiastic partisans and there was never any suggestion of Hessianizing these demonstrations until later. Mark Hanna commercialized them so that they came into disrepute. Up to that period, the men who proudly marched in such processions were volunteer political enthusiasts. They would have been insulted if offered pay and no one was permitted to march except those who chose that public way of manifesting their convictions.

From St. Louis, on the 25th of July, I telegraphed, "The Tar Heels are booming Henry Skinner for Vice-president. Bryan stands loyally by his running mate and will not now accept the nomination for President unless Sewall is also endorsed." That was Bryan's sincere position, and he made it known without any doubt that this was his earnest desire. He used all the influence at his command to secure the endorsement of Sewall, but he was not a match for Machiavelli Butler. Indeed, there was a very strong influence in the convention against nominating even Bryan, and newspaper men who talked freely to me at the St. Louis convention, or some of them, believed that Mark Hanna's agents were very active there and were perfectly willing to spend any amount of money to secure a division of the silver forces. Bryan was nominated by a vote of 1,042 to 331. The opposition to Bryan had been so loud-mouthed that the North Carolina Populists, who were for him, became very uneasy; and so, when his nomination was effected, I wired *The News and Observer* that Kitchin, Guthrie, Skinner, and Butler were delighted.

Butler, all along, professed to be doing everything he could, without having a split, to secure harmonious action of the Populist Party, and, toward that end, sought to convince them that it was a mere gesture to nominate Watson for Vice-president but that it was necessary to do so in order to hold his forces in hand; that many Populists were already saying he was trying to carry them into the Democratic Party, but, by God, they wouldn't go; that he really was the man who was using a solvent to unify, instead of destroy. Stone talked very plainly to Butler and told him the responsibility of the defeat of Bryan would be upon his head and the heads of the other men who were advocating the nomination of a Populist for Vice-president; that it would go out in the country that the silver forces were disorganized, opening the grounds for trades and traffic of all sorts and that it would prevent a harmonious campaign.

Some of them actually believed Butler, but I had had some previous experience with that gentleman, having been very close to him when he first came out of college and I believed in his sincerity. Later I watched him take the easiest way by sacrificing any views or principles he had professed. Jones thought I was too hard on him. Others saw that if Butler didn't lead, Tom Watson would, and that he would be about as easy to deal with as a bull in a china shop, whereas they could do business with Butler.

The convention, after much discussion and more oratory and much singing, drove a nail into the coffin of the Democratic victory when they refused to endorse the nomination of Bryan and Sewall and threw a discordant and demoralizing element into the campaign by the nomination of Watson. He was to be a thorn in the side of all the silver men from that day until the election. Nobody could quiet or silence him. He was obsessed by his ego and first demanded that he be given preference over Sewall. In fact, he first demanded that Sewall be taken down and that he be made the candidate for Vice-president and everything he did was injurious to the campaign and the cause. These were not Butler's tactics. He really wanted Bryan elected, or he made the leaders of the Democratic Party think so, although those who knew him best never fully trusted him.

It wasn't long before it was seen why he was so anxious to have a candidate for Vice-president. He wanted to trade, in the nation, as he had traded in North Carolina. Moreover, large sums of money, contributed to the Bryan campaign, were being put up by rich owners of silver mines and other Western Silver Republicans and Democrats. When Butler learned they had made large contributions to the Democratic campaign fund, he would ask for a like contribution to his campaign fund, and he would also call upon Senator Jones to help finance the campaign for the Populists, keeping two separate organizations with separate expenses and handling the money himself for the Populists. The rich Silver Republicans were afraid not to grant part of his request, and all during the campaign there was this dual necessity of money and the fear that, unless the Populists were helped, their leaders might not play fair. My opinion was then, and I told Senator Jones so, that through other people Butler was getting money from Mark Hanna, and there ought to be a detective on his track to see where he got his money and what he did with it. Nobody could see how he was spending any money, while Jones was spending all the money he could get and helping everywhere. A prominent Nebraskan, who had a position in Populist headquarters, James A. Edgerton, afterward told me that he believed Butler kept most of the money for himself. If he was right, that explained why, after the campaign, Butler, who had never had any money, blossomed out as a man of wealth. There was no law then requiring the publication of campaign receipts or expenditures, and no accounting was ever made to anybody of money received for the Populist national campaign or how it was expended. Suspicion might have done him great injustice, but many believed he feathered his nest out of that campaign.

In a number of States the question of fusing on electoral tickets was attended with much embarrassment and trouble. In North Carolina, for example, the State in which Bryan was particularly strong, Butler was playing a double game. He insisted on fusing with the Republicans on State issues and demanded that the Democrats fuse with the Populists on the electoral ticket. As to the electoral ticket, there was much to be said in favor of his proposition, and there was no other course to pursue. If he was sincere, it was clearly the duty of the Democrats to withdraw part of their electors and substitute for them Populists who were sincerely for Bryan. If he were insincere, it was all the more necessary to hold him to a joint electoral ticket for fear of losing the electoral vote for Bryan.

This complicated the situation in North Carolina greatly. Naturally, the Democrats distrusted the Populist leaders, because they were in a close compact of fusion with the Republicans on every office in the State from constable to senator. It was not easy to persuade old-time Democrats to vote for a Populist elector when Populists in their home county and district were actively supporting the Republicans for each county and State office. The bitterness was greater than can be described. I talked often with the Populist leaders, Butler and others. They always declared that they, personally, were perfectly willing to vote for the Democratic electoral ticket for Bryan but it was difficult to carry their people with them. I reported to Senator

Jones that the only way to insure the electoral vote in North Carolina for Bryan was to fuse with the Populists on electors.

That created a great division in the Democratic Party in the State. Some of the Bryan men were so bitter toward the Populists that they preferred to run the risk of losing the electoral vote of the State to having anything to do with Butler. All the Democrats who were not strong for Bryan at heart, although they openly were supporting him, were very willing to fight against any Populist on the electoral ticket. State Chairman Clement Manly was confronted with one of the most delicate and difficult situations that ever met any man in the State. On one hand were men like myself, and that included the bulk of the Democratic editors and leaders, who were confident that unless there was a joint electoral ticket McKinley would carry the State and that it was necessary to make concessions. On the other hand, there were strong men who held that you could not make a successful fight for the Populist and Democratic fusion on the national ticket, while Republicans and Populists were supporting the same State and county tickets. And there was very much to be said for their point of view.

Manly, from the first, saw that the State would probably go for McKinley unless there was fusion. He was for it and was using every influence diplomatically to bring about a feeling in the party that would justify fusion on the electoral ticket. When that was done he was confronted by the direct and flat refusal of some of the Democrats, who had been nominated as electors, to withdraw. While all the energies of the campaign ought to have been directed against the party's enemies, it was necessary for the party leaders to devote much time to conciliation. Finally, however, the diplomatic policy of the committee prevailed. Swearing they ne'er would consent, the recalcitrant electors did consent, and the electoral ticket was made up of six Democrats and five Populists. The Populists selected were the least objectionable to the Democrats of all who could have been put on the ticket. This showed that no matter what Butler was doing in other States he was playing the game squarely for Bryan in North Carolina, although a condition was imposed that in the electoral college the five Populists were to be free to support Watson for Vice-president while the six Democrats would vote for Sewall. In States like Nebraska, there was no trouble.

In North Carolina the agreement could not have been possible except for the fact that the Honorable Cyrus B. Watson, Democratic candidate for Governor, and Major William A. Guthrie, Populist candidate for Governor, were both so sincere and straightforward in their campaigns for Bryan and his cause that they were ready to make any sacrifice. In fact, if Populists like Major Guthrie—and there were many of them—could have had their way, they would have overruled Butler and Hal W. Ayer, the Populist state chairman, and would have endorsed the Democratic ticket for electors and eliminated the difficulties.

THE "YELLOW BELLIES" HOLD CONVENTION

The Gold Democrats held their convention in Indianapolis and nominated General Palmer and General Buckner. This convention was composed of men who had carried out the sitting bolt in the convention that nominated Bryan and of other Cleveland men and people who believed in the gold standard. I had known General Palmer very well when I was in Washington in the early days of the Cleveland administration. He was Senator from Illinois, had been a general in the Federal army, and after Appomattox had been assigned to duty in Raleigh. I talked with him often about his stay in Raleigh. He was highly regarded by Mr. Cleveland and by the country. He had been a brave soldier who, like Andrew Johnson and others, was inimical to the policy of Reconstruction and became a Democrat in a state where they were in the minority. He believed that the gold standard was right. Buckner, his associate, had been a general in the Confederate Army, and was likewise a man of high standing and character and undoubtedly sincere in his belief that free silver was a dangerous experiment. I do not recall whether North Carolina was represented in the convention that nominated them or not. It probably was. I know that Colonel Paul B. Means, who had been one of the three delegates to vote for Cleveland in 1892, stated publicly that McKinley would carry North Carolina. The Charlotte *Observer* was sympathetic with the ticket, and so far as its influence was concerned it was against Bryan; but it did not bolt and did not advise bolting because it was interested in trying to regain North Carolina for the Democratic Party. The Gold Democrats gave the name of "Popocrats" to the Bryan people, and the Bryan crowd retaliated by calling the advocates of Palmer and Buckner the "Boltocrats."

In North Carolina the nomination of Palmer and Buckner fell flat. The convention of gold Democrats was called at Greensboro to endorse the nomination, and a great sounding of trumpets was made. The gold Democrats predicted that there would be a great outpouring of the people. *The News and Observer* sent its special correspondent, W. E. Christian, to Greensboro to cover the convention. His report laughed them out of countenance and nothing more was heard of them. Only eight people outside of Greensboro attended the convention and at the election they had only a little more than five hundred votes.

An aftermath of such a vote by an honored Bishop in Raleigh, was this story told by Mayor Russ, the prince of humorists:

"When I reached the Mayor's office this election day I found a ward boss, a red-hot Democratic heeler, waiting for me. I saw he was excited or troubled. He opened up at once, saying, 'Mr. Mayor, I has come to call on you to exercise your jurisdiction.' I asked wherein. The ward worker said: 'At the election in my precinct. Bishop Cushi [Cheshire], the bishop of the white 'Piscopal Church, went to the polls and voted the Nigger ticket for McKinley. In a few minutes Dr. Hunt [Rev. A. B. Hunter, a white clergyman from the North, head of the Episcopal St. Augustine School for Negroes], came up and said: 'Give me a Bryan ticket and he plumped the white man's ticket into the ballot-box.' I asked my caller what jurisdiction that situation presented to the Mayor of Raleigh.

" 'It is this, Mr. Mayor: I want you to exercise your jurisdiction and change Bishop Cashi [Cheshire], who voted the Nigger ticket, from being Bishop of the white 'Piscopalians an' make him president of the Nigger school, and then to change Dr. Hunt, who voted the white man's ticket, to be Bishop of the white 'Piscopalians. The swap air necessary in view of today's voting."

The Mayor added that he told the petitioner that while he was an Episcopalian and he and Dr. Hunter had voted the white man's ticket together, and he disapproved of Bishop Cheshire's voting for a Republican, the law did not give the Mayor the jurisdiction to make the swap of positions requested.

The story was widely told. It created much amusement and campaign bitterness evaporated in general laughter. But Bishop Cheshire never joined in the merriment. He did not live to see President Roosevelt, an officer in the Episcopal church, shatter the gold standard fetish.

That year I had a convention habit but did not attend the Republican Convention. From the day of the famous Manly telegram, "God Almighty Hates a Quitter," it was evident that Thomas Brackett Reed, sturdy advocate of the gold standard, had no chance to secure the nomination. Two causes operated to nominate McKinley: (1) Mark Hanna had early rounded up the delegates for a likable protectionist who always voted in a way to enrich the big industrialists; and (2) it was thought that McKinley, having always voted with the silver men, "could work both sides of the street." Neither Hanna nor McKinley wanted a gold standard plank, but when Lodge and others pointed out that it was the way to secure big subscriptions Hanna was convinced and McKinley yielded. It was a well-greased machine, and after the Moneycrats, as they were called, had their way, including an unknown millionaire for Vice-president, all went well. The loss of the silver men was compensation for the big money that made coercion possible.

HOKE SMITH AND CLEVELAND AT THE PARTING OF THE WAYS

Hard words were the order of the day and the Democrats who had been close to Cleveland but who had been regular in their allegiance to their party in the 1896 campaign, were soon placed in a very embarrassing position. Mr. Cleveland was implacable. He said little but he had no toleration for any Democrat who held office under him who would not oppose Bryan and Seawell.

No man of that day had to meet quite so serious a Gethsemane as Hoke Smith. He was a Georgia Democrat. Cleveland had appointed him as Secretary of the Interior, largely, and perhaps chiefly, upon the recommendation of Lucius Q. C. Lamar, long Senator from Mississippi, Secretary of the Interior in Cleveland's first administration, and later appointed by Cleveland Associate Justice of the Supreme Court. Lamar was intellectually perhaps the ablest Southern Senator and one of the most lovable men who ever lived, a dreamy, scholarly man who mastered any subject to which he put his mind. When Cleveland was making up his Cabinet, after the election of 1892, he appealed to Lamar to suggest the best man in the South for a Cabinet portfolio. There had been a bitter contest in Georgia over the election of delegates to the National Convention in 1892. Then, and for many years, the two elements of the Democratic Party in Georgia were represented by the two leading papers of Georgia, the Atlanta *Constitution,* which had been given national reputation by Henry Grady and was then controlled by the Howells, and the Atlanta *Journal,* controlled by Hoke Smith. In the campaign for delegates, the *Journal,* supporting Cleveland, called the *Constitution,* supporting David Bennett Hill, "The Hillstitution," and there was a furious fight, with Hoke Smith as the victor. Cleveland, of course, knew all about that fight and knew Hoke Smith had won for him over what had long been the dominant faction in Georgia. Hoke was not backward in letting Cleveland know, during the whole time, what he was doing for him. He was young and progressive and vigorous and had won the warm friendship of Justice Lamar. He was unknown in national politics.

I knew at once, as soon as Bryan was nominated, and everybody knew, as soon as Palmer and Buckner were nominated, that Hoke Smith's position was an impossible one. I had kept in close touch with him after resigning my position in the Interior Department and we were devoted friends. He had great personal regard for Mr. Bryan, but he had come to believe that bi-metalism was impracticable and he had stood with Cleveland, though at first with some trepidation, in his advocacy of the gold standard. But there was quite a difference between advocating the gold standard inside the Democratic Party and bolting the Democratic ticket in the State of Georgia. In the first place, he believed in regularity. In the second place, he had personal esteem for Mr. Bryan and, while he had given all the offices in the Interior Department to J. Sterling Morton to be awarded to Morton's friends in Nebraska, he never did it willingly, but because Cleveland would not recognize Bryan in any way after his attack upon his position on the money question.

I knew at first hand the conflict in the mind of Hoke Smith in 1896. He was the only member of Cleveland's Cabinet who supported Bryan. He received a severe lecture from Cleveland. Smith was greatly disturbed over his position and opened his heart to me. He had spoken against free silver and was committed to the gold standard. He hated to leave the Cabinet. My advice was to "Stick to your party. Cleveland is going to aid the party of high tariff. You would be going with a party that would not only prevent tariff reform but would also humiliate the South. Whatever others do, we Southern Democrats must abide in the ship." For a time he was mistrusted by both silver men and Clevelandites, but later his ability and courage were recognized. Georgia elected him Governor and Senator.

In his letter of resignation, August 5, 1896, Hoke Smith did not recant his previous gold standard advocacy, but placed his support of Bryan upon local considerations, adding: "I would strike my own people a severe blow if I repudiated a nominee of a regular Convention, thereby setting a precedent for disorganization."

Cleveland's answer showed his disapproval. "I was astonished and much disappointed by your course and I am by no means relieved by the reasons you present in justification of it." He combated the soundness of Smith's reasons and added, "It is due to our countrymen and to the safety of the nation that such an administration [as ours] should not be discredited or stricken down." He virtually told Smith he had deserted his colors and associates and, as to his argument, declared, "It seems to me like straining at a gnat and swallowing a camel."

The rebuke cut Smith to the quick. He had led the fight that gave Cleveland the vote of Georgia in 1892. Cleveland had said when he was named, "Hoke Smith is a very able representative of the New South."

Hoke Smith was a forthright and downright man of vigor, force, and ability. He thought he was thick-skinned, but he wasn't, not any more than Cleveland, whose letters to his confidential friends prove that he was wounded by the hard things said about him. There are no thick-skinned men in public life. The one thing that got under Hoke Smith's skin was the almost daily ridicule by Dana's *Sun*. It was Dana's habit to make some public man in each administration the butt of ridicule. Cleveland had felt his barbed sarcasm when he was Governor of New York. From 1893 until the end of his life, Dana and Dana's young men made Hoke Smith their target. What they said about him didn't hurt so much as the fact that the *Sun* always printed his name as "Hoax Myth." It often treated him as both a myth and a hoax—not a real Cabinet officer but a sort of hoax upon the American people. There was nothing Smith could do about it and he essayed to laugh it off, but the grins were very dry ones.

"I never ridicule a man in my life unless I like him or feel he has won a place where ridicule won't hurt him," Dana once said when a serious and solid public-spirited Philadelphian sent word to Dana "that his darts wounded him." That ought to have been a consolation to Hoke Smith (Hoax Myth) but it wasn't healing.

So far as his political fortunes were concerned Hoke Smith acted wisely by following his convictions. He knew that regularity was the supreme political rule of action in the South and that if he bolted the regular nominees his political career was ended.

XIX

SWINGING THE CAMPAIGN CIRCUIT WITH BRYAN

THERE WAS NEVER any hotter weather or hotter political atmosphere than in New York City on August 13, 1896, when Bryan formally accepted the nomination. Scores of North Carolinians went up. The rank and file of the Democrats of New York State seemed to be for Bryan. They were tremendously enthusiastic. Few of the leaders from New York had said anything after the nomination of Bryan, and their delegates had all taken part in the sitting bolt. A little while after the convention a newspaper man had asked David Bennett Hill if he was still a Democrat, and all of the newspapers, with many a comment, printed his reply: "Yes, I am still a Democrat, and very still." That was the attitude of the bulk of the leaders of the Democratic Party in New York when Bryan made his speech of acceptance. Senators Hill and Murphy later came out for his nomination in a perfunctory way. Richard Croker, boss of Tammany, was to come out for him more strongly, but all this was in the future.

The men who had been at the front in the Cleveland regime were against Bryan, although many of them had not yet come out openly. The New York papers were all against him, except the *Journal,* which had recently come under the ownership of William Randolph Hearst. Hearst had gathered around him on the staff of the *Journal* gifted young writers and was making the paper virtually the Eastern organ of the Bryan wing of the party. His writers soft-pedaled on silver, although they printed articles from Morten Frewen, the distinguished British bi-metalist, and articles daily from capable Americans favoring free silver; but their emphasis was upon Bryan's labor record and his criticism of the Supreme Court for turning down the income tax decision and what might be called social welfare measures. The *Journal* was then militantly progressive, and each day in the metropolis which Bryan called "the enemies' country," this paper pilloried Mark Hanna editorially, but chiefly through the Davenport cartoons. The one representing Hanna with dollar marks in a checked suit became almost the Democratic trademark of the campaign. Everywhere you went, the smaller papers copied this cartoon of Davenport, and Mark Hanna was represented to the people as a great big overgrown man, with heavy jaws and thick neck, with dollar marks all over him. This was tremendously effective because it soon developed that the campaign was to be one in which there was to be such lavish expenditure of money as had never been dreamed of in the United States.

The *Journal* correspondents accompanied Mr. Bryan everywhere, printed interviews and stories about him, and made him a popular figure with its readers. Simultaneously the circulation of the *Journal,* which had been one of the smallest papers in New York, went into the hundreds of thousands. Although undoubtedly it did not gain in advertisements because of its Bryan support, this gave it an immediate circulation which it could not otherwise have obtained. Since it was the only paper in any big city in the East supporting Bryan, the Bryan people subscribed to it and looked to it for leadership. The Hearst of 1896 was young and either felt something of the urge for the average man, such as was incarnated in Bryan and Tom Johnson, or got on the bandwagon to give his paper circulation. I thought then that he was sincere. His father had been a Democratic Senator from California and was one of the earliest free silver advocates, and young Hearst had been brought up in that atmosphere. He was invited to attend a meeting of the Democratic National Committee. This was the first time I ever saw him. Senator Jones asked him to make any suggestions that he thought would be valuable in the campaign. I remember to have been greatly surprised at his very low voice, his timidity, and his apparent modesty. He seemed not able to express himself, and in the very few words that he uttered disclaimed any ability to make any suggestions except that he thought Mr. Bryan's speeches were attracting great crowds, and inasmuch as the press was, as a rule, against Bryan, the *Journal* was the only means by which he could get publicity. The Bryan people throughout the country were enthusiastic about Hearst's support and welcomed it, for without it they would have had no voice in the papers of the Eastern metropolis.

The Bryan reception in New York was enthusiastic, and the rank and file of Tammany seemed to be truly Democratic. The National Committee and Democratic leaders left New York after the meeting with a feeling of perfect confidence that victory was in the offing. They judged by the enthusiasm of men who toiled. They did not

Left, Benjamin Tillman, Governor and United States Senator from South Carolina, who was enthusiastic for Bryan. *Right,* Thomas E. Watson, of Georgia, Populist leader and United States Senator.

THE CAUCASIAN.

RALEIGH N.C. APRIL 2 1896

AYER

STATE AUDITOR

We don't believe in the honesty of any man who says he is a Populist and then says he is willing to vote for a Goldbug. He may be honest but we don't want to be mixed up with any such honesty as that. A man may be a good fellow in his WAY, but it might be a very proper thing to damn his Way. Editorial in Caucasian April 2

N.E. Jennett

HE CAN'T RUB IT OUT

A cartoon by Jennett in *The News and Observer* of October 30, 1896, pointing out the inconsistency of the Populists, as seen in the statement of Hal W. Ayer, head of Butler's paper, *The Caucasian,* and their later political alignment in the 1896 presidential campaign.

know that the screws were to be applied later. They did not sense the tremendous power of the Eastern press, the voice of opposition to the young Lochinvar, and the fear of the silver dollar, and more than all, the antagonism to putting a man in the White House who would regard New York City as "the enemies' country."

The weather in New York was unspeakably hot. The old Fifth Avenue Hotel, where my wife and I and most of the committeemen were gathered, had only one cool place. That was the large bar room. It was kept at a low temperature, and it was here that most of the members of the National Committee held their conferences. My wife later often told the story that, for the first time in her life, she had to tell people calling to see me that they would find me in the bar room. It was a famous room. It was the same hotel in which Senator Platt always held his "Amen Corner" breakfasts. It had not generally been Democratic headquarters in New York City, but the crowd was so great that the old Hoffman House was filled with New York politicians. The visiting Democrats foregathered at the Fifth Avenue. It was the best hotel that I ever visited, and furnished the best food. For four dollars a day you could get a room with bath and three meals a day and a supper at bedtime. The dinner alone, with such variety, would cost you ten dollars now.

THE SITUATION IN NORTH CAROLINA

Bryan and Senator Jones were deeply interested in the situation in North Carolina. Bryan knew all about the political situation, the fusion between the Populists and Republicans. It was regarded as the only Southern state in the doubtful column. I pointed out to Bryan and Jones that it would be essential for Bryan to come to North Carolina. Jones agreed that he ought to go, and Bryan promised to come later in the campaign. I was able to return home and assure the Democratic campaign managers that in September Bryan would make a trip through the State, speaking at a number of points.

Immediately after Bryan's acceptance, the situation in North Carolina became more acute. The Populist Convention was held in Raleigh two days after Bryan's speech. It was composed of heterogeneous elements. There was great rejoicing in that party when Colonel Oliver H. Dockery, who had inherited from his father the leadership of the Republican Party of Eastern North Carolina, had left the Republican Party and come out as a staunch advocate of free silver and joined the Populist Party. He never got over his hatred of Russell, not for Russell's defeating him for Governor, but because he felt Russell had stolen the nomination; and he used somewhat the same language about it that later Theodore Roosevelt used about Taft, when he employed the most vituperative language in denouncing his former Secretary of War. The Populists nominated Major W. A. Guthrie for Governor, Dockery for Lieutenant-Governor, William H. Worth for Treasurer, and Cyrus Thompson for Secretary of State.

The first break between the leaders occurring in this convention was that between Butler and Harry Skinner, but Butler won out. However, it was a pyrrhic victory, for in the next Legislature Skinner was to have his innings. The question in the convention was whether they would fuse with the Republicans or not. The idealistic Populists, free silver Populists, those who had left the Democratic Party because of Cleveland's opposition to free silver, had no heart to unite with the Republicans, but those who wanted an office saw no choice if they wanted a slice of pie, and Hal W. Ayer, head of Butler's paper, declared for the fusion with the Republicans in State matters.

Shortly after his nomination, Guthrie challenged Watson, the Democratic candidate, and Russell, the Republican candidate, for a joint debate, and for a time it looked as if there were going to be a three-cornered debate throughout the State. Guthrie did this of his own accord. Butler and the Populist managers were still figuring on fusion and were ready to sacrifice any of their candidates if they could make a fusion which would insure half of the offices in the State to themselves. They were considering taking Guthrie down, if thereby they could assure the success of others on the State and county tickets. Guthrie, who was always an independent and pugnacious man, upset all their calculations. It was suggested, day after day, and it came from Populist headquarters, that part of their ticket would be taken down and overtures were made to Guthrie. He was adamant and gave out interviews declaring that, under no circumstances, would he come down; that he was in the fight to the finish. He warned the Populists if they voted for any gold bug they would disgrace themselves. This threatened to prevent fusion and delayed the plans for some time. In the end the Populists had to proceed in fusion, with two candidates for Governor against the Democratic ticket.

Guthrie and Watson were good friends and they sought in every way possible to secure such a situation as would separate the Populists from the Republicans. Guthrie and Watson each was ready to come down in the interest of the other if they could insure the electoral vote for Bryan and prevent the Republicans from carrying the Legislature. The joint campaign between them was seen to be a sort of love feast in which they both advocated the same thing. Watson became ill in the campaign and had to retire from it.

In the middle of September, at a meeting of the Bryan forces in Washington, Butler gave assurance that, whether there was fusion or not in North Carolina, the electoral vote of the State could be counted upon for Bryan, and said, "It is like the case of two women who appealed to King Solomon to settle the dispute as to the motherhood of the child. Neither one of us can afford to have the child killed to settle the dispute." Guthrie made his plea to the Populists: "Do not vote for any candidate for the Legislature unless he pledges himself not to vote for Pritchard or any other gold man for United States Senator."

BRYAN SPEAKS IN NORTH CAROLINA

Before Bryan reached the State, Captain W. H. Kitchin, who, although he had joined the Populist Party under resentment for Cleveland's anti-silver views, was always a Democrat at heart, demanded that the Populists should withdraw Watson as Vice-president and throw all their strength for Bryan and Sewall. Shortly thereafter, Mr. Bryan reached North Carolina. An electoral ticket of six Democrats and five Populists had been agreed upon, so that when Bryan reached North Carolina the two groups united in his reception. It took much delicate diplomacy to effect this without friction. Senator Jones telegraphed me that Bryan would reach the State on September 17 and asked me to meet him in Knoxville, take charge of his speaking through North Carolina, go with him through the Middle States and New England, and represent the National Committee on that trip.

Up to the time Bryan reached Asheville he had been speaking throughout the West and had always travelled in a day coach on his day trips. He refused to have a private car, and he reached Knoxville in a hot spell, weary and tired. His voice was not good. The North Carolina committee determined that it was not humane to subject him to the hard trip and many speeches, without such comforts as could be provided, and Chairman Manly therefore engaged a private car. General Julian S. Carr, Major E. J. Hale, and I met Bryan in Knoxville. The crowd greeting him in Asheville was so large that there was no thought of trying to have the meeting in any building, and Bryan spoke to a great multitude who thronged the mountainside in a sort of open air amphitheater. I do not know how many thousand people were there, but it was as enthusiastic a crowd as ever Vance spoke to in his old home. Bryan placed himself in touch with the crowd by his reference to Vance, rejoicing to be in the old home of the man who had been the prophet of tariff reform and free silver. "I have a reason for coming to North Carolina," he said, "which is personal, aside from my interest in the electoral vote of the State. It was the State of North Carolina which, at the Chicago Convention, before I became a candidate and before my home State had taken any formal part in placing my name in nomination, by resolution decided to give me the unanimous vote of their delegation in the Convention."

This recognition made the North Carolina supporters feel they had a particular interest in his candidacy. It was a triumphal march through the State, Bryan speaking at Asheville, Hickory, Statesville, Charlotte, Salisbury, and Greensboro, before he reached Raleigh. The train was crowded with politicians. One of the most interesting things of the trip was the attention to him by the two United States marshals, O. J. Carroll, of the Eastern District, and Thomas J. Allison, of the Western District. Bryan suffered from the intolerably hot weather. These men would take turns fanning him between stations. They were both very large men and they would fan and sweat, sweat and fan in the drawing room, and the politicians in the car were saying they were both straining themselves to earn a reappointment if Bryan should be elected. They hadn't anything to say about Cleveland, but if Grover could have seen "Jud" Carroll and Tom Allison fanning Bryan and paying such devotion to him, they would have lost their jobs before November.

Mr. Bryan's tribute to Vance was in these words:

"I am glad the canvass of this State opens in this county, which was the home of one of the grandest public men given to this nation—not alone by North Carolina, but the entire country— Senator Vance. He was a man whom I delighted to honor, and I am glad that I stand among his neighbors and friends advocating the same cause that he so eloquently advocated. I cannot more than impress upon your memories the words of his last speech: 'The great fight is on. The money power and its allies throughout the world have entered into this conspiracy to perpetrate the greatest crime of this or any other age, to overthrow one-half of the world's money and thereby double their wealth by enhancing the value of the other half which is in their hands. The money changers are polluting the temple of our liberties. To your tents, O Israel!'

"He foresaw the struggle in which we are now engaged. He realized the magnitude when many others did not. Those words came from him as words of command, 'To your tents, O Israel.' And the command was heeded by the Democratic Party."

Some of his hearers believed that the mantle of the great North Carolina Commoner had fallen on the Nebraskan.

The "Bryan Special" train moved through the center of North Carolina from the mountains to the coastal plains, and in the two days' tour he spoke at a score of places to hundreds of thousands of enthusiastic supporters. His strenuous campaign had left Bryan hardly an opportunity for a bath and he greatly enjoyed that comfort in the luxurious home of General Carr at Durham. At Raleigh he was introduced by Hal W. Ayer, Chairman of the Populist State Committee. Some old-time Democrats resented this honor being given to a Populist at the State's Capital, but the Democratic State Chairman, Clement Manly, knew that victory in North Carolina depended on the Populist votes and wisely did everything possible to secure that support. Bryan had been speaking in Nash Square but a few minutes under an electric light when a great bug with fangs entered his throat and he was compelled to seek the assistance of a surgeon to remove the clawing bug. Consternation ensued until the "varmint" was removed and Bryan was able to continue. He set forth his position that he would not urge Democrats who believed in the gold standard to vote for him because he would not have supported "for president a man who would in the presidential chair continue the present financial policy and mortgage the United States to English bondholders." That declaration strengthened Bryan with the Populists, but old-time Democrats who were denouncing gold Democrats as "bolters" did not approve. Concluding, he said that while he "did not dispute the right of any Democrat to vote against the Chicago ticket, if he thinks its success will imperil the country," he had "a right to ask that the men who had been pretending to be Democrats shall now, when the Democratic Party has been rescued from the people's despoilers, leave the name and not attempt to take that name with them into disgrace." At Goldsboro, Bryan was introduced by Charles B. Aycock, later elected Governor. People debated whether Bryan or Aycock was the more eloquent. At Wilson (my home in boyhood and young manhood), Bryan took occasion to say pleasant things about me to my old friends.

At Rocky Mount, Congressman Bunn, who had served with Bryan in Congress, brought us enough lunch for a big company, with delicious scuppernong grapes. Writing of his tour in *The First North Carolina Battle,* Bryan said:

> "This State is credited with the largest contribution to my assortment of rabbits' feet. Total number received, nearly thirty— North Carolina's quota about ten. The first foot was presented to me as I left the Chicago Convention, just after my speech in support of the platform, donor unknown. These were all declared to be of the 'left hind foot' variety, but even with the aid of horseshoes and four-leaf clover stalks, they were impotent to secure for me the Presidency."

His trip through North Carolina had made a greater impression even than Clay's visit when he was a candidate for President, which up to that time had been the standard of measurement for crowds. The enthusiasm which the Populists had shown convinced any of their leaders who might have been willing to throw Bryan overboard for the State ticket, that it was a dangerous thing to do. When the train pulled out of North Carolina for Virginia I saw, and so informed Bryan, that his trip through the State had cinched it, and no matter what fusion might be arranged as to State offices, the electoral vote was safe. I doubt whether the situation could have been made certain if he had not visited North Carolina. The people, particularly those who were strong for silver in both parties and some Republicans, though not many, attended the meetings more as though they were going to religious revivals than to political meetings. Bryan introduced Biblical phrases into his speeches, which recalled the sort of campaigning Vance had done.

SWINGING AROUND THE CIRCLE

I went on with Bryan then through Virginia, Maryland, Delaware, and the New England States, and back. I shall never forget the reception in Richmond. Bryan spoke at night from the balcony of the Jefferson Hotel. He was introduced by Senator John W. Daniel. They made a great pair in appearance. You could scarcely find two more distinguished looking men than Daniel and Bryan. The moon was shining so that it was almost like day. Back of Bryan and Daniel, in the rotunda of the hotel, was a marble statue of Jefferson. That gave Daniel the suggestion for his introduction. I hope it has been preserved. I thought, at the time, I never heard any equal to it. It may have been that my enthusiasm was such that I was in a mood to enhance its greatness. Daniel said, in substance, that as he stood looking at the statue of Jefferson and recalled his philosophy and teachings and then turned to look at Bryan, understanding what he stood for, he could not suppress the thought that, suddenly, this statue of the Sage of Monticello had come to life and was speaking, through the Nebraskan, the immortal truths which the founder of Democracy had formulated. It took Daniel fifteen or twenty minutes to develop that likeness in classic language and the crowd was at the highest pitch of fervor when Bryan came out. He swept the audience even more than Daniel had.

He was to speak the next morning at Fredericksburg and then at Washington. We had to leave on a very early morning train without breakfast. Arriving at Fredericksburg, we visited the home of Washington's mother and other historical scenes. Bryan used, for the text of his speech, the old story, then new to me, that Washington at that place threw a silver dollar across the Rappahannock and that nobody else had been able to do it. The reason for his accomplishment of this feat was that a dollar would go farther in those days than it would now.

At Wilmington, Delaware, as at some other places, Bryan was entertained by an old friend and I was also included in the invitation. It was a beastly hot night. Arrived at the home of our host, he almost collapsed. For a time the host and I feared for his life. Nurses rubbed him part of the night with alcohol and the doctor attended him. Next morning, however, he was as fresh as a daisy. I do not think it was so much the speaking that overcame him as what happened that afternoon. The news came to him that the Democratic State Convention in New York had nominated for Governor John B. Stanchfield and the candidate had repudiated the Chicago platform.

Bryan had previously accepted an invitation to go to New York to speak and he requested me to get in touch with the Democratic State Chairman of New York, Elliott F. Danforth, so that he could talk to him over the telephone. I talked to Danforth and made an appointment for Bryan. He confirmed the report that the nominee had repudiated the Chicago platform, whereupon, Bryan told him that unless the candidate was removed from the ticket and a candidate for governor nominated who would advocate the Chicago platform, his self-respect would not permit him to speak in New York, that he should denounce the action of the New York Democrats and decline to fill his engagement. He was very much excited, deeply outraged, and highly indignant. Later in the campaign the candidate who had refused to endorse the Chicago platform withdrew, another candidate was nominated, and later Bryan went to New York and took part in the campaign. However, he had called it "the enemies' country" and the newspapers played it up so much that New York retaliated by voting against their "enemy," as they regarded him.

The crowds that turned out to hear Bryan in New England were record-breaking, and the Republicans began to fear that the Democrats were going to win their strongholds. When Bryan reached New Haven, it was arranged that he should speak on the Yale campus. There was a sharp division of opinion in New Haven; most of the students were anti-Bryan and most of the Bryan men, led by Alexander Troupe, were mechanics and laboring men. Bryan had not been speaking more than five minutes before he called out, "Hold that man! Catch him!" From the stand he had seen a pickpocket put his hand in a man's pocket and take out his purse. This created some diversion. When somebody threw an egg at Bryan, pandemonium broke loose. It was supposed to have been thrown from a body of students who had been very noisy and had greatly outraged Bryan's supporters. At one time, there threatened to be a general conflict.

"If the syndicates and corporations rule this country, then no young man has a fair show unless he is the favorite of the corporations," declared the Nebraskan. Bryan's carrying voice announced a sound doctrine to many hot-headed youths of the privileged class. They yelled and hooted. For a time he could not go on, but he came back bravely, saying, "People have been terrorized by financial institutions until in some instances it is more dangerous to raise your voice against the ruling power in this country than it is in an absolute monarchy."

The shot went home and the jeering youths broke out afresh. A brass band from a distant part of the campus came in to take a blaring part in the noise, playing loud tunes while the Yale boys shouted "Ho-ax, Ho-ax," and surged to and fro around the stand, the rear part having fallen in while the chairman was trying to speak.

Bryan finished his speech with difficulty. The jeering by the students and the replies by Bryan's friends were such that at one time I thought there would be blows. I do not know whether he shortened his speech, but I think he did. The Democrats of the city were so much outraged that they denounced the Yale students. Perhaps there would have been a conflict but for Bryan. At first he was very indignant but said:

"Do not blame the boys. You could not expect much more of some of them. Their fathers, some of whom have gotten rich by the oppression of the poor, have threatened their employees with discharge if they vote their convictions. When older men who have gotten rich by governmental favor, see the people who have made them rich rise up and demand equality of government, and resort to methods of boycott and intimidation to keep their ill-gotten gains and increase them, how can you expect their sons to treat the advocates of equality with respect?"

That of course infuriated the Yale boys, and they became more uproarious. Then, turning from his philippic, Bryan smiled and said he had been familiar with college boys, had been one himself, and their pranks must not be taken too seriously. As the news of the meeting went all over the country it outraged the Bryan people throughout the West, and they sent indignant protests to Yale and to New Haven denouncing the ruffians of "the effete East." The Yale *News* condemned the "horse-play," and the President of Yale mildly regretted the incident, saying, "Boys will be boys." The New York *Sun* said, "They ought to have done it and the sentiment to which they gave utterance was honorable to them." That commendation was offset by a resolution by the Choctaw Indians in Oklahoma, which said, "We admonish all Indians who think of sending their sons to Yale that association with such students could but be hurtful alike to their morals and their progress to the higher standards of civilization."

As we travelled through the industrial towns of Connecticut and Massachusetts, I remember giant placards which almost covered the fronts of factories reading, in big letters: *"This factory will be closed on the morning after the November election if Bryan is elected. If McKinley is elected, employment will go on as usual."* These big signboards, in various phrasings, seemed to blot out the horizon, and when Bryan would denounce in the most vigorous language this attempt to intimidate the employees, many of them would cry out and tell him to "Go on. The employers may reduce us and our children to starvation but they cannot control our votes." It wasn't politics. It was war. At some places the employees would hear Bryan as if he were a crusader for them, as he was, would listen to him quietly, evidently wishing to applaud but hesitating to do so because of the report that there were spotters through the crowd sent by the employers, and the employees were afraid to show their approval for fear they would lose their jobs. It was a reign of terror in industrial communities, the like of which never was seen before in this country.

I had never seen a crowd on the Boston Commons before. It seemed to me that the whole creation had gathered that night when Bryan spoke. I thought I had seen enthusiasm in the South, but it was nothing like Boston. The Commons was crowded—thousands and tens of thousands were massed. Every sentence by Bryan was punctured by the sort of enthusiastic applause which one gets from an emotional and sympathetic audience. Although, when the vote came, many of the employees did not vote their convictions, the warm reception they gave Bryan was something that those who witnessed can never forget. I telegraphed *The News and Observer* that the people of Boston were "wild with enthusiasm."

From Boston Bryan went to Bath, Maine, speaking at the home of Arthur Sewall, Candidate for Vice-president. We spent Sunday there. The bulk of the people of the town were Republicans by inheritance and belief, and yet they turned out in great shape to hear Bryan. The Republican editor told me they did it as much out of compliment to their townsman as to hear Bryan. The Sewalls had been residents of Bath since the town was built. The father of the candidate had been a shipbuilder and he had followed the same calling. The Sewall ships had carried commerce when a merchant marine in America brought wealth to the New England coast. He was a typical New Englander, large of figure, with a big head, frank and sincere. He entertained not only Mr. Bryan and his party but the large staff of correspondents who represented various press associations and daily newspapers, who were in the Bryan party.

At Bath and elsewhere in New England, I met choice spirits on every side, men of distinction and ability, who had never surrendered their Democratic politics, and I obtained a better appreciation of the devotion to principles which had kept them in the Democratic ranks in a section where victories were rarely won by their party.

Bryan's day of rest at Bath set him up and we turned southward. By the time we had gotten down to West Virginia, in accordance with the scheme, another member of the National Committee met him and took charge of the campaign through the Middle West.

Bryan then thought he was sure to win and I had been heartened to find so much enthusiasm in "the enemies' country." As I was leaving, he said to me, "If you think you have seen enthusiastic people you ought to go with me to Ohio, Indiana, and Kansas. These people have given us great welcome in the East, but the West is on fire." And it was, at that time. Before I got back to Raleigh, the first of October, on my return from Maine, I stopped in New York and saw Senator Jones, Senator Gorman, Senator Faulkner, and other prominent Democratic leaders. I wired *The News and Observer* that Bryan would be elected President by an overwhelming majority of the popular vote and would have a large majority of the electoral college. We certainly were a bunch of optimists. I never doubted and Senator Gorman always believed, if the election had been held then, the prediction I made would have come true. The intimidation campaign had just been started in New England and had only made its first faint appearance in Ohio and the Middle West, where later money and intimidation got in their perfect work.

FEDERAL OFFICE-HOLDERS OUSTED

On the day I returned home the papers announced that the District Attorney for the Eastern District of Virginia had been compelled to resign because he had been a member of the committee to meet Bryan in North Carolina and escort him through Virginia in his campaign through the Old Dominion. That, and other resignations and dismissals, sent terror to the hearts of the office-holders through-out the country, and some of them who had up to that time preserved their regularity came out for the Palmer-Buckner ticket, because they knew their official heads depended upon such action. In the strong Democratic states, like North Carolina, most of the office-holders felt it prudent to make no public utterance, although I think practically all of them supported Bryan. In fact, Aycock and Glenn, who were United States District Attorneys, were active on the stump, and if they ever had any intimation they should be silent I never heard of it.

A chorus of clerical wolves snapped at Bryan's heels during the campaign, satisfying their love for notoriety and making first page in opposition journals. Among those who quit preaching the Gospel to slander a character of whom Franklin Lane said, "Bryan is the truest Christian I have known," was Thomas Dixon, Jr., of North Carolina. Then a sensational pulpiteer in New York, he described Bryan as "a mouthing, slobbering demagogue, whose patriotism is all in his jaw bone." He won praise from the *Tribune* and the *Sun* which were in his class of vilifiers, and Wall Street welcomed Dixon as a partisan who was an adept in throwing the bull of bil-lingsgate at a man they could not defeat except by defamation.

Election day was one of nervous anxiety. In Wake County we felt the Fusionists had the best chance but we figured that the Democrats would carry part of the legislative ticket. We were perfectly con-fident that N. B. Broughton, candidate for the House, would defeat Jim Young, Negro candidate. But even that certainty turned out to be an uncertainty, for when the returns came in the Negro Young had beaten Broughton by ten votes although the county had gone fusion by a large majority. The full Fusion State ticket had been elected, including Russell for Governor. The Legislature was Fusion by a large majority, which insured that Senator Pritchard would be reëlected or a Populist put in his place. The Senate was composed of twenty-four Populists, nine Democrats and seventeen Republicans. The House of Representatives had forty-nine Republicans, thirty-five Democrats, thirty-four Populists, and two doubtful. In the whole State Palmer and Buckner received only 572 votes. The Supreme Court was Fusion, and Fusionists had elected nearly all members of Congress from North Carolina.The Bryan electoral ticket had won by a large majority.

Bryan never doubted that he was elected in 1896. I am certain that he was the victim of frauds as outrageous as those which kept Tilden out of the White House. The difference between 1876 and 1896 was that the Mark Hannas got in their dirty work before the election, and, twenty years before, it was perpetrated after the polls were closed. If labor had not let McKinley's plea of "protection to labor" deceive so many workers and if they had been fully organized, the result would have been different. Still, in spite of intimidation by threats of losing jobs, and the use of more millions than had ever been used before—and in a year of financial distress—Bryan won the election. It was stolen from him by padding registration, buying election officers, and every method known to political chicanery. Every crook, ready to sell out, got his price. Even then, Bryan won.

On the face of the returns he needed only 142 votes to carry Kentucky, where General Buckner and Colonel Watterson aided in giving its electors to McKinley. A change of 962 votes would have given him the electoral vote of California. He needed 9,000 to get Indiana, 1,000 in Oregon. Ohio's registration was so large as to indicate padding, much larger than before and afterward, and honest returns would have put Maryland and West Virginia in the Bryan column. I was confirmed in my belief that Bryan was elected by admissions of Republicans in the months that followed and by newspaper comrades who knew, but could not prove, the methods employed to effect another 1876 stealing of the presidency.

In a book published shortly after the election Governor Altgeld undertook to prove that Bryan was fairly elected, citing instances where there were more votes counted than there were voters. I never heard his figures questioned. A number of Washington correspondents, some of them Republicans, admitted after the election that if the votes had been counted as cast in California, Kentucky, Indiana, Ohio, Maryland, and West Virginia, Bryan would have won.

Mark Hanna had a campaign chest of over sixteen million dollars while the Democrats had less than a half million dollars. It is said that, since 1868, the party that expended the most money elected its candidates for President. Bryan made no public claim. It would have been unwise. Hanna's money and "blocks of five" had worked so smoothly that proof of the skulduggery was not obtainable. Claims, unsupported by proof, would have done Bryan no good. Hanna had destroyed the evidence.

Most of the anti-Bryan papers behaved very decently after the election but the Bryan people were outraged by an editorial appearing in the New York *Tribune* a few days after the election. *The News and Observer* copied it and asked "Isn't it time to quit?" As showing the character of the campaign that Bryan had to meet, this extract from the *Tribune* editorial will give the infamy of it better than any words I could use. The *Tribune* said:

> "It is a sorry day for the burglars and bum-throwers and mail robbers and railroad train wreckers and all anarchists and criminals in general in Illinois and elsewhere. It is a day for rejoicing for the nation, giving the assurance that there will be no reproduction in the White House and not much longer for an anarchist [Governor Altgeld] in the executive chair of the empire state of the West."

With that kind of a statement after the election, the type of campaign Bryan had to meet before the election can be imagined. The allusion to Governor Altgeld was particularly offensive to me. At the Chicago convention and afterward during the campaign I came in close touch with him. I heard him speak, discussed him with men of sound judgment in Illinois, and entirely changed my opinion about him. Some people said he was the brains of the Bryan campaign. Altgeld was a profound student of political economy and had reached his conclusions by much study. He had a bitter tongue and he talked about the Mark Hannas as viciously as the *Tribune* could write about him. It was a sight to see him in action, stirring the multitude. I heard him once at the Chicago stock yards speaking to thousands of working men, and I have hardly in my life seen men so stirred as he arraigned what he called the "moneycrats" who were seeking to bring about the same class rule as that which cursed Europe. I remember, in New York, when Bryan made his speech of acceptance, I was sitting with Willis J. Abbott, who was then the chief editorial writer of the New York *Journal* and an ardent Bryan supporter. We were talking about the leaders of the Democratic Party, and Abbott's wife asked me if I didn't think Governor Altgeld was "the loveliest man in the world." The question struck me between the eyes. I had once thought Altgeld an anarchist and a dangerous man. At first I had rather resented his prominence in the Bryan ranks. Mrs. Abbott went on to tell me about Altgeld's family life, the beauty and unselfishness of it. And later I talked to Brand Whitlock about him. Brand had quit the Republican Party as a youth because of its sordidness and had become a friend of Altgeld because of his vision of social justice. Through these and other channels I found that the Altgeld of my former appraisal was not the real Altgeld, but that he had a passion for justice and fairness and wished particularly to give the underprivileged man in America a chance.

Perhaps the one person of the opposing party who saw best the significance of Bryan's campaign was Mrs. Henry Cabot Lodge, whose husband never felt the crusading power of the Great Commoner so clearly as his wife. Describing, after the election, the campaign in a letter to her friend Cecil Spring-Rice, Ambassador from Great Britain, Mrs. Lodge gave this graphic word-picture:

"The great fight is won. It was a fight conducted by trained and experienced and organized forces, with both hands full of money, with the full power of the press—and of prestige—on one side; on the other, a disorganized mob at first, out of which burst into sight, hearing and force—one man, but such a man! Alone, penniless, without backing, without money, with scarce a paper, without speakers, that man fought such a fight that even those in the East can call him a crusader, an inspired fanatic, a prophet! It has been marvellous. Hampered by such a following, such a platform—and even the men whose names were our greatest weapons against him deserted him and left him to fight alone—he almost won.... We had during the last days of the campaign 18,000 speakers on the stump. He alone spoke for his party, but speeches which spoke to the intelligence and hearts of the people and with a capital P."

That the wife of Lodge, surrounded by those who believed that her caste was born booted and spurred to ride on the backs of others, could sense the fright "the Heaven-born Bryan" threw into the ranks of the privileged class, attests to the appreciation by his foes of his matchless appeal to his countrymen. Mrs. Lodge evidences, in spite of underestimating the character of Bryan's supporters, that down beneath her partisanship she realized that a real man, with a certain noble afflatus, had stirred the country and frightened the party of which her husband was a leader.

XX

BATTLE ROYAL BETWEEN A STATE AND A RAILROAD

THERE IS NEVER a dull day in a newspaper office. Scarcely had the excitement of the 1896 election died down before *The News and Observer* was in another fight. Two days after the election it was announced that Governor Carr had made up his mind, without advertisement, to lease the Atlantic and North Carolina Railroad. My paper said that, without giving everybody a chance to bid on it, the lease ought not to be seriously considered. The matter of a lease had been carried on in secret. When asked to give the public the terms of the proposed lease, the Governor declined, but said it was to be leased to a Goldsboro syndicate and he favored it because it would take the railroad out of politics. *The News and Observer's* attack upon the lease of the railroad created a diversion from the election and stirred up the bulk of the people who had not become reconciled to Governor Carr's lease of the North Carolina Railroad to the Southern Railway in 1895.

The North Carolina Railroad, running from Goldsboro to Charlotte, of which the State owned three fourths of the stock, had been leased in September, 1871, for thirty years, to the Richmond and Danville Railroad at a rental of 6 per cent per annum on the stock. In 1894 the Richmond and Danville was reorganized as the Southern Railway. When the suggestion of the lease of the North Carolina Railroad to the Southern Railway first came to my attention, six years before the thirty-year lease would expire, *The News and Observer* in its issue of August 1, 1895, declared that there was no need to consider the lease at that time and printed the proposition which Colonel Andrews of the Southern had made to the directors of the North Carolina Railroad in conference in Raleigh. The Southern proposed to re-lease it for ninety-nine years at 6½ per cent on the stock for the first six years and then for the rental to increase to 7 per cent. *The News and Observer* pointed out that the present lease did not expire until September, 1901; that three sessions of the Legislature would be held before the expiration of the lease, and that the directors would

Upper left, Judge Alphonso C. Avery, member of the North Carolina Supreme Court. *Upper right,* James A. Bryan, leading business man of Eastern North Carolina, who opposed the lease of the Atlantic and North Carolina Railroad. *Lower left,* Henry W. Miller, popular official of the Southern Railway. *Lower right,* A. F. Hileman, Populist Speaker of the House during the turbulent session of 1897.

Left, Dr. John Spencer Bassett, Trinity Professor, who roused a storm of indignation in the State press by his statement concerning Booker T. Washington. *Right*, Thomas Dixon, preacher and author of books and plays touching on the Ku Klux Klan.

make a blunder that would be equal to a crime if they should make any lease without first submitting it to the people. The Charlotte *Observer* reprinted *The News and Observer's* article and advised against the lease and said that the Seaboard Air Line Railroad officials would like an opportunity to bid on the lease of the railroad if opportunity was offered. *The News and Observer* declared, "We are shocked that the Governor should countenance a proposition so unjust to present and future generations," and said "The lease is a blunder without excuse, it is a crime without palliation." Day after day, hoping to arouse sentiment that might cause the next Legislature to take steps to annul the lease, my paper continued to criticize it, denouncing it as a desperate and dangerous defiance of the people's wishes by a corporation long entrenched, and comparing the rental with what the Southern paid for the Southern Atlanta Airline of $500 a mile per year more than the State was securing from the North Carolina Railroad, much of which was an integral part of the through system of the Southern from Washington to Atlanta.

In great headlines, *The News and Observer's* story from Burlington about the lease was headed, "A Crime of a Century." It was pointed out that with the stock at 140, the State was not getting 6 or 7 per cent as alleged by the Governor, but only 4.86 per cent if leased for fifty years, whereas under the old lease it got 6 per cent.

When I came back to Raleigh in 1895 to edit *The News and Observer,* I never heard Governor Carr refer any more to the fact that he was free from influence of the Southern or make mention of Colonel Andrews, but I observed there were close social and friendly relations between the executive mansion on one corner and the home of Colonel Andrews diagonally across the street, and my observations made me fear that the old railroad influence was getting in its work. When it was first rumored that a lease was being considered, I went to see Governor Carr and asked him about it. He refused to talk about it, turned red, and showed indignation that anybody should be inquiring into the affair, said nothing had been done; and when I recalled his statement about Colonel Andrews, made early in his term, he resented it. I knew then he had gone over to the enemy.

Failing to prevent the lease by private argument to the Governor, I hoped to build a fire that would make it so hot he couldn't go on with the deal. *The News and Observer* had quite a controversy with

Governor Carr. He defended his action on the ground that the Southern Railway could almost parallel the North Carolina Railroad and that it would do so unless it secured the lease at that time. Undoubtedly, this threat had been held over him so long that it influenced him, but his big argument was the fear of Fusion looting. As a matter of fact, the Southern Railway had dictated its own terms.

Governor Carr went out of office a saddened and dejected man, and a very indignant one. Having been flattered for four years and shown so many courtesies, social and otherwise, by the Southern Railway and its entourage, he saw himself neglected and even forgotten by those who had appeared to be his best friends, as the days of his term drew to a close. When he had been inaugurated, he was not highly esteemed by the Southern Railway people, who had much to do with social affairs in Raleigh. When Russell came in, the despised Russell, the Republican Russell, who was elevated largely by Negro votes, all the people who had been fawning upon Carr left him, and not one of them called to say good-bye as he was leaving the Capitol. He drove away with nobody but his family and a few old friends to say a kind word for him. Most of his best friends had been shocked by his leasing the railroad and had held aloof, and those who had used him now had no more time to devote to him. They feared that the lease could be upset and they set their influences in motion to capture Russell.

Immediately after Russell had received the certificate of election as Governor, he made several statements: first, that when he reached Raleigh he would allow the cows to graze on the grass around the executive mansion; second, that Josephus Daniels would not be permitted to enter the mansion during his term; and third, that he would bend every power, personal and official, to annul the lease of the North Carolina Railroad.

I was strongly in favor of all three propositions and found myself most unaccountably in perfect accord with Governor Russell in his first three *pronunciamentos*. As to the first, I had no cows. I did not live near the Governor's mansion, and the flies, always incident to keeping cows, could not trouble me. As to the second, I had no desire or intention to have any relations whatever with Russell, having no confidence in him and no admiration for him. As to the third, I stated that he had gotten on *The News and Observer* platform and could not crowd me off, but would find the paper coöperating with him fully and completely in any and every attempt to secure the annulment of the midnight lease.

As to his third proposition, Russell said, "The North Carolina Railroad is the golden link; the lessees must buy the road or bust, and the price must be fixed by the State." His price was $5,300,000, whereas the railroad had been leased to the Southern Railway upon a basis of $4,000,000, but he said his views, "like the reports of the cotton markets, were subject to change without notice with reference to the price," and he wound up his statement with two original and skyscraping remarks about "the cannibals of Wall Street." Replying to the threat that the Southern Railway would parallel the North Carolina Railroad, if the lease was touched, he said it would not be allowed to do it if the Legislature was equal to its duties. "We will not *now* express any doubt of Russell's earnestness," said *The News and Observer,* emphasizing the *now.* "The people who have all along been in favor of evoking jury settlement, hoping that the lease will be annulled, will be glad to have those in authority secure what they, in their private capacity, have been unable to accomplish," and added, "If Russell will follow the lead of *The News and Observer* in all matters, after his inauguration, as he seems to be doing in his pre-inaugural address, it will be an agreeable surprise." The Democratic advocates of the lease made sport of the fact that Russell, the Republican, and the Democratic *News and Observer* had gone to bed together. They felt that my approval of Russell's position would injure the paper and would strengthen them in the party. I believed Russell sincere, but it was the sincerity of a man who lacked staying qualities. In the early days no man could have been so violent as he was toward the advocates of the lease unless he was ready to fight. Russell drew down upon himself the opposition of powerful influences which believed him sincere. Later, they were to thwart many of his plans and finally break him when he was in financial distress.

The Capital Club of Raleigh, of which Colonel Andrews was the leading spirit, tendered a reception to Russell upon his inauguration in 1897, the first one it had given to an incoming governor. It created a storm of criticism in the city and in the State. The unterrified Democrats, who had fought Russell to the finish, saw through the pretension that it was being done to the office of Governor and not to the man. It did not assuage them. Russell saw through it, too, and instead of being mollified or influenced to soft-pedal on the

North Carolina Railroad lease, he hurled defiance and swore in his wrath that, above everything else, he would bring all the power of the State to bear, in order to upset that midnight fraud upon the people of North Carolina. He started at it in a manner indicating that he was terribly in earnest. In the early days of his administration he engaged competent counsel, appointed directors of the North Carolina Railroad who were in sympathy with him, and in every way threw the influence of his office, his legal ability, and his powerful vigor into upsetting the lease. But the time came when he surrendered.

I can never forget the setting and effect of Russell's inaugural address in January, 1897. I had a seat in the House of Representatives at the reporters' desk within a few feet of him. His manner was that of a man who had come to a place where he could heap vengeance on his enemies. There was pent-up fury about him. His eyes flashed a baleful fire and you could feel that he regarded himself as, after long exclusion from power, having the opportunity to glut his long-stored hate and get even with his political enemies. The Republicans were full of enthusiasm. They cheered Russell as in political campaigns. The Negro members were particularly vociferous and the Populists, who had been awarded the Speakership and saw an equal distribution of patronage, were almost as enthusiastic. There were some who were as quiet as the Democrats. They were the sort of Populists who were later to come back to their old party.

Russell opened his address with the quotation of a sentence which Vance had used in 1876 in his inaugural address: "There is retribution in history." The use of that sentence made Russell's supporters wild and put ire in the soul of the Democrats.

The daily *Caucasian* had not proved profitable and had ceased publication. The Fusionists felt the need, when the Legislature met in 1897, of having a daily organ at the capital which should uphold their Fusion policy. The Southern Railway and others wishing to uphold the lease and control the Fusion Legislature in the interest of favoritism, also desired an organ. A new paper, the *Daily Tribune,* was established. It was current gossip that a Republican trust magnate and people close to the Southern Railway put up considerable money. It was started with a flourish of trumpets; it had fine equipment and was well printed. Its sponsors imported as editor

W. W. Haywood, a native of Missouri, then editing a paper at Hendersonville, N. C. He was the greatest ballyhoo artist and "snollygoster" Raleigh had seen. He could write more muck-raking stories, employ more billingsgate, and sling more mud than any other newspaper man in the State. He was a swashbuckler of Swashbucklerville, a stuffed-shirt in appearance, with a genius for abuse of decent people. The paper was militantly Republican and in the first days of its existence drew to its support the Fusionists, both Republicans and Populists. It was established as a Republican organ to hold the Republicans in line, as the *Caucasian* had held the Populists in line for the Fusion. The list of stockholders was not given, but C. Kenyon, business manager, said, "Although we will not now divulge the names of the stockholders, they are wealthy and practical business men of North Carolina and, if necessary, a large capital can be easily raised." While preaching Republican doctrine and praising McKinley and Pritchard, the paper, as was soon disclosed, was established to defeat Russell's fight to annul the lease. That was its real objective. It was also the mouthpiece of the Tobacco Trust. Early in the year litigation had been begun in some states to dissolve that trust. The Populists and Democrats generally opposed the trust. Editor Haywood knew that the direct road to the heart and pocketbook of people who were backing the paper was coarse denunciation of *The News and Observer* and its editor. Day after day, week after week, as long as this publication continued, slime oozed from its columns. It overshot the mark because it had neither decency nor truth.

All Fusionists at first hailed the paper because it did not disclose its real purpose and they were all glad to have a paper that would answer *The News and Observer*. A little later they saw that its Republicanism was only skin-deep but its devotion to its railroad and trust masters was whole-hearted and undivided. As soon as Russell employed attorneys, some of whom were Democrats, to fight the lease, the *Tribune* turned upon him for appointing Democrats to office, holding that retaining such lawyers in litigation as Judge Avery and Judge McRae, who were influential Democrats, was turning the administration over largely to the Democrats. I never saw either Haywood or Kenyon except on the street. When they first came to Raleigh and made announcement of the paper, they gave it out that they were going "to give *The News and Observer* and

Josephus Daniels hell," and it was "norated" around that they had an abundance of money behind them. One of their pressmen, in the freemasonry of labor union brotherhood, told *The News and Observer* pressman that Mr. Washington Duke had bought and given them the press. My friends advised me to look up Haywood's record, which, they said, was very unsavory, and to expose him. *The News and Observer's* attitude toward the *Tribune,* after it had started, was one of ignoring it.

Soon the *Tribune* had to take a public stand between Russell and Andrews. Colonel Andrews, who had been a Democrat and had exerted influence in selecting Democratic officials, had voted for McKinley in 1896 and was violent in attacks upon Bryan. He was credited with giving help to the *Tribune.* Russell had at first thought the paper was truly Republican without any strings tied to it, but when he began his attempt to undo the railroad lease he found the *Tribune* was not a Republican paper primarily, but a Southern Railway paper. In the bitter conflict that followed, in and out of the Legislature, the *Tribune* became almost as offensively vicious toward the Governor as it was toward *The News and Observer.* There was therefore the singular situation in Raleigh of the *Tribune,* the Republican paper, praising Republican policies and denouncing the Republican Governor because he was trying to undo the North Carolina Railway lease, while the Democratic *News and Observer* was denouncing Fusion policies and having no relation whatever with the Governor except to denounce him upon his general policies, while earnestly supporting his policy to annul the lease.

It was not more than two or three months after the Legislature adjourned that the *Tribune* was sold out by the sheriff. It had done the dirty work for which it was established, in dividing the Populists and Republicans and defeating Russell's attempt to secure the annulment of the lease. After that, the interests which had put up the money to carry it along had hoped that it would become self-supporting. When it was a drag and its influence was nil and its vulgarity had brought it into contempt, the men with money withdrew their support and it went on the rocks, unwept and unsung. But if it was unwept and unsung by those who had established it, when it was sold out by the sheriff the full story of its banality became public. Its effects were sold at public auction. Its physical property was bought by the afternoon paper, but the most important thing it had, so far as *The News and Observer* and the public were concerned, was its letter books and files, which were also sold at auction and purchased in bulk for a song by Joseph H. Weathers, with other stuff. Weathers sold the letter books to *The News and Observer* for ten cents. It was the best investment we ever made. It returned large dividends in its revelations which helped to drive nails in the coffin of the Fusionists. These letter files proved what *The News and Observer* had asserted when the *Tribune* was founded and what it had denied with all the lurid language and denunciation which a pastmaster in coarseness and indecency could employ. The public was familiar with its calling everybody a liar who said that Colonel Andrews or the Southern Railway or the Dukes or the American Tobacco Company had any hand in it. The documents in evidence told of the rise and fall of the *Tribune;* they showed that Colonel Andrews not only had a block of stock in it but that the Southern Railway had violated the law in discriminating in freight rates in favor of that paper; they showed it had a "divvy" with Barnes, a Populist of Raleigh who had the public printing; they showed the Dukes were stockholders, and the books revealed the management as cheap grafting crooks. The paper had sought to add to its receipts by charging $7.50 a head to Negro politicians and other Negroes who wished to be made prominent. The publication of the information about the ties greatly strengthened the position of *The News and Observer* with those who had previously not accepted its statements that the *Tribune* was established as an organ of monoply.

The backers of the *Tribune* had supposed that a divided patronage for a Raleigh daily would bankrupt *The News and Observer*. If the *Tribune* had been able to effect a substantial division of patronage for the Raleigh morning daily, this expectation would have been realized. It may be that if the exposure had not been made when it was established, the *Tribune* might have imposed upon the people, for except for its editorial abuse, it was a good newspaper, having the Southern Associated Press telegrams, a bright local editor, Willis G. Briggs, a talented young man of Raleigh of an influential family. However, *The News and Observer* tagged it on the day it started. The more it squirmed and swore it had no connection with the Duke and Andrews interests, the more people felt it did protest too much. When the letter files proved conclusively not only that all my paper had said was true but that these big interests actually owned stock as well as contributed money, the wisdom of the course of my paper was justified.

When the stuff was sold at auction, the big men who had put up the money had been so disgusted they decided to have nothing else to do with it. They never thought about the internal evidence of their connection or of how *The News and Observer* could use it. Some of their henchmen, immediately after finding that Weathers had sold the books and records to my paper went to him and tried to persuade him to get them back, but Weathers was about as glad to have the exposure as *The News and Observer* was, and told them he had sold it in good faith and had no claim upon it as it was no longer his property.

Immediately after the inauguration there was a contest on between Governor Russell in the Governor's office and Colonel Andrews in the Southern Railway office, to see who could capture the most Fusionist members of the Legislature in the bitter lease fight. Quite a number of the Democratic legislators (some of them railroad attorneys or agents) had already lined up to uphold the lease of the North Carolina Railroad to the Southern Railway, and the fact that Russell was fighting it caused others to favor it—they didn't want Russell to win.

In that contest for legislators who could be influenced either by office or money, Russell had little success in his attempts to control legislators by patronage. There was in the Senate a Republican from Yancey County by the name of John B. Hiatt. He was a partisan of Pritchard. In that contest Pritchard threw all his influence, as he always did, with the Southern Railway. The Governor believed it important to get Hiatt because, while not a man of much influence, he was forceful. I happened to be passing through the anteroom of the Senate Chamber one morning and stopped to look at the Journal of the last Legislature for something I wished to use in the paper. As I stood, with my back to the window, I heard voices, very low at first, and then I heard a man swear and say he would be "damned" if he would do it. I turned around and saw that Hiatt was denouncing James E. Alexander, private secretary to the Governor, saying his vote could not be bought with office. Alexander, when he saw me and found that Hiatt was denouncing him in loud terms, beat a retreat. Hiatt told me that Alexander had offered him a position as president or secretary of the North Carolina Railroad if he would stand with

COL. ANDREWS' STEAM CALLIOPE.

A cartoon by Jennett in *The News and Observer* of August 22, 1895. Colonel Andrews, who secured the lease of the North Carolina Railroad is sitting playing the steam calliope. The man with the heavy moustache nearest him is Governor Elias Carr, who made the lease. The others are directors appointed by the Governor who approved the lease.

EVEN THE MAN IN THE MOON IS AGIN 'EM.

"There is down in my county a man of long and strong vision who tells me that during the Fusion Legislature of 1897 he used to see the moon hold its nose every night as it passed over the capitol at Raleigh." From a speech by Hon. Claude Kitchin.

A cartoon by Jennett in *The News and Observer* of July 12, 1900.

the Governor in the fight to annul the lease and I printed his statement with the details of the incident. It created a sensation. The railroad crowd was glad of the publication. Russell was furious. It was freely talked that the Governor was trying to buy votes with offices and that the Southern Railway officials were buying them with money and passes and my story substantiated one part of the report.

The bitterness between Russell and Andrews created two camps. The *Tribune* stood by the Southern Railway and fought their battle as a true hireling with every weapon of indecency, while Russell had no newspaper support, except that at the time he was standing on *The News and Observer's* platform although he had no speaking acquaintance with the editor of that paper. One of the attorneys engaged by Russell to fight the lease was Judge A. C. Avery, who had been Supreme Court Justice a long time and a Democrat of Democrats. Avery had been, from the first, an opponent of the lease. He kept in touch with the progress of the litigation and from time to time gave me the inside facts which enabled me to aid in the fight. However, I was with the Governor only in his attempt to annul the lease. In all other things *The News and Observer* was vigorous in denunciation of his administration. How Russell could hate and how he could fume! But he was an amateur and a novice in dealing with legislators. Colonel Andrews was a past master. He knew all the leads that touched men. The Southern Railway had made it a practice to retain a multitude of attorneys. Any lawyer who wanted a free pass, which was worth much money to him in his professional duties since he could travel from New Orleans to Washington and all over North Carolina without cost, could be an attorney of the Southern Railway if he would render either villein service or be shut-mouth and take no position on any policy antagonistic to the Southern Railway.

The bill urged by Russell for the repeal of the North Carolina Railroad lease had been drawn by Judge Avery and, said *The News and Observer,* embraced three propositions:

> "First, to compel foreign corporations to be subject to State laws and State courts. (This would have prevented any railroad operating in North Carolina unless it submitted to the courts and laws of North Carolina.)
> "Second, to carry the question of the validity of the lease to the courts for settlement;
> "Third, to prevent monopolism."

After Russell's vigorous message urging the Legislature to repeal the North Carolina Lease, Major Hiram Grant, of Wayne, introduced a resolution which was understood to be done at the suggestion of the railroad officials, calling for an investigation of the making of the ninety-nine year lease. The purpose of this investigation was to secure delay and give opportunity to sidetrack the bill to annul the lease. Governor Russell and Grant had been intimate friends from the time Grant came to North Carolina as one of the leading carpet-baggers in Eastern North Carolina. Russell was greatly outraged at Grant's deserting him in the matter nearest his heart and he denounced him in true Russell vitriolic language, saying, "Grant is a Hessian who betrayed his constituents in order to get the favors and smiles of the monopolists and he is one of the sneaks and traitors whose existence and safety attest to the liberality and toleration of the decent people among whom he lives."

Governor Russell's then most brilliant lieutenant in the West, Marshall Mott (afterwards an eloquent revivalist), son of Dr. J. J. Mott, long the "iron Duke" of the Republican Party, who in 1896 had become a silver Republican, called Grant "an old pie-hunting alien, a stupid skunk, a coward and knowingly a liar." He named him "Major Hy Pha Lootin Grant." Such expressions as this about Grant and Abbott show the heat of the times and illustrate how Russell and his associates denounced those who went back on them. All the same Grant's resolution was passed, causing a hold-up. It was believed by the opponents that they could bring about what actually did happen, a stalemate, with nothing done. The hearings on the lease were initiated for the purpose of delay. When they began, having had very much to say about the lease, I was summoned to give testimony in the hearing. About the time the hearing began a telegram was received from R. J. Reynolds, head of the R. J. Reynolds Tobacco Company and also one from Eugene E. Gray of the Chamber of Commerce of Winston-Salem, urging that the lease be annulled. This was followed by a proposition from Mr. Reynolds offering to lease the road himself, arguing that the price at which the road had been leased was too low. The charge had been widely made that the stock in the North Carolina Railroad had come down because of agitation about the lease. It had been run down to $109 and Mr. Reynolds offered to buy the stock at $112.

While the fight was raging *The News and Observer* said that

Colonel A. B. Andrews of the Southern Railway was the moving power controlling the Legislature and that his assistant, Henry W. Miller, who had begun work in the company as his stenographer and, though a very young man, had come to be the most influential man in the Southern Railway organization, was more regular in his attendance upon the sessions of the Legislature than any member. No committee could meet that had consideration of any bill with reference to the railroads that Miller was not present. He knew all the legislators and was agreeable and popular. I had a real regard for him personally and it was reciprocated. He distributed free passes plentifully and he had a winning way. *The News and Observer* declared that "all sense of shame has been lost by the corporations and Miller, as private secretary, directs openly which bills shall or shall not be considered," and added: "Electors of the once sovereign State of North Carolina, you know the owners of your Legislature. Have you no blushes for them?"

When I was on the stand, many railroad lawyers were in the room. In my statement I said the lease had been executed for ninety-nine years at midnight without the knowledge of the people; that it was inimical to the interest of the State to make the lease without competition fifteen years before its expiration; that, if it was to be leased at all, consideration should be taken of the fact that the railroad was worth very much more than the four million dollars of the stock outstanding. I gave, in substance, the arguments which *The News and Observer* had printed from day to day from the time the lease was made. Mr. Henderson, brilliant chief counsel of the railroad, conducted the cross-examination. By many questions designed to trip me he sought to weaken my testimony. Every time he would ask a question that sounded as if he were making headway, the railroad men filling the lobbies would volubly give evidence of their glee. F. B. Arendell of the staff of *The News and Observer,* who had been at Burlington on the night of the leasing of the road, was also examined. He substantiated the stories the paper had printed—that the lease was consummated at midnight under such circumstances as to indicate haste and unwillingness for discussion of the question.

After offering to buy the stock and showing his good faith in his belief that the North Carolina Railroad had been leased at too low a figure, R. J. Reynolds offered 10 per cent for the lease instead of the 6 and 7 per cent at which it had been leased. About the same time,

Mr. Reynolds sent me a check, saying the people were behind *The News and Observer* and to keep up the fight and he and others would stand back of it. I returned it, whereupon Reynolds subscribed for twenty copies to be sent to his friends. The Reynolds offer greatly stimulated the opponents of the lease. The Seaboard offered to pay $120,000 a year more than the Southern was paying. The best of the argument was all with the people who said that the price at which the road had been leased was too low.

After the long investigation, which did not throw any new light on the lease question, the Senate passed a substitute for Russell's bill which approved the lease but reduced the term from ninety-nine years to thirty years. I urged the House to approve the Senate substitute with an amendment raising the rent to $400,000.

The fight over the lease overshadowed everything else for a time, and when the Senate Bill got to the House the bitterness was beyond description. The railroad program had been carried out according to previous arrangement, which was for the Senate to hold it for weeks pending pretended consideration and not let it reach the House until a few days before the Legislature must adjourn. It was clear to the railroad lobbyists that they could not secure legislative approval. What they were fighting for was to prevent any action, so that the lease would stand. Russell, of course, preferred no action, rather than disapproval of his bill. When the bill came up in the House *The News and Observer* said the disgraceful rioting in that body was as bad as that in the 1868-69 Legislature and that bribery, corruption, usurpation, and radicalism were the legitimate fruits of the Fusion.

The rioting in the House of Representatives was so disgraceful that the Speaker made an appeal to the police force of Raleigh to come to the Capitol and restore some semblance of order in the chamber. At one time some of the members, wishing to break a quorum, sought to leave the House. The doorkeepers locked the door and fist fights ensued between two or three members and officers of the House. There was such pandemonium as I have never witnessed before or since. The Speaker, who had no experience in parliamentary law, A. F. Hileman, Populist, of Cabarrus County, was unable to secure even a semblance of order or to obtain a vote. Four or five were speaking at one time. Some were crying that they would kill the doorkeeper if he attempted to interfere with the legal rights of the legislators.

In the midst of all this bedlam would rise the imperturbable and inimitable J. Frank Ray, of Macon, who never favored anything but always opposed every proposition of the Fusionists. He got the body so tangled up in a parliamentary maze that Hileman looked around helplessly to some lawyer to tell him what to do. During that session I saw Frank Ray deadlock the House hour after hour by parliamentary superiority. When everybody else was mad and swearing Frank was calm and placid and would, in the most loving voice, say, "Mr. Speaker, I was merely rising for a parliamentary inquiry." Then he would proceed to speak for a half hour while the Republicans were demanding that the Speaker put the question. Of course the Democrats threw all the fuel on the flames possible in order to make the Legislature ridiculous and contemptible. And some Democrats were as subservient to the railroads as the Republicans. As long as the Fusionists could coöperate they were able to carry their measures through, but the breach between them on the Pritchard election and the lease question had separated them. The Populists who were fighting the lease believed that most of those who had bolted were in the pay of the railroads and did not hesitate to say so. Amid scenes of uproar and denunciation and bitterness, the Russell lease bill with the Grant amendment went to the table. Forty days of the 1897 session had been consumed on a measure which failed, and when it failed both sides rejoiced.

Immediately after the adjournment of the 1897 Legislature, Governor Russell undertook to obtain control of all the institutions in the state. The first act was to remove the directors of the North Carolina Railroad. Inasmuch as the directors, appointed by Governor Carr, opposed the annulment of the lease, Russell wished to have a board in favor of his policy. The Southern Railway had either brought an injunction or was threatening to do so to prevent Russell's carrying out his threat to annul the lease. On March 11, Russell wired Judge Charles H. Simonton, Federal Judge: "The proxy on the part of the State and the eight directors on the part of the State, named in the bills filed in the circuit court at Greensboro by the Southern Railroad and General Trust Company of New York, have been lawfully removed by me with the approval and consent of the State. Any consent by said proxy or either of said directors to an order in either cause will be unauthorized, collusive and fraudulent."

Shortly before that time, Judge Simonton had been in conflict with

Governor Tillman of South Carolina. He had issued injunctions against Tillman's control of the railroads. Tillman gave out a statement to North Carolinians, in vigorous Tillmanesque style, in which he said: "I see you are all in a devil of a muddle about railroad matters. Well, you may expect Judge Simonton to give the Southern anything they want, for they own him, body and soul."

That was the opinion of Simonton held by the people who had been fighting for railroad regulation. Right or wrong, his injunctions had been against the State authority. In fact, *The News and Observer* had said that his appointment was dictated by the Southern Railway and, for a long time, he was a storm center and the subject of much criticism and denunciation.

In July Judge Simonton rendered a decision in the lease of the North Carolina Railroad. It was sweeping, and to the effect that the directors of the railroad had the right to make the lease and that it was executed in conformity with the requirements of the charter. The application of Governor Russell to try the case in the State courts was denied. The Judge left open the question as to whether there was fraud in securing the lease and appointed the Honorable Kerr Craige, of Salisbury, to take evidence as to fraud. *The News and Observer,* commenting on this decision, said, "Judge Simonton's decision is just exactly what it was said by the Southern Railway officials here it would be. It is truly wonderful how accurately some people can guess on some matters. If they could foretell the result of a horse race with as much certainty as they can Judge Simonton's decisions in a railroad case, they would wear diamonds."

When *The News and Observer* was seeking to undo the ninety-nine year lease of the North Carolina Railroad to the Southern Railway, the Seaboard Air Line, of which Captain Day was then Chief Counsel, made an offer to lease it at a much higher price. Captain Day was then very warm in praise of *The News and Observer's* position; in fact, so much so that while that fight was in progress he came down to *The News and Observer* office to see me and this conversation ensued: "How much money are you making on *The News and Observer?*" asked Captain Day. "We are not making any money. We are having a hard time to make ends meet," I replied. He said "My God! That is a shame! Here you are making the fight for the people and not making any money. I will tell you what I will do. I will make the Seaboard Air Line buy you a press and help you out in any way you want so that you can carry on the people's fight." I thanked the Captain because his motive was friendly but told him *The News and Observer* was in no sense advocating that the railroad be leased to the Seaboard or any particular road—that it was advocating undoing the midnight ninety-nine year lease and compelling the lessee to lease the Atlantic and North Carolina Railroad along with the North Carolina Railroad and to put the lease up to the highest bidder. The Seaboard was ready to do this and felt that if the question was reopened, it would have the best chance of securing the lease. I told Captain Day I was not fighting the Seaboard's fight, that I appreciated his kindness in the matter but I could not accept anything from the Seaboard Line or anybody else.

For several days Captain Day insisted upon my accepting money from the Seaboard and thought I was "a damn fool not to accept it." Later he got in touch with F. B. Arendell, who was then advertising manager of *The News and Observer* and Arendell went with him down to Norfolk. They were great cronies. At Norfolk, Captain Day took Arendell around to see Mr. St. John, President of the Seaboard Air Line Railroad, and St. John told Arendell he was very anxious to adopt the same policy in North Carolina that he had adopted when he was in control of Western railroads; that was to make the railroad a developer of industrial and agricultural interests along the line of his road; that the Southern railroads could not pay unless new industries were established on their lines. He said he wanted Arendell to visit the towns along the road and write articles about their agricultural and industrial progress. Arendell could then get the people of the towns to advertise in the issues in which these industrial articles appeared. He said the Seaboard would buy $100 worth of every such edition. Arendell made the contract promptly and wrote about eight or ten articles, and the Seaboard bought one hundred dollars worth of each of such issues.

When *The News and Observer* criticized the Legislature for permitting Mr. Miller to use the Southern Railway whip to drive them, Colonel Andrews made a statement that my paper's opposition to his policies was due to the fact that he had cut off the passes which had heretofore been extended to it in return for advertising in its columns. My paper asked: "Does Andrews think he can buy opinions of those who ride on passes upon the Southern Railway?" *The News and Observer,* like all other papers in North Carolina, had been receiving passes for its editor and agents in exchange for printing the schedules of the railroads. No account was kept of the value of the passes or the value of the advertising, and that of the passes was generally in excess of the advertising. There was no way of travel in North Carolina then except by train, and newspapers having travelling agents felt they could not send them about the State if they had to pay railroad fare. The possession of a pass was deemed as valuable as the ownership of an automobile, plus gasoline, in later days. After *The News and Observer's* strictures about the midnight lease, with a gesture as if it would put *The News and Observer* out of business, Colonel Andrews withdrew the passes from the paper and gave out that this had been done because it had been unfairly critical of the policy of the railroad.

For years *The News and Observer* had been fighting the giving of free passes to public officials and urging the prosecution of railroads for so doing and the Supreme Court was to uphold the conviction of the Southern Railway in issuing a free pass to P. N. Haliburton, door-keeper of the House in 1897, and was to approve the fine of a thousand dollars for the violation of the law. This was hailed as putting an end to the free pass bribery in North Carolina, and it did lessen it very much. But thereafter, when lawyers even more than ever had come to control the politics of the State, any lawyer of political influence who wished it could obtain a free pass by being placed on the roll of attorneys, many of them never being given any legal business.

XXI

SOWING THE WIND TO REAP THE WHIRLWIND

B UTLER HAD SAID, in the campaign of 1896, that the Populists would not stand for the election of any gold bug to the United States Senate, and although he had fused all over the State with legislators who were going to support Pritchard, he made up his mind that he must destroy Pritchard if he himself was to be the leader of the opposition to the Democratic Party.

When Butler came out in a philippic against Pritchard and declared he must be defeated (1897), it created a great sensation. Pritchard's friends declared that by solemn agreement the Populists were to have one Senator and the Republicans one, and that Butler was guilty of treachery and bad faith. Butler denied that and pointed to the Populist platform and his declarations for free silver and said any Populist who voted for Pritchard would be denying his faith and proving treacherous to the people who had trusted him. Those who first thought it was a sham battle and that Butler was just talking to hold his followers, soon found out it was a real fight. Pritchard had been able to seduce leading Populists by office and promise of office, and those who had ambitions saw that if the Republicans and the Populists quit fusing, the Democrats would come back into power and they would be dead ducks.

In the Legislature the Democrats voted for Rufus A. Doughton for the Senate. Butler, who didn't overly like Cyrus Thompson personally, because he feared him as a rival, threw his strength to Dr. Thompson, Secretary of State, though his election would have given both senators to the East, violating an unwritten law that one should come from the East and the other from the Western part of the State. Seven of the Populists would not vote at all. Pritchard was reëlected, receiving 88 votes to Doughton's 33 and Thompson's 43, a clear majority over the Democratic and Populist candidates. The day after the election Butler and his associates prepared a list of the Populists who had voted for Pritchard and marked them for slaughter. Early in the session, when the real fight came on, nineteen Populists who intended to vote for Pritchard walked out of the Populist caucus, which foreshadowed Pritchard's victory. The files of the *Progressive Farmer* and the *Caucasian* will show the bitterness of the fight against Pritchard by the Populists and their hatred of Colonel Harry Skinner, whom they characterized as Pritchard's "pie distributor."

The day after he was elected Pritchard announced, as if he had the right, that Colonel Skinner was the future leader of the Populist Party. The Democrats had no regret about Pritchard's election, seeing that he would be bitterly attacked by the two Populist papers in the State, which had a large circulation with the rank and file of the Populists. Their strategy was to win the Populists back to the Democratic Party, their former home. The election of Pritchard put an end to any hope of securing legislation desired by the Populists and silver Democrats. It foreshadowed the defeat of Russell's attempt to annul the lease of the North Carolina Railroad. Most of the Populists who bolted the Populist caucus for Pritchard had really become Republicans and henceforth, whenever they were needed, most of them were ready to vote along with Pritchard and the railroad.

The Republicans in the Legislature set out to gerrymander the towns and cities so as to put them under the rule of Negroes and their cohorts. They succeeded, under the drive of Governor Russell, in his home city, Wilmington. The government instituted in that chief seaport in the State became so corrupt and unable to give protection to its people that it proved the undoing of what was called "Russellism" in North Carolina. Some other cities and towns suffered to a less degree, but enough Populist members balked at the gerrymandering bills to prevent the passage of some and to amend others so as to save other cities from the fate of Wilmington.

The sum total of the legislation of the session of 1897 had to its credit the passage of the abolition of the fellow servant law, a relic of ancient days, and substituting in its place a law suitable for modern conditions. For a long time the engineers, conductors, and firemen had been advocating the abolition of the old rule that, if an accident occurred, damages were well-nigh impossible because of the presumption that the principle of fellow servant took away the responsibility from the owners of the railroad. B. R. Lacy, afterward, for a long time, State Treasurer, and a committee from the railroad brotherhood were busy urging the passage of this act. The railroads had killed it several times. *The News and Observer* joined hands with the Railroad Brotherhood in the fight. While the railroad attorneys and managers were so busy fighting the lease and opposing the reduction in railroad rates, the bill was passed before they could get in their usual effective efforts against it. They regarded it as of little importance compared to defeating Russell's plan to annul the lease and reduce rates. When the legislation was enacted the Railroad Brotherhood committee wrote me a letter of warm appreciation of the part *The News and Observer* had played in securing the legislation. It created a bond of friendship between me and the Brotherhood that endured.

The legislation to turn over the insane asylums and other hospitals to the Fusionists was so poorly drawn that the Democrats determined to take the matter into the courts. When the new directors selected a new superintendent for the Western Insane Asylum at Morganton, Dr. Patrick Murphy, who had been the head of the institution since its establishment and had made it the foremost hospital for the insane in the South, ordered the Fusionist selected as superintendent out of the building when he tried to take charge. *The News and Observer* praised Murphy's courage and devotion to the insane. When the case came before Judge Adams, a Republican Superior Court Judge, he held that the legislation had not been legally enacted. So the hospitals were saved.

Not so, however, with the penitentiary and the Agricultural Department. Positions in these had generally been given to political workers. Russell gave the penitentiary to his old and intimate friend, John R. Smith, of Goldsboro. Smith had more friends among the Democrats than anybody else in the Russell entourage. He wanted to be friendly with everybody and do every man a favor. He didn't know how to say no to the gang, and he himself had no high ideals of public service. He made the mistake of appointing his son as prison physician. The general tone of the prison management was so bad, so inefficient, and so low that it began to be a stench; and *The News and Observer,* through the sources of news which it established, was able to acquaint the people with the scandalous conditions there. The paper proved that there were officials in charge of the prisoners who were guilty of more criminal conduct than the convicts. I felt very sorry for John R. Smith. In Goldsboro, where he lived, although an active Republican he had always been a warm friend of Governor Aycock and my brother and was their client. He was of the type of a number of the Fusion officials, neither moral nor immoral, but he was surrounded by a lot of people who were so bad and so incompetent that the penitentiary management became a blot on the State administration and Governor Russell came out in an interview suggesting that the wisest thing that could be done was to lease out the convicts and the whole penitentiary so that it should no longer be a public institution but should be run by private individuals. It is hard to depict the mixed imbecility and rottenness which characterized that institution in the early months of the year. Among other things, a man was appointed to the chaplaincy of the penitentiary named the Reverend T. W. Babb, a very active Populist worker. He had written and spoken much for the Fusion movement and had some talent. In his early days, he had given promise of usefulness as a Baptist preacher. After he was appointed to the chaplaincy in the penitentiary and his apppointment was widely heralded as that of "a prominent Baptist divine," Rev. R. T. Vann, of Raleigh, honorable and high-minded Baptist preacher, felt it his duty to give the record of the Reverend Mr. Babb, who had been driven out of his pulpit and expelled from his church for conduct unbecoming a minister. Babb was so fond of whiskey that he could not keep sober. All his doings were published in *The News and Observer,* which overlooked no peccadillo of the members of the new government. Babb was really a pitiful sight. Starting out right, he had slipped and slipped until he had lost his grip. He became the easy prey of his appetite and brought increased disgrace upon the Russell administration.

It was somewhat better in the Agricultural Department, where Russell appointed J. M. Mewborne, of Lenoir, as Commissioner. Mewborne, himself a Populist, was personally money honest, and his private life was all right. Into that department were dumped men who had no fitness for office. Soon its inefficiency and lack of service to the farmers became such that *The News and Observer* called it "the Russell Manure Pile," and by that name it went. The penitentiary was in such bad shape and the Agricultural Department stunk so that Russell had to do something. He was devoted to John R. Smith and could not turn him out in the cold, and he had great faith in Mewborne because he believed he was honest. He decided on a swap and made Smith Commissioner of Agriculture and put Mewborne in as superintendent of the state prison. The swap was regarded by the public as an admission that what *The News and Observer* had been saying was true. My paper, day by day, pointed out that the only improvement that could be made was to clean out both institutions and get new men. Just before the Legislature adjourned, although Mr. Leazar, who had been superintendent of the penitentiary under Governor Carr, reported that the institution was self-supporting and needed no appropriation, Russell secured a fifty-thousand-dollar appropriation, evidently distrusting the ability of his appointees to get along as well as Leazar had done, but this was only a drop in the bucket of the money that was needed as time went on.

The legislators had hardly reached home before *The News and Observer* pointed out that the revenue bill was defective and litigation was begun to determine that question. The Supreme Court declared that it was not legally enacted and remitted the State to the revenue bill of 1895. The State Treasurer, seeing that this would reduce the revenue and wishing to avoid a deficit, assumed the right to say what appropriations he would pay and what he would not pay, and this was supported by the Governor and the Council of State. *The News and Observer* criticized this assumption of power and this virtual veto of the acts of the Legislature as "high-handed." Treasurer Worth's response was that, in an emergency, it was his duty to hold the money for the hospitals for the insane and like institutions. While he had no legal authority for this, his motives were undoubtedly of the best.

Among other good legislation enacted by the 1897 Legislature was the passing of the law forbidding free passes to public officials. A bill to that effect had been before Legislatures for years and at this session it was opposed by railroads but passed the Senate by a vote of 21 to 19. *The News and Observer* rejoiced.

One of the last acts of the Legislature was to elect Dr. D. H. Abbott, carpet-bagger from Pamlico County, as railroad commissioner to succeed Eugene Beddingfield, whose term had expired. Dr. Abbott was a close friend of Governor Russell, but, like Major Grant and other carpet-baggers, he always genuflected toward money and power. He had not long been on the commission before it was apparent that he sided with the railroads, or it was so believed. He was soon to be put to the test. Turning over to his lawyers a large part of the business of carrying on the litigation of the lease but putting himself into it every now and then with vigor, Russell turned toward securing a reduction of railroad rates. Inasmuch as the Populists and Republicans now controlled the majority of the commission, it was believed that it would reduce railroad rates. An attempt had been made to get the Legislature to do this. It had failed. Those opposing such legislation had said that the Railroad Commission was created for that purpose, had full power, and ought to reduce the rates. In the summer the matter was pressed. On July 13 I wrote a letter to the commission at some length, pointing out that the taxation on railroads was too low and they were not assessed at their true value, and showing by comparison of the figures for Virginia and South Carolina that in those two States the Atlantic Coast Line, Southern, and Seaboard, which systems covered part of North Carolina, Virginia, and South Carolina, were assessed 50 per cent higher than in North Carolina. I also pointed out that North Carolina had the highest freight rates of all the states in the Union and called attention to the fact that manufacturers and shippers had effected an organization seeking to put a stop to the discrimination in rates against North Carolina. At the same time a letter was sent to the commission from Ceasar Cone, head of the big Cone manufacturers, cotton commission house and exporters. He pointed out how the textile and other industries in North Carolina were injured by high freight rates and discrimination against the State.

Russell urged a reduction of rates. My recollection is that he personally went before the commission in stressing the necessity of an increase of assessment and reduction of rates. I am certain that he brought every pressure to bear to secure the same thing Judge Clark and I had urged upon the commission. In fact, some of the railroad papers said that a new party was being organized in North Carolina headed by Russell, Clark, and Daniels. They sought to lessen the weight of the arguments by claiming that Clark and I were standing by Russell and Russellism and our politics might not be without taint. The fact that Clark had been nominated by the Fusionists for Justice of the Supreme Court and that Butler and others, when they were Democrats, had supported me for Public Printer when I was elected by the Alliance Legislature, were paraded in their columns as evidence that Clark and I were more ór less Populistic.

The commission decided against the reduction of rates. This was a great disapppointment to the manufacturers and business men and farmers of the State, particularly the Populists and liberal Democrats who were aroused. The action was denounced generally throughout the State. On the day that the Railroad Commission decided against the reduction *The News and Observer* said Russell had been "bitten by his own dog," Dr. Abbott. Immediately upon the refusal of the commission to reduce rates, Russell gave out a statement denouncing its action in strong terms.

Russell was so outraged with the decision, which was made by Major J. W. Wilson, Democrat, S. Otho Wilson, Populist, and Dr. D. H. Abbott, Republican, that he presently took steps and removed both the Wilsons from office. He wanted to remove Abbott and his denunciation of him was lurid, but he felt he had no grounds for such removal.

S. Otho Wilson went on the commission as a loud-mouthed Populist. He denounced his predecessor because he had not reduced the railroad rates. He soon became one of the commissioners upon whom the railroads could depend. What he got, nobody ever knew, but there was a suspicion that he had sold out and had been well paid for it. This may do him an injustice but it was brought out by *The News and Observer* that there had been put in operation since Otho Wilson went on the commission a "Railroad Commission Hotel." It said in its issue of July 29: "The hotel is owned by Major James W. Wilson, Chairman of the Board, and it is operated by Commissioner S. Otho Wilson. It is the Southern Railroad's pet and all trains stop there to take dinner." It came out that this Round Knob Hotel was owned jointly by Colonel Andrews and Major Wilson. *The News and Observer* said that the railroads ought to give Dr. Abbott the Weldon Eating House, where all trains stopped for dinner, so as to give him equal compensation for his villein service, as the Wilsons were getting "their'n" from the Round Knob Eating House. Four days later *The News and Observer* pointed out that the railroad eating house at Round Knob did not belong to Major Wilson and Colonel Andrews but the hotel and furniture were respectively the property of Colonel Andrews, Major Wilson, and S. Otho Wilson. It never called him S. Otho Wilson but "Sotho Wilson." On August 26, Governor Russell ordered the Railroad Commissioners, James W. Wilson and S. Otho Wilson "to ·show cause why they are not disqualified from acting as railroad commissioners by ownership and operation of Round Knob Hotel." Under the law the Governor had the power and was required to suspend commissioners for an interest in any railroad property. *The News and Observer* day after day printed all the sidelights about the Round Knob Hotel. On September 24 the Governor suspended both these commissioners and appointed L. C. Caldwell, Populist, of Iredell County, in place of Major Wilson; and John H. Pearson, Democrat, of Burke County, to succeed S. Otho Wilson.

Pearson belonged to a Burke family that had long been influential in public affairs. His brother had been a prominent Republican of Burke. Pearson was an ardent silver man and a devoted admirer of Bryan. He was elected to the House from Burke by the combined vote of the Democrats and Populists. Russell made the appointment because Pearson was well regarded among the Populists and silver Democrats and had influential Republican kin. It may be that he was also influenced to it by Judge Avery, who was his chief counsel in the annulment of the lease fight. Whatever his motive, it was a good selection. Pearson made an honest and honorable commissioner.

Caldwell, of Iredell, who was appointed chairman, had been Democratic mayor of Statesville. He was an eloquent speaker and a good lawyer. These two new commissioners increased the valuation of railroads for taxation and took forward steps to secure better freight and passenger rates in North Carolina. Their act was in striking contrast to the do-nothing policy which had marked the conduct of the two Wilsons after S. Otho secured the lease of the Round Knob hotel for his mother.

The newly appointed railroad commissioners, seeking to get to the bottom of the lease of the Round Knob Hotel to S. Otho Wilson, summoned Andrews to testify. It was regarded by railroad influences, which were then very powerful, as something like *lèse-majesté* for anybody to ask Colonel Andrews to do anything he didn't want to do. He treated the Corporation Commission with contempt; he and his clerks declined to answer any questions and were held in contempt. Among the questions they wished to ask Andrews and his clerks, in addition to those about the Round Knob Hotel, was whether the Southern Railway gave S. Otho Wilson a special rate on his freight. Andrews' refusal to answer these questions resulted in suits being brought against him for $40,000 in eight civil actions for five thousand dollars each for failure to give evidence. After the new commissioners were sworn in, a lawsuit was begun to restore the old commissioners to their former positions. Russell's indignation knew no bounds when his own man and virtual appointee, Dr. Abbott, announced that he would recognize the Wilsons as his associates on the commission until the courts decided whether Russell had the power to suspend them.

Russell's denunciation of Abbott was about as severe as that he had made of Hiram Grant, a brother carpet-bagger, who had deserted him in his fight to annul the lease.

The litigation about the appointment of John H. Pearson to succeed S. Otho Wilson came up before Judge Robinson, close friend of Russell and Republican from Goldsboro. He decided that Pearson, and not Wilson, was entitled to the office of railroad commissioner. Wilson appealed to the Supreme Court, which affirmed the lower court's decision.

There was again an attempt to reduce the appropriations to the University of North Carolina and other institutions for higher education supported by the State. "Little Bill" Bryan, of Chatham, came forward again with a bill to take all the State appropriations away from the University. Columbus Durham was dead. Dr. Kilgo was going about the State proclaiming that education in State institutions was destructive of Christianity.

As a side issue of renewing discussion about the larger appropriations for the University there was an attack on Professor Charles W. Toms, newly elected head of the Department of Education at the University, by Dr. John S. Bassett of Trinity College, who in those days was backing up Kilgo's attacks on the University. Among other things, Bassett wrote that if President Alderman had aimed to enthrone deism above Christianity, he could not have gone about it more sagaciously than by employing a man to disseminate the views contained in Professor Toms' report. Toms had said, in his report on character-building in the public schools of Durham, that they wanted to teach children to look through nature to nature's God, which Dr. Bassett characterized as unchristian. This was so far-fetched that it created no impression. Mr. Toms was a sincere member of and leader in the Methodist Church, and Dr. Alderman an elder in the Presbyterian Church. Their lives incarnated Christianity at its best.

A LIKABLE REPUBLICAN

One of the most interesting and likable men who loomed large in the Russell administration was Colonel J. C. L. Harris (everybody called him "Loge"). He and Russell had long been personal and political friends and were alike in some respects. It was to secure his aid in litigation and in the desire to reward his friends that Russell made him his right hand man and attorney extraordinary. He had seven attorneyships for State institutions and State positions, and soon it became accepted in Raleigh that the only way to get the ear of Russell was to retain his close friend, Colonel Harris, who became known by newspaper men as "the god of War" because he had been given a position by Russell, which entitled him to be called "Colonel." He was a unique character. His father had come to Raleigh from Rutherford County in the Reconstruction days as Commissioner of Public Works and his son read law and became a leading young Republican. Later he held positions on the staff of several Republican newspapers that were established and flourished for a time in Raleigh. In the meantime, he had some law practice. He was universally "cussed" during campaigns by Democrats and liked at all other times. He had a kindness of heart and a friendliness so pervasive that nobody could dislike him.

It was sometimes hard for militant Democrats who came into *The News and Observer* office at night and saw Colonel Harris with his coat off, reading proof and editing telegrams, to understand how the paper could roast him and still be on such good terms with him. The truth is that nobody could be on any other sort of terms with him, for he never carried hatred and he regarded politics very much as a game. He played it as many men play a game of chess, or any other game. He had been pretty poor and had had a hard time educating his large family before the Fusionists won, but with the election of Russell he blossomed out. The finest silk hat that could be had in New York was his first purchase and from having dressed in the ordinary every-day sort of clothes, like most people in Raleigh, the Colonel became a paragon of fashion. His long frock coat and silk hat marked him as a man of style. In fact, he was the Pooh Bah of the administration. Russell hated most Democrats, particularly lawyers who had been active in politics, and it soon became understood—it was one of those pervasive things that was acknowledged without any proof—that if you wanted to get a pardon from Russell it was a very helpful thing to get Colonel Harris to share in making the application. Getting fees from his seven attorneyships under the Russell administration, getting fees from litigants who wanted to have the ear of the court, obtaining large fees from people who wanted pardons, and adding other clients who would like to stand in with the powers that be, Colonel Harris became the most prosperous of Raleigh lawyers. He was sought after by everybody who wanted a favor from the Russell administration, and his kindness of heart made him wish to help everybody.

There were several pardons during the Russell administration that came in for very sharp criticism. About the time of Russell's financial difficulties, when he surrendered his fight against the North Carolina lease, there was a prevalent belief, for which nobody ever offered any proof, that he and Colonel Harris would divide the fees paid to Colonel Harris for pardon applications in cases where parties were willing to pay a large sum to get their relatives out of the penitentiary.

The scandal of pardons reached high-water mark in 1899. *The News and Observer,* on July 20, said editorially "We have, from time to time, taken notice of the indiscriminate way in which the executive pardons have been granted in this State—often in a manner so mysterious and inexplicable that the most charitable view to be taken of the matter was that the Governor of the State was thus petulantly revenging himself upon the public, with which he quite well understands he is not a prime favorite. This pardon business has gone merrily forward until it has attained not only the bad odor of a public scandal but the proportions of a menace to law and order." It further said that the Governor had hit upon a new scheme to "turn prisoners out without pardoning them and at the same time put good fees into J. C. Logan Harris' pocket." A few days later the paper again said, "Do you want a pardon? Then employ Marshall Mott, J. C. Logan Harris or Spencer Adams to get it for you. They have got the only nickels that fit the slot machine." It was pointed out that pardons were made secretly, and newspapers were denied any news about them. When reporters sought to find whether the pardons were granted at the executive office in Raleigh, they were denied information and the only way news of pardons or paroles trickled out was when the person pardoned turned up at his old home.

XXII

THE BISHOPS AND OTHER CLERGY IN POLITICS

AFTER the election of 1896 the element that had been fighting appropriations for higher education in North Carolina felt they now had the opportunity to win. As soon as the returns had been compiled, the Reverend John E. White, Secretary of the Baptist State Mission Board (this position really gave a man as much authority as a bishop in other churches), who had succeeded Dr. Columbus Durham, backed by Josiah W. Bailey, editor of the *Biblical Recorder,* made the statement that there would be a hundred Baptists in the Legislature; and at a session of the Baptist State Convention on November 17th, a resolution was adopted renewing the war, which had been begun by Dr. Durham in the Baptist Church and Dr. Kilgo in the Methodist Church the previous year. At the Baptist State Convention, over the open opposition of only one member, Professor J. W. Gore, of the University faculty, the following resolution was adopted:

"Whereas, the state aid to higher education by taxation is wrong, unjust and unwise, a wrong against the people who cannot receive the benefit of such opportunities; unjust to private and corporate and denominational institutions voluntarily supported; unwise because the people of North Carolina are not now adequately provided with public schools for their children and need every cent of their taxes which can be spared for their children:

"Therefore, resolved: That the Baptist State Convention of North Carolina affirm its opposition to state aid by taxation for higher education."

Only two votes were cast against the resolution. Dr. White's statement that there were one hundred Baptists in the Legislature was taken to mean that they were expected, as legislators, to vote in accordance with church affiliations. During the campaign there had been an attempt on the part of some leaders of the opposition to the University, State College, and other State institutions, to secure the nomination of legislators who were in sympathy with their views.

They had a measure of success. Shortly after the action of the Baptist Convention, the same question came up in the Western North Carolina Conference of the Methodist Church, and the committee on resolutions reported a resolution somewhat like that adopted in the Baptist Convention, sponsored and advocated by President Kilgo, of Trinity College. It was expected to go through as easily under Kilgo's chaperonage as the like resolution had passed the Baptist Convention, but it struck a snag and it was defeated by a vote of 84 to 54, after quite an exciting debate, in which opposition to the resolution was voiced by presiding elder Charles W. Byrd, Charles W. Tillett of Charlotte, Professor D. Matt Thompson, a fine, old-type educator, for whom the high school at Statesville is named, and Rev. R. S. Webb, brother of "Sawney" Webb of the Bellbuckle School in Tennessee.

The defeat of this resolution was a great surprise to Dr. Kilgo, who had informed his Baptist associates that his church would join them in the campaign. In his Thanksgiving sermon Dr. Kilgo made an attack on the opponents of the resolution and the newspapers that supported them. He likened them to Voltaire and said they sought to enthrone the politicians above the preachers and the platform above the gospel and they would have us worship the State instead of the Son of God.

At the Eastern North Carolina Methodist Conference at Kinston, Dr. Kilgo proposed a resolution in line, but modified, with that adopted by the Baptists. The one that passed was much milder than the speeches made by Dr. Kilgo. Even so, there was considerable opposition to the Kilgo resolution. Two presiding elders, Hall and Swindell, opposed it, and attempts were made by Dr. Cyrus Thompson, recently elected Secretary of State on the Fusion ticket, and the Reverend N. H. D. Wilson to get the floor and discuss the question; but the previous question having been called, they had no opportunity.

Was Jefferson a monster? That question was again debated in the early part of 1899 and was precipitated by a continuation of the denunciation of Jefferson by Dr. Kilgo. He virtually demanded that no Methodist send his sons to an institution supported by the State, declaring him to be disloyal to his church if he did so. Dr. Kilgo sought to justify his position by claiming that the origin of the State institutions of higher education were born out of infidelity. In an address on January 23 he was more vicious than usual in his denunciation of

Jefferson, interlarding it with tributes to wealth. He declared that Jefferson was an infidel and that the sort of education he would give to the youth of America would make them despise religion. He said Jefferson was a demagogue and a leveller, who had declared that commerce had done more to civilize the Orient than Christianity.

Shortly after *The News and Observer* published Kilgo's denunciation of Jefferson, he was answered by Dr. William E. Dodd, professor at Randolph-Macon College in Virginia (a Methodist institution). Dr. Dodd wrote an illuminating and informative article in *The News and Observer* headed, "The Religion of Jefferson—He Was Not An Atheist As Charged." This was followed by an article written by Dr. N. B. Herring, of Wilson, an able liberal thinker, who used quite as vigorous language in going after Kilgo as Kilgo used in going after Jefferson.

During the controversy over adequate appropriation for the University, Josiah Bailey, in the *Biblical Recorder* encouraged Kilgo and, on July 21, 1897, said, "All the bourbons, all the political tricksters, all the lobbying educators combined cannot stop the tide that is rising in North Carolina for Christian education." He wrote Kilgo: "I want to caution you to be as careful as possible. You know I want you to be aggressive; you must be; but guard your utterances. The Pharisees are watching you." He had previously cautioned Dr. Kilgo that Judge Clark was his enemy. At that time Bailey and Kilgo were singing a duet of adoration of trusts, when not opposing decent appropriations to the University and other State educational institutions.

Dr. Kingsbury (a Methodist), of the Wilmington *Messenger,* severely attacked Kilgo, with whom he had a spirited controversy. He called Kilgo an "Ambassador of the Devil." Kilgo replied in kind, but his severest critic was the Honorable John R. Webster, a Methodist, graduate of Trinity College. Webster pictured Kilgo as spokesman of the Tobacco Trust and sought to prevent his election to the bishopric. On October 10, 1901, Webster declared that Dr. Kilgo had been transformed by Duke influence from a ripsnorting Populist to a "goldbug and trust apologist and we are reliably informed that he voted for McKinley in the last election." On another occasion Webster wrote that, in a chapel lecture, Kilgo had said a man who would vote for William Jennings Bryan was not worthy of the elective franchise. In 1904 Webster declared that Trinity College was "rapidly becoming a training school of Republicanism and mongrelism and is designed to bring up a race of Trust champions and apologists." When, on January 21, 1900, in a sermon in Raleigh, Kilgo referred to Thomas Jefferson as "a religious monster" Webster's Weekly said "We repeat, it is Jefferson's political principles that are an offense to Dr. Kilgo and the Dukes, whose mouthpiece he is, and not the great man's doubts and fears upon religious matters." Later, when Kilgo published a pamphlet dealing with Jefferson's religious belief, Webster wrote: "The Dukes (who are dyed-in-the-wool Republicans) are probably furnishing the money for this attack on Democracy, as the dead Jefferson cannot sue them for libel."

After Kilgo was reported to have said in Roxboro that "a man could take a diamond ring and lead the average woman anywhere," Webster wrote: "Is a man who holds such views, that the average woman can be led anywhere with a diamond ring, fit to preside over a Christian college? It would be interesting to know the reason for this college president's low estimate of women. How many of the sex has he tempted with a diamond ring?"

In December, 1907, when Kilgo said that "trusts and monopolies are not the awful curse to society that we are led to believe by demagogues," *The News and Observer* excoriated him, saying, "Whose bread I eat, his song I sing," and added, "The more Kilgo praised the Dukes, the more money they gave. His defense of the trust was a case of priming the pump—he poured a dipperful of sweetened words in the pump and gushes of gold poured forth."

In order to sugar-coat their hostility to the University, Dr. Kilgo, Bailey, and others began, belatedly, to champion publicly more money for public schools, though they never did anything effective for public education and at one time Kilgo wanted the church to have control of all education. He even took the ground that "higher education is the privilege of the few." He opposed any aid for youths for college education. He thought this type of aid was wrong and said "A pauperized manhood is a poor substitute for a college diploma," and, further, that any youth who accepted a scholarship in a State institution "is laid under every obligation to every tax-payer from the old Negro who pays on a raccoon dog to the millionaire who pays on diamonds and bonds." "I do not believe in free higher education by church or state," was an early declaration. He demanded that all Methodist preachers should influence members "to select a Christian college instead of a secular institution."

CIGARETTES REGARDED AS A SOCIAL EVIL

In the late eighties and the early nineties *The News and Observer* in concert with many preachers and some editors (the manufacturers were not then advertising in a large way) waged a hot warfare against the use of cigarettes. My paper declared that they were "coffin tacks" and their consumption injured the health and tended to weaken the intellect of those who smoked them and that therefore no religious organization ought to condone their manufacture or use. Not a few physicians said they were injurious to health. Arthur Brisbane, in the Hearst papers, waged a war against cigarette smoking. In 1897 the Methodist Conference of Western North Carolina had passed a resolution denouncing the use of cigarettes, and in the conference of 1898 a similar resolution was introduced which created much discussion and aroused much feeling. The ablest man in the conference, Rev. Dr. Charles W. Byrd, of Asheville, supported the resolution on social evils, which included one denouncing the use of cigarettes, and he said that if it was not passed it would be interpreted to mean "that we have been bought off by the Dukes." The particular friends of Dr. Kilgo moved to strike out all references to cigarettes, and, after a heated debate, the conference reversed its action of 1897 and struck out its action against cigarettes by a vote of 65 to 62.

No woman smoked then and the sentiment was so strong against their doing so that no lady would think of smoking in a hotel dining room, in a restaurant, or even at a private dinner. It took years and millions of money spent in advertising to break down that taboo. If any smoked—as they probably did—it was secretly done.

XXIII

RALEIGH PAPERS WAR TO THE KNIFE

IT WAS NOT long after the daily *Tribune* was sold out before there were rumors, and *The News and Observer,* on July 18, 1897, said, that a new daily paper was to be started in Raleigh but its politics would be a sort of Joseph's coat affair, and added: "It is further understood that the same forces that were back of the *Tribune,* the Southern Railroad, American Tobacco Company officers, and a few rich politicians, would again put money in it under the new management."

Toward the end of that year *The News and Observer* installed a new press, a Cox duplex, the prettiest I ever saw. Prior to that time every sheet of paper had to be fed into the press by hand, and only one side of a sheet could be printed at a time. This meant that somebody's hands must feed into the press ten thousand sheets every day. With a large circulation, this became increasingly difficult. To catch the mails and meet the larger circulation, the new press was purchased. This enterprise was hailed by the paper as a big event, as indeed it was. It was the first paper in the State to have a perfecting press; that is, one that would print the whole paper from a roll. It had been the first paper to install linotype machines in North Carolina. One reason for this purchase, aside from the need of increased facilities of the paper and the fact that it would enable us to make a better paper, was the threat of opposition.

All during that summer and fall, reports persisted that a new daily was to take the place of the defunct *Tribune.* The corporation Democrats in the State, foreseeing victory for the Democrats in 1898, wished an organ to enable them to carry out their purposes. Having used the Fusionists to their own ends and to the undoing of the Fusionists, who were now on the down-grade, they planned to desert those they had seduced and to dominate the white supremacy party.

My paper, thundering day by day against Russellism, demanded reduced passenger and freight rates and juster assessment for taxation of railroads. It also vigorously advocated prosecution of the Tobacco Trust and like illegal combinations in restraint of trade. Its policy invited opposition from the monopolies. All during that summer and fall I sensed it was coming. Colonel Andrews, of the Southern Railroad, who was resolved to control the State at any hazard for the benefit of his company, supported by other public service corporations and monopolies, resented deeply the fact that the only morning paper in Raleigh, his home town, was daily opposing the plans and policies which he thought he had a right to carry through and which he had carried through in large measures in the preceding years. These influences now established the *Morning Post*. The distinct declaration was made privately that those who were putting up the money for it were resolved "to destroy *The News and Observer*." Southern Railroad men and allies, in various ways, spent many thousands of dollars to publish the *Post*. They at first believed that, within a few months at the most, they could drive out *The News and Observer* and control the field. They purchased good material and good presses, and they obtained as editor Robert M. Furman, who had large personal popularity. He was agreeable and pleasant to everybody and had had long experience in newspaper business and in Democratic politics.

The News and Observer, from the time the American Tobacco Company was organized, had been against the Tobacco Trust. It was not at all difficult to induce Duke to fall in with the plan of a paper at Raleigh that would portray the American Tobacco Company as a benevolent and philanthropic institution and combat *The News and Observer's* contentions that the Company was getting much of its prosperity by putting down the price of the tobacco which it bought from the farmers.

The *Post* secured as city editor a young man who had made some reputation in getting local news on the afternoon paper, Thomas J. Pence. He had a better nose for news and a greater capacity for getting scoops than any other newspaper man in Raleigh. The same thing was true of him when he went to Washington as correspondent of the *Post* and, later, as correspondent of *The News and Observer*. He had a winning and attractive personality and could worm a story out of men without seeming to do it, better than any other man I knew. He made the local page of the *Morning Post* very bright.

The News and Observer, in announcing the fact that the men who undertook to control politics in North Carolina, having made a failure of a Republican paper, would establish a new paper, said that it was as true in 1897 as Blow-Your-Horn Billy Smith had said in 1870 that "you cannot publish a paper for a party that can't read." *The News and Observer* staff, particularly the travelling correspondents, were instructed to tell all the subscribers that the *Post* was being established with railroad and trust money with the avowed purpose of "running *The News and Observer* out," to get control of the Democratic Party for their own selfish ends. By the time the first issue of the *Post* was printed, it was pretty well understood who owned it and for what purpose it was established. The fight between my paper and the Southern Railroad people, which had begun with the agitation for a Railroad Commission in 1887 and with my refusal to become editor of *The News and Observer* when Colonel Andrews offered to buy it and let me edit it on the condition that I would say nothing about a Railroad Commission, was accentuated. The antagonism was heightened by my fight against the midnight lease of the North Carolina Railroad. It was increased by *The News and Observer's* opposition to the giving of passes and its continued demand for reduction of railroad rates and increase of assessments of their property. If they could kill *The News and Observer* and on its remains establish a railroad organ, they thought the money invested would earn a good dividend. The editorial which I wrote at that time was widely copied and commented upon. It was entitled "Mordecai at the Gate." It made a great hit with the public and infuriated the owners of the railroad organ. I was Mordecai, Andrews was Haman, and the prophecy of Haman's fate for the *Post* was scriptural.

From its establishment on, the *Post* frequently made it a point to take some extract from *The News and Observer* which it thought could be used adversely and to comment on it. The reply that I usually made was, "The wheezy old railroad organ down the street is earning its stipend which it gets from the railroad by abusing *The News and Observer* [so many inches or columns] yesterday." Every once in a while, some Democrat who wished everything to be harmonious would come to me and urge me in the interest of party harmony to have no controversy with the *Post*. I would always reply that he was advising me to go out of business and to surrender the Democratic Party to Andrews and the Dukes, so that they could make it subservient to their interests. I declined to sacrifice myself or the principles of which *The News and Observer* was the only spokesman at the State capital. The *Post* showed wisdom in everything except in its open and notorious subservience to the Southern Railway and the Tobacco Trust. If it could have camouflaged its ownership, it would have injured *The News and Observer* more than in proving I was right in calling it a railroad mouthpiece by advocating everything the railroad wanted and denouncing everybody who criticized the policies of monopoly and railroad rule. My designation of the paper stuck. The great bulk of the people in the State, when they bought the *Morning Post,* would say, "Give me a copy of the wheezy old railroad organ." Then and always, the strength of *The News and Observer* was that people relied upon it to champion their cause and could not be separated from it. Our agents would report that Southern Railway employees felt they must take the *Post,* and some of them did, but they had *The News and Observer* sent to their homes.

When I declined to help the railroad bosses cut my throat by agreeing to furnish the *Post* the Associated Press news, the management of that paper sent its local editor, Thomas J. Pence, to Washington as its correspondent and made arrangements with the New York *Sun,* which was not then a member of Associated Press, to furnish its news service. Pence, bright and quick, got in touch with other Washington correspondents and sent out daily on a special leased wire from there, the best service that could be had outside the Associated Press. However, it cost the *Post* very large sums of money, much more than *The News and Observer* was paying. In world news, *The News and Observer's* service was so far superior that the *Post* had a difficult time with subscribers who were interested in the latest and most accurate news. As long as the *Post* lasted, it was a war to the knife. While it was losing money heavily all the time, it was taking considerable business from *The News and Observer,* enough to make it have a hard time to make ends meet. I spent every morning in the business office looking after advertising and directing the business end of the paper. My afternoons and nights were devoted to writing editorials. The members of our staff were on their mettle, all of them working long hours and everybody feeling it was a fight to the finish and ready to make any sacrifice to win the battle.

As an illustration of the fight between the two papers for business, this incident is an example: My biggest advertiser was the National Biscuit Company, which had recently been incorporated and had been dubbed the Bread Trust. It was putting on its famous Nabisco and other brands and had merged into the company pretty much all the makers of crackers and breads. Not long after the *Post* was established, the company annulled its contract for advertising in *The News and Observer* and turned it over to the *Morning Post*. This cut a big hole into a very slender income from foreign advertising. The Biscuit Company's advertisements were the most beautiful that appeared and it cost nothing to set them up. The profit was therefore good. The loss of that contract was not only serious in the amount of loss it involved, but it gave a certain prestige to the *Post* to claim that the biggest advertiser had come out of *The News and Observer* and gone into their paper, indicating that it was being recognized as the best advertising medium in Raleigh.

I always thought I did a pretty good piece of work when I wrote to the President of the Biscuit Company telling him that it had been stated in Raleigh—and that was the truth—that the reason the National Biscuit Company's advertising had been taken out of *The News and Observer* and put in the *Morning Post* was because that paper upheld the trusts, whereas *The News and Observer* had opposed monopoly in every form; that I hesitated to accept and publish this statement about his company without giving him an opportunity to deny it, and I wished he would please write me whether the editorial policy of my paper had caused him to discriminate against it in placing his advertising. The business manager of the *Post* had made that representation. In a few days I received a long letter from the president of the National Biscuit Company in which he hotly disclaimed that his company ever considered the editorial policy of a paper when it came to making advertising contracts; that they would regard it as unworthy of any American corporation to try to control the utterances of a newspaper by giving or withholding advertisements. I had sensed such would be the answer, for no concern could publicly admit that it used its advertising to control editorial support. I had advised our advertising agents to keep in touch with the National Biscuit people. Within a few days after receiving this letter from the president of the company, *The News and Observer* received a new contract for all the advertising of that company. It was the worst blow that had ever struck the *Post,* for it stopped its boasting. It had been hoist with its own petard. This incident shows how the two papers worked against each other to get business and how hot the fight was. About half the Raleigh merchants would recommend to foreign advertisers that they use the *Post* and the others rooted for *The News and Observer*.

When the fight was the hottest and *The News and Observer* receipts and expenditures were about even, Raleigh suffered a moderate epidemic of smallpox. It was confined to the southern section of the city. People who had the disease were taken out to improvised buildings south of the city in what was called the pest house, where they were kept isolated from the balance of the town. Smallpox was raging that year in Norfolk and other places also. *The News and Observer* printed each day the number of fresh cases, the total number and how many had been taken to the pest house. The *Morning Post* did not know there was any smallpox in Raleigh, judging by its columns. Business was very dull in Raleigh that spring. Men who had bought large stocks had them on their shelves and were very blue. What should they do? Holding a meeting one day, one prominent merchant suggested that the reason business was so dull was because out-of-town people were afraid to come to Raleigh to trade because of the printed reports that there was an epidemic of smallpox. It was suggested that the people in the country would not know there was any smallpox in the city if *The News and Observer* did not print it.

One morning shortly after I had gotten down to the office and was talking to Fred Merritt, I heard what seemed like a cavalcade, coming up the stairs. It turned out to be a score of merchants, in fact nearly all of those who advertised in the paper. They filed into the office and said they had come to tell me the reason business was so bad in Raleigh that spring was that *The News and Observer* was saying smallpox was so prevalent that if people came here to trade they might catch the disease. The *Morning Post,* they said, had never printed anything about it, and the only information people had was from my paper. The spokesman of the merchants, Sherwood Higgs, who ran the biggest advertisements in the paper, said, "We have had a meeting, Mr. Daniels, and we have come to say to you that, unless you will promise us not to print another line about smallpox in your paper, we are all going to withdraw our advertising from *The News and Observer*." I tried not to show what a solar plexus that would be. The paper could not run without the advertising that was given it by the men in that room. I paused long enough to look about and see that among the number were some of my best friends. Others spoke up and confirmed what Mr. Higgs said. Others said nothing. I let them go on and talk before I said anything. Merritt started to speak, to say that a newspaper wouldn't be a newspaper that didn't print the news, but I told him to let the gentlemen state their position. After they had made their threat, very direct and very terrifying, I decided what I ought to say. When Mr. Higgs added, "Will you make us the promise?" I answered:

"Gentlemen, every dollar I have in the world is invested in Raleigh, and all the money I owe is owed in Raleigh and all the business I have or hope to have is here. I am as much interested, therefore, as any of you in what will contribute to the welfare and prosperity of the city, but you must see that no editor could maintain his self-respect or be worthy to be an editor of a paper if he permitted even his best friends and associates to dictate the policy of his paper. If you have come to talk to me as a citizen of Raleigh as to what is best for the town and to confer about it with the understanding that we all have a mutual interest, I shall be very glad to take up the matter with you and discuss it, but if you have come to say what it shall or shall not print, then you must see that no self-respecting editor could hold a conference with such a threat over his head."

When I had finished, I arose and said, "Gentlemen, I would like for you to think about this. I will go down to the business office and let you discuss it among yourselves and I will return when you have made up your mind fully what you wish to do." And so, Merritt and I went below. My heart was in my throat because I knew some of the visitors were *Morning Post* people, and I had a notion that the suggestion had come from the *Morning Post* or through its partisans. However, I knew some of them were friends of mine. I heard them talking upstairs, some in loud tones, and after what seemed an age to me one of them came to the foot of the stairs and asked me to come back. They said they had thought about it seriously and they had reached the conclusion that they would like to discuss the situation with me as a citizen and a friend without any threats. We debated for a long time as to what was best for the city. I told them that my news from Norfolk was that its business was much worse than in Raleigh; that the papers there had not printed a line about smallpox and rumors had gone out all over that section and in Eastern North Carolina that smallpox was raging in the city and, from the lack of facts, people thought it was ten-fold worse than it was, whereas *The*

News and Observer had printed the facts exactly as they were, show-ing that smallpox was confined to a very small section of the southern part of the city. I had explained that all those who had the disease had been removed quickly under the superintendence of competent Thomas P. Sale, health officer, who had, with the same sort of spirit that actuated men who had been given medals of honor, gone into the pest house and looked after the people; that, in my opinion, the only wise thing to do for the business of the town was for the papers to print the facts exactly as they existed. There had been only thirty-five cases in Raleigh for a month and the paper had printed exactly where they were, not one of them north of Cabarrus Street, and the people who came to Raleigh to trade all transacted their business north of that street. By giving the facts, just as they were, there had been no chance for the people in the country to feel there was any widespread epidemic, but if we stopped printing the facts, people would jump to the conclusion that Raleigh was a pest house and it would be boycotted. Some of the merchants took the other side. We had a warm debate, some maintaining that we ought to suppress the news entirely. The final result was that the meeting adjourned with the understanding with most of them that *The News and Observer* would be careful not to magnify but to print the facts day by day.

When the conference was over, I was "all in," because, while I had put up a pretty stiff fight, the threat had in it the possibility of severe injury to the paper. I knew that one third of the merchants would have loved to see *The News and Observer* go under. It was interesting and heartening that afternoon, as one by one, a number of merchants who had come in the morning under the leadership of men in a militant mood, called personally and said that they were not in sym-pathy with the threat; that they didn't like to refuse to come down, but they never had any intention of boycotting the paper. That was knowledge after the fact. Our local reporters and others on the paper had evidence, which they thought was correct, that the whole thing had been engineered by some of the *Morning Post* people. At any rate, my paper had met that local crisis and won out in a way to com-mand the respect of most of the business men, even those who were antagonistic, and was made stronger thereby. Of course, the visit be-came known and that knowledge helped my paper. We continued to print—and we were the only paper in Raleigh that did—the facts about smallpox and how well Mr. Sale handled it.

He was a rare sort of man, Tom Sale was. He was, for a long time, the political boss of Raleigh and on the side of the politicians I was fighting, but he was always a warm friend of mine. In the smallpox matter and like affairs, he had the stuff in him of which good officials are made. He felt he must go with the crowd that won in city politics because he was poor and needed his job, but by comparison he was a shining light of efficiency and capacity and integrity. I later recommended him for steward at the State Prison and he afterward became warden. In that position he demonstrated ability of so high an order that he ought to have been promoted.

As the campaign of 1898 drew near, there was quite a division in the Democratic Party as to what its policy ought to be. The *Post* was very vicious in its denunciation of the Populists and very mild in its criticism of the Republicans. Its policy tended to keep the Alliance men voting with the Republicans by virtually telling them they could return to the Democratic Party only on their knees. *The News and Observer,* believing that the bulk of the Alliance men had joined the Populist party because of the distress and poverty on the farms and that the bulk of them had no sympathy with the Russell administration, wanted to make it easy for them to come back to the Democratic Party. As the time for the State Convention drew near, *The News and Observer* suggested that it would be wise to nominate some Populists of high character for positions on the State ticket and to unite white men of the State in the supreme and difficult task of defeating the Fusionists. The *Post,* on the other hand, denounced *The News and Observer* as at heart a Populist paper for wishing to hold the olive branch out to those who had voted against the Democrats in 1894-96. It was a delicate and difficult situation. In the first place, those of us who wished to hold the door open for honest Populists to come back had to meet the charges that these very Populists had fused in 1894 and 1896, and were in some sense responsible for the ensuing evils. Also there was no assurance that an olive branch would be received by enough former Democrats who had joined the Populists to win success. The bulk of the leaders of the Democratic Party were opposed to overtures. The Wake County Democratic convention had by almost unanimous vote, declared in favor of the policy recommended by *The News and Observer.* Such party leaders as Colonel Davidson, Judge Avery, Judge Peebles, Captain Mason, Rufus

Doughton, Congressman Kitchin, and many others believed the Populists should be invited to return home.

When the convention met the matter was discussed by the committee on platform and resolutions, of which I was a member. The committee met in *The News and Observer* office and spent an entire afternoon. The opponents of any overtures to the Populists were in the majority. Only three, W. W. Kitchin, R. A. Doughton, and myself, favored making overtures. The others all favored a platform for free silver and along the lines of most of the policies which the Populists advocated. The committee made its report at night. The minority, Kitchin, Doughton, and I, decided to yield to the judgment of the majority, headed by Governor Jarvis and Senator Overman. When Governor Jarvis presented the report, a sort of smile went all over the convention when he called upon me to read it, because the delegates knew that I had favored going further than the committee had gone.

The resolution, which I read as the recommendation from the committee, was adopted as follows:

> *Resolved* 1: that the proposition for fusion submitted by the Populist Committee be and the same is hereby declined;
> *Resolved* 2: that the Democratic Executive Committee be, and the same is hereby instructed to entertain no further propositions.

As a matter of fact, I had acted as secretary and Jarvis wasn't certain he could read my writing. The platform was adopted unanimously. The fact that many Democrats had wished a reunion softened those Populists who were disgusted with Russell. It made it easy for many to support the Democratic ticket. We were able to show that the Democratic platform in all the matters which had separated the Democrats and Populists were in agreement. However, as the campaign progressed, little was heard except the issue that unless the ignorant Negro could be eliminated from politics good government could not be attained.

It was recognized that *The News and Observer* must be depended upon to influence the Populists to return to the Democratic ranks. Chairman Simmons raised money to circulate as many copies of my weekly *The North Carolinian* as could be printed to be sent to Populists. I sold the paper to the committee at actual cost. It went into most of the sincere Populist homes and its arguments induced many of them to come back to the party.

One of the New Year's gifts in 1898 to *The News and Observer* was a letter from a Republican from Hillsboro, N. W. Brown, who asked that we discontinue his subscription to *The News and Observer,* saying the *Police Gazette* was more worthy of the patronage of decent people. The announcement of the discontinuance of his subscription was made by Brown in other papers, and *The News and Observer* said that for Brown to stop taking the paper was a decoration of honor, for he was an old McKinleyite who had tried to break up a Bryan meeting in 1896, and that if *The News and Observer* was as bad as the *Police Gazette,* it was because it was recording daily the doings of the Fusionists in office and what they did was an offense to decent people.

JOSEPH P. CALDWELL AND THE CHARLOTTE OBSERVER

In the years from 1896 on, there was a continual controversy between the Charlotte *Observer* and *The News and Observer,* accentuated when the Charlotte paper fought the nomination of Bryan. Editor Joseph P. Caldwell of the Charlotte paper was a close friend of Ransom and, when in 1896 Senator Vance made his great free silver speech in Charlotte, Caldwell wrote a very critical editorial in which, in essence, if not in words, he called Vance a demagogue. He used his facile pen to ridicule free silver advocates, presaging the bolt he was later to lead against Bryan. This was the beginning of the break of a strong friendship between Caldwell and myself. Caldwell was editing the Statesville *Landmark* when I began editing the Wilson *Advance.* After I moved to Raleigh, I saw him often and, if I do say it myself "as hadn't ought to," we were the leading newspaper exponents of two schools of thought in North Carolina. In 1887 I had visited him at his home in Statesville, and he never came to Raleigh that he did not take dinner or supper at my home. His sister, who was a gifted teacher, had taught a school attended by my wife's relatives and they were devoted to her. That and our mutual interest as editors of weekly papers drew us together.

Outside of our interest in journalism, however, we looked at life from very different angles. His idea of politics was the Ransom idea. The first suggestion of a difference between us came in 1889, when Ransom was elected Senator. Three of my best friends in the Legislature were from Iredell County, Senator W. D. Turner, later Lieutenant-Governor, Augustus Leazar, afterward Speaker of the House, and

John B. Holman, called the "Watchdog of the Treasury." They all voted against Ransom for the Senate although the county convention had passed a resolution instructing them to vote for Ransom. Caldwell charged them with breaking faith. Leazar told me that he attended the convention; that he did not leave the courthouse until he thought everything was over and that, unknown to him or the candidates or most of the delegates, Caldwell offered a resolution on the shank of the meeting to instruct for Ransom; that it was not mentioned during the campaign; that everybody knew he was opposed to Ransom and he did not regard the instructions as representing the will of the people. Caldwell demanded that they vote according to his resolution. Leazar and other Iredell legislators resented his criticism.

Caldwell always sneered at prohibition. In his early editorial career he was not interested in public schools although later, largely due to the influence of McIver, the Charlotte *Observer* espoused the cause and gave it good support. When D. A. Tompkins, of South Carolina, bought the Charlotte *Observer,* he offered a half interest in it to Caldwell and persuaded him to go to Charlotte where he could have a free hand in a larger field. Caldwell hesitated about going. At Statesville, and always, he was the old-fashioned editor who read all his exchanges, wrote locals and editorials, and was the master paragraphist of the press. He could put into a few lines more than any of his contemporaries and he had a humor and satire that gave the Charlotte *Observer* wide reputation. He loved to work at night, loved to supervise the make-up, to look over the locals and, in a word, was like Peter Hale in that respect. Whatever else he was, he was never dull, and dullness is the only crime for which an editor ought to be hung.

Tompkins, who put up the money, was one of the leading captains of industry in the South. He had a cotton mill in South Carolina, wrote interestingly about industrial progress, sold cotton mill machinery, was interested in agricultural and industrial education, was a trustee of State College in Raleigh and a leader in the awakening industrial life. He was ambitious. He saw that a daily paper with a brilliant editor like Caldwell would help him advance his ideas and increase his business. He might be called the apostle of the new school of materialism in the South.

Caldwell had no ambition for office. He declined the appointment as collector of internal revenue which Ransom offered him. Many people believed that he entertained a secret ambition to be Governor. I doubt that. He was wholly wedded to journalism. How much influence Tompkins' practical materialism had upon him, I do not know—he thought, none at all, but the Charlotte *Observer* made its appeal to the element, then growing, which had a contempt for the policies that, under Vance's tutoring, were dominant in the State. Ransom hypnotized Caldwell. When the criticism of Cleveland for vetoing the silver bill was almost unanimous in North Carolina, Caldwell's paper approved it, and this rallied behind his paper a large number of the more prosperous business men in the State.

In addition to that, his was the first paper in the State that had enough money, thanks to Tompkins, to enable him to employ gifted writers. He had a genius for discovering and encouraging them. Among his "boys" were John Charles McNeill, the Scotland County poet, whose untimely death cut short a career of promise; Isaac Erwin Avery, member of the distinguished Avery family of Burke, who had a rare gift at writing and knew how to touch the hearts of his readers; H. E. C. Bryant, who became a star reporter and added to his reputation as a Washington correspondent of the New York *World* and of North Carolina papers; and Howard Banks, who later became connected with the *Sunday School Times* at Philadelphia, and went with me to Washington as my secretary when I became Secretary of the Navy. Caldwell was such a prodigious worker himself and had a style that was so effective that he stimulated these and like young men, who aided him in making the Charlotte *Observer* a popular paper. These elements, with Tompkins' business judgment, gave that paper prestige and the largest circulation in Western North Carolina.

In the spring of 1896, *The News and Observer* and the Charlotte *Observer* began a long controversy. When the Farmers' Alliance was organized, the Charlotte *Observer* was bitter in its denunciation of it and of its advocacy of free silver and other policies. It was contemptuous of Vance's advocacy of like measures—so much so that in the early part of 1896 *The News and Observer* said:

> "The arrogance, abuse and intolerance of Alliance men by the Charlotte *Observer* from 1892 until 1894 gave to the Populists more recruits from the Democratic ranks in strong Democratic counties in which its circulation was the largest than the combined efforts of all the Populist papers and propaganda."

Aforetime the Charlotte *Observer* had been a silver advocate, and *The News and Observer* was referring to its flop. Caldwell was urging the nomination of Cleveland or some gold standard man for president in 1896 and *The News and Observer* was urging the nomination of a standard bearer who believed in bi-metalism. *The News and Observer* said, "Since Caldwell's profession of faith in the gold standard, water is at hand. Why shouldn't John Sherman baptize Mr. Caldwell?" And the Charlotte *Observer* replied in kind and denounced *The News and Observer* as Populistic. That controversy became so acute that it caused a breach which was not healed until toward the end of Caldwell's life.

As a young man Caldwell had been city editor of the Raleigh *News* when its policy against using convicts to build the Western North Carolina Railroad was directed by Walter Clark, a stockholder, whose control of the paper was not generally known. After Caldwell gravitated toward the right and Clark toward the left, the *Observer* was very critical of "stockholder Clark," as Caldwell always called him. His barbed paragraphs about Clark had pith and point and they stung.

We both attended the editorial convention at Winston-Salem in the heat of the controversy. In those days editors were entertained in private homes, at their gatherings. The local committee, assigning the editors to their homes, took cognizance of the attitude of Caldwell and myself and the hosts. I was assigned to be the guest of Dr. Dick Dalton, leading physician of the town and strong silver Democrat, and Caldwell was the guest of W. N. Reynolds, who took the Caldwell side in the controversy. These gentlemen had married sisters. There was much talk in the town and in the convention about how this paper and party division had cut into families and communities and into the press association. In fact the controversy later became so bitter that, after I had published a communication from Dr. McKelway, editor of the *Presbyterian Standard* of Charlotte, who had ferociously denounced Caldwell, alleging that his paper was always on the side of the liquor crowd, Caldwell announced that he would go to Raleigh next day for two days and intimated that there might be a physical combat between us. He came to Raleigh, went up to the capitol. I never saw him. He did not call to see me and returned to Charlotte, nothing being said about an encounter. The feud between Caldwell and McKelway later resulted in a libel suit, and as *The News and Observer* was in hearty accord with McKelway's advocacy of prohibition, it printed, from time to time, statements from him. This brought increased estrangement between the two papers.

At the editorial convention held at Hendersonville, Caldwell and his wife and daughter attended. I took two of my sons to the convention and on a mountain trip. The relations between Caldwell and myself were still strained and we did not speak to each other, but I had known his wife before they were married and, during the entire convention and on our trip to the mountains, my son Jonathan and Caldwell's little daughter, Adelaide, played together all the time, to the surprise and interest of all the other editors. His second wife, who was Miss Addie Williams, an accomplished newspaper woman, believed he was the greatest man in the world and almost worshipped him. Praise from him, even before their marriage, was to her the crown of life.

I have said that Caldwell was not ambitious for public office. He was not, but he had rendered for a long term of years continuous and signal service to the state as unpaid chairman of the Board of Directors of the North Carolina Hospital for the Insane at Morganton. He was devoted to Dr. P. L. Murphy, a distinguished alienist, the able head of that institution. Caldwell supported him with enthusiasm and never missed a meeting of the Board of Directors. Caldwell was beloved by all in the institution and the sorrow's crown of sorrows was that, when his health became impaired and he was unable to continue writing and the power of speech was gone, he spent his last days in that institution, not because of mental trouble, but because he loved it better than any other place. Its officials and all of its employees gave him the tenderest care and showed appreciation for his long and valued service. Before his affliction, for he lingered long, we had not spoken for years. When we met, which was seldom, he never saw me and I never saw him, although we might have been in the same small room. But, visiting Morganton, I went over to the hospital to call on him. He could speak, but not easily. I did not know how he would receive me but I recalled our early friendship and deplored the break that had come. I didn't wish him to pass away without knowing that I had for him the same feeling I had had in the early days before political differences brought estrangement. He received me very cordially. We talked about the delightful visits I had made in his home when we were both editors of weekly papers and we parted with friendly greetings. Even before his illness, his last years in Charlotte were sad ones. He had literally burned the candle at both ends and his physical vitality was broken down. Caldwell had little money sense and little ambition about money so that, with his death, the paper passed out of the control of his family. His ability had been the great asset of the paper.

XXIV

THE NEWS AND OBSERVER FIGHTS RUSSELLISM

I N 1897-98 THERE was much discussion of the situation at the Blind
Institution in Raleigh. It had been turned over to a board of directors of which Jim Young, the Negro politician of Raleigh, was the
leading spirit. The board of directors made an inspection of the institution. Cartoonist Jennett, in *The News and Observer,* had pictures
of Jim Young inspecting the sleeping apartments of the young blind
white girls and of the election of a defaulter as steward. My paper was
severe in the denunciation of the management of the institution. Dr.
Charles F. Meserve, President of Shaw University, a Negro college
in Raleigh, was a member of the board of directors. He resented the
strictures of *The News and Observer* upon the methods of the board.
Being a Northern man and president of a Negro college, he did not
understand the intense feeling which was aroused by the appointment of Jim Young on a board of directors of a white institution for
the blind. He was an honest man and keenly interested in having the
institution run properly. Later, when he realized that his fellow directors were more interested in jobs than in the education of blind
children, he protested but was unable to do anything about it. He,
therefore, resigned, saying that he could not remain with self-respect
since "political pull" had taken the place of efficiency and moral character. A new building was erected and on the cornerstone the names
of the directors of the institution were cut in marble. In view of the
scandals that attended the management of the institution and the
sense of outrage that a Negro should be appointed as leading member
of the board of an institution for white blind children, indignation
rose to white heat.

On the day after election in 1898, when the Fusionists were driven
from power, an enthusiastic celebrating crowd of Democrats visited
the institution and, by torch-light, cut the name of the Negro trustee,
Jim Young, off the cornerstone. The fact that this was done, and
done by citizens who could not, at other times, have been guilty of
what some called vandalism, evidences the temper of the times. The

white supremacy advocates were resolved to leave no vestige of the administration which for four years had humiliated the State.

During the session of the Legislature, as in almost every Legislature since, there were suggestions of improvement in the law relating to the working of women and children in the mills. Some of the Fusionists had denounced the Democrats during the campaign because they had not enacted such legislation. A bill was introduced to reduce the working hours to ten in the textile mills. It was promptly tabled in the Fusion Legislature as it had been in the Democratic Legislature, showing that the conscience of the people of neither party was awake to the duty owed to women and children in industry. Many of the mill workers had voted with the Fusion Party. In the counties where they were strong, the Fusionists had been very severe in denouncing the Democrats for doing the bidding of mill owners. When they came into power they followed the same unenlightened policy. That course was another nail in the coffin of Fusion. The forgotten men who had helped them to office resented the betrayal, although even then, as in other times, these forgotten men and women were not able to make effective their protest because they had no organization and lacked leadership. Following the defeat of the measure, however, the discussion caused some improvement.

W. A. Erwin, head of the chain of cotton mills at Durham, which later extended into Davie and Harnett counties, issued an order that no child be allowed to work in their mills unless they could read and write. This was in advance of the later legislation that required compulsory attendance at schools. The Odells of Concord had adopted that policy some years before and it was approved by a number of the mill owners, though put into effect by only a few of them. I remember having talked at Concord with the Odells before they adopted that policy. It was an innovation. Some of the more hard-boiled mill men predicted it would not work well. Later, when the Odell mills failed, they sneeringly said that this policy was partly responsible for it, although the great success of Erwin's mills, which had put it into operation, disproved the claim.

The appointment of Negroes on the school committees, the Fusion plan being to appoint two white men and one Negro, had aroused a storm of resentment all over the State. It was argued, on the part of the Fusionists, that they expected the Negro to look after the Negro schools and the two white men to look after the white schools. Many

Democrats appointed on these school boards refused to serve. I remember talking about the matter with Robert W. Scott, who had been a member of the House, and Senator from Alamance. He was the leading practical farmer of that section. He really did more in the nineties for agricultural diversification than any other farmer in the State. It was Scott, as member of the House, when money was being put into other uses, who compelled the appropriation of money for the Agricultural Building at the Agricultural and Mechanical College. It was hailed at the time as an important victory. It ought to have been called the Scott Building. If there had been proper gratitude and appreciation for his services, Scott would have been Commissioner of Agriculture. He told me that, while attending the Presbyterian Church at Hawfields one Sunday, Senator S. A. White, Republican, came to him and told him that he had been appointed member of the school board. Scott asked him the names of the other members. He was informed they were White, a white Republican, and a Negro. Scott declined to serve. Although he and Mr. White were elders in the same church, the old man grew white with rage and, for a long time their relations were very much strained. White declared that a man could not be a Christian who was unwilling to serve on a board with a Negro to help in public education. "Afterwards," said Scott, "when I was nominated to redeem the district, I was very glad that I had been wise enough to decline to be a party to Fusion plans. We rescued the schools and improved them by the Democratic plan."

The News and Observer, every now and then, had a story about the holding of the magistrate's courts by Negro magistrates and of one or two cases where white women had been called into these courts to be tried by Negro magistrates. The people of the State greatly resented the appointment of Negro magistrates. This, together with the increase in crime on the part of Negroes, heightened indignation against the Fusionists. Whenever there was any gross crime on the part of the Negroes, The News and Observer printed it in a lurid way, sometimes too lurid, in keeping with the spirit of the times. For example, in its issue of June 16, the headlines read: *"Burned to Ashes, the Black Devil, Riddled with Bullets First, a Righteous Judgment, Ravished and then Killed a White Lady, Paid the Penalty for his Crime, an Outraged People Chased the Fiend for Two Days and When They Caught Him Made Short Work of Him."* Another headline in the same paper said: *"Attempted Rape. Another Candidate for the Hemp Route to Glory."* The increase in crime of that character was widely printed and commented upon. An apprehensive feeling of danger on the part of the women who lived in the rural districts pervaded some parts of the State. Farmers who had been accustomed to go to town and come back in the night ceased doing so. The indignation over cases of assault and rape of white women by the Negroes, though these were few in number, was such that women in the country who at first had been strong for the Populists, now convinced that Fusion had some part in the increase of attacks, began to turn against the Fusionists. One day a Populist farmer from Rhamkatte, near Raleigh, during the campaign of 1898, came to my office and demanded that *The North Carolinian,* which was the weekly paper of *The News and Observer,* no longer be sent to him. The Democrats had raised a fund to subscribe to this weekly paper to be sent to Populists who had formerly been Democrats and his name was on the list. I told him I thought he had called to express thanks to me for sending him the paper without charge, that I was sure he would like it and was surprised that he wasn't enjoying it and asked him what was the trouble. "Trouble!" he said. "My wife gets scared at the pictures you print and she has about turned Democrat." This illustrates the feeling of fear of the women in the country. It was one of the factors which, in 1898, caused many farmers who had joined the Populists in 1894 to help drive the Fusionists out of power.

While *The News and Observer* was calling upon the honest Populists and all the other people who believed in white supremacy to join hands, it was waging war on those Populists and Republicans who were responsible for the disgrace that came to the State under the Fusion administration. That propaganda was having good effect and winning Populists. *The News and Observer* printed a statement furnished to it by the Rocky Mount *Argonaut,* alleging that Marion Butler who, in spite of his fight on Pritchard during the Legislature, was still devoted to continued fusion with the Republicans, had said, "If colored men commit outrages, the Democrats pretend to be terribly shocked in public but when they get behind a wall, they laugh until they grow fat and if the outrages are not frequent enough they hire worthless Negroes to commit them." This statement was played up by the Democratic papers. It was accepted as true and Butler was roundly denounced all over the State. Butler denied that he had said the Democrats hired Negroes to commit rape, said he was in favor of white supremacy but other things must go with it. My paper, replying to Butler, printed affidavits furnished by W. A. Campbell, editor of the Rocky Mount *Argonaut,* declaring that Butler did use the exact language attributed to him.

About that time *The News and Observer* also printed that the white and Negro convicts at Caledonia Farm of the State Prison ate together and that social equality was in effect more or less among the employees at the State Prison. When the Reverend Mr. Babb, or, as *The News and Observer* called him, the "Rev. Altogether Righteous Babb," charged with drunkenness and other offenses, was dismissed as chaplain, it was announced that a Negro preacher would be made chaplain at Caledonia and would preach to the white as well as colored convicts. More outrages on women were committed, and, on December 1, not many days after Butler had denied his statement, the State was outraged by an incident that came up from Pamlico County. *The News and Observer* called it "the fruit of Fusion," and said, "social equality had been put in practice among the Fusionists of Pamlico County." A Fusion official (giving his name —for no one was spared) of that county declared that a Negro politician was the father of his daughter's child. My paper said the official had neglected his family and affiliated with the Negro during the campaign; that the Negro tenant ate and slept at his house and that this Negro gave medicine to the official's daughter to bring on an abortion, but the child was born, was a mulatto infant, and the daughter said that the Negro (name given) was its father. About the same time a jury in Vance County, composed of nine white men and three Negroes, convicted a Negro of assaulting a white woman, and the jury was out only seven minutes. All these cases of miscegenation, rape, and outrage, followed up by the reports of drinking and immorality in the State Prison, which were duly printed day by day, shocked honest Populists as well as the Democrats of the State and drove more nails into the coffin of Fusion. About that time, when the race feeling was very tense and growing worse, day by day fuel was added to the flame by the publication of a book by Bishop Gaines, colored, who asked the question, "Will the black race ultimately blend with the Caucasian?"

The News and Observer undertook to number the scandals under the Fusion administration. In 1898 it had uncovered five, each one of which was sufficient to drive the Russellites out of power; and now, on the New Year, it printed conspicuously what it called the sixth and greatest scandal. One of the choice plums of an administration in North Carolina, when the Atlantic and North Carolina Railroad was operated by the State, was the presidency of that road. It did not pay a great deal, but it gave its recipient a pass on all the railroads in the United States and put him in the class of the railroad executives. It also gave him political influence, and he himself could give passes to anybody he chose. Russell appointed as president Robert Hancock, of New Bern, who had long been a Republican leader in Craven County. He was nearly always able to control the solid Negro vote and to hold a few white men in line. Early in January, Robert Hancock was charged by his wife's niece, aged seventeen or eighteen years, with seducing her on trips on which he took her to New York. The girl and her father brought suit against Hancock for ten thousand dollars. *The News and Observer* said that Hancock would probably be indicted for rape and there was fear of violence toward him in New Bern. When the girl told her mother of Hancock's treatment of her, Hancock put her out of the house, got her sister fired as teacher in the school at New Bern, and threatened to have her father's pension stopped. The publication, in *The News and Observer* of this sixth and greatest scandal, created a sensation throughout the State. The New Bern *Journal,* published in his home town, said that Hancock was guilty, and the girl wrote to Governor Russell that the charges were true, though the charges in court had been withdrawn without her consent.

It was developed that, under the legislation passed by the Fusionists in 1895, Hancock and two Negroes had the power to name all the teachers in the New Bern schools, and the sister of his victim had been dismissed by them. After publishing all this scandal from its own correspondents and quoting the New Bern *Journal* and showing up the indignation of the State expressed in many ways, Governor Russell told Hancock he must disprove the charges or he must resign as president of the Atlantic and North Carolina Railroad. Hancock wrote the Governor denying the charges, saying they were invented by enemies who were persecuting him and that he would be able, and shortly would present evidence, to prove all his contentions. At the meeting of the directors of the Atlantic and North Carolina Railroad shortly thereafter, made up of Hancock's friends, they decided to give him another chance. The impression prevailed for a short time that the Governor was willing to wash his hands of the matter and let the directors take the responsibility. That was not true, for a little later Hancock was put out. Thereupon he made a public statement in which he asserted that Russell had told him if he would "get a horse-whip and go to *The News and Observer* office and beat up Josephus Daniels," he would be reappointed. "I was your servant," wrote Hancock to Russell, "but when you delivered your ultimatum on the 13th day of January that I should make a violent and personal assault upon Josephus Daniels, editor of *The News and Observer* and retain my position, otherwise I would lose it, I felt that you were trespassing upon sacred grounds." Hancock said he was unwilling to be the instrument for satisfying Russell's thirst for revenge; that Russell lacked self-respect and he would not become an assassin to hold his job. Governor Russell came out in a vitriolic attack upon Hancock, saying that he was a plain liar, that he could bring no proof, and that he cared nothing about Hancock's statements. "The statement that you can make for me," said Russell to a reporter in a midnight interview, "is that I never said anything to Hancock about assaulting Daniels or anybody else." Hancock was removed and brought suit, but he was not reinstated and he ended his pyrotechnics in defense by demanding that Russell be impeached.

The charges against Hancock were accepted as true, but his dismissal by Russell did not cost him his leadership of the Republican Party in Craven County or his ability to control Federal offices in his part of the State. Of course, the Republicans could not give him an office because the charges might have prevented his confirmation, but they did the same thing, indirectly, when his son was appointed post master. *The News and Observer* said that, instead of being punished for his conduct, Hancock had been rewarded.

I had known Hancock a long time and some of his kinsmen were very popular and were fine men. They felt that Hancock had become a Republican because Craven County had a Negro majority and it would give him prominence. He was a political boss for many years in that county and in the district, and was a regular attendant at the Republican conventions, where he was given credit for being one of the best gum-shoe politicians in the Second District. He was thin and wiry, and the contrast in appearance between Hancock and Russell was about as great as could be between two physical bodies. He had been very helpful to Russell in securing the nomination.

Then came scandal number seven. Rev. Dr. T. W. Babb, who had been chaplain of the State Prison, concluded that, since he had been discharged he would turn State's evidence against his fellow officials in the State Prison. He unbosomed himself to a *News and Observer* reporter with a tale involving most of his political associates. He charged that a number of those holding high positions were guilty of immoral conduct with female convicts, and there was so much truth in it that several of the prison officials had their heads taken off. Babb attributed his dismissal not to his own lapse, drinking and immorality, but to the fact that he did not stand by the Governor in his attack on the lease of the North Carolina Railroad. He charged that the warden of the prison had taken his favorite woman out of the stockade and had a room fitted up in his house for her, and that she was the same woman with whom Dr. Babb himself had gotten into trouble. His story was illuminating and gave names, places, and times; and it was so revolting that *The News and Observer,* in printing it, could not claim that it was not in the *Police Gazette* class. Not long after Babb's interview with *The News and Observer* he disappeared. News came from Washington that he had received a nine-hundred-dollar job in one of the departments at Washington. He passed out of sight but, before passing, his testimony had been a sinker to the party which he had supported.

The Republicans, having no newspaper organ in Raleigh, in the early part of 1898, created two organizations to print a paper, one a Republican and the other a Populist, but the real organ of the Fusion administration then was the *Progressive Farmer,* edited by J. L. Ramsey. For a time he was one of the most influential writers of the Fusion administration. He had something of the viciousness and vigor of S. Otho Wilson, wielded a wicked pen, and wrote about the Democrats as vigorously as *The News and Observer* did about the Fusionists. He invented the term that was applied to me during all the days of 1895 to 1898 by the Fusionists, "the State Saviour." Ramsey was a queer product. He was a genuine Populist and came into the editorship of the *Progressive Farmer* upon the death of Colonel Polk. He managed to have several suits brought against the paper by Democrats whom he had denounced, and otherwise obtained prominence in the party. He became secretary of the Board of Agriculture and held that office along with his writing for the *Progressive Farmer*. *The News and Observer* always called him "Secretary of the State's Manure Pile," and said that the color of his dude shoes, very yellow, was a reflection of the barnyard where he lived. He blew into politics off a farm and added to the gaiety of the situation by vehemence and vigor and not a little ability.

Concurrently with the exposure of the numerous scandals of the Russell administration, there came from many quarters demands for the impeachment of Governor Russell. This demand grew with each exposure and was urged from two points of view, each powerful. The first was from the standpoint of the Democrats, who were chiefly moved thereto by the bad government in Eastern North Carolina towns, in the State Prison, in the Agricultural Department, and elsewhere, coupled with the fear that had come to women living in the country—a fear caused by increased lawlessness, the marked increase of crime being shown in the report of the Attorney General, a Republican official. The second element demanding the impeachment of the Governor was made by those who resented Russell's vigorous fight to undo the lease of the North Carolina Railroad. Under the leadership of Colonel Andrews, their demand became strong.

On February 20 there was a paragraph in the personal column of *The News and Observer,* the significance of which was not seen by many people. The headlines read that an old college friend of mine, "Sol C. Weill, is visiting the Governor." This able young lawyer had been a partner of Russell when he began to practice law in Wilmington. Although Weill was a staunch Democrat, they were good friends. Weill soon went to New York and succeeded in the practice of law. I sensed that something was up because Weill had never been to Raleigh before that he didn't come to see me first thing. The fact that he was staying with Russell at the mansion made me wonder at the cause of his visit. When *The News and Observer* said again on March 12, "Sol Weill is visiting in the Governor's mansion," I began to make inquiry. I learned that he not only was a guest at the Governor's mansion but had visited the office of Colonel Andrews at the Capital Club. What they talked about, I did not know. Weill did not come to see me until just before he was leaving town. I asked him what he was doing in Raleigh. He smiled broadly and said he was "here on legal business." I sensed by his manner it wasn't "legal business." Events moved rapidly in March and April. There is no doubt that the fear of impeachment haunted Russell. He believed *The News and Observer* would be very glad to see him impeached and would throw all its weight toward that end. He knew that the Southern Railway influences, added to *The News and Observer's* and the charges that might be sustained, would make it difficult for him to escape conviction.

Russell thus lived in the shadow of the fear of impeachment, first suggested by Southern Railway attorneys. He was a blustering but not a courageous man. The possibility of disgrace unnerved him. It was generally believed, and no doubt was true, that Ricaud and Weill used that as one of the big arguments to induce him to withdraw his suit to annul the lease. More than that; it was generally talked that the Southern Railway had something on Russell, something that would ruin him. Their lobbyists confided to politicians and newspaper men that if they should choose to show their hand they could damn Russell any minute.

The inside story of how Andrews and the Southern Railway captured Russell, secured his capitulation, and made him a creature of contempt with most people and of pity with some, will never, of course, be told. He had two intimate friends, Democrats, who had moved to New York to practice law. Assuming that he was in financial difficulty and that he was in mortal fear of being impeached, the natural thing for a man of his temperament would have been to appeal for advice to these former partners. Undoubtedly, that is what brought Sol Weill to Raleigh. It was currently reported and believed, a little later, that Mr. Weill had been retained by the president of the Southern Railway. The owners of the road were tired of the litigation and controversy and desired to bring about an end of the fight to annul the lease. If so, Weill would have had two motives for making peace: first, the desire to relieve Russell's financial and other embarrassment; and, second, his desire to serve his clients. At any rate, the truth undoubtedly is that, through the New York end and by Weill's acting as attorney and friend as well as liaison officer, an arrangement was effected which caused Russell to quit fighting the Southern Railway lease.

Russell had dismissed the Wilsons from the Railroad Commission because they did not reduce the passenger rates. He favored Caldwell and Pearson because they not only reduced rates but had also reduced the telephone and telegraph rates and increased the assessment of the railroads for taxation. These things troubled the Southern Railway officials because it had the most mileage in North Carolina and they feared that the decrease of rates and increase of tax assessment might stand in the courts. In fact, they knew these measures would stand if they were settled upon their merits. Therefore, in trying to adjust things with Russell, they were ready to trade with Russell if he would agree to tell his railroad commissioners to take the back track and restore the high railroad rates. In return, they would allow him to save his face by not withdrawing the suit to annul the lease but to secure his agreement that if Judge Simonton held the lease valid, he would make no further fight. They knew what Simonton would do, or thought they did. Referring to one of Judge Simonton's injunctions, *The News and Observer,* in March, said, "If we continue tamely to yield to every usurpation which Simonton makes, he will go further and further and this judge who rides to his court in Vice-President Andrews' private car will be more completely master of the State than this sovereign State is disposed to be his servant."

On that very same day, the commissioners met and decided to stand by the reduced passenger rates in spite of Russell, and I, personally and in the paper, strongly commended Pearson and Caldwell for their firm stand and defiance of Russell's flop. In the deal which Weill had arranged, the annulment of the decrease of rates was a part of the consideration. *The News and Observer,* next day, printed that the Andrews-Russell deal had fallen through because Russell could not control his commissioners. Later Pearson stood firm. Long before he had been appointed, he had been a leader in his section and had written articles and made speeches in and out of the Legislature in favor of railroad reductions. He was a pioneer in the advocacy of that and other reforms. But Caldwell wobbled. He would—and he wouldn't. One day it would be reported that he was going to stand firm and the next that he was going to break down. Finally, he tendered his resignation and then tried to recall it. However, Russell accepted it, even though he had a string tied to it. But, before he resigned, on the last day of March, Caldwell voted to restore the high rates and, as Abbott was always with the railroads, Russell had been able to assure the Southern Railway people that the deal would go through.

On March 24, it was reported that the North Carolina Railroad lease case had been stricken from the Circuit Court calendar and *The News and Observer* said of Russell, "Another Esau parts with his political birthright for a mess of pottage," and, "It looks like Caldwell is going to go over to the railroads too." At that stage of the affair, Butler came into the picture and gave out a public statement that he favored the reduction of rates. The end of March saw the end of the lease fight and the consummation of the Andrews-Russell deal. Russell and the directors of the Railroad met in secret and agreed to stop the fight against the lease. There was tense interest in Raleigh, and elsewhere, as to what they would do but *The News and Observer* publication had prepared the people to expect what really happened. Russell went over to the railroad, as the paper said, "bag and baggage." The contempt cases were abandoned, the free pass cases and other suits against Andrews, and all the various sidelights of litigation and threats, were abandoned. When the contempt cases came up, Solicitor —— Pou exposed Russell and denounced him for desertion. The whole State, except those who were in the deal, or who approved it or acquiesced in it, was up in arms. *The News and Observer* thundered and exposed it in every detail. Nobody actually knew whether Russell got money or not, but it was believed that he had his debts paid by the Southern Railway. If so, it was all done in New York. The opinion of unbiased people in Raleigh was, on the one part, that Russell had been frightened by the impeachment demand into surrender, and that *The News and Observer* was as much responsible for this as the railroad; and, on the other, that his financial condition had been such that he was willing to sell out. My own opinion, and that of many unbiased people, was that both happened. Russell stood baffled, defeated, and lonely, with hardly an influential friend in the State.

Fortunately for Russell, at that time the *Maine* was blown up in Havana and the attention of the people was so engrossed with the coming Spanish-American War that political questions, for the moment, were forgotten. Most of Russell's appointments to military positions were non-political. In a sense, he reinstated himself with many people by his organization of the North Carolina regiments to take part in the war. For example, he appointed to high military positions Colonel W. H. S. Burgwyn, member of the distinguished family and prominent Democrat, brother of a noble Confederate General, and Colonel J. F. Armfield of Statesville, son of Judge Armfield, one of the leading Democrats in the West, and other capable men, regardless of politics. He coöperated in every way with the Federal government and with the National Guard toward making North Carolina's part in the Spanish-American War effective.

In the hot campaign of 1898, when the Red Shirts rode the highways and when passion was at its height and "Down with Russellism" was a word to conjure with, he was isolated. The denunciation was more of Russellism than of Russell. He had almost faded out of the picture. He made no speeches in the campaign. When he was denounced, as he was on every stump, and his administration was held up as disgraceful and rotten and every vile epithet that could be devised was applied to him, he never took the stump in defense of what he had or had not done. Of course, in his whimsical and vicious way, he would now and then denounce his critics, but he had neither the nerve nor the backing to throw himself into the campaign.

Governor Russell was a rare character. He came of a large slave-holding family in Brunswick County and stood high in his class at the University. Even there, however, he showed the hot temper and bitter invective which increased in later life. He was among the most ardent Confederates and early entered the Army, where he was promoted to be Captain and assigned to duty at Fort Caswell. It was not long, according to D. McCallum—he said Russell was "vicious, violent and vindictive"—before Russell's temper got him into trouble with his Colonel for disobedience of orders. Approaching the Colonel from the rear Russell struck him a severe blow. Only the intercession of George Davis, later Attorney General in the Confederate cabinet, saved him from a court-martial and expulsion from the Army.

After the war, he was elected to the State Senate, where he was popular with his associates and showed ability. As a lawyer he commanded a good practice. Later he became a Republican in Reconstruction days and defeated the eloquent Alfred Moore Waddell for Congress. He was consistently inconsistent, growing more bitter as he felt the semi-ostracism that was the portion of white men who belonged to the Republican party in eastern North Carolina.

XXV

THE SPANISH-AMERICAN WAR

T HE BLOWING up of the *Maine* stirred the country as nothing else had done in many years. The people in North Carolina and elsewhere had followed the civil war in Cuba with much interest and had been shocked by the cruel and inhuman conduct of the Spaniards in herding the Cuban insurgents into camps.

North Carolinians' first personal interest was aroused when the report came that the *U. S. S. Winslow,* on its way to Key West, had experienced a tough time on heavy seas but had proven seaworthy. When, on February 1st, Ensign Worth Bagley, of the *Winslow,* came to Raleigh on a visit to his mother and told of the terrible trip and the courage of Commanding Officer Bernadou. With the blowing up of the *Maine* on February 15, and the drowning of two hundred and fifty-three men and officers, the feeling in Raleigh and all over the country ran high. McKinley's serious attempts to secure adjustment of the difference between this country and Spain were both denounced and approved. In North Carolina the sentiment was much divided, but as the conviction grew that the blowing up of the *Maine* was due to Spanish treachery, and with the reports of increasing cruelty to the Cubans, the sentiment for intervention grew in North Carolina, as elsewhere. When war was declared, North Carolina was among the first of the States to furnish its quota. Two of the most earnest advocates of war, in Raleigh, were Justice Walter Clark, who had been the youngest brigadier general in the Confederate Army, and who said, in an interview, "There will be no war if millionaires can prevent it," and Colonel John W. Hinsdale, another Confederate, who declared that "the money-bag crowd controls the press." *The News and Observer* said there were plenty of jingoes in Raleigh, but when Spain's answer was unsatisfactory, the war feeling in Raleigh, as in Washington, swept all before it.

The first Monday morning issue of *The News and Observer* was on April 4. It apologized for breaking the Sabbath and excused itself for this Monday publication, and justified it, by referring to the critical situation facing the country. On April 7, *The News and Observer* came out strongly for intervention, saying:

"It is now fifty-one days since two hundred and sixty-six American sailors were murdered in Havana Harbor by Spanish treachery. The people have been told for fifty days 'to wait.' For what? So that Spanish diplomacy may gain advantages and Wall Street speculators get rich on tips furnished by those close to the administration?"

On the next day it headed its editorial "Get Your Knapsacks, Boys."

ENSIGN WORTH BAGLEY

I suppose the attitude of the paper was more influenced than I knew by the letters which my wife's brother, Worth Bagley, wrote to his mother and which I read. When the *Maine* was sunk, his indignation, like that of most naval men, blazed, and he thought the only thing to do was to fight the Spaniards who had been responsible for the murder of his fellow shipmates. When Worth was in Raleigh en route to the Caribbean waters, from which he was never to return, I talked to him about the outlook for war. I did not then share his feelings that war with Spain was the only answer, but with the youthful naval spirit that resented the sinking of the *Maine,* he had not the shadow of doubt that it was done by the Spaniards. He was eager for war. That spirit animated the Navy from top to bottom and the younger men felt it more deeply than the older ones. In fact, Worth said in one of his letters to his mother what was in the heart of other young men who were trained for efficiency in war, that the chance for glory lay along the war with Spain. The following extracts from letters to his mother illustrate the spirit of the young naval officer in the spring of 1898:

"[Extract from letter April 3, 1898 (written from torpedo boat Winslow)] It looks as though we were to have war.... The Spaniards will be easy prey for our Navy, which is in the most efficient condition. ... If the Spaniards back down now, it would be the source of the very bitterest disappointment. They will have to kneel and crawl in a manner that history has never before seen. Why did they blow up our Maine? No matter what pretext any or all of the members of Congress can give for war, *we must have it*. The cause of war lies in a set of American colors blown up in an explosion, and with the colors the men who served to protect them; blown up at night while asleep—evidence in itself sufficient to show that a contemptible Spaniard did it. The blood almost fills my head when I think of this; it makes me almost wild with anger....I shall write you another letter soon, certainly before any fighting takes place....

"[Extract from letter April 14, 1898 (from torpedo boat Winslow)] You must not fret about me. In the first place, there may be no war; this is very probable I am afraid. In the second place a Spaniard couldn't hit an honest American at pistol range; the Dago is too much a coward for that. The war, if it comes, will be very easy. The adversary is too poor an adversary for much glory to be gained for our flag. But it is to be hoped that we may sink some of their ships in return for the poor Maine.

"[April 21, 1898 (written from Key West, Fla.)]...For your sake I might almost wish there would be no war; on my own account, I am very happy that chance is offered me for distinction....Our boat is in splendid condition, and officers and men are well and anxious for a fight. We have good men and faithful ones and our chances for success are the very best....

"[May 4, 1898 (from Key West)]...You need have no fears about me for there is no danger for us now. There may be when the Spanish fleet comes, but I am sorry to say that I fear that will never be. A war comes only once in a generation, and it will be very hard if I can get no chance to do some unusual service, so it is very disappointing to have no tangible enemy to meet....

"[Off Matanzas, Cuba, May 7, 1898]...The nation as a whole, from the tenor of the papers, has realized that the Navy is our defense, our real fighting body....The navy has shown its worth; we may trust hereafter that politicians will cease to prate as they did six months ago, about our 'expensive gold-laced luxury.' Our nation, a first-class power supposedly, should at the present moment feel shame that our navy is not such a one that the war should even now be over. To me it seems a disgrace that the United States should be fighting an apparently lengthy war with a nation poor in defense as well as finances. How can the ordinarily well-informed man, although he may have some pride of country, tingle with it as he should, if such conditions last? It is the 'rope-rein' politics advanced by dishonest 'leg-pulling' demagogues, that keeps us as a nation from gaining and gaining glory 'till we forget.' I have almost spoken my thoughts on paper, and have forgotten that I am writing a letter...."

The height of enthusiasm, which is indescribable, stirred the country when the news was published on the morning of May 2, that on the previous day Admiral Dewey had crushed the Spanish fleet off Manila and, on the next day, that he had made another attack and had taken Manila and that the Spanish rule in the Philippines was at an end.

The first permissive naval order on record was given in person by Commodore Dewey (promoted to The Admiral of the Navy after the victory at Manila Bay) to Captain Charles V. Gridley, commanding the flagship *Olympia*. As the ships approached the Spanish vessel (2½ miles distant) Dewey turned to Gridley and said: "You may fire when you are ready, Gridley."

I used these words of Dewey as the text of my address, years afterwards, when the monument to Gridley was unveiled at Erie, Pennsylvania, and stressed that it showed Dewey's greatness in placing confidence in Captain Gridley. Military officers give direct commands. Dewey had statesmanship as well as naval leadership.

On May 9, a "vest pocket" battle occurred off Cárdenas in Cuba. The papers told how the little torpedo boat, *Winslow,* and three tiny Spanish gunboats engaged in the first fight in Cuban waters and that the *Winslow* had gained valuable information for the naval forces.

A little later came news of the death of Worth Bagley and of how the *Winslow,* sent (May 11) into Cárdenas Bay to reconnoitre, had been fired on by the Spanish guns behind masked batteries and the first blood in the Spanish-American war was shed.

In his *History of the Spanish-American War* Henry Watterson gives this graphic account of the fighting at Cárdenas, in which Ensign Worth Bagley and four sailors were the first Americans to seal their courage with their lives:

"The first American sailors to find in death the baptism of heroism were killed in a battle between small ships in Cárdenas harbor, on the north coast, the 11th of May. The gunboat *Machias,* the torpedo boats *Winslow* and *Foote,* and the revenue tug *Hudson* were blockading Cárdenas in the harbor of which were three Spanish gunboats. On the 11th the cruiser *Wilmington* arrived off the harbor and Commander Merry of the *Machias* and Captain Todd of the *Wilmington* decided to send the torpedo boats into the harbor and cut out or destroy the Spanish craft which were coming out and menacing our boats. The *Wilming-*

ton could not enter on account of her draught and the presence of mines in the main channel. The *Winslow* entered the harbor at full speed after a Spanish gunboat, and immediately the vessels of the enemy and a shore battery opened a raking fire upon her, to which the *Winslow* and the *Wilmington* both replied. The Spaniards concentrated their whole attention upon the *Winslow*.

"There followed forty minutes in which American heroism and courage rose to splendid heights as described by the reports of the fight. The first shot from the enemy fell among the buoys in the harbor. The next tore through the flimsy hull of the torpedo boat, wrecking the steam steering gear forward and rendering the boat unmanageable. The Spanish trap had caught its victim. The decoy gunboat had lured the fierce little fighter to within range of the shore guns. The red buoys marked the range. The *Winslow* could not escape, and it was a fight then to the death. Her three little 1-pound guns began to hurl back missiles at the gunboat, which was now adding its share to the firing.

"Again and again shells crashed into the *Winslow*. A splinter flying from the deck struck Lieutenant John J. Bernadou, the brave commander of the little craft, just below the groin in the right leg. He wrapped a towel about it, using an empty 1-pound shell for a tourniquet, and went on with his duty as commander. When he found that his steam steering gear was gone he rushed aft to arrange the hand gear. A shot wrecked that, too. Steam was already pouring out of a perforated boiler below and the men were coming up. Another shot and the port engine was wrecked. Then went the forecastle gun. But still the brave men kept firing with their two remaining 1-pounders.

"Help was coming, for the little *Hudson* was steaming in at full speed, and the *Wilmington's* 4-inch guns were dropping shells all about the murderous battery ashore.

"Amidships, near the ammunition stand, was Ensign Worth Bagley calling down to the engineer to back and go ahead with his one remaining engine in an effort to spoil the Spaniards' aim. All the electrical contrivances were wrecked, so the others went by word of mouth. By the Ensign were working a half dozen of his men. No one had yet been killed, although the craft had been riddled through and through. Then came a shell that struck squarely on the deck and exploded as it fell. The *Hudson* was by this time so close that her crew could hear the words of the men as they went to their death.

" 'Save me! Save me!' shouted one poor fellow, with his face all torn, as he staggered back and all but fell into the sea. Some one reached an arm to him, caught him by a leg, pulled him back, and laid him on the deck, dead. Ensign Bagley had thrown his hands into the air, tottered forward, and fell against the signal mast, around which he clasped his arms and sank slowly down in a heap. They did not know he was dead until they went to carry him below.

"Besides Bagley those killed outright by the shell were two service sailors, and two others, who, mortally wounded, died within an hour....

"The death of Ensign Bagley and the four sailors brought to the United States the first realization of war. Not a man had been killed at Manila. Bagley was the first to give his life to the cause. He was appointed to the Naval Academy from Raleigh, North Carolina, in 1891, and had been in the service but three years. The five men who were first to lose their lives in the war, fighting against the Spaniards, were buried with martial honors. At the funeral of Ensign Bagley at Raleigh, a great concourse assembled to do honor to his memory. The city was draped in mourning and the first display of patriotic sorrow and homage was equally complete and significant."

I first heard the news of the death of Ensign Worth Bagley on the morning after he was killed. I was eating breakfast when the telephone rang. Mayor Russ was at the 'phone. He said he wanted to see me on an important matter and did not wish to come to the house, but requested me to come to a little grocery store about a square from our home. I went over and he handed me a telegram which had been sent to him from Key West, which said that, in the fight at Cardenas, Worth Bagley had been killed. Somehow, I had never associated him with death. He had talked so enthusiastically about the necessity of going to war and had written his mother letters to cheer her up and to relieve her of any possible uneasiness, that it had not occurred to me that this shadow could fall upon his home. I loved him as well as if he had been of my own blood, for I had married his sister when he was twelve years old, had gone with him to Annapolis when he entered, and had dropped in to see him often during the years when he was a cadet there. After the first shock, my only thought was how the news could be broken to his mother and sisters. I do not think they had suspected anything when I was called out on business and I had not sensed the import of the message. I feared the shock would kill his mother. As soon as I could gather myself together, I went back home and told my wife. In addition to her deep love, she had great pride in him, and the news of his death shook her to the foundations; but, as is always the case with noble natures, the desire to help soften the blow to others sustained her. We did not dare to tell her mother until we could summon the family physician, and so, when Dr. Hubert Haywood arrived and had been told of the tragedy, it was communicated to her. We had underestimated the anxiety under which she had lived, for she had feared it from the first and had, in her dreams, felt that he would not come back. Therefore, while the news prostrated her she had, in a sense, been more prepared for it than the rest of us. Mother love runs ahead and shares with those it loves any tragedy that may come.

If universal sympathy has any solvent or any healing, it came to the family then, for hardly had the shock come, when messages poured in from all over the country and the people in Raleigh, always tender in trouble and thoughtful and sympathetic, seemed almost as much touched as Worth Bagley's immediate family. The State was, "like Niobe, all tears." There were thousands of young men in the camp at Raleigh training for the war. He was the first young man to be killed, he of our very own, and it fell like a pall over the camp. The story of the brief engagement, Lieutenant Bernadou's account of the short and quick battle, of young Bagley's courage in dying at the post of duty, all combined to give a glory to the tragedy, and the Ensign's mother had the consolation of sympathy that served to nerve her to endure the shock. Moreover, she took out his letters, in which he had told her of his earnest desire for war and of his confidence in its holy purpose, and had entreated her, if he should fall, not to sorrow for him, and her telegram from "Fighting Bob Evans," who had known Worth well, saying that he "envied the lad his death"—these were some of the things that softened the blow. In the camps where the young men were training, the death of Ensign Bagley strengthened their courage and increased their determination that North Carolina give its united support of the war. All felt that his death was a consecration.

At first, we did not know how death came or whether his body had been rescued. It was some alleviation to learn that the body had been taken to Key West and embalmed, and to receive telegrams and letters from friends there who had attended the religious service, con-

Ensign Worth Bagley, of Raleigh. The first (and only) American Naval Officer killed in the Spanish-American War. He was killed in action at Cárdenas Bay, Cuba, May 11, 1898.

In foreground, Theodore Roosevelt, Colonel Leonard Wood, and General Joseph Wheeler (distinguished Confederate Veteran), in the Spanish-American War (Underwood and Underwood).

ducted by a preacher who had known and loved him, and the long letter from Lieutenant Bernadou telling of the fight, with tributes to Worth's valor when he looked death in the face, unafraid. I shall never forget the night his body arrived. No such storm had come to Raleigh in the history of those living. Bridges were washed away and the lightning flashed as his body was borne by soldiers who had his own zeal to hurry to the front, the zeal that had possessed him in the early days of the war. The flashes of lightning were such that it was light as day as, after midnight, his body was borne up the steps into the home where he was born.

The funeral was held in the open, in the south end of the Capitol Square, attended by the two thousand soldiers in training and by the whole community and hundreds from all over the State, with tributes and flowers from Washington and Annapolis. He was buried with the honors of a brigadier general. The body was interred at Oakwood Cemetery. Four men had been killed in addition to Bagley, who was the first officer to fall, and his mother's first thought was of the mothers of these lads, and messages of condolence were sent to them by her. Immediately a spontaneous movement was begun for funds to erect a monument, suggested in a letter in the Morning *Post* by Captain N. W. West, calling on everybody to send one dollar for the monument fund. This fund was swelled by gifts from outside the State and a sufficient sum was secured to erect the statue which stands in the Capitol Square in Raleigh. When it was unveiled tributes were made by two other heroes of the Spanish-American War, Richmond Pearson Hobson and Victor Blue.

The sculptor of the statue, F. H. Packer, poured all his enthusiasm into his task. It was his first statue. He had only photographs and the recollections of the Ensign's family to aid him in fashioning an excellent piece of work. My wife had several photographs taken in his naval uniform, of our seven-year-old son, Worth Bagley, who unveiled the statue of the uncle for whom he was named. His grandmother, observing how long the boy looked at his pictures said, "Worth, if you keep looking so much at your picture people will believe you think you are good-looking." Nothing abashed, the lad replied, "I am, Granny."

Bagley, from an early age, had his heart set on a naval career. He greatly admired a relative, Captain Peter Humstead Murphey, commanding a Confederate naval force at Mobile Bay. Learning that

Murphey, an old classmate at Annapolis, was in command of a Confederate ship which had been captured, Captain James Edward Jouett, U.S.N., sent his launch to bring him over. When Murphey came aboard, the old classmate slapped him on the shoulder, saying, "You old rebel, I'll bet you haven't had a square meal for a long time. Wash up and let's go to breakfast. I told the cook that I'd bet you were hungry and ordered him to have the best breakfast ever served on this ship."

In 1889, Congressman B. H. Bunn, from the Fourth District, had an appointment to make to the Naval Academy. Among the applicants was young Worth Bagley and a dozen more of the brightest youths in the district. Not wishing to select from so many worthy applicants, Captain Bunn decided to give the appointment to the applicant who made the highest marks in a competitive examination. A committee of three well-known educators, Professor A. G. Wilcox, of Nash, chairman, Professor E. W. Kennedy, of the Durham public schools, and Professor Purrington, of Wake Forest College, were appointed to conduct the examination. After taking the examination, but before knowing the results, Worth went to Chapel Hill, where he passed the entrance examination so that if he failed to get to Annapolis he would enter at the fall term of the University. He won in the competition, was appointed June 30, 1889, and, writing to his younger sister, Ethel, signed himself, "Worth Bagley, U. S. N., Lord High Admiral to His Majesty Ben Harrison's Fleet." His joy knew no bounds. On September 7 he telegraphed his mother, "Passed mentally and physically." His letters to her cheered the whole family and kept them in touch with what he was doing and thinking. In one letter he told how a visiting admiral, speaking to the cadets, told them that "in any strait you should grasp with one hand high up on the nearest rope and with the other still higher up for the Government." Worth added, "I heard a pretty wild fellow say, 'Government be damned if I ever fall overboard!'"

Hazing was in vogue at the Naval Academy. Worth was summoned by the officers after he had been severely hazed and ordered to give the names of the hazers. He replied, "I have been taught that it is dishonorable to tell on a schoolmate. I mean no disrespect or disobedience to authority but I would regard myself as doing a dishonorable act if I were to tell. That I cannot do." The answer was "Unless you obey orders and give their names you will have to go on the Santee" (the ship where the cadets were sent for punishment). For eighteen days he suffered the punishment and he was released only when the cadets, who did the hazing, confessed and asked for his release. In the 1891 spring examinations he was deficient in one study, receiving a mark of 2.42 when 2.50 was required and he was dropped. When his mother appealed to the Congressman who had appointed him, Captain Bunn gave him another appointment. Grateful, he wrote expressing his appreciation, and added, "I hope you shall never have cause to regret the appointment."

When our first baby, Adelaide, was born, Worth wrote his mother, "Kiss Addie a thousand times for me and tell her I have a great notion to try to get sick leave just to go home to see the baby. I bet $50 she is not any more proud of it than I am." When his first nephew was born, Josephus Daniels, Jr., he wrote the following letter, which his family prized as a model of loving advice from an uncle to a new born nephew:

> "Annapolis, Md.,
> "Sunday, Aug. 2nd, 1894
>
> "Commodore Josephus Daniels, Jr.,:
> "My dear young (?) Nephew:
>
> "I am making an early reply to your letter announcing your most welcome arrival, in order to show my appreciation of the honor you have conferred in allowing me to be the first to receive a letter from your hand.
>
> "Your handwriting is strangely like your father's; you will be lucky, sir, if you resemble him in other traits and qualities of heart or mind—I came within an ace of adding 'looks,' but I love you little one already, and shall wish you no such hard luck.
>
> "I shall help to bring you up in the right way when I am at home. Do not cry when I inform you that you must eat hardtack and salt horse from now on so that you may get used to the diet. Worse yet you must have a copy of Luce's Seamanship right at hand even while sleeping and eating. Then on your first-class cruise you won't have the trials to undergo that your uncle is now passing through.
>
> "Above all, you must learn to be self-reliant. You must be a man at fifteen: it won't be hard for you to accomplish it. Never ask any favors if you can help it. Be a lady's man but don't tell each and all of them that you love them; at first some of them will believe you which will be sad for them, afterward none of them will believe you which will be sad for you.

"Study hard and, until you enter the Naval Academy, don't pretend to know a thing until you do know it. Don't be a bookworm or a hot house plant but take the proper exercise and make yourself a strong man. Don't tell a lie, even at the Naval Academy. Love your father and mother and obey orders. It is as bad to disobey orders from the proper source as it is to tell a lie.

"Keep this letter and I will keep yours, then some day we will compare. You will laugh then and wonder if your uncle kept all these things.

"He didn't, that is the reason he wants to warn you beforehand and make an officer of you; you won't have the faults he had.

"But he will repeat to you what was said to him and the rest of the Navy team last year before the game with West Point which we won 6 to 4. Mind it wherever you may be. It is: 'For God's sake keep your nerve, and show the stuff you're made of!'

"With every good wish, and the hope that your life begun in a bed of roses will suffer only enough thorns to make a man of you in the time of danger and necessity, I am

"Your loving uncle,
"Worth Bagley"

All went well with the cadet until May, 1895, when he wrote home, "have been recommended to be dropped physically on account of my heart. Last year the doctors found that the apex of my heart had shifted to the left about two inches due to violent exercise." One doctor advised him not to play football but another doctor said playing would not hurt him. The Secretary of the Navy (Mr. Herbert) granted a re-examination after I had presented the matter to him and he was held over for final examination at the end of the two year cruise.

It was as fullback of the Navy football team that he became famous in Navy and football circles. In December, 1890, he wrote, "We have the satisfaction of knowing that we walloped West Point in the dust, 24 to 0—I made the winning touchdown and goal for the class of '93, though I suffer from a pain in my leg." Of the game at West Point (1891) when the Navy lost, he wrote that the Army players "averaged nine pounds more than ours," and added, "I felt exactly as I imagine I would feel in battle, threatened with defeat and carried away with excitement. Not a thought of danger entered my head." In the Thanksgiving game of 1892 Bagley won honor, as his prowess enabled the Navy to win, but it was the 1893 victory he won for Annapolis that put his name at the head of the football heroes. Casper Whitney, of *Harper's Weekly,* placed Bagley as the fullback on the "All Star America" team. During the game his mother, arriving late with a friend, was looking for her seat when an admiral, learning who she was, said, "Take my seat, Madam, for I've won $100 by your son's brilliant playing." She was never quite so happy as when she saw him carried, at the end of the game, off the field on the shoulders of his mates amid resounding cheers, the hero of the hour. "His punt broke the record," said experts. He received a trophy, a gold football made by Tiffany, to be used as a watch charm, on which was engraved, "Worth Bagley, Fullback, 1893."

THE POSITION OF THE STATE IN THE SPANISH-AMERICAN WAR

The Spanish-American War was declared. Wars were declared then. It was only in later years that undeclared wars were fought. *The News and Observer* said that North Carolina could furnish 248,-000 volunteers if needed. When the call came, and only volunteers served, there were more people in North Carolina who wanted to enter the war than could be enrolled and equipped.

For the first time Negroes were formally inducted into military service, and James H. Young, chief Negro politician of the State, was authorized by Governor Russell to raise a Negro regiment, of which he was made Colonel. These Negro troops were mobilized at Fort Macon, which was called Camp Dan Russell, and there they were trained before they were sent to Florida. There was a feeling on the part of many that Russell had made a mistake. It was pointed out that the Federal government always put white officers over Negro troops and that Governor Russell ought to follow that precedent—that he was playing politics in doing otherwise. Certainly Russell had done little enough for the decent Negroes, of which there were many in North Carolina, and they demanded this recognition. The result showed that they largely measured up to it. James H. Young, as Colonel, and Jim Hamlin, as Lieutenant-Colonel, both intelligent Raleigh mulattoes, made much better soldiers than anybody had expected, and they were seriously desirous of securing such morale in the Negro troops as to increase the standing of the Negroes in the State. General Cowles was quoted as saying that some of them were guilty of cowardice. This was undoubtedly true of some but not of the major portion. *The News and Observer* was pretty severe, however, in criticizing Colonel Young of the Negro regiment, when he left his regiment, while in training, to come to Raleigh, as the paper said, "to boss the Wake County Republican Convention." Some of the Negroes afterwards joined the regular Federal Army and served creditably in the Philippines.

The North Carolina people who, in the main, had been zealous for the war after the sinking of the *Maine,* followed its fortunes with the deepest interest. It seemed that, as in so many other wars, the important events occurred on Sunday and people could not wait for a Tuesday paper to get the news. The Dewey victory at Manila stirred the State as it did the world. I praised Admiral Dewey, not only for his brilliant feat but for his statesmanship in telling the German naval officers where they got off, and for his attitude toward Aguinaldo and the Filipinos, who had been fighting Spanish bad rule. I remember how thrilled we all were at the cruise of the *Oregon* and how, day by day, the people read eagerly every line the papers printed about its record-making speed from California around the Cape, hurrying to strengthen the American fleet in Cuba. The *Oregon* was then the brag ship of the Navy and Captain Clark became a national hero as he annihilated distance and made the trip from California to Cuba in 68 days, a distance of 16,000 miles, arriving in time to take part in the war. Among the young officers was Zeb Vance Johnson, of Lincoln County, who was worthy of his distinguished name. Later, when I became Secretary of the Navy, I recalled the thrill that Captain Clark's name gave us all in this historic voyage. I came to know him well and to find that he was in every way worthy of the honours which had been given him in the Spanish-American war days.

By the middle of May the North Carolina troops training at Camp Bryan Grimes in Raleigh were ready to go to the front. The chief thing that *The News and Observer* printed then was the doings of the soldiers. We kept in touch with them and almost every home in Raleigh was open to them. They were all "our boys." As the time approached for their leaving most of them had made so many friends in Raleigh that it was like breaking home ties. Moreover, Raleigh had become so much interested in them and the war that other things were forgotten. When they entrained Raleigh was a very lonesome place. I had visited Camp Grimes often, knew the officers well and many of the men. I often lunched with them and, half a dozen times lunched with Captain Beavers' company from Raleigh. It is singular what war does. Before the war Captain Beavers was a young man in Raleigh, little known, who had been a member of the Governor's Guard. He turned out to be a superior drill master and soldier. He had the stuff of making a big soldier in him. For his own career, it was a pity the war ever ended or that he did not go into the regular army. Some men are born to be soldiers and peace does not afford them the opportunity for the kind of service for which they seem to have been born.

When the boys were getting ready to go to Florida, preparatory, as they thought, to going on to Cuba, I decided that the biggest piece of news that the paper could print would be the daily doings of the North Carolina troops. It was a big event and a big adventure for *The News and Observer* to undertake to send a special correspondent with them. They left Raleigh about May 22, and the first of a series of daily stories about their doings appeared in a telegram from Fred L. Merritt, the city editor, who had been detailed to go with them, as the war correspondent. There fell a gloom over the city when his telegram told that the train bearing the North Carolina troops to the South had been in a wreck and two of the soldiers killed. The position of honor on the front page of the paper, printed in double column measure, was assigned to Merritt's correspondence. He did a fine piece of work, interlarding war news with stories, the news and activities of the members of the various companies, so that every day readers of the paper read about some officer or boy in the regiment. If one of them was sick, *The News and Observer* gave the news; if there had been any infraction of the rules, the news came. It was indeed an epitome of the daily doings of the North Carolina troops. For a paper of its income, *The News and Observer* had perhaps the best stories of the troops of its own State of all the other papers in the country.

Merritt lived in camp and won the regard of the Irish General who was in command. He wrote much about him and about all the visitors to the camp in Jacksonville, stories of Jacksonville, stories of escapades, of courage,—stories of all sorts. Great bundles of the paper were dispatched every day to the troops. One of the chief events of the day with the North Carolinians in Florida was to read *The News and Observer*. People always like to read about themselves, and seeing that whatever Merritt knew got into the paper, many of these officers and men became assistant correspondents and helped him out. Although the General was fond of Merritt and treated him well our correspondent kept his independence, and when days and weeks went by and the troops were not paid off and had no money, Merritt roasted the authorities for their lack of consideration and justice to the boys who had volunteered to serve, had left their homes, and could not get the paltry pay which the government promised them and which they needed. In fact there was almost an insurrection in that regiment and others because of the delay in paying the men. About that time General Julian S. Carr, of Durham, patriot and generous citizen, visited the camp. He was given a great ovation. He had furnished them tobacco as they left the State and had given a purse to the officers to add to the comforts of the troops. When he learned that they had not received a cent of money since they reached Jacksonville, he sent a red-hot telegram to Governor Russell and to the War Department denouncing in undiplomatic language the lack of appreciation of the brave heroes who had left their homes to serve their country and were being forgotten and outrageously treated. Getting no satisfaction from his telegrams, he offered to advance $25,000 so that the soldiers might be paid off, but there was so much red tape about it that the General's offer was turned down, much to his indignation and that of the soldiers. Merritt reported that if General Alger, Secretary of War, had been present, they would almost have mutinied.

Whether the indignant telegrams and General Carr's offer to advance money had anything to do with it or not, after the troops had been at Jacksonville some weeks the money was forthcoming. The best story Merritt wrote from the seat of war was the story of the celebration of the soldiers on pay-day. They felt that they had been waiting ages for it. They were hungry for some cash; and so, when it came, they did as soldiers so often do, spent much of it on larks. They bought alligators and made them mascots and pets. They rushed to Jacksonville and the money went fast and furiously. They hadn't had anything to drink, and what some of them imbibed was stronger than beer. The story evident between the lines indicated that many of them had a high old time and some of them got into trouble. Merritt stayed with them until the end but they never got to Cuba.

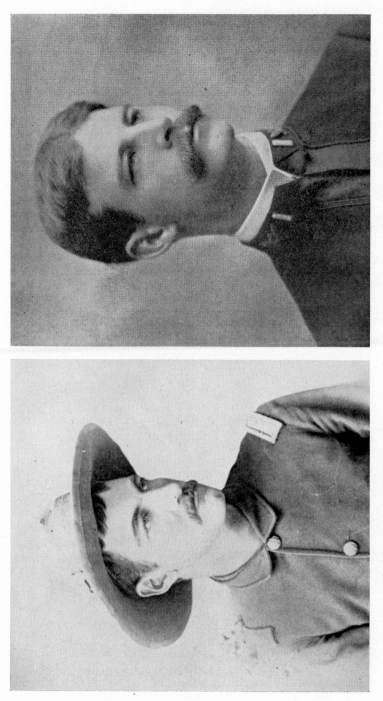

Left, Lieutenant William E. Shipp, North Carolina officer killed in Cuba, in whose honor a monument was erected in Charlotte. *Right*, Richmond Pearson Hobson, distinguished hero of the Spanish-American War, grandson of Chief Justice Pearson.

Left, Statue of Zebulon Baird Vance, erected in Capitol Square, Raleigh. *Right*, Statue of Ensign Worth Bagley erected in Capitol Square, Raleigh.

BRYAN AND THE WAR

They had all left home promising to "drive the dirty Spaniards out of Cuba," and for that to be done without their participation they regarded as a great injustice. Indeed, they had a feeling that they had been given the same sort of treatment that Bryan's friends thought had been administered to him. *The News and Observer* contrasted the opportunity the McKinley administration gave to Roosevelt with that given to Bryan and denounced the administration for favoritism, pointing out that Bryan had been marooned in Florida and his regiment, which was trained by experienced officers, had been denied any place where they might render real service, while the Roosevelt Rough Riders had been immediately taken to Cuba and given the opportunity, which Roosevelt embraced, to make war what General Grosvenor had said it was on the floor of the House, to wit: "a Republican war."

"The Republican administration," wrote Charles Willis Thompson, "was taking no chances on Bryan's getting away with any military glory, and it marooned him in Florida until after the war."

The War Department had given General Fitzhugh Lee and General Joseph Wheeler every opportunity, and for this the South was very appreciative and was enthusiastic about the things that Wheeler and Lee did. However, the Bryan men always felt that, deliberately and with forethought, the Nebraskans were shunted to one side because the administration was afraid that if Bryan won any glory it would put him in the White House. They were resolved that whatever glory came out of the war should inure to the benefit of the Republican Party. They never lost sight of that from the beginning to the end, although it was the Democrats in the House and the Democratic newspapers that forced McKinley's hand and compelled him to declare war when he really was trying to keep out of it.

Interest in the war was heightened in the South because Fitzhugh Lee and Fighting Joe Wheeler, of Confederate fame, added to their distinction under the Stars and Stripes. When General Wheeler signified his purpose to fight against Spain, his daughter trying to dissuade him said: "Father, you surely had enough fighting to do from 1861 to 1865." He answered: "Daughter, if a fish had been out of water thirty-three years and suddenly came in sight of a big pond, he'd wiggle a little at any rate." Going into action in an ambulance at the battle of Santiago, when things were not going well, he mounted his horse and led the charge, shouting: "The Yankees are running; they're leaving their guns," adding, "Oh, damn it, I didn't mean Yankees, I meant the Spaniards." Lee also won his spurs wearing the blue as he had done in the gray uniform.

WILLIAM E. SHIPP

In North Carolina people were stirred by the sinking of the *Maine,* by the death of Worth Bagley, and by Hobson's heroism. This feeling was heightened when the news came that another young North Carolina officer of bravery and fine spirit had been killed. On July 10 Lieutenant William E. Shipp, member of a distinguished Lincoln County family, had been killed in action leading a charge at San Juan. In Raleigh this tragedy came very close to the people because he had married one of the most brilliant and beautiful young women of Raleigh, Miss Margaret Busbee, who later won a reputation as a writer of short stories and was universally beloved. She served until her death as the North Carolina member of the Board of Regents of Mount Vernon. Immediately after the death of Lieutenant Shipp, a movement was begun to build a monument to him, as had been done for Bagley. The suggestion was made and widely approved in Raleigh that a statue of Bagley, representing North Carolina's supreme sacrifice in the Navy and of Shipp as its supreme sacrifice in the Army, should be erected on Capitol Square. A movement to that end was begun, but the relatives of Shipp preferred that he be buried in the soil where his ancestors had lived. A monument to his memory was erected. Two sons, Fabius Busbee and William Shipp, followed in the father's footsteps and became honorable Army officers.

AFTERMATH OF WAR

The news was hailed everywhere with gladness on July 27 when Spain sued for peace and the war was over. Yet it was a long time before the soldiers were all mustered out. The North Carolina troops were brought back to Camp Bryan Grimes to be mustered out and the slow process irked them. When war is on, soldiers are ready enough to stay away from their homes and to endure any hardships, but when the necessity of their mobilization is over they want to get out the next day and are rebellious if they cannot go home. The aftermath of the war among the North Carolina troops in Raleigh showed so much disorder as to bring criticism on that part of the regiment which was guilty of it. Some soldiers beat up Negroes; two soldiers beat a Negro woman, and there was laid the foundation for race trouble. On the night of September 20 a white man was shot on East Martin Street. Twenty shots were fired, and while the shooting was going on soldiers arrived and orders to shoot Negroes on sight were heard. *The News and Observer,* which had been practically the organ of the North Carolina troops, pointed out that there had been trouble and many fights ever since the return of the troops, and sought to give advice to the soldiers and Negroes to prevent clashes. When a drunken provost-guard on Wilmington Street held up Negroes and made them get off the street and threatened to run them through with a bayonet, he was arrested by several civil police but was turned over to Federal authorities. In October a lieutenant of the Second North Carolina Regiment had a fight with a bell-boy at the Yarborough Hotel. The officer was cut. It is interesting in this day, when no names are suppressed, to recall that *The News and Observer* did not give the name of the officer but condemned him and took the part of the bell-boy, who claimed he did not have a knife but that some of the officer's friends had it and, when they started to cut him, cut the officer instead. Drink was at the bottom of it. The trouble reached high-water mark on October 20, when the soldiers celebrated pay-day; some of them went up Hillsboro Street shooting out electric lights, and another Negro was cut. There was a sense of relief on the part of the officers and most of the soldiers, when the troops were finally demobilized.

BRYAN'S GREAT MISTAKE

Senator Hoar, Mr. Bryan and others, were greatly outraged at the war which followed in the Philippines. They believed that it could have been averted by giving to the Filipinos the same sort of government and the same sort of help and friendship that was given to the Cubans and they urged it, but without avail. However, later, when McKinley's "benevolent assimilation" program in the shape of a treaty with Spain came up in the Senate, to the surprise of the whole country Mr. Bryan, who said he had resigned his place in the Army in order to fight imperialism, suddenly appeared in Washington and, in a conference with Democratic senators, advised them to vote for the ratification of the treaty. He contended that this would end the war in the Philippines and after the war was ended the issue of imperialism would be clear-cut and the American people could be mobilized to compel the withdrawing of the troops and to give the Filipinos their independence. At that time Bryan had commanding influence and was able to convince enough senators that he was right to defeat the vigorous opposition to the ratification of the treaty which Senator Gorman, Democratic leader of the Senate, was waging. Senator Gorman told me that the Democrats and the anti-imperialists in the Republican Party had the treaty defeated and that, if Mr. Bryan had not personally urged Democratic senators to make the mistake of voting for ratification, the way would have been opened to prevent any imperialistic policy in the Philippines. "Once let the treaty be ratified," Gorman said "and it is an iridescent dream to suppose that Mr. Bryan can win his fight. The only way to win it is to hold up the treaty." Even with Bryan's urging it had a majority of only one vote.

XXVI

THE WHITE SUPREMACY CAMPAIGN

I n 1898 North Carolina people were engaged in two wars, each waged with such fury as to make it sometimes difficult for the readers of *The News and Observer* to tell which was the bloodier, the war against Spain or the war to drive the Fusionists from power. The latter war may be said to have been opened on May 10 at Laurinburg. In any other year since the Civil War, if a political meeting had been staged on Memorial Day it would have been regarded as profanation. However, because they believed they were engaged in a righteous struggle, something far above politics, a sort of protection of home, which was the principle that sent so many North Carolinians into the Confederate Army, the white supremacy people staged their first speaking at Laurinburg on that hallowed day. The most impressive voice raised early in the year for the character of the campaign to be waged was Henry Clay Wall, of Rockingham, a quiet and able business man who beneath his very mild exterior had the spirit of revolution against what he believed to be wrong. Hector McLean was the moving spirit of the Laurinburg meeting although he was only one of a number composed of practically every white man in Scotland County. The eloquent arraignment of Fusionism, with such lucidity and power as to attract the attention of the whole State, was made by Charles B. Aycock, afterwards Governor. Hardly second to his speech in impressiveness was that of Locke Craig, of Buncombe, afterward elected Governor. These two leaders of the movement, Aycock from the East and Craig from the West, had been schoolmates at the University of North Carolina and were devoted friends throughout their lives. Singularly high-minded, loving literature, profoundly versed in Emerson and Carlyle, whose style could be seen in their speaking and writings, they lifted the campaign above mere denunciation and abuse.

In the Democratic State Convention of 1898 the platform, the speeches, and the invitations were all along the line of trying to secure for the Democratic nominees the support of all men who believed in white men and white metal. The ability of Senator Simmons and his success as chairman in 1892, caused the party leaders to turn to him to lead the fight. Senator Simmons was a genius in putting everybody to work—men who could write, men who could speak, and men who could ride—the last by no means the least important.

Early in the campaign I was requested by Chairman Simmons to get up a carefully considered document about Fusion rule, which could be printed and sent over the State. He suggested it would be much better if it could be gotten out in the form of a speech; so I went down to Lemon Spring and made the speech which I put in type. When I arrived, the Populists were already there in great force, more Populists than Democrats, demanding a division of time, which was granted. We had quite a field-day of debate; and, of course, the prepared speech was never delivered as written but was printed as it had been written. I was compelled to meet the attacks of the Populist speaker. I was happy that Duncan McIver, who had been State Senator and my warm friend, went out with me. It was the first time I had made a speech in the campaign. I wasn't much on speaking. That speech was circulated all over the State and was about the first document sent out that gave the full story of the Fusion misgovernment. Later I spoke in other counties, but when Aycock saw that I was advertised to speak, he sent me a telegram virtually ordering me to quit making speeches. He said any man could make speeches if he would read *The News and Observer* but my job was to furnish the material. "You stay in Raleigh and let the rest of us do the travelling about," he said. It is strange how many people feel they would like to do something they cannot do as well as the thing they are doing. I had a desire to get out in the campaign, whereas there were scores of men who could make better speeches than I could, and my forte, if I had any, was to forge the weapons in *The News and Observer*. Aycock well understood that. Simmons did, too, but not being so intimate he would not be as frank as Aycock, whose advice was very good. I took it, except in two or three places where I had already committed myself. Acting in concert with Senator Simmons, I got out supplements for the Democratic papers of the State, containing Jennett's cartoons and all the scandals of the Russell administration, with every act and argument that we thought would serve to influence the white people who had been Democrats. *The North Caro-*

linian, my weekly paper, printed one hundred thousand copies of one issue and sent them broadcast to names furnished by the County and State Democratic committees.

The Republicans organized with A. E. Holton as chairman, and Dr. Cyrus Thompson was the Populist chairman. Thus the two parties put forward the most astute and able men in direction of their campaign. When the Republican State Convention met in July, it helped dig the grave of Fusion. There were very many Negroes who were delegates, more than at any other time probably, and they were demanding equality in every way. Russell's policy was unanimously endorsed, and plenary power was given the executive committee to fuse. The sensation of the convention was the speech that was used most effectively by the Democrats in the campaign, that of the Negro congressman from the second district, George H. White. He had been elected solicitor of the district and was then in Congress. He was thick-set and very black, and he spoke with an effectiveness which could arouse his Negro hearers to the highest pitch. Having been solicitor and congressman, he believed that the Negroes should have their fair share of the offices, and upon all occasions he had demanded this. The Negroes back of him were threatening the party unless they had recognition. Before the convention *The News and Observer* printed a list of all the Negroes in office in the State. In his speech to the Convention, which created more enthusiasm among the Negroes than any other, Congressman White took up *The News and Observer's* statement about Negroes holding office and said, "I am not the only Negro who holds office. There are others. There are plenty now being made to order to hold offices. We don't hold as many as we will. The Democrats talk about the color line and the Negroes holding office. I invite the issue."

It was in August, 1898, that *The News and Observer* printed in great headlines the story which finally sealed the doom of Fusion. It told in detail the result of Negro control in the city of Wilmington. It described the unbridled lawlessness and rule of incompetent officials and the failure of an ignorant and worthless police force to protect the people. It gave incidents of housebreaking and robbery in broad daylight and other happenings under Negro domination. Its staff correspondent who went to Wilmington to look into the matter said that there were murmurings of vigilance committees for the protection of the homes of the citizens. Just a few weeks thereafter the event happened which stirred the state from mountain to sea and finished digging the hole into which Fusion was to fall. A Negro by the name of Manley was publishing in Wilmington a paper called the *Record*. It had a good local circulation and was also circulated to some extent in the State. It had become the Negro organ and chief advocate of Fusion. In its issue of August 21, the *Record* said, "The morals of the poor white people are on a par with their colored neighbors." The next week this was followed up by another statement which *The News and Observer* called *"Vile and Villainous,"* in black type, and said it was an outrageous attack on white women by Negroes. Editorially Manley said:

"We suggest that the whites guard their women more closely, as Mrs. Felton says, thus giving no opportunity for the human fiend, be he white or black. You leave your goods out of doors and then complain because they are taken away. Poor white men are careless in the matter of protecting their women, especially on the farms. They are careless of their conduct toward them and our experience among poor white people in the country teaches us that the women of that race are not any more particular in the matter of clandestine meetings with colored men than the white men with colored women. Meetings of this kind go on for some time until the woman's infatuation or the man's boldness brings attention to them and the man is lynched for rape. Every negro lynched is called 'a Big Burly Black Brute' when in fact many of these who have been thus dealt with had white men for their fathers and were not only not 'black and burly' but were sufficiently attractive for white girls of culture and refinement to fall in love with them as is well known to all."

That editorial by a Negro political editor inflamed the white people of the State. They blazed their indignation. The quiet, law-abiding, and respectable Negroes saw what it meant, and the next day Frank Dednam, a representative of a well-to-do Negro family of Raleigh, said in *The News and Observer,* "Not a word of Manley's editorial expresses the sentiment of the colored people in North Carolina. I was never so shocked in my life. I shall not be surprised to hear that violence has been done Manley by either whites or negroes." *The News and Observer* said in an editorial that the statement by Manley was the legitimate result of the political situation and that the white people of the State of North Carolina would not stand for such things; that people reaped what they sowed and that the slanderous article of the Wilmington Negro had so aroused the people that a race riot was imminent in Wilmington and was only averted by the coolness of the whites; that instead of the Negro politicians' generally taking the position of Dednam, the Raleigh good Negro, some of them came to the defense of the paper.

White people surrounded the office of the *Record* the night following. Manley received anonymous letters counselling him to leave Wilmington at once. So bitter was the indignation aroused that two days later a special telegram from Wilmington said that the Negroes were riotous, a demonstration was held by a mob on Princess Street, and there were angry mutterings against the whites. The policemen finally persuaded the Negro mob to disperse. On August 26, *The News and Observer* contained an editorial in which it said that Republicans were responsible for the slander of white women, and printed a story to the effect that some Negro preachers were backing Manley. The Manley statement went like wildfire from house to house, particularly in the rural districts. The women and their husbands were righteously indignant. The Democratic speakers made that attack upon the white woman of the country districts the burden of their song; and that, together with White's statement about Negroes' holding office, was declared to be the natural fruit of Fusion. My paper said the only way to teach such men as Manley and such officials as had been guilty of corruption the lessons they needed was to drive out of power, in disgrace, every man who had defended Russellism.

Correspondents from all over the State and some out of the State went to Wilmington to investigate the matter, and they all wrote of a reign of inefficiency. The Charlotte *Observer's* correspondent, H. E. C. Bryant, wrote the story of "The Dirty Town Under Negro Health Officers." He said that Negroes and other Fusionists were so busy playing politics that no attention was given to the streets or to health matters. Early in September the Wilmington *Messenger* printed a story of young white women in Wilmington being pushed off the sidewalks by Negro policemen on their beats. The New Bern *Journal* printed that in that town a Negro man struck a young white girl in the face. Greene County was excited by burglary and attempted rape by a Negro. While *The News and Observer* was printing the stories written by F. B. Arendell, member of its staff, from towns under Negro rule, the situation in Wilmington became so critical that vigilance committees were appointed. Ministers of the Gospel and citizens of high standing were organized into squads, and every block in the town was patrolled at night by prominent citizens with guns. A reign of terror was on. About that time *The News and Observer* printed a picture of a member of the Legislature, a Negro from Craven County, who was twice convicted of forgery, and, at the same time, a picture of the trial of a white woman before a Negro justice of the peace in New Bern. *The News and Observer* printed, on September 21, in a box on the front page, the following:

> "Should be Lynched. The negro candidate for senator from Edgecombe will help lynch any negro who votes the Democratic ticket and he gave this advice to negroes: 'Go to the election well armed with rocks in your pockets, clubs in your hands and carrying your pistols, and don't let any officer arrest you after you have registered until the day after the election unless you have stolen something or killed somebody. Come to see me if they get after you.'"

A Negro deputy sheriff in Wake County served subpoenas on leading white men including the mayor. Another article told that the Negro school inspector made an official inspection of a white school in Barton's Creek Township in Wake County. The next day on the front page in a box in *The News and Observer* was the following: "Afro-American Council want to repeal laws forbidding marriages between negroes and whites."

About that time *The News and Observer* had a cartoon and quoted Sheriff Hahn, Republican, of Craven County, saying he brought "a batch of convicts to the penitentiary yesterday. I brought the only Democratic Populist in Craven County among the number and when I got ready to leave, I picked out the blackest negro in the bunch to chain him to." George White came into the picture again. He attended a circus in Tarboro, and when objections were made to his sitting with the whites, he said he was as good as white folks. When made to move from the seats reserved for the whites, he left the circus. Another cartoon was printed showing Jim Young, director of the white Blind Institution, in a classroom where white blind girls were being taught, and also inspecting the bedroom of a white woman teacher of the Blind Institution. A story appeared of the Negro deputy sheriff at Wilmington drawing his pistol on the street-car conductor, who had refused to give him a free ride.

When the Manley statement aroused the people to white heat, Fusionists answered that Manley was an irresponsible man and had no right to speak for the Republicans. Denying the statement of the Republicans that Manley was an irresponsible upstart and mischief-making simpleton, an affidavit was sent all over the state signed by B. G. Worth, R. W. Hicks, C. E. Borden, W. L. DeRossett, and John C. Springer, leading business men of Wilmington, who said that Manley was appointed deputy register of deeds under the Republican administration in New Hanover; that George T. Howe, travelling agent of the *Record,* was elected to the Legislature by the Fusionists in 1896 and served in the 1897 session; and that Manley's paper was the recognized organ of the Republican Party of that section.

The denunciation of having Negroes and whites on the same school committee was so great that State Superintendent Charles H. Mebane, who had been elected as a Populist and who had made an excellent officer, came out publicly recommending that each race control its own schools. He later won the confidence and respect of the school people of the State of all parties. Afterwards he quit the Fusionists and became editor of a Democratic paper, which he edited until he died.

In the 1876 campaign the greatest indignation had been aroused when Republicans in Jones hired out poor white people to Negroes; in this campaign the people of Jones County were aroused when a Negro school committeeman inspected a white school at Maysville. In September *The News and Observer* printed that white ladies in Vanceboro were compelled to go to a Negro to list their taxes, and a white insane man had been brought to the State Insane Asylum by a Negro deputy sheriff. The Fusionists in Wake renominated Jim Young for the Legislature. This recalled his membership on the board of the white blind institution, and it was all brought out again in the papers. The Reverend O. L. Stringfield, who had been travelling all over the State for the Baptist University, in a speech at King's Mountain Baptist Association declared that "not one-half of the horrors of Negro domination had been printed in the papers." The Democrats used with great effect an article written by Frank

Weldon of the Atlanta *Constitution* saying that if the Fusionists should carry North Carolina, Negroes from other states would flock to North Carolina and make it a Negro state, a black commonwealth, a refuge for the race. Early in October, it was printed that the Wilmington Negroes were trying to buy guns; that they had sent an order to the Odell Hardware Company for twenty-five Winchester rifles, but the Odell Company after investigation, had refused to send them.

The situation was so bad at Wilmington that W. H. Chadbourn, the Republican post master, wrote to Senator Pritchard telling him of the race danger, suggesting that all Negroes turn over to white people all offices they held and assuring Pritchard that the race trouble was not "the usual political cry." Toward the end of the campaign the Fusionists made some headway by saying that if the Democrats won they would disfranchise the illiterate white people as well as the Negroes, that the Democrats had made up their minds to disfranchise the illiterate voters.

The campaign speeches of all parties were attended by great crowds of people. The Fusionists were as much excited as the Democrats. In some places violence was attempted, and in many it was feared. Butler had been rotten-egged at one or two places, as had a few other Fusion speakers. *The News and Observer* counselled against any violence. In an editorial headed "Let Them Severely Alone," it opposed rotten-egging or rocking of Fusionist speakers. This was based upon an incident that happened at Middleton. Henry Covington, white Republican at Laurinburg, who made an incendiary speech, was made to retract it. He was quoted as saying that the Negroes were the best race of people on earth. It was printed that he told the Negroes that when white girls returned from colleges and schools, Negroes were usually employed to look after them and drive them about over the country, and that he added, "If I were in your place, I would put my arms around them." At Mason's Cross Roads near Old Hundred, three hundred white citizens forced him to stand up in a buggy and apologize, and he was then told to hit the grit, which he did. A leading Republican of New Hanover County, Colonel F. W. Foster, following the action of the post master, said the Republicans ought not to put up a ticket in the county. This was Governor Russell's home county. Republicans like Foster said they were as much outraged by the excesses as the white Democrats. The

Wilmington *Record*—Manley's Negro paper—published an appeal by "colored ladies" as follows:

"Resolved, that every negro who refuses to register his name next Saturday that he may vote, we shall make it our business to deal with him in a way that will not be pleasant. He shall be branded a white-livered coward who would sell his liberty and the liberty of our whole race to the demons who are even now seeking to take away the most sacred rights vouchsafed to any people. We are further resolved to teach our children to love the party of manhood's rights and liberties, trusting in God to restore order out of the present confusion, and be it resolved further that we have these resolutions printed in our daily *Record,* the one medium that has stood for our rights when others have forsaken them."

This was signed "an organization of colored ladies."

As an evidence of the acute conditions, the Democratic Club of Winston-Salem passed resolutions requesting the tobacco manufacturers and other employers of labor to use all reasonable efforts to give white men positions instead of colored in their places of business and to extend the same privilege in all patronage. At Ashpole near Lumberton, an armed body of Negroes was forced to retire by a larger body of armed white men. After they retired, some of the Negroes in the mob, who had promised to go home, fired on the guard and three white men were shot. A telegram from that place said, "The ring-leaders of the black mob are known and a crowd of one hundred white men heavily armed are after them. More trouble is expected. The negroes have been inflamed by incendiary speeches and the white people are armed to quelch it, if possible, in its incipiency." On its editorial page, *The News and Observer* compared the affair at Ashpole to the first shot fired at Lexington and told the people in the State that the incendiary speeches of radical leaders had borne their logical fruit and the welfare of the State was at stake in the election to be held in November. It declared that there was a limit to the forbearance of even the law-abiding Anglo-Saxon, and that if pushed beyond that limit and trouble came, the responsibility for it would rest upon the heads of the white scalawags and the ignorant and vicious Negroes. It was reported that Russell and Pritchard had asked for troops to control the election in North Carolina, and a special from Washington said that the matter had been discussed in the

Cabinet. Toward the end of the campaign, another Negro paper, the Kinston *Searchlight,* printed an editorial which was widely reprinted by the Democrats. It said, "You can look for the burly negroes on the eighth of November at the ballot box in a solid phalanx animated by the negresses." It urged every Negro to stick to the Republican Party because it had freed him, and closed by saying, "Adhere to the teaching of the Republican and Fusion Parties. If you don't, hell will catch you to the delight of the Devil." The first public barbecue given by the Fusionists in Wake County was at Marshburn's Mills, and the whites and the Negroes made a disgraceful scramble for the barbecue. Social equality prevailed.

THE RED SHIRTS

Toward the close of the campaign, Red Shirts appeared in the counties adjoining the South Carolina line. The State chairman and the leaders welcomed every volunteer movement that promised victory. They coöperated with the Red Shirt brigades by sending speakers. A Macedonian cry was sent from Robeson County over the border to Senator Tillman, who had been a Red Shirt leader in South Carolina when Hampton had been elected Governor in 1876. Tillman responded, and wherever he spoke he was attended by a cavalcade of men who would meet him at the station and ride through the county with him, riding through the colored sections of the towns, all wearing red shirts, shouting white supremacy. Some of them carried shotguns and would shoot in the air. They created terror. I had read about Red Shirts but had never understood how three hundred men on horseback, wearing red shirts, with pants tucked in their boots, and carrying guns, could make such a terrifying spectacle as I saw at Pembroke one afternoon just before sunset. The members of the Red Shirt brigade had escorted Senator Tillman through Robeson County to the depot where he was to take the train. He had spoken violently and had followed somewhat the same line of Colonel Waddell, saying that the white folks of South Carolina would chunk enough Negroes in the river before they would permit their domination. His speech had created such feeling in the hearts of those who heard him as nerved them to follow the South Carolina plan. Tillman himself, a swarthy man with one eye, looked like a veritable leader of a revolution, not unlike that which dominated France for a period. The train stopped for ten minutes as the cavalcade, with Tillman at the head, rode up to the station. If you have never seen three hundred red-shirted men towards sunset with the sky red and the red shirts seeming to blend with the sky, you cannot conceive the impression it makes. It looked like the whole world was carmine. I then understood why red-shirted men riding through the country, even if they said nothing and shot off no pistols, could carry terror to the Negroes in their quarters.

There were no Red Shirts until after the Manley editorial. There were no Red Shirts until after the reports of violence and the speeches of George White and the declarations of the colored leaders of Wilmington and the threat of the Senator from Edgecombe to lynch any Negro who voted the Democratic ticket. Violent language begets violent language and violent action begets violent action. As the campaign neared the end, both sides were desperate and, "You are a liar, a perjurer and a villain"—with every other possible epithet that could be employed by public speakers—was used. White supremacy club members all over the State were vigilant, riding by day and by night; public speakings were held on every hustings. Business was forgotten and the one business of the white people of the State was to redeem it, and the one business of the Fusionists was to hold on at any hazard. In the matter of election machinery, the Fusionists had the advantage. In the counties where they had a large Negro vote they would have won but for the Red Shirts and white supremacy men and the determination of the white men that at any cost they would redeem their counties from Fusion rule. Many Populists who would not come over and vote against the Fusionists remained at home.

The more militant members of the party rode the county by day and by night and summoned their followers to go to the polls ready to meet force with force; but, as always happens in the South when there is a contest of this kind and the white people are greatly aroused, ready to wear red shirts and to carry pistols, many Negroes felt that the contest was unequal and stood aside. The terrible part about it was the effect of it upon the law-abiding respectable Negroes. They had been placed between the upper and nether millstones. They had themselves been humiliated by the conduct of the wicked and lewd members of their race; they had been driven by the corrupt Fusion white politicians, who cared only for spoils; and not a few of them were wholly indifferent to the result because the rule of Fusion had disillusioned them. They had great contempt for Russell, for whom they had voted.

Toward the end of the campaign, correspondents from other parts of the country came into North Carolina to study the situation. I remember one of them, Harry L. West, who had been one of the three commissioners of Washington City appointed by Cleveland. He visited all the counties along the South Carolina line to study the Red-Shirt movement. After his survey of that situation, he came to Raleigh and spent a day with me. Somebody had given him a red shirt and a rifle such as had been used in one of the Red-Shirt brigades. He was persuaded to dress up in it and have his picture taken. Of course the picture wasn't used. In a bantering vein, I told him if there was any congressional investigation of the Red Shirts in North Carolina I would prove he was the leader of the whole movement by filing his picture wearing the red shirt and carrying the rifle. The red-shirt wearers did not injure Negroes in their bodies. Undoubtedly, if the Negroes had resisted, there would have been bloodshed in Robeson, Scotland, and Richmond; but when the Red Shirts marched, they marched in large numbers. They usually rode horses and had weapons, and their appearance was the signal for the Negroes to get out of the way, so that when the Red Shirt brigade passed through the Negro end of a town, it was as uninhabited to all appearances as if it had been graveyard. That was the psychology of the Red Shirt parade. It effected what it undertook, because while the Negroes would not have been influenced much by speakings or even denunciations, they had grown up in a sort of terror of Red Shirtism in South Carolina, and they accordingly made themselves scarce. The result, of course, was as the local people had foreseen, that many Negroes either did not vote or made no fight in the affected counties on election day.

In that campaign, every white man who could talk was on the stump; every white man who could write was writing, and every white man who could ride and could influence a vote was enthusiastically at work. By the middle of October, they didn't need much speaking and didn't need much organization. The fire was kindled and there was a vigorous determination to carry the State that swept everything before it. For the first time the women of the State attended public speakings in large numbers. This was particularly true in the rural districts, and many women whose husbands had been

Populists and some whose husbands were Republicans were enlisted. Of course, they could not vote, but when the speakers would tell of the horrors and read the Manley letter and repeat the stories of well authenticated outrages, the people would be aroused to fever heat.

The News and Observer was the printed voice of the campaign. Of course other papers were vigorous, and nearly all the newspapers in North Carolina were straining every nerve and printing everything that could bring victory, but *The News and Observer* was relied upon to carry the Democratic message and to be the militant voice of White Supremacy, and it did not fail in what was expected, sometimes going to extremes in its partisanship. Its correspondents visited every town where the Fusionists were in control and presented column after column day by day of stories of every Negro in office and every peculation, every private delinquency of a Fusion office-holder.

By the first of October the Party was one solid mass, organized like an army, and word sent out from headquarters was taken up with zeal in the whole State. Not a Fusion conference could be held in the State that *The News and Observer* didn't get it, sometimes by its own correspondents, but it had voluntary correspondents, too, vigilants who were keen to watch every movement in every county and district and telegraph or telephone that a conference was on. Almost every Democrat was not only a fighting man but he was also a sort of Sherlock Holmes on a small scale. Fusionists found that whatever they did leaked out and *The News and Observer* would print it next morning. For instance, a Fusionist council of war was held in Raleigh and a member spoke about the principles of the Populist Party, when Otho Wilson got up and said, "This is no time to talk of principles." Generally the Fusionists would map out their plan at a night meeting, and sometimes a disgruntled Populist would in a surreptitious way convey the information, and sometimes a Republican small man who wanted to get in the limelight would on the sly give us the story. Day and night we worked, for I rarely went home until two or three o'clock in the morning, getting the news and writing the editorials and conferring with Democratic leaders. Never a day passed that two or three or four county chairmen did not come to Raleigh to secure speakers, report, or give suggestions. We would meet at Democratic headquarters or they would come to my office, and every one of them had a story of something they thought would tell against the Fusionists. We were never very careful about winnowing out the stories or running them down. The things we knew were so bad that when these county chairman and local leaders would come in with terrible stories, they were played up in big type. Whether all of them could be sustained in a court of justice or not, the Fusionists called them *"The News and Observer's* lies" even when they were authenticated by affidavits. As an illustration of their denial of the truth, several of the Fusionists got together in Raleigh and issued a statement that the Manley editorial was written by Democrats and circulated by Democrats; in the rural districts they said there was no such man as Manley; that it was all a *News and Observer* concocted lie to defeat the Fusionists. So superheated were many of their followers that they really believed it was a lie. In fact, the people on every side were at such a key of fighting and hate that the Democrats would believe almost any piece of rascality and the Fusionists got into the habit of denying everything. Toward the end of the campaign, the Fusionist speakers were almost beside themselves with baffled rage.

AYCOCK AND GLENN AROUSED THE PEOPLE

The two men on the stump in that campaign of 1898, as in the campaign of 1896 and 1900, who did most to stir the people and to bring about victory, were Charles B. Aycock and Robert B. Glenn, both of whom afterwards became Governor. They had been electors for Cleveland in 1892, and they canvassed the State from end to end in 1898. Every county and every township holding meetings would wire to Simmons in Raleigh to send Aycock or Glenn. They traveled and spoke day and night. There were no automobiles then and no good schedules for travelling by train, no good roads, no aeroplanes, and the strain upon them in that campaign and in the succeeding ones undoubtedly shortened their lives. They were about as unlike as any two men who have lived in the State.

Glenn was larger, more vigorous, quite as vibrant—what you would call a "gully-washer." He spoke with every muscle in his body and could tell a story of Fusion outrage in a way to excite his hearers, so that if any Fusion office-holder had been present he would have feared for his life. He rarely spoke less than two hours, and if the day was hot, when he finished he didn't have a dry rag on him. Sometimes he would take off his coat and collar and when he would get half through, if he hadn't taken off his collar, the people having heard that at some other place he had done so, would cry out: "Bob, take off your collar and give 'em hell," which he proceeded to do to the cheers and hurrahs of the great body of people. He was tremendously effective in his sledge hammer blows. Whenever it was announced that Glenn and Butler were to have a joint speaking, as often happened, the crowd was measured by acres and it was an all-day contest. Butler was more adroit; he was more incisive; he could play upon the passions of his hearers but in nothing like the effective way that Glenn could do, but no matter how deep a hole Glenn thought he had dug for him, Butler was able to keep from falling in. Glenn said that in a debate with Butler he had to be on his guard in order not to let Butler get the best of him. These speakings resulted in each side making their followers more enthusiastic and determined. Glenn had the best of the argument and was on the offensive. To hear him read the Manley letter and to comment on it and to hear his tribute to the women in the rural districts, which he delivered in a voice that could be heard almost in the next county, was terrible and terrifying. Nothing Butler could say could undo that, so that the Manley letter and incidents of that kind which Glenn handled in a sledge hammer fashion gave him the best of the debate and a less skillful debater than Butler would have been annihilated by Glenn's handling of the letter and the scandals of the Russell administration.

Glenn used a meat axe; Aycock used a rapier. Glenn spoke two or three hours; Aycock, rarely over sixty minutes. Aycock left something to the imagination of his hearers. Glenn never left out a detail or an incident. The average man was more moved by Glenn, but the Aycock speech was a classic. It was so perfect that if you were to omit a sentence, or a word from a sentence, it would bleed. He marshalled his facts with precision and told his stories inimitably. With the possible exception of Vance—and even that is doubtful—no man could tell a story that would illustrate a point so perfectly. He impressed his hearers with his essential courtesy and fairness. He never seemed to abuse anybody. In fact he disarmed criticism by his very absence of the sort of invective that Glenn used so effectively and yet he secured the same effect, and often a greater one, by proving the iniquities of the Fusionists rather than by denouncing them. You felt that he did not like to do this. When you heard Glenn, you felt that he was revelling in telling the stories of crime, and when you heard Aycock you felt that he was ashamed to do it and was doing it only from a high sense of public duty. Glenn made the Republicans mad by vigorous denunciation. Aycock made them feel that he was showing up their iniquities and was sorry for the good ones who had been mixed up with the scoundrels. It was inimitable—he made no enemies among the Republicans and yet no man ever converted so many Republicans or Populists. He was ingratiating, and at first the Democrats thought he was going to be lacking in the knock-down-and-drag-out methods which the campaign demanded. But as he went along, he showed such a gift for getting under the very cover of the Republican policy and exposing it that when his speech was ended you felt that unless a surgeon should come and remove the corruption the whole body politic would be destroyed. And yet you never knew exactly how he did it. His favorite story in that campaign, which he told in such a way as to get hold of the people, was that one morning as he was taking the train out of Raleigh about four o'clock and was travelling with Dr. B. F. Dixon, who was afterwards State Auditor, a man came in and sat down in the seat before them. Dr. Dixon asked the man how old he was and he said he was thirty-five years old. Aycock commented, "That is impossible, Dr. Dixon. No man can get as dirty as that in thirty-five years." He used this incident to illustrate his great surprise that any party could produce such a dirty and filthy administration in a few years as had happened under the Russell administration. This incident was told in a droll way, and the effectiveness of it was greater than a long recital of the deeds which he would bring in as if they were samples of a long reign of corruption.

As to the other Fusion speakers in the campaign, they fought shy of speaking with Glenn and Aycock, except Dr. Cyrus Thompson, and there again was a debater. I always thought he was better than Butler. Butler had no eloquence. Butler had much of insinuation and invective, but Thompson had eloquence and vehemence, he was tremendously interesting in his sidelights and stories, and he had an originality and a quaintness that were attractive. He didn't talk like anybody else, even in private conversation, and on the stump he had an original way, and my, how he could enthuse the Populists!

I had an engagement to speak in Duplin County in the Chinquapin section when my friend Benjamin Aycock was running for the Senate. He was an older brother of Governor Aycock and a man of

Upper left, Locke Craig, Governor of North Carolina, 1912-1916. *Upper right,* Charles B. Aycock, Governor of North Carolina, 1900-1904. *Lower left,* R. B. Glenn, Governor of North Carolina, 1904-1908. *Lower right,* Judge Francis D. Winston, Lieutenant-Governor who was host to President Theodore Roosevelt.

Upper left, Judge George Rountree, leader of the Wilmington Revolution. *Upper right,* H. C. Wall, pioneer worker in the White Supremacy campaign. *Lower left,* John C. Scarborough, State Superintendent of Schools. *Lower right,* Colonel A. M. Waddell, eloquent orator and militant fighter for White Supremacy; Congressman and Mayor.

rare judgment and sterling qualities. As State Senator he was the staunchest leader for right policies; as Corporation Commissioner he measured up to the high duties and compelled railroads to pay just taxes and reduce excessive rates. He was elected State Treasurer in 1908. The morning I arrived in Duplin there came a message from the Populists' chairman asking for a division of time with Dr. Cyrus Thompson. It was accepted and the program was that I was to speak first and then Thompson. When I arrived, there were about fifty or seventy-five Democrats present, and perhaps twenty-five or thirty Populists. There were very few Republicans in Duplin except Negroes and there were not many of them present. A few were on the outskirts. Thompson was there and a few of the faithful, but about the time I finished speaking and Thompson was about to speak, after a brass band number, two or three hundred Populists rode up shouting and took possession of the meeting. They hadn't come to hear me, but they gave Thompson such a reception as that section had never seen before, nor since, I suppose. I had made my long speech to the Democrats and a few Populists. The Populists had arranged a spectacular demonstration. All carried cornstalks and waved them, and when Thompson got up to speak, they gave him such an ovation as might have been staged in a National Democratic Convention. From the beginning of his speech, he never made a threat or told a story that they didn't all rise up and cheer. It was terrible. Our small body of Democrats, faithful and true, did the best they could for me but they were outnumbered six to one. The Populists had been drilled and it looked more like a crusade than a campaign on their part. I always had great respect for Cyrus Thompson's speaking ability after that day, although while he was Secretary of State he was quite venomous toward *The News and Observer,* and I must say he had good grounds for it.

THE WHITE SUPREMACY CONVENTION

Toward the end of October, while the Democrats were vigilant and organized, it was apparent that the opposition was straining every nerve, and that something more must be done to insure the defeat of the Fusionists. In Democratic headquarters it was debated how the miasma of the corruptions and the ills of Negro rule could be brought home to the people of the whole State in such an impressive way as to utterly rout the Fusionists. It was felt by all that some supreme thing must be done. Jarvis, Aycock, Glenn, and pretty much all the leaders first and last conferred with Chairman Simmons about the situation. It was determined to ask the people of all Eastern North Carolina to come together at Goldsboro to declare the conditions that existed in the East and to make an appeal to the whole State, somewhat like that made in 1876 to the Center and the West to come to the rescue of the Eastern brethren. It was well understood that such a meeting would primarily stir the East to a more militant attitude for its own preservation. The result of these conferences was the calling of a White Supremacy Convention in Goldsboro. To show the temper of the meeting, after Chairman Simmons opened it with the statement of the serious situation in North Carolina and the necessity for more vigorous action in order to rout Negro rule, Major William A. Guthrie of Durham, who had been the Populist candidate for Governor in 1896, was made temporary chairman, in order to rob the meeting of any semblance of being a purely Democratic rally. Major Guthrie called upon the Reverend N. M. Jurney, a Methodist preacher who gave as much of his time to politics as to preaching, to pray, and his prayer partook of the feeling of the times. "Let us feel this day," he prayed to the Lord, "the vibrations of our coming redemption from all wicked rule and the supremacy of the race destined not only to rule this country but to carry the gospel to all nations and maintain civil and religious liberty throughout the world." Then he added the petition that "there will be no riot or bloodshed."

Major Guthrie began his address by reading from the Scripture, and he compared the present situation with the period when the Hebrews were in subjection. He declared that the present conditions in North Carolina had been brought about by the uniting of one hundred and twenty thousand Negroes and thirty thousand white men "at whose bidding these one hundred and twenty thousand Negroes go to the polls in a solid phalanx and cast their ballots." He praised the thirty-two thousand honest Populists who had voted for him for Governor in 1896 and severely chastised "those five thousand renegades who under the leadership of a few traitors of their party and their principles had gone out and voted for the Republican Governor and thereby helped to saddle Negro domination on the good old state." This, mind you, from a Populist who had been a Republican since 1868 up to the time he joined the Populist Party. It was all the more effective because of his political antecedents. "The Anglo-Saxon," he declared, "planted civilization on this continent and wherever this race has been in conflict with another race, it has asserted its supremacy and either conquered or exterminated the foe. This great race has carried the Bible in one hand and the sword in the other and with these emblems of religion, we say to the nations of the world 'Resist our march of progress and civilization and we will wipe you off the face of the earth'."

Colonel Alfred Moore Waddell's speech, which was in line with Guthrie's—they were the high-water marks of the convention—was mainly devoted to vivid word pictures of conditions in Wilmington. He detailed the intolerable conditions which compelled even ministers of the Gospel to patrol the streets at night to protect their homes. "We are going," declared Colonel Waddell, "to protect our firesides and our loved ones or we will die in the attempt, and I don't say that for the purpose of winding up an oratorical flight. That determination is in the minds of the white men of Wilmington and we intend to carry it out." He declared that the Wilmington people would drive out the Manleys and the Russells and the horde of corruptionists "if they have to throw enough dead Negro bodies in the Cape Fear to choke up its passage to the sea." In ordinary times Waddell was one of the most graceful and classical of speakers, but on that day he was an American Robespierre, as indeed he had been in the early seventies when he redeemed the Wilmington district and was elected to Congress. He was the sort of man who in political revolutions and in war came to the front by sheer audacity and courage. But, when things were moving quietly and smoothly, he was to be found in his library reading, and seemed more or less of a dilettante. It required conditions such as existed in 1898 to bring him to the front. His speech electrified the Convention. Portions of it were printed and sent all over the State. His defiant utterances were quoted by speakers on every stump. The cause of Wilmington became the cause of all.

The resolutions adopted by the eight thousand men focused into a brief space the spirit of the white supremacy movement. Nobody in that meeting mentioned the Democratic Party; in fact, during the last days of the campaign, the White Supremacy Party was the term employed by all speakers who were fighting the Fusionists. The resolutions, which better than any other expression epitomized the conditions, were, in part, as follows:

"That as a consequence of turning these local offices over to the negroes, bad government had followed, homes have been invaded and the sanctity of woman endangered, business has been paralyzed and property rendered less valuable, the majesty of the law has been disregarded and lawlessness encouraged.... We have contemplated no violence but we are determined to use all proper means to free ourselves of this negro domination which is paralyzing our business and which hangs like a dark cloud over our homes.... It is not our purpose to do the negro any harm. It is better for him as well as for us if the white man shall govern and while we propose to protect and encourage him in all his rights and duties of citizenship, we affirm that North Carolina shall not be negroized. It is of all the states of the union particularly the home of the Anglo-Saxon and the Anglo-Saxon shall govern it."

At that time the threat of Federal troops being sent to the State was hanging over the people and the resolutions went on to say "No such conditions exist in the state as to justify Senator Pritchard in calling upon the President to send troops to the state or the governor in issuing his brutal proclamation."

After that conference, the only fear was that Federal troops would be ordered into the main centers. The Fusionists were depending upon that help, and the white supremacy advocates feared it, not so much for what the troops would do but because the people were so wrought up that they feared bloodshed would follow. On October 25, *The News and Observer* printed from Washington under headlines, "To Invoke Bayonet Rule," the story of the discussion in the Cabinet of the request of Russell and Pritchard to have Federal troops sent into North Carolina to control the election. Attorney General Griggs was reported as strongly denouncing the situation in North Carolina and ready to send troops if it should be found necessary.

About that time there was printed a story in Washington, which *The News and Observer* called Pritchard's "ghost story," to the effect that the life of Governor Russell was threatened and race riots in the State were imminent. Russell issued a vigorous proclamation against the Red Shirts, but it was very clear and was made plain to Pritchard, Russell, Butler, and the rest that the coming of troops would not avail their party; that the white heat that dominated the white supremacy leaders and the rank and file of the people was such that it would have taken Grant's Army to have held them back; and that, instead of strengthening their position, it would have routed the Fusionists except in the places where the troops were able to take charge of the polls.

Jennett's cartoon on Russell followed a Davenport idea. Whenever Mark Hanna appeared in Davenport's cartoons he wore loud clothes with big checks and every check was a dollar mark. Every time Jennett drew a cartoon of big-jowled Russell he gave him the same checks that had been given to Hanna, but instead of dollar marks he drew a repulsive, very black, kinky-headed Negro. It was horrible-looking, and Russell raved every time he saw it. I never blamed him. It advertised the fact that it was a white supremacy campaign which was being waged and that its main objective was the getting rid of the big Negro vote.

Russell was in terror for his life. He feared he might be assassinated. Returning from Wilmington on the night of election day, he was jeered and made sport of and ridiculed and denounced by a crowd assembled at Maxton. The conductor knew that a little later, when the train came into Hamlet, there would be a crowd there, for Hamlet was the center of southern North Carolina and South Carolinians would come over to get the news. The South Carolinians, having participated in the Red Shirt parades, thought they had as much to do with the election as the North Carolinians. In fact not a few of them naturalized themselves for a few days in order to vote, which swelled the majorities in the counties bordering on their State. Knowing all this, the railroad people feared that when Russell reached Hamlet some violence would be done him. It was therefore suggested to Russell that, instead of riding in the regular car en route to Raleigh, he take a seat in the express car or baggage car and remain there while the train was shifting and the passengers were getting supper at Hamlet. He was glad to do this and to pass through the funnel of Red Shirts without being seen. When the train reached Hamlet, the people, having heard Russell was on the train, surrounded it. "Where is Russell? Where is the Governor? Bring him out! Let us get a look at him!" All sorts of uncomplimentary expressions were heard, and undoubtedly if he had been visible he would have been subjected to more severe treatment than he had received at Maxton. Railroad men feared he might receive personal injury, and if he had resented the jeers of the crowd, such might have happened. All the cool-headed people were glad that the railroad men had smuggled him through the town. He reached Raleigh in safety. He was very glad a little later to get out of office, unwept, unhonored and unsung.

The most exciting event after the Goldsboro meeting was the issuing of a bench warrant by Justice W. A. Montgomery of the Supreme Court for the arrest of Captain Buck Kitchin, of Halifax, his son, his son-in-law, and three of his close friends. This warrant was issued at the request of Republican State Chairman Holton upon the allegation of B. B. Steptoe, a Negro politician, who charged that Captain Kitchin and his party came to his house in the night, broke in, and with threats and guns forced him to resign as registrar. Captain Kitchin might be called the original advocate of white supremacy and the father of the expression and the organization. I remember as a boy hearing him speak in the courthouse at Wilson. When nobody else could get an audience or stir the people, he could bring them to white heat, and the burden of his speech, from the early seventies until his death, was white supremacy. He believed that a white man in Eastern North Carolina who wasn't a Democrat was a traitor to his race, and he believed it so deeply and preached it so consistently that he thought suppression of the vote of Negroes was doing the Lord's own service and that the methods should not be inquired into too carefully. What Kitchin asserted, probably the bulk of the white people in the Second District and the Negro counties believed. They did not think the ignorant Negro had any right to vote and most of the Negroes were ignorant. Captain Kitchin was bold to rashness, open and frank in his advocacy of the suppression of the Negro vote and he had little patience with white associates who were not quite so willing to suppress the vote except by indirection. He believed if the white people were aroused, mobilized, and united, their mobilization would make the Negroes afraid to exercise their franchise. Others suppressed the Negro vote in the black districts by methods which were not so open. Sometimes the ballot boxes were made away with, and sometimes tickets were printed wrong, and sometimes the vote was not counted as it was cast. Captain Kitchin preferred the bold and open declaration that the Negroes had no moral right to vote and that it was the duty of white people to control and govern by using any weapons that God and nature put in their hands.

So believing, with this long record and the leadership which he and his sons had in Halifax County, he and the other white men of the county determined to wrest Halifax from the control of Negroes. The Fusionists had control of the machinery and Steptoe was a registrar, and it was charged that he was registering sixteen-year-olds and dead Negroes. Certainly he was very active in putting every Negro possible on the books. He came to Raleigh and laid before the State Republican chairman the situation in Halifax County and said unless something was done the Fusionists would be routed. He made an affidavit that on a certain night, led by Captain Kitchin, a half-dozen men had broken into his house and forced him to resign as registrar. Kitchin denied vigorously that he had ever gone to Steptoe's house, and while it was generally believed that some of the white supremacy men had gone to Steptoe's house, as Steptoe alleged. Kitchin's boldness and reputation for doing things in the open led most people to believe that Steptoe had charged Captain Kitchin with doing something which others had done and that the Republicans thought, if they could tag the crime on to Kitchin and his sons, who were the leaders of the white supremacy movement, it would be more effective. However that may be, his arrest overshadowed everything else in the State for days and served to incite the white supremacy people to greater indignation than ever. They rallied around Kitchin and denounced his arrest as a high-handed piece of Jeffreyism.

Judge Montgomery, who had issued the warrant, lived in Warren County and had been a Democrat until he joined the Populist Party. I remember the first time I ever heard him make a speech. It was at a Baptist State Convention in Raleigh. I went to the convention with that old Roman, John C. Scarborough. Montgomery, who was a Baptist and who had been disappointed in his political ambition, was making a speech. This was before he had joined the Populist Party. He recited the religious proclivities of public officials in North Carolina and declared that while the Baptists outnumbered practically all the other denominations, yet they were discriminated against when it came to recognition in high positions for which they were well qualified. He sought to arouse the Baptist State Convention to demand more offices for Baptists. Old John C. Scarborough, who despised demagoguery, sitting under the shadow of the sanctuary, grabbed me by the arm and said to me in a whisper of disgust, "They ought to put the damn son of a bitch out." His language was always so free from such expressions that I was astonished. It showed such indignation and such use of swear words as I never dreamed possible for him.

I daresay it was the only time he ever used that word. There wasn't a stauncher Baptist than John C. Scarborough or braver Confederate soldier or a truer man. He had been elected Superintendent of Public Instruction repeatedly, not because of his religious affiliations but because of his worth and character. He felt Montgomery was using the church gathering to bolster his own ambitions. His pioneer work for public education laid deep and broad the foundations upon which our public school system rests.

As soon as Montgomery issued the warrant, Captain Kitchin took the first train to Raleigh and demanded a hearing. He declared that the statement of Steptoe was a lie from beginning to end, that he had never visited his house or broken into it or made any threats. The papers took it up and Kitchin declared that Holton had gotten Steptoe to make the affidavit against him and that it was a conspiracy hatched out in order to furnish a pretext for bringing Federal troops into the State. I shall never forget the tenseness in the Supreme Court room when the case came on to be heard. Kitchin, who was very dark of complexion, with black hair, and eyes that flashed, and who did not fear the face of man or devil, was so outraged that his boys and neighbors feared he would lose his case by the kind of denunciation of Montgomery which all thought he would make. There came with him from Halifax scores of men who were ready to stand by him to any extent. I didn't see any guns but I have no doubt that in that court room there were plenty of them in hip pockets. The white supremacy leaders counselled Kitchin to restrain himself. Outside the court room, he denounced Montgomery and the whole crowd in such adjectives as Billy Sunday never dreamed of, but when the case came to be heard his evidence and that of those with him and his alibis were so clear and so perfect that the case fell down utterly, with the result that it was another nail in the coffin of the Fusion campaign.

After the charges against Kitchin and his associates were dismissed, Steptoe disappeared utterly as if the earth had swallowed him up. He did not go back to Halifax County. It probably would not have been safe for him. Every attempt to locate him failed. Afterwards I learned that he spent all these days and nights within a square of my home in Raleigh. He never left the house in the daytime and was closely guarded and protected by his colored friends, who feared for his life. A colored neighbor of mine told me afterwards where Steptoe spent those days and said he had advised him that he would be safer in the square adjoining my house than in any other place in North Carolina; that nobody would expect to find him there; and that if any trouble came, he knew I would do everything to protect his life.

Everybody approached election day with nervousness and anxiety. It was well known that the Negro vote would be small in some counties, but there was deep anxiety lest race riots or trouble at the polls should mar the day. As a matter of fact, however, while there was tension at the polls, there was no violence. At some places in the black districts, guns were fired and the white supremacy people surrounded the polls in great numbers. They were directed to be there early and late. In the places where the Negro vote was large, the impression prevailed among the Negroes that it was not safe for them to make any show of resistance. Many of them did not go to the polls to vote. Some of the quiet ones told their neighbors that Russell and his crew had betrayed the Negroes and it wasn't worth risking their lives to keep in a crew that was ashamed of them and would not stand up for them. On the night before election day all the saloons were closed at seven o'clock and were compelled to remain closed until five o'clock on the morning after the election.

The election resulted in a sweeping Democratic victory. Two-thirds of the Legislature was Democratic and there was a twenty-five-thousand majority for the ticket. With great enthusiasm old-time celebrations were carried on all over North Carolina. As an aftermath of the celebration and the only place where there was violence, Wilmington, had a day of blood. The white supremacy people determined to expel Manley from the city, and to set fire to his building and burn it as a lasting evidence that no vestige of the Negro who had defamed white women of the State should be left. His building was gutted and burned but Manley escaped. How the eleven Negroes were killed, how three whites were wounded, and how the riot began, there was never any well authenticated evidence. The white supremacy people declared that the Negroes precipitated the riot by firing on the white men. If that is the true statement, they did not fire until four hundred armed white men led by Colonel Waddell marched to the *Record* office to destroy it. Some of the papers said it caught fire in an unaccountable way, evidently meaning that nobody knew who applied the torch. The probabilities are that many applied the torch. In fact, it was an armed revolution of white men of Wilmington to teach what they believed was a needed lesson, that no such defamer as Manley should live in the city and no such paper should be published. *The News and Observer* said, referring to the revolution and conduct of the Wilmington white people, "If any reader is inclined to condemn the people of Wilmington for resolving to expel Manley from the city, let him reread the libel upon the white women of the state that appeared in the *Daily Record*." Six companies of militia were ordered to Wilmington at the request of Lieutenant Colonel Walker Taylor. After the burning of Manley's building, the board of aldermen resigned and the city came under the control of a white supremacy government with Alfred Moore Waddell as Mayor. As soon as he emerged from the position of private citizen to public official, Colonel Waddell's fiery spirit changed and he became the protector of peace and order. He put guards around the jails to protect Negro prisoners and declared that no more violence should be tolerated. It was the end of violence and the end of trouble. The result of the election was accepted. The politically-minded Negroes either returned to their work or left the city, and the quiet, industrious Negroes who had all along been made the tools of white and colored leaders, rejoiced that the end had come. Colonel Waddell even went so far as to warn unruly whites that no disorder would be tolerated.

On November 11, almost immediately after the election, the Wilmington people determined to be rid of the men who had conducted a government bordering on anarchy. They—the Cape Fear Vigilantes, though they did not give themselves that name—gave notice, after eleven Negroes had been killed and nine Negroes and white men wounded, that the men who had been responsible for the bad government and race troubles should leave the city. Among these was G. Z. (Gizzard) French, white carpet-bagger, who had been State Senator, the author of the law that put the Wilmington government under the rule of the Negroes and their allies. He and the others were escorted to the train by a squad of white militia with fixed bayonets. It was believed that French went to Washington. Before he reached the station a rope was thrown over his head and several strong men were hanging him to a beam, when influential citizens, led by Frank H. Stedman, a white supremacy leader, interfered and saved his life. Carter Beaman, colored, went to South Carolina; Tom Miller, Pickens Bell, Aaron Bryant, and Rev. I. J. Bell were put on the train and told never to return. This was done by soldiers. They also ran out of town Trial Justice R. H. Bunting, ex-Chief of Police John R. Melton, Charles McAllister, Isaac Loftin, colored, and an ex-policeman. These men went to New Bern but were not allowed to remain there and had to move on. Bunting was said to have lived with a Negro woman for many years. His paramour and several other Negro women who had been talking too much were ordered to leave town. Loftin and McAllister had sold fire arms to the Negroes. R. B. Reardon and W. E. Henderson, Negroes, fled before being run out of town. Some of them who were driven out of Wilmington located at Richmond and the Richmond authorities notified them that they were not wanted. The only way they could get into another town was to change their names. Manley was said to have gone to New Bern but could not be found there. He seemed to have disappeared off the face of the earth, but later the Washington *Star* published an interview with a man claiming to be Manley, who denounced the Wilmington people and the people of North Carolina in vigorous terms. It probably was Manley. It was later printed that Manley intended to establish his *Record* in New York. In December William L. Jeffries, associate editor of the *Record,* made application for a place in the Hall of Infamy by claiming that he wrote the famous editorial about the white women of the State and that Manley did not write it. There were many aftermaths, among them the Negroes denounced John C. Dancy, a Negro collector of the customs at Wilmington, because he had denounced the extreme conduct of members of his race. Parson Leak of Raleigh advised the Negroes to stay out of politics and to ally themselves with good white people. He declared himself in favor of the disfranchisement of all illiterate Negroes and favored the Jim Crow car law. He blamed Russell for the Wilmington trouble and the other ills which had brought on race bitterness.

As a result of the white supremacy feeling, the corporation commissioners were asked to issue an order compelling railroads to have separate cars for whites and Negroes. This brought protests from all the railroads. They said it would impose a heavy burden on them and there was no need of compelling them to carry additional cars. The Railroad Commission refused to order Jim Crow cars. Agitation was begun to compel the Legislature to do so, and when it met it did order separate cars for the races and required the commission to see that equal service was afforded to whites and Negroes on the trains.

As soon as it was clear that the Democrats had won, there were many suggestions that some public position should be given to me because of the service rendered during the campaign. In reply to these suggestions in the press, some editors suggesting one position and some another, I printed a statement in *The News and Observer* saying that the editor of *The News and Observer* would not be a candidate for any position in the gift of a Party and added:

"The editor of *The News and Observer* has never had but one ambition, and that is to publish a strong and useful, influential newspaper free to condemn the wrong and uphold the right. The only public positions he has held in the past were accepted at times when the income was necessary to pay the expenses of his newspaper and the pay received therefrom was devoted to that purpose. He congratulates himself that the income from *The News and Observer* is now sufficient to make office-holding, distasteful to him under any circumstances, not necessary."

Following the white supremacy victory, there were celebrations all over the State, but the big State celebration was staged in Raleigh. A meeting was held there to arrange for the celebration, at which I presided; and at that meeting the motion was made to thank *The News and Observer* for its leadership in the fight. I said that this ought to include all Democratic papers, but the meeting unanimously overruled the chair and the motion was unanimously adopted, with a shout of approval after Norman Jennett, the clever cartoonist, had been included. Some of the older people deprecated the holding of a big celebration, fearing it might result in trouble, but *The News and Observer* took the ground that the celebration ought to be held and that it meant no harm to the Negroes; that the Democrats were their friends and not enemies; and that the speeches made and the whole celebration would serve to bring about a kindly feeling between the races. However, there was much apprehension lest the conservative people could not keep the celebration in hand. Shouting Democrats came from all parts of the State, a few of them wearing red shirts, and they were welcomed at *The News and Observer* office. Its building was illuminated and decorated with brooms, emblematic of the sweeping victory, and with a rooster in electric lights. I presided at the meeting and speeches were made by distinguished men. The speaking was held in Nash Square, and by arrangement certain speakers were to address the marching crowd at various points as they passed in the procession. One of the most humorous incidents occurred when Judge Francis D. Winston, organizer of the white supremacy clubs, arose to speak at the Capitol Square on Fayetteville Street. The marchers did not even stop but walked on by. The great crowd assembled was more interested in seeing the marchers than in hearing the speaking. After a few sentences, seeing that everybody was marching by and shouting and not listening to him, Winston made his speech in pantomime. As the crowd marched, for fifteen minutes without saying a word Winston made gestures. Of course, the crowd beyond his voice thought he was speaking, but those near, seeing it was a pantomime and not an address, grew hilarious. It was the funniest incident of the celebration.

Only one incident, already mentioned, indicated anything out of the way that night. During the speaking, quite a company of young men marched to the Blind Institution. They took with them a skilled stone mason and cut off the name of Jim Young, Negro leader, from the cornerstone of the institution. During the campaign his activities on this board had been denounced and speakers had declared in the heat of the campaign that when the Democrats came into power the last vestige of Negro direction of white institutions should be ended, and that they would erase the name of Young from the cornerstone of the Blind Institution. Outside of that act, nothing was done at the celebration that indicated bitterness.

A day or two after the election, the Negro State Fair was held in Raleigh. The Negro manager had invited Governor Russell to open the fair, but he declined the invitation. On the morning of the opening of the fair, its president, Parson Leak, Methodist preacher who had been a Republican leader in 1894 and 1896, but who had broken with Jim Young and the other Negro leaders in 1898, came by and asked me to make the speech opening the fair. I told the parson that in view of my activity in the white supremacy campaign, I felt that the Negroes might not relish my addressing them. "On the contrary," he said, "this old rascal who is up in the Governor's mansion, who has gotten everything he has had from Negroes, has been ungrateful. They have no respect for him. They know that at heart you are their friend and they need somebody who was a leader of the white supremacy campaign to give them assurance of friendship and protection. You are the very man they want." And so I went out and opened the Negro Fair. The Negroes had assembled in great numbers. I tried to voice to them the genuine friendship which the leaders of white supremacy felt for them and pointed out that it was a campaign not directed at the law-abiding and industrious Negro but at the Negro slave-drivers of which Russell was the head, and assured them that the day of election for them was really a day of emancipation from corrupt party leaders; that Lincoln's emancipation proclamation had struck from their hands the shackles of physical slavery and the defeat of Russellism had struck from them the shackles of political slavery to an office-holding crowd who were ready to use them for their own enrichment. The Negro leaders followed—Professor Bruce, of Shaw University, and John C. Dancy, collector of the customs at Wilmington, and other wise Negroes—and counselled peace and acceptance of the situation, so that within a few days the State was as quiet as if there had never been a heated campaign.

The big question that now loomed was the best plan of withdrawing from the ignorant Negroes, who had been used as tools for the bad government that cursed the State, the right of suffrage. Booker Washington made a statement in which he urged the Negroes to think more of work and saving and efficiency than of voting, and other Negro leaders spoke along the same line. There was a strong sentiment in favor of holding a constitutional convention, but when the election returns were tabulated and it was ascertained that, after the putting forth of militant efforts, the Democratic majority was only 17,938, the feeling grew that it would be wiser not to risk the opposition that a general reform of the constitution would invite. Therefore I took ground against a constitutional convention at that time and favored submitting a suffrage amendment, leaving the matter of further amendments to the constitution for a time when the Democratic Party would be more safely entrenched in power. There were differences of opinion as to the sort of amendment that should be adopted in North Carolina. There were advocates of the South Carolina plan, the Mississippi plan, and the Louisiana plan.

XXVII

IN THE WAKE OF THE WHITE SUPREMACY VICTORY

T HERE WAS quite a contest in the Legislature of 1899 over the speakership. There were three candidates, men who were afterward to hold commanding positions in North Carolina, H. G. Connor, of Wilson, Lee S. Overman, of Rowan, and Locke Craig, of Buncombe. The vote of the Western Democrats was divided between Craig and Overman, the latter getting 26 and Craig 14. Connor, the only Eastern candidate, received 46. Overman, when Vance's private secretary, lived in Raleigh. He married in Raleigh, the daughter of Chief Justice Merrimon. Armistead Jones, chairman of the Wake County Democratic Committee, assured Overman he would get the Wake County support, on which he was counting. But all the Wake County members voted for Connor, and Overman did me the honor of attributing their so voting to me. He gave me too much credit, though I had done everything I could to bring that result about.

The Democratic harmony which had welded all the varying elements of the Party into one common force during the white supremacy campaign was doomed to a temporary break in the early days of General Assembly of 1899. For thirty days the question of what to do with the Wilsons, Major Jim and S. Otho, who had been removed by Governor Russell, caused a bitter conflict. It could not be settled on its merits. Russell's statement in his message as to why they had been removed and why they ought to have been removed had no effect. It was as if a woman of easy virtue was preaching continence. People felt that Russell had started as a crusader against corporate domination and had sold himself for a mess of pottage. Therefore his advocacy of any cause injured it and his opposition made friends for it. A special committee was appointed to investigate the removal of the Wilsons. After the evidence was taken, Chairman Frank I. Osborne held that there had been an agreement between Major Wilson and the Southern Railway to make Round Knob Hotel, which he owned, an eating house, and it was accepted without question that, having made this agreement with the Southern Railroad, Major

313

Wilson entered into an agreement with S. Otho Wilson, his co-commissioner, that the eating house should be leased to Otho's mother at a nominal rent and that the Southern Railway would transport her freight and baggage and employees to and from Round Knob Hotel without cost to her. Those who had approved the removal of the Wilsons held that this was a corrupt arrangement and that both Wilsons should have been removed. They had all the facts and they had everything but the influence and the votes. If the men had been removed by a Governor who had the confidence of the people and if the political feeling had not been so strong, they would never have been reinstated. However, many Democrats came to Raleigh determined to undo everything Russell had done, and for them the fact that Russell had removed the Wilsons was reason enough that they ought to be reinstated. "Down with Russellism and everything that Russell did," was the cry. Politically, most of the Democratic leaders took this position. Moreover, a contributing reason that operated in Major Wilson's favor was the fact that Major Wilson was the son of Alexander Wilson, one of the most distinguished early teachers in North Carolina. Another was that he had been chief engineer in the construction of the Western North Carolina Railroad and was credited with a great feat of engineering in carrying the railroad over the mountains around Round Knob. Also, he had been an influential Democrat since the Civil War. He never made a speech and was not in the public eye, but in everything relating to the construction of the Western North Carolina Railroad, which was the dominating desire of Western North Carolina, he had been prominent. He had long been a Democratic leader. In fact, from 1868, three men in Burke County might have been called the Democratic triumvirate of Western North Carolina, or certainly a large part of it. People in that section who didn't like them, used to call them "the Burke Triumvirate," referring to their control of the Democratic politics of the West. They were three remarkable men and as long as they pulled together they got everything they wanted for themselves or for their friends. This triumvirate was composed of Alphonso C. Avery, Samuel McD. Tate, and James W. Wilson, all Democrats and Presbyterians. As young men, they went into the Confederate Army and all won titles. Avery's father had been a distinguished leader of the Democratic Party. The fact that his middle name was Calhoun told the story of how the Averys at Charleston and Baltimore had been leaders in the move-

Upper left, George H. White, of New Bern. North Carolina Negro Congressman from the Second District, 1897-1901. *Upper right,* James Hunter Young, Negro leader of Fusion Days, member of the Legislature from Wake County, and Colonel of colored troops in the Spanish-American War. *Lower left,* Reverend R. H. W. Leak, Methodist preacher and prominent Republican leader in Fusion days. *Lower right,* Henry P. Cheatham, Negro Congressman from the Second District, and later, to the end of his life, superintendent of the Negro Orphanage at Oxford, North Carolina.

Above, a cartoon by Jennett, in *The News and Observer* of August 14, 1898. *Below,* a cartoon by Jennett in *The News and Observer* of September 30, 1898. The checks in Governor Russell's coat contain Negro heads.

ment against Douglas, with the resultant split in the Democratic Party. Judge Avery's brother, Isaac Erwin Avery, had won immortal glory by his famous charge and glorious death at Appomattox. The whole family for almost a century had been prominent in public affairs. Later, the County of Avery was named for the family. Judge Avery became Superior and Supreme Court judge; Major Wilson, chief engineer of the Western North Carolina Railroad and Railroad Commissioner; Samuel McD. Tate, chairman of the board when the Western Hospital for the Insane at Morganton was constructed, and afterward State Treasurer. These offices were incidental. Little happened in North Carolina politics in which these three men did not have a hand.

The Round Knob Hotel had been built primarily as an eating house where travellers on trains to and from Asheville could stop for meals. It had been closed for some time. As told in an earlier chapter, Major Wilson wished to reopen it, and so he and Colonel Andrews planned that the trains should stop there if they could get a hotel proprietor to furnish good meals. From the time S. Otho Wilson went on the Commission, while he was denounced by all the Democrats, Major Wilson treated him with great consideration. He made up his mind to capture him. Learning that Otho's mother had kept boarders, he pretty soon came to terms, by which the mother of the Commissioner should lease the Round Knob Hotel. Major Wilson knew very well that the day Otho's mother entered his hotel Otho would go along with him. Otho thought he was very smart, but in comparison with the diplomacy of Major Jim he was a baby. When the big question came up in the commission as to the reducing of railroad rates, the two Wilsons voted together. It would be more nearly true to say that Major Wilson voted against reducing the rates and took Otho out of his pocket and registered his vote. The Round Knob Hotel lease had done the work.

Russell was then vigorously fighting railroad rule, and when he learned of the Round Knob Hotel scandal he removed the Wilsons from office. The Legislature would now render the final verdict. Major Wilson had enough friends and kinspeople to turn the scale. The committee, headed by his lifelong friend the Honorable Frank I. Osborne, former Attorney General, of Mecklenburg, brought in a report that the Wilsons had not done anything improper. It was adopted by a vote of 83 for the vindication of Major Wilson to 56 against it and 74 for vindication of S. Otho Wilson and 58 against. It is a rather remarkable fact that many of the legislators were so disturbed in their mind as to their position that seven senators and twenty-five representatives were absent when the vote was taken. Most of them felt that the Wilsons were guilty but did not wish to register a verdict on the side of Russell. The sentiment in the State was that they were both guilty, certainly of questionable conduct.

I knew from the moment the committee was appointed what Osborne would do. He was the most brilliant lawyer of the day, the most plausible and seemingly the fairest, never bitter, always free from invective, stating the side of his opponent with such fairness, or apparent fairness, as to disarm any suggestion of partisanship, and yet I knew, and everybody in the Legislature believed, that when the report was made Frank Osborne would stand by the Wilsons and that he would find a way to do it that would be so plausible and expressed in such terms that it would take a Philadelphia lawyer to pick a flaw in it.

In the debate over the report of the special committee, which did not terminate until three o'clock on the morning of March 2, it was interesting to hear the speech of Senator R. B. Glenn, afterward Governor. He had not indicated how he would vote. He had talked to everybody about it, expressed his great trouble, and indicated that he was giving it conscientious consideration. I knew all the time he would vote for the Wilsons even when he seemed to talk as if he could not do it. He said he wanted to vote for Major Wilson but wanted to kick the scoundrel Otho out. I knew that he had too long been the attorney of the Southern Railway to kick clean out of the traces, and yet it hurt his conscience. He had all the pains and agonies of childbirth and was a most miserable man for the two weeks before he had to vote, but when the time came to act he made a "gully-washer" speech. The chief burden of it was his picture of old Major Wilson, who in youth had donned the gray uniform and responded to the call of the State and jeopardized his life in a cause in which his own father had fought. The crowded lobbies cried as he pictured Wilson's Confederate valor. He then drew a picture of Western North Carolina shut off from the world, that great people with no outlet, the engineers of all Christendom unable to pierce the mountains, when Wilson, the young Confederate soldier, taking up the battle of peace and with a splendid vision, constructed the greatest piece of engineering in all the tide of time, for which he received no compensation except sufficient to support his large family in a most humble way. Glenn then came to the incident which he did not defend, but saw nothing immoral about it; Major Wilson thought that he was really doing a good thing and that, while Otho was a vile creature, Major Jim had been influenced only in trying to help Otho's poor mother, who wanted a boarding house where she could make her bread. It was a speech long to be remembered, delivered with energy and power of the perfervid kind. I had talked much with Glenn about the case; he had unbosomed himself to me as being in great doubt, until he began his speech. He told of his mental and moral troubles in reaching a conclusion, said it was a sort of Gethsemane to him, but that he "never could vote to condone any act of that arch traitor to North Carolina, Daniel L. Russell."

The News and Observer every day printed argument upon argument why the Wilsons should not be reinstated. It asserted that the whole defense depended upon technicalities. When it was all over everybody felt relieved. It had brought to Raleigh hundreds of people, and the temperature around the Yarborough House was sometimes so high that it would have broken any thermometer.

After the vote on reinstatement, Otho Wilson resigned. The tender of his resignation, which was widely known before the vote was taken, insured the verdict in his favor. Every legislator who voted to reinstate Otho Wilson did so with the knowledge that he would not resume service on the commission. Major Wilson's term was to expire in about a month. Those who voted for reinstatement did so with the knowledge that his days on the commission were numbered. The Wilsons received six thousand dollars for back salary, and the very next day the Legislature abolished the Railroad Commission and set up the Corporation Commission with three new commissioners: Franklin McNeil, an able lawyer who had been solicitor of his district, of proven ability and high character; S. L. Rogers, a business man who had been clerk of the court in Macon County and who afterwards was appointed by President Wilson as Director of the Census; E. C. Beddingfield, who had been one of the first railroad commissioners and had gone out when the Fusionists came into power. He had been secretary of the State Farmers' Alliance and had served from Wake in the House and Senate. Of course, to save his face, Otho Wilson made a proclamation that he was still a commissioner, but he passed out of the picture. No flowers. No tears.

At the end of the 1899 Legislature, the *Progressive Farmer* said:

"Thus the people's money is being divided out to pay political rewards. There is no help for it now. But the tax-payers of North Carolina will speak in thunder tones at the polls when there is another election. No party, no man, has ever been able to run roughshod over the people of the State but a short time. 'There is retribution in history.'"

When it was suggested that Russell would call a special session of the Legislature, the *Progressive Farmer* said:

"Please don't, Governor Russell. We can endure famine, pestilence, drouth, war, but don't inflict any prolonged agony on the State, such as an extra session. If they don't do anything, let them go home."

FIGHT ON UNIVERSITY RENEWED

During the campaign of 1898 practically nothing had been said in public about the appropriations for the University and other State institutions of learning. Talk of white supremacy had swallowed everything else, but the opponents of enlargement of these institutions were not idle. In the campaigns of 1894 and 1896 some opponents of the University's growth determined to keep down appropriations and had believed they could win by helping the Fusionists. But when Major Guthrie, Governor Russell, and Marion Butler, in the famous contest, took grounds for enlarged appropriations for institutions of higher education, the University's opponents turned upon the Fusion leaders and sought to win, not by public discussion or denunciation, but by diplomacy. They sensed, perhaps earlier than the Democratic leaders, that the white supremacy campaign would win and attached themselves to it. Josiah William Bailey, editor of the *Biblical Recorder,* who held a position as member of the State Board of Agriculture under Russell and had lost influence by so doing, resigned his position and in the campaign came out in a vigorous denunciation of Fusionism and in favor of disfranchisement of the Negro, thus throwing his influence in favor of a victory for white supremacy. The Reverend John E. White, his classmate, joined Bailey. White was then Secretary of the Baptist State Convention, a position of commanding influence. He had always been a Democrat and had not been a party to helping Fusionists, although his father joined the Fusion Party while his brother was a militant leader of Democracy in

Franklin. In fact, if he had tried, he could not have been anything but a Democrat, for he was a nephew of one of the most ardent Democrats and best men North Carolina has produced, Sheriff Ellington, of Johnston County, who was not only an efficient officer but one of the most influential Democrats in the State.

Bailey, White, Dr. Kilgo, and others who had taken up the fight upon the death of Dr. Durham, decided they could win more by trading than by an open fight. When the white supremacy campaign, in the early stages, seemed critical and the leaders were doubtful of the result and were seeking to bring to their aid every possible influence, Bailey, White, and others held a conference with State Chairman Simmons and Governor Jarvis, one of the elder statesmen whose influence was very great. As a result of this secret conference, Jarvis and Simmons agreed that if the opponents of increased appropriations would throw their influence toward victory for white supremacy, they would guarantee that the Legislature to be chosen would make no increases in the appropriations for the University or other State institutions of learning. This agreement being secured, Bailey, White, and the others fought the Fusionists. Bailey's vigorous denunciation of Russell was widely used. It was heralded as a statement of a man who, seeking to serve the Agricultural Department of the State had accepted a position as member of the State Board of Agriculture under Russell, and had felt impelled to resign his position because of the rottenness of the Russell administration. This internal evidence of the corruption of Russellism helped to bury it. The Fusionists said Bailey had voted for McKinley in 1896, had sought the position under Russell, and had not resigned until he saw the ship was sinking. There were more than a few Democrats who severely criticized Bailey for lending aid to the enemies of the Democratic party. Nobody outside of Jarvis, Simmons, White, Bailey, and Kilgo heard of that agreement during the campaign. It was kept a profound secret. I never heard of it, nor suspected it.

Early in the session of the Legislature my close friend, Dr. Charles McIver, head of the State Normal School at Greensboro, which was doing a monumental work on almost shoestring appropriations, came to see me about its necessities. He showed that young women were knocking at the door for entrance; that many of the public school teachers were inefficient and the only hope for better teachers was to enlarge the facilities of the State normal schools. He expressed great surprise that I should have been a party to a secret political agreement in the campaign to deny any expansion of the University, the State College at Raleigh, and the Woman's College at Greensboro. I asked him what he meant, and then he disclosed to me evidence which permitted no doubt that Jarvis and Simmons, undertaking to speak for the Democratic Party, had promised Bailey and White during the campaign that appropriations for state educational institutions would not be increased.

"Do you believe, Charles," I asked, "that I could have been a party to any such arrangement?" He answered, "I could not have believed it except from what you have been saying in the paper. Every indication pointed to your being a party to it by opposing increased appropriations. We could explain your action only on the ground that you were so concerned in carrying the election that you had consented to the agreement because you thought it absolutely essential to win in November." I was as indignant at the secret agreement as he was and saw then how the policy of the paper had seemed to show I was a party to it. It left me in a very peculiar situation. I ceased advocating that policy and sought to find ways by which such an unholy agreement could be thwarted. It seemed to me that, while Senator Jarvis and Senator Simmons were undoubtedly actuated by fear and duress, that the party could not be bound by such a secret agreement. When the matter was talked of among members of the Assembly and it leaked out—in fact Bailey and White made no bones of saying to the legislators that there had been an agreement, of course saying it in confidence and not publicly—all of us who were in favor of strengthening the University and other State institutions sought means to prevent the carrying out of an agreement extorted in critical stages of the campaign. Only lack of funds prevented larger appropriations than were voted, but an increase was made and I supported even larger ones than were voted.

After McIver told me about the secret agreement and showed his indignation about it, I asked Governor Jarvis if he had been a party to it. He admitted that, in the stress of the campaign, when it looked as if success were in doubt, he had been approached by the opponents of State education and along with Simmons had said that, as white supremacy ought to be the supreme issue, he was opposed to any policy that could possibly stand in its way. He therefore had agreed with Bailey, Kilgo, and White to use his influence against increasing appropriations until a suffrage amendment was adopted. He didn't want to talk about something he had agreed to in a time of stress. In fact, he was ashamed of it, but he felt bound by it. I think at heart he was very happy when an increase was made and he would have been much happier if he could have been free to urge it. It was one of the incidents of the campaign which left a bad taste in the mouth. Jarvis and Simmons never said so, but they felt that they had been held up. They had been made to "stand and deliver." As to Simmons, he had never taken much interest in educational policies or appropriations. Politics was his passion, and educational problems had not received from him much consideration. Having been educated at Trinity College he always had a sense of loyalty to it. Therefore it was easier for him to make the agreement with the President of Trinity College and others than for Jarvis, who had been, although he never got full credit for it, the pioneer while in the executive office for universal education and had never failed to ring true for public education, high and low. He was later to be a leader in securing the establishment of the Eastern North Carolina Training School at Greenville and, as Chairman of the Board of Trustees, to establish it upon a sound basis. The fact is that in the later years of his life that school was his child. He saw every brick that went into it, made every contract, had much to do with the selection of its faculty, and fathered it in its early days, leaving it a legacy of love and service that will never be forgotten.

In his memoirs Simmons says that "in order to win the 1898 campaign I felt it necessary to make two promises which later became somewhat embarrassing," and added:

"I promised the various denominational colleges, which were then rather hostile to state institutions, that I would not increase the appropriations for the latter during the session of 1899. Through Jarvis I also promised the large corporations that their taxes would not be increased during the bi-ennium. Colonel Samuel A. Ashe explained those promises in his Democratic Hand Book of 1898, but after the Legislature had been in session a short time a railroad bill was introduced. The railway representatives complained to me and I went to the chairman of the committee which had the bill under consideration—a Baptist representative from Iredell County (John B. Holman, 'the watchdog of the treasury' as he was called)—and told him the promise must be kept. The matter was settled to the satisfaction of the railroads but the Baptist representative was angry. Later the executives of the State University and the Woman's College were aroused because of the promise relative to the appropriations for the state schools. This was especially true of McIver of the Woman's College. But I told him I had made the promise and must keep it. McIver was greatly irritated. He said: 'You have sold us out.' But the Baptist from Iredell was delighted. He exclaimed, 'By heavens, Simmons, hold them to the promise!' I was bitterly criticized for these promises but I felt then, and I now feel, that they were necessary. If we were to win, every controversy which tended to divide the Democratic vote had to be held in abeyance."

That trade was akin to secret treaties, which have never wrought good. I thought then, and think still, that the promise by Simmons and Jarvis was indefensible. They assumed the right of campaign managers to usurp secretly the powers of legislative bodies. The defense by Simmons does not justify the secret agreement. It convicted railroad executives and church leaders of taking advantage of politics to obtain ends the people would not grant after open discussion. How much money the railroads contributed to the campaign chest was not disclosed. There was then no law requiring publicity. Simmons and Jarvis thought the end justified the means, and many legislators felt bound by their promises, but most of them resented the position in which they had been placed.

When the hearings came before the committees on appropriations the argument for increase was made by Dr. Alderman, President of the University of North Carolina, and Dr. McIver, President of the North Carolina College for Women; and the argument against it was made by Dr. John E. White. None of them referred to the discreditable agreement. It was a battle royal. Alderman was easily the prince of public speakers. McIver was called "a steam engine in breeches" and was the most powerful and influential leader in public education and the foremost pioneer in the higher education for women and the training of women teachers. White was a very forceful and eloquent speaker but at a disadvantage because he could not publicly disclose the agreement. Its existence embarrassed him because his sense of propriety did not permit him to defend a secret agreement made during a campaign. I heard the debate with great interest and with great partisanship. White and I had been friends since his boyhood and in later years it was renewed and strengthened. I had heard him speak at Wake Forest when he graduated, as handsome a youth as ever stood upon platform, with eloquence, with athletic prowess, with powers of leadership hardly paralleled. In athletics he was the best baseball player of his day. His first pulpit service was in Wilson, where he was pastor of the Baptist Church. In the years which brought division, although we were as far apart as the poles, our friendly relations were never broken although sometimes they were strained. He loved the State profoundly although he was to live most of the time out of it. His ability and his attractiveness in the pulpit called him to Atlanta and other cities. At his best there was no preacher in the State who was his superior. I remember his coming back later to Raleigh and preaching a joint Thanksgiving Day service when the Teachers' Assembly was in session. That sermon stands out in my mind as one of the truly great pulpit utterances by North Carolinians of his day. At his invitation I delivered the commencement address at Anderson College when he was president of that institution. We talked of old days and contests and rejoiced that the old issues that divided us no longer existed. His early death was a sorrow to me and a great loss to the South.

An appropriation of $100,000 from the general fund was made to lengthen the public school session. This bill was introduced in the House by John B. Holman, of Iredell, and in the Senate by McIntyre, of Robeson. McIver and Alderman believed that its inception was largely inspired to prevent any increase in appropriations for their institutions. Hitherto the public schools had drawn all their incomes from taxes in the counties, from fines and forfeitures, and not directly from the State treasury, though in 1895, in my salutatory as editor of *The News and Observer,* I had declared that "the public schools should be supported by the State funds, divided between the poor and rich counties in proportion to the children of school age." McIver and Alderman pointed out that while they favored $100,000 and a million dollars and all that could be had for public schools, this was so small a sum that it would only add a few hours to the public schools and might deny the opportunity of training teachers for public schools by withdrawing the $100,000 for the necessary training. Therefore most advocates, who used it as a means to hurt the State institutions, sought to convince the legislators that McIver and Alderman were more interested in their own institutions than in the poor children in the State. There was much bitterness in the controversy. I sensed danger that in the public mind McIver and Alderman would be put in the attitude of opposing larger appropriations for public schools, whereas they had done more and were ready to go further than any advocate of this particular appropriation, or any dozen men in the history of the State. I took strong ground in favor of the $100,000 appropriation as superior to everything else and called upon the educators and legislators to appropriate it and then to give quite as large a sum to the University and other institutions. And this was the policy that prevailed. When the bill passed Dr. McIver gave an interview warmly approving it and predicted that in a few years that sum would be increased to $500,000. That was a day of comparatively small things. It was not a great many years before that $100,-000 was increased to more than three million, and later the policy of State support advocated in 1895 by *The News and Observer* was adopted, though most of the rich counties fought it.

THE SUFFRAGE AMENDMENT

The big duty of the Legislature of 1899 was to garner the fruits of the white supremacy victory. After the November election I had printed interviews showing how South Carolina, Mississippi, and Louisiana had achieved that result. These interviews, together with the constitutional amendments and laws of those States were all printed, or the substance of them, in *The News and Observer,* and when the Legislature met, its members had all the data from these three States. A special joint committee composed of the ablest lawyers in both houses was named to frame a suffrage amendment. The chairman of the committee was George Rountree, of Wilmington, a lawyer of marked ability.

Day by day and night by night this committee wrestled with the problem. At first there were two points of view. There was an element advocating the Mississippi plan. That law put it into the hands of the poll holders in each precinct to determine the eligibility of a voter. No man could vote in Mississippi unless he could read the constitution or make an intelligent interpretation thereof. That made it possible for the judges of election in any precinct to say, without appeal, whether a Negro voter possessed those qualifications. That was the simplest way of insuring Democratic success. But leaders who had seen the evils of suppressing the Negro vote by local election officials often not guided by justice, wished to base the suffrage upon a principle and not upon the whim or decision of election officials. Some who wished the Louisiana Grandfather Clause plan desired to insert a provision enabling a person to vote if he owned a certain amount of property. An argument in favor of the Louisiana method, which I had printed in *The News and Observer* and which had great weight, was that shortly before his death President Lincoln had approved a new constitution for Louisiana which admitted the newly enfranchised Negroes to suffrage only when they should demonstrate their capacity either by education or ownership of land or other property, without changing the provisions of laws as to white voters. I urged that if we followed the plan that Lincoln approved it would have weight if the amendment was tested in the courts.

A large portion of the time of the committee was taken up considering whether the Grandfather Clause was constitutional. Many feared that it would be set aside, and there was serious doubt along this line. Senator Caffrey had told me in Washington that Louisiana legislators believed it essential to fix a near date in the constitution for registration under the Grandfather Clause so as to make it certain that white voters, as well as Negroes coming of age later, should stand upon the same terms. He thought it ought not to be left open longer than a year. As the consensus of opinion was in favor of the Louisiana amendment, the question then rose as to what date should be fixed, beyond which a white man could go on the permanent registration and so insure his perpetual right to vote. The members from the West, led by Senator Mike Justice, of Rutherford, and Representative Ray, of Franklin, and others, were apprehensive that one part of the amendment might be declared constitutional and another part unconstitutional, whereby the uneducated whites might lose their suffrage along with the uneducated Negroes. This was the crux of the matter. It was well understood that to submit an amendment to the people which, by any possibility, would disfranchise old white men, could not receive a majority of the votes.

While discussion was going on, Judge George H. Brown and some others urged that no amendment be submitted to the people but that a constitutional convention be called clothed with power to enact a constitution which should go into effect without submission to the people. They feared that any debate upon a suffrage amendment might arouse such suspicion among the uneducated white voters as to doom it to defeat, whereas if it was enacted and put in operation it would soon be seen that it would disfranchise no white men. That proposition received little favor. I favored submission of the suffrage amendment without any other amendment to the constitution. This position was in line with Speaker Connor, Chairman Rountree, Senator Simmons, Judge W. R. Allen, Locke Craig, Charles B. Aycock, and other leaders of the party.

When this constitutional amendment is read, it is seen to be so simple that it is hard to realize a month was consumed in day-and-night sessions before it could be perfected and unanimously reported. In the end there was a dormant fear of the constitutionality of the Grandfather Clause. It was realized that there was no other way, unless the determination to submit the most honest suffrage measure was abandoned. Every Republican in the Legislature voted against its submission. The Populists divided, and the vote of the Populists on this question forecast their future political alignment. It was a clear-cut issue between those who wanted to remove the great bulk of ignorant Negroes from the exercise of suffrage and those who wanted to continue them. Pritchard and Butler saw, in the elimination of the ignorant Negro vote, their undoing. They were ready to go to any length to defeat any plan that denied the ballot to every Negro, even the most ignorant. *The News and Observer* called it "a history-making day when the House, on February 18th, passed the suffrage amendment by over a three-fifths majority," and praised "the great speeches of Rountree and Winston." The crowded galleries applauded and there was a feeling that deliverance had at last come. The next day the bill was taken up in the Senate and passed by a vote of 42 to 6, Senators Fields, Glenn, and Travis making the leading speeches in favor of it. "The people will speak next," said *The News and Observer.*

The next business was passing an election law, and here there came a sharp clash. One day Judge Connor, Speaker of the House, sent for me and said he was in great trouble; that the Legislature was about to do a thing that would have the effect of making nugatory all the attempts to have an honest amendment and honest election; that a number of the members of the Legislature, and some politicians outside, were insisting upon a sort of election law that would still leave the question of whether elections were honest in the hands of local poll-holders. They had proposed sections of a bill that were utterly inconsistent with the guarantee of the constitution. Judge Connor was very indignant and wanted me to join hands with him and others to see that the election law was in line with the spirit of the amendment. The law was an improvement, but not as perfect as Connor and I had tried to secure.

OUTLAWING THE TRUSTS

Next to the suffrage and education and political measures that commanded the attention of the Legislature, the matter of outlawing the trusts came up. Representative Stevens, of Union County, introduced a bill with teeth. It was earnestly supported by *The News and Observer,* which was joined by the Charlotte *Observer,* then edited by Joseph P. Caldwell, who said, "It has been suggested that the Stevens Bill is immoral in that it provides that no trust can collect a bill by law. . . . This is the bill's best feature. Desperate diseases call for desperate remedies. Trusts are, morally speaking, outside the pale of civilization. A law which will, in any degree, check their aggression, is its strength." Stevens, who had introduced the bill, was a rare sort of man, one of the best legislators of his day. He had a fine humor and a rare ability. He was a pioneer Progressive, with a capital P.

Trusts were then strong in North Carolina. They began the usual process of mining and sapping any bill having teeth. By the time the Senate got through with his bill Stevens could hardly recognize it. In 1899, as in other years, the opponents did not come out in the open but declared they "wished to perfect the bill, that it had some crude points." When they got through perfecting it they had taken out most of the teeth, so that when it was enacted and Senator Glenn, of Forsyth, had said it was a very good law, *The News and Observer* said it hoped he was right, but it feared that the amendments had well-nigh emasculated it, which turned out to be the exact truth.

When the anti-trust bill was up in the Legislature, it was stated and printed that Moses H. Cone, head of the Cone Export and Commission Company and of a corporation owning large cotton mills, had threatened to leave the State if the Legislature passed an anti-trust law, and had also denounced the proposition to establish a dispensary in Greensboro. *The News and Observer* commented upon the alleged threat to leave the State and said North Carolina welcomed capital and business men and everybody, but it didn't want any citizens who wished any special privilege or who wished immunity from the laws of supply and demand and competition. This brought from Mr. Cone a very interesting and delightful interview in which he disclaimed that he had ever made any threats of leaving the State. He said he opposed the dispensary in principle; he did not believe the anti-trust laws were needed.—As a matter of fact, he said, "I am a low tariff Democrat in spite of the fact that I am a manufacturer."

Mr. Cone was the same man who, in 1896, had been leading the business men in opposing the free coinage of silver, and at a meeting of the Editorial Association in Greensboro he had been one of the speakers. *The News and Observer* then was regarded as a leading Bryan and silver paper and the Charlotte *Observer,* edited by J. P. Caldwell, was the spokesman of the opposition to Bryan and silver. At that meeting Mr. Cone offered to pay the expenses of the trip if Mr. Caldwell and I would go to Mexico and make a study of the conditions in that country where the silver dollar was freely coined, and come back and tell the difference between the civilization and prosperity of Mexico under the silver standard and the United States under the gold standard. His proposition was received with interest by the editors, and he insisted that he was in perfect seriousness and wanted us to go. There were reasons enough why I couldn't go to Mexico as I had to stay at home and run the paper, and the same reasons kept Caldwell at home; but I told Mr. Cone that if the policies were changed and the United States had the silver and Mexico the gold, you could not compare the prosperity of two countries, or test it by their measurement of value as to primary money; that the kind of money each nation used, had very little to do with its progress and prosperity; that Mexico had been feudalistic while the United States had been democratic; and that Mexico's natural resources had been obtained by foreigners, and that its people did not even own the silver mines that furnished its circulating medium.

Mr. Cone fathered one of the largest textile plants in the State at Greensboro. He and his brothers began as selling agents for other mills and then became prosperous manufacturers. He established a magnificent country place near Blowing Rock and by the object lesson of his large orchard encouraged apple growing in Watauga and adjacent counties. He planned that his mountain estate would one day become a State Park. When he faced death he picked out as the spot for his burial the highest mountain peak on his large and beautiful acres. Like a greater Moses of his race, his body lies on another "Nebo's lonely mountain." He combined vision and love of the beautiful in nature with a genius for making money.

About the time the anti-trust bill was under consideration, the ladies of Raleigh were holding a Confederate bazaar, and business houses were making contributions. The cigarette trust sent three thousand cigarettes as a donation. The ladies to whom they were sent politely declined the gift, stating that under no circumstances could they be parties to the sale of cigarettes. This indicated the sentiment of 1899 on the part of the women, and many men, as to cigarettes. If anyone had indicated, in that year, that any North Carolina lady would ever smoke what was popularly called "coffin nails," it would have been regarded as slander of the good women of the State.

OTHER DOINGS OF THE 1899 LEGISLATURE

One of the incidents of the Legislature, which came as an aftermath of the white supremacy campaign, was that the Republican caucus expelled from its membership Isaac H. Smith, the Negro Republican elected from Craven County because of his alleged friendly words and acts approving Democratic policies as against Republican policies; and later, for the same reason, he was expelled from his church in New Bern and made a pariah of his race and party. During the campaign *The News and Observer* had printed a picture of Isaac. He was about the blackest man that ever came to the Legislature. He made a good deal of money in operating a bank in New Bern, where he loaned out money to his race at a rate of interest in keeping with loan sharks of all races. Isaac made a vigorous reply to the expulsion and declared that he refused to be muzzled; that he stood foursquare for decency in government. He closed his speech in the House by begging his white friends not to charge to the Negroes the mistakes and misrule of Governor Russell.

One of the most interesting and hard-fought battles in the Legislature was the creating of a new county, Scotland, by dividing Richmond County and making Laurinburg the county seat of the new county. The people of Richmond County were up in arms against it and Raleigh was crowded with people from both ends of the county, the lower section fighting for it as if it were a matter of life and death and the Rockingham people declaring that, if that rich part of the county was lost, Richmond County could not carry on. The victory for the new county was largely a matter of personality. Hector McLean, a "God-Blessed Mac," had been in the Legislature several times from Laurinburg and was one of the smartest Scotsmen and one of the best that ever came out of old Scotia. From the day he first entered the Legislature until Scotland County was created, he never had any thought about any bill except as to its effect on Scotland County. He made friends with everybody, and members just could not vote against Hector. He was not a lawyer and not a public speaker, but when he spoke about Scotland County it was as though he were pleading for the life of his baby. He made a personal matter of it, making friends with every newspaper reporter, every legislator, and everybody who came to Raleigh, until one of the big issues was, "Are you for Hector or agin Hector?" Of course he had the help of Judge Neal, Professor Quackenbush, M. L. John, A. L. James, and other leaders who were past masters in getting things done.

Previously the Legislature had passed a law repealing the Fellow Servant Act. It was shortly followed by another for the protection of humanity, sponsored by Chief Justice Walter Clark. Railroad accidents were frequent and attempts to compel the railroads to use safety appliances had failed. When a case of alleged negligence came to the Supreme Court, when a railroad employee had been killed, the Court held that it was negligence *per se* not to equip cars with automatic couplers. As I look back upon it, it seems singular that the railroad managers and other owners of industrial plants nearly always had to be compelled, by law or Supreme Court decisions, to protect the lives of their employees.

Excitement flamed up in that Legislature when one morning the Republican representative from Davie introduced a resolution to impeach Judge George H. Brown because, as he alleged, at a reception and dance given at the Capital Club, Judge Brown was intoxicated. It created quite a sensation. There were plenty of people who had been at the Capital Club, where the strong punch flowed freely, and perhaps there were plenty of them who imbibed too freely including not a few members of the Legislature. These members were anxious that this resolution should be quashed for fear that it might be enlarged and take in all legislators and judges who had looked upon the wine when it was red. Judge Brown affected to make light of it, but it gave him concern. He was quite confident that he was sober but quite ready to admit that he had partaken moderately. His friends managed, after a few days, to induce the representative to withdraw the resolution so that many members of the Judiciary, Legislature, and Capital Club breathed easily. At that time investigators lacked the skill that was obtained later, when they seemed to have a corkscrew with a facility for dragging out the secrets public men wished to hide. This incident about Judge Brown was recalled afterwards when his will was contested in Beaufort Superior Court. His relatives sought to set aside his will on the grounds that he was mentally incompetent to make a will. The attorneys for his wife sought to show that he was not crazy but under the influence of drink. The jury decided it was mental inability rather than drink and on that ground set aside his will, in which he had undertaken to give all his property to his wife. He was one of the ablest lawyers of his generation, combining business acumen with legal lore. Everything he touched turned to money and his wise investments made him a rich man. He was never a drunkard and the attempt to prove him one failed.

The Jim Crow Car Law passed by the Legislature was bitterly fought by the railroads; and, as usual in those days, the active fighting was done by the officers of the Southern Railway, the active man on the scene being Henry Miller, later to become vice-president of the whole Southern Railway System, and a very able one. After the law went into effect there was a feeling that the Southern Railway was trying to enforce it in such a way as to make it so unpopular that its repeal could be secured. *The News and Observer* said, "The Southern bit off a big chaw when they set out to make the Jim Crow law unpopular." Henry Miller was quoted as saying to the Corporation Commission that he had sooner have a Negro sitting by him than a great many white people, and *The News and Observer* made this comment: "The people of North Carolina prefer to ride as they vote, as they go to church, and as they send their children to school." The paper praised the Seaboard Air Line, which, it said, had accepted the law and was carrying it out in its spirit, whereas the Southern was bucking the legislative mandate and trying to make the law unpopular. *The News and Observer* demanded that the letter and the spirit of the law be carried out and said it was not enacted to injure the Negroes but upon the same principle that separate schools were established for white and colored people. The paper called upon the Corporation Commission to compel the railroads to give equal service to both races. The attempt to secure a repeal of the law by making it unpopular failed, and later on *The News and Observer* was to take up the cudgel to compel the railroads to give the Negroes better service. After the law was seen to be permanent, most of the railroads were indifferent to giving clean cars and equal facilities to their Negro patrons. The truth is that there was a good deal of indifference to giving the patrons in day coaches, whether they were white or black, good service, and the Corporation Commission was derelict in its duty of compelling such service.

FIGHTING THE SUFFRAGE AMENDMENT

Hardly had the Legislature adjourned before the opponents of the suffrage amendment began their work of opposition. The *Progressive Farmer,* which had been the organ of the Populists, now edited by Ramsey, who had become so embittered with the Democrats that he was practically a full-fledged Republican, joined hands with Pritchard, Russell, and the rest in a fight against the amendment. Early in April Governor Russell, accompanied by J. C. L. Harris, Republican lawyer, went to Washington, and it was generally believed that they had gone to try to secure an injunction against the constitutional amendment. When they had returned, Colonel Harris denied that such was their mission. It was believed that they had received a cold shoulder and therefore did not wish to bear the odium of having attempted to secure Federal intervention. Major William A. Guthrie, who had played a large part in the white supremacy campaign, came out strongly for the amendment. In the summer I. M. Meekins, who was later Republican candidate for Governor and still later was appointed Federal Judge, stated that he favored it. A few Republicans took the same position, but soon the party organized into a solid phalanx and the Republicans and Fusion Populists undertook to array the people against the amendment and particularly to inflame the uneducated white voters. For a time they had some success because it was hard to make a white man who could not read and write understand that an amendment demanding educational qualifications could protect him and exclude the Negro. However, the Legislature had incorporated in the amendment a provision that if one part of it should fail, then it all failed. A campaign of education was put on by the Democrats.

During the whole summer and fall *The News and Observer* printed articles every week about the constitutional amendment submitted. The first of these was a long two-and-a-half column article by Charles B. Aycock, and then a symposium of several pages from men of prominence of every county in the State. Thomas Settle, who had been the most brilliant Republican campaigner in the State, came out in a statement saying he expected to support the suffrage amendment. Later on, I asked him why he had taken this position, since he was about the only prominent Republican who had done so. He had been defeated for Congress in the Fifth District by Governor Kitchin and was out of harmony with his party. He had run up against Pritchard and had won out. He said that, as long as the Negro voted, his party could have no chance in North Carolina, but, if the amendment was adopted, giving the registration of voters to the party in power, if ever his party got into power one time, they could register all the Negroes they pleased and could permanently control the State. Of course he did not say this publicly. Settle and I had received our law licenses at the same time. While the paper was always very severe upon him on political lines, we always talked freely, and after his defeat for Congress he was rather cynical and contemptuous of his own party.

The other brilliant Republican in North Carolina who had earlier in the year declared for the constitutional amendment, Isaac M. Meekins, was thus referred to when *The News and Observer,* on November 31, said: "Isaac Meekins, who suddenly lost his voice just before the election of 1898, has recovered sufficiently to write a stump speech in favor of Negro rule which is published in the Negro organ at Asheville."

Toward the end of the year the question of who should be the Democratic nominee for Senator to succeed Senator Pritchard, whose time was drawing to an end, began to be debated and discussed. *The News and Observer* said, "The Senatorial question should be eliminated. Do not talk about the senatorship until after the constitutional amendment is adopted." It printed a statement from General Carr saying he would not make any announcement of candidacy at the time. *The News and Observer* also said, noting that the senatorial

race would be between Jarvis, Waddell, Carr, and Simmons, that
a primary ought to settle it and that discussion ought to wait until
after the 1900 campaign. Simmons, the Democratic chairman, admitted senatorial ambitions but said, "There is now pending over
the people the question that overshadows who shall fill that office or
any other office and, until that question is settled, there shall be no
dividing or detracting scramble over this office." Governor Jarvis
said he expected to be a candidate and favored holding a senatorial
primary on the day of the presidential election in 1900. Colonel Waddell said he would be a candidate for the Senate if a primary was
ordered, but that such primary ought not to be held until after the
August election and he would not be a candidate if the choice was
to be made by the Legislature and the people were to have no choice
in a primary.

The Republicans had little to say early in the campaign about the
amendment, except in the matter of organizing. Marion Butler had
been rather silent because he had been studying law. In the early
fall he obtained his license to practice. He had graduated from the
University in 1885, had been a school teacher, then editor of the
Clinton *Caucasian.*

In October a Republican meeting at Statesville was addressed by
Senator Pritchard, who laid down the plan along which the Republicans and Fusion Populists were to wage their big fight the next year
against the amendment. The burden of Pritchard's speech was that
the amendment would disfranchise the illiterates of both races alike.
While he said nothing about wishing to keep the ballot in the hands
of ignorant Negroes, his whole speech was one of deep solicitude for
preserving the rights of the illiterate whites of the State. He was
always effective on the stump and by that time was the undisputed
leader of his party, both Republican and Fusion Populists.

Shortly after this speech at Statesville, Senator Pritchard introduced a resolution in the United States Senate declaring that the
pending constitutional amendment in North Carolina was unconstitutional. I do not suppose that Pritchard expected to secure favorable action on his resolution, and it was regarded in North Carolina
as laying the foundation for litigation when the amendment was
ratified, as well as intended for national consumption.

As far back as the day after election, in November, Judge Avery,
in an interview to *The News and Observer,* proposed, in view of the

danger of attempted Federal control of elections, that North Carolina ought to have, as before the Civil War, its State elections in August. In order to make assurance doubly sure that the Federal Government had no right to interfere, it was determined to hold the election of 1900 in August and that, at that election, the suffrage amendment should be voted on and all State officers elected.

The News and Observer, at the end of 1898, had reached high water mark in circulation and boasted that, in one week, its two representatives, W. M. Rogers, in the Western part of the state and H. B. Hardy, in the Eastern part, had brought in, respectively, one hundred and seventy and one hundred and forty-seven subscriptions. It pointed out that its circulation, in two months, had grown from fifty-one hundred to sixty-two hundred. It boasted, "the people *will* have the best."

At that time it began to work upon what it called the Twentieth Century Edition of *The News and Observer* and sent trained men all over the State to prepare an edition of the paper that would show North Carolina's great industrial progress, give in full the story of the legislation enacted, and print sketches of men who had led in the white supremacy fight. The motif of this edition, aside from trying to make some money, which was needed to pay for the new press, was the prophecy that, with the end of political revolution and with the certainty of the adoption of the suffrage amendment, with peace and stability in its borders, the future industrial progress of North Carolina was assured. The coöperation of the people in getting out this edition was all that could be desired, particularly in Wilmington, where the people appreciated the great help that *The News and Observer* had rendered them in securing freedom from the body of death in their city government. They told our representatives they would do anything *The News and Observer* wanted. All over the State industrial and political leaders coöperated in enabling *The News and Observer* to print that year a newspaper containing 228 pages, which was, by all odds, the biggest paper that had been printed in the State, and it was called the largest single issue that had been printed in the world up to that time. The financial returns were gratifying but the big thing about it is that it pointed the way to the future industrial progress, based upon political calm and freedom from bitterness which had troubled the State for years.

At the emancipation celebration held in Raleigh on January 1, 1900, Dr. James E. Shepard, prominent Negro of Durham, delivered the address at the meeting, making an appeal to vote against the suffrage amendment. The resolutions declared that the Negroes were fitted for citizenship and that they paid taxes of over $245,000,000 anually and had 2,750,000 children in school, 37,000 teachers, 400 newspapers, several banks, and some factories. That address to the white people would have found more favor if the experience of North Carolina people in 1894 and 1896 had not shown that, while there were many Negroes who were qualified for citizenship, the race, almost as a unit, had been really political slaves to Russell, Butler, and other Fusionists. There were, in 1896, to my knowledge, a number of Negroes of character who were disgusted with their political taskmasters but they did not dare to take a stand apart from the bulk of their race. There was never any greater slavery with reference to freedom of action in politics than subsisted in the nineties among Negroes. Now and then one would cry out and denounce Russell and the leading Fusionists, but when they did they sealed their doom with their race. A few Negroes like Parson Leak did so. Our colored nurse, Aunt Sophie, belonged to his church, and my wife told me that our young boys always hailed him as "Brother Leak," which pleased the nurse and the parson.

The temperate and well worded appeal of the Negroes in Raleigh on Emancipation Day for consideration and regard of their rights by the white people was undone by the bitter and vicious speeches of such men as Congressman George White, colored. Within a month after Dr. Shepard's speech of appeal and reasoning, White came to the front again and declared that only 15 per cent of the lynchings were caused by rape. He declared that, if there were not so many assaults by white men on black women there would not be so many other crimes. The Negro paper, published at Asheville, also added fuel to the flames by its attack upon *The News and Observer* in which it upheld White in his policy. In May, after Judge Spencer B. Adams had been nominated for Governor by the Republicans, *The News and Observer* quoted Judge Adams, who was reported to have said, in a charge to the grand jury in Columbus County in August, 1898, that "nine times out of ten, if you will chase down the fellows who are trying to stir up race prejudice, you will find that the most vigorous one is sleeping with a negro woman." In the same charge, he said, "Rape is a lesser offense than seduction, the only difference being that one is committed by force and the other by fraud."

A scholarly Negro in Raleigh in the nineties who made a reputation was Professor Edward Johnson, leading historian of his race, who was the author of *History of the Negro Race in America; History of Negro Soldiers in the Spanish-American War; Light Ahead for the Negro;* and *Negro Almanac and Statistics.* He was a lawyer, Dean of the Law School of Shaw University, an alderman in Raleigh, and delegate to Republican National Conventions, but he was not very active in the bitter campaigns of 1894-98, in which race feelings ran high. He was well regarded by members of both races. In 1907 he moved to New York to practise law and was elected as a Republican to the Assembly at Albany, from Harlem, the first Negro elected to the New York Legislature.

A LIFE INSURANCE PROJECT AND OTHER MATTERS

The News and Observer, on February 5, 1899, printed the following notice, which was required by law to secure a charter for a life insurance company:

"NOTICE

is hereby given that application will be made at the next session of the General Assembly of North Carolina to incorporate the Carolina Mutual Life Insurance Company.

(Signed) Josephus Daniels."

I had been studying the large amount of premiums sent out of North Carolina for life insurance. Whenever a North Carolina enterprise was to be financed it was necessary to go out of the State to obtain the money, whereas ample capital would be available if the bulk of its insurance premiums were kept at home. At that time the insurance companies had not adopted the policy of loaning money in North Carolina. Policy-holders and others could not borrow money in a large sum or practically any sum from insurance companies. Between the excitement of the campaign of 1898 and the almost equal excitement of the campaign of 1900, my thought was turned to the necessity of North Carolina's entering into the insurance field. I argued that money paid for premiums should be kept at home, thus building up great financial institutions in the State. I therefore decided to organize a strong life insurance company and, for a time,

considered myself the one to take the active management of it. But
upon reflection I knew that I could not seriously consider anything
except running a newspaper and that if the insurance company was
to succeed some trained insurance expert must take the laboring oar.
I brought the matter to the attention of prominent men in North
Carolina, including General Julian S. Carr, J. A. Long, of Roxboro,
E. B. Borden, of Goldsboro, and others who agreed to become incorporators and to take stock in the company. General Carr, at that
time regarded as the richest man in the State, was very enthusiastic
about it and was willing to be the president of the company, to render
every assistance, and lend his influence, which was then very great.
After a meeting of the incorporators it was decided to seek James H.
Southgate, of Durham, as head of the company. He had built up the
largest fire insurance business in the State. He gave the invitation
consideration, and at first he was inclined to accept. When he refused
—that was where he dropped his watermelon. He was the nearest big
man of all the insurance men in North Carolina. He had graduated
at the University, was an eloquent speaker, and was devoted to reading the best books. He was well versed on insurance, particularly fire
insurance, and if he had listened to us and had become head of a
North Carolina life insurance company, he would have succeeded in
quite as great a way as afterward the Jefferson and other life insurance
companies succeeded, although of course it would have taken longer
in those lean years. I suppose I talked to him a dozen times about it,
and finally General Carr and I took the matter up with him to decide
and he said: "I have given the matter serious consideration and I have
come to the conclusion that the insurance business of this country is
in the hands of the people in New York and in Hartford, Connecticut, and that we cannot compete against them and could not make a
success of a home life insurance company." He sincerely believed
that, and I think most men in the insurance world and in business entertained that view. It was the result of a natural condition, whereby
the South then had an inferiority complex as to matters of fiscal
operation.

Later on there was organized in Raleigh the Jefferson Standard
Life Insurance Company, in which I was one of the first stockholders
and which *The News and Observer* promoted in every possible way.
Three young men in Wilson, my old home, P. D. Gold and C. W.
Gold, sons of Elder P. D. Gold, and Dr. Albert Anderson, a leading

surgeon of that town, conceived the idea that a State life insurance company could be made successful. I coöperated with them from the beginning. It was not long before they were able to secure as much stock as they wished, and the company was organized and began business in Raleigh as the Jefferson Standard Life Insurance Company. From the first it won success. The Golds came to Raleigh as officers and Dr. Anderson as medical director, with men like Joseph G. Brown and Charles E. Johnson as officers; the directors embraced some of the first business men of the State. I declined to be a director in pursuance of a policy which I had made never to be a director of anything in which it was hoped that money could be made. In a few years the Jefferson Standard was consolidated with the Greensboro Life Insurance Company and its headquarters moved to Greensboro, where it became the biggest insurance company in the South.

A curious incident showed the temper of the times. When the Golds came to Raleigh as officers of this company they brought the first privately owned automobiles that were used in that city. To ride in an automobile in that period was regarded as doing something as daring as flying in the days before Wright and afterward Byrd and Lindbergh flew about the world. The people of Raleigh, as they saw these young officers of an insurance company dashing by in automobiles, said to themselves, "They are high-flyers. You'd better not put your money in an insurance company where the officers ride in automobiles." Hearing this sentiment expressed and holding similar sentiments himself, Colonel Charles E. Johnson, one of the first officers of the new company, advised both the Golds that, if they wished to build up a life insurance company in a conservative town like Raleigh they must sell their automobiles and walk. They took his advice. That feeling was not confined to Colonel Johnson. I remember, about that time, hearing Mr. Ashley Horne, successful business man and manufacturer of Johnston County, saying he would not deposit money in any bank if the president and cashier owned an automobile. He didn't much care about their owning an automobile but thought it indicated they might be inclined to a fast life and not be conservative in their expenditures. A few years later, when I was talking to Charles Gold about selling his automobile at the earnest solicitation of Mr. Johnson, he said, "I never could get over Colonel Johnson's insisting upon my selling my automobile because folks would not take out life insurance policies in the company of which

I was an officer because it showed extravagance, particularly when, a little later, he was riding about Raleigh in one and did not lose the deposits in his bank."

STORY OF A ONE-MAN BANK

The Raleigh Savings Bank was the first savings bank established in Raleigh and one of the first in the State. It was established chiefly under the leadership of Mayor Wynne to encourage saving. At that time, no bank in Raleigh and I think, indeed, in North Carolina, paid interest on deposits. The organizers of this savings bank were fortunate in securing as its president Mr. Wynne and as its cashier John T. Pullen. Here was a rare man. For many years he was the best beloved citizen in Raleigh. He had large family connections, was a nephew of Stanhope Pullen, the bachelor benefactor of Raleigh who gave the land for the State College, presented Pullen Park to the city, and at the time of his death was buying land for a boulevard all around the city. Like his uncle, Mr. Pullen was a bachelor. In early life he had been a little wild, but from the time that he had attended a revival and joined the Baptist Church, his chief business was evangelism, and his chief effort was spent in loving and caring for the poor and in winning the love of children. In the bank and out of it, he always had one pocket full of religious tracts and the other full of candy, which he distributed equally to anyone he met. The candy he gave to children, and to grown-ups, the tracts. He built a church in the southern part of the city and had upon it a great sign "Prepare to Meet Thy God." Before our marriage my wife taught a class in Mr. Pullen's Sunday School every Sunday afternoon. Religion to him was the real thing and he preached it. Best of all, he practiced it. He devoted more time to going into the homes of the very poor and the submerged and the wicked than to his bank. He never thought that his religion was helping the bank, but people had such confidence in him that widows and many others who had a few pennies they wished to save, would deposit their money in "John Pullen's bank." That was the name the bank went by, and no one remembered that it was called the Raleigh Savings Bank. It was not, except on the official stationery.

Mr. Pullen conducted the funerals of the poor, attended their little social meetings, which he always opened with prayer. He had a gaiety and humor all his own and a rare friendliness. He was married to those who needed comfort in the way of religious advice or money to buy the necessities of life. He spent most of his salary for tracts, candy, and aid to the poor. He did much to keep up the Old Ladies' Home, took supper there one night every week (sending oysters or some delicacy for the meal), and made it a point to visit the poor who were in Rex Hospital and to leave them some token. When his uncle died and left him quite a sum of money, he did not change his mode of living, spending no more money on himself, but gave more to people in need. When he died he left a considerable estate, some of which went to the Pullen Church and some to the Old Ladies' Home, and he made other gifts of the kind that had characterized him in life.

The bank grew to be an important institution. James Litchford, a capable and active business man, went into the bank with Mr. Pullen as assistant cashier. He demonstrated his ability as a banker. The stock was owned, at first, in small shares by nearly everybody in town. I remember, when it was established, Mr. Wynne came to see me and I took $50 of stock. Gradually people on the inside of the bank, seeing how valuable it was becoming, bought it up, and Mr. Litchford purchased a large quantity. He was ambitious to control it. Captain Thomas, President of the Commercial National Bank, and Mr. Pullen owned nearly half and Litchford also owned nearly half and there was a contest to see who would control the bank. Litchford was anxious to own the majority stock, and one day he came to see me and offered me $100 for my wife's $50, which seemed a large amount to offer. When I hesitated, he said he would give more than anyone else and wished me to promise him that I would give him the refusal of it. I sensed some reason why he was so anxious to acquire that little stock. That afternoon I had a call from John Pullen, who was very much excited and said Litchford was trying to get control of the bank. "I don't know whether he wishes to get rid of me or not, but if he controls the bank I am at his mercy. I have never wished to control it, but I do not wish any other officer to make it so that I must stay in the bank or not, at his will." He went on, in a very modest way, to say that he had put his whole life in the bank and, without being presumptuous, he thought he had made the bank. I told him everybody knew that to be true; that I had no idea if Mr. Litchford owned the majority stock he would make any change in the bank officers; that he knew, as well as everybody else in Raleigh, that it was "John Pullen's Bank" and not the Raleigh Savings Bank. Pullen wanted to buy my wife's stock and said her two shares of $25 each, would carry the control of the bank. The ownership was so nearly even that her shares held the balance. That afternoon I talked the matter over with Captain Thomas, who confirmed what Pullen had said. He thought it would be a great blow to Pullen if Litchford, or anybody else, owned the controlling shares and could dictate how it could be managed. He also thought it would seriously hurt the bank if Pullen's activities and enthusiasm and interest were lessened. I then told Pullen I would do anything he said about the matter, but my wife preferred to hold the stock and to give him its voting power so that, under any circumstances, her stock would be voted for whatever he desired. This settled the fact that Pullen was the controlling element in the bank. He liked Litchford and Litchford, of course, admired Pullen. They were very different men, Litchford a careful and accurate banker with no interest in the things that were Pullen's life. His accidental death was a great loss to Raleigh because he was one of the most capable of the younger bankers and business men and had a successful future ahead of him.

After Pullen's death the Citizens Bank, having bought the majority stock, wished to buy it all, which it did in March, 1913. My wife sold her stock to Mr. Brown at the price he named, which was, I think, $175 for stock with a par value of $50. She invested it in stock in the Citizens National Bank, obtaining $400 in stock including the dividends she had received for her original investment of $50. It was deemed to be the best sort of investment, and it was until President Joseph G. Brown died.

XXVIII

"A PAPER THAT SPEAKS OUT IN MEETING"

N OT LONG AFTER Captain Day became Superintendent of the State Prison the news came from Washington that the hands and feet of three Negro convicts were frozen while at work on the Northampton prison farm. Other reports of cruelty to prisoners began to drift in and letters came to *The News and Observer,* some anonymous and some otherwise, to the effect that Louis Summerell, Superintendent of the penitentiary farms near Weldon, had been guilty of cruelty to the convicts. On May 9 *The News and Observer* had a story headed "Brutal Beating and Starvation." This was a charge made by the convicts that the Federal prisoners were made to work outside the prison walls and that one was whipped until he could not stand. "Captain Day does not deny the flogging but denies that it was extensive and says it was necessary." Later there came other stories from the prison farms and *The News and Observer* said that convicts who had been sent home were maimed for life, their toes were frozen off, and they had been unmercifully beaten on the Northampton farm.

Every time these charges of cruelty were made, prison authorities said most of this testimony came from convicts, who could not be trusted. When the charges continued to pour in, and when, in the latter part of August, D. S. Russell, brother of Governor Russell, testified to Summerell's cruelty to the convicts, C. P. Sapp, member of the editorial staff of the paper, went to Halifax to make an investigation. He reported that Summerell played sick when the committee arrived and the investigation was postponed. Sapp reported that Russell's testimony showed that one man was beaten to death. My paper printed seven columns of testimony, most of which was given by convicts, but the testimony of D. S. Russell, who had every reason, because his brother's appointees were in charge of the penitentiary, not to make a false statement, convinced the State that the conditions there under Summerell were unbearable and called for remedy. In his second story from Halifax Mr. Sapp wrote:

"To see this fellow Summerell is to remember him. His large and flabby person, his eyes baggy of the underlids like a man who has bad mornings and a bad conscience, his large hairy hands, his eyes that waver continually, his rasping drawl, all make him stick in the memory.

"He came out yesterday in patent leather shoes, white socks, and told his tale. He was meek enough, for Summerell browbeats where he can and bootlicks where he must. He does not look like a man who would habitually pull his wife's hair and twist his children's noses as a pastime; he does not look like a man who would, in a passion, break the neck of a harmless dog and kick a dog for holloring.

"He is a man with no control of his temper, a man who is utterly heartless in driving his men to labor, a man who coddles a few pets and abuses the rest of the defenseless men committed to his keeping.

"If the evidence of the men, whom others swore were not biased, is to be believed, then Summerell is a brute, a tyrant, and a subject for the grand jury."

Mr. Sapp went on to say that the only parallel to his brutality was Weilerism, comparing his acts to the brutality in Cuba which compelled the United States to enter the war against Spain to put an end to the most unspeakable cruelties. The paragraphs above are samples of a column or more of Mr. Sapp's pen pictures of the terrible conditions which he found on the prison farms. Even so, he said that there were prisoners who had been flogged who were afraid to speak, so great was the terrorism. It was pointed out that Summerell made friends of the rich planters surrounding the prison farms in Northampton and Halifax and furnished plenty of hands to pick their cotton on their broad acres while leaving the penitentiary cotton unpicked. The articles published in *The News and Observer* aroused the people of the State. The penitentiary authorities, although calling them lies and denouncing the paper, were compelled, a little later, to take notice of them and carry on a sort of an investigation, but this was not until after, in September, *The News and Observer* had demanded an investigation at the Anson farms, where things were not going well, and in a long article, under the headline of "More of Summerell's Brutality Revealed," denounced him and made it impossible for the prison authorities to shut the matter up.

They had a hearing and Summerell testified for himself, denying, in a sweeping way, all the charges of cruelty and brutality, saying only that he had been compelled to beat the prisoners who had refused to obey the prison rules and that most of this testimony was lies by prisoners to get sympathy. *The News and Observer* continued, day by day, to demand that the prison authorities dismiss Summerell and put humane men in charge of the prison. The authorities continued to pretend to do something, and did nothing.

Finally, in October, a secret session of the penitentiary authorities was held, and an attempt was made to whitewash Summerell. The whitewash did not stick and in an editorial a few days after, *The News and Observer,* under the headline "It Will Not Down," continued to voice public sentiment for protection to helpless people who had been committed to the State Prison. On October 22 this public sentiment for humanity was expressed in the strongest way in an able article in *The News and Observer* by Dr. J. D. Hupham, of Henderson, who wrote vigorously and from the standpoint of a Christian minister. Shortly after this, as nothing was done, Dr. Hupham wrote an article on the "State's Slave Pen and Summerell's Mistake." Most of the newspapers took the matter up. The whitewash administered to Summerell had failed, although vigorously applied by some who had received favors at his hands. The prison board took the matter up again, but they considered only one charge against Summerell and the worst ones were ignored. About that time the *Biblical Recorder,* edited by Josiah William Bailey, palliated the crimes of Summerell and sought to show that *The News and Observer* and others were influenced by political feeling in the exposure of brutality on the prison farms. Whereupon, Dr. Hupham, the most distinguished Baptist preacher in the State, wrote an article against what he called "The *Biblical Recorder's* most amazing defense of Summerell's brutality." This created great interest because Dr. Hupham and Mr. C. T. Bailey, father of the editor of the *Biblical Recorder,* had for many years been the most intimate friends. He had been a sort of father to young Bailey, and the article was written in a tone of regret that the young man should have been misled and should have permitted the Baptist paper to minimize cruelty to the convicts. His rebuke, although in a brotherly and regretful tone, was all the more severe.

The article by Mr. Sapp, in *The News and Observer,* excoriating Summerell infuriated him. I heard from various sources that he had threatened my life, had said that whenever he came in sight of me one of us would have to die. Not long afterward I was going to Norfolk, and just as the train pulled out of Weldon, a telegram was handed to me saying that the party I was to meet in Norfolk could not be there. I left the train at Garysburg and walked over to the nearest store to see if I could get a buggy to carry me to Weldon. The keeper of the store, who was a subscriber to the paper and a friend, said, "What on earth are you doing here? Summerell has sworn he is going to kill you on sight and he was here not five minutes ago, and he is liable to come back any minute. In fact, I think he is going to come back, and if he sees you he will be certain to shoot you, for he is armed. I strongly urge you not to wait for any buggy but to take the track and walk to Weldon as fast as you can." Although it was raining, I proceeded to take the advice of my friend. He sent me word afterward that, within a short time after I had left Garysburg, Summerell returned and someone told him I had been there. He swore and almost foamed at the mouth. The storekeeper sent me word that I had a very narrow escape with my life. In the meantime Summerell brought suit against *The News and Observer* for $100,000 for libel and engaged most of the attorneys at the Northampton bar, the chief of these being Robert B. Peebles, who was afterward Judge of the Superior Court.

Years before, when the silver question was uppermost, Peebles had been the most ardent advocate of free silver in his part of the State. He had led the fight in General Ransom's county against him because Ransom had stood with Cleveland. He was very enthusiastic for Bryan and was at Chicago when Bryan was nominated and supported him. He had also been very friendly to my election as national committeeman. For some time he had it in the back of his head that he might succeed to Ransom's power in his part of the State. He was an uncertain sort of man, a very good lawyer and relentless. He had become offended at *The News and Observer* after the campaign of 1896, and when Summerell engaged him to bring suit for libel he was happy to do it. In fact, the common reports around Jackson were that he was very willing to undertake the case and was quoted as saying he would "show up *The News and Observer* in its policy of hounding men it didn't like." While this suit was pending, I went to Weldon with a committee to meet William Jennings Bryan, who was to speak in Raleigh, and to escort him to the capital. With others of

Members of the editorial staff of *The News and Observer: Upper left*, Charles P. Sapp. *Upper right*, Edward Conn. *Lower left*, Edward E. Britton. *Lower right*, W. T. (Tom) Bost.

Left, William Henry Bagley, Business Manager and Director of *The News and Observer. Right,* Miss Mary H. Horton, Vice-President and Cashier of *The News and Observer* since May 29, 1900.

the committee I had dinner at the Weldon hotel. While we were at dinner I looked out the window and I saw a sight which I recall to this day with considerable blood curdling. Summerell stood with his face pressed against the window for at least a half hour. It seemed like one hundred years as he glared at me with all the baleful, fierce fire of hatred a man full of passion could put into his countenance. I never knew before how much of murder a man could express in his face without saying a word. If he had said to me in words, "I have a gun and I am going to shoot you when you come out of that door," he could not have said it more plainly. He looked exactly as Sapp had described him, with even more malevolence. Nobody else in the company noticed him except State Senator E. L. Travis, who knew him well and knew of his threats against me.

Presently Travis whispered to me, "Summerell is in town and was at the window a few minutes ago. Did you see him?" I told him I had. "Well," he said, "he has threatened to kill you on sight and he is armed to do so. General Ransom and the rest of us have tried to reason with him but it is impossible. He is as near crazy as a mad man can be, and when you go out he will shoot you unless you can evade him. He has left the window now and has gone to the door waiting for you. When the rest of us go out you go through the back door. He will be waiting for you at the front door with the crowd. I will see that the crowd does not leave until the train blows and when that happens you go out and get on the last car and go into the toilet and lock the door and don't come out until I come or send someone to tell you that he has left."

I followed his directions to the letter and he had mapped it out well. I got on the Pullman car and went immediately to the toilet and locked the door. It was well for me that the doors on the Pullman toilets are very strong and will stand the severest efforts to break them. I had been there but a few minutes when I heard a man saying, "Where is the God-damn scoundrel?" as Summerell came roaring through the train like a tiger. He had gone through every car until he got to the Pullman, as I afterward learned. When he came to the toilet of the Pullman he knocked on the door with some metal instrument and tried to force it. He didn't know I was in there, but he thought so, and did his best to knock the door down. I guess he had tried all on the train in the same way. At any rate, after a while, he ceased banging but stayed on the train until it had left the next station. I remained in my protected position about a half hour longer, when one of the party came and knocked on the door, saying that I might safely unlock it as Summerell had got off the train at the last station and gone back to Weldon. Several times in my life I have looked death in the face, but that night it grazed me closer than any other time. I had no weapon and no defense against the powerful man and I always felt that I owed my life to Ed Travis.

Summerell had not only retained Judge Peebles but also Captain Thomas W. Mason, who was the most eloquent man at the Northampton bar, but, unlike Peebles, Captain Mason had no stomach for the fight. He knew Summerell's power in the county. He was not popular but people feared him. The large planters were under obligations to him. Captain Mason all along advised Summerell that the only correct position for him to assume was to secure a correction of the extreme statements made about him by Mr. Sapp and that this would be better for him than to have long litigation, with its consequent bitterness. Peebles, on the other hand, told Summerell he was certain to win and ought to expose *The News and Observer* and give the editor what he deserved. It came to me from different sources that Peebles was resenting the attempt of my friends in Northampton County to settle the case out of court. General Ransom saw me several times about it and had several talks with Summerell. He was using every influence he had to delay the trial until Summerell could get over his hate. I think Ransom, Burgwyn, and Mason might have succeeded but for Judge Peebles, who had blood in his eye. I never exactly understood why, but I was well aware of it. Of course the position of my attorneys, Ben Gay, of Jackson, and Busbee and Gray, of Raleigh, was to postpone the case as long as possible. Most of the witnesses of Summerell's cruelty were convicts and the only testimony we had of importance was that of Governor Russell's brother, who, while he had testified to the cruelty, was not desirous of appearing as a witness for *The News and Observer*. The deeper we got into the case the more clearly we were convinced that everything we had said about Summerell was true but the more difficult it was to find witnesses who could testify to it. The convicts were poor, and those whose time had expired were scattered all over the State. Those who still remained in the prison were afraid to testify, and we could get no opportunity to examine them. It was a very desperate case, the most desperate of the many libel suits brought against *The News and*

Observer. My lawyer debated asking that the case be moved from Northampton County on the allegation that the paper could not get justice there. I vetoed that, not willing to say a Northampton jury would fail to give a just verdict. We debated every other avenue that seemed open, securing several continuances.

Finally the case was set for trial at the August term of court. Judge Peebles gave notice that the case would be tried and that there would be no continuance. In the meantime he had been nominated for Superior Court Judge of that district and would retire from practice of law and become judge on the first of January following. That term was the only court in Northampton County before he would go on the bench. Captain Mason was willing to postpone the case and General Ransom urged Summerell not to press it, but Peebles was hell-bent to try that case and, as he said, "give Daniels hell before a Northampton jury." It was a passion with him. I looked forward to the trial with fear that Summerell would obtain a verdict because we had few witnesses except men who had been convicted of crime. Moreover, I feared for my life. Friends told me that if Summerell should become enraged during the trial he was apt as not to prefer vengeance by shooting me in court than to wait for the slow process of trial.

In that ordeal the good fortune that followed me all my life came to me in an unexpected way. I had been troubled with eczema for some time, and two weeks before the court convened it became so serious that I could walk only with difficulty. My doctor, unable to check it, put me to bed. One day he said, "I think if you would go to Crockett Springs in Virginia and bathe your leg twice a day, or oftener, it would cure you. I have done everything I can here and I advise you to go." He told me of a patient who had suffered in the same way who had been relieved after a stay at Crockett Springs. I hailed his advice with more eagerness and enthusiasm than I dared show my physician, Dr. Hubert Haywood. After he had given me this advice, I told him about this case against me in Northampton County, which was set for the next week. He said, "I will write a certificate that you are under my treatment and unable to attend court," which he did, and taking my oldest boy, Josephus, with me, we left the next day for Crockett Springs. I never knew whether the water of that spring or my relief from not having to undergo that trial cured me. I did not desire that any improvement should take place until after the day set for the trial. I did not give myself the full treatment the first few days but bathed my leg very sparingly, fearing that Peebles might get the court to order a doctor over to examine me and, if I suddenly became well from the efficacy of the water, my prescription of absence from the State might not save me. As fortune would have it, Dr. Haywood had been the physician of Judge Peebles' wife, who was a daughter of Colonel Paul Cameron. She had long been an invalid and had spent much of her time under Dr. Haywood's professional care. When I told my attorneys about Dr. Haywood's orders they were even happier than I, and when I ventured to express the fear that the court might still order me there on a cot, if necessary, they felt sure that Captain Peebles would not dare to question Dr. Haywood's good faith. When the case was called, a letter from Dr. Haywood was read, saying that I was under his care with a very painful affliction and it was impossible for me to be present at the court. I heard afterwards that Peebles was very much annoyed at his defeat.

The Judge, of course, under the circumstances, ordered the case postponed until the next term. By that time Peebles had been sworn in as Superior Court Judge and was holding court in the Western part of the State and it was not difficult for my attorneys to take the matter up with Captain Mason and agree to what he had all along wanted, that is, a retraction by me of the charges that could not be established. We were very glad to do this and to pay the costs in the case and the fees of Summerell's attorneys. The case went off the docket. It was the closest call I ever experienced. I never saw Summerell again, or heard from him. One good thing the penitentiary authorities did in that year was to buy Caledonia Farm. Agricultural lands were selling at low prices and 7,290 acres were bought for $61,665.

There was a great deal of gossip in Raleigh to the effect that when the Supreme Court met for consultation the meetings were surcharged with passion and bitterness. Judge Clark was smarter than any of his associates. In a sense, at that time, the Supreme Court decisions on cases affecting public office were somewhat like political debates. If Judge Clark hit below the belt, as was charged, he did it with consummate ability. I suppose there was never any more bitterness in a court in the history of the world and no man was ever hated so thoroughly by his associates as was Clark in those days. In the language of the street, he often "made monkeys" of the majority. Certainly his dissenting opinions furnished material for Democratic pillorying of Fusionism. *The News and Observer* charged that the majority of the Supreme Court was so partisan that they upheld everything that would keep the Fusionists in office. The big question in the court was that of the famous decision of *Hoke* vs. *Henderson*. That decision, rendered before the Civil War, held that an officer elected for a given term could not be ousted from the office until the term had expired even though the duties might be changed or the office not deemed to be necessary. In other words, a man elected to public office had property rights in the office which could not be taken from him. That decision had been written by the distinguished Justice Ruffin and was relied upon by the majority of the Supreme Court as settling the question. Acting upon it they declared unconstitutional most of the acts of the Legislature which, for example, repealed the Railroad Commission and therefore took away the office from the railroad commissioners and elected instead a corporation commission to which the legislature had elected Democrats. There were a dozen like cases. *Hoke* vs. *Henderson* was held up as the law and the prophets by the Fusionists. There were not wanting Democratic lawyers who felt that the court was justified in following that decision under the doctrine of *stare decisis,* but Judge Clark took the ground, and argued it with great ability, that the right of the people to abolish an office when they did not think it was needed was superior to the right of an office-holder, and he illustrated that position in such plain every-day language that the man on the street could get the point. His dissenting opinions, published in *The News and Observer,* were among the few opinions of the Supreme Court that were read by the people. Lawyers might agree with *Hoke* vs. *Henderson,* but the average man was quick to see that putting the right of an office-holder and his salary above the necessities of government denied the right of the people to such government and such officers as they wished. It was a long controversy, which eventuated in the impeachment of justices of the Supreme Court and got into politics. Judge Clark was never too busy to write a dissenting opinion and to have opinions about everything going on. One day he would write a vigorous dissenting opinion about *Hoke* vs. *Henderson* and the next he would come out in an interview. I remember that about this time he gave an interview in favor of an income tax for public schools. A little later, when *The News and Observer* was advocating a franchise tax on public service corporations, Judge Clark made a study of how many countries and states imposed such a tax and advocated it for North Carolina. My recollection is that he put that point of view into a Supreme Court opinion. He sometimes went very far afield in his dissenting opinions to advocate public policies. The strict lawyers resented this, but it made him stronger with the people.

At this time there was great dissatisfaction among the tobacco farmers over the starvation prices the Tobacco Trust was paying for their tobacco, and they called a meeting in Raleigh to organize the North Carolina Tobacco Growers Association. A committee was appointed to consider the matter and they came to my office in a recess of the meeting to talk about who should be head of it. A little while before, J. Bryan Grimes, a young farmer of Pitt County, who was a tobacco grower, had made an address upon the necessity of organizing the farmers in order to protect them against the prices fixed by the trust. He was not known to these older farmers, and when they asked my advice as to who should be head of the movement, I said, "You must have a man who has a typewriter and has the time and money to give attention to the organization. I advise you to elect J. Bryan Grimes of Pitt County."

They elected Grimes, who showed organizing ability. Later, when Grimes was candidate for Secretary of State (1900), although he was opposed by a veteran campaigner, Daniel Hugh McLean, silver-tongued orator of Harnett County, who had the support of Simmons, Aycock, Glenn, and nearly all the leaders, the farmers in all the tobacco counties rallied to Grimes and made possible his nomination. He was so efficient in his office and attended to his duties so well that in all the mutations of politics he could not be defeated, and he held the office until the day of his death. He held it although he was a Clark man when Clark was fought by the political machine and although he was a Kitchin man when Kitchin was defeated by Simmons.

Grimes was ambitious to make the office of Secretary of State what it was in the days of Saunders when it collected and printed the Colonial Records. He was a member of the State Historical Commission and one of its leading members. Under him the office of Secretary of State was really the center of the historical interest before the large expansion of the State Historical Commission. He may be said to have done very much toward a revival of interest in North Carolina history. He wrote not a few brochures and pamphlets and spoke often of the need of preserving North Carolina history, particularly emphasizing its part in the Civil War in which his father, General Bryan Grimes, for whom he was named, had fought and played a distinguished part.

The Corporation Commission, having increased the assessment of the railroads for taxation, *The News and Observer,* noting that the railroads had obtained an injunction and would fight the increased assessment, on July 19 denounced in a long article the granting of such writs. It had headlines as follows:

"Simonton spawns nine injunctions. The Railroads must not pay more taxes. The Commission is enjoined. Assessment of last year will stand. Southern Railroad gets one huge blanket injunction for every foot of its lines, three injunctions for the Atlantic Coast Line and five for the Seaboard."

This was followed up with an editorial on "Judicial Usurpation," and during the year there was much discussion of what I regarded as an indefensible use of the railroad injunctions by a Federal judge to control the actions of a sovereign State. "Who owns the government, anyway?" *The News and Observer* asked. "The people who created it by their sacrifice of blood and treasure and who support it by their sweat and taxes, or the servants they have put in office?" Editorially I went on to say, "The United States Supreme Court has sinned far less against the people's sovereignty than the underling judges. The people move slowly but, when they move, their servants, although dressed in judicial robes, will learn they are but servants and subject to dismissal at the will of their masters." *The News and Observer* pointed out that the judicial hold-up cost the State of North Carolina $104,000 revenue in 1899, of which the schools would lose $25,000 needed for education of the children and the balance would be lost to the counties and cities since the railroad property would be undertaxed.

XXIX

BRYAN'S PRESIDENTIAL CAMPAIGN OF 1900

I N FEBRUARY, 1900, I went, with a committee of five others, to Richmond to meet William Jennings Bryan, who was coming to Raleigh at the invitation of State Chairman Simmons and myself. He arrived on February 14 and his first speech in Raleigh was made at the Johnston Street Station, the shops of the Seaboard. All the railroad engineers and mechanics were present and he was introduced by Henry Cole, a machinist. He spoke in the afternoon to an immense crowd in a tent on Centennial School grounds. The tent had been erected because there was no hall large enough to hold the crowds that came, and even the big tent was not large enough. Senator Simmons introduced Bryan, who spoke on "Taxation, Money, and Trusts." The Academy of Music was never quite so crowded as when he spoke that night. Leading people came from all over the State. I introduced him and said, in part, "In 1896 the Democratic Party, by a mighty struggle, freed itself from the control of men who had bound it to the body of death. It named for President the man who worthily wears the mantle of the Sage of Monticello. The money-changers who had polluted the temple of liberty compassed his defeat by denouncing him as a demagogue and stirrer up of strife. In 1900 the Democratic Party will renominate Mr. Bryan. Time has silenced and disproved the traduction of this great man and those that did not understand him will now support him with enthusiasm."

Simmons, in his introduction in the tent, had been quite as eulogistic, though he was not a strong Bryan supporter. He had been somewhat troubled lest, in coming to Raleigh, Bryan might have some foregathering with Butler and the Populists. They had supported him for President, and of course he looked to Populists for support again in 1900. Bryan did not want to drive them off. Some of the staunchest State Democrats insisted that Simmons and I urge Bryan to declare himself in favor of the suffrage amendment. For State purposes we would have liked that, but we decided that Bryan should not be asked to discuss a question which concerned only North Carolina. He steered clear of it. *The News and Observer* had two and one-half full pages devoted to Bryan's visit to Raleigh and North Carolina and its correspondents said the trip from Richmond to Raleigh was a "great ovation." At every station large crowds gathered, evidencing that he was even more popular than he had been in 1896. From Raleigh I accompanied Bryan to Chapel Hill, where he spoke to the student body and was received enthusiastically. He was greatly impressed with the spirit of the institution and gave a sum of money to establish a medal for oratory, which is permanent. My brother, a good judge, always said the speech in the Academy of Music that night was the best Bryan ever made, and others agreed with him.

Shortly afterward a meeting of the Democratic National Committee was held in Washington, and Kansas City was selected as the site for the National Convention. The meeting in Washington was a Bryan gathering. The *Post* story of this committee meeting said, "Daniels is the National Committeeman from the Tar Heel State. He wears a big, black soft felt hat and speaks in a voice that is typically Southern in its softness. He talks with emphasis too when he makes his predictions as to the outcome of the campaign." That paper also said, in commenting on its interview with the national committeemen, "Notice too that some of the Committeemen, like Daniels and Thompson, speak of the money question instead of the free coinage of silver. There will be less of silver talked and more about control of currency by the national banks."

During this visit to Washington, I dropped in at a meeting of the Woman's Suffragists and heard Mrs. Carrie Chapman Catt for the first time. In fact I think it was the first time I had ever heard a speech advocating woman's suffrage. I wrote an article for *The News and Observer* about Mrs. Catt and suffrage, saying her wonderful ability impressed me very much. From that time on I had great respect for her, which was heightened in later years, when during the World War I became associated with her when she was an active member of the Woman's Council for National Defense. She had not the moving eloquence of Anna Howard Shaw, but she was the most logical and convincing of all the women speakers for suffrage.

IMPERIALISM MADE PARAMOUNT

The North Carolina delegation to the National Convention in 1900 was instructed to vote for Bryan. It decided to present for nomination as Vice-President General Julian S. Carr. I was a member of the committee on arrangements in Kansas City and went out ahead of the delegation. The convention met on the Fourth of July. The meetings of the committee on platform were the stormiest and most long contested sessions in years. That was the year the Democratic Party made imperialism the "paramount issue," or sought to do so by their platform. To me it was a time of great distress of mind. It looked as if the Democratic Party had a good chance of winning. Bryan had secured the support of many thousands who had left the party in 1896, particularly men who were opposed to the imperialistic policy in the Philippines, and there was every indication that the bulk of the Palmer and Buckner gold men were ready to come back into the party and fight imperialism under Bryan's leadership. North Carolina was instructed for Bryan and the delegates were nearly all personally enthusiastic for Bryan. However, a majority of the delegates believed that, since the discovery of gold in the Klondike and Alaska, the necessity for the free coinage of silver had passed and as the money question was no longer acute because there was plenty of gold, the silver question should be relegated to the background and the supreme issue should be made upon hostility to monopoly and to imperialism.

As soon as I arrived in Kansas City I got in touch with some of Bryan's friends and talked to him on the telephone. It had been reported that Bryan had said he would not take the nomination unless the convention again declared for the free and unlimited coinage of silver at the ratio of sixteen to one. I tried to persuade him not to insist upon that plank and told him that it would be unwise to try to run a campaign again on that issue. He said if we did not put the silver declaration in the platform everybody would talk about it, but if it went into the platform as a secondary plank, we would show that we still stood by our colors but the other issues would be paramounted. Of course he still strongly held the view that silver ought to be a primary money and thought the increase of gold might not continue, and if it did not we would return to the same situation of distress as prevailed in 1896; that if we left it out people would say we were backing down and had been wrong and that we ought to stick to our colors. He said he was not in favor of making it the paramount issue as in 1896, but he did not tell me he would not run unless we declared for the sixteen to one ratio. The North Carolina delegation selected Judge Avery on the platform committee. I was reëlected National Committeeman.

Our delegation was disturbed, particularly when Richard Metcalfe, editor of the *Commoner,* at that time Bryan's spokesman, appeared with a declaration from Bryan that unless the sixteen to one declaration went into the platform he would decline the nomination. Pretty soon a tentative vote was taken in the committee, Judge Avery voting for the exclusion of the sixteen to one declaration. I was in the Kansas City Club, where the meetings were held, and I recall, in the early hours of the morning when the committee, having had no sleep for a long time, were blear-eyed, that Senator Tillman came out of the committee looking as black as a thunder cloud and seeing me came over and said, "By God, Josephus, when did you turn traitor and go over to the gold bugs?" Nothing but the threat of Bryan not to take the nomination put the silver plank into the platform that year. I had a hunch it was a mistake, but nobody could convince Bryan. By a majority of one in the committee it was voted to incorporate sixteen to one. They persuaded the convention to do what Bryan hoped the whole country would do—forget it, for when Senator Tillman read the platform in a voice that could be heard distinctly to the utmost recesses of the big convention hall, he stressed the declaration against monopoly, but when he came to the discussion of the Philippine question, he proclaimed in the loudest tones, "The paramount issue of this campaign is imperialism." The convention rose as one man and shouted a long time in approval, forgetting the money declaration.

Without spending a dollar Bryan had kept the leadership of the party in a marvellous way. He had no support from largely circulated newspapers, and no money. Though defeated, he still completely dominated the party. So we all left the convention and came home, feeling that the time for Mr. Bryan to win had come. We believed that tens of thousands of Republicans, who protested against the war in the Philippines and the introduction of colonialism in our government, would support Bryan, who made a remarkable campaign. The country was not stirred as in 1896 and it was impossible to arouse many people on a question so remote as the Philippines. Bryan never made better speeches. For a time it looked as though he was going to reach the White House, but after the campaign had proceeded for some weeks it became evident to observers who were not carried away by enthusiasm, that the American people could not be aroused by any wrongs done to people across the sea. The North Carolina delegation was particularly gratified at the nomination of Adlai Stevenson as Vice-President, when they saw that General Julian S. Carr could not win. Stevenson's father was born in Iredell County and Stevenson had many relatives in North Carolina.

The opening gun against Bryan, in the North Carolina campaign, was fired by the Charlotte *Observer*. It declared the people who favored white supremacy ought not to support Bryan because when he came into the State early in the year at the invitation of Simmons and Daniels to speak, he was requested to say a word in favor of the suffrage amendment but declined to do so for fear he would offend Butler and drive off Populists. The *Morning Post,* which *The News and Observer* always called "the Boast," or "the Wheezy Old Railroad Organ," did not go so far as the *Observer* in denouncing Bryan, but gave all the aid and comfort it could without bolting the ticket. Whereupon *The News and Observer* said this was a natural thing for "the Boast" to do because its father and controller and financial backer, Colonel Andrews of the Southern Railway, had voted for McKinley in 1896 and supported Pritchard for Senator later and was against real democracy at all times. As to the Charlotte *Observer's* fight on Bryan, *The News and Observer* answered it by saying, "No better could be expected from that paper since the chief owner (D. A. Tompkins) holds a $3,500 sinecure under McKinley." A full answer to the *Observer's* statement that Bryan had refused, when asked to say something about the suffrage amendment, signed by Captain S. A. Ashe, Chairman Simmons, Josephus Daniels, and Mayor Powell, of Raleigh, who had accompanied Bryan on his trip to Raleigh, was published. They said Bryan was not asked to say anything about the amendment. We agreed with him that it was his place to speak on national issues alone, which he did.

The Charlotte *Observer* and *Biblical Recorder,* then edited by Josiah William Bailey, denounced those Democrats who called upon all the men who had voted for white supremacy to stand for Bryan and the white metal. Bailey was quoted as saying if the race issue was injected into the national campaign he "would vote for McKinley" as a protest, and the anti-Bryan papers made much of this. *The News and Observer* said, "Bailey won't do it because until April he called himself an Independent and held office under Russell. He then entered the Democratic primary and bound himself in honor to the verdict." Bailey was then a frequent contributor to the *Morning Post* and in his communications to that paper and in the *Biblical Recorder* was very severe on *The News and Observer,* and there arose quite a controversy between Bailey and my paper. In its issue of August 18 *The News and Observer* charged that Bailey was an advocate of imperialism and a defender of trusts; that he favored the gold standard and was an upholder of corporate rule. All these charges Bailey denied, whereupon I called on him one day at the office of the *Biblical Recorder* and asked permisison to go over his files, which was granted. From these files I published a whole page which proved that he had gone much further in advocating Republican, imperialistic, and trust doctrine than he himself had supposed. I asked him to print in *Biblical Recorder* communications an answer to what he had published about *The News and Observer*. I wrote, "Your charges against *The News and Observer* are false, are made under hypocritical pretense and are intended and made for the purpose of helping to carry the state for McKinley. Your allies, the Southern Railway, the American Tobacco Trust, the Standard Oil Company and all other trusts and monopolies, are fighting the Democratic Party." I told him if he was going to advocate these doctrines it was better to call himself a Republican and continue his subservience to corporations under the right name. *The News and Observer* also said that, instead of coming out and taking his medicine since the paper's exposure of his advocacy of Republican doctrine, Bailey was trying to dodge by saying *The News and Observer* had made an attack upon the *Recorder* and the Baptist Church. For weeks the controversy went on. A nit-wit correspondent of the *Biblical Recorder* wrote that Bailey's writings were "inspired," whereupon *The News and Observer* made a great deal of it and wondered whence the source of this inspiration, ridiculing the thought that a man who had written so much Republican doctrine could have any inspiration. This ridicule got under Bailey's skin more than the previous denunciation. I added, "Bailey earned that booby prize." (It had been printed earlier in the society columns of *The News and Observer* that Bailey had won a booby prize at a euchre club party given at the home of Colonel Andrews, but he denied later that it was a card party, saying that it was a tiddledy winks affair.) *The News and Observer* concluded its advice to Bailey, "Avow yourself a Republican and advocate Republicanism as openly as you do slyly."

It was in May, 1900, that *The News and Observer* made the best news scoop of its history. Twenty-three people were killed in an explosion at the coal mines at Cumnock, North Carolina. The horrible death of these miners was told in every detail in *The News and Observer* within a few hours after it had taken place. The paper was able to boast, and did, because no other paper even mentioned it although it occurred within forty miles of the city at four-thirty o'clock in the afternoon before. This scoop gave the paper prestige. We owed the scoop to a good friend at Sanford, the telegraph operator, Tim Cobb. As soon as he heard about the explosion, Cobb called up the Raleigh Seaboard Air Line operator in Raleigh and gave him the information which enabled *The News and Observer* to score a great beat. This scoop would have been a great thing to glory in at any time, but just then there was competition in Raleigh between the two morning papers and the fact that *The News and Observer* came out the next morning with a big story telling how the explosion occurred and the names of the people killed and injured and all about it, while the *Post* did not even know that it had happened, gave me pleasure beyond expression. It is a singular thing about the newspaper business that writers, reporters, and editors receive a greater thrill from being able to put over a scoop on competitors than from anything else.

DEFEATING THE RING IN WAKE

In the Wake County Democratic Convention of 1900 was seen the first clear-cut fight on prohibition as it manifested itself in nominations for the county ticket. The Democratic organization in Raleigh, composed of those who made politics a business and who had most of the county and city offices, determined to nominate William B. Snow as Senator, a lawyer of ability and character understood to be against prohibition. "Wet and dry" was getting pretty exciting then and it soon became apparent that Snow was being supported by the Wake ring and by the wet people. In 1928, Snow told me prohibition was the best thing that ever happened in North Carolina.

It was apparent that in the Legislature of 1901 local option, dispensaries, and prohibition would play a large part. Those of us who were dry did not wish to bring it into politics. It was apparent that the saloon men were lined up with the Snow supporters. I had, up to that time, paid no attention to the senatorial campaign and was busy over State politics. One day Big John Thompson came to my office and said that Snow ought not to be nominated because of his affiliation with the ring element, and that we ought to nominate somebody else. It was decided by a small group that the wisest thing to do was to make a straight wet and dry fight and to bring out N. B. Broughton, who had spent his life fighting saloons and to whom a saloon was a red flag. It was only a few days before the primary that Mr. Broughton consented to run. W. N. Jones, John W. Thompson, E. P. Maynard, and I, and a few others, started a quiet fight to nominate Broughton. When the convention met in Raleigh the supporters of Snow, thinking he had a walk-over, were astounded when W. N. Jones rose and made the best speech of his life placing Broughton in the nomination. He was nominated. The convention adjourned with threats by the wets to bolt the ticket. The party in the county seemed split wide open. The saloon men said they would defeat Broughton at any cost, and there were twenty-five or thirty saloons in Raleigh. I became uneasy as they walked out of the convention, many of them breathing threatening and slaughter against Broughton. As the afternoon wore on there were more reports of a bolt. The printers in Raleigh were for Broughton, whether they were wet or dry. He had come up from the case. I obtained much of my information about the plans to defeat Broughton from the printers, particularly from Samuel Bogasse and Charles F. Cook, foreman and advertising man in our printing office. Both of them were members of the Board of Aldermen and partly owed their election to the wet interests. I conferred with Bogasse and after supper I said to him:

"Sam, I wish you would do a little political work tonight to help our friend Broughton. You have a habit at times of going around to the saloon and taking a glass of beer, a very bad habit that I wish you would stop, but if you are ever going to do it, I would like for you to do it tonight. I wish you would go to the saloons and casually say, but in a way that the owners of the bar and their retainers can hear, that you have just come from *The News and Observer* office and you heard me say that I had about come to the conclusion, and so had other temperance men, that the time had come to drive all the saloons out of Raleigh and establish a dispensary and that if the saloon men of Raleigh fought Broughton we would have a bill introduced in the legislature and passed to establish a dispensary in Raleigh without the vote of the people."

A dozen such bills had been passed in the previous Legislature and prohibition had been put upon several counties by legislative enactment. I added,

"I also wish, Sam, that you would tell the saloon-keepers if they support Broughton for Senator heartily and he is elected, we Broughton supporters will guarantee that no action will be taken about the saloons in Raleigh except by vote of the people, but if they fight him, they will go out of business without having a chance to vote."

I knew that would put the fear of God into their hearts. They believed they could carry the majority vote in Raleigh as they had generally done, but they knew at that time *The News and Observer* was very influential with the legislators and the prohibition sentiment was strong in the State. I did not go home that Sunday morning until about one o'clock. Within a half hour Bogasse began his tour carrying my position to the saloon-keepers. At least half a dozen of them, maybe more, dropped in the office to see me, and before I went home I had the assurance from the leading saloon men who took active part in politics that anybody who said they intended to fight Broughton had slandered them, that while they did not agree with him in his temperance views they had great respect for him as a man and, above all things, they were Democrats and would support the ticket heartily, which they did, and the saloons kept on in Raleigh until by vote of the people the dispensary put them out of business.

I went to Washington to attend a meeting of the Democratic Committee in September and gave out an interview in the Washington *Star* in which I said, "The State of North Carolina will always be Democratic." In August I went to Chicago to attend a meeting of the national committee and, after conferring with the leaders from the West, I went with Bryan through a number of towns in central Ohio, and telegraphed *The News and Observer* that "unless all signs fail, Bryan will carry Ohio." I was not a true prophet.

XXX

AYCOCK'S RENUNCIATION AND NOMINATION

THE STATE DEMOCRATIC CONVENTION met on April 12, 1900. It was the greatest and most enthusiastic political convention that men of that generation had ever seen. The people poured into Raleigh more like crusaders than partisans. They felt the hour had come when the State should be redeemed. It was more than a political redemption. It was a social and economic redemption which the Democrats thought they were going to achieve. There was an almost unanimous sentiment, from the mountains to the sea, in favor of nominating Charles B. Aycock, of Wayne, as Governor. I had seen it coming for months and had found that what afterward came to be known as "the Simmons machine" was very enthusiastic in organizing the movement for Aycock's nomination. I went to Goldsboro and sought to dissuade Aycock from becoming a candidate for Governor. I believed he was better suited to make a great reputation as United States Senator than as an executive.

It was clear that whatever high honors the party had to give would go to Aycock and Simmons. They had been the most outstanding and conspicuous leaders in the white supremacy revolution, Simmons as the chairman and strategist and Aycock as the orator, voicing, as no other man did, the desires of the great populace. People admired Simmons' astuteness, his successful organizing quality, his capacity to meet and conquer adverse conditions and to weld men of varying views into one solid phalanx, but nobody loved to hear him speak. He could write strong documents, which other people used, and he was the best organizer the State had known; but while the people looked to him with confidence and felt he was entitled to great reward, they did not love him as they did Aycock, who had garnered the love of the people more completely than any other man who lived in my day. He was the only man I ever knew whom people in his home town would rather hear than anybody else, no matter how often he spoke. As a rule an orator is beloved in his own community but after he has spoken there two or three times he will draw greater audiences away from home. It was not so with Aycock. Let it be known that he was to speak in Wayne County and the whole county would be there. That was so from the time he began to practice law until he was elected Governor and even afterward.

I wanted him to decline to run for Governor and to announce that he would run for Senator. His whole training and his whole capacity marked him as having the qualities that would enable him to grow into a great Senator. I told him that Simmons' friends were seeking to sidetrack him into the governorship, which would last only four years, while if he went to the Senate he would stay there for his lifetime. I said that we ought to give Simmons the governorship and he himself should take the senatorship. I shall never forget his reply. He said: "The people know what a man can do and ought to do better than he knows himself. From 1892 they have picked me out for Governor. Everywhere I have been if they have had anything to say about any honor that is to come to me, it is for the governorship. The average man in North Carolina thinks more of the Governor than he does of a Senator. He thinks it is the greatest office. He remembers that Vance was Governor twice and, while you and other friends think that the Senate is my place, and I would prefer it, you must pay deference to the superior ability of the people to pick their leaders. If they want me to be anything, it is Governor. I know that Simmons wants the senatorship and I am willing for him to have it. He has earned great honor and I wish no division in the party." He had faith in a sort of predestination, whereby the people would pick their leaders better than the leaders could pick their places. While he knew that some of Simmons' friends were pressing him for the governorship, in order to make it easy for Simmons to go to the Senate, he felt that this was an infinitesimal part of it and that the people had not been put up to it, but had selected him for the governorship of their own motion and that he ought to respond to their call. There was much in what he said, but I knew better than he did how the Simmons machine had helped to create that sentiment and had fostered it and organized it.

I did not know of Aycock's renunciation of his senatorial ambition until Simmons wrote his memoirs, in which he said:

"Aycock told me he wished to be Senator. He said he thought I would be a better executive and that his qualifications fitted him for the national post. I replied that the people had already decided the matter. Aycock finally acquiesced and became one of the State's great Governors."

Justice, who was devoted to Aycock and afterward was made Superior Court Judge by Aycock, put him in nomination in a speech that was equalled only by the seconding speech of Edward W. Pou. Both speakers stirred to highest pitch the enthusiasm of the delegates who packed the hall and filled adjoining streets. Not more than half the delegates could get into the hall.

The convention declared in favor of holding a primary for the selection of a Senator, for which, as the paper said, *"The News and Observer* has long contended." In fact it had long urged a primary for the selection of all officers. It won the fight, although the Simmons leaders fought it and accepted it only after they saw that the bulk of the voters were determined upon it. The convention instructed its delegates to vote for Bryan for President, and its platform on national matters was in keeping with the Chicago platform.

Shortly following this convention the Populists held their convention in Raleigh and nominated a ticket headed by Dr. Cyrus Thompson for Governor. It was controlled by the Federal office-holding element of the Populist Party, and as Butler's term as United States Senator was expiring he joined hands with them. Its chief purpose was to effect fusion with the Republicans. It was never the purpose of Butler or Thompson to make a genuine fight for their ticket. It was nominated for trading purposes.

On May 31, the Republicans met and nominated a ticket, also for trading purposes. It was headed by Spencer B. Adams, Republican Judge. It endorsed the administration of Russell, but without mentioning his name—it dared not do that. The day after the convention was held it was said that Russell was very indignant that the convention had shied off from endorsing him although it had, in a blanket resolution, endorsed what had come to be known as "Russellism." McKinley's administration was endorsed by name. They were not afraid to mention him although they dared not name Russell. Pritchard was urged for Vice-President on a ticket with McKinley, and some of the Republicans from Mitchell County actually thought he had a chance. Claudius Dockery was nominated for Lieutenant Governor.

The Democrats lost no time after their convention. The papers and speakers immediately began the fight. The whole campaign was carried on and everywhere writers and speakers based it on the plane of Aycock's great and broad speech of acceptance in which he had said:

> "We had a white man for Governor in 1898 when negroes became intolerably insolent; when ladies were insulted on the public streets; when burglary in our chief city became an every night occurrence; when 'sleep lay down armed and the villainous center-bits ground on the wakeful ear in the hush of the moonless nights'; when more guns and more pistols were sold in the state than had been in the twenty preceding years. Under that rule lawlessness stalked the state like a pestilence—death stalked abroad at noonday—the sound of the pistol was more frequent than the song of the mocking-bird—the screams of women fleeing from pursuing brutes closed the gates of the heart with a shock."

Answering the denial that Negro rule existed in North Carolina, he pointed out that the white men in office owed their election to the solid Negro vote and gave a graphic description of the intolerable conditions that had been brought about. The speech had a challenge and defiance in it and also had a winning pledge of justice. It was so different from the vehement denunciations which many speakers were using as to convince even the Negroes who did not vote for him that the Democratic Party was not vengeful and that under Aycock's leadership they would be fairly treated.

By July the campaign had gotten into full swing, and all sorts of charges and counter-charges were made. In some places there was danger of violence. In fact, in several places Fusion candidates and speakers were subjected to rotten-egging. Herbert Seawell, of Carthage, was given a shower at Shelby, and Butler at Rocky Mount and Wilson, and a Democratic speaker, Charles W. Gold, had rotten eggs tossed at him in Wilson. After Seawell had been rotten-egged, the Democrats of Shelby passed a resolution condemning it and said it was an act of irresponsible boys, but Seawell never got over it. It looked at one time as though the egg market would be exhausted when both parties began to use them, and the older the eggs the greater the market for them. *The News and Observer* declared that the egging of Fusion candidates could not be charged to Democratic leaders; that they were thrown by irresponsible parties and it was to be deprecated. The Populists declared, undoubtedly as truly as the Democrats, that the egg-throwers were young men acting on their own initiative. But the truth must be told that there was no Democratic resentment in the headquarters when the news came that Butler had been rotten-egged.

O. J. Carroll, United States Marshal, who was a familiar figure all over the State, and had been a drummer for many years and active in politics, had dubbed Marion Butler, Senator from Sampson, "Mary Ann" when he first fused with the Republicans. When Butler would start to speak people would call out, "Go it, Mary Ann. Give the gal a chance!" or, "How would she like a dose of eggs?" When it was found that this designation made Butler very mad, it was used pretty generally. However, it was never used by Simmons or Aycock or *The News and Observer*.

It is hard, in the quiet aftermath, when years have intervened, to understand the white heat of that campaign. The bulk of the white people of the State made up their minds to win at any hazard. A few weeks before the election, Red Shirts made their appearance in the southern counties. By the middle of July it was apparent that the house of Fusion was to be demolished. However, State Chairman Simmons organized as thoroughly as in the previous campaigns, and the speakers on the stump, led by Aycock and Glenn, aroused the people to fever heat. Simmons denounced the pernicious activity of Federal office-holders. *The News and Observer* denounced Russell for the mobilization of troops in the armory at Raleigh and declared that impeachment was too good for Russell, who had tried to put troops in Smithfield. Declaring that the Democrats in Wake County were getting ready to disfranchise their voters, Marion Butler secured the arrest of registrars. Simmons countered by saying he would arrest any person who arrested a registrar. The Democrats thought, up to the last minute, that Russell might attempt the use of troops, but Russell had learned his lesson in 1898 and was not willing to jeopardize his personal safety. Hundreds of thousands of copies of *The North Carolinian,* my weekly paper, were sent out all over the State to Populists and Republicans. Thomas Fortune, a Negro editor in New York, was quoted as saying "Negroes will get at the throats of white men." It was very evident that during the campaign the Republican and Populist leaders were keeping the Negroes in the background. They were advised to "lay low." That advice was followed.

Butler was the foremost speaker of the Fusionists. As an example of his methods of campaigning, when he spoke at Morganton, he brought a ten-year-old child upon the platform and undertook to prove that the child would be disfranchised when he became of age if the suffrage amendment was adopted. The effect of that object lesson was not only destroyed but became a boomerang when *The News and Observer* printed in big type that the white child Butler was shedding tears about was a mulatto. Butler and the Fusionists swore that was "a Democratic lie," but the Morganton Democrats replied by offering evidence that it was true. At any rate it destroyed Butler's argument and no more did he take a child upon the platform.

On the front page on July 25 *The News and Observer* printed in a box that J. M. Barrow, Fusionist, of Randolph County, had said that Confederate soldiers ought to have been disfranchised. That and like statements were paramounted and drove nails into the Fusion coffin. When Aycock spoke in Duplin County, a mile of Red Shirts met him and escorted him to the speaking stand. When he reached Clinton the town was full of Red Shirts welcoming him.

Election day was looked forward to with deep anxiety. It was feared that there would be trouble at many voting places, but, as generally happens when people are afraid of trouble and are prepared for it, it did not come. In the big Negro counties many Negroes did not even come to the polls. The Red Shirt parades had intimidated them. In other sections some of them were so disgusted with their own leaders that they did not care anything about voting. On the night before the election, Colonel Waddell, in a fighting speech at Wilmington, said:

"You are Anglo-Saxons. You are armed and prepared and you will do your duty. Be ready at a moment's notice. Go to the polls tomorrow and if you find the negro out voting, tell him to leave the polls and if he refuses, kill him, shoot him down in his tracks. We shall win tomorrow if we have to do it with guns."

The day before the election *The News and Observer* predicted that Aycock would be elected by a 40,500 majority. Looking back upon it, I wonder why we didn't say 40,517. As a matter of fact, the majority for Aycock was 60,352, and when it was announced, *The News and Observer* printed a picture of Aycock and said he was elected Governor by the largest majority ever given a candidate for the office of chief executive of North Carolina. He ran 5,000 ahead of the amendment. A few days after the election Butler came out in an interview in the Washington *Post* saying the Democrats stole 20,000 votes. My paper called Butler "a dirty bird" and said, "Butler's purpose is plain. Having been repudiated by the people of North Carolina in a manner that leaves no doubt of their contempt for him, Butler proposes to follow in the footsteps of all defeated Southern Republicans and say defeat was brought about by fraud and force and intimidation. Thus, he is befouling his own nest."

The next day *The News and Observer* said, "Butler is a Judas Iscariot, a Benedict Arnold, who tried to debauch the politics of North Carolina," and added,

> "He has never had a friend he did not betray. He has never advocated a principle that he didn't trample under his feet for gain. In the present campaign he desired to obtain the confidence of honest Populists and Democrats in order to betray their secrets to Hanna's party which furnished him the money on which he led the two campaigns."

In August of 1900 the statue of Governor Vance was unveiled in Capitol Square and the largest concourse of people Raleigh had seen was present. It was a fitting time, for Aycock, the new Governor, was to receive it. *The News and Observer* published in full what happened on that day and devoted nineteen columns to the address of the Honorable Richard H. Battle on Vance, and to the other addresses. Mrs. Vance was in Raleigh. The oration of Mr. Battle was really a comprehensive story of Vance's life. Mr. Battle had been private secretary to Vance when he was Governor during the War Between the States, had known him as a student at Chapel Hill, and had always regarded him as the greatest man he had known. He had been with Vance in critical times, and they had been young Whigs together. Both of them had opposed the war of the sixties, but when Lincoln called for troops they stood with the Confederacy. Through life there was an intimacy between them, although two more different men never lived. Vance was vigorous, strong, combative; he loved the people, believed in them, trusted them. He successfully got over Whig doctrine and traditions and became as true a disciple of Jefferson as ever Andrew Jackson was. Mr. Battle never changed.

He became a conservative in 1868. He was so clean and honorable that the corruptions of that time drew forth his condemnation.

Upon the appointment of Furches as Chief Justice, to succeed Chief Justice Faircloth, who died late in 1900, Russell appointed Charles A. Cook, of Warren County, as Associate Justice. The selection of two Warren County men as associate justices on the Supreme Court of North Carolina during the Fusion rule was out of the usual order. Many years before, the two, Cook and Montgomery, had been Democrats in Warren County. They had been contestants for small offices and for leadership, and when Montgomery attained the ascendancy Cook left the Democratic Party and became a Republican. It was always believed that he did it because he did not feel he had received proper consideration. Later, when the Populist movement became strong in the County, Montgomery joined the Fusionists. Old-time bitter rivals in the Democratic Party, both later found themselves serving on the Supreme Court bench as members of the same party. Politics makes strange bedfellows. Cook was a remarkable looking man, the only man, I believe, with the exception of Redfield in Wilson's Cabinet, I ever saw wear a red beard. He had unquestioned ability. He had been a staunch friend of Russell, having helped to nominate him for Governor, and having stood by him in his fight against the lease of the North Carolina Railroad. He was fiery in temper but had many fine personal qualities. He was the son of an old-time Methodist preacher. The father was in demand in the country districts as a successful revivalist and many stories were told about him.

I recall one which was told following a revival he had held in Nash County, after which many converts joined the church. Some time after the revival, Preacher Cook was at Nashville during court week. In those days everybody went to the county seat on Tuesdays of court. As Cook was standing in front of the court house a man came staggering up and said, "How do you do, Brother Cook?" The preacher not remembering his name, the man asked, "Don't you remember me, Brother Cook? Don't you know me? I am one of your converts." The preacher replied, "I have no doubt you are. You are acting just like a man I might convert. If you had been one of the Lord's converts you wouldn't be drinking."

At one time Preacher Cook held a position in the Revenue Department and his business was to ride through the country and arrest illicit distillers or people who were manufacturing liquor without paying tax. Uncle Sam had to keep an army of what Vance called "revenue doodles" to travel the country-side to cut up illicit stills and prevent the making of liquor without license. As Cook went about this business in which he was engaged, if he would hear of a revival within riding distance he would be certain to go and lend a hand. The story is told that, after cutting up several stills in Hickory Mountain, he went over to a near-by church in Chatham, where they were having a revival. A noted revivalist, he was fervent in prayer. For a few days he quit the revenue business and devoted himself to saving souls. He was not doing the preaching but was doing the exhorting. Finally, every person in the neighborhood had been converted except one young man. The story is unsupported but runs that one night at the meeting Preacher Cook had gone in late and was sitting on the back seat. Friends were exhorting the young man to go to the mourners' bench. His mother and sister and all the good people were crowding around him, urging him to go up and confess, but his resistance was strong. They didn't want to close the meeting until they had plucked him as a brand from the burning. Finally Preacher Cook leaned over and said, "Young man, I want to speak to you a minute. Don't you want to be a Christian?" "Yes," said the young man, "I would like to be a Christian." "Well," said Cook, "Don't be a damn fool. Go up and get religion." None of the other appeals had had any effect upon the young man but this semi-profane admonition hit him at the place where he lived and he marched up to the altar and soon the church resounded with shouts that every person in the neighborhood had been saved.

SIMMONS WINS SENATORSHIP

The State Convention in 1900 ordered a primary for the purpose of determining who should be Senator. The Simmons forces had at first opposed a primary. All the candidates except Simmons united in demanding a primary and it was ordered. Simmons didn't like it, but he always had the political sagacity to make a virtue of necessity. Soon the candidates began to announce themselves, first, Governor Jarvis, then Colonel Waddell, and General Carr. As each made his announcement I wrote an editorial about him, stressing his strong points and particularly his service to the State and the party. It was not long before Colonel Waddell saw the handwriting on the wall. He had no organization and his health was not good. After making a few speeches, he withdrew. It was not long before Governor Jarvis did likewise. Shortly the contest was between General Carr and Chairman Simmons. From my boyhood General Carr had been my warm friend, and my affection for him and my gratitude for his many evidences of friendship were such that I went to Durham to talk to him about his candidacy before he made his announcement. I told him that I did not believe it was possible for him to win, for Chairman Simmons had led two successful campaigns and the people generally favored his election. I said that it would cost him a large part of his fortune to secure an organization. I tried to dissuade him from entering the race, but he had received letters from hundreds and thousands of people all over the State urging him to run.

In Durham, although there had been some antagonism between Carr and the Dukes, there was unanimity in his support, and the primary returns showed that he practically got the unanimous vote of Durham County. His friends in Durham and elsewhere were enthusiastic for him to enter the race. In all the counties around Durham, in all the places where he had spent much time and had many acquaintances, he carried a large vote, but he had practically no strength in the mountains and little east of Raleigh. His vote in the central part of the State, considering the momentum of Simmons' leadership in the two previous elections, was remarkable. In Wake County, where he spent much of his time, although Simmons was a resident of Wake at that time, the vote was very close. Neither of the candidates made a speaking campaign, although they spoke occasionally. General Carr travelled about the State and in half its counties he had effective organization. He was generous and liberal and, I suspect, spent a considerable amount of money. It was alleged he did, but it was never alleged that he spent any money in an improper way.

His manager and chief associates insisted that *The News and Observer* editorially support General Carr as a candidate and throw all the weight of its influence to his election. I felt that *The News and Observer* did not belong to me; that whatever influence it possessed had largely come from the fact that it had been the leader in the Democratic campaigns and every Democrat had a right to a hearing in its columns; that it ought not to be turned against any Democrat

in favor of another; that personal friendship and personal relationship ought not to control the policy of the paper. Some friends of
General Carr went to him and told him he ought to request me to
throw the paper editorially to his support, but he never did it, and
when I explained my position he acquiesced in it. At that time there
was no such thing as charging for political advertising. We had not
then become commercialized. My paper published many communications from advocates of each candidate, perhaps more for Carr than
for Simmons because more were sent in, but they were all signed by
the writers and the paper did not take sides. Simmons won the fight
by something like 60,000 majority and carried 80 counties out of 96.
Although it was a great disappointment to Carr he came up with his
usual buoyancy and was the first to congratulate Simmons. The contest left no sting, although it had been the dream of Carr's life to
be either Governor or Senator. Carr's manager in that campaign was
Howard A. Foushee, afterwards State Senator from Durham and
Judge of the Superior Court, a man of sterling qualities whose untimely death was a genuine sorrow to me, because we were warm
friends. Simmons' manager was Charles M. Busbee, a leader of the
Raleigh bar.

XXXI

I VISIT THE ACADIANS IN LOUISIANA

S HORTLY AFTER THE Democratic State Convention, 1900, when Aycock had been nominated for Governor and the platform had made white supremacy the leading issue, I made a special trip to Louisiana to make a study of the operation of the Louisiana amendment. I wished to ascertain for my own information and for the enlightenment of the voters of North Carolina the details of its operation and determine whether the conditions were so much like those in North Carolina that we could reasonably expect it to work well in our State. On May 8, en route to Louisiana, I stopped at Montgomery, Alabama, to attend the conference on the race problem of the South, where distinguished men spoke. In *The News and Observer* I wrote the first of a series of articles from the South and gave the history of the operation of the suffrage amendment in Alabama and said in the article, "People in that state are determined to let nothing stand in the way of elimination of the negro vote." That was a day when managing editors did not use the blue pencil and my article, written from Montgomery, Alabama, was four columns long. It was not too long for that day, because the consuming interest of North Carolinians was in the suffrage amendment. People eagerly looked for everything that could throw light upon it. My letter was not only published in *The News and Observer* but was copied and extracts from it were widely circulated by the Democratic Committee, as were the succeeding letters from Louisiana. *The News and Observer,* editorially, said that I had gone to Louisiana "to make a calm study of this question."

As soon as I arrived at New Orleans I first sought an interview with Judge E. B. Kruttschnitt, who had been the leader in the Louisiana Legislature and head of the lawyers who drafted and stood sponsor for the Grandfather Clause in the Louisiana constitution. I had a letter to him from his former classmate, R. O. Burton, prominent lawyer of Raleigh. He received me courteously and gave me the story of the conditions that prevailed in Louisiana before the adoption of the amendment and the argument in favor of its constitutionality. His point of view was that inasmuch as it had largely followed the line of Lincoln's Louisiana plan, keeping intact the suffrage laws prior to the enfranchisement of the Negroes, providing that the Negro should vote as he demonstrated his capacity, and making the law applicable alike to white and colored, after a given date, the law would stand because ultimately it looked to no racial discrimination. He said he believed it was essential to fix the date of registration on the permanent roll at the time of the adoption of the amendment. That is to say, if it were left open for some future date to say when a man was a legal voter, the courts might hold against that provision, and he strongly advised that North Carolina follow the Louisiana plan. After talking with him, I talked with the editors of the New Orleans papers, the city attorney, and a number of others. On May 9 *The News and Observer* printed my letter, giving the interview with Judge Kruttschnitt, in which I said the ablest lawyer in Louisiana gave his views and "declares that the Grandfather Clause is perfectly valid and Louisiana has placed it in a form safe from judicial attack." I quoted him as saying, "It does not deprive anyone of the right to vote on account of race, color, or previous conditions of servitude but it catches the ignorant Negro just the same."

On May 10 my second article appeared. It contained statements of Jerry Gleason, practical politician of Louisiana, who pointed out that their suffrage amendment had eliminated the Negro from politics but it guaranteed every white man the right to vote. The testimony from all these people in Louisiana was that the suffrage amendment had purified the politics of the State, that the elections were now absolutely fair, and that the choice of the people was elected. I quoted Republicans as saying it was a good thing. State officials told me, and I put this in the article, that it took two years to convince the people of Louisiana that the amendment would not deprive the white people of the right to vote but after the election they saw that their vote was protected and this ended opposition to the amendment on the part of the illiterate white people. I also pointed out that the only white men the amendment disfranchised in Louisiana were the foreigners, mostly Italians, who had not been naturalized. They had come into Louisiana after 1868 and therefore it could not insure them the ballot, any more than it could insure the Negroes, except through their ability to read and write.

After talking to other leaders of the State, including judges and others, I determined to make a visit to see how the Acadians liked it, or, as they were called in Louisiana "the Cajuns." These Acadians, descendants of the French people, were driven out of Nova Scotia and made famous by Longfellow's "Evangeline." They make up a material part of the population, nearly all of it, in one section of Louisiana. They are nearly all Catholics. Many of them served in the Confederate Army and many of them speak a broken English, partly French, but a French that could not be understood in Paris. Very many of them were illiterate. The problem that confronted the makers of the amendment in Louisiana was how to protect these uneducated voters as well as other uneducated voters in northern Louisiana of old American stock. The bulk of the white voters desiring protection were the Cajuns.

As in North Carolina our desire was to protect the white men who were not educated, so in Louisiana people wanted to protect the Cajuns. I sensed that conditions in that part of the State were somewhat like parts of North Carolina. It was really to see how the amendment worked there that I desired to visit the Cajuns. I had formed a strong friendship, while in Washington under the Cleveland administration, with Andrew Price, a member of Congress from that district. His father-in-law, Mr. Gay, had been the first Democrat to be elected to Congress from that district after the war, and Andrew had succeeded him. He was a handsome man, very well esteemed, an able leader of his party. He had retired from Congress and had been a member of the constitutional convention that had drafted the suffrage amendment. I found that he was living at Thibodeaux. Wishing to be certain that he was at home before making the trip, I telegraphed him that I would be in Thibodeaux the next day, from New Orleans, and wished to see him. When I reached there Mr. Price met me at the train with a number of prominent Democrats, most of them Acadians, and arranged a luncheon so that I might have an opportunity to learn all that I could at first hand about the working of the amendment. He had read in the New Orleans *Picayune* about the purpose of my visit to New Orleans and he was good enough to ask these gentlemen to meet and aid me in my survey. I talked with Judge L. P. Caillonett and Thomas B. Bibadeaux and other Acadians. Another one of the most intelligent gentlemen I met told me that his father could not read or write, which was the case with quite a number. He said that neither he nor his people would have submitted to any amendment that would have denied suffrage to the Confederate soldiers who stood against the reconstruction measures. He gave me plenty of evidence to show that under the workings of the amendment all these people had voted, they were on a permanent roll, and their right to vote was protected just as firmly as his. Andrew Price and Sheriff Beary and others confirmed this. It was an interesting day. I had never before been in that part of Louisiana, and of course my imagination had been intrigued by the story of the wrench of the Acadians from their home in Nova Scotia. I was interested in seeing how they lived and what sort of people they were. The region is a big sugar district and Price took me to see some of the large sugar plantations and mills. From this visit I obtained material for a letter telling what North Carolinians really wanted to know. It appeared in *The News and Observer* under the headlines "Cajuns like amendment. It works to perfect satisfaction of educated and uneducated whites of the sugar district."

Before taking the train from Thibodeaux I said to Andrew Price, "Give my regards to your wife. I had hoped to see her." My wife and I had known them fairly well in Washington in 1893 and 1894. He replied with a laugh, "You must see her. I could not permit you to leave here without seeing my wife. It is necessary for my family happiness. When your telegram was received at my house stating that you were coming to see me upon an important matter, not naming it, I was away from home. My wife opened the telegram. When I returned that night she asked me, 'Andrew, who is Miss Josephine Daniels?' I told her I did not know any such person, and she said, 'Now, Andrew, own up. Who is this lady from New Orleans?' I could think of nobody of that name but I remembered I had a stenographer when I was in the constitutional convention in Baton Rouge and I rather thought her name was Daniels, but I wasn't certain. I told my wife I didn't know who it could be unless it was that girl who had typed for me. She teased me for a time, expressing her unbelief that I could not remember this lady and then handed me your telegram. The operator, instead of signing *Josephus,* had signed it *Josephine.* I didn't understand it at all and neither did my wife until I received the New Orleans *Picayune* and read an interview with you. Then it was all cleared up, or at least I thought it was, and told her you were a man, but it will be necessary for you to come home with me and assure her that Miss Josephine Daniels wears breeches." He had told this story at the luncheon, to the amusement of all.

The Price home was just off a bayou and was lower than the water, being protected by levees. Mr. Price said the reason he hadn't invited me to be his guest at his home was that they were raising the house. I saw that they were putting brick supports under it and raising it high enough so that if the levee should break at any time the house would not be inundated. I thought then I would not like to live in a country where the river running before your door was perhaps four or five feet higher than your house and any break in the levee would inundate you. Mrs. Price was very courteous, and we had much fun out of the telegram.

I went back to New Orleans, where I met Jared Y. Sanders, who had been Speaker of the House and was then Lieutenant Governor, one of the livest wires in Louisiana politics. He was a nephew of Senator Foster, the man who killed the Louisiana lottery. I had known Mr. Foster in Washington when he was Senator from Louisiana. Sanders was the soul of hospitality and courtesy, and when he found out what I wanted to learn he volunteered to go with me to Baton Rouge and aid me in getting all the material possible. We went up the Mississippi on a very delightful trip, where I met Governor Foster, Leon Jastremski, Commissioner of Agriculture, and other public men, who were good enough to tell me of the workings of the amendment in all parts of the State, particularly in the sugar belt, where the Cajuns lived, and in North Louisiana, where the people were very like the uneducated people of North Carolina. There were many things to see in Baton Rouge and much of history.

During the day I visited the University, walking in on an English class while my friend from North Carolina, Dr. C. Alphonso Smith, was teaching it. We had been good friends when he was teacher in Selma, and so were very glad to see each other. He adjourned the class so that we might chat about old times and new. He had made some study, as a teacher, of the suffrage amendment in Louisiana. He had lived some years in Johnston County of North Carolina as well as in his native city of Greensboro and knew the conditions in the State. He gave me the results of his study. I had already obtained information from pretty much all the political sources.

I wrote several letters from Baton Rouge, one of them headed,

"*Puts Politics on higher plane. The Grandfather Clause in Louisiana constitution has ushered in a new era in civil life and all troubles on farms and plantations have vanished.*" The importance of this was that before the amendment there had often been disorder and some killings at election times on the plantations where the Negroes largely outnumbered the white population. The next article, which I wrote was from St. Joseph, Louisiana, appeared on May 16, with headlines, "*How it looks in the black belt. The amendment leaves no necessity for fraud or force. Honest and peaceful elections secured.*"

The third article, from Baton Rouge, was under the headlines, "*How it looks in white counties. The amendment in Louisiana has caused the rank and file of the Populists to return to the Democratic Party.*"

This was an important sidelight of my investigation because the objective and goal of the Democratic campaign at that time was to induce the rank and file of the Populists in North Carolina to return to the Democratic Party. I emphasized how the amendment had operated in reuniting white people of Louisiana. While not nearly so many Democratic farmers joined the Populist Party as in North Carolina, still in the northern part of Louisiana the same influences prevailed as had worked in North Carolina, and the public men were very uneasy lest the Populists might follow the example of the Populists in North Carolina and vote with the Republicans. In Louisiana that would have been fatal to the Democratic Party, and I pointed out, by statements from prominent leaders, that the Populist Party had, almost *en masse,* returned to the Democratic Party and were pleased with the workings of the amendment. The last article I wrote from Baton Rouge was headed "*Women do not fear. The amendment hailed with joy by the women of the state who do not now dread elections.*" This article also had great bearing upon the situation in North Carolina for, during the Fusion rule in that State, there was always a dread on the part of the white women in the rural districts that bad Negroes, feeling that they had license because their party was in power, might resort to brutality.

The survey which I had made, partly on my own motion and partly at the request of State Chairman Simmons, was widely published and widely read. These articles formed the basis of much of the argument which followed in the campaign when the suffrage amendment was adopted. As a matter of fact, I could not well have made this survey if I had had to pay my own expenses. The actual expenses of the trip were borne by the State Democratic Committee, which published in pamphlet form extracts from my letters particularly emphasizing that by the practical operation of the amendment no white men had been disfranchised, that it had resulted in a unified white party, and that race troubles and fear on the part of women had vanished in Louisiana.

A little later the Fusionists circulated in Raleigh a statement to the effect that white people had been disfranchised under the amendment, and the Governor of Louisiana wrote to Chairman Simmons so clearly and so plainly denying the truthfulness of that story that from that time on the Republicans were not able to make any headway. The Louisiana experiment and its results in working out perfectly what was desired in North Carolina caused the Fusion speakers and writers to shy off from any discussion of the Louisiana experiment.

The Legislature of 1899, which had submitted the suffrage amendment, having in mind the fact that Senator Pritchard might secure debate of it in the national Congress and that it might get into Federal court, possibly necessitating some change to meet any judicial snag it might encounter, did not adjourn sine die but adjourned to meet again on June 12. It directed its committee to be prepared with any amendment to the election law or the constitutional amendment. The day after the special session of the Legislature met, the changes were made in the election law and *The News and Observer* said that these changes left no chance for fraudulent voters to register.

XXXII

THE BEGINNING OF A NEW ERA

A YCOCK WAS inaugurated Governor on the 15th of January, 1901. It was, as *The News and Observer* said, a notable occasion. No such gathering had been seen in Raleigh at an inauguration, not even in Vance's day. People came in great numbers. There was no building in Raleigh large enough to hold one-tenth of them. The inauguration took place on the east front of the Capitol. Aycock arrived from Goldsboro in the early morning, accompanied by what seemed to be the whole population of his County. It was a gala day, a sort of celebration of the victory, as well as the heralding of a new day. It was indeed the beginning of a new era. As Vance had set the standards for twenty years following Reconstruction, so Aycock erected a high standard for chief executive, which guided his course and which all of his successors have emulated.

"We meet under extraordinary circumstances," Aycock declared, when the cheering, which had the echo of campaign enthusiasm, had died down. "A new constitution greets the new century."

The State waited for his address. He had been elected in a campaign in which white supremacy was the slogan. What would be his attitude now toward the Negroes? In his speech of acceptance of the Democratic nomination for the governorship, he had declared that an era of good feeling must be the outcome of the contest and had said,

"Then we shall learn, if we do not already know, that, while universal suffrage is a failure, universal justice is the perpetual decree of Almighty God and that we are entrusted with power, not for our own good, but for the Negro as well. We hold our title to power by the tenure of service to God and if we fail to administer equal and exact justice to the Negro whom we deprive of suffrage, we shall, in the fulness of time, lose power ourselves, for we must know that the God, who is love, trusts no people with authority for the purpose of enabling them to do injustice to the weak."

Called to the highest office, would he remember these words? He graphically told the story of North Carolina's emerging from poverty after the Civil War, and how, in its poorest days, it had cared for the helpless and defective Negroes as for the whites, and whatever of bitterness had followed in the campaign had been due more to the men who led the Negroes than to the Negroes themselves. He pledged the party, of which he was leader, to the education of white and black alike and declared of the suffrage amendment which had been adopted, "It takes no step backward. It distinctly looks to the future; it sees the day of universal suffrage but sees that day not in the obscurity of ignorance, but in the light of universal education." He continued, "We shall provide for and agree upon a system of schools that is designed to reach every citizen," and then he unfolded his conception of the duty of the party in power for honest elections. He declared that he had come to the highest office "with a humble heart, to be Governor of all the people without regard to party, color, or creed." He had not failed to ring true on the promise he had made when he was a candidate of his party.

His administration showed that in every act and word he was a leader, without political bitterness or race antagonism. The Negroes of the State came to look upon him as their best friend. Later, when he was getting ready to run for the Senate in 1912, he received a letter from a Negro in Henderson, which he prized as highly as any letter he ever received. It was illustrative of the feeling of the Negroes in North Carolina toward the Governor.

Henderson, North Carolina,
February 29, 1912.

Dear Boss:

I am writing to tell you that I sho am for you, and if you, don't get ellected, it will be because the most folks have got less sense than me. I have been on the staff of several governors but am for you all the time and if I don't vote for you it will be because they will not let me vote for anybody. I don't want to vote for anybody else for anything nohow.

Your servant and respectful nigger,
James Gill, the barber.

The Legislature organized with Walter E. Moore, of Jackson, as Speaker, and Henry A. London, of Chatham, President pro tem of the Senate. Senator Simmons was elected on a joint ballot by a vote of 124 to 26, Richmond Pearson receiving the Republican vote. Fusion was ended. Those early Populists who had been disgusted with the Fusion government had come back to the Democratic Party, and the Butlerites had gone to the Republican Party. Butler was then in bad odor with the Republicans because he had fought Pritchard, and so they would not give him the courtesy of a complimentary vote to succeed himself. Pearson had served in Congress and had been Minister to Persia. I remember the first time I ever saw him. The North Carolina Press Association was being held in Asheville. Vance made the address of welcome. It was a classic of his love for the mountains, and I remember his saying, "The first music that ever fell upon these infant ears was the ripple of the mountain streams gurgling as they made their way down the mountain side," and a like sentence about the sun rising over the hills and making pellucid the waters of the Swannanoa. The editors were entertained by Richmond Pearson, then a Democrat, at his palatial home called Richmond Hill, named after his father's home in Yadkin County. The editors were divided into two classes as they went to the spring on the farm where drinks and refreshments were served—there was a buttermilk brigade and a champagne brigade. Someone recalled the ancient story that buttermilk cost Mr. Pearson as much as champagne, indicating that he was not a real farmer but an agriculturist.

In the Legislature previous to 1901 an amendment to the divorce law had passed letting down the bars and two bills were introduced to make divorce still more easy in North Carolina. *The News and Observer* opposed any and all bills that would add new causes for divorce and in 1901 called upon the Christian people of the State to come to Raleigh and mobilize, not only to kill the bills that had been introduced, but to repeal all bills that had passed since the codification of the laws in the seventies. There was a fine response to this appeal, and the leading ministers, headed by Bishop Cheshire, and the editors of the religious papers of all denominations and influential laymen came to Raleigh. At the meeting there were two suggestions. One was to demand a law that would allow no divorce except such as was authorized in the Bible. The other was to recognize the statutes of the divorce law as it had been in existence in North Carolina for many years. It was finally determined that the status quo ought not to be changed, and a bill was drawn repealing all the additional causes that had been incorporated since 1876. I devoted column after column demanding the enactment of this law and published communications from all parts of the State. There was a hearing on the bill and the room was crowded. "Every departure from the biblical rule is a step from good sound morals and good public policy," said *The News and Observer*. I remember during the discussion—and it was one that aroused great interest—having a talk with a young lawyer, for whom I had warm friendship. He was opposing the bill and was being criticized by the preachers and others in his county for so doing. I asked him why he was taking so much interest in the matter and with great frankness he said:

"You will not find many young lawyers who are standing with you on this matter. My biggest fees come from people who want divorces. In all other cases people higgle over fees and it is impossible to get them to agree to pay what we lawyers think we ought to have, but when people want a divorce, they will pay a young lawyer as big a fee as the most distinguished lawyer in the state receives for the greatest case. We are not going to pass a law, if we can help it, that will take away our bread and butter."

The legislation was enacted and remained unchanged until the debacle of war times when other weakening amendments were adopted. I charged that loose divorce advocates wanted to make Raleigh as easy a place for divorce as Reno.

During the bitter political contest from 1894 to 1900, when *The News and Observer* was going after the Fusionists and charging them with all sorts of things from pitch and toss to manslaughter, it had been compelled to defend a large number of libel suits. While it always believed that its publications were true, in the heat of the campaign it printed statements that could not always be substantiated. At one time it was the defendant in libel suits aggregating four or five hundred thousand dollars, most of them growing out of the heated political exchanges of the day. There had been no change in the libel law in North Carolina since the time of the Indians—or at least the colonial government. As a matter of fact, there was a maxim, "The greater the truth, the greater the libel." The editors of the State did not have a fair chance to be relieved from honest mistakes. The matter of securing more enlightened libel laws had been considered by the North Carolina Press Association for some years. A committee, of which I was a member and of which Major H. A. London of the

Chatham Record and W. C. Dowd of the *Charlotte News* were also members, had appeared before the Legislature in 1899 asking a better libel law. It had received a favorable report but the committee of lawyers to whom it was referred had pigeon-holed it and buried it. At the session of 1901 the editors came back with a law which was drawn in my office, chiefly by Major H. A. London. The editors of the State united in pressing its passage. At that time the newspapers had more influence than they have ever had, before or since. In the campaign of 1900 they had been really the spokesmen of the Democratic Party. Editors had talked with their representatives during and after the campaign and asked relief from the sword of Damocles which hung over their heads. Major London's argument before the committee, backed by mine and Dowd's and others, caused a favorable report, and the most modern and best libel law in the Union was enacted. It did not permit any newspaper to evade the payment of actual damages which any person sustained by reason of the publication, but it recognized the impossibility of editors' substantiating by legal processes every statement published in the haste of daily journalism. It permitted them to make amends for a statement that was not true and, when such amends were made, permitted the recovery only of actual damages. A paper, to escape punitive damages, was required to apologize for the mistake and retract the statements complained of, and the apologies and retractions must be published in the same-sized type and in as prominent a place in the paper as the article complained of. This was a wise provision because as a rule an editor does not wish to make an apology. In a way some editors feel that it is a reflection upon them to admit they have ever made a mistake.

In the 1901 Legislature, in acordance with the provisions of the suffrage amendment, legislation was enacted to secure a permanent registration of all the older white men who were protected in their suffrage. When this legislation was enacted, guaranteeing this right, *The News and Observer* said that it answered and destroyed the argument of the Fusionists that the passage of the amendment would disfranchise white men as well as illiterate Negroes and said that not one white man was disfranchised. The Republicans voted against the measure with the sort of stupidity that marked them all through those years. They had protested on the stump that they were the friends of the illiterate white voters and had declared that they opposed the suffrage movement, not because they wished the Negroes to vote—oh, no! That was farthest from their thoughts!—but they trembled with fear lest some illiterate white man should lose his vote. Now with the permanent registration act, which insured every aged white man the right to vote provided he registered within a brief time, they all voted against it, showing that, at heart, their real opposition to the suffrage amendment was that it would disfranchise the uneducated Negroes.

When Aycock came into office, it was developed shortly that, in the preceding year, there had been a deficit of $170,000 in the taxes. "Where shall it come from?" was the question *The News and Observer* asked, and to which the Legislature sought to address itself. Judge A. W. Graham, of Granville, proposed that the money be derived by taxation upon the gross income of the railroads, and his measure passed the House. It did not get by the Senate. *The News and Observer* argued that a reassessment of railroad property ought to be ordered; that the former assessment was very much below the true value. Whereupon the *Morning Post* denounced *The News and Observer* as wishing to persecute and injure the railroads, which were doing so much to develop the State, and said that the attempt to saddle upon them heavy taxation was Populistic. While this discussion was going on, Raleigh swarmed with railroad attorneys and officials, so much so that Representative Willard of New Hanover, introduced and secured the passage of a bill in the House to compel all lobbyists to register. While that measure was being considered, the lobbies of the House were filled with railroad attorneys, and a score of them occupied seats on the floor of the House by reason of the fact that they had formerly been members of the Legislature. One of the perquisites of being a member of the Legislature of North Carolina in those days, and there has been little change, was that it gave a lawyer lobbyist the privilege of the floor, and this was used by attorneys to earn large fees. I supported Willard's bill to register. After passing the House, it found a sarcophagus in the Senate. During the debate in the House a Raleigh attorney opposing it demanded that "if lobbyists were to be excluded from the floor Josephus Daniels must be excluded, too, because he is the most persistent lobbyist in Raleigh," and Willard replied that his bill would exclude every man who was lobbying for pay and if Mr. Daniels or anybody else was lobbyist in the pay of any corporation or person desiring legislation, he must be registered. When the members proposed that I be branded as a lobbyist by name, the glee of the railroad attorneys in and out of the Legislature was expressed by loud applause. I did lobby but never received a penny.

Shortly after Aycock was inaugurated it became necessary for him to appoint a Solicitor for the Fourth Congressional District. Solicitor Pou, having been elected to Congress, tendered his resignation. The two candidates for the position were Armistead Jones and W. C. Douglas. Aycock was inclined to appoint Douglas and ought to have done so. During the campaign of 1898 and 1900 in Wake County, where the fight was a difficult one and I was very active in it, Armistead Jones had been the county chairman, and he made an appeal to me as did William M. Russ, Clerk of the Superior Court, formerly Mayor, to go with Russ to Governor Aycock and recommend the appointment of Jones. I hesitated about it, but my action then was based upon Vance's dictum that "The horse that pulls the plow ought to have the fodder." It overbore my hesitation and I went with Russ to see Aycock to persuade him to appoint Jones as solicitor because of his political services as county chairman. I never regretted it but once—that was all the time. Afterwards I told Aycock that if ever I criticized any act of his he might well say that the most regrettable appointment of his administration was the one he made on my recommendation.

In the Spring of that year there was a strike by the mechanics of the Seaboard Air Line Railway, and in the early days of the strike there was a minor explosion at the round house. Immediately the railroad officials and attorneys called upon Governor Aycock and showed him the section in the North Carolina code which gave the railroads the authority with the approval of the Governor to employ deputies in case of labor troubles. They asked Governor Aycock to make a blanket approval of the appointment of as many deputies as they felt were necessary. They were to pay the bill. They pressed this very hard upon the Governor, and were backed, of course, by the *Morning Post* and the railroad influences of the State. The Governor refused the permission and *The News and Observer* approved his action. The Governor told the applicants that the State of North Carolina was a sovereign State and that it was able to preserve order. He did not believed in subletting the sovereign right to a private corporation, saying the law was not mandatory but permissive. He declared that the property would be protected; that if necessary he would call upon the city and county and if they were unable to protect the property he would call out the State Guard; that no destruction would be allowed but he would not, while he was Governor, allow any private interest to usurp the functions of the State. This decision infuriated the railroad officials, and *The News and Observer* said that the law was not passed for the purpose of making the State take sides with employing railroads in the case of a strike, as it would be doing if the Governor acceded to their request. It said further, "The strikers have shown themselves peaceable and law-abiding and the railroad property is not in danger." It declared that the proper course to pursue was one of arbitration, and that the railroad officials and the strikers ought to agree upon arbitration. Some days afterwards *The News and Observer*, under the headline, "Say Scabs Stole," said that the men brought to the city by the Seaboard to supply the place of the striking machinists were getting in hot water and were showing up as hard customers. Most of them, indeed, were hard customers, and in a few days *The News and Observer* had another story in which it said the scab machinists had sued the Seaboard Air Line Railroad for their hire. The railroad strikers made themselves regular Sherlock Holmeses and knew every movement made by the strikebreakers. A few of them went to extremes, and one scab was tarred. The answer of the railroad officials was to cut down the shop force in Raleigh and to drop sixty men. It was a hectic summer in Raleigh in railroad circles and the railroad employees had a hard time.

Early in the year, after State Treasurer Lacy came into his office, it was discovered that Major W. H. Martin, Chief Clerk in the office, was short in his accounts to the sum of $16,550.53, during the term of William H. Worth as State Treasurer. Worth was a Populist, and in accordance with the general Fusion agreement his chief clerk was to be a Republican. The Republicans had urged him to appoint Major Martin, who had come to Raleigh with the Northern Army and was regarded as a skilled accountant. Mr. Worth knew nothing about him, but, finding him competent, trusted him fully and went out of office without the slightest suspicion that Martin had been stealing all the time. When State Treasurer Lacy discovered this, Martin, of course, was dropped and was indicted and sent to the penitentiary for ten years. *The News and Observer* said that as the truth came out more and more, the people saw they were justified in defeating the Russell administration, even in turning out of office a man who, personally honest like State Treasurer Worth, was surrounded by crooks and thieves.

At the next session of the Legislature, a bill was introduced to repay the amount of money which Major Martin had taken after State Treasurer Lacy came into office. It created controversy. The Republicans demanded that if Lacy was reimbursed Worth ought to be reimbursed also; that both of them were honest men and neither had connived at Martin's peculations. The political feeling ran high, and Lacy contended, with sound reason, that he had not appointed Martin and was not responsible for him; that he had followed the usual custom of retaining in office for a few weeks officials in order to give assistance to his new employees; and that the State ought to thank him for discovering the fraud and giving the evidence to convict the culprit. The legislature reimbursed Mr. Lacy, but only after a good deal of discussion, and some legislators opposed it because it did not reimburse Mr. Worth. Periodically for twenty years attempts were made to reimburse Mr. Worth, and in 1927 upon the representation that Mr. Worth was now an old man and needed the money, that he had been personally honest and that his only sin was association with crooks whom he did not know to be crooks, the Legislature reimbursed him, and properly so, as an act of mercy to a kindly Quaker who believed that Russell, Martin, and the rest were as honest as he was. When the shortage was discovered in the treasury, Mr. Worth turned over everything he had to his bondsmen.

In the first half of Aycock's administration there were three lynchings in the State, and in Anson county a Negro was run out of the State for "talking too freely about the lynching of Luke Hough." These lynchings were for the crime of rape, and *The News and Observer,* under the headline, "Lynching Must Be Stopped," took strong ground that the men charged with the crime should be brought into court. Several newspapers, however, and not a few people, took the ground that in a case of rape, where there was no doubt of guilt, lynching was the only remedy. Governor Aycock was humiliated by these lynchings and offered a very large reward—the largest that had ever been offered for the apprehension of lynchers—but I do not recall that the rewards brought any arrests.

There had been a great scandal about the issuance of pardons in Russell's administration. Up to that time there was no publicity attending the granting of pardons and no news was given out about them. The first thing people knew about a man's pardon was when he appeared in his home. Governor Aycock inaugurated the plan—and I think he was largely influenced by my urging it—of protecting himself and the public by surrounding the pardon with somewhat the same sanctity as a hearing in the court. In the first place, he announced he would not consider a pardon unless an application was made and printed in the paper published in the county in which the crime was committed, thirty days before the application was made. This would give notice to the people in the vicinity where the crime was committed, so that if they desired to be heard they could oppose the pardon. He also made the rule that, when a pardon was granted, it should be announced from the Governor's office and the reasons therefor assigned. I am not certain as to whether this has been made a part of the law, but if so, Governor Aycock's rules broadened the law, and thenceforth, even when people were opposed to extreme clemency, as under Aycock and Bickett, who were most free with pardons, they were compelled to say that they had had the opportunity, if they had wished to embrace it, to protest against a pardon and to give reasons why it should not be granted.

About the middle of Aycock's administration there was much criticism of his frequent granting of pardons and issuing of paroles. Friends sometimes imposed upon his warm heart and his aversion to punishment, and he made not a few pardons which were deserving of criticism. When criticism of what they called "abuse of his pardoning power" (which I also called it in *The News and Observer*), was at its height, there was an amateur minstrel show in Raleigh, which Governor Aycock, and pretty much all the people in public life, attended. One scene was of a man dressed as Governor, making his round of inspection of the penitentiary. As he reached a cell door, a convict stumbled against the Governor and, turning, said, "Beg pardon, Governor," whereupon the man acting as Governor ran his hand in his pocket and handed the convict a pardon and the man went out of the prison scot free. This was regarded as a palpable hit and caused great amusement. Some of the people thought it would make Aycock mad and protested against it, but he enjoyed it more than anybody else, and when we talked about his pardoning too many people, he always said, "Very well, maybe I do, but did you ever know any man who ever lived who is remembered for his hardness or loved for it? You and a few other hard-hearted legalists may object, but the people with good hearts will forgive a Governor for making mistakes when they would not love him if he did not lean to the side of mercy."

My paper had always inveighed against what I regarded as abuse of the pardoning power by the executive and was critical of judges, solicitors, and juries who asked the Governor to constitute himself into an appellate court and overturn their finding and sentences. When Governor Aycock issued many pardons my paper criticized his actions, holding that an executive should use that highest prerogative only in rare and exceptional cases where the courts, for some reason, had not been in possession of later discovered facts, or when some exceptional reason for clemency existed. Aycock's friends were irked at my criticisms, and one of them asked him, "What's the matter with Josephus? Has he gone back on your administration?" The Governor lighted his pipe, took a few whiffs and said, "No. Joe and I are as good friends as ever. The trouble is that he long ago committed himself to a hard doctrine and, to be consistent, thinks he must roast me for pardoning poor devils who have suffered enough. The only thing that troubles me is, not that I do pardon, but those punished too severely are not pardoned." He continued to pardon and I continued to criticize, without any break in relations. He was that way. He kept friends without capitulation or without expecting one hundred per cent agreement.

The Legislature of that year imposed a State income tax. It was not a large one. *The News and Observer* was the only paper in the State that printed the names of the people who gave in income tax and the amount they gave in for taxation. In Wake County there were only seventy-three people who gave in income tax, which meant that not more than this number received, or acknowledged they received, an income of more than $1,000. There was an exemption of this amount, and all above that sum had to be listed. Those who gave in the biggest incomes in Raleigh were the following: Colonel A. B. Andrews, $20,730; Dr. James McKee, $5,000; Ernest Haywood, $4,400; Dr. Hubert Haywood, $4,291; J. C. L. Harris, $4,000. These were all the large incomes. It may be noted that Senator Simmons' income was only $1,000 above exemption and mine was the same. In June, about tax-listing time, the judges of the Supreme Court, feeling they were not liable for the tax or desiring to escape its payment, probably both, asked the Attorney General to give an opinion as to whether judges and other state officials were liable for the income tax. The Attorney General, Mr. Gilmer, replied by quoting an opinion given by acting Attorney General Joseph B. Batchelor some dozen or more years previously, holding that the salary of a judge, or other state official, could not be taxed. He stressed the old English rule that by taxation the King could destroy a judge by imposing so large a tax upon his salary as to make him subservient, and said that there grew out of this the principle that a judge's salary could not be decreased during his term of office. This opinion was widely criticized. *The News and Observer* denounced it vigorously and said it had no foundation in reason or sound law; that, of course, if the Legislature had undertaken to fix a different rate of taxation upon judges and other officials than upon other citizens, it would have been unconstitutional because taxation should be imposed on all alike; but that, as the salary of a judge was taxed exactly like that of a lawyer, farmer, or anybody else, it was stretching special privilege to exempt the tax-eaters from a burden imposed upon all the tax-payers. This word "tax-eaters" greatly offended those enjoying freedom from taxation. It caused the first serious difference between *The News and Observer* and Judge Clark. I pointed out that Judge Clark had always rung true against the least semblance of special privilege and said the judges ought not to take advantage of this opinion, which would defeat the just law. There was a division of opinion among the judges, Judge Connor of Wilson and other judges, while not passing upon the question, gave in their income for taxation, saying that they did not wish to stand on a different basis from the other citizens. Very few of them did this and even those who did objected to its being printed because it might look like a reflection upon their fellow-judges. Still *The News and Observer* printed it whenever it found it out and contrasted their willingness to help pay the government expenses to the attitude of other officials who drew their salaries legally but were willing to let other people bear the burdens which they ought to share.

The publication of the names and incomes of Raleigh people who paid income tax was resented by tax-dodgers and those "opposed to publicity of private affairs." But again in 1902 *The News and Observer* printed the list of the persons in Wake County who gave an income tax, and the amount. Several of my friends came to me before it was published and insisted it was giving publicity to matters that were entirely private and protested against their personal affairs being given such publicity. I pointed out to them that the number giving income tax had increased considerably over the previous year; that most people had given in a larger amount than the year before; and that publicity was the only way to secure the fairest giving in of incomes for taxation. Only two Negroes gave in incomes for taxation: Professor Edward Johnson, who later went to New York and made a reputation as a writer of books on Negroes, and James H. Young, who had served in the Legislature and was a colonel in the Spanish-American War. *The News and Observer* not only published this list but it printed the list of those who gave in incomes in the previous year or failed to list any income for that year. It was no respecter of persons. Agitation was begun to keep income taxes secret, and succeeded. There is no more reason why an income tax should be secret than the tax on a cow or a farm.

The News and Observer was continuing its fight on smoking cigarettes. Its issue of May 25, 1901, in an editorial headed "Poison Mind, Body and Heart," said, "The Duke cigarettes not only destroy the mind and body and home but give this country a bad name abroad." It quoted a Chinese missionary who said, "The nude picture attachment makes the cigarette poison the mind, body and heart and blocks the way of the Christian missionary." Shortly thereafter, Dr. Kilgo, who did not then agree with my paper's viewpoint on cigarettes, apparently in reply to the missionary whom we had quoted, made an address in which he said, "The broadest spirit in this country today is the business spirit, not the religious or political spirit. Civilization is now engaged in a great fight for supremacy in the Celestial Empire. I tell you that God will go into China through the cotton factory, the railroad and the telegraph quicker than through the prayer-meeting." *The News and Observer* commented in condemnatory terms upon this statement by Dr. Kilgo and said it was because the cigarette trust was invading China and carrying its pictures of naked women that he ought to condemn it, but he was refraining from doing so because of the large gifts which the Dukes were making to the institution of which he was head.

Toward the end of the year, a suit was brought by South Dakota in the Supreme Court asking it to compel the state of North Carolina to sell the North Carolina stock to pay the holders of $388,000 worth of Western North Carolina Railroad bonds. When these bonds were issued, the Legislature undertook to secure them by a lien upon the stock held by the state in the North Carolina Railroad but this act had been repudiated by the Legislature when it came to adjust the State debt in the early seventies. On the 19th of November the Supreme Court granted South Dakota leave to sue North Carolina to collect these bonds. The State feared that the suit might be the opening door, as indeed it was intended, to compel the payment of all the reconstruction bonds. It was regarded as a test suit, although the bonds on which South Dakota brought the suit had a lien upon specific property owned by the State, whereas the great bulk of the bonds had no such security. The suit created the deepest interest. The State was very poor then. It was difficult to get enough income to pay the ordinary expenses of government. Governor Aycock took steps to contest the suit of South Dakota and engaged Judge Shepherd, Judge Merrimon, and George Rountree to defend the state in the action. Then the case was tried in the newspapers of North Carolina. The *Caucasian,* Marion Butler's paper, argued that the State of North Carolina was dishonest because it would not pay the bonds, and warmly approved the editorial of the *Morning Post,* urging that the State pay these bonds without contest. The State's attorneys believed that the Supreme Court had no jurisdiction, inasmuch as the bonds had been given to South Dakota for the purpose of procuring it to use its sovereign right to sue another State and, in reality, this was a fraud upon its jurisdiction. This contention was made very strongly. The Supreme Court did not see fit to go behind the acquisition of the bonds and granted South Dakota the right to sue. It was not at first known how South Dakota came in possession of the bonds. It did not develop until later that this case had been actually initiated when Russell was Governor. Some of these bonds were sent to State Treasurer Worth and he was asked to pay them. He consulted Governor Russell about it. Shortly thereafter, Russell took the matter up with Marion Butler, Senator from the State, and he, through his fellow-Populist or Silver Republican colleague, Senator Pettigrew, arranged that a certain amount of these bonds should be given to South Dakota, if that State would bring the suit. Of course, if the suit was won for South Dakota, the holders of the other three hundred thousand dollars or more of the bonds would also be able to collect. There was a belief that Russell and Butler, who were engi-

Upper left, Moses H. Cone, textile manufacturer and leader in industry. *Upper right,* W. A. Erwin, mill owner, in advance of his time in humanitarianism. *Lower left,* J. J. Thomas, President of the Commercial Bank in Raleigh. *Lower right,* John T. Pullen, Raleigh banker and city almoner to the poor.

Upper left, Major Henry Armand London, Confederate soldier, for forty years member of the Democratic State Committee; State Senator. *Upper right,* Judge Robert Martin Douglas, member of the North Carolina Supreme Court. *Lower left,* Judge W. S. O'B. Robinson, brilliant Fusion Judge who lost out with the Republican Party because he refused to eat with a Negro National Committeeman. *Lower right,* Judge Robert Bruce Peebles, who held the whole Robeson County Bar in Contempt of Court.

neering the matter, were acting for the holders of the Reconstruction bonds, and that behind the South Dakota suit a scheme to compel the State to pay the many millions of fraudulent bonds which would have bankrupted the State. *The News and Observer* said, "Russell and Butler are both in Washington in the interest of the South Dakota suit against North Carolina. They are a precious pair of decoy ducks, put up by certain manipulators who inaugurated and are behind the whole piece of deviltry." When the case came to final settlement the Supreme Court held that the stock in the North Carolina Railroad was pledged for the payment of the bonds and directed the payment. The question then arose as to how the State could be compelled to pay. Could the court put the property up at auction on the capitol grounds in Washington if the State refused to pay? Some lawyers held that it could not, and that the Supreme Court decision had no binding effect. Governor Aycock took the ground that, whether the Supreme Court of the United States could take the State by the neck and order it to sell the stock, was not a question to be considered; that, inasmuch as the constitution provided that one sovereign State could sue another, every State was in honor bound to respect this decision and that to do otherwise was to substitute anarchy for law. The State borrowed the money and called in all the bonds of that type.

The papers in the summer were full of statements, which have since been almost annual, that cotton mills would be moved from New England to the South. In August *The News and Observer* had an editorial on cotton mills and child labor laws, in which it said, "If any mills are coming from New England in the expectation of employing child labor, the South does not welcome them" and added that the South was getting ready to enact laws against child labor, for shorter hours and better wages. I have never ceased fighting for this essential trinity for diversified prosperity.

XXXIII

FROM FUSION JUDGES, GOOD LORD DELIVER US

T HE FUSION SUPREME COURT by a vote of 4 to 1 had declared unconstitutional important measures which the Democratic Legislation had enacted in 1899 and had upheld Fusion legislation enacted
in 1895 and 1897. Prior to the session of the 1901 Legislature there
had been talk of impeaching some of the Supreme Court Justices.
Certain decisions of that court had outraged the Democrats, and
many of them believed that the court was governed in its opinions by
purely political considerations. When suggestions of impeachment
were first made, Pritchard, Linney, and Pearson declared that the
transparent purpose of those advocating impeachment was to pack
the Supreme Court in order to declare the suffrage amendment constitutional. Members of the Supreme Court declared that Justice
Clark had originated the suggestion for their impeachment. They
had resented Clark's vigorous dissenting opinion and detested him.
This was interpreted by the Democrats as meaning that if the suffrage
amendment ever came before the Supreme Court, Furches, Douglas,
and other members would declare it unconstitutional. The bitterness
of the suffrage fight had not died away. Underneath the actual impeachment proceedings, the partisans pro and con may have been influenced by the knowledge that the final settlement of that question
might come before the court.

Not long after the Legislature of 1901 met, a resolution for impeachment, which had been drawn up by the leaders of the House of
Representatives, Craig, Allen, Rountree, and others, was offered in
the House and adopted by a very large majority. I was in accord with
the action and had advocated it personally and in my paper. The
resolution introduced in the House from this committee was offered
by Locke Craig, of Buncombe, afterward Governor, on the first day
of February, and called for the impeachment of Chief Justice Furches
and Associate Justice Douglas upon the following grounds:

1. Violation of certain sections of the Constitution in causing
an illegal mandamus to be issued.

2. Intending to bring the General Assembly into disrepute and violating the provision of the Constitution respecting the issue of illegal process.

3. Ordering payment of money which the Legislature had forbidden to be paid.

4. Unlawfully issuing writs (five separate specifications).

5. At various times in their decisions, destroying and defeating the action of the General Assembly in violation of the Constitution.

The resolution also condemned State Auditor Ayer and State Treasurer Worth. The House was crowded when the resolution was offered and the feeling was tense. It was known that Judge Connor, member of the House from Wilson, and perhaps the ablest Democrat in the House, felt that Furches and Douglas deserved censure but did not feel that they should be impeached. He proposed a resolution of censure as a compromise between impeachment and no action at all, but he had a small following. *The News and Observer* said editorially, "The question of impeachment is only a question of whether Furches and Douglas performed an act in violation of the constitution and laws of the State." It was the first impeachment proceeding brought against judges in North Carolina in the lives of any men then living. The bulk of the people of the State, who had felt that the Supreme Court was the bulwark of Fusionism, strongly favored impeachment; but there was a very strong element of members of the bar and a portion of the press, a conservative class, some of whom sided with Judge Connor in favor of censure while others did not believe that Furches and Douglas had been actuated by partisan considerations. When the vote on the Craig resolution was taken in the House, it was 62 to 33. Every Republican voted against it, 62 Democrats voted for it and 13 against it. George Rountree, of New Hanover, who had been rather slow to espouse the cause of impeachment, after making a study of the decisions and conferring among the leaders for impeachment, Craig, Allen, and others, became convinced that the judges had been actuated by partisanship and had violated the law and the constitution. The high-water mark of the contest was the debate between Connor and Rountree. The people of the State at large had the highest regard for Judge Connor's conviction and courage, but they felt that his own judicial service and his kindliness, in a way, warped his judgment and made him too tender toward judges who had been recreant. Rountree attacked his position with great ability, declaring that Connor stood for an utterly indefensible position; that either these judges were guilty and ought to be impeached or they were innocent and ought to be acquitted; that it was a *brutum fulmen*—and Rountree used the word a hundred times during the course of the trial—merely to declare a censure of officials who had violated the law and constitution. He said that for himself he couldn't see any justification for censure. If they had not violated the constitution they ought to be commended, and if they had violated it they ought to be impeached. The middle course of Judge Connor he held to be begging the question. After the passage of the impeachment resolution, following the brilliant debate in the House —the Republicans left the laboring oar to Judge Connor, although they did not agree to his resolution of censure—the Speaker appointed as the managers on the part of the House before the impeachment court the following: William R. Allen, Locke Craig, George Rountree, A. W. Graham, R. H. Hayes, J. F. Spainhour, B. B. Nicholson, F. M. Shannonhouse, and A. A. F. Seawell, easily the ablest lawyers in the House.

During the long trial, following the adjournment of the Legislature, these gentlemen, acting with the eminent counsel engaged, devoted themselves to presenting a case which they, and the bulk of the people of the State, believed justified impeachment. When the trial began all the galleries and the floor of the Senate were crowded. The counsel engaged to appear for the judges under trial were ex-Governor Thomas J. Jarvis, F. I. Osborne, C. M. Cooke, W. P. Bynum, Jr., F. H. Busbee, B. F. Long, and J. Lindsey Patterson. The counsel advocating impeachment was composed of Cyrus B. Watson, W. A. Guthrie, Theodore F. Davidson, C. M. Busbee, and James H. Pou.

The wives of most of the attorneys on both sides and of the managers of the impeachment were in Raleigh. It was an interesting sight, when the court was convened every morning, to see sitting on the right side of the Senate Chamber the women whose husbands and friends were advocating impeachment, while those of the advocates for the judges sat on the left. These ladies were quite as partisan as their husbands, and social amenities were adjourned during the trial. Nothing else was discussed in Raleigh. I rarely missed a session, and by the time the trial began I had published an account of the Holden impeachment trial, which had been the only other such trial in many years in North Carolina. When the impeachment defense began *The News and Observer* had an editorial headed, "From Fusion Courts Good Lord Deliver Us," and the paper strongly supported the impeachment, while the *Morning Post* in Raleigh and the Charlotte *Observer* opposed it. *The News and Observer* charged that these papers, the first of which was owned by the Southern Railway, were favoring these judges because Colonel Andrews and the Tobacco Trust opposed impeachment. There was a running controversy between the papers and much denunciation backward and forward, which added to the intensity of interest on the part of the people of both sides during the trial.

At first there was great confidence that the judges would be impeached, but as the days went on, a doubt about it developed. When the vote was taken the Senate Chamber was packed, and the interest was so tense that you could have heard the fabled pin drop. The presiding officers, all dignified, warned against any outburst of applause or otherwise. There were eleven Republicans in the Senate, and they all voted against conviction on all of the five articles. Twelve Democrats voted against impeachment. On the first article the vote was 27 to 23 for impeachment; on the second and third, 24 to 26, and on the fourth, 25 to 25. Impeachment, therefore, failed, but the advocates of impeachment felt that, since on the first article they had a majority of four, the vote was a moral victory for them, whereas the friends of the judges regarded it as a vindication. On the day the vote was taken, Senator Mike H. Justice, of Rutherford, declared the judges were guilty of the charge, and *The News and Observer,* in a two-column editorial headed, "Judges Not Vindicated," declared that they were morally convicted. The State breathed freely again, and with the tension over there was a feeling on the part of those who advocated impeachment that the trial had brought a salutary lesson. The result was not unlike Franklin Roosevelt's attempt to reorganize the reactionary United States Supreme Court. The battle was lost, but the war was won.

Somewhat in the nature of an aftermath, in June, 1901, Fabius H. Busbee, who had volunteered to defend the Supreme Court Justices in the impeachment trial, gave notice that he would make a motion in the Supreme Court for a reargument of the Coley case. My paper more than intimated that Mr. Busbee's zeal to defeat impeachment was to gain favor with the court in railroad litigation. It also said that, in giving a new trial in the Kilgo-Gattis and like cases, the judges were paying the debt they owed to the American Tobacco Company and the Southern Railway for zeal in saving them from impeachment. The Coley case became a *cause célèbre*.

Engineer Samuel Coley had been given a verdict of $12,000 for personal injuries by the Southern Railway. Coley had many friends who felt that a $12,000 verdict was not too large for the loss of his arm. The Southern Railway attorneys, evidently thinking this might make a precedent for large damages, were resolved, if possible, to have the verdict set aside. On one side the railroad employees were lined up and on the other side the railroad attorneys. Naturally, as of every other disputed question in that day, *The News and Observer* and the *Morning Post* took opposite sides very vigorously, and sometimes very abusively. Referring to an application for a re-hearing, my paper said:

> "Without a hint to the outside world, it is published exclusively in the *Morning Boast,* along with the schedules and other matter furnished that paper by the Southern Railwayites, that the Supreme Court has ordered a rehearing in the Coley case."

and added:

> "Although the *Morning Post* runs on a slow freight schedule as to everything else, it is a lightning express with reference to everything concerning the Southern Railroad management in North Carolina. It scores a scoop on its contemporaries in knowing the mind of the North Carolina Tar Heel magnates. It can publish that long in advance of official publication of the status of railroad cases before the courts—in these matters, it is a 'scooper' from Scooperville, and no mistake, and always blows the whistle when the conductor pulls the bell cord."

It should be added that the Supreme Court affirmed the decision in the Coley case and he got $12,000, although the case went off by a vote of 3 to 2, Cook and Montgomery dissenting.

In June, in a case in which the Southern Railway had been sued in Iredell Court, Judge Brown in his findings held that the Southern Railway officials at Statesville had tried to tamper with the jury and *The News and Observer* said that it wondered why the *Morning Boast* had failed to print Judge Brown's findings. That was another incident in the continuous controversy between the two papers.

XXXIV

AGAINST LYNCHING, LIQUOR, ILLITERACY

I N 1902, as in every year, there were strong editorials in *The News and Observer* and other papers, in the effort to prevent lynchings in North Carolina. The early part of the year was marked by a horrible one at Salisbury. Two boys were lynched for killing Miss Cornelia Benson. Governor Aycock offered a reward for each person in the lynching party, a sum aggregating $30,000, and *The News and Observer* said it was not lynching, but was premeditated murder. Governor Aycock directed Solicitor Hammer to proceed to Salisbury and make a thorough investigation, and to leave no stone unturned to apprehend the culprits and bring them to justice. In March, a Negro, charged with poisoning the family of Dr. David Tayloe, of Washington, was taken from the jail at Williamston and lynched, and in August a Negro who was being taken to jail in Edenton for assault, was shot down as he was being carried from the jail. In August also Tom Jones, a Negro alleged rapist, was lynched near Kinston, and a Lenoir County jury formally made its findings as to the lynchers by saying the man was lynched "by parties unknown to the jury, obviously by an outraged public acting in defense of their homes, wives, daughters and children. In view of the enormity of the crime by said Tom Jones, alias Frank Hill, we think they would have been recreant to their duty as good citizens had they done otherwise." *The News and Observer* said the mob should have placed the criminal in jail, applied to the Governor for a special term, which would have been ordered at once, and lawfully hung him on the gallows. It also said that Governor Aycock had done more to prevent lynchings than any other Governor in the country and nothing distressed him so much as that lynching should disgrace his administration.

Early in 1902 was organized what later came to exert powerful influence, the Anti-Saloon League, of which N. B. Broughton was president. This organization embraced in its membership many of the strongest men in the State. It held meetings in Raleigh during sessions of the Legislature and promoted State prohibition. Upon its organization, *The News and Observer* said, "With the education of the people, the temperance spirit will spread and the day will come when the saloon will no longer be open in North Carolina. It will come step by step, as public sentiment demands it and is ready for it." This proved to be a good prophecy. It did not come until over one third of the counties of the State went dry and many of the towns had voted out the saloons, and in a dozen or more towns the saloons had been displaced by the dispensary.

I was surprised, seeing that I generally lived up to a policy of refusing to accept liquor advertisements, to find in going over some old files that *The News and Observer,* in July, 1895, carried an advertisement of the Salisbury Liquor Company, whose copy read: "Fine Old Corn Whiskey A Specialty," and also an advertisement of "Old Nick" which had been manufactured in Yadkin County for a century. I was all the more surprised, seeing that later when I was a strong advocate of State prohibition there was a sharp clash with the distiller who had inherited the Old Nick distilleries, which were put out of business by the State prohibition law. He sought to have his distillery exempted by trying to incorporate it as a town, as is told in more detail in another connection.

A SCHOOL HOUSE A DAY

Upon the death of General Toon, Superintendent of Public Instruction, Governor Aycock appointed James Y. Joyner, a classmate and friend at the University, who had, as superintendent of the graded schools in Goldsboro and as second in command, under McIver, at the State Normal and Industrial College, shown ability and vision. *The News and Observer* warmly praised the appointment and declared that the day of an educational era of good feeling had come. It supported Aycock and Joyner in the many measures which were put into effect to secure a sound and vigorous public opinion for better school houses and longer terms. The administration was characterized by the statement that a school house was built for every day in the year. It was a constructive administration as well as a progressive one. Dr. Joyner was one of the half-dozen educators with vision and constructive ability, who made the late eighties and nineties and the period covered by the Aycock administration the most revolutionary in changing public sentiment and strengthening it for public education. Recognition of his leadership came to him while in the office of the State Superintendent by election as president of the National Education Association. The first real movement toward consolidation of public schools began in 1902 and on March 21, *The News and Observer* said, "There are too many schools and too many districts. Let there be consolidation with wisdom and common sense."

In the same month *The News and Observer* had a leading editorial on "A Road Tax or a Mud Tax," in which it pointed out that the mud tax in North Carolina, both in money and in preventing transportation and progress, was heavier than any tax that might be imposed. Early in the year my paper issued a "Good Roads Edition," the first paper of the kind to be printed in North Carolina. It was issued in honor of Good Roads Week, which was observed by a conference in Raleigh. To this conference came leaders in the creation of public sentiment, which later crystallized into the construction of the best roads in the South. When a suggestion was made that the State ought to issue ten million dollars of bonds to build good roads, it was deemed to be so wild a thought that it received no consideration from the conservative men who were sincerely devoted to road construction. If they could have been told that twenty years later the State of North Carolina would issue more than one hundred million dollars of bonds, they would have said that the prophet was entertaining iridescent dreams. I urged that the mud tax stood not only in the way of proper consolidation of country schools, for children from a large area could not come to a public school because of the bad roads, but it also was a barrier against the extension of the rural delivery system. I went to Washington to see the Post Master General and to urge an extension of the rural delivery in North Carolina. This was after one of his assistants had attended the road conference in Raleigh and had told the people that the reason there were no more rural delivery systems in North Carolina was because of the bad roads. I took issue with him in *The News and Observer,* saying that while both of us were agreed that we ought to have good roads the lack of them was no justification of the Post Office Department in denying as many rural delivery routes in the State as in a State like Iowa, for example. North Carolina, I said, was about the same size and the same in population as Iowa and the people were entitled to mail delivery whether they had good roads or not, provided rural carriers could be found who would furnish their own conveyances and carry the routes for as low a price as they did in Iowa.

OLD NICK AND OTHER DISTILLERS OUSTED

Before the session of the Legislature of 1903 opened I began an agitation for an act forbidding the sale or manufacture of liquor except in incorporated towns and revoking the incorporation of certain cross-roads controlled by distillers. I also advocated legislation providing for referendum as to whether a town wished prohibition, dispensaries, or saloons. It was pointed out that it was more difficult to deal with the distilling curse, but one thing was evident: the people demanded the abolition of the distilleries and would not much longer tolerate their demoralizing and debauching influence.

In December State Chairman Simmons made his first declaration as to temperance legislation, and on December 3, 1902, *The News and Observer* quoted him as saying that the manufacture of liquors should be under State control. *The News and Observer,* quoting this, wrote an editorial on the headline "The Distilleries Must Go." Later on, my paper, along with Aycock and Simmons, approved the legislation which was enacted in 1903, known as the Watts law, which prevented the manufacture of liquor in North Carolina and the sale of it except in incorporated towns. The bill, offered by Mr. A. D. Watts, of Iredell, had been broadened from his original conception. Watts had no primary interest in prohibition or temperance. He was a consummate politician who knew the situation in Western North Carolina and saw that the Republican workers were generally people employed by the Federal revenue department. There was no limit upon the number that could be appointed and it had been the habit of the Republican Party to select men quite as much for political work as for running down illicit distilleries. They indeed constituted the Republican working force in a score or more counties. Watts' idea was that if you could separate these men from a Federal salary, they would lose interest in politics and the Democrats would carry these counties much more easily. I sympathized with his point of view, as did Simmons and Aycock, and we got behind the Watts bill. It had the effect that Watts predicted. As soon as nobody could manufacture liquor in North Carolina, the Federal government appointed very few inspectors. The Watts law was thus a very good Democratic measure, but it went much further than Mr. Watts had expected. It became a good temperance measure and later, aided by the Ward (of New Bern) bill, which prevented any sale of liquors except in incorporated towns (and said towns must be real towns and not crossroads) at one blow made a large part of the State dry, so that it was easy later on for the prohibitionists to carry the State.

When the legislation was pending in the Senate in 1903, there was a hearing which brought to Raleigh hundreds and maybe thousands of people. I do not recall ever before seeing great multitudes of women in the legislative halls wearing their badges and telling legislators that prayer meetings were being held all over the State. The champions of the two sides in this debate were Charles W. Tillett, of Charlotte, for the temperance forces, and Cameron Morrison, of Rockingham, for the distillers. Mr. Tillett had begun the practice of law at Rockingham, and Morrison then lived there. Richmond County came down in full force, headed by Senator Everett, who was as straight in life as he was straight in figure, tall, erect. He had been a Confederate soldier, and after the war, in a very quiet way, had been looked up to by his people as a leader. He resented the fact that Cameron Morrison had accepted a retainer from the Hamlet liquor dealers and distillers to fight the measures, not so much because he objected to Mr. Morrison's taking a fee, as because Mr. Morrison, at the time, was chairman of the Democratic Executive Committee of the county. Captain Everett held that he ought not to use the influence of that position, given him by all the Democrats of the county, in behalf of keeping Hamlet the central place of manufacture and sale of liquor in Southern North Carolina. When Morrison reached Raleigh on the day of the hearing, *The News and Observer,* in a double-column editorial, demanded that he either resign his place as chairman of the Democratic Executive Committee of Richmond County or decline to represent the rich distillers of Hamlet. The editorial was printed in black type. It infuriated Mr. Morrison. The real reason why he was so furious was not because of what *The News and Observer* said but because, at home, Senator Everett and the temperance forces were making it very uncomfortable for him.

Tillett spoke in the spirit of his father and as a result of his upbringing in a Methodist parsonage. His father, the Reverend John Tillett, Methodist circuit rider, was one of the pioneer temperance advocates in the State. He felt he could not preach the Gospel without preaching against liquor. Upon every charge he served, he was the center of temperance agitation in a day when temperance agitation was unpopular. Preacher Tillett was the author of a saying which became famous in North Carolina, in the days when the temperance battle was some fight. He was preaching at Burlington, then called Company's Shops, which, like all other towns in North Carolina, had many saloons and where Saturdays and Saturday nights were often turned into drunken saturnalias. Beyond sermons against it and occasional denunciations, the temperance forces were helpless, but the Reverend John Tillett thundered in his pulpit and in private urged people to mobilize to drive out the saloons. He denounced them and the saloon business so frequently and vigorously that the operators regarded him as their chief foe. Toward the end of the year, when he was going to conference, his church had not raised the full salary promised. I daresay it wasn't more than six hundred dollars and he had a large family. As he entered the post office one morning—in those days the post office was the club and rendezvous—a crowd had assembled and was waiting for the mail to be opened. By evident prearrangement, the leading saloon-keeper of the town (and usually these saloon-keepers were pleasant and agreeable and many of them were charitable) approached Mr. Tillett and said, "Mr. Tillett, I know you are the enemy of my business and want to destroy it. I have here a twenty-dollar bill which I made selling liquor, selling something which you say sends a man to damnation. I wish to offer you this money, made out of this traffic, to pay on your salary or for church purposes if you can take the money by a traffic that you have denounced." He handed over the twenty-dollar bill, which Mr. Tillett took, opening it in the palm of his hand, smoothing it out, and looking at it for several minutes, before he said a word. The saloon-keeper thought he wouldn't take it, but would call it tainted money. After a few minutes the reverend gentleman, looking at the bill and stroking it, said, "Old twenty-dollar bill, you have served the devil many years and served him faithfully. I now pronounce you converted and will put you into the service of the Lord," and he put it in his pocket.

The speech made by Mr. Charles W. Tillett, son of the old preacher, made a profound impression. He was in his prime. When he had a cause in court or before the Legislature, no man could be more effective, more eloquent, or more able. The spirit of his father sat upon him as he stood in the chamber surrounded by white-ribboned women, preachers, and temperance workers. He was cool and collected, while his opponent, Mr. Morrison, was excited and furious. Mr. Morrison said that in spite of his plain statement that he was the paid attorney of the liquor men, *The News and Observer* had seen fit to misrepresent his position. He begged them to consider this cause on its own merits and not to be swept away or influenced by Aycock, Daniels, and Simmons. He then turned to me, as I was sitting near Mr. Tillett, and said, "I don't mean to make any threat. I have always voted your way and Mr. Simmons', but if you don't stop talking about me the way you do, I may not keep on voting for you." He declared it was not fair to saddle S. Otho Wilson on them, and, again turning to me, he said, "There seems to be a desire to monopolize Democratic leadership in this matter. No, the trouble is [turning to me] we have crossed your imperial will and we have questioned your mighty judgment." *The News and Observer* had an editorial discussing lawyers who appeared for whiskey interests. It was pretty severe upon them, claiming that in a great moral issue lawyers ought to be citizens and voice their convictions and not lend their influence to an unholy cause for fees, particularly instancing Mr. Morrison. When the bills came up in the Legislature, the galleries were crowded again with temperance workers. The Watts bill to close up the distilleries was passed by a vote of 78 to 38, London's measure to shut up the saloons passed by a good majority, and Richmond County was made dry.

After the measure became a law that no liquor should be manufactured, except in incorporated towns, the Senator from Yadkin introduced a bill entitled, "An Act to Establish a Graded School at Yadkinville," which, when examined, showed that it was incorporating a town three miles square in order to make it possible for Glenn Williams to continue the manufacture of Old Nick Liquor. For several generations the Williams family, rich and well connected, had manufactured Old Nick Whiskey in Yadkin County and sold it all over the South. It was never poisoned. It was made of good material, and many people who wished to keep a little in the house for snakebite and other purposes (chiefly for other purposes) sent to Yadkin County and purchased it by the gallon and barrel. It was one of the biggest industries of that section for many years. In this connection, I recall that when the letters and papers of Governor Jonathan Worth were printed by the State, one of his granddaughters was very much shocked when she read, for the first time, a letter from Governor

Worth to Nick Williams, making a trade by which he obtained a barrel of brandy in exchange for the clip of his sheep. It was quite common for Old Nick to swap his liquor for wool or anything else he could turn into money. Naturally, his son, Glenn Williams, who had inherited a large plantation and the distilleries, thought it was a great outrage to destroy his business. His father had been a responsible citizen and, in that day, the making of whiskey was not regarded as bad. In fact, he never lost caste by it except with a few prohibitionists. He was esteemed as having added to the happiness and enthusiasm of his generation, and the younger Williams came to Raleigh to protect his interests. He was the only man in the city who, on week days, wore a Prince Albert and a shiny silk hat and put on what the boys called "lugs." He was the best dressed man in town, had his rooms at the leading hotel, and brought to bear every influence. He didn't realize that a new order had come.

One of the queerest legislators in the history of the State was Long, of Cabarrus. Frank Rogers, a popular drummer and politician given to practical jokes, was credited with electing Long as a joke. Rogers was the author of a widely quoted saying in North Carolina that "nobody in Cabarrus County ever voted for anybody; that on election day the populace rose as one man and went to the polls and asked, "Who is the fellow I want to swat today?" They always voted *against* somebody. The boys in Concord urged Long to be a candidate. He announced his candidacy on the platform of "more liquor and better liquor." He declared the State of North Carolina thought more of the land than of the man. He said no farmer could put fertilizer on his land unless it was analyzed to see that the ingredients were pure, but said he, "They will allow men to sell liquor to good citizens of the State which has poison in it and the overshadowing issue in North Carolina is to adopt the same rule as to protecting men who drink, as farmers are protected from frauds in fertilizers." He was a curious sort of fellow, loved his dram, and wanted it free from poisonous substances. The young fellows in Concord hurrahed about him first as a pure joke; then the Republicans endorsed him as a candidate, which insured his election if he could get a few hundred Democratic votes. He got them and was elected. Frank Rogers and the drummers of the State who wanted to have a lot of fun persuaded Long that he must address the House on his great reform of "more liquor and better liquor." At a given time, it was announced, Long would speak. The galleries were crowded and when he made his impassioned appeal that the stomachs of the men of North Carolina were as much entitled to protection from adulterated liquor as the land from adulterated fertilizer, the galleries and lobbies applauded out of derision and out of fun, and Long thought he was the greatest statesman of the day. It was one of the most ridiculous scenes as his hearers crowded around him and told him he had made the greatest speech of a generation. The old man believed them. They assured him his bill would pass; that he was the only seer in the State who saw the necessity of protecting the stomachs of whiskey drinkers. His idea was to have chemists in the Agricultural Department analyze intoxicants as they analyzed fertilizers. After the hurrah and the guffaw, nothing more was heard of Long's bill or of Long.

XXXV

WALTER CLARK AND THE JUDICIAL CONTESTS

I N THE YEARS following the rout of the Fusionists, I found myself
in the centre of two contests for high judicial stations. As a rule
the selection of judicial officers was not political, but when the Supreme Court annulled laws from political bias and railroads and big
interests wished to keep progressives off the Supreme Court the people demanded a change in the court. It was laymen who improved
British justice. Lawyers as a rule stand for the status quo. These
opposing views conflicted in North Carolina in 1902 and came to a
head in the selection of Chief Justice of the Supreme Court.

Early in that year there began a very heated contest as to who
should be the Democratic nominee for Chief Justice. James E. Shepherd had been Chief Justice and had been defeated by the Fusionists.
His friends thought that he ought to be returned to the post he had
filled with credit. Associate Justice Walter Clark, who had been on
the bench for some years, aspired to the chief justiceship. He was
strongly supported by the farmers and what may be called the more
progressive element. The result might have turned out differently if
Judge Shepherd had not been hampered by the ardent and unwise
support of him by the chief counsel of the Southern Railway, Fabius
H. Busbee, and chief counsel of the Seaboard Air Line, W. H. Day.
They hated Clark intensely. They said he could not do the railroads
justice and that, while Shepherd held the scales evenly, he would give
them and the people a fair hearing. They began early to organize for
Shepherd, but they said one word for Shepherd to fifty words against
Clark. That created an atmosphere which was injurious to Shepherd's
chances. The railroad attorneys, almost in a body, organized to
nominate Shepherd, and Clark was a good enough politician to let
this be very widely known.

In January, Henry A. Page, president of the Asheboro and Aberdeen Railroad, a railroad somewhat longer than it was wide, built
by his father as a lumber road, and afterward extended into three or
four counties, took up the cudgels against Clark in *The News and*

Upper left, J. Y. Joyner, Superintendent of Schools in the administrations of Aycock and succeeding Governors. *Upper right,* Wilfred Dent Turner, Lieutenant-Governor during Aycock's administration. *Lower left,* J. Bryan Grimes, Secretary of State and a pioneer in tobacco farmer organization. *Lower right,* Benjamin R. Lacy, State Treasurer during the administrations of Aycock and five succeeding Governors.

Upper left, Charles M. Busbee, director and attorney of *The News and Observer;* Simmons' manager; a leader of the Raleigh Bar. *Upper right,* Richmond Pearson, Republican leader; member of Congress; and Minister to Persia. *Lower left,* Judge Howard A. Foushee, manager of General Julian S. Carr's senatorial campaign. *Lower right,* Claudius Dockery, Republican leader in 1894-1901.

Observer. He was a brilliant writer. I sometimes thought, if he had devoted himself to it, he would have been a more brilliant writer than his brother, Walter Hines Page. He wielded a trenchant pen and wrote interestingly and vigorously, and in those days, he was talking about *The News and Observer* viciously. He reformed later. He was so much abler as a writer than any other railroad official or attorney that the big railroads were glad to stand aside and let him carry on their fight. His railroad was small and there was no prejudice against him such as was entertained against the spokesmen of the big roads. He therefore became for a time the voice of the railroads of the State. If Day and Busbee had been wise they would have kept out of the controversy for Chief Justice, but neither one of them ever saw a day when he had wisdom. They had ability, brilliance, in fact; but they had the fatal defect which comes to men who can say bright and sharp things. They would ruin their cause, in order to turn a sentence that would sting or burn or to secure a laugh or applause. Page took up the cudgels in my paper against Clark and excoriated him and my paper. I had not taken sides up to that time but felt compelled to defend Clark, because, in the railroad questions uppermost at that time, *The News and Observer* had, for years, been advocating the position which Judge Clark had maintained as a citizen and judge. Every time Henry Page threw a stone at Clark, he was hitting *The News and Observer,* and he loved to do that.

My own personal preference in the matter was for Shepherd. He was a citizen of Washington, North Carolina, and that alone would have made me partial to him. He had married Miss Brown, also from that town, and had been, since his early manhood, a close friend of my mother. When he was studying law he supported himself as a telegraph operator in Wilson and boarded with my aunt. Influenced by the charm which drew people of all sorts to her, he became a very warm friend of my mother, and their friendship lasted as long as he lived. He had looked after the sale of the land on which she was born in Hyde County and handled a few matters of business for her, for which he would not take a fee. He never went to Wilson without going to see her. Later, when he was on the bench and she visited Raleigh, he always called to see her. In the great crisis of his life in 1888, when Captain Laughinghouse assailed him when he was candidate for Associate Justice, I had been deeply interested and active in his support, and had a part in helping him during the campaign.

When it was over, he wrote me a letter of appreciation and sent me a present of a beautiful Bible, which I have always kept near me. I preserved it more religiously than I have read it or followed its precepts. For these reasons and because of his judicial qualities, I naturally would have been in favor of his nomination. However, at that time, the conflict between railroad control and the people who wanted to regulate railroads and prevent their domination of politics, was uppermost. The question was whether the people or the railroads should control the State. Shepherd was not a partisan. He did not love a fight. Clark would rather fight than eat.

I resented deeply that Judge Shepherd's campaign was being managed by Day and Busbee. They were the brightest lobbyists of the railroad interests in the State. They were for Shepherd not so much because they cared for him, but because they were against Clark, who opposed railroad control of the State. Of course, along with these men was James H. Pou, who was counsel extraordinary for all the railroads in any matters coming up in Raleigh in the courts or in the Legislature, although he did not always appear. At another time I said in my paper that the other lawyers had attained distinction as attorneys for corporations and railroads and had received large fees, but Mr. Pou had made a new rule in that he fixed the fee not on the basis of services rendered but on the basis of the mileage of the railroads he represented. I cannot say that I blamed him for not liking that editorial comment.

About February these lawyers, and others, some of whom were railroad attorneys and some who were not, went to see Governor Aycock and pointed out to him that the party was about to be involved in a bitter conflict over the nomination of a Chief Justice, which was unseemly; that judicial position should be awarded because of learning and no extraneous considerations ought to be involved. Aycock was a warm friend of Shepherd. He had made the convincing speech in the convention when Captain Laughinghouse had assailed Shepherd, and he knew of his ability and integrity. His callers persuaded the Governor that, as head of the party, it was his duty to prevent the injury to it which would be caused by a fight between Shepherd and Clark.

One day I received a telephone message asking me to come to the Governor's office at a certain hour. He laid before me this situation and told me of the men of high standing and having no connection with the railroads, who had urged upon him the high duty of seeking to prevent the threatened damaging contest by renominating Judge Clark as Associate Justice and Judge Shepherd for the position of Chief Justice, which he had filled satisfactorily. I asked the Governor if Captain Day, Mr. Busbee, and Mr. Pou had talked to him about this matter. He said they had. I told him that, in my opinion, these railroad lawyers had effected an organization to defeat Clark because Clark could not be used by them; that, while I entertained the same high opinion of Shepherd that he did and, personally, wanted to support him, I could not do so because of the company I would have to be in; that I could not join hands with the railroads who were trying to defeat Clark because of his virtues and not because of his failings. I told the Governor, also, that I believed most of the people who had seen him had been urged to do so by the railroads. Then I said, "Governor, this poker is hot at both ends. If you will take my advice, you will tell Bill Day and Fab Busbee and Jim Pou, if they want that poker handled, one of them will have to take hold of one end and one of the other and let them get burned. But, Governor, keep your fingers free." When he saw that I was convinced, in spite of my affection for Shepherd, that it was my duty to stand by the man who had opposed railroad manipulation and domination, he ceased trying to persuade me to follow that course. I think he told the gentlemen that it was a matter in which the Governor of the State ought not to intervene. Thereafter, Judge Shepherd let it be known that he would not enter the race.

A short time after my talk with the Governor, Judge Clark, who somehow got wind of everything that took place, requested me and State Treasurer Lacy to call at the Supreme Court Building. Upon our arrival, he said he had written an article for publication and he wished to consult us about it. The article charged that the railroads had conspired to compass his defeat because he would not do their bidding. He went on to say, virtually, that Governor Aycock (calling him "a former railroad attorney," though Aycock represented one railroad only in court cases), was in league with the railroads. He assailed the action of the Governor in relation to a railroad tax case originating in Washington County. The article was violent and unjust and was inspired by Clark's resentment that Aycock was opposed to his promotion. Clark always struck hard and quick and, sometimes, viciously. Lacy and I listened to the reading without comment. I was seething with indignation at the unjustified attack on Aycock but held in until the reading was finished. Clark turned to us and asked, "What do you think of it?" I showed my feeling by saying, "If you print that uncalled for and unjust criticism of Aycock I will publicly oppose your nomination." I was mad clear through. Turning to Lacy, he said, "Ben, what do you think?" Lacy answered that he felt just as I did. Clark took out his pencil and erased all to which we had objected, saying, "I asked for your frank counsel and I am taking it." It took me some time to cool off. I never spoke to Aycock about it. My support of Clark was based upon my belief that he was standing with my paper against corporate domination.

In the early days, before Shepherd had declined to permit the use of his name, there appeared what became a frequent feature on the editorial page of *The News and Observer,* an article in editorial type credited to the *Rhamkatte Roaster.* This article showed, from the standpoint of a countryman who could not spell, how the corporations were fighting Judge Clark and ridiculed Captain Day and Mr. Busbee, who were opposing him because he would not run on the schedules fixed by their railroads. Being something new in the line of journalism, the article created interest and was particularly resented by Captain Day, who made it a point, so I learned, to denounce the paper very loudly upon every occasion, so much so that everybody who heard him was all the more convinced that the chief opposition to Clark was engineered by the railroads. Later, all through the years, whenever any matter of controversial interest came up and I wanted to comment in a vein not serious, I would write the article and credit it to the *Rhamkatte Roaster.* There was no such paper, but some people reached the conclusion that there was such a paper and that it must be a very bright sheet and quite original. Many persons wrote they would like to subscribe for it.

On June 29, *The News and Observer* had an editorial headed, "What the Test Shows," and said: "The Southern Railroad organ has for many weeks been trying to defeat Clark and said Wake County was against him. Yesterday Wake County unanimously endorsed Clark." It also said, "That vote clearly gauges the influence of the *Morning Post* in the councils of the Democratic Party in Wake County." In the State Convention Clark's majority was overwhelming.

After Judge Shepherd declined the use of his name, Thomas N.

Hill, of Halifax, announced himself as a candidate for Chief Justice, but, good lawyer as he was, he never made any headway because it was believed his nomination had been sponsored by Day and Busbee. *The News and Observer* said, "Nobody is backing Hill but Palmer and Buckner supporters." He received a very small vote in the Democratic Convention, not even that of his own county, for he and Clark were both Halifax men. Later, the Republican Convention endorsed Judge Hill for Chief Justice. *The News and Observer* said this showed that it had not been wrong in saying that the opponents of Judge Clark were ready to go to any length to compass his defeat. There was really no doubt about the election. My paper had this editorial on the following day: "Dead and Very Dead. Fabius H. Busbee, at his voting place yesterday, said 'I intend to vote for Thomas N. Hill for Chief Justice. He is a dead straight man.'"

I had a part in one of the closest contests in the history of the State for the position of Associate Justice. The candidates were H. G. Connor, of Wilson, and George H. Brown, of Beaufort. Both had served with ability and acceptability on the Superior Court bench. Brown was then on the bench and Connor was practicing law in Wilson. My relations with both of them were such that it troubled me greatly, though I had no difficulty in deciding between the two and threw every influence that I could command for the nomination of Connor. He was nominated by a majority of five and one third votes out of more than one thousand votes cast in the State Convention, and it was nerve-racking while the tellers were counting the vote. Judge Brown felt that I ought to have kept hands off in the contest seeing that he was from my birthplace and Connor from my old home at Wilson. He was sore, for a time, because my brothers and I had been so active for Connor. The prohibition question was not invoked, but most of the prohibitionists were for Connor, while the opponents favored Brown. The only public mention of drink was that, at the convention a bibulous supporter of Connor from Wilson, so drunk he could hardly navigate, buttonholed delegates, telling them they ought not to vote for Brown because "he drinks too much." The spectacle caused many a laugh at its incongruity.

Brown was holding court in Buncombe County and immediately upon the announcement of the vote, I sent him this telegram: "Connor was nominated by a majority of $5\frac{1}{3}$ votes. You will be nominated unanimously two years hence, as Associate Justice." This telegram showed him my personal feeling and prevented strained relations. The prophecy came true two years later.

In July, 1902, I attended at Rocky Mount a convention which was an unhappy experience in my political life. Governor Aycock had appointed my brother, Charles C. Daniels, as solicitor of the Fourth District. The convention was called to nominate a judge and a solicitor. The most influential politicians of the district had effected an organization deemed to be invincible for the nomination of Jacob Battle, of Rocky Mount, as judge and R. A. P. Cooley, of Nash, as solicitor. Franklin County put up the Honorable Charles M. Cooke for judge. The fight in the convention was clear-cut for Cooke and Daniels, on the one side, and Battle and Cooley, on the other. In Wilson County, where my brother lived, he had some strong opposition, but the great bulk of the county was for him as were Franklin and Vance; both of them gave most of their votes for him and for Cooke. If Edgecombe and Nash could have been made solid for Battle and Cooley, as it seemed in the early stages, they would have been nominated. Battle had strong support in Wilson, some of it by political enemies of my brother, who believed if Battle was nominated for judge it would defeat Daniels for solicitor. They had given assurance to Battle's friends that he would get a part of the Wilson vote. If he could obtain one fourth of it, as seemed probable, he would be nominated. That would defeat my brother. Fortunately the Democratic plan of organization contained a clause, which had rarely been invoked, that, in a precinct meeting, any Democratic voter could demand a poll of all present as to the candidates, and that the friends of the candidates would have the right to select delegates in proportion to the votes so cast. My bother's friends in several precincts in Edgecombe and Nash split the vote enough to nominate him if he could carry Franklin, Vance, and practically all of Wilson, his home county. In order to be forehanded, before the township meeting I had received a ruling from State Chairman Simmons that if the vote were taken at a precinct meeting before delegates were elected, the minority was entitled to name its own delegates. They had done this but had been challenged. However, with this ruling, the unit rule attempt was doomed.

I arrived at Rocky Mount early and called upon my friends who were supporting Battle and got the lay of the land before the dele-

gates from Wilson arrived. I found that they were depending upon
Battle's getting enough votes out of Wilson to defeat Cooke, and I
saw that victory depended upon a practically solid vote in Wilson for
Cooke and Daniels. When the Wilson delegates arrived I ascertained
that a number had committed themselves to Battle before Cooke became a candidate, and they felt honor-bound to vote for him. Some
of these were sincere, but most of them used that as a feint to defeat
my brother without voting directly against him. It was all that Fred
A. Woodard, Sid Woodard, and other friends in the Wilson delegation could do to hold the Wilson people in line for Cooke. In fact,
when the convention opened, it did not look as if that would be possible. Early in the morning I had a conference with two of the best
politicians in the State, Captain Bill Yarborough, of Franklin, and
J. A. Thomas, editor of the Louisburg *Times,* and with some Vance
friends, and I found that Vance and Franklin were solid for Cooke
and Daniels. Cooke could get no votes in Edgecombe or Nash and it
would be necessary for Wilson to cast nearly its solid vote for Cooke.
Martin County, whose political leaders were in league with the opposition to Cooke and Daniels, had assured the Battle and Cooley
forces that Martin would vote for them. However, the county convention, instead of electing delegates, passed a resolution that any
Democrat in the county who desired to attend would be a delegate.
When the train reached Rocky Mount from Williamston it looked
like an excursion train. Almost every Democrat in Martin County
seemed to be on that train. My brother had many friends in the
county, and of course Battle and Cooley had influential friends. It
was now clear that Martin County would divide its vote. When the
roll was called to nominate a judge, Wilson came last. I was sitting
next to Sid Woodard, of Wilson. We had counted up the vote of all
the other counties and saw it would be necessary for Wilson County
to cast all its votes, except a very few, to nominate Cooke. When Wilson was called Woodard arose and announced its vote, giving Cooke
just enough to nominate him and Battle a few. Such an uproar followed as I have never heard before or since. Lawyers and politicians,
who were generally self-contained, rose and denounced the Wilson
delegates as traitors, scoundrels, and thieves. Some of the Wilson delegation wanted to resent the insults. It looked as though the convention would break up with personal violence and riot. However, the
calm and suave Fred A. Woodard, who always managed to control

politics in Wilson County without seeming to do it, quietly said to those who wanted to fight: "Keep your seats. Never mind what they say. If they call you 'sons of bitches,' don't say a word. Let the others rave. We have the votes." And they raved for half an hour or more. The chairman could not secure order. He saw the only thing to do was to let the storm run its course. Bitterness grew out of that convention that lasted a lifetime. Men who had been my best friends became my bitterest political enemies. I never expected to get out of Rocky Mount that day without being assaulted. I had been very active, and Governor Aycock had done all he properly could to help my brother's nomination. But as I was on the spot, not a resident of the district, resentment of my activity went beyond all bounds. Some of the speakers requested that I, an interloper, be requested to leave the hall and cease cracking the whip and using carpet-bag methods to direct action in a district in which I was not a resident. The Wilson delegates sat quietly in their seats as unruffled as if nothing had happened. After a time quiet was restored and Cooke was declared nominated. Presently Frank Spruill obtained the floor and put my brother in nomination amid such jeers and cat-calls and abuse from the opposition as can hardly be described. Spruill, a Franklin County delegate, and perhaps the best speaker in all Eastern North Carolina, was undeterred by the jeers. He would stop every now and then and say with provoking coolness: "Gentlemen, when you have made yourselves hoarse I will proceed. We are here to nominate Cooke and Daniels and we are going to do it if it takes until Christmas." Finally the roll was called and Daniels was nominated by about the same majority as Cooke, and the convention adjourned.

I had been editor of the *Rocky Mount Reporter* some years before and spent one day in each week there. My paper, the *Wilson Advance,* before that had gone into the homes of almost everybody in Rocky Mount and Nash. Although these people had been among the best friends I had, political rancor such as existed was deadly to old friendships for a time. But time healed the sores and old friendships were renewed.

Left, Senator Lee S. Overman. *Right*, Senator Furnifold M. Simmons.

Upper left, Major John W. Graham, candidate for Congress. *Upper right,* S. M. Gattis, of Hillsboro, Speaker of the House in 1903. *Lower left,* David M. Furches, of Iredell, Chief Justice of the North Carolina Supreme Court. *Lower right,* Owen H. Guion, Speaker of the House in 1905.

XXXVI

HOW OVERMAN GOT TO THE SENATE

THE GENERAL ASSEMBLY of 1903 was the last body to have free choice in the election of a United States senator. Pritchard's term had expired, there was no provision for instruction by a primary, and the law for the election of United States senators by the people was in the offing. Pritchard had grown in the appreciation of his people and the Republicans supported him solidly. The fifty thousand Populists were no more. Butler had gone into the Republican Party with his Sampson neighbors, and quite a number of others had followed him or were taking no part in politics. Many, however, had returned to the Democratic Party and acted as if they had never left it, regarding their recent political attitude as a mere vigorous protest against Cleveland and bitter attacks by local Democrats. And with many that was the real situation.

Returning to power after hard struggles, the Democrats had an abundance of able senatorial material in the contest for senator, and it was a battle royal extending into weeks. Each candidate had his headquarters and his manager and his runners, and the whole State was stirred from end to end. Every night the supporters of each candidate would hold a caucus, and if any of their supporters happened to be absent, he was sent for and lined up as if in an army. Any man missing a single caucus was suspected. It looked, at one time, as though there would be a permanent deadlock. Early in the year, Robert B. Glenn, who was later to be Governor, had announced his candidacy, but withdrew in favor of Cyrus B. Watson. In the State at large, among the people, Watson was the favorite. He had been candidate for Governor in 1896, when it was hopeless. He had fought the Tobacco Trust with vigor and power. In the end that stand defeated him. He was always a free man and a poor politician. He made no alignments but carried his sovereignty under his own hat and said what he thought, which sometimes robbed him of support. Still, if a vote could have been taken in the State by the people at large, he would have been elected. Craig was the popular favorite of the mountains and would have carried Western North Carolina almost unanimously. His fight in 1894 and 1896 in Buncombe was without parallel, when he put his life in jeopardy. Overman was very strong in his own section and had warm friends all over the State. He had served in the Legislature where he had been Speaker. He had a good record. He was one of the first advocates of a railroad commission in the State, had been Vance's private secretary and had married Merrimon's daughter. He had a faculty for making friends and was strong with the influential politicians. He was handsome and very attractive in manner and bearing. He had been educated at Trinity College and was in sympathy with Mr. Duke, Mr. Odell, and Dr. Kilgo in the great fight when Cyrus Watson was appearing for Gattis and securing verdicts against Duke and Kilgo. Overman had never said anything about the Tobacco Trust. He would have voted in the Legislature for an anti-trust bill but he would not have offended the men who opposed it. He had, as a director of the North Carolina Railroad, by direction of Governor Carr, voted for the lease of that road to the Southern, although he had never been a railroad attorney. The railroads had no ties on him. He was the most consummate politician of them all and became one of the most influential and popular senators—a career that ended only with his death. He had the distinction of bearing that one associates with the toga. The truth is, he was one of the few men in North Carolina who never failed to get all he wanted, except once. He was defeated for Speaker by Judge Connor. He always charged that up to me. General Julian S. Carr had a large vote in his section of the State, but in this race, as in his other political races, he was unfortunate. He had the most ardent friends. If a vote had been taken by the people, he would have received a very large vote, but he was no politician, was known chiefly for his philanthropy. He was the first of the candidates to withdraw. He was so agreeable he didn't like to run against anybody anyhow. S. B. Alexander, of Charlotte, who had been head of the Farmers' Alliance and had served long in the State Senate and in Congress, had good support from the farmers but was never really a contender. Judge W. A. Hoke, who later became the able Chief Justice, was preferred by many thoughtful men, but never developed much strength.

During the preliminary senatorial contest, Craig challenged Pritchard for a joint debate and Pritchard accepted the challenge. The other candidates for the Senate criticized Craig for this challenge, saying that he had no right to regard himself as the champion of the Democratic Party, that, in doing so, he was assuming he would be the opponent of Pritchard when the real opponent of Pritchard could not be selected except by a caucus of Democratic legislators. I remember well the debate in Raleigh. Craig was not as good a debater as Pritchard. He was a better scholar. He had lived in Carlyle and Emerson as a college student and afterwards. His sentences were beautiful, his speeches ornate, and he had fire and oratory. Most Democrats thought that Craig upheld the Democratic doctrines ably but Pritchard presented his position with such force that about the best that could be said for the debate was that it was a drawn battle.

In the early days of the fight, there was more or less bitterness. During the heat of the contest my wife and I invited all the candidates to dine at our home and they all accepted. This was the first and only time they came together during the fight. With them were Governor Aycock, Lieutenant Governor Turner, Speaker Gattis, and R. A. Doughton, the latter doubtless invited because, in a previous contest, he had been the Democratic caucus nominee for the Senate. At first there was a little stiffness at the dinner, but it was removed when they all got to talking about the senatorial contest by way of badinage, and it was turned into a delightful evening mainly by Mr. Watson. By inheritance, he was a Quaker. My wife and a remote ancestor of Mr. Watson were kin. They began to talk about the Quakers in North Carolina. He told some stories about his Quaker ancestors and my wife told some about hers and shortly Mr. Watson was the center of the conversation and the life of the party. If he had gone on the stage, he could have imitated almost anybody and he had rare humor. For most of the more than two hours he kept the floor, telling stories, sometimes at the expense of an opponent, in a good-natured way; the others joined in now and then, but Watson was the star. At a late hour, he finally arose and said, "Gentlemen, we must be going. It is time for me to be building my fences." And the party broke up with good feeling and fellowship. Most of those present congratulated me afterward that my wife and I had done a good service in bringing together these excellent men who were drifting apart.

The vote went on from night to night in the Democratic caucus, with very little change, Overman first in the lead and then, when there were withdrawals, Watson in the lead; and as each would have the largest vote, their friends would come to Raleigh by the score. A member of the Legislature could hardly attend to his business because of being lobbied by friends in behalf of a candidate. Finally, Overman received the majority and was nominated.

Throughout 1903 the anti-saloon forces continued active in and out of the Legislature. As evidence of the deep feeling among religious people, *The News and Observer* said the First Baptist Church of Wilmington had passed a resolution to excommunicate all members who served "King Alcohol." By serving King Alcohol they meant the people who did not vote for prohibition. In the summer of that year, agitation began in Raleigh for an election to drive out the saloons and establish a dispensary. It was a battle royal, and *The News and Observer* had an editorial headed "Impotent Boycott," saying the liquor dealers had announced they would boycott all business men who signed dispensary election petitions. Concurrent with the oppositon to the dispensaries, the liquor dealers retained a number of lawyers to manage the campaign against the dispensaries. In an editorial on "The Ethics of the Legal Profession," *The News and Observer* declared that any lawyer who would accept such retainers was selling himself and that he could not follow that course and be an honorable lawyer. It added that nobody would respect an editor who took that ground, and a lawyer was entitled to no more respect than an editor.

There were numerous elections that year for dispensaries in various places in the State and also for prohibition. In some of these places the advocates of the saloons were in control of the election machinery, and in order to carry the election they were registering illiterate Negroes who had no right to vote. In the election in Raleigh, this was done in my ward, and there was a very interesting time on the day of election. Finding that the registrar, a saloon advocate, had registered Negroes regardless of their ability to read and write, I looked over the registration books and challenged every Negro who was registered, except the school teachers and preachers and those known to have education. The news got out that all were to be challenged, and on the day of election hundreds of people were surrounding the polls in that ward near Shaw University. Half a dozen lawyers were employed to represent the wet Negroes, some of them influential Democrats. Every Negro who came up to vote, having been challenged, was compelled to stand in the middle of a ring with scores of people looking on and read parts of the constitution. None on trial knew what an *ex-post facto* law was and none could correctly pronounce "Lieutenant Governor." There were plenty of white voters who, with a curious and critical crowd looking on, would have been embarrassed by that public test. I justified my act by reflecting that these Negroes were being used by the liquor forces to their own undoing in the debauchery of their race. I fortified myself by the fact that they and the white registrar were violating the law. But it was cruel. When they failed, they were disqualified and had to stand aside. After a dozen had made the attempt and failed, the other uneducated Negroes did not seek to vote.

THE NEGRO ISSUE AGAIN

In previous elections, the Republicans had championed keeping all the Negroes, ignorant or otherwise, in possession of suffrage. Just before the 1903 Legislature assembled, Senator Pritchard, whose term was expiring, replying to Democratic criticism in *The News and Observer,* said that the Negro delegates in the Republican Convention of the previous summer, who were elected and attended, did so at the instance of Democratic manipulators in order to injure the party. He also said that a majority of Negroes who were permitted to register and vote under the amended constitution, had voted the straight Democratic ticket in 1902. *The News and Observer* said that Pritchard had been very free in appointing Negroes to office as long as they could vote but, after the Democrats had forced limited suffrage upon his party, he had opposed the appointment of a man simply because of his being a Negro and *The News and Observer* said that this was not sincere. This was brought up by reason of the fact that Sam H. Vick, a Negro at Wilson, who was recommended by his party for appointment as post master, was making a fight at Washington to secure the position, and Pritchard was opposing him. I had known Sam Vick when we were boys in Wilson. I was some older than he. I knew his father, as reputable a colored man as ever lived, who had the confidence of the whole community. Sam had grown up as a straight-living colored youth, had gone off to college, and was the real leader of the Republican

Party in the county. When he was first appointed post master and when he had previously held office, his bond had been signed by George D. Green, Mayor of Wilson, a leading Democrat. While the Wilson Democrats opposed the appointment of any Negro to that position, after Pritchard's party had appointed him, the white people endorsed him as a colored man of high character. *The News and Observer* said that Pritchard's opposition to him could have no basis except the fact that the Republican Party now, since the Democrats would not let all the Negroes vote, were trying to make favor with the white people by refusing to let any Negroes be appointed to office. Pritchard retorted that *The News and Observer* had changed its colors and was advocating the appointment of Negroes to office. Of course this was far from the truth and Pritchard knew it, and we had an interesting controversy about the false issue. The matter became of nation-wide interest. Vick had been a student at Lincoln University in Pennsylvania, and the faculty and alumni of that institution, knowing that Vick was a Negro of character, resented that he should be denied recognition because of his color. Berryman, then the young and unknown, but rising, cartoonist, printed a cartoon in the Washington *Star* entitled, "What North Carolina is laying on the doors of the White House." It was discussed in New York papers, and Negroes of the nation took it up and said it was a question of whether they ought to be repudiated by the party to which they had given their suffrage, quoting *The News and Observer's* statement that he had always been a staunch Republican, chairman of the Executive Committee, and the best Negro in the United States; that while the Wilson people didn't want a Negro post master, there was no argument against the Republicans' appointing him, except on account of his color. The controversy became so widely discussed that the President came out in a statement that he would appoint Vick unless it could be demonstrated that he had voted the Democratic ticket. He got the job, and Pritchard all the time wanted him to have it but was laying the foundation of a "respectable" white Republican Party in the State and felt he must offer up, on the altar of such an impossible thing, the best Negro in the State.

Aycock's administration was noted as one of friendliness to the Negro. He had advocated taking the right to vote from the ignorant, because they were being used to keep in power men not fit to govern.

But he never indulged in any anti-Negro talk. However, even after the suffrage amendment, which was approved to remove the big ignorant Negro vote, there were still some Democratic speakers who insisted on singing the old "white supremacy" song. John Charles McNeill, the gifted poet of Scotland County, where the white supremacy campaign was launched, wrote these lines:

> "I cannot see, if you were dead,
> Mr. Nigger,
> How orators would earn their bread,
> Mr. Nigger.
> For they could never hold the crowd,
> Save they abused you long and loud
> As being a dark and threatening cloud,
> Mr. Nigger."

A TAR HEEL JOAN OF ARC

In February, 1903, an event occurred which enabled *The News and Observer* and Governor Aycock to render a great service to education. Greensboro Female College, which was the oldest woman's college in the state, had been established many years before by the Methodists. It had been successful for a long time, but in later years it had been kept alive by means of contributions of a number of influential Methodists, particularly the Odells, Julian S. Carr, Col. Alspaugh, R. T. Gray and a few others. The land on which the college was located was valuable, being in the heart of Greensboro. The college was in debt and some of those who had been giving money to support it felt it was a hopeless undertaking. They decided to sell the land on which it was located and close the college. In the crisis, a Joan of Arc appeared, a fine young lady stenographer, Miss Nannie Lee Smith. She came to Raleigh, hoping to get help to save the college. This modern Joan of Arc interested us very much. I went with Gray and Miss Smith to see Governor Aycock to enlist his interest. It was not difficult to do. The Governor said, "No educational institution shall close in North Carolina while I am Governor." He agreed to go to Greensboro to speak and try to stir the friends of the institution and city of Greensboro to come to the rescue. Speaking at a mass meeting in the City Hall on the night of July 8, 1903, Aycock compared the young champion of her alma mater to the Maid of

Orleans, when bishops and other leaders were hopeless. As a result of his speech, Aycock discovered other Joans of Arc—and the college was saved. Aycock's eloquence and earnestness and *The News and Observer's* stick-to-it-iveness and the bringing in of the romantic idea that a modern Joan of Arc was leading the cause, stirred the imagination of the people and saved the day.

XXXVII

I AM HUNG IN EFFIGY

I N THE LATTER part of October, 1903, Booker T. Washington came to Raleigh. He spoke at the Negro State Fair to a great audience of white and colored people and made a profound impression. *The News and Observer* declared he was the greatest man of his race in the achievement of leading them in the right lines. I went out to hear him speak. He was very unlike the old-time eloquent Negro orator such as Fred Douglass or Joseph C. Price. They were old-fashioned orators who made people weep and cry. Booker was modern and more like a professor or business man than an orator. He had humor too, but of a sort all its own. He left no bitterness. He greatly pleased men of both races. The substance of his address was to urge upon his race the necessity of efficiency in whatever they undertook. He deplored the fact that too many of them were willing just to get through with a job so that it would pass. He illustrated it in this way: "A few years ago you would travel from Richmond to New Orleans and you would not find any white barbers or white-washers anywhere, but now in the cities of the South, these two trades, which had been monopolized by the Negroes, are being invaded by the white people." He told the Negroes they could retain these trades and hold their places as brick masons and in other trades by doing their work so well that the Southern people would not feel compelled to patronize newcomers. He urged industrial education. He said that the future of the Negro race depended upon the relations of the Negroes and the white people in the South. With wisdom, he counselled each to trust the other, to be mutually helpful and to understand that the destiny of the Negroes in the South was to be worked out through understanding between the races who were to live in the South. He counselled the white people to help the Negroes, pointing out instances of white men who had shown great interest in improvement of the Negro race in education and trades. It was a refreshing and wholesome speech, and ever afterwards all who heard him felt that he was indeed, not only a practical apostle to his race, but also a friendly adviser to the white people.

I met Washington first in 1894 when I was chief clerk in the Interior Department. He called with reference to Tuskegee's getting part of the appropriation under the Morrill act. All educational matters were under the direction of the Interior Department. Hoke Smith had known Washington before and received him cordially. He highly approved of the work Tuskegee was accomplishing. I had liked Booker Washington then because he early showed himself the ablest leader of his race. We were friends ever after, and I accepted an invitation to make an address when his statue was unveiled at Tuskegee after his death.

In the same issue of *The News and Observer* that commented on Booker T. Washington in 1903, was an editorial on "The Evolution of Abe Middleton." In the Fusion days Abe had been the leader of the Negro Republicans of Eastern North Carolina. In the Legislature and elsewhere he had taken a prominent part in Fusion politics. There was a strong feeling against him among the white people of his county because he had organized the Negroes for fusion. In its editorial *The News and Observer* said that he was no longer Abe, but Abraham, the father of the new Negro agricultural progress in North Carolina; that, since he had retired from politics and had given his time to farming, he had become a successful farmer and as president of the Negro Fair was leading his race along the lines which alone could bring it prosperity and usefulness.

The day after Booker T. Washington was in Raleigh and *The News and Observer* had an editorial headed "Can Do Nothing But Good," and praised Washington's speech, a storm broke, the echoes of which resounded for many months in North Carolina and created long controversy. In its issue of November 1, 1903, in great head-lines *The News and Observer* had the following:

"PROFESSOR BASSETT SAYS NEGRO WILL WIN EQUALITY."

"HE ALSO SAYS BOOKER WASHINGTON IS THE GREATEST MAN SAVE GENERAL LEE BORN IN THE SOUTH IN ONE HUNDRED YEARS."

"SOUTHERN LEADERS SLANDERED."

"DIRE PREDICTIONS OF COMING CONFLICT BETWEEN THE RACES."

"STRUGGLE WILL GO ON AS LONG AS ONE RACE CON-
TENDS FOR ABSOLUTE INFERIORITY OF THE OTHER."

"DARE NOT NAME END."

Under these headlines my paper printed an article by Dr. John
Spencer Bassett, a professor in Trinity College, which had appeared
in the *South Atlantic Quarterly*, October, 1903, issued at Trinity
College, in which the writer said Booker Washington, "take him
all in all, is the greatest man, save General Lee, born in the South
in a hundred years." He suggested the equality of the races and
predicted there would be a conflict between the two races, saying
that "the struggle of the negro will not be so unequal as now," adding
"I do not know just what form the conflict will take. It may be
merely a political conflict; it may be more than that."

In printing this article *The News and Observer* printed all the
sensational sentences in caps. It had an editorial headed, "Stir Up the
Fires of Race Antipathy." It had three columns about the matter,
called Bassett (bASSett) a freak, quoting, as fitting Bassett, what
Senator Joe Brown, of Georgia, had said of Ingalls, he was "a right
smart fellow, but he hain't got no sense." The paper named all the
great Southerners of the past hundred years and asked, "Will Trinity
College applaud the statement that Booker T. Washington is greater
than Craven, its founder, or Duke or Kilgo?" and asked, "Does he
[Bassett] pray with his face turned toward Tuskegee?" It admitted
that Booker T. was, as it had said only two days previously, the
wisest and greatest leader of the Negro race, but it denied him the
position which Professor Bassett had given him. On the next day, it
had another long article with the following headlines:

"KINDLED FLAME OF INDIGNATION."

"THE PEOPLE FEEL THAT PROFESSOR BASSETT'S UT-
TERANCES ARE AN OUTRAGE."

"EAST AND WEST AROUSED."

"AN IMPASSIONED EDITORIAL IN THE ARGUS."

"CAPTAIN J. B. EDGERTON, LEADING CITIZEN AND
METHODIST OF GOLDSBORO, WRITES 'IF I HAD A SON
UNDER PROFESSOR BASSETT, I WOULD WIRE HIM TO
PACK HIS TRUNK AND LEAVE ON THE FIRST TRAIN'."

"DENUNCIATION AT DURHAM."

In the continuing days, *The News and Observer* printed, under
"The Spirit of the Press," editorials from most of the newspapers
denouncing Bassett's appraisement of the great men of the South.
They were practically unanimous in their disapproval. Communications poured into *The News and Observer* by the score and the
storm increased in violence. On November 10, Professor Bassett
printed an article in the Durham *Herald* in which he undertook to
explain:

> "Between the races is a wide gulf and I should be the last man
> to try to bridge it. I had no thought of social equality in my mind.
> I was thinking only of the industrial and civic outlook of the
> negro race....
> "The word 'greatest' as used by me has been given a meaning
> which I did not have in my mind. I had only reference to one's
> capacity to break over fearful impediments and achieve success."

The News and Observer said his explanation was sorely in need of
crutches and added, "Professor bASSett doesn't make it any worse.
We feared, when he came to explain, that he would regret excepting
General Robert E. Lee, but he lets it stand that Lee is greater than
Booker. Small favors thankfully received."

Outside of Durham, every paper in North Carolina, except the
Charlotte *Observer,* the *Biblical Recorder,* the *Caucasian,* and the
Progressive Farmer, vigorously condemned the Bassett article, and
many of them demanded that he should retire. Even the North
Carolina *Christian Advocate,* organ of the Methodist Church (Western Conference) said, "We think, however, that duty demands that
we express most emphatically our disapproval of some utterances of
Professor John Bassett." The Raleigh *Christian Advocate,* edited by
Rev. Dr. Ivey, said, "For the life of us we cannot see the remotest
connection between the affair and the question of free speech." It
called for the earliest attention of the Board. Later Dr. Ivey criticized
those who were using the Bassett utterance "to injure Dr. Kilgo."

Some churches passed resolutions condemning Bassett's utterances
and the papers were full of denunciatory comments by many citizens.
The News and Observer, on November 13, printed interviews with
the county superintendents of the State, who were holding a meeting
in Raleigh condemning Bassett, and in its issue of November 15 had
an article with the following headlines:

"Kilgo Will Stand by Bassett—Three Preachers Fail in Efforts to Secure Meeting of the Trustees of Trinity College. What Trinity Now Needs. The Great Majority of the Methodist Laymen Think the Time Has Come for Dr. Kilgo To Retire with Dr. Bassett for the Good of the College."

A day or two afterward, in its news columns, *The News and Observer* said that Dr. Bassett would offer to resign and that his "letter of resignation is written for special meeting of the trustees called for Tuesday to consider Bassett's article." On the 20th it said, "Bassett Resigns." On December 2 the headlines of *The News and Observer's* news story were:

"Rejects Bassett's Offer to Resign. The Trustees of Trinity College Were in Session from Seven-thirty Last Night to Two-Forty this Morning. Little Was Given Out and It Was Known the Meeting Was of Deepest Interest and Filled with Discussion, but Beyond What Is Quoted Above, Nothing Can Be Said Except That the Trustees Will Give Out a Statement Today."

On December 3, the headlines of *The News and Observer* were as follows:

"Eighteen—Seven—Thus They Voted. Senator F. M. Simmons and Dr. T. N. Ivey Led the Fight against the Retention of Professor Bassett. A Burst of Applause. Dr. Kilgo Loosed Vitriolic Floods upon the Press of the State and upon *The News and Observer* in particular. Begun Reading Headlines from the Latter and These Aroused the Only Unanimous Applause of the Trustees."

President Kilgo and the members of the faculty sent a communication to the trustees, the concluding paragraph being as follows:

"The undersigned, therefore, members of the faculty of Trinity College, in all sincerity, with all the emphasis they can command, urge upon your honorable body to decline to accept the resignation of Professor Bassett. We urge you to say of Trinity College what Thomas Jefferson, the founder of American democracy, said of the institution which he established: 'This institution will be based upon the illimitable freedom of the human mind. For here we are not afraid to follow the truth wherever it may lead nor to tolerate error so long as reason is left free to combat it.' "

Each member of the faculty presented a sealed envelope containing his resignation if Bassett was asked to resign. The trustees, in a statement, made the following declaration: "It clearly appears the faculty and the students disagree with certain of Professor Bassett's opinions so far as we can ascertain, unanimously. Neither do we agree with them."

They declined to accept Bassett's resignation on the ground, as set forth at length, of devotion to "academic liberty" and at the same time passed a resolution of "absolute confidence in Dr. Kilgo."

For years Kilgo had gone about the State, in many sermons, addresses, and statements denouncing Jefferson and all his teachings in most vicious language. For example, in a sermon in Raleigh in 1900 he called Jefferson "a religious monster." Colonel Webster (Methodist), former Speaker of the House, in his paper said, "It is Jefferson's political principles that are an offense to Dr. Kilgo and the Dukes, whose mouthpiece he is, and not the great man's doubts and fears upon religious matters." Kilgo followed up his denunciation of Jefferson in Raleigh by publishing a pamphlet dealing with Jefferson's religion, and Colonel Webster wrote, "The Dukes (who are dyed-in-the-wool Republicans) are probably furnishing the money for this attack on Democracy, and the dead Jefferson cannot sue them for libel."

And in a crisis, Kilgo had no argument or plea except to invoke the doctrine of the much denounced Jefferson! Shades of Monticello!

The day after the meeting of the trustees, some students of Trinity College, imbibing the idea that *The News and Observer* had attacked the college and inspired by the criticism of the paper by President Kilgo, lynched, on the campus, a stuffed figure labelled "Josephus Daniels." *The News and Observer* said that was "an evidence of the liberal spirit prevailing at Trinity College under Dr. Kilgo."

The next day *The News and Observer* had an editorial saying that Bassett had committed the unpardonable sin and that Dr. Kilgo, in his speech, had read an editorial in *The News and Observer* on the expulsion of President Andrews from Brown University because he stood for bi-metalism, an editorial in which *The News and Observer* had denounced Brown University because of this proscriptive policy. My paper said that the complaint of thousands of Trinity College people was that the President and Dr. Bassett permitted their opinions to be shaped by rich trust magnates either to defend or apologize or overlook the illegal or wrong methods of the cigarette trust company, that they spoke to please the trust, and free speech was not involved. "The rich men give large sums to the college," it said, and "That differentiates them from Brown." The paper asked further if anybody ever heard of Dr. Kilgo or Dr. Bassett having an opinion that clashed with the opinion of the head of the tobacco trust. Two days later the North Carolina Press Association held a meeting and denounced the action of the students of Trinity College in hanging the editor of *The News and Observer* in effigy. The next day *The News and Observer* had an editorial, "Completely Boxed The Compass," in which it said that for months Dr. Kilgo had gone through the state denouncing Jefferson as "a monster," and now his whole defense is based upon declarations quoted from this "monster." Dr. Kilgo and his associates had tried to make the people believe, particularly the Methodist people, that *The News and Observer* was the enemy of Trinity College and I wrote an editorial headed, "The Enemies of Trinity College," in which I said:

"As the president of Trinity College, Dr. Kilgo has made blunder after blunder, denounced good man after good man, exhibited a spirit of venom and proscription to this and that leader, spit upon this tradition and shown contempt for that sentiment dear to the hearts of old-fashioned Methodists. Those who are determined to stand by him at all hazards, finding that his course could not be successfully defended, have fallen back whenever he was criticized to the untrue and stereotyped reply, 'Oh, he is an enemy of Trinity College.'

"Who are the enemies of Trinity College? They are the men in the faculty who write and speak things that are false, absurd, fantastic, egotistical, malicious—give utterance to the sentiments that shock the best sentiments of the state; students at the college who sing of hanging an infirm Methodist preacher on a sour apple tree and are guilty of lynching; trustees who, shutting their eyes to the demand of a great church that has entrusted them with the management of a great college, use their positions to keep at its head and in its faculty men who will destroy the usefulness of the institution by making it alien to North Carolina Methodism and North Carolina policies; patrons and preachers who, from a false conception of loyalty and caring more for upholding Dr. Kilgo and Dr. Bassett in a wrong cause than to broaden the usefulness of a great institution and to bring men in touch with the heart of the great Master of the Church which established it. . . .

"The friend of Trinity College is he who would apply the remedy necessary, not failing to use the knife. A surgical operation separating Dr. Kilgo and Dr. Bassett from all connection with the institution will save it to the state and to the Church. This paper has always been the friend of Trinity College."

The echoes from the Bassett letter and resignation went over into the new year. On January 7, 1904, the quarterly convention of the Hertford Methodist Church passed resolutions endorsing the minority of the trustees of Trinity College in demanding Bassett's resignation and condemning an article in the Boston Evening *Transcript* which, they said, insulted the preachers. Presiding Elder Underwood, who was present, tried to prevent the passage of the resolution but could not do so. It was referred to in *The News and Observer* next day as follows:

"So far as known, Mr. Underwood is the only presiding elder who has sought to aid in the attempt to 'destroy the *News and Observer*.' He hastily stopped his own subscription and is understood to have advised other preachers to do likewise. He also wrote a long article published in the organ of the cigarette trust and Southern Railroad, formerly called the Raleigh *Tribune,* and now called the *Morning Post,* attacking *The News and Observer*. It is in his district that his policy is first repudiated, a healthy sign."

Shortly after the Hertford resolution, the Raleigh *Christian Advocate,* which had been greatly offended by the article in the Boston Evening *Transcript,* said its editor was one of the trustees who voted that Bassett ought to retire from the professorship at Trinity College. The pro-Bassett article infuriated him and had the effect of greatly strengthening the position of *The News and Observer* in the Bassett-Kilgo controversy.

After the storm blew over, Dr. Bassett actually resigned and the resignation was given and accepted with a feeling of relief. He went to Smith College, where he won high position both as a teacher and as an author. Away from the pro-trust environment and anti-Jefferson policy then permeating Trinity and approved by the Dukes, Dr. Bassett was never heard afterward to give expression to antagonism to State universities and to other ideas which, in the atmosphere in

Durham in the early nineties, caused him to win criticism. Instead, he developed into an able teacher of history and sound economics, such as Jefferson and Jackson and Wilson incarnated. His *Life of Andrew Jackson* is his great work and is by many regarded as an authoritative life. During the Wilson administration in his new environment he was one of the ardent supporters of Wilson's progressive policies and one of the ablest advocates of the League of Nations. He took such strong and able leadership in the fight for the League that he was proposed by many Democrats as candidate for United States Senator from Massachusetts on that issue. I did not see him after he resigned from Trinity College, except in Washington on one occasion, until he came to Raleigh some years later. I called on him at his hotel and went with him to the Governor's mansion to call regarding some matter relating to historical research in which he was engaged. There was no stiffness in the meeting and no reference to his article which had created such an uproar or to my being hung in effigy by his students. I asked Dr. Alderman, who was a teacher of Bassett at the University, about him, and he said that at Chapel Hill he had observed Bassett's abilities but that Bassett had eccentricities and sometimes felt, in his young manhood, that he must be against the prevailing sentiment. So when he was opposing the majority opinion in North Carolina he felt that he must be right.

It would be impossible to appraise truly what happened in those days without understanding the atmosphere of the period. Only a few years previously North Carolina had been governed by a political combination in which Negroes furnished the largest part of the vote. Under the Russell administration such things happened as infuriated the white people of the State and caused them to organize Red Shirt brigades to drive out Fusion. When they had attained victory, they had disfranchised the illiterate Negroes and the question of whether this disfranchisement would stand made anything that touched upon it a matter of great importance politically. The people who had won this victory at such great price felt that Dr. Bassett's article would have the effect of reopening the race question, and all of us were more intemperate in denunciation of it, because of the surrounding conditions, than we would have been at any other time. The vigorous denunciation by Dr. Kilgo of Jefferson, his tirades against Bryan and the organization of the farmers who believed that the Duke tobacco trust was impoverishing them—all these things contributed to make a state of mind into which Bassett's article threw the match that lighted the fires of indignation, which stirred the State.

As usual in those times, whenever any matter came up for discussion, Josiah William Bailey, editor of the *Biblical Recorder,* got into the controversy. Bailey, taking up the cudgels for Bassett and Kilgo, made a statement that *The News and Observer* was "trying to take captive the Bride of Christ" and "hectoring the religious denominations"; that "it would invade the Church and dictate to them"; that "it has coolly assumed that neither officials, boards nor churches have rights which it must respect"; and that *"The News and Observer* had put forth a terrible and desperate effort to lord it over God's heritage." Bailey called *The News and Observer* a "paper red-handed with personal and political persecution, reeking with the smell of personal ambition to rule," and added, "The people must destroy this attempt to take captive the Bride of Christ or they themselves will be destroyed." *The News and Observer,* replying to Bailey's criticisms, quoted from his praise of the paper in the temperance fight, showing that he was an echo of Dr. Kilgo in the fight on the paper, and said:

"Nine-tenths of the Methodist laymen are tired of Kilgo and Bassett and will not be quiet while their fantastic, vicious and incendiary sensationalism is injuring the college that is dear to them. The contest that is going on in the Methodist Church is to decide whether Trinity College shall be a Methodist and Southern Institution or an annex to the cigarette trust, alien to North Carolina Methodism. The *Biblical Recorder* joins the Southern Railway, Cigarette Trust, whiskey ring and the Kilgo-Bassett crowd to destroy *The News and Observer* because it will not wear any yoke, corporate or ecclesiastical. ...

"Bailey's animosity toward *The News and Observer* is political and is based on nothing but politics. It goes back to several years ago when this paper exposed his truculency to the cigarette trust, the Southern Railway's attempt to dominate North Carolina politics and his insidious attempt to advance the interests of the Republican Party in North Carolina.

"Through manipulations, this would-be-dictator of his Church and this political boss actually got a Baptist association somewhere in western North Carolina to pass a resolution that *The News and Observer* was 'an enemy of the Baptist Church.' For what? Solely because I exposed his political duplicity.

"I defied his assumption then to destroy *The News and Ob-*

server. I defy him now in his second attempt to have it boycotted and annihilated.

"Bailey was office-holder on Russell's manure pile, took his per diem, but although he lived here, actually drew three dollars a day for subsistence, but offered to pay it back in the face of investigation.

"Everybody in North Carolina knows that editor Bailey in politics runs with the Charlotte *Observer,* the *Morning Post* and other anti-Democratic journals."

The circulation managers of my vociferous competitor, the *Post,* about that time were boasting that its circulation was piling up. *The News and Observer* countered by showing that, while there were twenty newspapers printed in Raleigh going out as second class mail, *The News and Observer* paid more postage than all others combined, and this statement was given officially from the Postmaster.

TOBACCO GROWERS AROUSED

In the period of the Clark-Kilgo controversy, with the Tobacco Trust always in the background, the tobacco growers were indignant because of the low price the trust was paying for their crops. "It is not Duke's money that is making Trinity College rich," the growers of the weed said, "but our money. The Dukes withhold fair payment for our crops and get the glory of benevolence to an educational institution. We are the real donors."

In February, *The News and Observer* printed an article by Andrew Joyner, who had made a careful study of the amount of money paid for tobacco on the various tobacco markets in North Carolina. This showed that the Tobacco Trust had cut tobacco prices in half and the article pointed out that $5,000,000 had been lost by the farmers through the Tobacco Trust, the exact shortage being $5,178,395.00. Editorially the paper said that the law of supply had nothing to do with the reduction of the price; that the trust fixed the price at its own sweet will.

That summer, the farmers held a great meeting in Rocky Mount, with three thousand present. They passed resolutions against the tobacco trust, which were called by *The News and Observer* "a new declaration of freedom." The plan of the campaign was outlined by Colonel J. Bryan Grimes and the farmers were determined, if necessary, to organize to buy their own tobacco on the markets. The whole

State was agitated by the starvation tobacco prices. Jesse Brake, the leading farmer of Edgecombe County, said, "Four hundred and fifty pounds of tobacco bring $14.65 and the American Tobacco Company is confiscating the farmers' tobacco. It has put up the cost of the manufactured articles three cents. It has had a six-cents tax taken off, yet it puts the farmers' tobacco down one third." Chief Justice Walter Clark compared the trust to war and famine. *The News and Observer* said, of the meeting at Rocky Mount, "But the sleeping lion will be aroused and the American people will yet be delivered from their present slavery to the men whose dishonest dollars now dominate."

XXXVIII

THE FIRST NORTH CAROLINA REUNION
AND OTHER MATTERS

IN OCTOBER, 1903, the most significant gathering in the history of the State, the First North Carolina Reunion, was held under the leadership of Dr. Charles D. McIver and a committee of patriotic men in Greensboro. They staged a reunion to which were invited all the native North Carolinians who had won prominence in other States. It was a remarkable gathering, native sons attending from thirty states, embracing the Chief Justice of Nevada, the Governor of Montana, senators and distinguished divines and, among others, Murat Halstead, editor of the Cincinnati *Commercial,* who had been named as Ambassador, but had been turned down by the Senate because of his roasts of certain senators. His family had moved from Eastern North Carolina when he was a small boy, and he had never been back to it until McIver discovered he was a North Carolinian. In fact, that reunion discovered many such men who had gone away, either sons or grandsons of the State. Mr. Halstead could speak, as well as write, and the spell of his mellow and inspiring message long remained with me, having about it the tang of the salt sea of his native Currituck County and the lilt of the seafowl, whose cries, as they flew low over adjacent waters, were his first lullabies.

In keeping with the religious spirit of the State, the opening of the notable events of this historic reunion was marked by sermons (October 11), by three distinguished ministers born in North Carolina, who had won fame in other commonwealths: Rev. Dr. Walter W. Moore, Presbyterian, of Richmond, Virginia; Rev. Dr. Charles W. Byrd, Methodist, of Atlanta, Georgia; and Rev. Dr. Clarence Dixon, Baptist, of Boston, Massachusetts. At one time seven bishops of churches in America were natives of North Carolina, and five senators. Eloquence by a score of orators charmed the great gathering, which was presided over by General Matt. W. Ransom, who set the pace for a feast of patriotic oratory. It reached high-water mark in the welcoming address of Governor Aycock, which stirred the great assembly and has become a permanent North Carolina classic of State history.

PUTTING LIQUOR-SELLING OUT OF POLITICS

The dispensary election in Raleigh took place early in October, 1903. On the Sunday previous to the election *The News and Observer* had three pages of campaign matter in favor of it and its editorial was headed, "Give the Dispensary the Benefit of the Doubt." It was an arraignment of the saloon as a great evil and an argument in favor of trying out the dispensary as an improvement. I said people who believed in prohibition should give the dispensary a trial, in order to get rid of the debauching saloon. It was pointed out it would do away with the money lure in the traffic and take the saloon out of politics. For months *The News and Observer* had been trying to get the board of aldermen to close the saloons at eight o'clock and to have some effective regulations, all to no effect. My paper severely denounced what it called the "big nine" in the board of aldermen and said, day after day, they were doing the bidding of the saloon interests. One strength of the saloons in Raleigh was not only that they were active in politics and put up money for political campaigns, but they paid higher rental than anybody else, and some people who owned buildings occupied by them did not wish to lose good paying tenants. Some business men believed that if Raleigh shut up its saloons, trade would go to other towns.

When election day came, the argument for giving the dispensary the benefit of the doubt probably had more weight than the argument of those who advocated it as a permanent solution. The vote was 677 for the dispensary to 483 against it. Only one ward, and that was the ward in which I lived, and one precinct in another ward, were carried by the wets. At the same election, the proposition was submitted whether Raleigh would permit distillers to operate in the city. The vote was 751 against and 187 for. The victory won, *The News and Observer* and temperance advocates rejoiced and thought that the end of the fighting was over, but they were very much mistaken. The interests that fought the dispensary were still in control of the board of aldermen. They undertook to put in charge of the dispensary an ex-saloon-keeper and two other commissioners who did not have the confidence of the community. If they had carried out their policy, the dispensary would have become not only a place of debauchery but it would have become the center of graft and corruption. The attempt raised a storm of indignation, and the more reputable men who opposed the dispensary joined with its advocates in denouncing the selection of men who would not, as they believed, administer the dispensary honestly as a temperance measure. There was, therefore, a break in the big nine, and they elected as the managers of the dispensary W. N. Jones, W. N. Snelling, and W. P. Batchelor.

It was not easy to induce strong prohibitionists to accept the service. Mr. Jones was president of the Baptist State Convention, an ardent prohibitionist, who hated the liquor traffic. He had been chairman of the committee, which was composed of himself, N. B. Broughton, W. J. Young, Josephus Daniels and Ed Johnson (Negro), to conduct the campaign for the dispensary. When he was approached and asked to be dispensary commissioner, he threw up his hands and said he never could consent to be a member of a board that sold liquor. Mr. Snelling, who was a devout Methodist, hesitated before he would accept. Mr. Batchelor had favored the dispensary, not as a prohibition measure but as a measure of getting more revenue for the city, and he said if the church people could vote to establish the dispensary, he didn't see why they couldn't carry it on decently and honestly. Finally, we persuaded Mr. Jones and Mr. Snelling to accept. Mr. Batchelor was the active manager and Mr. Snelling the financial head. It was conducted with scrupulous honesty and freedom from attempt to secure large sales. Still, while it was in existence, the profit on the dispensary was so large that the city tax rate was reduced. This was held by many as a reason why the dispensary should be made a permanent institution. Inasmuch as Durham had voted dry, the people of that town made frequent pilgrimages to Raleigh on business and often went back with a little black satchel, not filled with what Doheny gave Fall, but a bottle full of liquor purchased at the dispensary. I remember being at the station one day when quite a number of Durham people were returning home. A gentleman came in with a black bag, rather sagging because of its weight, and Colonel Charles E. Johnson held up his bag and said to the Durham citizen, "I will drop my bag on the floor if you will," intimating the Durham man's bag was full of liquor.

Instead of injuring trade the dispensary rather increased it, for people came from the dry surrounding territory to get their wet supplies, and the bigger the business of the dispensary the more those of us who had advocated its establishment worried about it. We had hoped that it would greatly lessen the consumption of intoxicants. It did, of course, lessen the habit of treating and convivial and social drinking, and rid the city of much of the saloon evil that had cursed it, but the business was much larger than we desired. Every now and then, Mr. Jones and Mr. Snelling would drop in and berate me for having induced them to take a job so distasteful to them, but Mr. Batchelor rejoiced in the expansion of the business, and his salary was raised. He earned it all and proved a capable and honest manager.

Shortly after the dispensary was opened, *The News and Observer* declined a large advertising income. The dispensary, of course, bought the kind of whiskey and brandy people wanted, careful to see that it was as pure as could be made. One of the benefits of the dispensary was that whatever was sold there had been analyzed, and no poison was dispensed. Every manufacturer of liquor wanted to create a demand for his product, knowing that if there was a great demand the dispensary would buy. For that reason *The News and Observer* was deluged with proposals and offers of advertising and a pot of gold was in view. Times were hard and advertisements scarce. "If you could advocate a dispensary," said one of the big distillers who wanted to begin with a whole page of advertisements, with pictures of his brand in bottles and testimonials of its fine quality, "I don't see why you cannot let us put advertisements in your paper, advising people to buy the best." He thought I was a fool to turn down all the advertising. He and others said if Mr. Jones and Mr. Snelling, as sincere prohibitionists as I, could be commissioners, there was no reason I should not accept advertising for what the dispensary sold. After the dispensary became a profit-making institution, the members of the committee who had urged its creation were as anxious to get rid of it and put prohibition in its place as they had been for the dispensary, having regarded it as a halfway house from the saloon to prohibition. It had done one good thing: it had defeated a political machine with a big voting strength, but that was temporary.

POLITICIANS MOBILIZE TO ELECT A BISHOP

In October, 1904, the Episcopal Convention of the Eastern Diocese of North Carolina met at Goldsboro. It was a strange sort of meeting and had before it the business of electing a Bishop. The most popular and esteemed minister of that church was the Reverend Robert

Strange. He was a prince of men, evangelical, on close and intimate terms with ministers and laymen of all the churches, interested in social welfare and in every way contributing to causes like prohibition and coöperating with other churches in every good movement. The laymen of the district were not only unanimous for him, but aggressively so and mobilized for his election. Quite a number of the clergy thought that he was entirely too Low Church, and that he had never won distinction outside of North Carolina. In fact he had spent all his life in this State and the clergy preferred the election of another. Most of them looked askance at the preferment of Mr. Strange. The laymen voted for him, the clergy against him at first. There was as much interest among the public men of Eastern North Carolina about the selection of a Bishop as about the election of a United States Senator. Dr. Strange was the candidate of the Democratic Party and his campaign was managed by Colonel Wilson G. Lamb, the most astute Democratic politician in Eastern North Carolina, aided by Francis D. Winston and a score of other such men who were quite as prominent in politics as they were in church affairs, or even more so. The first few years I lived in Raleigh Dr. Strange had been the rector of the Church of the Good Shepherd and we had our meals together at the same table in the Yarborough House. My brother Frank had been his classmate and admirer at the University. I had formed ties of strong friendship with him in Raleigh. Very often in the afternoon I would go with him to see some of his sick and poor parishioners. We took many long walks together, and when the contest came on for Bishop, *The News and Observer* turned Episcopalian for the time being and advocated him as earnestly as if it had a right to a voice in the sacred business of apostolic succession. In Goldsboro, where the convention was in session, Governor Aycock, my brother Frank, and all the politicians made it their business to lobby the delegates, and when Strange was finally elected, it was hailed as a great victory for the kind of religious evangelism and breadth of fellowship with all denominations which Bishop Strange incarnated and of which, later, Bishop Darst became a leader.

A staunch Episcopalian, an officer of St. James Church, writes this recital of an incident that occurred just preceding the election of Bishop Strange.

"I sat in St. James church on the north aisle when some clergyman (whose name I have forgotten) walked to the front of the chancel and proceeded to read a letter saying something like this —'I have a letter from Bishop ——— in which he says that Reverend ——— is eminently fitted by a list of qualifications to become the Bishop of Eastern North Carolina.' This letter was quite strong and from what he read it enrolled the Bishop definitely in the anti-Strange group.

"At this point Reverend Richard Hogue, Rector of St. James church, walked out in front of the minister and demanded that he read the entire letter. It was a dramatic moment, and it was not until the Reverend Mr. Hogue pressed home his point that the minister reluctantly read the first part of the letter which said that Robert Strange was 'the man for the church, qualified in every way to fill the position—but if they were unable to elect Robert Strange,' that this other minister was qualified.

"It proved the minister reading this letter to be telling a half truth and that the writer of the letter definitely approved of Strange—wanted Strange, that he was first choice, but in the event they could not get him, the men mentioned in the latter part of the letter was No. 2 choice."

There was indignation at the attempt to advance the ambition of another to the detriment of Strange by suppression of the important part of the letter. Even so, Strange was elected by only one vote majority. He did not spare himself, dying August 23, 1914, not quite ten years after his ordination, mourned by the whole State. In his holy office he served with the same fidelity as marked the career of his distinguished grandfather, United States Senator and Democratic leader.

BOOSTING CIRCULATION

In February, 1904, H. B. Parker, Jr., of Goldsboro, brought suit against the Southern Railway for $25,000, and Fabius H. Busbee, attorney for that railroad, asked for a continuance of the case on the ground of the great influence of *The News and Observer*. Whereupon *The News and Observer* wrote an editorial headed, "Fabius Will Have to Quit," saying, "If Mr. Fab Busbee does not intend to try any cases where *The News and Observer* circulates, he will have to quit practicing law in North Carolina." Nobody helped *The News and Observer* quite so much those days as the attorneys for the Southern Railway.

DUKE AND THE OUTLAWS OF COMMERCE

In April, 1904, the news came from New York that J. B. Duke had decided to enter politics personally and would go as a delegate to the Republican National Convention. *The News and Observer* said, "This is funny. As head of the trust, he has been in politics ever since the trust was organized. Personally he has been behind the scenes and pulled the strings. Always a Republican, he has had Democratic associates to try to control the Democratic legislators and officials." About that time some of the supporters of Parker, including the *Morning Post* at Raleigh and other North Carolina newspapers that had fought Bryan, talked about having a plank in the Democratic platform against bad trusts, aping the Mark Hanna idea that there were good and bad trusts. Whereupon *The News and Observer* said, "It would be about as sensible to warn sinners to fear falling into the hands of the bad devil. A devil must be a satan. A trust is essentially evil, for every trust that does business is an outlaw of commerce."

FURMAN'S KINDLY NATURE

On May 12 Robert M. Furman, editor of the *Morning Post,* dropped dead at Beaufort. He had been in bad health some months. At the suggestion of E. C. Duncan and W. H. Bagley, directors of the Atlantic and North Carolina Railroad, President James A. Bryan furnished a special train to bring the body of Furman to Raleigh. The next day I had an appreciative editorial on Mr. Furman in *The News and Observer*. The controversy between the *Morning Post* and *The News and Observer* had been painful to me because of the kindly nature of Mr. Furman. He was so gentle and sweet-spirited that you could hardly associate him with being the editor of a paper which I had regarded as so vicious. All during the controversy I had refrained from any personal criticism of him, holding that the *Post* was the organ of the Southern Railway and dominated by Colonel Andrews. I always thought it was very irksome to Mr. Furman to be in any sort of controversy. He loved the quiet, easy way, and whatever he accomplished was always accomplished by the personal equation. He was a master of quiet diplomacy more than he was a master of the pen. His death made no difference with the policy of the *Post,* which he had never controlled. Furman's personality brought it friends. When this personality was withdrawn, the paper lost its best asset.

XXXIX

"ADJUDGED GUILTY OF CONTEMPT OF COURT"

I WILL NEVER PAY a cent. I will rot in jail before doing so."
These were the words I literally hurled back at Judge Thomas R. Purnell in the Federal Court at Raleigh when he announced that he had found me guilty of contempt of court and fixed as the punishment a fine of $2,000. My retort discourteous made the Judge mad and disturbed my lawyers, who sought to silence me by a loud whisper: "Be quiet. You will add to your punishment." The Judge rapped severely, saying, "The defendant will be in the custody of the Marshal until the fine is paid." This was on May 30, 1904. The court room was packed when the news was circulated that I had been ordered to appear to show cause why I should not be punished for contempt for editorials in *The News and Observer,* which virtually charged that, in appointing receivers for the State-owned Atlantic and North Carolina Railroad, the Judge in a recent visit to Norfolk had conspired with W. H. Day and V. E. McBee to take over the railroad.

Some days before my criticism of the Judge, a gentleman called and warned me to be careful in what I said about Purnell, adding, "Judge Purnell says he intends to take the first opportunity to haul you into court for contempt of court." Another gentleman warned me that Purnell had said he "was just waiting for a chance to send Daniels to jail." In answer I said, "Better men have been in jail. Bunyan wrote *Pilgrim's Progress* in jail. I have never yet written anything that would live. Perhaps if I were sent to jail I might be able to do it."

After the Democratic victory in 1898, which swept out of office practically all the Fusionists except those who had been elected for a long term, Governor Russell, who had broken with Pritchard and the leaders of the Republican Party, having lost the confidence of the people of the State, sought to regain it by appointing some Democrats to office. Among the most fortunate of his appointments was that in connection with the Atlantic and North Carolina Railroad, which was owned by the State. The small-bore politicians, to whom he had given control, had been incompetent where they were not corrupt. To that board he appointed some Democrats and, in 1899, made James A. Bryan, of New Bern, president of the road. Russell knew that Bryan was a friend of Aycock, who would be elected Governor in 1900. Bryan was reputed to be the richest man along the line of the railroad and owned considerable stock in it. He was politically ambitious and something of a Warwick. However, to be president of the Atlantic and North Carolina Railroad was his chief ambition. He had wished the appointment when his cousin, Washington Bryan, was appointed by Scales.

When Bryan took charge of the road he found it was in very bad condition. He felt it his first duty to put the road-bed in first-class shape and to secure equipment. To that end he immediately stopped payment of dividends and devoted all his energies to improving the road and increasing its revenues. To obtain this there was no way except by an additional mortgage on the road. The stockholders, however, disgruntled at the stoppage of dividends, passed a resolution against additional mortgages for any purpose. They urged that the railroad be leased. This recommendation was made to Governor Aycock soon after his inauguration, and the Governor made known that he would receive tenders for the lease of the road. The highest rental offer for the first ten years was only 2½ per cent on the capital stock, and Governor Aycock announced he would not lease the road for less than 3 per cent annually for the next ten years and 6 per cent annually for the following twenty years, and the lessees would also have to pay off the floating debt of the company of $48,000 and build fifty miles of new road to connect with it.

The News and Observer declared that the time was not ripe to lease the road and said the fact that the once despised Mullett Road was greatly desired by four separate syndicates "means something." V. E. McBee, who had been with the Southern and Seaboard roads, made an offer of a seventy-five year lease meeting the Governor's terms and increasing it to 7 per cent for the last twenty-five years. A short time after making this bid, McBee withdrew it and, simultaneously, K. S. Finch, of New York, claiming to be the owner of forty-seven shares of the Atlantic and North Carolina Railroad stock, filed a bill in the United States Circuit Court for the Eastern District of North Carolina, asking for the appointment of a receiver for the company. He alleged that the company had never paid any dividends, except at the expense of maintenance, and that the road was in an unsafe condition and was badly managed.

While in Norfolk Judge Thomas R. Purnell, District Judge of Eastern North Carolina, appointed V. E. McBee temporary receiver of the road until April 4, 1904, when answer was to be made before him in Raleigh. *The News and Observer,* which had opposed leasing the road to McBee on the ground that he was a Dugald Dalghetti in railroadism and was in close touch with W. H. Day, of Raleigh, who was a Dugald Dalghetti in politics, opened up in earnest against Judge Purnell's order. In February it ran a story with these headlines:

"Conspire to grab the A. & N. C.? Judge Purnell makes 'Butch' McBee Receiver Under Application of New Straw Stockholder from New York. Others Surprised. K. S. Finch of New York Recently Came Into Possession Of a Few Shares And Now Complains That The Road Is Badly Managed. How Capt. McBee and Col. Hinsdale Went to Norfolk, Saw Judge Purnell and Brought Back the Order Yesterday Morning."

On the same day the paper carried an editorial headed, "A Blow That Endangers Rights of All Corporations," in which it hit hard at Purnell and said that the Governor would take steps to protect the rights of the State which owned 12,666 of the 17,972 shares. On February 27 the road was turned over to McBee, who ordered all agents to make immediate settlement of the affairs under the old administration. President Bryan, in answer to the Finch charges, declared that McBee's cuts in the employees would endanger the safety of the road and that the business of the road was ample to pay the debts and yield a surplus.

At that time *The News and Observer* and the Raleigh *Morning Post* were in controversy on almost everything that came up, always on opposite sides. The *Post* said the receivership was imposed precipitately, but approved the grab. *The News and Observer* said this proved there were sinister motives behind the receivership. Judge Simonton agreed to come to Raleigh on March 10 to hear the case. Upon the basis of the stories printed in *The News and Observer,* Governor Aycock became convinced that some sort of conspiracy lay behind the Finch suit. It was a well laid plan to take the control of the road out of the hands of the Governor and to deny the State's right to operate a road of which it owned most of the stock; and it was based upon a charge of incompetency of Aycock's administration.

When he became convinced that it was a conspiracy and that Finch had bought the stock for no purpose except to throw the road into the hands of a receiver, Governor Aycock made application to Chief Justice Walter Clark to issue a bench warrant for the arrest of McBee and Finch. This created a sensation. It stirred the State from end to end. There had been no great love lost between Governor Aycock and Chief Justice Clark, but the Governor knew that Clark was a man who, if the conspiracy was shown, would show no quarter to the perpetrators.

McBee was brought to Raleigh as a prisoner and charged with "fraudulently, maliciously and unlawfully conspiring with K. S. Finch to injure, damage, and impoverish the Atlantic and North Carolina Railroad." This was done on a warrant sworn out by the Attorney General on behalf of the people of the State. *The News and Observer* declared that the warrant for the arrest of McBee and Finch, followed by McBee's arrest, was the boldest and bravest act of a generation. This unexpected charge of conspiracy, with the Governor of North Carolina as the prosecutor, was not expected by Finch, who "hollered out loud for help." Judge Purnell was asked for permission to amend the complaint, but he passed the cry of distress along to Judge Simonton, and that day *The News and Observer* announced that Finch was to pay par for the stock. It disclosed a contract to pay $100 a share for the stock to Ed Chambers Smith for forty-seven shares of stock, but Smith stated that he did not know the purpose of the purchase until later. The stock was then selling for not more than twenty-five cents on the dollar, and a man from New York who would purchase such stock at par must have had some ulterior purpose. The selling of it to Finch and the taking of his note for ninety days, having nothing but the stock for collateral, for a time caused people to think that Ed Chambers Smith was in the conspiracy, but although he was a pretty good friend of Day and McBee he had no relations with Finch, and, as he testified, when application was made to pay him a hundred cents on the dollar for his stock, he was very glad to sell it. He was probably influenced by his friendship for Day and his desire to sell the stock for a much larger sum than it cost him. The hearing before Judge Clark in the Supreme Court chambers packed that room with as tense an audience as ever heard a case before a Chief Justice. The Governor and the State administration officials, the directors of the railroad and *The News and Observer* staff, and others who were in sympathy with its fight on the conspiracy, ranged themselves on the one side of the chamber. The prisoner, McBee, and his counsel, Day and Hinsdale and others, backed by certain influences in Raleigh which always sided with any railroad grab—and they were numerous—and the *Morning Post* and its backers, were grouped on the other side. McBee was a member of an influential family in North Carolina, was related by blood and marriage to distinguished people, and of course they took his side, so that the crowd in the Supreme Court chamber, when the Chief Justice called the case, might be said to have been pretty evenly divided, with the possible preponderance of vocal sympathizers with McBee, Day, and the looters.

The Chief Justice held McBee for probable cause of an attempt at fraud but only after hearing evidence, over strenuous objections by McBee's counsel, which *The News and Observer* said "disclosed revelations showing the most outrageous attempts at fraud in North Carolina," and added the testimony was "a stench." The hearing disclosed that W. H. Day and J. W. Hinsdale had acted as counsel for McBee in his plan to secure the Atlantic and North Carolina Railroad. It had appeared to them that the best way to secure this was to throw it first into the Federal Courts. For this purpose a citizen of another State was needed. Finch was sent for, and in order to enable him to qualify as a stockholder he and McBee bought forty-seven shares of Atlantic and North Carolina Railroad stock from Ed Chambers Smith at par.

McBee was placed under bond—"A prisoner under bond," my paper said—and added, "He wants to drop his receivership as if it were a red-hot stove." Judge Simonton gave a solar plexus blow and ordered the road back into the hands of its owners, assessing McBee with the expenses of receivership, while Finch and his sureties were saddled with court costs. The Wake County grand jury found a true bill against McBee. Judge Brown denied an application to quash the McBee and Finch indictments.

Six weeks later the matter was all reopened by an action very similar to the Finch suit. On May 2 John P. Cuyler, of New Jersey, holder of thirty-seven shares of the A. and N. C. Railroad stock, filed a bill in the same court making practically the same allegations as had been made in the Finch suit. On May 3 *The News and Observer* carried the story under these headlines:

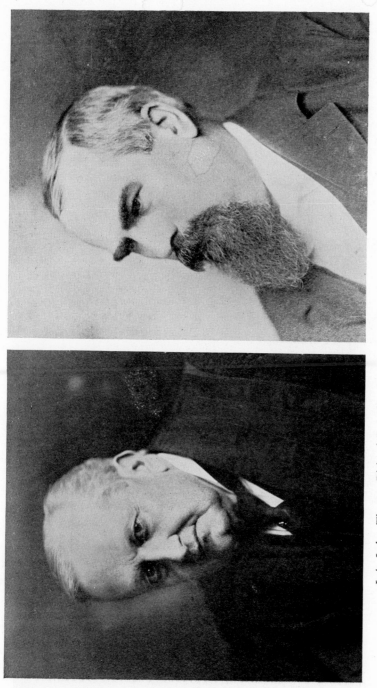

Left, Judge Thomas Richard Purnell, of the Federal District Court of Eastern North Carolina, who found Editor Daniels "guilty of Contempt of Court." *Right*, Henry C. Dockery, who held Editor Daniels in custody for Contempt of Court.

Left, Judge Robert W. Winston, able jurist, who fought for freedom of the press in North Carolina; leading counsel for Editor Daniels in Contempt of Court proceedings. *Right,* Jeter C. Pritchard, United States Senator and Judge of the United States Circuit Court, who heard and dismissed the Contempt of Court case.

"The Expected Has Happened. John P. Cuyler of New Jersey Asks for Receivership of A. and N. C. Railroad. Hearing set for May 21. Complaint filed by Capt. Day And Judge Purnell Issued Order To Show Cause Yesterday. The Bill of Complaint a Conglomeration of The Same Old Story Alleged by Finch and Affidavited by McBee."

On May 7 the paper printed the news that Captain W. H. Day had attacked, with a stout walking cane, Edward Britton of *The News and Observer* staff in the Yarborough House lobby, without any provocation. *The News and Observer* said Britton had never written a line about Day. Every creditor and nearly every stockholder joined with the State in opposing a receivership and said that during Bryan's administration the earnings above the expenses and fixed charges amounted to $295,863.85, which was invested in the betterment of the physical condition of the road.

The News and Observer carried a red-headed editorial, "Syndicate of Pillage and Plunder," and on Sunday, May 29, commenting on Purnell's granting a receivership for the Atlantic and North Carolina Railroad, said:

"THE LATEST ACT IN THE A. & N. C. R. R. RECEIVERSHIP MATTER"

"The fourth act of the A. & N. C. R. R. receivership play took place in the Federal Court Building in Raleigh yesterday afternoon, when Judge Purnell appointed T. D. Meares as receiver.

"The first act took place in Norfolk when Judge Purnell appointed V. E. McBee receiver upon the application of Finch, who did not own a share of stock in the road.

"The second act took place in the Federal Court Building in Raleigh when Judge Purnell, saying that his order in Norfolk was illegal because made outside of the jurisdiction of his court, ascended the bench and made the order over again.

"The third act was pulled off with the same scenery some weeks later when, after the conspiracy proceedings, the judge being 'highly indignant' the receivership was vacated, the story of the McBee-Finch game of 'Bunco' having been exposed.

"The fourth act in the same play drew a crowd to the Federal Court Building yesterday afternoon. It was at once apparent that the judge had determined to appoint a receiver and after permitting the lawyers to talk a little, he made the appointment. Mr. Meares, who was first appointed receiver, is the man who was to assist McBee, who was first named as receiver. Finch, who is now said to own his stock, was made a party. So we see that yesterday's appointment was but the finishing up of what was begun in Norfolk, for McBee and Meares are so close together that if one should be called Tweedledee, the other would appropriately be called Tweedledum.

"The State of North Carolina owns two-thirds of the stock in the A. & N. C. R. R. and under the law the Board of Internal Improvements, of which the governor is chairman, is charged with the management of the property. Whether they manage it well, or otherwise, they are responsible to the people, whose servants they are, and not to any federal judge. The federal court had no call to intervene. There is not an instance of a receivership of large property in this state that has not resulted disastrously. Can we expect any other result in this instance?

"As evidence that Cuyler did not bring his suit to protect his $3,700 stock (if indeed he has any stock at all) the state offered to put up a bond in any sum to guarantee him against loss. In the state courts a receiver will not be appointed for property if the owners in charge give bond to save a minority stockholder or creditor from any possible loss by reason of continuing in charge. The federal court ought to, in matters relating to receiverships, follow the rules of the state courts. No stockholder, up to this hour, has ever complained to the Board of Internal Improvements of any wrong action. Cuyler has voted for every act criticized. Does he own and can he control the stock upon which his suit is predicated? Nobody believes this suit was brought for the correction of any evils, but for an ulterior purpose not now disclosed.

"Judge Purnell graciously stated that a meeting of the stockholders to agree upon a lease would not be considered an act of contempt of his court, provided the lease they might agree upon were submitted to him! The day will never come when his permission will be asked by state officials as to how they shall perform the duty imposed upon them by the Legislature. There is not a decent citizen of North Carolina who would ever forgive the Governor of this commonwealth if he humiliated it by submitting a lease to any federal court....

"Of course the state appealed. The appointment of a receiver was expected and the state was ready last night with the papers and the bond. The matter will be heard before the Circuit Court of June 28th. If the owners of three-fourths of a piece of property have rights superior to that of one $3,700 stockholder in a company of $1,800,000.00 the property will be restored to its owners. Wrong may triumph for a time, but right will eventually be established. The men who are laughing now will be found weeping when the real truth is brought to light, as it will be as sure as God reigns in the heavens."

The paper also had a number of editorial paragraphs which were repetitions or suggestions along that line or were virtual charges that Judge Purnell had conspired with W. H. Day and V. E. McBee to steal the A. and N. C. Railroad.

The Federal court opened on Monday. Between twelve and one o'clock a member of the Grand Jury from Warren County came into *The News and Observer* office to pay a subscription and told me that Judge Purnell had taken up a good part of his charge with practically demanding that the Grand Jury bring a bill of indictment against me for criminal libel, referring to the editorials which appeared in *The News and Observer* on Sunday. This member of the jury remarked that it would be a "cold day in August" when Purnell could get that jury to bring in a true bill against me. That was the first I heard of Purnell's charge and of his intention to invoke the judicial power against my paper. Having made the statement to a number of people that all he wanted was a chance, he availed himself of this opportunity, and if he had not carried out this promise the enemies of *The News and Observer,* the railroad crowd and their sympathizers, would undoubtedly have called him a coward. Later on Monday Judge Purnell, evidently seeing that the jury would do nothing in spite of his vigorous charge, cited me to appear before him on the next day for contempt of court as evidenced in the editorials quoted above.

On May 30 the headlines in *The News and Observer* were these words:

"The Last Straw Put On The Load. Judge Purnell Issues Rule On Josephus Daniels for Contempt of Court Because of Sunday's Editorial. Mr. Daniels Is Ordered To Appear In Court This Morning At Ten O'Clock To Show Cause Why He Should Not Be Attached For Contempt Of Court On Account of Editorials in Sunday's News and Observer. Expressions of Greatest Indignation Heard Everywhere All Yesterday And Today."

On the same day *The News and Observer* had a story with these headlines:

"Norfolk Job Bears Its Fruit. McBee Indicted For Felony Is Co-Receiver. Prophecy Is Fulfilled. Indignation Rises To Highest Pitch When It Was Learned That McBee Was Appointed. Receivers Will Run Hash-House Now."

On Tuesday morning at ten o'clock I was arraigned before Judge Purnell for contempt. The court house was crowded and there was great tensity. The railroad crowd knew what Purnell was going to do and were anxious to see him railroad me to jail. People from many parts of the State crowded in. Purnell was visibly very nervous and excited when the case was called. Judge Robert W. Winston made my defense. Of course the editorial had appeared and there was no disputing it. He stressed the freedom of the press as protected by the Constitution of the United States and made an able and learned argument along that line. Often brilliant before the Court, he was at his best and made a speech which convinced me that I had done exactly right. Immediately after he had finished, Purnell, showing his nervousness and with evidence of hostile feeling, hammered on the bench as he said: "The defendant is fined $2,000 for contempt of court and is remanded to the custody of the Marshal until the fine is paid." To the great horror of my attorneys, I spoke in a loud voice and said: "I will never pay a cent. I will rot in jail before doing so." The judge showed great indignation and rapped on the bench for order. Scores of people came up and handed me twenty-dollar bills and other offers of money to pay the fine. There was almost a run on the banks by my friends to offer me money. Several volunteered to pay it all and it would have been very easy to have paid the fine several times over. I remember Ed S. Abel, lawyer of Johnston County, was in town that day, and he rushed over to the bank and brought over a great roll of bills and was very much distressed when I would not accept the money. Frank Borden, of Goldsboro, was there too and came over and said, "I will get the money at once and pay it." Herbert W. Jackson brought over a bag of money, sufficient to pay the whole fine. The Misses Reese, Milliners, sent $100. Quite a number of others made tenders of money and offered to pay the fine, but I declined to permit the fine to be paid.

Shortly after the sentence I was taken by the Marshal into his room in the Federal Building and remained there until court adjourned. Friends by the score and the hundred came in to see me, all proffering aid and many endorsing my position not to pay the money but to fight it out to the finish. To those who offered money I expressed my gratitude, but said, "Suppose I take your money and pay this two thousand dollars. I will write another article tomorrow of the same tenor and Purnell will impose another fine and it will be an endless chain of editorials and fine-paying, which will exhaust all the resources of myself and my friends. I will never pay it."

When court adjourned, the Federal Marshal, Henry C. Dockery, came in and said: "Are you ready to go to jail?" I said, "You are the man to determine when I go to jail." "I hate like the devil to put you in jail," he said, "as much as I dislike your politics." He was a strong Republican and *The News and Observer* had had enough to say about the Dockerys, his father, brothers, and himself, in political battles, to cause him to feel pretty sore about the paper, but personally we had been on friendly terms. He was an agreeable man and did not carry bitterness or hate. Moreover, as I learned later, he had no respect for Purnell and there was no love lost between them. When he found that the fine would not be paid, he said, "I think maybe you will change your mind before night and so I will take you over to the Yarborough House for dinner and bring you back to the court house until time to take you to jail." When he took me to the hotel it seemed as though pretty nearly everyone in the State was there. Judge Peebles of the Superior Court had issued orders citing practically all the members of the Robeson County bar for contempt of court, because they had set a docket so that they would try no important cases before him. John D. Shaw, Jr., who was in Raleigh at the time, having been brought to the city by Judge Peebles, who charged him with contempt of court, said that Judge Purnell had confided in him, "I am having a hell of a time, Shaw." The Robeson bar, their witnesses, and many other lawyers, were present, and there were many who had been drawn to Raleigh by my arrest, so that, as we went in, almost everybody stopped me to speak to me, most of them to congratulate me. The Marshal said, "You are the first prisoner I ever had that received an ovation for being sent to jail. It is a new experience." Telegrams began to come in from all parts of the State approving the stand I had taken.

The feeling was tense—a State Judge holding a score of lawyers in contempt and a Federal Judge sentencing an editor for contempt; a Chief Justice finding railroad officials guilty of conspiring to steal a railroad; thousands of people crowding the court rooms; orders ready to call out the State guards and a clash imminent between State authorities and Federal authorities. Young Charles Busbee, now a colonel in the U. S. Army, told his father that his history lesson at school was covering the era of the French Revolution and what was happening in Raleigh resembled so nearly the incidents in Paris that he couldn't tell one from the other.

While I was at dinner in the custody of Marshal Dockery, a rather singular thing happened. Dockery's younger brother, Oliver H. Dockery, then a captain in the Army, was in the dining room with his bride and he brought her over to introduce her to me, saying that she had told her father in Ohio before she left that I was the one man in North Carolina she wanted to meet, but she never supposed she would have to go to jail to make my acquaintance. It was a pretty interesting story. Toward the end of the Fusion administration in North Carolina, Dockery, a rather dashing and vigorous political speaker, moved to Raleigh to practice law. He had served in the Spanish-American war. He ran for solicitor of the district and made the sort of campaign that his father, Oliver H. Dockery, Sr., made, the Dockery kind of campaign always creating enthusiasm with the Republicans and arousing the resentment of the Democrats. Probably no public man in the State aroused more hatred among the Democrats than this young man's father, for whom he was named, although personally the Dockerys were well liked except during political campaigns. As candidate for solicitor young Dockery had infuriated the Democrats and had organized the Negroes. *The News and Observer* had cartooned him unmercifully. He was defeated. Most of his speeches toward the end of the campaign were bitter denunciations of both the paper and its editor. Naturally, he felt that the last quarter in the world from which he could receive any kind consideration would be from the editor of that paper. Shortly after his defeat he secured a commission in the Army and left Raleigh to take up his life work as an army officer, abandoning the practice of law. I had not seen him since that time. A few months before my arrest a gentleman called at *The News and Observer* office one day, a fine looking business man, who brought letters of introduction to me from his friends in Ohio, among others one from Governor Pattison, whom I had known in a political way. He said he had come on a very delicate mission; that he had an only daughter who was the first object of his affections; that a young army officer from North Carolina, who had been stationed near his home, had met his daughter and paid her marked attention, and had addressed her, but he did not know anything about the young man and had come to North Carolina to try to find out something about him before the matter went any further; that he thought his daughter's heart was engaged and he was anxious that she should make no mistake; that the young man was attractive and agreeable and rather good looking. He then told me that the young man was Oliver H. Dockery. I looked at him a minute and asked: "Did Mr. Dockery refer you to me?" He said: "No, I never mentioned the matter to him. He doesn't know that I am here on this mission. I have come on my own accord, and very quietly, to investigate for myself." Then I told him the story of the Dockerys' political career as it was, even showing him some of the cartoons, and told him that politically Oliver H. Dockery had, as a young man, followed his father and his family, and, in the bitter campaigns that had preceded, had himself been vicious, and *The News and Observer* had roasted him very severely. I did not know much about him personally aside from politics but said that Justice Walker of the Supreme Court had married his sister, who was a fine lady, and Marshal Dockery had married one of the finest ladies in Rockingham. Although politically the Dockerys were despised in Richmond County, the new generation was connected by marriage with some of the best families in the State; that the young man was attractive and good looking and I knew nothing to discredit him except the part he had played in politics.

The father of the girl told me that he was a Republican but a great friend of Governor Pattison and had voted for him for Governor; that of course the man's politics would not affect him at all but it was his personal character and standing that he was interested in. I introduced him to some people who were connected with Richmond County people and to Judge Walker, who had married a near relative of Dockery. I told him good-bye and that was the last I heard of the matter until the day I was in custody. Dockery, in the meantime, had married the girl, who had come over to thank me for what I had said about her husband, which had satisfied the father that her lover was worthy to be admitted to the family.

After dinner at the Yarborough House, Marshal Dockery took me back to the Federal Court building and left me in one of the large rooms with P. A. Mitchell, assistant Marshal, as officer in charge. All the afternoon the room was crowded with people coming and going. Governor Aycock, other state officials, Chief Justice Walter Clark, Judge Henry Groves Connor, and other judges of the Supreme Court, and prominent citizens from all parts of the State came up to see me, some of them congratulating me, others sympathizing. Telegrams continued to pour in from all over the State saying, "Stand firm. We are with you." Most of the lawyers who called were interested in the argument which Judge Winston made that morning before Judge Purnell, in which he quoted the law on contempt, which was that contempt of court in a Federal court inferior to the Supreme Court in Washington must have been committed within presence of the court or near enough to interrupt or trouble its proceedings. Very few lawyers had ever examined this statute and the history of it was interesting. It was drawn by James Buchanan, afterwards President of the United States, when under a Whig President's administration an editor in Missouri was haled before the court for contempt. The contempt grew out of an editorial criticism of the Judge. The case became one of more or less national importance. It created the greatest indignation and bitterness among the Democrats of the country because the editor had been fighting the party's battles and the Judge had been acting in a partisan way. After that incident in Missouri, no other editor had been haled into court for contempt by a Federal judge because the statute denied the Judge the old right of punishment for contempt except in the court room or near enough to be disturbing. Judge Winston stressed the distance of *The News and Observer* office from the Federal Building, which forbade that anything going on in that office would interrupt the proceedings of the court, and argued that an editorial in a paper was not such an interruption as justified punishment of the editor.

As night came on the question was still open as to what Judge Purnell would do with me. I was in the Federal court room in the office of the Marshal in the custody of an Assistant Marshal. Dockery was more worried than I was, and when the court adjourned he came in and said, "I want you to pay that fine. Money is flowing all around the court house here. It won't cost you anything if friends will pay it and it will get me out of trouble." I told him it was final, that it would not be paid. "I hate to take you to jail," he said, "but I guess I will have to do it. I hate like the devil to do it, as much as I dislike your politics." I told him I understood he was an officer of the court and I did not ask any favors of him for he must do his duty as he was ordered by the court. Then he left me and went over to the court house. He found my brother, Judge Daniels, seated in front of the court House and Judge Purnell talking with him. Afterward my brother told me the Judge expressed his great regret at being compelled to uphold the honor of the court by this punishment, that he held my brother in high esteem but I had acted in such a manner that it was necessary to act as he did. Before night Marshal Dockery called Judge Purnell aside, so he told me afterward, and told him that I had refused to pay the fine and asked him what he should do with me.

The Judge said, "Put him in jail."

"Very well," said Dockery, "Please give me that order in writing."

"Why do you wish it in writing?" asked Purnell. "He is in your custody and you need nothing else."

Dockery replied, "The reason I want it in writing is because if Daniels goes to jail, neither you nor I can sleep in safety tonight. When the crowd comes to get me, as it will do, I want to show them that I have written instructions for the jailing process and then, instead of getting me, they will get you."

Purnell looked very grave, Dockery told me later, and seemed surprised that there was so much indignation and then turned aside and said, "He is in your custody. Do what you please, so that you keep him."

Dockery replied, "You understand, Judge, if he is in my custody he will stay at the Yarborough House with a Marshal sleeping with him and I will construe that to be in custody."

Purnell walked off without a word, and so Dockery took me back to the hotel for supper and then put me in Room 28. It had happened that this was the very room I had occupied before I was married. It seemed to me a good portent. After supper, Mr. Mitchell, the Assistant Marshal, whose son had been, for a brief time, on *The News and Observer,* was very kind and asked me if I would like to go for a walk. He said, if I wished, he would take me home to see my wife. He had learned that night that my wife expected to be confined within a few days and he was as considerate as possible. So we went down on South Street, where I spent some time at home, and then he took me back to the hotel where Mr. Mitchell slept in the room with me.

In the meantime I had found time to write an editorial which appeared in *The News and Observer* the next morning. This long editorial, filling several columns, was, in part, as follows:

> "*A personal word from the editor in custody.* In custody of the United States Marshal, Room No. 28, Yarborough House. To the People of North Carolina":

It began by thanking the people for their kindnesses and saying that the editor had never had any ambition but to be an editor and went on to say:

> "As a school boy in Wilson, as a volunteer correspondent of Hale and Saunders' *Observer,* I was made happy by a word of commendation from those two noble editors and from that day until I became editor of *The News and Observer* my sole ambition was to edit a daily paper at the capital of my native state.
>
> "My criticism of Judge Purnell was true. It was moderate. It was plain as language could make it. Before I would retract a solitary sentence of that editorial or abase myself, I would rot in a dark dungeon all my days.
>
> "The matter is far above any personal one. It is comparatively a small matter what becomes of me. It is a vital matter whether the press shall be free."

I had not eaten my breakfast the next morning before my brother Frank and Judge Winston were in my room greatly excited over the editorial. They said, "Here you are in jeopardy of your freedom, the case pending in court, and you are adding to your offense. You must promise us not to write another line until this case is settled." And they said much more along that line in true friendly advice of counsel to client. I said, "Boys, you are representing me in the court to see that I get my legal rights but you have not been retained or asked to have anything to do with the editorial policy of *The News and Observer.* I am the sole judge of that and I shall write in it every day exactly what I choose to say, no matter what happens." They gave me up as hopeless.

My two oldest sons, small boys, Josephus and Worth, came every morning to see me. Worth, who was as expert at climbing as a squirrel, spent his time climbing up on the radiator pipes and sliding down, much to the consternation of his Uncle Frank. He was not old enough to understand my situation, but Josephus was older and took my sentence to heart, never having known anybody in durance vile except those guilty of stealing. My wife, as always, was calm and courageous.

After Judge Purnell had denied an appeal with vigor and some feeling, or, as *The News and Observer's* local story put it, "The pale and nervous Judge Purnell gripped his chair, his head down and chin lowered, while a look of fixed purpose swept across his face." He would not even hear Judge Winston in an argument for appeal, thundering "no appeal lies." That night R. T. Gray, who had been my personal friend and attorney and for a long time attorney for *The News and Observer,* James H. Pou, a leader of the Raleigh bar, and ex-Governor Jarvis went to Washington to make appeal to Chief Justice Fuller for a writ of habeas corpus. The Chief Justice told them he would go to Raleigh with pleasure to hear the application but that he had his bags packed and reservations made to leave that night for Maine for a much needed vacation. Even so, he would hear it except for the fact that it was not necessary; that Mr. Pritchard had been appointed Circuit Court Judge of the District embracing North Carolina and that he could hear it just as well as the Chief Justice. Then he said: "The Judge in North Carolina was in error in denying the appeal because at this very session of the court, on May 16th, in the case entitled *Edward E. Bessett* vs. *W. B. Conkey Co.,* it was held 'plainly, clearly, unmistakably and boldly that an appeal lies from the Circuit and District judge in contempt proceedings to the Circuit Court of Appeals.'" A unanimous opinion was delivered by Justice Brewer. *The News and Observer* said:

"The question therefore arises by what authority is Daniels now in durance vile. Is he illegally restrained of his liberty? Is Judge Purnell to nullify, abrogate and destroy the act creating the Circuit Court of Appeals? Is he higher and mightier than the Supreme Court of the United States?"

Application was also made to Chief Justice Fuller for an order to set the receivership aside. He granted the request and held that an order appointing a receiver for the A. and N. C. Railroad be suspended and that the properties of the road be left in the hands of its owners until further order of the United States Court of Appeals.

On the very day that the application was made to the Chief Justice for habeas corpus, Judge Jeter C. Pritchard had taken his oath of office in Richmond as Circuit Court Judge. My attorneys saw him and filed application for habeas corpus and said they would appear before him any time or place where the hearing could be held. Mr. Gray told him that a new arrival in my family was momentarily expected and because of that Judge Pritchard said, "I will come to Raleigh day after tomorrow and hear the application for habeas corpus." He did so. Our youngest son, Frank, was born four days after I was released. He just did miss seeing his father in custody. He was named for my older brother, Frank Arthur Daniels, Judge of the Superior Court. The name Frank is the favorite one in my family, there being five bearing that name. As a matter of fact, they all ought to bear the name Franklin, for my father gave the name to my older brother because of his admiration for Benjamin Franklin.

In the meantime I was kept in custody, being taken by the Marshal or Assistant for my meals to the Yarborough House and sleeping there with the Assistant Marshal, spending a part of the time in the room, being allowed to walk home once a day and also to *The News and Observer* office, and in the marshal's office at the Federal Building having time to write editorials dated, "Room No. 28, Yarborough House."

I was kept quite busy answering telegrams and letters. Pending the appeal *The News and Observer* and other papers were full of stories about the arrest and punishment, and before leaving for Washington, James H. Pou said to a reporter, "The only thing definite is that if Mr. Daniels is put in jail he will be made Governor of North Carolina." A number of papers came out and said I ought to be nominated for Governor, but in an article in *The News and Observer* I said that I had no political ambitions and I gave no ear to these suggestions, which came from many quarters.

After my attorneys had gone to Washington to see Chief Justice Fuller, Walter Watson, one of my attorneys, looking up the authorities, ran across some advance sheets from Washington in Purnell's office, containing the court's decision in the Conkey case, and brought it to the attention of Judge Purnell, who stated that upon application Mr. Daniels could appeal his case and he would hear the argument, indicating that in view of this decision he would grant an appeal, which he had so peremptorily declined on Tuesday, refusing then even to hear authorities on the application for appeal. I told my lawyers that inasmuch as Mr. Gray, Mr. Pou, and Governor Jarvis had seen Judge Pritchard, and he was coming to hear the case at Raleigh, and since Judge Pritchard had already at that time issued a habeas corpus, we would not make application to Judge Purnell or accept anything from him; so no attention was paid to Purnell's suggestion that he would grant an appeal. Most of my lawyers were agreed that, under the circumstances, it was our duty to await Pritchard's coming.

On the next day, at three o'clock, Judge Pritchard heard the application in the United States Federal court room in Raleigh. The District Attorney, Colonel Harry Skinner, had no desire to appear in the case. He had been an applicant for the judgeship when Purnell was appointed and felt that he ought to have received it. He had very little more respect for Judge Purnell than had Marshal Dockery, but Judge Pritchard told him it was his duty as District Attorney to appear for Purnell. Carrying out that duty, Judge Skinner merely stated the facts but made no argument. Judge Robert W. Winston made the argument before Judge Pritchard, which was widely read and quoted all over the country. The hearing took place before a crowd that filled the room and overflowed into the lobbies. Judge Pritchard, when the argument was concluded, said that he had great respect for Judge Purnell and had no doubt that he "acted from conscientious motives and in all sincerity," but said he failed to find anything to warrant the imposing of a fine on Josephus Daniels and dismissed the whole action. As he stated his decision, the court had to suppress a spontaneous rising demonstration, and thus the case ended.

The Chief Justice, having remanded the A. and N. C. Railroad to the control of the State until it could be heard in the Circuit Court, the matters that had excited the State were both disposed of, and I had my liberty without paying any fine or making any apology or retraction.

Judge Pritchard was applauded and praised all over the State. When it was announced in *The News and Observer* that Judge Pritchard was coming to hear my case, some of my good Democratic friends in the country, who remembered how the paper had roasted Pritchard in the campaign of the nineties, were greatly disturbed and came to me and asked me if I thought I would get a fair hearing.

They thought Pritchard, remembering many hard things *The News and Observer* had said about him in political campaigns, would be inclined to stand by Purnell. I knew he had no love for Purnell. He had secured his appointment but had regretted it many times afterward because after being elevated from the position of United States Commissioner to a Federal Judge, Purnell had gotten the swell-head so that he would not even listen to his benefactors. I also felt that Pritchard would be glad of an opportunity to show that as a Judge he had no political rancor although in the political campaign, beginning away back when he was opposing the railroad commission and *The News and Observer* was advocating it, we had clashed many times and the paper had done everything it could to prevent his election to the Senate. However, our personal relations had always been more friendly than that existing between me and any other Republican leader. I knew that while, from early manhood, he had been attorney for the Southern Railway and looked at railroad matters from the point of view of his early training, he was a life-long Republican from principle, fair, open, and above board, a political fighter without hate, not in the large class of pie-hunters who had joined the Republican Party for office. He grew in the Senate and on the bench, and his death was sincerely mourned by all North Carolina.

Shortly after my wife's brother, Ensign Worth Bagley, had been killed on the U. S. S. *Winslow* in the Spanish-American War, Judge Pritchard, then United States Senator, took the Ensign's mother to call on President McKinley. He asked the President to appoint the younger brother, David Worth, as a cadet to Annapolis, which McKinley was very glad to do. Naturally this fine spirit won the gratitude of the whole family and, political opponents though we were, strong personal friendship was cemented that endured. In the days to come we were to be closely associated in the campaign in 1906, when we canvassed the State for State prohibition, and to his death we were friends. The last time I saw him was when I spoke in Asheville at a reunion of the Thirtieth Division. He went to the auditorium to hear me and afterwards I called on him at his home in Asheville. He was then marked for death. I had a very delightful conversation with him and went away rejoicing that, after the stress and strain of the heated days of the nineties, we both had forgotten all the hard things we had said of each other.

The lawyers who had appeared for me—and they all volunteered—after the trial was over declined to accept any fee, were R. T. Gray, James H. Pou, Charles M. Busbee, T. B. Womack, J. N. Holding, W. L. Watson, T. S. Fuller, of Raleigh, ex-Governor Jarvis, of Greenville, Fred A. Woodard, of Wilson, Robert W. Winston, and Victor Bryant, of Durham.

The News and Observer editorial paragraphs, day by day, showed that it was not troubled very much by the trial, as this one indicates:

> "The business management of *The News and Observer* is said to be troubled to know how Judge Purnell found out that he had been criticized in this paper. He does not subscribe to the Old Reliable and this seems to have been an aggravated case of borrowing one's neighbor's papers."

I was in custody three days and a little over three hours. The morning of my release my editorial headed "Good-bye Room No. 28," was very severe upon Judge Purnell and reviewing the matter, I said, "A weak tyrant is a public contempt. A truckling judge, grasping at power, fails to play the game," and asked, "What would have happened to Editor Daniels had he lacked the resources of his friends?" It went on to discuss the perils of humble suitors in Purnell's court. It was very severe upon the Judge, calling him an "ignorant pigmy, a tyrant, a clown, nothing more than Tom Purnell, puffed, distorted, craven, truckling, a puppet king, laughable figure, a constant menace," and added, "This is the judge whose confessed ignorance of the law is a constant menace to the humble suitors in his court, whose lack of knowledge of the proprieties of his position led him to insult and attempt to nullify by trickery the writ of his judicial superior. A pigmy, for a moment in the arena, would presume to draw a feeble blade against the freedom of the press."

Shortly after Judge Pritchard said he found nothing to justify my arrest or punishment and dismissed the suit, my wife came down and, in the joy of freedom, we went to ride in the country. Just as we were turning the corner at the Supreme Court Building, a colored man, Lunsford Davis, who had been in the employ of *The News and Observer* for many years, stopped the horse in great excitement. Lunsford was at once the happiness of the whole office and the despair. He would do anything for anybody at any time, but about every few weeks he would "tank up" and beat his wife and each

Monday morning thereafter I was called upon to get him out of jail, where he had been placed the previous day for punishment of his conjugal partner. He had been in jail many times and I had secured his release as many times. He stopped the horse and ran up and took my hand in both his, as if we were partners, and said, "'Fore God, Mr. Daniels, I suttinly is glad to see you is out of jail. I know how it feels. I'se been there myself," and I often said that Lunsford was really the only person among the hundreds and thousands who showed their friendship to me, who could do so out of the fullness of bitter experience.

The tenseness of the situation in Raleigh and in some parts of the State while I was in custody made itself felt in many ways. Telegrams came in, offering to send bodies of Red Shirts to inflict indignities on Purnell. I learned afterward, and on good authority, that toward night on the day Purnell had haled me into court and fined me, his original program had been to have me taken on the midnight train to Atlanta and put in the Federal prison. This secret design became known to a few men and a number of them banded themselves together to prevent it. To my great surprise I learned afterward that one of the most substantial, quiet, and law-abiding men in the city, Mr. Thomas B. Crowder, commission merchant and neighbor of mine, was the head of the movement, and the news had gotten to Purnell that if any attempt was made to take me to Atlanta it would not be wise for him to sleep at home that night, for they would take him out and tar and feather him. Mr. Crowder never talked about the matter. He was the sort of man who always acted without talk, but when I learned it was such quiet men as himself who were most indignant I appreciated the tense feelings all over the town and in the State. My best-informed friends believed that it was this threat to Purnell which caused him to consent to let Marshal Dockery hold me in custody and keep me wherever he would.

While the State was aroused these days and the great bulk of the people were indignant at the action of Judge Purnell, the Charlotte *News* lamented that "in the midst of praise the three papers which are rivals of *The News and Observer* should add discordant notes to the chorus." The Raleigh *Post,* which was founded by the Southern Railway officials in order to destroy *The News and Observer,* was the chief spokesman of the discordant chorus, but the Charlotte *Observer* was not far behind. *The News and Observer* and that paper had had bitter controversies growing out of the Bryan campaign and then out of prohibition. It defended Purnell in his action and declared that the case involved defense of license, not freedom, of the press, and that Purnell could not be expected to submit patiently to the detractions of Josephus Daniels. The Raleigh *Caucasian,* organ of Butler's party, and the Hickory *Times Mercury* (Populist), joined in along this same line. They were the only four papers that did not ring clear in what was not personal, but was an attempt to strain the law to prevent real freedom of the press in North Carolina when an arrogant Judge, dressed in a little brief authority, would have destroyed it.

Shortly after Judge Pritchard's decision, the committee—R. T. Gray, Henry A. Page, and W. T. Lee—appointed by Governor Aycock to coöperate with the Board of Internal Improvements in making a thorough investigation of the A. and N. C. Railroad, with a view to ascertaining to what extent, if any, the allegations of mismanagement of the A. and N. C. were true, made their report. It was that President Bryan had used large sums of the company's revenue for making permanent improvements but that many items had been charged up to extraordinary improvements which should have been included in operating expenses. This report was well received and Governor Aycock later reappointed Bryan and the other officers. Among other things that this committee criticized was the use of annual passes. They found that the proxy committee, for example, consisted of thirty-five men of whom fourteen were not even stockholders, and they said the use of passes was inspired by a desire to give favors to large shippers so as to secure business for the road. They also criticized the fact that annual passes were given to thirty-four attorneys. They concluded that the best and most economical operation of the road could not be obtained under State control and advised a lease. In August the road was leased to a company headed by R. S. Howland, and after all the turmoil about the management and litigation and investigation, the general public approved Governor Aycock's leasing the road, but I was not in favor of it.

No evidence was ever produced that Judge Purnell had any financial interest in ordering the receivership of the A. and N. C. Railroad. There was a feeling that he was one of the conspirators and *The News and Observer* intimated as much, but neither then nor afterward was there any proof that he had received any money or was to receive any money.

Judge Winston, long afterwards, wrote me:

"Your brother, Frank Daniels and I, sat up until three o'clock preparing the case, having been allowed only twenty-four hours for the work and only one speech of sixty minutes. When you retorted in the court to Purnell's offer to 'call off his dogs' if *The News and Observer* would do the like, 'I'll rot in jail first,' that was real contempt and we attorneys shivered to our very spines. You recall that Purnell experienced pain and sorrow when he sentenced you and said he was your friend and had as an Odd Fellow, sat up all night at your sick bed only recently, you answered back, 'No one asked you to.' In a word, you were more confident than your lawyers and much bolder, a trait you often (if not always) manifested when sure you were right, unless boldness would disrupt the Democratic Party. One difference between you and H. G. Connor and myself was in the approach to reform. You availed yourself of any weapon, we would use gentler means. You were an apostle of righteous discontent. Connor in a letter to me greatly deplored this phase of yours and pleaded for 'Here a little and there a little.' Perhaps you were right, for 'Better a dissatisfied Socrates than a satisfied pig,' or as Untermeyer sings:

> "'From compromise and things half done
> Keep me with stern and stubborn pride
> And when at last the fight is won,
> God keep me still unsatisfied.

"Your triumphant acquittal by Judge Pritchard began a new era in North Carolina's social and political history. As old man Roger Gregory at the end of the case said to me of Purnell, 'Bob, you didn't kill the turkey, but he won't roost so high.' Railroads and corporations saw the handwriting on the wall and became aware that they had better get out of politics. And soon they did!"

XL

STATE AND NATIONAL CAMPAIGNS OF 1904

T HE DEMOCRATIC State Convention of 1904, held in a big and noisy warehouse in Greensboro, resulted in the nomination of Robert B. Glenn for Governor, defeating Major Charles M. Stedman. There was gossip that Stedman had the support of the Tobacco Trust and that Glenn, an attorney of the Southern Railway, had its backing. If so, the one support offset the other. Glenn was nominated because in three hotly contested campaigns against Fusionism he had won the people by his eloquent and scathing arraignment of Russell and Butler and the rest. That Convention witnessed the high-water mark of the inspirational eloquence of Governor Aycock. Upon his inauguration in 1901, after he had led the fight to disfranchise illiterate voters in the white supremacy campaign, Governor Aycock had declared for universal education and committed his party to that policy.

Before he became Governor, Aycock thus summarized the duty of the white man, the Negro, and the State:

"Let the Negro learn once for all that there is unending separation of the races; that the two peoples may develop side by side to the fullest but they cannot intermingle; let the white man determine that no man shall by act or thought or speech cross this line, and the race problem will be at an end.

"But I would not have the white people forget their duty to the Negro. We must seek the truth and pursue it. We owe an obligation to the man in black; we brought him here; he served us well; he is patient and teachable. We owe him gratitude; above all we owe him justice."

During his term of office Governor Aycock had given proof that he was the sincere friend of the Negro and had urged better school facilities for children of both races, emphasizing the duty of the white race in that regard. His policy met the opposition of an element in the party that did not wish to be taxed for the education of the Negro and those who thought education would cause the Negro not to "know his place." They had brought forth a plan under which taxes collected from the whites should be employed for white schools and the Negroes should have only such public schools as could be supported by money collected in taxes on property owned by Negroes. The opponents of Aycock's policy were organized, and had given it out that the Greensboro Convention would repudiate Aycock's course. They had militant and forceful leaders. Some of Aycock's friends were disturbed; some weak-kneed ones even wished him to make no allusion to the question in his address giving an account of his stewardship. Shortly before going to the convention he asked me to come to the Governor's Mansion to confer upon the forthcoming convention. He read me portions of his address. As we sat alone and he read the noble utterances which were the very marrow of his convictions, I was thrilled by the words that breathed the noble spirit behind them. "Do not change a word; do not dot an 'i' or cross a 't'," I told him when he had finished reading what was to enthrall hearers and drown the opposition.

In his address opposing giving the Negro only the school fund derived from taxation on property owned by Negroes, Governor Aycock said:

"The proposal is unjust, unwise and unconstitutional. It would wrong both races, would bring our state into condemnation of a just opinion elsewhere and would mark us as a people who have turned backward. Let us not seek to be the first state in the Union to make the weak man helpless. This would be a leadership that would bring us no honor but much shame.... Let us be done with this question for, while we discuss it, the white children are growing up in ignorance.

"I am perfectly aware that there are men, good men, and many of them, who think that the experiment of educating the Negro has been a failure.... I find in the State men who think that the Negro has gone backward rather than forward and that education is injurious to him. Have these men forgotten that the Negro was well educated before the war? Do they not recall that he was trained in those things essential for his life work? He has been less educated since the war than before. It is true that he has been sent to school, but his contact with the old planter and with the accomplished and elegant wife of that planter has been broken. This contact was in itself a better education than he can receive from the public schools, but shall we, for this reason, say that he is incapable of training? Ought we not, on the contrary, to study the conditions and realize that the training which he needs has not been given to him since the war in like manner that it was before?"

It was a terribly hot day, the gathering noisy, and his opponents cocky. Aycock had not been speaking five minutes—he was a master of assemblies—before you could hear the proverbial pin drop, so tense was the interest as his hearers hung upon his words. The effect was electrical. Men who had come to denounce were converted and remained to applaud. Some of the strongest opponents sought to rally their scattered forces. Once again Captain Laughinghouse, who had opposed Aycock in the convention that nominated Shepherd, came out as the champion of the anti-Aycock forces. He never feared the face of man and was ready to meet any opponents in any contest. But Aycock had so completely won the convention that not even the eloquence of a Bryan or a Kitchin could have stemmed the tide. Instead of condemnation, there was enthusiastic commendation. While scattered voices were now and then raised against fair provision for schools for the Negroes, the opposition to the Aycock doctrine, which was warmly supported in my paper, never again raised its head in North Carolina. Instead, North Carolina led all Southern states in giving a chance for education, primary and other, to the Negroes of the State.

In this day of air-conditioning and microphones and comfortable auditoriums where great audiences can hear, it is a far cry to the conventions of other days when big gatherings in the summer were attended with physical discomfort and when most speakers could hope to be heard only by a portion of the audience, whose chief participation was in loud cries of "Speak louder!" I recall the following story by a brilliant correspondent, H. E. C. Bryant, about that convention, which shows how attempts to cool the air in Greensboro mystified delegates:

"When Glenn was nominated for Governor of North Carolina in 1904, many of the Democratic stalwarts attending the state convention in Greensboro had never in their lives seen a modern water supply system.

"For their comfort, while they wrangled all night, their Greensboro hosts poured constant streams of water on the roof of the warehouse which served as the convention hall. There was no warning of this novel plan for cooling the building, and, seeing the eaves drip hour after hour, some of the participants in that memorable meeting thought the water was coming from the clouds. One farmer, who had taken a long nap in his seat, said on waking:

"'Well, durned if I care if the convention did last all night, 'cause the way it's raining I couldn't plow today if I was at home.'

"J. Harry Myrover of Fayetteville, one of the most learned newspaper men of his day, a quiet, frail man, went to bed rejoicing that the Lord was blessing the land with a much needed rain. Going from the hall to his hotel, to protect his new straw hat from water he carried it under his arm. With trousers rolled high, he was stared at as he hurried through dusty streets.

"The next morning, as he started back to the convention, which was still under way, he met Thomas Allen Sharp, an old University man, then residing in Greensboro, who inquired as to his health.

"'I'm getting better, but my nerves are out of tune,' he said. 'I had a strange experience last night and still feel the effects of it.

"'I was not ill, but completely befuddled. I had two queer attacks. During the progress of the convention I became drowsy, walked over to a window to get a breath of fresh air, and much to my surprise found it was pouring rain. I drifted back to the Cumberland delegation, wondering how I could get to my hotel, since I had no umbrella and did not want to get my straw hat wet.

"'Well, sir, when the convention recessed for breakfast, I rolled up my pants, turned up my coat collar, wrapped my hat in a newspaper and set out. After I had gone about a hundred yards I saw that I was travelling in dust about an inch deep. There was no sign of recent rain, and I was puzzled.

"'I had been taking some new medicine—mixed with a little whiskey, but not enough to hurt. The whole thing must be a dream, I thought. I slept an hour or more and then returned to the convention. Busy with my delegation, I never gave the rain another thought until I approached a window and saw the same sort of torrents that I had seen before. I went out and saw no clouds, or other signs of rain.

"'By that time I was really worried. I wondered if the medicine and whiskey had gone to my head. I was faint and afraid.

"'A doctor told me to go to bed and rest. I did, and now I

am out again, but that downpour is beyond me. I never was in that fix before.'

"Mr. Myrover was astounded when Mr. Sharp explained the 'downpour.'

" 'Well, thank the Lord, my mind is at ease; I feared I was going mad,' he said.

"Marcus Erwin had to soothe a back-country delegate who was mystified by the constant pour of water. The Buncombeite, becoming tired and sleepy, went out to wet his head. The stars were shining, and the ground was as dry as a bone. Pressing his head between his hands, he returned to Mr. Erwin for an explanation.

" 'Mark, is that rain I see falling out yonder?' he asked.

" 'No,' said Mr. Erwin, 'I do not see any rain.'

" 'Mark, my boy, are you telling me the truth?'

" 'Yes, you are mistaken about the rain.'

"The man collapsed and Mr. Erwin stretched him out on a long seat. He soon fell asleep, and when he waked the convention had adjourned and the rain had ceased."

BRYAN WINS HEARST'S HOSTILITY

An attempt was made in the Democratic State Convention of 1904 to instruct the North Carolina delegation to the national convention to support Parker. Those of us who did not look favorably upon the nomination of Parker had no candidate. However, I took the floor and opposed instructions, but the speech of W. W. Kitchin— the best ever—captured the convention. A few days before, Bryan had given out a statement vigorously opposing the nomination of Parker. Some of us preferred to go free rather than to be instructed. In taking that position, I jeopardized my election as a member of the National Committee. When the convention met, however, I was reëlected without opposition. The North Carolina delegation voted as a unit for Parker. When Parker's telegram repudiating the platform came, some of the North Carolina delegates felt that it made victory impossible.

A St. Louis paper said, "Mr. Daniels has attracted some attention by his advocacy of a tariff plank in the platform providing tariff for revenue only. He holds that a plank for conservative tariff revision will be heralded by the Republicans in the campaign as a free trade plank and the Democrats might just as well declare for this kind of plank as they will get just as many votes by it." Almost at the last moment, with delegates from California, Illinois, and other States, an attempt was made to nominate Hearst. He sent a mutual friend to Bryan asking the Nebraskan to place him in nomination. Inasmuch as Hearst had supported Bryan in 1896, the New York publisher was asking a return of favors. Bryan would have been in an embarrassing position if a short time before he had not promised to place Senator Cockrell of Missouri in nomination. That saved him, but Hearst believed that Bryan favored Cockrell, who had no chance, because he wanted an excuse not to nominate him. Inasmuch as Cockrell had been a Confederate soldier, Bryan's action silenced Hearst men afterwards, who charged Bryan was anti-South. I telegraphed to *The News and Observer,* "If they [the Hearst leaders] had relied more on plans and less on boodle, there would have been a different story." Although Bryan had no influence in the early part of the convention, when, rising from a sick bed against the doctor's orders, he came before the convention and made his speech declaring, "You may say that I have finished my course and am ready to be offered up, but you cannot say I have not kept the faith," he completely won the convention. Bryan always believed that was the high-water mark of his oratorical successes because he converted a convention hostile to him into one that gave him a larger measure of applause than he ever received, before or afterwards. I thought that Mr. Parker should have spoken earlier and not waited for the party to adopt a platform and then ask it to retrace its steps, in order to secure his acceptance.

Early in the campaign I received a telegram from Chairman Taggert asking me to come to New York. Upon my arrival he confided to me that he did not like the looks of things and he wished me to stay at headquarters and suggest ways to put life in the campaign. The next day I had a talk with James Creelman, brilliant journalist, who told me that the campaign was petering out and that unless something was done to put life into it we might as well throw up the sponge. Attending a meeting of the Executive Committee, August Belmont, who was furnishing the money, asked me what should be done to increase interest. I suggested that the first thing was to secure more active support by the press, which had at first approved Parker but which was now printing little because little was being done. "How can they be enlisted?" he asked. My reply was that they be invited to New York, given a banquet, and taken on an excursion up the Hudson to "Esopus," the home of Judge Parker, where he would give them a "pep" address. The idea met with favor. "It shall be carried out as you suggest without regard to the cost if you will take charge of arrangements," was the response.

I had worked myself into a hard job in the heat of the summer. But I was game. All editors favoring Parker's election were invited, a magnificent banquet at the Waldorf-Astoria was held, with eloquent speeches made by enthusiastic editors, and all embarked next morning on a river steamer for "Esopus." It looked like the beginning of a winning campaign. My ardor was not decreased even when an editor from North Carolina, unused to champagne, came near missing the ship. (I should say that Henry Watterson and Herman Ridder selected the liquid menu.) It was a lovely day on the beautiful Hudson and the several hundred editors were in high spirits as Judge Parker welcomed them, clean and serene after a swim in the Hudson. They pledged their support of him in a stirring address, but Judge Parker responded in almost as dull and stolid a speech as ever made a dry summer day feel more siccant than seemed possible. Enthusiasm and confidence oozed out as the Judge read on and on without a sentence that breathed. Returning on the river, we were a dispirited gathering. En route to the city, the editors, in appreciation of my organizing the expedition, presented me a beautiful loving cup on which was inscribed:

Presented to
Hon. Josephus Daniels
Chairman
National Editorial Conference
By the
Democratic and Independent
Editors of the United States
Esopus, Sept. 8, 1904.

The chief purpose of the pilgrimage was achieved. On one day the papers gave front-page stories, with pictures and speeches of the banquet, and the next day printed Parker's speech and good stories of the event. Belmont and Taggert and DeLancy Nichols were pleased with the good press and felt that the campaign had got its good second wind. Parker's speech, if not calculated to inspire those who heard it, made a good impression as printed. Predictions of victory were heard, and Democrats, easily made so, became assured they would win. I returned to Raleigh to take part in the State campaign with hope but not confidence. Parker had the support of large money interests in New York City and there was plenty of money to run the campaign.

At first it looked as if Parker might win, but that optimism did not last very long. It flopped when before the election Parker came out in a sensational and specific charge that the big moneyed interests, which had been assumed to be against Roosevelt, were spending unheard-of sums of money to elect him. Roosevelt replied demanding proof and denouncing the charge in Rooseveltian language. Parker was utterly annihilated when he was unable to furnish the proof of his virtual charges of criminal conspiracy between Roosevelt and the big interests to buy the presidency. The Democrats were humiliated and embarrassed by Parker's failure to substantiate the charges. They went to the polls in gloom and received the disappointing election returns without surprise. It was later learned that Parker had made the charges on the authority of Daniel Lamont, who had been Secretary of War under Cleveland, and was regarded as one of the most astute politicians in the country. He was closely connected with what was called Big Business in Wall Street. The information he gave Parker was true and he had the facts. However, when Parker called upon him to furnish evidence to substantiate the serious charges, Lamont declined to do so, saying it would ruin him financially if he did. That left Parker high and dry.

It later turned out that Parker was right and that Roosevelt had written a letter to Harriman, the great railroad king, saying, "You and I are practical men," and soliciting Harriman's support. The proof that Roosevelt had been financed by the big interests, when it became known, did not seem to hurt him. He had a way that enabled him to get away almost with murder in politics. Whereas Parker was colorless and made no appeal to the imagination, Roosevelt was colorful and dominant. Although Roosevelt afterwards acted, with reference to the Tennessee coal and iron matter, in a way to justify Parker's estimate of him, and permitted all manner of special privilege to go on, he had a strong hold on the popular admiration. Roosevelt disliked Speaker Cannon and roasted him. He was opposed to crude materialism. He was perfectly free from the money devil. He did many fine things and had marked talent for paramounting the big things he did and making folks forgive his mistakes and errors. Any other man who had called as many honorable men liars as he did, would have been destroyed, but Teddy had such an indefinable popularity that it destroyed the men he denounced sometimes most ruthlessly and without foundation.

The North Carolina campaign was carried on under high pressure because of Glenn's robustness and because he had a very taking way with the voters. During the campaign of that year the Republicans dropped ex-Judge W. S. O'B. Robinson from membership on the National Republican Committee. He had committed what *The News and Observer* called three unpardonable sins. First, at a dinner in Washington City, given to the members of the National Republican Executive Committee, Judge Robinson refused to eat with the Negro members of the committee and his refusal caused a scene. Second, he opposed a plank in the Republican State Convention abusing Aycock. His personal affections were deeper than political beliefs and he and Aycock were devoted friends; when the Republican Convention denounced Aycock, he denounced the convention. And third, he voted for prohibition in the Republican Convention. These three unpardonable sins prevented his retention on the committee and so, as *The News and Observer* said, he was kicked out. The wide publicity given to Robinson's expulsion and the reasons for it did not help the Republicans in North Carolina. As a matter of fact there was no doubt of the result and Glenn upheld the banner in such a way as to give enthusiasm where it was needed.

LOSS TO THE "OLD RELIABLE"

On September 2, Wiley M. Rogers died. He had been travelling agent and correspondent of *The News and Observer* before I purchased it and had remained with it afterward. I was devoted to him. He was one of the choice souls of the earth, modest, industrious, loyal to the paper and everything it stood for. He always called it the "Old Reliable." In the days of stress he was a strong right arm. He could go into a county without ever seeming to ask questions or take interest in politics and sense the situation better than any man I knew. Every Saturday, when he came in from his trips, he would give me the low-down on what was going on, and he was a genius for getting new subscribers to the paper. He was also chief book-keeper of the paper and devoted four days of the week to the road and two days in Raleigh to this work. For months he knew he was doomed to die. Greater cheerfulness and resignation I never knew in a man. I was in New York when he died. *The News and Observer* never had a man on its staff to whom I was more devoted and who was more capable and efficient or who had a more beautiful life.

XLI

IN GOVERNOR GLENN'S ADMINISTRATION

Governor glenn, elected by a large majority, was inaugurated in January, 1905. The Aycock administration had been marked chiefly by a greatly awakened interest in public education, stimulated by his eloquence and zeal, and the foundation of legislation was enacted on which the great structure of the succeeding years was built. At the close of his administration he reported that the State Prison operation had enabled him to turn over a surplus of $132,867.36 to his successor. Under Julian S. Mann, Superintendent of the Prison, it was conducted with business efficiency and the convicts were well cared for. Taxation on railroads had been increased, public affairs were free from even a hint of graft or scandal, men called to public office had high ideals, important temperance legislation had been enacted, outlawing all stills except those in incorporated towns, foreshadowing the future outlawing of all the manufacture and sale of whisky in North Carolina. It was an administration of steady progress, the central idea being that the future prosperity of the State could be stimulated and secured only by the education of all the people and equal facilities in the public schools for children of both races. After the era of Red Shirt brigades and race conflict, it was four years of good feeling between the races, and larger justice in the courts, and, as Aycock retired, the whole State shared a feeling of "Well done."

Owen H. Guion, of Craven, an old friend, was Speaker of the House in 1905. Controversial legislation was certain to come up and I feared the railroad members would control the committee on railroads. One day, before announcement of the committee, I said to the Speaker, "Owen, I would like to see what members of the House you are putting on the railroad committee." He answered, "Come up to my room and I will show you the list." Nearly every member on the list was a railroad attorney or had such relation to the railroads that made me ask if Bill Rodman (the Speaker's brother-in-law and a railroad attorney), had helped make up the committee. "Of course not," he said. "I asked all members of the House to indicate the committees on which they wished to serve and these men all asked to go on the committee." Only railroad men had asked such assignment. The people were asleep.

"When it is announced," I said, "the people will say the railroad committee was picked by railroad men and I would be compelled to say the same thing, and everybody will think your brother-in-law had a finger in the pie." The Speaker was free, had no tie-up with any interests. He asked my suggestions. I said, "Tear up the list and put on other men." He said he could not do that because he had promised these men to put them on the committee. "There is no fixed number on any committee," he said. "I want to be fair. You give me an equal number of names you feel sure will see that the right thing is done, and I will add them to the list." I did so, heading my suggestions with Captain J. J. Laughinghouse and A. D. McGill, who could be relied upon to see to it that the railroads should get no underhold.

There was much agitation for a repeal of the loose divorce laws and the last interview Governor Aycock gave before leaving Raleigh was upon that measure, in which he said: "It is better that a few individuals should suffer for being unhappily married than that the public viewpoint with reference to the sublimity and permanence of the marriage relation should be in the slightest degree weakened." The Legislature strengthened the divorce laws and *The News and Observer* urged, editorially, that they should be made to conform with the laws of the Bible. The preachers of the State, and most of the newspapers, stood for this legislation and it was enacted, but not without a great fight.

The second legislation that came up and created the greatest discussion and hardest fight was the bill introduced by Senator D. L. Ward, of Craven, to prevent the sale of liquor outside of any incorporated town, and the size of a town was defined in the act. This act had been shown to Governor Aycock and he had favored it, and Governor Glenn gave it his warm and enthusiastic support, as did Senator Simmons. The opponents resented it when Senator Simmons came out in a strong statement in favor of the Ward bill, and *The News and Observer* said he was undisturbed by their threats. It also said the seven leaders against the Ward bill, who had sent out the letters against it, had "swunk" to six, and compared them to "Private

Mulvaney, Corporil wanst but rejuced." The bill passed both houses by a large majority, the vote in the House being 69 to 23.

In the previous year an attempt had been made to drive out the stills and saloons at Hamlet, Richmond County, but the owners of these stills, who were making a great deal of money, some of them defrauding the government and dividing their profits with Federal officer holders, had been able to defeat it. At this session of the Legislature, Captain W. I. Everett, State Senator, introduced a bill to make Richmond County dry. While this legislation was pending, the Anti-Saloon League held its convention in Raleigh. It was very largely attended, particularly from Richmond and all the adjoining counties. Hamlet was the strategic center of the liquor forces in North Carolina. The passage of the Everett bill by the Senate was hailed as destroying the stronghold, and the day after the Legislature passed the bill for prohibition in Richmond County, a fire broke out in the barrooms of Hamlet at dawn. *The News and Observer* said, "The cause of the fire is not known, but it has the look of incendiarism."

In January, 1905, *The News and Observer* obtained the inside story of the South Dakota bonds. It had been believed before that Russell and Butler obtained the employment in this case by reason of information Russell had obtained by virtue of his office. However, it was not positively proven until January, when *The News and Observer* printed the story of how the owners of these South Dakota bonds had sent them to the State Treasurer for payment and had inquired about their status; that State Treasurer Worth had taken them to Russell and asked his advice about them and had been told to leave them with him and he would look into it. He did "look into it," and the next heard of these bonds, about which the owners had written to the State Treasurer, was that eight of them were in possession of South Dakota, and suit was being brought against the State. Having succeeded in winning big fees while in office, Russell and Butler put an advertisement in the New York *Evening Post* asking for other Southern bonds, which they said could be collected. *The News and Observer* reproduced that advertisement, signed by W. N. Coler and Co., R. F. Pettigrew, D. L. Russell, and Marion Butler, Committee.

Governor Russell was very indignant at the criticism, and in an interview in the *Post,* said:

"We shall not seek to enforce against North Carolina any bonds that were not honestly issued nor will I attempt to collect from the state the proceeds of bonds that were fraudulently disposed of by the state or railroad officials except to the extent of such amount as went into the treasury of the state or of the railroad companies and were used for the benefit of the state in railroad construction and otherwise. I am confident that ex-Senator Butler will concur with me in this statement. The bonds which the North American Trust is collecting are generally those of states other than North Carolina."

The News and Observer, commenting on this, said:

"Bear in mind that this statement comes from a man who, while Governor of North Carolina, betrayed his trust and prevented the state treasurer's redeeming certain bonds offered for redemption at twenty-five cents on the dollar *in order to compel the state to pay more than it had received.* He is the same man who conspired with Butler and Pettigrew to induce South Dakota to sell its sovereignity in order to compel North Carolina to pay for bonds on which it had received only twenty-five cents on the dollar. There is no parallel in history to this infamy on the part of Butler and Russell—the one the governor of the state and the other the senator from the state—taking advantage of positions given them by the state to conspire to make it pay bonds that it had always been willing to pay on the basis of every cent received. If the matter had been discovered before Russell's term as Governor had expired, steps would have been taken to bring about impeachment."

It concluded by calling Russell and Butler "these two traitors," and went on to say that Russell and Butler "and their allies here in North Carolina, who keep in the background, are the logical bond descendants of Littlefield and Swepson—no whit better."

The first day the General Assembly met, *The News and Observer* wrote an editorial on the need of child labor legislation under the head of "Do Not Grind Up the Seed Corn," but the sentiment for the humane law was seen not to be strong when the labor law was defeated in the House Committee.

Governor Glenn began his administration under most favorable auspices and supported measures of public welfare. Although he had been an attorney of the Southern Railway he soon made it clear that, as Governor of North Carolina, he owed no obligation to these former clients. He was very sensitive about it. I remember on the night when he was inaugurated, at the reception he took me to one side and said, "You opposed my nomination because you thought I would be influenced by Andrews. You will see that, as Governor of North Carolina, I have no strings tied to me." The paper and the Governor were on very good terms most of the administration. In fact, they were in such hearty accord, particularly on all temperance matters, that it drew us very close together.

The question of freight rates was much discussed in this year and *The News and Observer* had quite a controversy with Henry A. Page, Ceasar Cone, and J. Elwood Cox. Mr. Page was president of the Aberdeen Railroad, which had been constructed as a lumber road and afterward was used in regular railroad business. He became, for this year and during the active agitation for railroad rate reduction, the spokesman of all the railroads and we had some right sharp tilts. In the course of one of his arguments he said that although *The News and Observer* had grown, it hadn't reduced its subscription rates; yet it was demanding that the railroads cut their freight rates. To this the paper replied that he was mistaken; that it had reduced the rates from seven to six dollars a year and asked the railroads to make a similar reduction.

In a news story *The News and Observer* asked, "Why are the Cones for higher freight rates and why do Ceasar Cone of Greensboro and J. Elwood Cox of High Point, leading business men and manufacturers, declare they are opposed to giving any government commission the power to fix rates on railroads?" The paper also asked, "Are the hearts of certain big shippers touched via directorships and free passes on the Southern?" It ascertained and printed that both Mr. Cox and Mr. Cone had free passes. At that time the Southern Railway owned little roads like the Chapel Hill branch, High Point and Asheboro branch, and a number of other branches, and it was their policy to give important shippers positions as directors of these roads, which carried with them a pass on the whole Southern system. *The News and Observer* charged that the activities of these "pass toters" in opposition to railroad rate reduction was due to the fact that they carried passes. Ceasar Cone replied in the same tone that *The News and Observer* had used and denied that he had ever flopped and that he had never believed in government regulation of rates. For a long time, and particularly when J. Elwood Cox was candidate for Governor in 1904, *The News and Observer* made a habit, on Mr. Cox's frequent trips to Raleigh, of saying in its local column, "Mr. J. Elwood Cox of High Point came to Raleigh yesterday on business. He rode on a B pass of the Southern Railroad." Cox was a Quaker and a very warm friend of Herbert Jackson, secretary and treasurer of *The News and Observer* and cashier of the Commercial Bank. When Jackson asked Cox about this pass he said, with a smile, "I don't object to *The News and Observer's* printing the fact that I ride on a pass but I do resent their making the statement about the kind of pass. I am riding on an A pass." Cox was the best of all the Republicans, a successful banker and manufacturer and a man of excellent private character, whose Republicanism came out of his Quaker training in opposition to slavery.

In the latter part of May the Southern Railway announced that its train going west from Raleigh would leave the city about midnight and, commenting upon it, *The News and Observer* said:

"This is another attempt to injure *The News and Observer* and cause loss of subscribers west of Raleigh. Such a course, it is believed, will help the Raleigh *Times* [succeeded to the Raleigh *Post's* subscription list] and Butler's subsidized *News* in Greensboro. We appeal to the people of Western North Carolina not to permit the unfair attempt to prevent the wide circulation of the only morning daily published in the state's capital. The change was foreshadowed in December. It is ordered now for no other purpose except to injure *The News and Observer* in the West because it will not bow the knee to Baal. The establishment of the *Morning Post* by the Southern Railroad folks, having failed to injure the paper, this is another blow beneath the belt. The train has been held in Raleigh until morning over twenty years to carry papers into the West. There is no good reason to make it leave here before midnight."

Next day *The News and Observer* said, "Sooner than be silent when the Southern Railway crowd tries to control the next State Senate, *The News and Observer* will come out monthly and go by ox-cart, but when it comes it will blister those who seek to run the Democratic Party while helping to elect Republicans." In discussing the change of schedule, *The News and Observer* pointed out that the profit on the North Carolina Railroad, leased by the Southern, had increased $805,113 in ten years. The suggested schedule change created resentment in Western North Carolina. A. F. Sams, afterward Senator from Forsyth, called it "nothing less than an outrage." Petitions were signed in every town in the west against the change. At the same time *The News and Observer* demanded that the tax assessment of the Southern Railway be increased by over one hundred and fifty thousand dollars. On June 10, after the petitions had come in from all over western North Carolina, the Corporation Commission, on a formal complaint filed by Duncan McIver, of the firm of McIver and Seawell, of Sanford, issued an order suspending the change of schedule going west until after a hearing on its merits. *The News and Observer* said that unless the Commission had taken this action the contemplated wrong would have been put into effect before the hundreds of complaints and petitions could have had their day in court and that it was then up to the Southern to submit to a square deal on the evidence or attempt to defy the evidence. "Which will it do?" *The News and Observer* asked. Two days after, my paper said, under the heading, "Snuggling on the Bosom of Purnell," that the Southern Railway had defied the Corporation Commission and then had run to the Federal court for protection. "Spite Schedule On" described the order which would have assured all parties a square deal, and said, "Yesterday, fearing the consequences, attorneys hastened to Purnell to prevent the Commission from enforcing the order and punishment for contempt and the judge came to time as per usual." The paper also said, "The Corporation Commission cannot maintain its self-respect without serving a rule upon Colonel A. B. Andrews to show cause why he should not be attached for contempt"; and in an editorial, headed "Cannot Stop *The News and Observer*," I wrote, "The change in the schedule imposes heavy expenses upon the paper but we intend to send out a good paper on the early train no matter how extreme the expense," and added:

"This paper will live to print the funeral of sheets which the Southern Railroad seeks to favor, to denounce political control of North Carolina by the Southern Railroad or any other railroad and to demand a square deal for the people of North Carolina. The Southern Railroad's belief that it can 'kill and make alive' can be carried too far. In the meantime Mordecai is 'still sitting at the King's gate' and a good and honest edition of the paper will reach its readers in Western North Carolina."

Referring to the Purnell order, *The News and Observer* asked:

"Is Colonel Andrews bigger than the state? Can he spit upon legal orders with impunity? If the Southern Railroad can snap its fingers in the face of orders of the Corporation Commission and treat its orders with contempt, the claim of Colonel Andrews that he is bigger than the law will seem to have some basis. Judge Purnell's injunction shop is often patronized by the Southern Railroad. If the Judge wanted a recommendation, the Southern Railroad could say: 'We have tried injunctions from several federal judges when we wished to defy the state law and the mandates of the people, but yours are the easiest to get of any we have yet tried.'"

Next day my paper said, "The Federal judiciary has wrought more ruin in this state since the war than Sherman's invasion. It has been, in nine cases out of ten, when the railroads are interested, the haven of taxdodgers and law-breakers."

The next day the Southern Railway filed an answer to the Commission, and the paper said it was a great show of respect for its powers. After they filed that petition, Commissioner Rogers went to Waynesville to confer with Attorney General Gilmer. The following day the editorial referring to a comment of some opposition paper that this was a fuss between the Southern Railway and *The News and Observer,* said, "It is not any such thing," and outlined the main points of difference between *The News and Observer* and the Southern Railway.

In a hearing before the Corporation Commission, R. T. Gray, of the counsel for the petitioners against the Southern Railway and Purnell, read a statement in which it was declared that since the Commission appeared to be unable to enforce its orders they would desist and withdraw their petition before a powerless Commission against an all-powerful Federal court. *The News and Observer* had an editorial on "A Powerless Commission on One Side And an All- Powerful Federal Court, Generally With the Railroads On the Other," and also said that the Corporation Commission was genuflecting to a powerful Purnell and that the Corporation Commission admitted its impotence. The Commission's conduct was so generally denounced that suggestions were made that the Commission be abolished, but *The News and Observer* had an editorial, "Reform It —Do Not Abolish It." Referring to the victory of the railroad *The*

News and Observer said, "If you are the Big Boss, Railroad, you can practice anarchy and ride rough-shod over the law and the Federal judge will make the parties obeying the law pay the costs of your anarchy. Who said 'There is nothing new under the sun'?"

At the State Democratic Convention *The News and Observer* said that the Democratic platform declared, among other things, that the powers of the Corporation Commission should be enlarged so as to give it full and adequate power to regulate all public service corporations in the State and make them subject to its jurisdiction. That was a bitter pill for the railroad officials and politicians to swallow.

In the summer of 1906 there was a very warm contest for the State Senate in Wake County. The railroad and city political organization brought out as their candidate for the Senate, John C. Drewry, who at that time owned the Raleigh *Times,* the policy of which was against everything that *The News and Observer* regarded as Democratic. It had been the tool of those who wished to injure the cause of temperance; had praised Purnell and McBee in the Atlantic and North Carolina steal; had denounced Chief Justice Clark regularly because his decisions were not pleasing to the railroads; had denounced the Laughinghouse bill for railroad rate reduction; had been the organ of insurance companies; in fact had inherited and carried on the worst Billingsgate and subservience that had characterized the Raleigh *Tribune* and the *Morning Post,* but the use of money in the primaries and powerful railroad and machine support nominated Drewry. At that time *The News and Observer* did not have the evidence which it obtained later that the *Times* was in receipt of a subsidy from the Southern Railway.

The tense opposition to *The News and Observer* by the Southern Railway was evidenced in a remark made by Engineer Hay of that road. Someone asked him why he fought *The News and Observer* and would not let it go into his home. He said, "I fight it because it fights my meat and bread." *The News and Observer* made this answer: "The way this newspaper fought the meat and bread of the engineers of the Southern Railroad and other railroads in North Carolina is that it was chiefly responsible for the passage of the fellow-servant law which did more for the engineers and firemen than all the Southern railroad officials. They pay them a salary for hard work. *The News and Observer* saw to it that if any were killed his family didn't suffer."

In July Taft, then Secretary of War, made a remarkable speech at Greensboro which was to be used effectively for many years to injure the Republican Party. Tom Pence, Washington correspondent of *The News and Observer,* when it was printed that Taft was going to Greensboro to speak, upon the invitation of Spencer B. Adams, quoted Taft as saying, "I do not know the Adams mentioned in this dispatch. The truth is that I am going to North Carolina at the invitation of my old friend, Ex-Senator Marion Butler." The fact that he was coming on Butler's invitation damned him before he arrived. For Taft personally the people had great respect, but that he should come into the State at the invitation of Butler injured him not only with the Democrats but with the Republicans who despised Butler's attempt to get control of their party. Pence also telegraphed *The News and Observer* that Taft was coming to Greensboro to launch his presidential boom. Taft's speech delighted the Democrats and infuriated the Republicans. Inasmuch as the gathering he addressed was composed mainly of Federal officers and their henchmen, his speech was received with silence and indignation on their part, and the powers-that-be in the Republican Party never loved Taft.

Mr. Taft made this indictment of the Republican Party in the South:

"I do not wish to seem ungracious, but I must be candid. In my judgment the Republican Party in North Carolina would be much stronger as a voting party if all the Federal offices were filled by Democrats. As long as the Republican Party in the Southern states shall represent little save a factional chase for Federal offices in which business men and men of substance in the community have no desire to enter and in the result of which they have no interest, we may expect the present political conditions of the South to continue."

In the course of his address Mr. Taft said that Southern men had a genius and talent for public service and their absence from the councils of the Republic was a distinct loss. He then made an appeal to the young men of the South who wished a voice in the government of their country, to join the Republican Party where they would be welcomed to an equal voice and participation. He told them as long as they remained in the Democratic Party they cut themselves off from positions which they were eminently fitted to fill.

Commenting on Mr. Taft's invitation in my paper, under a heading "Respectfully Declined," I told Mr. Taft that the young men of the South could not be induced to desert their Party and their principles in the hope of obtaining office. He was thanked for the courteous way he offered the bribe of office if they would desert their principles. I declared that principles governed them more than pie and they could not be seduced from allegiance to the party of their faith by the tender of Federal jobs.

Years later, when I was Secretary of the Navy, Mr. Taft, in a personal conversation, referred to his Greensboro speech and said he was perfectly sincere. I replied that I knew he was sincere and asked, "Do you think if I had accepted your invitation to join the Republican Party in order to get office I would now be a member of the cabinet?" He gave a famous Taft chuckle and said he guessed my course was the wisest one.

DR. KILGO AND THE BISHOPRIC

In May of that year at the General Conference of the Methodist Church in Birmingham, Dr. Kilgo, President of Trinity College, received a very large vote for Bishop. However, he was not elected, although he led in the early balloting. His defeat was due to the fact that Colonel John R. Webster, former Speaker of the House, wrote a vigorous article against his election, giving to the delegates the gist of the evidence in the Kilgo-Gattis case and some of the violent speeches made by Dr. Kilgo, particularly denouncing Gattis, whom Webster called "an aged and honorable preacher whose only crime was trying to defend his character from assault." A few other Methodists joined Colonel Webster in this protest against the election of Dr. Kilgo. Colonel Webster asked me to join him in this protest, which I declined to do. I had been as severe in criticism of Dr. Kilgo as John Webster but I did not doubt Kilgo's personal integrity and did not wish to carry a fight about litigation or politics into the church body. Colonel Webster said if I had joined him and Judge Clark and others in circularizing delegates against Dr. Kilgo he would never have been elected to the bishopric. I declined to have any part in blocking the worthy ambitions of a truly brilliant preacher. At the next Conference he was elected and in the high office he greatly impressed those who heard him with his deep spirituality and evangelistic consecration. Even when I felt, and declared in all sincerity, that his zeal to secure more money for the college from the Dukes caused him to be too subservient to their political beliefs and business methods, I never let an opportunity to hear him preach go by. He had a winning appeal and a style all his own.

As a preacher, Dr. Kilgo was *sui generis*. He was one minute an old-fashioned circuit rider upholding, with a rare gift of eloquence, the simple faith that carried the Wesleyans far in the new world. In the same sermon he was the modern champion of commercial penetration of the world, lauding the men who carried trade into the Orient as doing more for the spread of Christianity than the missionaries. His artistry was so perfect that most hearers did not perceive the incongruity. As a word-painter and a maker of pictures in his discourses he was a past-master. Perhaps his best word-painting was his story of the debt he owed his horse—he loved him as much as Lee did Traveller—who was his companion and friend when he rode the circuit. Between them was such intimate association that he described how his faithful horse saved his life by fording a turbulent stream. You felt you could almost hear the horse neigh and see him shake his mane as he came out of the rushing stream, rider and ridden united in a bond which Dr. Kilgo described as a lasting partnership in the spread of the Gospel. As the climax of this sermon, which made you feel like saying, "My kingdom for a horse" (such a horse) the preacher would conclude with a description of how, when he entered through the pearly gates, he would be riding his faithful steed, closing with real drama as he declared, "And I would not wish to be in heaven if my horse were denied entrance." It was all done with such artistry that you felt with the preacher that the horse who carried him to safety had won a title to glory.

Dr. Kilgo loved to make sensational statements, as, for instance, in one of his sermons he declared: "I am bigger than any State; bigger than Texas—bigger than North Carolina is." When criticized for the statement he explained that he was undertaking to show that "man is a divine creature and that it is not the divine idea to make a tool of the State," that any man is bigger than the State. He loved to excoriate Bryan and free silver along with Jefferson, saying more than once, "There are men in the land idling away their time, shirking work and sending their wives to the field or the factory, while they, themselves, saunter around, talking 16-to-1, who ought to have 'sixteen lashes' if you please—to their backs." To a class he said, "You ought to deport yourself so you could look any man in the face and tell him to go to hell."

After he was elevated to the bishopric, in Asheville in 1910, Bishop Kilgo became the most spiritual of preachers, omitting all the defense of monopoly or praise of monopolists, holding up the old Methodist doctrine and traditions with a spirit so sweet that he won many hearts. Shortly after his ordination, he resigned as President of Trinity College. He was not to live long, dying August 10, 1922, mourned by his church.

MY WIFE PREVENTS CHANGE IN THE STATE CAPITOL

In Glenn's administration, a movement obtained headway to modernize and enlarge the State Capitol building. Chief Justice Walter Clark, State Insurance Commissioner Young, and Senator John C. Drewry were the three leaders in this movement. They engaged Frank P. Milburn, as architect, to draw plans to erect wings on the northern and southern sides sixty by one hundred feet and a west portico wing of forty-five by seventy-five feet. The architect stated that the present architectural structure would be preserved and the building would be even more beautiful. This proposal was hailed with satisfaction by many who felt that the Capitol was too small and by others who thought any new construction an improvement. Progress was the watchword of those who favored the additions to the Capitol and those who were opposed to it were called old-fogies. It was a battle royal in Raleigh. The influential officials were on the side of enlargement. By the time the Legislature met, the members from Wake County and Governor Glenn had been brought around and the bill was drawn and approved by the legislative committees to issue bonds to enlarge the Capitol.

When it looked as though the bill might pass, the opponents got into action and called to their aid—and it was necessary—legislators who did not believe in any bond issues for any purpose. *The News and Observer* called the enlargement "vandalism" and said the proposed addition would make the stately building a monstrosity. It said the building was already as large as it should be on the existing acreage. It urged the purchase of the two squares north of the Capitol so that the Capitol Square could be doubled in size and that additional buildings needed be erected on land to be purchased. It was impossible to secure legislation to buy that land. Those who wanted to enlarge the

Capitol opposed it, and those who were opposed to any bond issues joined with them. After a very ardent fight, in which my wife, whose chief civic pride was the State Capitol, threatened, in a somewhat facetious talk to the promoters, to take a gun, if necessary, to prevent a stone's being disturbed on that sacred edifice, the effort failed.

Some time before, Harry Bacon, architect of the Lincoln Memorial in Washington, had been in Raleigh. In a conversation, he had said to my wife—they had been school friends—that the Capitol in Raleigh was one of the three perfect pieces of Doric architecture in America. Fortified by this opinion from an eminent architect, the opponents were able to induce Governor Glenn to recede from his active advocacy of the project. I remember very well talking with Chief Justice Clark about it. He was a born iconoclast and innovator. He was very influential at that time and had thrown his influence along with the Insurance Commissioner and State Senator from Wake in the fight. He ridiculed as back-numbers everybody who opposed the enlargement, but said he was "out-generaled" by my wife. She was happy in having a hand in preserving what she believed was the State's chief architectural possession. In showing visitors about Raleigh, she would stop at the Capitol to let them drink in its beauties. If the visitor shared her enthusiasm, she admired his or her wisdom. If, however, the luckless visitor lacked admiration of her favorite structure, such party fell low in her estimation. That was her touchstone and yardstick by which she measured everybody.

THE TOBACCO TRUST AGAIN

On July 18 my paper stated that the American Tobacco Company had taken out life insurance on its employees, payable to any person who had served the company continuously for one year, applicable only to those receiving fifty dollars a week and under. After commending the American Tobacco Company for its action my paper printed, "What the Trust Has Done To The Tobacco-Growers," and said that in 1875 the average price paid on the Danville market for tobacco was $20.45 per hundred pounds, in 1885, $13.54 per hundred pounds, and in 1906, $7.79. The next week *The News and Observer* had an editorial, "Trust Dodges Tax," and stated that the American Tobacco Company had paid four million dollars for the Blackwell's Durham Bull Tobacco Company but it was on the tax books of Durham County at only $680,385 and added, "If that tax valuation is right, then the American Tobacco Company was swindled when it paid four million dollars for the property." When litigation was undertaken in the State courts, the Tobacco Trust received an injunction from Judge Purnell, who held that the company was not a State corporation and could be tried only in the Federal courts.

OFFICIALS VIGOROUS AGAINST LYNCHING

On August 6 of that year occurred one of the most dramatic lynchings in the history of the State. While court was in session at Salisbury, thousands of people stormed the jail and lynched three Negroes who were charged with the murder of the Lyerly family of Salisbury. The murder had been committed three weeks before, the man, his wife, and two children had been killed. The military company which had been called out was powerless against the mob, and *The News and Observer* story said the militia, not having authority from the Governor to shoot, left the scene. After that the mob got the Negroes over the sheriff's protest and there was much promiscuous shooting by the mob. Senator Overman and Judge Long, who was trying the Negroes, and Solicitor Hammer, addressed the mob on the jail steps. When the Governor was notified he sent more troops, who scattered the mob. The leader of the lynchers was George Hall, an ex-convict with a long list of crimes to his credit. Before the lynching the mob cut their victims' fingers, toes, and ears off as souvenirs and the bodies were badly mutilated. Hammer told the mob, "God Almighty reigns and the law is still supreme. This court will not adjourn until the matter is investigated." Investigation was begun at once. *The News and Observer* said that at a very early hour on the morning of the lynching, Misses Matildie and Aggie Lyerly, the only surviving members of the murdered family, were driven to the scene and viewed with awe the three bodies swinging from a limb. The girls held up well, and it was stated that it was believed they would survive the shock, which was at first doubted. *The News and Observer* called it a war on the State and said the lynching of the three Negroes at Salisbury was a piece of anarchy without justification or excuse.

Governor Glenn called out all the troops near the scene and declared everything should be done to bring the mob to justice. *The News and Observer* printed a horrible picture of the Negroes hanging to the tree, unquestionably real. It was a terrible photograph. A special to *The News and Observer* from Salisbury said, "The men who perpetrated Monday night's crime are afraid to allow their colleagues to remain in jail for the reason that someone might turn state's evidence and implicate them all. Judge Benjamin F. Long and Solicitor Hammer rose to the occasion, and Governor Glenn personally went to Salisbury to give every aid possible to prevent further violation of the law and to back up the Judge and Solicitor in seeking the punishment of the parties guilty of the lynching. Within a few days the case was heard and George Hall, lynch leader, was convicted and sentenced to fifteen years in prison. This was the maximum sentence under the law. *The News and Observer* said, "This is the first instance in the history of the State when the prisoner charged with aiding in lynching was convicted and it is a distinct victory for the court and the law." It also added, "The Rowan mob was insolent as well as vicious. It has asserted that lynching cannot be punished." To show the state of mind in Rowan at that time, a few days after the Negroes had been lynched, the Lyerly barn was burned by Negroes. *The News and Observer* said the Negroes were evidently moved by a spirit of revenge for the lynching at Salisbury.

In October of that year President Roosevelt came to Raleigh and spoke at the State Fair. He made a fine impression and spoke on the Northern Securities case and the regulation of railroads. I never knew exactly why it was, but supposed it was because *The News and Observer,* in the previous year, had been pretty hard on Roosevelt, that I was not invited to the luncheon given to him in a tent on the fairgrounds. There was a struggle among the socially prominent as to who should be invited. The number was limited and I don't know whether it was because I was not socially prominent or that I was politically undesirable, but my wife and I were about the only people who were accustomed to go to such places who were left out. That did not prevent my leading the applause for Roosevelt when he made a vigorous speech for the regulation of railroads and against the malefactors of great wealth and having a satisfactory conversation with him. Mrs. Roosevelt was with him and they reached Raleigh after a long journey, stopping at many places. The only flowers Mrs. Roosevelt received upon her arrival in Raleigh were sent by my wife. The newspaper men from the North, who were with him, gave a rather severe roast of the Raleigh reception, particularly criticizing the luncheon given at the tent on the fairgrounds. They called it a "Peanut and Pickle Luncheon" and contrasted it with the very elegant luncheon served at the leading hotel in Richmond by the Virginia people, indicating that North Carolina had country manners. That night Roosevelt attended the meeting of the State Historical Association and presented the Patterson Cup to John Charles McNeill, then toast of the State, as a brilliant young poet and writer. He was a lovable and delightful young man whose early death, like that of Young Avery on the Charlotte *Observer,* was widely lamented. I wrote an editorial the next day on the President's good example, praising him for paying the expenses of his train and saying, "He does not travel on a pass."

An annoying incident occurred when the Roosevelt train came into the depot. Governor Glenn was out of the State and Francis D. Winston, Lieutenant Governor, was the official host. Governor Winston, in all the pomp of office, called to see the President and pay his respects at the special car in the Union Station. There were so many secret service men around that it was some time before Winston and his staff were received. Members of his party were indignant when a secret service man patted the Governor all around his body to see if he were armed. *The News and Observer* denounced the secret service nuisance and said that Roosevelt, being a man of personal courage, ought to be relieved from the secret service men who surrounded him. The law, not the men, is at fault.

In his message to Congress, President Roosevelt urged amendments to the anti-trust law to make it more effective and said the fight was on against the Standard Oil Company. He recommended the prohibition of child labor and said, "It is time to prepare for tariff revision." So far as I can recall, that is the only time during his campaign for the presidency or during his incumbency in the White House, that he made reference to the tariff. He always side-stepped that question. In his early life, he had sneered at the high protective tariff of his party and at one time had vigorously denounced it, but after he became a candidate he said he realized that he could do almost anything with the Republicans if he didn't touch the tariff; that it was a fetish with them and so he chose, rather, to hold his place and carry out other reforms than to open a question in which he would be impotent.

RAILROAD ORGAN GIVES UP THE GHOST

On November 12 there was a death in Raleigh which *The News and Observer* did not deplore. It announced "The *Morning Post* Gives up the Ghost," adding that it had been absorbed by the Raleigh *Evening Times.* That was a local story. *The News and Observer* carried no editorial about it, no tears, no flowers, but it was not long before the *Times* secured as its editor R. W. Simpson, who was to unleash his slanderous pen and abuse *The News and Observer* with more virulence and bitterness than even Haywood, of the defunct *Tribune.* Shortly after *The News and Observer,* under the heading "Is The Prophecy To Be Fulfilled?" said the program of the Southern Railway, which had lost money on the *Post,* but had decided to "kill *The News and Observer*" in a new way, through the *Evening Times* in Raleigh and the *Industrial News* in Greensboro.

In the early part of 1906 litigation was begun against Samuel Spencer, president of the Southern Railway, for getting control of the Atlanta *News,* of which John Temple Graves was editor. Graves alleged that Spencer had illegally obtained control of the *Daily News* for the Southern Railway and the Central of Georgia Railroad. *The News and Observer,* in an editorial asked, "Why Railroads Own or Subsidize Newspapers," and answered its own question:

"Because they wish to continue charging more passenger and freight rates than conditions justify; because they wish to continue to pay taxes on under-valuation; at this time they are paying only 60 per cent on the true valuation in North Carolina and only 40 per cent in Georgia; because they wish to slip their agents into public positions to defeat legislation giving further regulation and to prevent laws requiring them to give prompt and equal service; because they have an ambition to be lords paramount in every state where they have railroads, requiring ambitious men to receive their O. K. before they can get promotion and to politically kill brave men who ring true against extortion, favoritism, neglect of duty to the public, bribery through passes and otherwise. These are the main reasons. In North Carolina the same crowd subsidized the Raleigh *Tribune* to advance their interests when the Republicans were in power and afterward established the *Morning Post* when it was thought the Democrats would be returned to power."

The agitation for the repeal of the mail subsidy, given to the Southern Railway for carrying fast mail from Washington to New Orleans, became an issue in North Carolina. The subsidy had been supported by the North Carolina senators of both parties and by most of the North Carolina delegation in the House, but W. W. Kitchin, afterward Governor, congressman from the Fifth District, denounced it in Congress and in other speeches. *The News and Observer* had long been declaring that it was a pure subsidy and that the Southern Railway was enabled by the receipts of this subsidy to carry on its political propaganda, and it denounced subsidies of all kinds. Kitchin's speech was a very able one and attracted wide attention, not only in North Carolina but throughout the country. It became the tocsin of the war against subsidies.

FIRST MILITARY COURIER TO RIDE IN AN AUTOMOBILE

In August Governor Glenn detailed John Park of Raleigh, who had the State agency of the Ford automobile, to take a trip as military courier to Morehead City. The trip was made, accompanied by another machine, with the expectancy of its completion in a day and a half. It was the first undertaking of its kind in the State. On the first day Park and his chauffeur, Tom Harris, made ninety-six miles, leaving Raleigh at 5 A.M. in a 15 h.p. Ford roadster, and when they reached Dover they had to wait for new batteries. It was the first automobile of any kind that had been seen in Morehead City. They reached Camp Glenn at 9:20 P.M. on August 6, after having left Raleigh August 1. Harris was arrested for driving across the board walk. In the latter part of that year the first automobile club was organized in Raleigh.

XLII

"THE GOD-BLESSED MACS SAVE THE DAY"

N O LEGISLATURE has assembled in North Carolina in my day in which the members were so evenly divided and the contest over legislation was so bitterly fought as in 1907.

The News and Observer, in the early part of the session, outlined, as the first important measure that should be enacted, one compelling lobbyists to register. Raleigh literally swarmed with them. Ex-legislators by the dozen, with railroad passes and railroad fees in their pockets, were there to fight any railroad legislation. The second piece of legislation I strongly urged was an anti-trust law with teeth. This brought trust attorneys to Raleigh in large numbers. The third big issue which my paper advocated was reduction of railroad passenger rates to two cents per mile. A two-cent rate bill had been enacted in Illinois. The railroads had conceded it in Virginia and that was the rate in operation in most of the forty-eight States. Therefore in pressing a two-cent rate I was advocating that North Carolina do what had been done in practically all the States not under railroad control. The railroads were selling inter-state mileage at two cents generally. The fourth action urged by *The News and Observer* was a law prohibiting the railroads from giving passes or mileage to editors of newspapers.

The measure to compel the lobbyists to register drew first blood. Its opponents denounced it as a great outrage that reputable gentlemen should be compelled to register as lobbyists when, as they claimed, they were acting in the public interest, even if they did receive fees. The bill passed the House, but was defeated in the Senate. In nearly all of the legislation of that session the House rang true, while the Senate, by a narrow margin, either reversed House action or so amended the reform measure as to cut the heart out of it. This victory of the lobbyists greatly cheered the opponents of the legislation of which Mr. E. J. Justice was the leader in the Legislature and *The News and Observer* was the leader on the outside. A *News and Observer* headline read "Put the Lobbyists in the Sunlight." When the

Senate defeated the bill, the paper said that some men prefer the shelter of darkness.

Mr. E. J. Justice introduced important railroad bills, the initial one of which was the reduction in passenger rates to two cents a mile. Bills to reduce freight rates were to follow. The railroad presidents and officials rolled into Raleigh in their private cars. They declared that the legislation introduced would destroy the prosperity of the railroads and of the State. Hearings were largely attended. Every railroad official or attorney denied the right of the State to fix rates on the basis of earnings, except President Gannon of the Norfolk and Southern. He admitted that the rates ought to be based upon the earnings per train mile. His was a small road and was not earning much. As usual, when railroad legislation was up, Henry A. Page, president of the Asheboro and Aberdeen Railroad, took the laboring oar for the railroads.

In one of his speeches, Page said, "The railroads have no more monopoly in North Carolina than has *The News and Observer*." "At least five thousand of its subscribers," he added, "don't want to take it but have to." While this legislation was in the most heated state the Southern Railway went before the Corporation Commission and made full surrender in its fight on the Selma Connection Case. The Southern had broken a long connection with the Atlantic Coast Line. My paper had in season and out of season demanded that the old convenient connection be restored. Franklin McNeill, chairman of the Commission, had ordered the connection restored, and the Southern had resisted.

The Greensboro *Industrial News,* which my paper called the *Daily Subsidized News,* declared that the legislation would be a menace to the State, and the Raleigh *Times,* then owned by the Southern Railway, through its relations with State Senator John C. Drewry, took the same ground. At one session Mr. Winborne, of Hertford, denounced as "infamous and libelous" an article in the *Times* headed, "Will Pump Mr. Page Because He Offended The Party's Boss Here. Daniels Does That and Still Protects Two Powerful Railroads. Wood Pile Negro Comes Out At Last." It said,

"Through the efforts of Daniels the new bill will force the Aberdeen and Asheboro Railroad to reduce rates but provides for no reduction on the Norfolk and Western and the Louisville and Nashville lines. Page's road only five miles over limit. Fine

Italian hand gets in its work because Page was guilty of disrespect toward the king. Likely that some warm talk will follow."

Winborne said that the article, attributing control to Daniels, reflected upon the conference committee. He denounced the editor of the *Times* as dishonorable because he had declared that the conference committee was "dictated to and dominated by Josephus Daniels." The committee proceeded to run down the false charges of the *Times,* and Page denied that he had had anything to do with the charge or the article. Editor Simpson refused to answer questions but filed a written statement prepared by his attorneys. He said that to answer would be violating newspaper ethics. The Charlotte *Observer* had printed the story from the *Times,* but H. E. C. Bryant, correspondent, testified it was merely a comment on the *Times* story. Locke Craig appeared as counsel for the committee and James H. Pou as attorney for the *Times.* The committee investigated the charge of the *Times,* and in its report said that it found Simpson's refusal to answer to be "a subterfuge to which he had resorted to conceal a slanderous and false charge made by him; that the charge repeated by the Reverend Plato Durham, minister, from his pulpit in Charlotte, had been made without any investigation as to the truth of the matters charged, and that he was unable to justify or excuse his conduct in making said charges."

The lobbyists and railroad attorneys were vocal in their approval of the false charges in the Raleigh *Times.* The Reverend Plato Durham, Methodist preacher of Charlotte, intimate friend of President Kilgo of Trinity College, was summoned to Raleigh by the committee investigating the Raleigh *Times* charge that the legislative committee was controlled by *The News and Observer.* Durham had repeated the Simpson charges and when he came to Raleigh *The News and Observer* headlines about his testimony were as follows, "Plato Durham Saves His Goat. Ninth Commandment Fails to Open His Lips." The paper said further, "He refused to answer—The remark of editor Simpson is taken up by preacher of bossism sermon. He declared that Mr. Daniels is an unprincipled man." My paper had also said that Durham had preached a sermon on bossism founded on a false and slanderous report and said, "He will probably preach next Sunday on the robbery of the Tobacco Trust," the intimation being that Dr. Durham, being a disciple of Kilgo, was a defender of the Tobacco Trust.

The report of the committee declared that the editor of the *Times* had printed a falsehood and the preacher had repeated it, without justification.

Dr. Durham was a son of Plato Durham, leader against the Reconstruction party, and inherited the talent and combatativeness of his brilliant father. He was a scholarly professor in Trinity College at the time when its president was pro-Tobacco Trust and anti-*News and Observer*. The younger man became a champion of his president and in that championship felt impelled to criticize *The News and Observer*. He had married the lovely daughter of one of my best friends and one-time pastor, Rev. John N. Cole, of sainted memory. Presently he was called to a chair at Emory University, Atlanta. When I was invited to speak to the students, Dr. Durham welcomed me with gracious courtesy, as did his charming wife. We forgot former disagreements and passages at arms. Like Professor Bassett when at Trinity, he stood with Dr. Kilgo in his fights. The atmosphere at Trinity in those years was pro-trust and anti-Democratic. In other atmospheres Bassett and Durham fell under the influence of Woodrow Wilson's leadership and returned to their early Democratic faith.

It was not until after the middle of February that it was possible to get a vote on the Justice bill for railroad reduction of rates. Rufus A. Doughton, former Speaker of the House, and afterward Commissioner of Revenue and of Public Roads, was the floor leader against reduction of rates, and Justice was the leader for reductions. They were trained parliamentarians, Justice having the advantage of being animated by a crusading spirit which urged the wresting of North Carolina from the domination of the railroads and trusts. Every parliamentary advantage was taken by opponents first to secure delay. It often happened that in a single legislative day a vote was taken on a dozen collateral questions. Neither side absolutely knew that it had a majority in the House. When the vote finally was taken the interest was tense. The galleries and lobbies were crowded, and when the vote was announced Justice had won on all the recorded votes by majorities ranging from 61 to 63 against 57 and 58. The interest was so tense that every member was in his seat. It is difficult, after the lapse of time, to convey any impression of the tremendous interest in the outcome. For thirty days little else had been talked about in the papers or by the people. Members had been deluged by telegrams and letters from home instructing them how to vote, and every influence which the railroads controlled were gathered in Raleigh, either in person or by lobbyists. The victory for those favoring rate reduction was hard won. It was the most brilliant victory in the history of legislation in North Carolina, in all the time I have observed Legislatures, and Justice won it by sheer force of his ability to make the people, in and out of the Legislature, see that it was a just cause.

The next morning *The News and Observer* announced the vote in headlines going across seven columns in red ink which read, "THE GOD-BLESSED MACS SAVED THE DAY," and its editorial was headed, "Dinna Ye Hear It? God Bless the Macs in the House and May Their Clan Increase." There were seven Macs in the House.

Some of these men had been besieged and all of them, like other legislators, had to run the gauntlet of railroad lawyers and lobbyists and those shippers enjoying special privilege. It had been dinned into their ears that railroad reduction meant no more railroad construction in North Carolina. That was the big argument. Every legislator who lived in a county desiring a new railroad was promised one built by his house or to his county seat if the bill failed, but if the passenger rates were reduced there would be no more railroad construction. This frightened a number of them.

The hard-won fight in the House, however, was but the first skirmish, and the railroads had secured a larger vote than I had expected. Their mining and sapping had been effective and a dozen members who came to Raleigh favoring railroad reduction had been induced or seduced to vote with the railroads. All eyes turned to the Senate. The leader in that body for railroad reduction was Reuben Reid of Rockingham. He was the son of the late Governor David S. Reid, the first Democrat to be elected Governor of North Carolina after the Whig Party became strong. His election was due to his wisdom in following the advice of Stephen A. Douglas, "the little giant of Illinois." Douglas had married a Rockingham County lady, a kinswoman of Governor Reid. Reid had been the Democratic candidate for Governor in the year previous to the visit of Judge Douglas to Rockingham County and had been defeated. Douglas told him that the Democrats in North Carolina would always be defeated until they found a popular issue. He advised Reid to run for Governor and make his issue the repeal of the law which permitted only landowners to vote for senators. He said that it was un-Democratic and un-American, and that an advocate of repeal would stir the people of the State and make him Governor. ·

Influenced by the advice of the great Northern Democratic leader, in his speech of acceptance, delivered at Beaufort, when he was re-nominated, Reid came out vigorously for universal suffrage and denounced the disfranchisement of men who were not landowners. However, in doing this, he had invited much opposition from a large slaveholding element in the Democratic Party—but he won.

In the 1907 session Senator Reuben Reid, with the political wisdom of his father, but a more fiery debater, upheld the cause of rate reduction against a battery of able opponents led by Neil Arch McLean, Senator from Robeson County. Before the fight came on the Senate floor *The News and Observer* had daily praised the "God-Blessed Macs." This was sincere praise of the members of the House. Senator McLean saw in this praise that denunciation would come to him as the leader of the railroad forces in the Senate. Every time any praise of the "God-Blessed Macs" appeared he went up in the air. *The News and Observer* said that, of course, he did not like the praise because he was not of the same clan; that he was division counsel of the Atlantic Coast Line and was representing that road on the floor of the Senate and not the people of Robeson County. This infuriated McLean and he rose on question of personal privilege and denounced *The News and Observer* as a sheet voicing the opin-ions of the mob and its editor as a self-appointed autocrat who cracked the whip and demanded that the legislators do his bidding.

Reid, champion of railroad reduction, and McLean, champion of the railroads, had been roommates at Bingham School and were close friends. I think they roomed together during the session of the Senate. One night, at a dinner, attended by both men, Reid, in a friendly way, berated McLean for abusing *The News and Observer* and told the little company he had been trying to find out why McLean did this and had ascertained the real reason. He said that "Neil Arch" had found out that the paper kept books on public men in North Carolina; that it had a ledger on which every man's name was recorded; that on one page it had the names of the "God-Blessed Macs," which were led by the seven members of the House who voted for railroad reduction, and the other page was devoted to the "God-Damn Macs" and that McLean's name led all the rest on the "God-Damn Macs" page. The company diners laughed hilariously at this and it was repeated all over Raleigh, so that during the contest the close friends of McLean rallied him as a "God-Damn Mac."

In his personal-privilege speech Senator McLean denounced a story which appeared in *The News and Observer* as false, and said he would cow-hide Edward L. Conn, who, he claimed, had written the story about some Robeson County bills. The next day *The News and Observer* said that McLean's threat to cow-hide Conn would not be carried out for two reasons, first that Mr. Conn had not written the article about the Robeson County bills, which was written by J. A. Parham, another member of the staff, a native of Robeson County, and, second, that Parham knew that the Senator from Robeson was trying to enact some legislation not desired by the people of that county. The prediction was verified.

The discussion in the Senate over the Justice bill was, if possible, more dramatic than in the House, and much of it was devoted by the opponents of the bill to a denunciation of *The News and Observer* and criticism of Mr. Justice for spending most of his time in the Senate. He and I were abused as being the most pernicious lobbyists in the State, and McLean demanded to know of the president whether we had registered as lobbyists. McLean was a brilliant speaker, eloquent and classical, rather more classical than logical, and the duel between him and Reid was well worth hearing because Reid had greater fire and more logic, while McLean was more eloquent and dramatic. Moreover, Reid was championing what the people wanted, and McLean, although he may have believed that the legislation was wrong, was weakened in his argument by the fact that he was a highly paid attorney of the Atlantic Coast Line Railroad. He had to spend much of his time defending himself. The outcome of the legislation was that the bill finally signed reduced the fare to two and one fourth cents a mile and not to two cents a mile, as in the Justice bill. However, in view of the powerful influences exerted by the railroads in the State Mr. Justice, *The News and Observer*, and others in the fight, believed they had won a victory—as indeed they had—over the combined influence of most of the leaders of the Democratic and Republican parties, for in this fight the Republicans lined up almost solidly on the side of the railroads, as they always did for the big interests, whether railroads, trusts, or cotton mills. If the Republican leaders had not carried free passes in their pockets and been subservient to the railroads, they had a great opportunity in the Democratic division to have made the same sort of appeal to the plain people which Governor Reid had made in the fifties when his party was in the minority. But they were already herded into the railroad camp.

Senator Reid had able support. The ablest and most vigorous of his assistants was State Senator James A. Lockhart of Anson, who not only voted for this and other like legislation but, together with Mr. Justice, is entitled to the first credit among legislators for laws that later put the water power companies under the control of the Corporation Commission. Justice and Lockhart led this fight and were defeated by the interests in the first contest, but later they won the victory.

From the time the legislature reduced the passenger fare on railroads to two and one fourth cents there had been intimations that the railroads would carry the question to the Federal court. On the 2nd of April Circuit Court Judge Pritchard gave a hearing at Asheville on the application of the Southern Railway for an injunction against the legislative act reducing the passenger fare on that road. A few days later he granted the injunction, as *The News and Observer* had predicted.

Whereupon, the paper wrote an editorial headed, "Judge Pritchard Is Bigger than the State." His decision suspended the reduced rate and ordered the taking of evidence. The next day *The News and Observer* said that the "act of the Illinois Legislature reducing passenger fare to two cents went into effect yesterday. They didn't have a Federal Judge in that State to set aside the action of the General Assembly." A few days after Judge Pritchard's decision, the paper printed a ringing interview with Speaker E. J. Justice on railroad contempt of State laws. He declared that the time had come when officers of the State "must choose between obeying Federal decisions and their oaths to enforce the state laws." He pointed out that the Legislature gave far more consideration to the case than did the Federal Judge who suspended the operation while admitting he was not satisfied with its unconstitutionality. Much discussion and many hearings went on. *The News and Observer* called upon the solicitors of the State and grand juries to indict violators of the law and to pay no attention to Judge Pritchard's illegal injunction.

Early in June superior court opened in Wake County with Judge

B. F. Long, of Iredell, presiding. He instructed the jury of Wake County to indict railroad employees who sold tickets in excess of the two-and-one-fourth-cent rate. Writing about the opening of Wake court, my paper had an editorial headed "Judge Long Makes Great Charge to the Grand Jury." The jury acted promptly and brought in four indictments against Thomas E. Green, passenger agent of the Southern at Raleigh, for violation of the rate law. The big question involved was that of sovereignty. Governor Glenn employed ex-Governor Aycock, Speaker Justice, and S. G. Ryan to prosecute the case in Wake County. The issue became acute when Green was arrested and placed under bond of $100. The Southern Railway attorneys advised him not to give the $100-bond and he went to jail. *The News and Observer* said that habeas corpus would be asked and the railroads trusted the Federal Judge to get him out of jail, but Judge Long, understanding what the railroad attorneys were up to, ordered Green out of custody of the sheriff and into custody of the court, thus disarranging the habeas corpus plans.

The next day it was announced that Judge Pritchard was coming to Raleigh to hear the Green case and would assume the right to over-rule Judge Long. The city and the State were full of great excitement. Pritchard arrived. He saw, but went back to Asheville without issuing any writ. The next week, in the Asheville City Police Court, District Passenger Agent James H. Wood, and O. C. Wilson, ticket seller for the Southern Railway, were convicted of violating the two-and-one-fourth-cent rate law and sentenced to thirty days in prison. That made no difference. The next day *The News and Observer* said Judge Pritchard came to Raleigh on the same train with Colonel W. B. Rodman, division counsel of the railroad, both registering at the Yarborough in Rooms 11 and 66. Judge Long fined the Southern Railway $30,000 for violating the law. Tom Green, an agent who had at their direction been permitting himself to be made the scapegoat, decided to submit himself to a nominal fine of $5.00. The dignity of the State was vindicated by the verdict of the jury, and the sentence was pronounced upon the railroad, which was, of course, the offending party. It had been necessary to indict Green because he was the only official of the railroad who could be reached who had actually violated the law. *The News and Observer* said it was presumed Mr. Green had lost his job by submitting to the court and promising to obey the law. However, it was stated the next day that he could have kept his job but that he had decided to go into the furniture business.

At this stage of the proceedings, Governor Glenn, having employed lawyers to prosecute the case, declared that the railroads must obey the State law or the suits would go on. As he had long been an attorney of the Southern Railway, this rather surprised many people, but it proved the truth of what he had said when he was inaugurated—that he had appeared for the railroads only as an attorney, but as Governor he appeared for all the people. He gave an ultimatum to all the railroads and said, as chief executive, he would stop all indictments and cease bringing suits against the railroads if they would sell tickets at the legal rate and withdraw the injunction.

The day after the Asheville men were arrested and fined, Judge Pritchard, of the Federal court, released them. Judge Long issued an execution to collect the $30,000 against the Southern. There was much talk of a truce between the State and the railroads. It was telegraphed from Asheville that an agent of the Federal government was there to compromise the issues between Judge Pritchard and the State courts. It was said that President Roosevelt was ready to support Pritchard; that telegrams had been exchanged between Asheville and Oyster Bay; and that Attorney General Bonaparte had advised an investigation of the situation in North Carolina. The next day the papers printed that Roosevelt would take a hand and said Attorney Sanford had been sent to North Carolina as moderator between Judge Pritchard and Judge Long. While this attempt to secure a truce went on, there was a set of wholesale indictments, and there was much speculation as to whether the State could win, or the Federal Judge. The railroads and their partisans were backing Pritchard; most of the newspapers and State government officials were enlisted to see that the State law should be carried out.

The News and Observer said at this point that it seemed inevitable that an extra session of the Legislature would be called to compel the railroads to obey the law. On July 27 I printed a statement under an eight-column heading, "The Governor Will Not Budge," and seven leading stories across the front page all dealt with the clash of State and Federal courts and urged the Governor to call an extra session of the General Assembly unless the railroads would obey the laws of the State. On July 28 came indictments of the "higher ups." My paper had been declaring every day that it was all right to indict Agent Green in Raleigh and Agent Wood in Asheville, but that the real violators of the law were men higher up, President Finley and Vice-president Andrews. On July 27 Finley was arrested on a warrant of the Asheville Police Justice for violating the State law but was released at once on habeas corpus writ issued by Circuit Court Judge Pritchard. The next day the railroads surrendered. The Southern and Atlantic Coast Line accepted Governor Glenn's ultimatum and announced they would put the two-and-one-fourth-cent rate into effect on August 8. Under an editorial headed "Mr. Finley and Mr. Green," *The News and Observer* pointed out that the railroad attorneys left Green in jail but got Finley out double-quick, and also said that Finley was trying to make it appear that the Southern was being coerced and the Federal Court denied lawful jurisdiction.

While all this litigation and excitement was going on in North Carolina over the two-and-one-fourth-cent rate, the very railroads that were operating in North Carolina, the Coast Line, Southern, and the Seaboard, had agreed, without litigation, to accept a two-cent railroad fare in Virginia. When the truce was arranged, *The News and Observer* said "Peace between the Southern and the State depends alone on whether or not the Southern wishes to continue to fight or is willing to deal with the people on fair terms," and in its issue of August 8 big headlines in red ink, eight columns wide, announced,

"North Carolina's Sovereignty Conceded by All.
"Today With All Railroads Obeying The Law, North Carolina Can Say 'God's In His Heaven, All's Right With The World.'
"Railroads Amenable As Citizens.
"Beginning this morning the Southern Railroad and Atlantic Coast Line, having been clubbed into obedience of the law, must sell tickets at the single rate of 2¼ ¢."

While all this discussion was pending, and there was much bitterness, an accident occurred on the Southern Railway near Raleigh, and *The News and Observer* said of the Southern Railway: "The rotten ties and rickety car gear road is the only road in the world where passengers have to raise umbrellas in coaches to keep out of the rain," and quoted the coroner's jury report confirming its statement that gross negligence and carelessness had caused the wreck. In its issue of August 25 the paper printed a story from Tom Pence, Washington correspondent, showing that the Southern was making money by the barrel, its biggest profits coming from its North Carolina lines. It declared, in another article, that the Southern Railway was guilty of bad faith and was not acting up to its agreement to expedite the case growing out of the rate reduction, and added:

"The Southern Railroad expert swearers in this state are giving the lie to the sworn statements made by that company now on file with the Corporation Commission. North Carolina gave for a song the Western North Carolina Railroad to the Southern in a day when wisdom had abdicated. In a worse day, when wisdom had turned into folly, it leased for ninety-nine years the North Carolina Railroad. The state is ready to relieve the Southern Railroad of both pieces of property that its experts say are burdensome upon them."

The article continued, saying, "Surrender the lease or quit advertising the state a pauper." As proof that the railroads were not acting in good faith, Governor Glenn called the act of Chief Attorney Rodman another piece of bad faith when he objected to the transcript of Wake County being sent to the Supreme Court and severely criticized the railroad attorneys for making an attack on Judge Long in the Southern Railway affidavit filed with the Supreme Court.

The taking of testimony in the case occupied weeks, and most of the evidence was taken in Washington where the records of the Southern Railway were kept. Standing Master Montgomery ruled that the records of the railroad must be kept available to the State's attorneys. Speaker Justice and the Honorable Fred A. Woodard spent two weeks in Washington looking through the books and Tom Pence, our Washington correspondent, kept the people of North Carolina fully informed of what was discovered in the examination. The order that the State's counsel could make a private examination of the books incensed the Southern officials, who expressed their indignation in strong terms, but Woodard and Justice went about the matter in the most methodical and thorough way and brought out many items of information which more than justified all the statements *The News and Observer* had been making about the railroad's employment of attorneys, paying money to newspapers, and spending money to control politics.

One of the first pieces of information Pence sent out was that the Southern Railway had paid James H. Pou, who was not listed as the chief counsel of the Southern, $675.96 for each of the first three quarters in the last fiscal year and in the last quarter $682.58, as well as also several expense accounts, the largest of which was $264.93. The next information that came out was the salaries paid the officials of the Southern Railway. Up to that time neither the Interstate Commerce Commission nor the Railroad Commission had been able to discover the overhead or the salary which the Southern paid to its officials. It was disclosed that President Samuel Spencer received $40,000, Vice-president Andrews, $11,000, second Vice-president Finley, $35,000, etc. The fact that Colonel Andrews received so small a salary and the others received so much more caused discussion, and the *Rhamkatte Roaster* wrote a vigorous article "agin discrimination agin Colonel Andrews," declaring, as he was chief political manipulator of the railroads, it was an outrage upon North Carolina not to pay him more money than that paid other officials who had not leased the railroads and run politics to put money into the Southern Railway coffers. But it turned out that Colonel Andrews' $11,000 was only part of what he received, that his chief salary was as president of the little railroads, that his chief business was to take care of the political affairs and the taxation of the railroads, and that it was best for his salary to be divided among the little railroads.

In *The News and Observer's* issue of September 11 Tom Pence, Washington correspondent, had the following as the head of a story about the investigation at Washington:

> "Pou Lobbyist for Southern—Lawyers and State Can Prove It. Railroad attorneys Mad At the Charge. Ex-Congressman Woodard says: 'If I can't prove That The Southern Through Its Lobbyists Has Spent Money To Kill Legislation at Raleigh, I will Quit This Case.' "

Governor Glenn held a conference with lawyers on rate hearing and declared that the State's cause was just and was sure to win.

In September the appeal from Judge Long's fine of $30,000 on the Southern for violating the passenger-rate law came before the Supreme Court. Edwin J. Justice made what *The News and Observer* called the great argument. The Washington correspondent continued to send information of what was discovered by Attorneys Woodard and Justice in going through the railroad books, and on September 24 the paper, with two lines in red ink, each eight columns

Upper left, James A. Lockhart, Senator from Anson County; militant leader in liberal legislation. *Upper right,* Edwin J. Justice, Speaker of the House; leader of liberal forces in the Legislature; prosecutor in California of those trying to destroy the Naval oil reserves. *Lower left,* Senator Neill Arch McLean, who led the fight against reducing the railroad rates. *Lower right,* Senator Reuben Reid, who led the fight to reduce railroad rates.

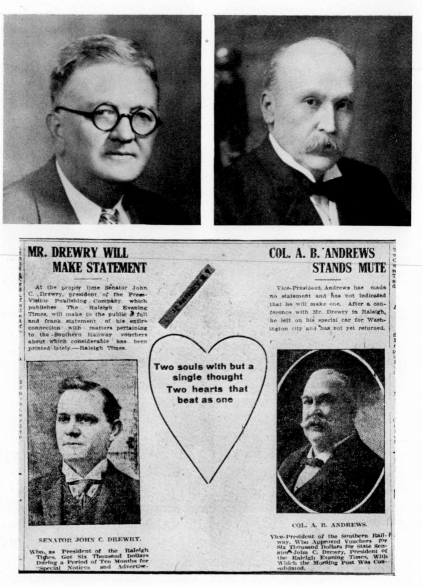

MR. DREWRY WILL
MAKE STATEMENT

At the proper time Senator John C. Drewry, president of the Press-Visitor Publishing Company, which publishes The Raleigh Evening Times, will make to the public a full and frank statement of his entire connection with matters pertaining to the Southern Railway vouchers about which considerable has been printed lately.—Raleigh Times.

COL. A. B. ANDREWS
STANDS MUTE

Vice-President Andrews has made no statement and has not indicated that he will make one. After a conference with Mr. Drewry in Raleigh, he left on his special car for Washington city and has not yet returned.

Two souls with but a
single thought
Two hearts that
beat as one

SENATOR JOHN C. DREWRY.

Who, as President of the Raleigh Times, Got Six Thousand Dollars During a Period of Ten Months for "Special Notices and Advertise-

COL. A. B. ANDREWS.

Vice-President of the Southern Railway, Who Approved Vouchers for Six Thousand Dollars for State Senator John C. Drewry, President of the Raleigh Evening Times, With Which the Morning Post Was Consolidated.

Upper left, Thomas E. Green, of Raleigh, who was sentenced to jail by Judge Long for refusing to sell tickets to passengers at the rate prescribed by law. *Upper right,* B. F. Long, Judge of the Superior Court, who imposed heavy fines and punishment on Southern Railways officials. *Below,* pictures of Senator John C. Drewry and Colonel A. B. Andrews, Vice-President of the Southern Railway, which appeared on the front page of *The News and Observer* of September 27, 1907, showing the influence of the Southern Railway in defeating legislation.

wide, had the following headlines: *"$6000 paid to John C. Drewry By the Southern Railroad."* This was followed, two columns wide in black ink, by, the following: *"$6,000 paid Senator Drewry's Paper,"* and *"Southern Railroad Pays Raleigh Evening Times That in Eleven Months." "Something Rotten in Denmark. The Charlotte Observer Gets Only $21.85 per month for printing schedules, etc., while Senator J. C. Drewry's paper in Raleigh has received $600 per month for a period of ten months."*

My paper printed, side by side, pictures of Colonel A. B. Andrews and Senator John C. Drewry. It said the Washington *Post* received only $89.90 a month and they made detailed statements of the advertising done, whereas the Raleigh *Times* made no statement whatever. In its issue of September 25, in an eight column streamer in red ink, my paper said, *"Times Got None of Money Paid Jno. C. Drewry, Says Crater."* George B. Crater, part owner and business manager of the *Times*, said his paper received not a penny of it. *The News and Observer* said people were not surprised at the corruption but at the negligence in permitting the matter to become public. The next day it printed Drewry's and Andrews' pictures on the front page and asked "What Was The Money Paid For?," and said the columns of the paper were open to Vice-president Andrews to explain why he approved vouchers of $6,000 to State Senator John C. Drewry for advertising. It also said that the files of the Raleigh *Times* showed that $2,000 of the Southern money went for 175 inches of space and said the vouchers disclosed that on July 30, 1906, Drewry "received $2,000 in full for advertising in the Raleigh *Evening Times* to Aug. 1st." In addition to plenty of passes in the four months after the previous settlement in full, in April the *Times* published Southern Railway display advertising 62½ inches and notices 122 inches, a total space of 175 inches at $11.43 an inch. This was sure-enough metropolitan pay, four times the highest rate of the New York *Herald*. An editorial in my paper on September 25, under the heading "Just Vindication" said, "In a long history *The News and Observer* never but once felt it to be a public duty to take ground against the nomination of a candidate for public office in Wake County." It went on to say that it opposed the nomination of Drewry for the Senate because of his close connection with the Southern Railway and the trust, and because he was elected by them, plus the biggest campaign fund ever spent in Wake County. It declared that the exposures showed *The News and*

Observer to be vindicated. The controversy as to whether the *Times* got the money came up. Crater denied it, but Colonel Charles E. Johnson, president of the bank, and F. H. Briggs, cashier, said it did get the money.

In the meantime my paper still continued to print a facsimile of the check and pictures of Andrews and Drewry side by side and offered them space to explain. A day or two later it printed their pictures with a heart between them and quoted, "Two souls with but a single thought, two hearts that beat as one." While all this discussion was going on Business Manager Crater changed his views, following the statement of the bank officials, and *The News and Observer* asked why he flopped. A day or two later the *Times* said Mr. Drewry and the paper would make a frank statement, and *The News and Observer* replied, "Mr. Drewry will not make any statement, frank or otherwise, in connection with his vouchers." It declared that the evidence adduced showed the methods used by the Southern Railway to defeat legislation. It said that the money was paid with the expectation of some illegal or secret returns and declared it was proof of the need of a law of publicity whereby all expenditures by public service corporations should be regularly published in detail. "If so insignificant a paper as the *Times*, controlled by so obscure a man as John C. Drewry, bore a relationship to a corrupt policy that made them worth $6,000, and probably more, in ten months, is not that evidence to show that, in the effort to carry out the large operation of the greater corruption, the six thousand dollars is but a drop in the bucket?"

I printed the pictures of Andrews and Drewry and a *facsimile* of the check on the first page every day for a considerable time, virtually charging that Andrews had bought the vote of Senator Drewry for $6,000. Learning, by the grape-vine route, that every time it appeared Andrews and Drewry would get hot under the collar, I kept it up until a friend asked me to cease daily publication because he feared its daily appearance was enraging Andrews to a point where it might cause him to have a stroke. Having served its purpose, it was then withdrawn.

Late in September, *The News and Observer* had a headline on "Senator Drewry's Humiliating Confession." It said he was forced to confess that his paper was subsidized by the Vice-president of the Southern Railway, although he submitted a lame and impotent plea. All during his campaign for the Senate, Drewry said he didn't get any cash from Andrews. Now, he said he did. He said he had agreed to print clippings designated by Colonel Andrews. These clippings were references to rate reductions, ridiculing those who favored railroad regulation. He printed a fulsome praise of Colonel Andrews as an editorial in the *Evening Times* on November 6, 1905. Sanford L. Rotter, who had been on the editorial staff of the Raleigh *Times,* resigned his position and said he had not known he was editing a subsidized paper.

On November 14 *The News and Observer,* under the headline, "Helps the Railroads," had the following:

"The result of the three months' trial of 2¼ ¢ as the maximum rate in North Carolina has been to increase the cash returns of the railroads on passenger business 10 per cent. The travel would have been larger if the maximum rate had been 2¢."

When the reduced rate case came before the Supreme Court, that body upheld Judge Long in the jurisdiction and in his decision, but did not sustain the fine of $30,000 put upon the railroad; Justice Clark concurred in the decision but he wrote a vigorous dissent to the opinion of the court that the railroad should not pay the fine.

A compromise arranged by Governor Glenn with the railroads required legislative approval, and the governor called a special session of the Legislature for January 21. He and the attorneys of the State, Aycock and Ryan, and others united in welcoming a settlement of all the matters in dispute upon condition that the railroad would sell mileage books at from two to two and one fourth cents and have a flat rate of two and one half cents for passengers and would pay the expense of litigation.

This dog-fall compromise was generally approved, *The News and Observer* acquiescing in it only because of the long-drawn-out litigation and the Federal court injunctions making it impossible to enforce the act of the Legislature for a two-and-one-fourth-cent fare. It said that the reduction in passenger rate from two- and three-fourths cents and three-and-one-fourth cents to two-and-one-half cents, and reduction in the price of mileage were the first fruits of the fight to control the railroads and added, "It has been established, once for all, that the policy of North Carolina, when it undertakes to enforce the laws, is to say to the Federal Courts 'Hands off.'" The fact remained, however, that the railroads had won as much as the State. I gave notice that a future fight would be made for a two-cent rate. It came later.

AN ANTI-TRUST BILL WITH TEETH

The Justice anti-trust bill, as introduced in the Legislature, had teeth. Therefore it was opposed by nearly all the same interests that fought the railroad reduction measure. In fact, the interests desiring privilege, no matter how wide apart in some things, always lined up for each other and united in opposing the anti-trust bill. They also united in opposition to Justice's bill for enlarging the power of the Corporation Commission. The House passed Justice's anti-trust bill but, as usual when legislation of this kind reached the Senate, it met an opposition which, though not declaring itself against an anti-trust bill, proceeded to extract its teeth. A substitute bill was offered by Senator James S. Manning. *The News and Observer* said of it, "Mr. Manning is candid and does not claim that his bill would reach the tobacco trust." When the Senate extracted Section A, *The News and Observer* said the House had proclaimed, by its action, that the Tobacco Trust must not escape, whereas the Senate had said that the Tobacco Trust must escape and had given it immunity by removing section A. The House replaced Section A and the fight went on. Finally the trust won by a majority of one in the Senate. *The News and Observer* declared that, in effect, the bill read "All trusts are evil except the Tobacco Trust. We mustn't do anything to it. It is our home trust." But my paper, praising Justice for his masterly fight, declared that the State had not approved the Tobacco Trust and it hoped it was possible, under the provisions of the bill, to reach that and other monopolies.

Early in the year more information came out about how the Raleigh *Times* was subsidized. *The News and Observer,* in its issue of Jan. 12, printed that State Senator Drewry confessed that W. W. Fuller, general counsel of the American Tobacco Company, owned half of the press on which the *Times* was printed. It said it should be remembered that, during the Legislature, Senator Drewry had voted against all anti-trust measures which had teeth in them, to please the American Tobacco Company. It also said that Fuller had been trying to sell his interest to Crater, the business manager. Crater was thrown out and Drewry sold some of his stock to J. V. Simms of Charlotte, who became business manager on January 13. On February 26 the *Evening Times* went into a receiver's hands, upon the application of H. J. Brown Coffin Company for the balance due on a coffin which the *Times* had purchased for a member of its staff. *The News and Observer* gave the history of the career of the *Times* and said it was not known who were then the owners but pointed out that when the *Morning Post* gave up the ghost, the *Times* had succeeded to its subscription list and to its policy of subservience to the Southern Railroad and the Tobacco Trust.

In April *The News and Observer* printed a story from Tom Pence, its Washington correspondent, saying that in talks with newspaper men President Roosevelt said he had entered North Carolina politics, where, he claimed, he had enemies; that he knew the Tobacco Trust wanted a tobacco delegation sent to the National Convention and had sought Pritchard to be a party to sending such a delegation. He was quoted as saying that the Tobacco Trust had spent large sums to defeat his nomination but that, after he was nominated, it wanted to contribute $70,000 to his campaign fund in the general election, which he had refused to permit Chairman Cortelyou to accept. After that interview, *The News and Observer* printed, as it did now and then when it wanted to shoot folly on the wing, an article on "Duke's Tainted Money Spurned," and credited it to the *Rhamkatte Roaster*.

In its issue of May 16 *The News and Observer* had another article headed, "Teddy About to Jump on to Buck. The Tobacco Trust Will Hear Thunder." This was an article sent to the paper by Tom Pence, and the editorial said, "The people do not merely want convictions and fines. They want an end of the trust's extortion." The paper warmly approved Mr. Roosevelt's denunciation of the monopoly and declared that he had done much to educate the country to the necessity of regulation. During all of the time Mr. Roosevelt was demanding regulation of railroads and beginning litigation against the Tobacco Trust, the paper supported him. In its issue of August 8, *The News and Observer* said of the trust:

> "Its desires are modest. All it wants is the earth with a barbed wire fence around it. The tobacco trust is a hog and wants all the swill. The tobacco crop is short this year. It ought to have brought 12¢ a pound but the trust fixed it at 7¢ or 8¢ and that is all that is being paid."

THE NEWS AND OBSERVER'S HOUSE-WARMING

On June 2, 1907, *The News and Observer* gave a housewarming to all its friends, upon the completion and opening of its new building on Martin Street. Before this long-anticipated and great event in the life of the paper, it had been published on South Fayetteville Street, half a square from the city auditorium, in a building not at all adapted to its purposes, which had been built by Littlefield for his organ during Reconstruction. We had purchased the Martin Street lot in the preceding year for $4,250. After the purchase of the property, when I was trying to borrow the money to build, I had a call one day from J. B. Blades, of New Bern, a lumber king and a staunch fellow Methodist and prohibitionist. He said that, in view of the fact that the paper had always stood strongly for temperance and all good causes, he would be glad to lend me the money to erect the building and I could repay it at my convenience. This offer was as great a surprise as it was an answer to the need. Borrowing $30,000 at that time would have been difficult and probably could not have been done except at a premium. This was a hard year for *The News and Observer*. The purchase of a Hoe press and completion of the building and installation were expensive and business was bad. In fact, at hardly any time in the history of the paper was I so depressed. Every dollar had to be counted twice, and although the Jamestown Exposition was held at Norfolk that year, I did not attend it because I did not feel able to spend a penny except for the bare necessities of living and for moving into the new plant. As the Exposition was held so near Raleigh I expected to get good business out of it, and we did issue a Jamestown Exposition edition, but it was not profitable. However, dull times did not prevent *The News and Observer* from keeping a stiff upper lip and boosting itself. The construction of the new buildings was a big event for the Daniels family, particularly for our sons. All four of them took part in the breaking of the ground.

In making the plans for the building, Henry Bagley, my wife's brother, the resourceful business manager, who had the duty of planning and supervising construction and did it well, told the architect to arrange so I would have a quiet office in the rear of the building. He showed me the plans and said, "You are interrupted so often by many visitors, some having no business, that you should not be troubled with callers who take up so much of your time." He was trying to protect me, and was following the plans of city newspaper establishments where the editor is hidden in an office on the 'steenth floor and sees very few visitors. I replied, "The plan is all wrong. Put my office in the front, with the door wide open, so that anybody can see me at any time. No man can edit a paper in a town like Raleigh or a folksy State like North Carolina unless he is in close touch with all sorts of people, the more the better. And put this sign on my door: OFFICE HOURS BETWEEN 9 A.M. AND 12 O'CLOCK MIDNIGHT. CAN BE SEEN AT ALL OTHER HOURS BY ANYBODY BY CALLING TELEPHONE 90. And that was that. I often think the editors of big city newspapers would write better if they were not excluded from the common touch. Never a day passed that I did not get an idea or information from a visitor who did not realize he was helping to inform my writing. And I jotted down news items and interviews for the paper as well in addition to writing editorials, sometimes writing the news story and also an editorial comment so that both would appear in the same issue. An editorial writer ought to read news stories before they are printed so that the reader can follow up the story with comment upon it in the same issue.

The housewarming was an affair of statewide importance. We printed a large special edition, containing a history of the paper, with articles from all the living men who had been, at any time, connected with the paper. Included among these were articles by Chief Justice Walter Clark, who had at one time been chief editor of the *Raleigh News,* Captain S. A. Ashe, who had long been editor of *The News and Observer,* Peter M. Wilson and Fred A. Olds and W. P. Batchelor, who had been city editors, and others. There were also pages of articles by prominent men in all parts of the State written in appreciation of the paper's service, and with congratulations upon moving into a home of its own. There were sketches of such distinguished men as William L. Sanders, Josiah Turner, Peter M. Hale, and others, who contributed much to its early life. I wrote an article for that edition on "Twenty-seven Years in Harness," containing a history of my newspaper experience, and defined my idea of what an editor should be.

Upon the opening of the new building we inaugurated the printing of the first colored comic pages by a North Carolina newspaper. They consisted of two pages in blue, white, and pink. One was "Mary and

Her Little Lamb," another, "Sambo and Funny Noises," and the third was "Uncle George Washington Bings, the Story Teller."

On the night the plant was opened hundreds of visitors came. Following an inspection refreshments were served by my wife and the wives of the members of the staff. Speeches were made by Governor Glenn, Chief Justice Walter Clark, and others. An interesting incident was that the building was dedicated in much the same form as that used for churches, the dedicatory prayer being offered by the Reverend Harper Whitaker, the oldest editor in Raleigh, who had printed a temperance paper from the time of the Civil War and was then a Methodist circuit rider. He had, for a long time, contributed a weekly column to *The News and Observer,* of rare homespun philosophy, containing reminiscences and humorous incidents, as well as some good preaching of a kind that greatly pleased the readers of the paper. We always referred to him as "Chaplain of *The News and Observer,*" an honor which he appreciated. He belonged to the Whitaker family who were among the early settlers of Wake County. He had a remarkable memory. While he had often been on the sidelines, he had kept in touch with everything that happened in Raleigh, in a newspaper way, from the days of the Civil War.

He told me a characteristic story of his experience as pastor of a circuit containing several churches in Franklin County. He had held a revival at which a number of people had professed conversion. He announced that, at the next monthly appointment, he would receive members into the church. He returned to Raleigh. Some time later he held another meeting at that church with the same results, but each night, after the revival services, he would open the doors of the church for members and make this quaint remark, "Last year, after we held our revival and I had gone to another church to preach, the Baptists went around to see some of our converts and induced them to join the Baptist Church before I could get back for my next appointment. I made up my mind that should never happen again and therefore we string the fish as we catch them."

AGAINST CIGARETTES

As President Roosevelt was beginning his attack upon the Tobacco Trust, which was to run its length until the Trust was ordered dissolved by the Federal court, Governor Glenn took a hand and seized millions of cigarettes which were on route to Great Britain, alleging

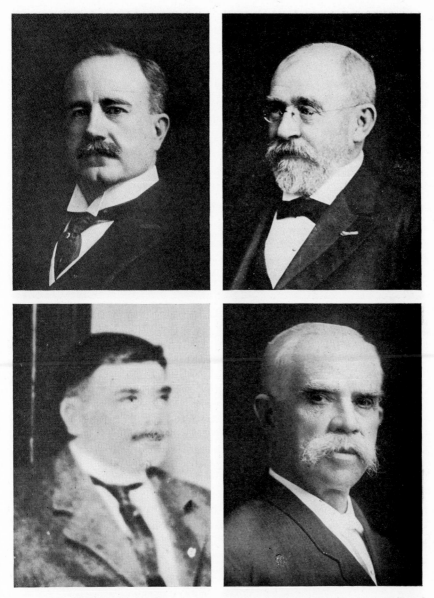

Upper left, John Skelton Williams, President of the Seaboard Air Line Railroad and Comptroller of the Currency in Woodrow Wilson's administration. *Upper right,* Dr. St. Clair McKelway, distinguished journalist, editor of the *Brooklyn Eagle. Lower left,* A. D. ("Aus") Watts, Legislator and active political leader in the Simmons campaign. *Lower right,* Ashley Horne, successful captain of industry and candidate for Governor.

Upper left, Governor William W. Kitchin, 1908-1912. *Upper right,* Claude Kitchin, Democratic Chairman of the Ways and Means Committee. *Lower left,* J. B. Blades, leading lumber man, who financed *The News and Observer* building. *Lower right,* Hugh G. Chatham, Senator, Chairman of the Democratic Committee, liberal industrialist.

that they were being sent over for monopoly purposes and that the two Companies, British and American, were combining to violate the law. At the same time J. O. W. Gravely, who had long been in the tobacco business, made a calculation and announced that the farmers in North Carolina had been robbed by the Tobacco Trust in the sum of $148,000,000. As to the sentiment in North Carolina at that time, two bills in the legislature are indicative. They were to forbid the manufacture or sale of coca-cola or pepsi-cola in North Carolina and *The News and Observer* suggested that, inasmuch as more young people were ruined by cigarettes than by whiskey, the sale of cigarettes to young people should be forbidden.

One of the most interesting visitors to Raleigh that year was Dr. St. Clair McKelway, editor of the *Brooklyn Eagle*. He had accepted an invitation to deliver the anniversary address at Chapel Hill and spent two days with me in Raleigh, going and coming. He had had many interesting experiences and told my wife and me some incidents which had never then been printed. They were informing and rather thrilling. He told us how he had been instrumental in securing a conference between General Grant and General Lee, shortly after the Civil War. He said that interview, which was strictly secret, had this result: whereas the other Southern states had to undergo the horrors of Reconstruction, Virginia escaped it.

XLIII

PERSONALITIES AND CAUSES IN 1908

T HE POLITICAL waters began to flow in 1908. Senator Simmons announced that he would not desire reëlection as chairman of the State Executive Committee, and Hugh Chatham was elected to succeed him. Hugh Chatham had a genius for friendship, and he combined political acumen with sound business judgment. My relations with him were most cordial, and his early death was a genuine sorrow. He served as president of the North Carolina Railroad under both Aycock and Glenn and was State Senator in 1914. Nothing made him so happy as adjusting differences between people he liked. Hugh was a model conciliator as well as an attractive and lovable man. As an example of his zeal in composing differences, he worked to end the long fight between *The News and Observer* and the Southern Railway when it was at its height because of the attempt of the Southern, by the change of a schedule carrying the paper to Western North Carolina, to injure the paper. He talked to Colonel Andrews and to the members of the Railroad Commission, and he secured a return to the old schedule, which was helpful to *The News and Observer*. He had no interest in this except his love of composing differences and trying to bring people he liked together.

NO MORE LIQUOR SALES IN RALEIGH

Toward the end of the year, the sentiment against the dispensary in Raleigh had grown to such a point that an election was called to substitute prohibition for the dispensary. Run without graft, without advertising, without trying to sell liquor, the demand for liquor, from Raleigh and all the surrounding country, had become so great that the dispensary was making money hand over fist. The temperance people, who had set it up as an improvement over the saloons, saw that the time had come to take the next step and to shut up the dispensary, as they had shut up the saloons. The dispensary had taken in, in the three years and ten months of its operation, $854,-358.14. Advocating prohibition for Raleigh, *The News and Observer* said that this money, under prohibition, would go mainly for provisions, clothing, hardware, and better homes for the people. The *Times* took the ground that this money was needed for city purposes and attacked the prohibition committee as being composed of hypocrites. It was a rather peculiar situation. The men who, four years before, were fighting to keep the saloons open, were now fighting to keep the dispensary and, in the main, the men who had fought to drive out the saloons by means of the dispensary, were now fighting to destroy their own creature and put an end to the sale of liquor in any legal way in Raleigh. When the election took place *The News and Observer* announced the results in red ink headlines, eight columns wide, and said that every division in every ward voted dry, the dry majority in the city being 547 out of 1,313 votes cast.

NORTH CAROLINA VOTES PROHIBITION

As soon as Governor Glenn issued his call for a special session of the Legislature to conclude the railroad conflict, agitation was begun to induce the legislators to pass a State prohibition act. In their gatherings the Baptists and Methodists had called for it. The executive committee of the anti-saloon league held a meeting and called a mass convention in Raleigh. *The News and Observer* said, "State prohibition is inevitable. Why wait?" and answered the argument that State prohibition would hurt the party. Agitation for State prohibition at this time was given impetus by ex-Governor Thomas J. Jarvis who pointed out that, a majority of the counties having of their own accord voted prohibition, the time had come when the Legislature should pass a blanket law and make the whole State dry. After the anti-saloon league had asked a prohibitory act without the vote of the people, John A. Oates, chairman of the prohibition forces, called to see me and requested *The News and Observer* to come out strongly for such an act. I told him that prohibition ought not to be a party issue and that if Governor Glenn, ex-Governor Jarvis, Aycock, and *The News and Observer* should unite in an appeal for it, the Republicans would take grounds against it, and the anti-prohibition vote, plus the solid Republican vote, would make the State doubtful in politics. I also told him that before *The News and Observer* would say a word about it I thought it would be wise for him to go to Asheville and see Judge Pritchard, who had long been the most influential leader of the Republican Party, and who lived in a dry county and was known to be strong for State prohibition. I also advised him to see Colonel Lusk, of Asheville, and other Republicans of influence in Western North Carolina, getting them to write strong letters advocating that State prohibition be passed by the Legislature. I also urged him to see Judge Robinson, of Goldsboro, and a few other Republicans in the Eastern part of the State and get them to do the same thing. As a rule the Republican leaders in the mountains were for prohibition. Except Judge Robinson and a few others, the Republicans in Piedmont and Eastern North Carolina were against it and believed they could carry the State if the Democrats enacted a State prohibition law. Oates thought I was right and took the train for Asheville, bringing back with him strong letters from Pritchard and other Western Republicans urging the special session of the Legislature to pass a prohibition act for the whole State. He also got a few other letters from other Republicans.

The News and Observer published Jarvis' letter one day and Pritchard's the next, and sandwiched in letters by Democrats and Republicans in order to show that prohibition was not a party question. A short time afterward Governor Glenn came out very strongly for State prohibition. A majority of the Democrats were unwilling to pass an act but decided to submit a prohibition measure to the people to go into effect the following January if the majority of the people voted for it. That was a wise action. The General Assembly passed the Long-Dowd bill and called for an election on May 20, 1908.

From then on, until the election in May, *The News and Observer* gave much of its space to advocacy of State prohibition. Its correspondents went all over the State and wrote up the meetings. We conducted the campaign for prohibition with as much vigor as the political campaign of 1898 or 1900, always holding that prohibition was not a political issue. Governor Glenn and Senator Pritchard spoke from the same platform as did other Democrats and Republicans.

One of the best services rendered by the paper during the campaign was the story from Salisbury. A meeting had been called of the liquor-dealers to organize the campaign, and about that time a mass meeting of the anti-prohibitionists had been called at the same time and place. It was heralded as a coming big event. It turned out to be a dud. Only three men of any importance turned up at the meeting, and *The News and Observer* contained an account of the "large and enthusiastic meeting" held by these three men, and compared it to the time when the nine tailors of Tooley Street in London passed resolutions declaring, "We, the people of England." The flash in the pan of this meeting, the prominence given to the few public men who took part in it, and the ridicule heaped upon them gave much encouragement to the temperance forces. A correspondent of our paper made great sport of the fact that he spent all the morning trying to find the convention and was sent from place to place to locate it. He indicated, without saying so, that the reason for this was that some of those who had started for Salisbury had fallen by the wayside. This story caused great amusement and made some very staunch enemies for the paper.

While the anti-prohibitionists had very few speakers—and most of them were imported—the prohibitionists had able men in the campaign, who spoke in all parts of the State. Judge Pritchard and Governor Glenn, ex-Governor Jarvis and ex-Governor Aycock spoke with effect. *The News and Observer* announced that eight out of ten Democratic congressmen were for prohibition and also Senators Simmons and Overman. It was a great change of front, or seemed so to some people, as *The News and Observer* gave warm praise to Judge Pritchard when he spoke in Raleigh.

On May 13 *The News and Observer* printed what it called a roll of honor, giving a partial list of volunteer speakers for prohibition in North Carolina. It embraced most of the men in public positions in the State. On May 10 it printed an editorial called "Elder Hassell on Prohibition." As a rule the Primitive Baptists in the State had not favored legislation on this question, but such leaders as Elder Hassell and Elder Gold were always on the side of driving out the saloons. I rejoiced to print Elder Hassell's statement because I had been his pupil when a boy in Wilson, and he was held in the greatest veneration by all members of his church and by the members of other churches as well.

Toward the end of the campaign there came to the State a Reverend Mr. Wassen, posing as an Episcopal clergyman. He spoke at Salisbury, which was a center of the anti-prohibitionists. During an anti-prohibition speech in Salisbury, according to an account in *The News and Observer,* "suddenly from a tough in the crowd came the vile expression, 'That preacher is the son of a bitch.' A voice cried,

'Don't say that, my friend. It is an insult to the dog.' " The story said that the toughs insulted, with vile language, ladies riding in temperance parades. The liquor men held a meeting in the court-house square while over five thousand heard George Stewart and Rev. Mr. Ham in the Tabernacle tent. The toughs cried, "We will make rotten sandwiches out of Ham," and declared, "Stewart's face is a map of Hell." Coming up close to the carriages containing ladies in the parade, the roughs asked, "Why in Hell don't you women put on breeches?" and said, "You are a damn set of hypocrites." "They ought to be down in the slums where they belong," and more of the same kind. This report from Salisbury, printed under big headlines, stirred the State and created a great controversy in Salisbury. Mayor Boydon denied that it was as tough as reported, but did not deny the "son of a bitch" incident. Whereupon, T. H. Vanderford, of Salisbury, member of the Democratic Congressional Committee of that district and leader of the temperance forces, said *The News and Observer's* report was literally true, and added to it that a policeman assaulted him by pushing him off the sidewalk. The temperature was so hot at Salisbury that it sizzled. *The News and Observer,* in a way, apologized for printing the Salisbury story and said that such language had never before appeared in the paper and was given only to show the depths to which the liquor forces were resorting. The day before the election, the whole paper was devoted to stories of meetings and parades. On election day women surrounded the polls in many of the voting places and many of them used their carriages to take voters to the polls. In some places prayer meetings for the temperance cause were held at the polls.

Undoubtedly the disgraceful affair at Salisbury helped the prohibition cause and on May 27, in eight columns of headlines, *The News and Observer* said, *"Prohibition Sweeps the State. North Carolina Is the First Southern State To Vote Prohibition By Popular Vote,"* and called it a new day for North Carolina. The majority for prohibition was 43,018. Governor Glenn came out in a congratulatory message and declared that prohibition would be enforced. The majority for prohibition, however, did not lessen the regret over Wake County. Here most official leaders of the Democratic Party lined up with the liquor dealers and other anti-prohibitionists. They had plenty of money, and Wake County went wet by 743 votes, but Raleigh proper went dry by 84 votes.

The day after the election *The News and Observer* said that the next victory the good people of North Carolina must win was one that would put a stop to the use of money in elections.

There was a strong sentiment for the enforcement of prohibition. In opening court in Raleigh, Judge J. Crawford Biggs said that he would send all operators of blind tigers to the roads.

During the State prohibition campaign Chairman Oates, in order to stimulate interest, had offered and designed a banner to be given to the county that cast the largest proportion of its vote for prohibition, and on June 20 there was observed in the Capitol, what was called by *The News and Observer* "a historical event," when Governor Glenn signed the State prohibition proclamation and the banner was presented to Yancey County. I made an address, the text of which was, "Let us look unto the hills whence cometh our help," pointing out that, in the election, every mountain county had given a large majority to prohibition, with Yancey in the lead. The banner was accepted by Ellis Gardner, a lawyer of Burnsville, who had been chairman of the campaign in his county.

A THREE-CORNERED GUBERNATORIAL CONTEST

Early in 1908, the fight between Kitchin, Craig, and Ashley Horne for governor began to warm up. In February Ashley Horne gave his platform. In one plank he favored prohibition and in another he opposed allowing railroads to earn dividends on watered stock. Ashley Horne had come out of the Confederate Army without means, but because of rare ability and versatility as farmer, merchant, manufacturer, and banker, he had amassed a fortune. In memory of his mother and as a tribute to the women of the Confederacy, he gave the money to erect the figure of the Confederate mother in Capitol Square in Raleigh. He was public-spirited to a high degree and generous to many good causes.

In February Craig and Kitchin held a debate in Anson County which was characterized by personalities. Both were brilliant orators but Kitchin was the more effective debater. He was the most suave public speaker, winning, in the first part of his addresses, by his moderation and sweet spirit (which he got from his mother, a kinswoman of Nathaniel Macon, and a most attractive woman), while in the last part of his speeches he would lash his opponents with great vigor and sometimes vituperation, arousing his hearers to the highest pitch of enthusiasm and indignation (a quality inherited from his militant father, Captain Buck Kitchin).

In all of his speeches, without saying that Craig was the candidate of the American Tobacco Trust and the Southern Railway, Kitchin would show that certain men and certain influences, close to these interests, were supporting Craig. He would then call upon Craig's supporters to demand that Craig refuse their support. This infuriated Craig and his supporters, who replied by saying that Kitchin was using this as a smoke-screen because he himself was receiving the support of the most influential men in the American Tobacco Trust; that his campaign was being managed by James S. Manning, an attorney of both the Southern Railway and the American Tobacco Company; and that the Fifth District, embracing Winston and Durham, where the Tobacco Company had the greatest influence, was almost solidly for Kitchin, which would not be so if he were really fighting the Trust. Manning denied that he had ever been an attorney for these companies, but he could not deny that he had secured a change in the Justice bill, which virtually exempted the American Tobacco Company from its provisions. However, as the controversy went on, Kitchin won out, and largely because he made the rank and file of the people believe that his fight against the Southern Railway subsidy in Congress and his opposition to the Tobacco Trust would give them a Governor who would put an end to trust and railroad control in North Carolina. They expected him to scotch the Tobacco Trust in short order. The truth about it was that neither Kitchin nor Craig belonged to anybody. They were both clean, high-minded men in their private life as in their whole public career.

Early in the campaign Senator Simmons, who had long been State chairman, and Governor Aycock, both declared for the nomination of Craig, and gave as their reason that in the great white supremacy campaign Craig had led the fight and really put his life in jeopardy for the cause; and that there had been no Governor from the mountains since Vance. Aycock and Craig had been classmates and devoted friends at the University and intimates all the succeeding years. Kitchin made the most of the fact that these two leaders, who had been given high honors, were seeking to perpetuate their domination by selecting the Governor. Aycock hadn't any machine and wouldn't have known how to use it if he had. He was like Vance. He always made his appeal direct to the people. Simmons, in his long term as chairman, had effected a cohesive organization which was loyal to him and which was employed to help Craig.

The mountains were solid for Craig, the Fifth District practically solid for Kitchin, and all the balance of the State was a field of contest. In Wake County Kitchin received 11 state convention votes, Horne 9, and Craig 4. Feeling ran high when the convention met in Charlotte, and the contest was the most long-drawn-out in the history of the State. It was also the high-water mark in oratory. Rarely have I heard three nominating speeches quite up to those placing these three men in nomination. Aycock's speech, nominating Craig, set the standard so high that it seemed impossible that any other speaker could reach it. Charles W. Tillett followed, placing Kitchin in nomination. He had not Aycock's reputation for oratory, but on that day excelled himself, and when he had finished the Kitchin men had reached the highest peak of enthusiasm. Many said his speech had been even better than that of Aycock. This high record having been set by the two earlier speakers, friends feared for Thomas W. Bickett, who was to nominate Horne. He was unknown except in Union and Franklin counties. He had seen no public service, except as a member of the Legislature, where he had served with ability. He had not spoken long, however, before he had the already aroused convention in the hollow of his hand. He had an original way of saying things and a quaint and delicious humour, and he took advantage of the fact that he was less known than either of the two distinguished men who had preceded him, and that his candidate had not the brilliant qualities of Craig or Kitchin. He had come, indeed, like David with his sling, to fight for a great farmer, great merchant, and great private soldier who, laying down his gun at Appomattox, had done more to build the State on solid lines than all the politicians and all the orators. He did not express it as bluntly as that, but with more finesse, so that when he had finished his speech, while he had not won Horne's nomination—which was not in the stars—he did secure his own later selection as Attorney General, and in 1916 he became Governor. The effect of his speech on his political fortunes was comparable to Bryan's taking the nomination for the presidency at Chicago.

On the first ballot the vote was, for Kitchin, 375.86; Craig, 334.88; and Horne, 147.14. The vote went on with little change for three days.

It became evident on the fiftieth ballot that Craig could not be nominated and his leading supporters then determined to nominate Horne. Bitterness between Kitchin and Craig people was so great that Craig and his supporters were willing to retire if they could also retire Kitchin. It was a sort of Smith-McAdoo fight in Madison Square Garden.

The Craig forces might have succeeded in nominating Horne if there had been no W. T. Crawford in the convention. Crawford had been a member of Congress from the mountain district for a long time. In the previous Congress his seat had been contested by his Republican opponent and his cause had been advocated by Kitchin, then a member of the House of Representatives. Kitchin had handled it with such consummate ability as to secure Crawford his seat, and they had become devoted friends.

After the balloting had gone on for three days and nights, everyone was weary. I went to see Mr. Horne, who was one of my best friends. While I never owed him any obligation except the $100 stock he took in *The News and Observer,* he had told me that any time I needed money he would be glad to help me. I told him the time had come when the good of the Democratic Party required somebody to make a sacrifice and that he ought to withdraw his name. His partisans strongly advised against it and he asked, "Do you know what will happen if I withdraw?" I said, "Yes, Kitchin will be nominated." "Well, do you want that to happen?" he asked. "You know," I told him, "I have taken no part in this campaign. I am not a partisan of either of the candidates but I am a partisan of the Democratic Party and if this bitterness goes on many more days it will work great injury to the party. I have not talked to you about it before because I would have been happy for your ambition to be gratified, but your nomination is impossible. The Craig people have tried to effect it, but they cannot do it. Somebody must get out. You are the lowest man and you cannot win. I do not think it is your duty to Craig or anyone else to tie up this convention indefinitely when at the end you will be in no better position than you are now." He felt that I was telling him the truth, but because the Craig men had sought to nominate him he felt he was under obligation to them. He held on for a while but, after the sixtieth ballot, he withdrew his name and enough of his votes went to Kitchin to nominate him.

If hard feelings prevailed they were soon overcome when Governor

Aycock, an ardent Craig supporter, in generous words moved that the nomination of Kitchin be made unanimous. In the campaign, all friction disappeared and Kitchin received the whole-hearted support of the people.

Writing to *The News and Observer* about the convention, I said, "From the day the gavel fell, on Wednesday, until the vote was announced, I have never believed any result possible except the nomination of Kitchin when the deadlock should be broken." On the last ballot, before Kitchin was nominated, the vote was: Kitchin, 399; Craig, 322; and Horne, 134. On the next ballot on which Kitchin was nominated, the vote was Kitchin, 467; Craig, 390; and Horne, 1. The convention instructed the delegates to the National Convention to support Bryan for the presidency and renominated all the State officers except that it named Bickett for Attorney General and B. F. Aycock as Corporation Commissioner.

In the State campaign that year, Kitchin followed the example of Aycock and Glenn, and with an eloquence that neither of them surpassed, made a canvass from the mountains to the sea, winning by a large majority. The Republicans nominated J. Elwood Cox, a prosperous banker, and my paper declared that Cox was the candidate not only of the Republicans but of the Tobacco Trust and the Southern Railway, and proved that he had stood for high freight rates and had opposed regulation of railroads, and that he was a typical Republican, in that he stood for privilege in both State and national matters.

PREACHER AND JUDGE ENGAGE IN MUD-SLINGING

The most sensational speech of the 1908 campaign was that made in Raleigh by Judge W. A. Montgomery, who began life as a Democrat but left the party in Warren County because of differences with other Democrats and because the party had never recognized him in the way he thought his deserts justified. He joined the Populist Party and was elected Associate Justice of the Supreme Court in 1896. In this campaign he was the most violent of all the speakers advocating the Republican nominees. In fact, he was the only man who injected real bitterness into it. Early in October he made a speech, presiding at a Republican meeting in the Academy of Music in Raleigh, in which he made a violent attack upon the Democratic Party. The report of his speech was very inadequate, the speech being much more venomous, I was told, than the report in the paper. Part of the report was as follows:

"Reverting to the days of 1868-69, the times that the Democrats say the carpet-baggers and scalawags set a low order of morals and broke into the natural order of things," Judge Montgomery gave utterance to words as startling as unusual. He praised the work of the reconstructionists, lauding the results of their legislation in this State. He eulogized the Northern people for their 'magnanimity to the people of the South, considering the peril into which they had been put by the South and the great Southern army that threatened the destruction of their civilization.' 'Was there ever,' he asked passionately, 'such a spectacle in all history?' He said that 'not even one Southern man was prosecuted by the North after the war.' (Is the Judge's memory failing so badly that he does not remember the arrest and persecution of President Jefferson Davis?)

"Judge Montgomery denounced the Ku Klux Klan, read passages in which the members of that organization were denominated murderers, and speaking of it in this State exclaimed: 'The Ku Klux Klan was to incite the people of North Carolina and the South against the national government.' He said the people 'never hear a Democrat condemn the Ku Klux Klan and their outrages,' and referred to them as a 'delectable set of gentlemen,' and to their character in the words, 'the ineffable meanness of the gang.'

"Judge Montgomery spoke with the greatest contempt for the play 'Traitor' which will be in Raleigh one night next week. 'A play is being engineered,' he said, 'the only purpose of which is to revive old feelings, and its hero will be probably one of those Ku Klux leaders,' his reference being to the gallant Randolph Shotwell. Continuing, the Judge said: 'For all I know it is a means used by the other party to inflame the feelings of the people just on the eve of an election.' Speaking of the author of the play, Thomas Dixon, Jr., Judge Montgomery said: 'He puts his picture in the paper (holding up a paper with a picture of the author). Ah! There is not a child that would not run from that face. It's the face of an old hyena fattening on the spoils of a churchyard. He is the man nursing the hatred and passions of the men of the South.'

"In conclusion Judge Montgomery defended the protective tariff and discussed the panic, and speaking of the latter declared: 'Who did that mischief I can't say.' "

The day after, returning from Democratic headquarters in Chicago, where I had been all summer, I learned from a Democrat who had heard Montgomery's speech, that Democrats were greatly outraged and indignant and wondered why *The News and Observer* had not printed what they called his "incendiary utterances." It was the only time the paper fell down in its reporting. I proceeded to secure extracts from his speech and to talk with prominent Democrats who had attended the meeting, and I wrote an article headed "Unspeakable in Its Virulence," in which I pilloried Judge Montgomery's speech, saying, in part:

"White men of North Carolina, what are you to say to men who approve of utterances which vilify the dearest traditions of your past? They are an insult to the men that are dead and the manhood of the living. The Republican Party, hawking such sentiments about the State, falls to even lower depths and the verdict of the white men of North Carolina will be that again the Republican Party has shown that it is unworthy of confidence and respect and by their votes will cast it into outer darkness. . . .

"The sure road to getting a piece of Federal pie if the Republicans control in Washington is to qualify by abusing one's neighbors, praising Carpetbag government, and denouncing Southern sentiment. . . .

"The day will never come when the South will forgive any man who calls William L. Saunders, Frederick N. Strudwick, Randolph A. Shotwell, and men of that high type of courage and patriotism 'ruffians and bullies.'. . . the 'defenseless' men they punished were rapists and knaves who were protected and encouraged by the carpet-bag governments. . . .

"The writer of these lines was taught in school by a man who belonged to the Ku Klux Klan—as knightly a soul and as true a lover of justice as has lived in the State. The man who calls him and the other men of like spirit 'ruffians' and 'bullies' may get a Federal office, but his name will be contemned in North Carolina while he lives and forgotten when he dies."

I added, "Judge Montgomery is now qualified for a seat on the Federal bench."

The morning after I arrived from Chicago, the headline, in large black type and the editorial on Montgomery filled a large part of the editorial page. Colonel Thomas M. Argo, a brilliant Republican, came up to town that morning and, meeting a friend of mine, asked, "When did Joe Daniels get back from Chicago?" The gentleman said, "I didn't know he had returned." "Oh, yes," said Argo, "he is back. Hell broke loose this morning. Didn't you see *The News and Observer?* Everything goes quietly in North Carolina as long as Daniels stays away and you can always tell when he is in town because the devil is to pay."

Colonel Argo was a real character. He had a Daniel Webster head and eloquence. Before a jury he had few equals. In a political campaign when he was a Republican candidate for solicitor my paper had severely attacked him—too bitterly. It left a sting for a time, but this did not last. A short while after his defeat, he was talking on the street with my wife's brother, who was a schoolmate and a close friend of Colonel Argo's son. The Colonel loved his dram, and when in his cups spoke sulphurically. When my wife had passed, Colonel Argo turned to her brother and said: "There goes the very finest woman in Raleigh, but I never could understand why she married that damned blatherskite Josephus Daniels."

That editorial on Montgomery's speech stirred the Democrats and made the Republicans very mad, and Montgomery walked about the streets so infuriated that he could talk about nothing except to denounce *The News and Observer.* I cut out the editorial I wrote about Judge Montgomery, with some extracts the paper had printed, and sent them to Tom Dixon in New York, because Montgomery had, in his speech, flayed Dixon, his book, and his plays, and had charged that they were incendiary and calculated to incite race riots. Tom Dixon replied in the issue of October 16, with a letter that put Montgomery's virulence in the shade. Nobody could ever use the English language with quite such intensity as Tom Dixon. He wrote always in an oratorical way. When he read how Montgomery had scored his book and plays, he took out his pen and wrote with as much vitriol as Montgomery had spoken. His article, under big headlines on the first page of *The News and Observer,* October 16, 1908, was as follows:

"THOMAS DIXON ROASTS EX-JUDGE MONTGOMERY"

"We Drove the Carpet Bagger From Our Midst, But the Scalawag, or Native Product, Has Always Remained in the South to Fatten on Corruption and Breed Death to Society."

"To the Editor:

"I am delighted to see that ex-Judge Walter Montgomery does not like 'The Traitor' or its author! If he did like me I'd be ashamed to shake hands with myself—even in the dark! If my books or plays ever meet the approval of a Southern scalawag or traitor, I'll withdraw them from circulation.

"I am always proud that I'm a Southern white man until a sneak of the Montgomery type bobs up and begins to foul the memory of the brave men with whom he once fought—then the more I see of such men, the better I like dogs.

"Every decent citizen in America today, black or white, Democrat or Republican, North or South, is ashamed of the foul record of Reconstruction—except the native skunk who still lives in the South and habitually betrays his race for office. This man has always stood forth unique and shameless in his degradation. Hell was made to consume such leper trash, but if I were the Devil I wouldn't give them hell-room—I'd make a brush heap outside.

"The Republican party can never make any progress in the South until it ceases to honor these traitors. There are Southern white Republicans, descendants of the Old Whig, who believe something, stand for something, are something. Yet the moment a Judas Iscariot appears who is willing to foul the nest in which he was reared, they push these men of principle aside, acclaim the renegade a hero and give him an office as a reward for his infamy. The South owes a debt of gratitude to a few carpet-baggers, men of brains and conscience, who helped to stay the flow of corruption in the dark days of Reconstruction—but in all our history not a single solitary native traitor of the Montgomery breed has ever lifted his hand to do aught for his country except to draw his salary! We drove the carpet-bagger from our midst, but the scalawag, our native product, has always remained in the South to fatten on corruption and breed death to society—and a living death to the party which harbors him. For this man always stands for negro supremacy.

"The courage of the Celt, the nobility of the Norman, the vigor of the Viking, the energy of the Angle, the tenacity of the Saxon, the daring of the Dane, the gallantry of the Gaul, the earth hunger of the Roman and the stoicism of the Spartan are the heritage of the Southern white man by divine gift of blood from sire and dame through hundreds of generations and through centuries of culture! Yet when we face this native traitor who once

wore the gray and rose in darker days with the men who as
Clansmen led a successful revolution out of defeat and ruin and
tore the negro's hand from the throats of our women—when we
face this skunk and see him eagerly betray his own race to fatten
on their sorrows, how can we explain him? I am afraid that we
find here proof positive that with the brave and true men who
came to our shores from the Old World and created this Republic
here were mixed a few of low criminal origin. Blood will tell.
There is no other reasonable explanation of the continued phe-
nomena of the Southern scalawag.

"Ex-Judge Montgomery highly honors me in his denunciation! He can depend on it I tried to give him his dues in my play,
'The Traitor,' I tried, and I think I succeeded in covering him
and his tribe with everlasting infamy. This play I count the best
and most artistic piece of work I have yet done; for I have so
carefully constructed it and got my results so skillfully that I will
make the Northern Republican hiss and curse him with the same
enthusiasm as the Southern white man. And long after both of us
are silent in death, my books and plays will be telling the truth
to generations yet unborn.

"Thomas Dixon, Jr."

"New York, Oct. 14, 1908."

Dixon's letter made Montgomery see red. News came to me that
he had threatened to shoot Dixon and me on sight or give us a good
cow-hiding. For several days the folks who saw him said he acted
like a crazy man. If there was anything in the world Montgomery
took pride in, it was his honorable ancestors. He had always prided
himself that his forbears had been people of gentle birth and high
character, and when Dixon accused him of being descended from
the scum of creation, it is no wonder that he was mad. I suppose if
he had met Dixon or me on the street, while in his passionate anger,
there would have been one less living man. Instead of trying to get
redress by attempting to shoot or horsewhip, however, he decided to
bring suit against Dixon for libel in the U. S. District Court for $50,000
and named *The News and Observer* as a co-defendant. Dixon was
reputed to have made a fortune from his books and pictures. Montgomery thought he would have a better chance in the Federal court,
and, as Dixon was a non-resident, he had a right to sue in that jurisdiction. Dixon and *The News and Observer* retained Governor
Aycock and Judge Robert Winston as their attorneys and Mont-

gomery had able lawyers. The case promised to be a *cause célèbre*. The · situation in the courts was such that there was no possibility of trying the case immediately. Governor Aycock, after reading over the pleadings and Dixon's letter, which *The News and Observer* had published with virtual approval, saw that, unless Dixon could justify his charge that Montgomery's ancestors were crooks, the jury would be certain to give him some damages. While waiting for the trial of the case, therefore, Governor Aycock, who had always been admired by Montgomery, undertook to secure an adjustment, with little success at first. The only admonition he gave me was not to print anything that would aggravate the offense. In the meantime, Montgomery withdrew the libel suit against Dixon in the North Carolina court and announced it would be tried in New York. Later, as time wore on and Montgomery saw that he, himself, had lost his temper and been very violent in his speech and that Tom Dixon had some justification for his violent expressions, he was induced by Governor Aycock to express a willingness not to press his suit if Dixon would withdraw the charge reflecting upon his ancestry and if Dixon and *The News and Observer* would pay the costs incurred in the case. This was done, and the case went off the docket, *The News and Observer* very much gratified to escape paying money, and Montgomery having the right to claim vindication of his honorable ancestry. Of course Dixon very readily said that he ought not to have made reference to that because he had never heard anything about Montgomery's ancestors at all, and he had been informed and learned that they were all people of character and not all related to the gang that some historian said had been driven out of Virginia and had found refuge in North Carolina.

An interesting sidelight on the case was that after *The News and Observer* had severely criticized Montgomery in the 1894-96 campaign, he began to plant trees at his new home which he was building at Wilmont on the western suburbs of Raleigh, and decided to name the trees. He planted one tree and named it McKinley. Another he named Shepherd; others, Furches, Aycock, Faircloth, and so on, and, coming to a runt of a tree, he said "I will name this Josephus Daniels. It is just like him." For weeks he would take every visitor out and, pointing out the trees, would give their names, adding that he had named the little runt of a tree Josephus Daniels.

Time passed. It turned out that the runt tree he had named Josephus

Daniels grew to be the finest tree on his place, which caused him much trouble, for occasionally people would twit him about it. He didn't want to cut down his best tree just because it had a hated name.

RALEIGH SCHOOLS SAVED

April saw Raleigh taking a backward step. Its school fund was not enough to carry on and an election was called to increase the tax. The proposition failed to poll a majority and the schools were ordered to close four weeks earlier than in other States. The new school house which had just been built could not be used for lack of funds. *The News and Observer* commented that it was the greatest backward step in Raleigh's history. A number of Raleigh people would not accept the situation and a committee of men and women determined to carry on the schools and devised a way. Some personal contributions were made and another school election was called. I recall that my wife and Nick DeBoy, a professional politician in Raleigh, who always lined up for the faction that fought *The News and Observer* policies, took charge of the fight, in the southern part of the city, for longer school terms, and the old-time politicians had a lot of fun seeing these two, Nick and Addie, going around together, visiting the voters from house to house. It was such team-work that brought success.

In the summer one of the most disastrous manufacturing failures in the history of the State occurred, that of the Odell Manufacturing Company, doing business at Concord. It was regarded as the most substantial and solid textile institution in the State. Captain J. M. Odell, its head, had begun his career as a boy in the cotton mill industry on the banks of the Deep River in Randolph County, and mastered the business from running a loom to being president. His son, W. R. Odell, was regarded as able and efficient. Stock in his corporation was held all over the State. The Odells were leading members of the Methodist Church, and for years whenever a Methodist preacher saved a little money he regarded buying stock in the Odell Manufacturing Company as the safest investment possible. The banks also regarded it as a sound investment.

Growing out of this failure and the closing up of its affairs was an incident that brought *The News and Observer* into great disfavor with the receivers and attorneys. Although much of the money that was saved was due to aged Methodist preachers and their families and other investors who had put their little savings in the Odell stock, the winding up of its affairs was the most extravagant and outrageous on record. It was impossible for the newspaper men in Greensboro to get information of the allowances made to lawyers and receivers. Application was made, but failed. I then instructed Andrew Joyner, our correspondent in Greensboro, to make a formal demand upon the court to examine the records. He finally ferreted these out and found that one lawyer in the case had been allowed $20,000, another, a sum almost as large, and like fees had been allowed to the receivers and other lawyers. It created quite a sensation when *The News and Observer* printed this news. The lawyers were very indignant. The paper demanded that they return the money, calling it "blood money," taken out of the scant savings of women and children, and denounced Judge Boyd for his wanton approval of misappropriation of money belonging to people who sorely needed it. I do not recall that there was any redress, although the report was that the allowances made before the publication were only in part, but there were never any more, and but for *The News.and Observer's* giving publicity there doubtless would have been even larger rake-offs.

SERIOUS BLOW TO STATES' RIGHTS

In its issue of May 24 my paper said the United States Supreme Court had sounded the dirge of states' rights in its decisions in two cases, one from North Carolina and the other from Minnesota. These opinions grew out of rate reduction, the arrest of the Southern Railway agent at Asheville, and attachment of Minnesota's Attorney General for his contempt of Federal courts in obeying State laws. These decisions of the Supreme court held that the Federal court had jurisdiction to suspend State laws by injunctions and that penalties prescribed for violations of the law are unconstitutional because they operate in effect to make railroads keep out of Federal courts. Judge Peckham, who had been appointed by Cleveland as a Democrat, wrote this death knell of State control of its own affairs, and Justice Harlan, Republican, of Kentucky, wrote a vigorous dissenting opinion, pointing out the danger in the final elevation of the Federal jurisdiction over the State governments.

In August there occurred one of the biggest floods in the history of the State. Three thousand people were made homeless in Fayetteville.

The Neuse River was miles wide near Milburnie and people had to use canoes to get to town. Henry Bagley and Vick Moore, of *The News and Observer*, going out to reconnoiter on the extent of the damage done, were overwhelmed by the flood. The horses they were riding sank under the water, and it was a miracle that both of them were not drowned.

Upper left, John A. Oates, president of the North Carolina Anti-Saloon League when the State voted dry. *Upper right,* Charles W. Tillett, leading member of the Charlotte Bar and courageous advocate of good causes. *Lower left,* Captain W. I. Everett, State Senator, who drove whiskey distilleries out of the Southern part of North Carolina. *Lower right,* Rev. R. H. Whitaker, D.D., prohibition editor and chaplain of *The News and Observer.*

Upper left, Robert M. Furman, State Auditor; editor of the Raleigh *Morning Post.*
Upper right, Joseph P. Caldwell, editor of the Charlotte *Observer,* supporter of
Ransom and of Cleveland's gold policy. *Below,* J. B. Holman, farmer-legislator,
"Watch Dog of the Treasury," who led in the reëlection of Senator Vance.

XLIV

THE NATIONAL CAMPAIGN OF 1908

T HE DEMOCRATIC STATE CONVENTION at Charlotte was in session so long that the delegates to the National Convention had to go direct from Charlotte to Denver. All delegates were for Bryan. I was reëlected National Committeeman.

Bryan was nominated by acclamation and John W. Kern of Indiana was nominated for Vice-President. A committee was appointed to select the national chairman, of which I was a member. After the Convention we went to Lincoln to confer with Mr. Bryan. Herman Ridder, editor of *Staats Zeitung,* a great German paper of New York, told me he had stopped over at Lincoln and urged Bryan not to be a candidate, but he gave Bryan active support when nominated.

Governor Haskell, of Oklahoma, was with us at Lincoln. He was a Bryan supporter and had been much in evidence at the Denver convention. It was in his administration that the law had been passed guaranteeing bank depositors. Bryan believed it ought to be a national law and had secured its incorporation in the Denver platform. He stressed it as an important issue in the campaign but did not live to see it adopted by the Franklin Roosevelt administration. While at Lincoln, in a private conversation Bryan said to me that he wanted Haskell made treasurer of the national committee. I told him I did not think it would be a good appointment. He asked me why I objected. I really had no reason except a hunch, and the hunch was not my own, and so I told him that during the convention at Denver, when Haskell had seemed to think he had the convention in his pocket, my wife had said, "Don't trust that man!" I told Bryan her hunches were sound. Bryan didn't say so but I saw that he didn't think much of hunches. He insisted that Haskell, being Governor of a State that had adopted a law guaranteeing bank deposits, should be selected. That seemed, then, good logic and better than a woman's hunch.

Nearly all the delegates stopped at Lincoln to see Bryan. He was in fine spirits and the delegates left him with optimism and enthusiasm. Bryan had a way of irradiating confidence. He believed he would be elected. But there was one thing that gave him pause—a large element of the Catholics were inclined to oppose him. There was a current report that priests had criticized Bryan because he had omitted any reference to Catholic missions when writing of his visit to the Orient, but had, instead, praised the Protestant missions. Taft was favored because, when he was Governor General of the Philippines, his adjustment of the friar lands pleased the Catholics. After Dewey's victory at Manila the question of what should be done with the friar lands was uppermost. It was believed the Pope had taken deep interest in the adjustment, and our Ambassador at Rome had taken a hand, in consultation with papal authorities. The arrangements included payment of a large sum for the lands to the Catholic Church. Nothing was said about this in public but Bryan feared then what happened in November; namely, that for the first time a large element of the Catholic Democrats would vote for the Republican candidate. Bryan talked to me about it. He did not believe the disaffection extended far, but in organizing the committee he thought it might be well to select a Catholic for national chairman, believing that such an act would counteract any tendency the Catholics might have to support Taft.

It was decided it would be best not to select a chairman from the South. In both of Bryan's other campaigns James K. Jones, of Arkansas, had been chairman. Bryan thought it would be wise to secure a chairman from New York. Norman Mack, the national committeeman from New York wished the position and said so frankly to his friends on the committee. There was some discussion as to whether Mack would be acceptable to the New York Democrats. Assurances were received that his selection would please New York Democrats of all factions. The members of the sub-committee thought Mack was a Catholic. That turned out to be a mistake, though he was of a Catholic family.

In 1896, when he was editing the Buffalo *Times* in a city that was strong for Cleveland and anti-Bryan, Mack had made his paper the most aggressive advocate of Bryan's election in New York. In fact, as he often told me afterwards, he had jeopardized his financial life by taking that course, for all the banks and rich men in Buffalo were against Bryan. Bryan's eloquence had fascinated Mack and he was a devoted worshipper of the Nebraskan. Bryan knew this and he esteemed Mack highly.

Bryan wanted me to be secretary of the committee. I told him I much preferred to head the literary bureau, write the text-book, and look after publicity. I had always side-stepped being secretary of anything. I learned early that secretaries receive few promotions. Urey Woodson, of Kentucky, who was secretary of the committee, had been a devoted Bryan man in 1896. Afterward he had favored Parker, and Bryan did not feel that he was in full sympathy with his cause. However, when I declined to take the place, and urged Bryan to favor Woodson, he was elected.

The committee selected Moses C. Wetmore, a rich tobacco magnate of St. Louis, as chairman of the finance committee. He was one of the few millionaires who supported Bryan. Haskell was made treasurer. It was expected that Colonel Wetmore would be able to strike a rock from which money would gush forth. However, it soon became clear that, while he was willing himself to contribute liberally, Wetmore had no successful access to other large contributors. It was impossible, in the early days of the campaign, to pay the bills as they became due. Conferences were held night after night by the campaign managers to devise some plan to raise money. Finally Colonel Wetmore called a meeting saying he had devised a plan by which he would guarantee to raise all the money necessary. Chairman Mack, Vice-chairman John Lamb of Indiana, Haskell, the treasurer, and others of us on the executive committee met to hear Colonel Wetmore explain his plan which, he had given out, would get blood out of a turnip. He was very confident and enthusiastic.

The substance of his plan was set forth in a letter asking for a contribution, which he intended to send to every Democrat of importance in the country. The letter closed with a statement that at the conclusion of the campaign an elegantly bound book in permanent form would be laid on the desk of the President-elect when he took the oath of office and that this book would contain, as the roll of honor, the name of every Democrat who had made a contribution to the campaign fund. It was even a little more raw than that, the appeal being, rather bluntly, the clear suggestion: "If you contribute generously you are sure to get a job." When Colonel Wetmore had finished reading his letter with a flourish he turned to the committee expecting unanimous approval. He had already arranged to have 100,000 copies of his letter, signed by himself as chairman of the finance committee and all the executive committee and by Chairman Mack. "It sounds like a damn good proposition," said Norman Mack. "It will get the money," said another. I was sitting near Lamb, of Indiana, who was an able lawyer with much experience in Indiana politics. I whispered to him, "It sounds like an echo of the blocks of five in Indiana," referring to the old Republican method of paying men to carry people to the polls in blocks of five. I had said nothing aloud. Chairman Mack turned to me and asked: "Josephus, what do you think of it?" I said, "Before we consider it on its merits, let us see how we would feel when we see a fascimile of this letter printed on the first page of the New York *Tribune* and Chicago *Tribune* some morning. In my opinion it would damn the party from ocean to ocean. It would be held up as a sort of bribe and it would be regarded as pledging Bryan to give the offices to those who made the biggest contributions." This criticism got under Colonel Wetmore's shirt. "Well, why in the hell shouldn't it?" he asked. "The fellows who do the work and pay the campaign expenses ought to have the offices. That is exactly what we ought to say. Every fellow who gets this letter who wants a little country post office, revenue job, or an ambassadorship will read it over twice and will say to himself, 'If I put up in big style I will get the job,' and that will stimulate such generosity that you will see the money roll in."

The meeting did not adjourn until long after midnight and then with Wetmore in high dudgeon. He had worked for days and nights on that letter and he regarded his plan as 100 per cent perfect. Bills were piling up and he did not know where the money was coming from and, after long considerations, he had evolved this method of filling the larder. Therefore, when I voiced criticism and objection, he was as indignant as if I had killed his baby. Some of the members of the committee were not willing to turn it down and yet they saw how the Republicans would make use of it.

Finally, I said: "Very well, Colonel Wetmore. We will let this matter rest. I will send a copy of your letter to Mr. Bryan and to Mr. Kern. They are the men chiefly concerned and if they approve it I will make no objection." "Oh, Hell!" said Wetmore, "you know Bryan wouldn't approve it. He is too damn conscientious. He has nothing to do with running this campaign. He is running for President. It is our business to elect him."

Next morning Chairman Mack came to my room before I was up and said he had been sleeping on it and didn't want to send it to

Bryan. He said he would go to Wetmore and suggest another plan. Colonel Wetmore did not forgive me for killing his baby, and every time I would bring in a big bill for printing or expense of getting out the text-book and for publicity, he would swear at me in a good-natured way and say: "I would have had a million dollars if you hadn't stopped me. You ought to pay this bill yourself." But, if we didn't have much money we had faith and we went on ordering printing and lithographs and sending out speakers. Somehow the necessary money came in, mostly in small sums and often from quarters least expected. Much of it came from people of little education, men who wrote from the farms saying they were sending a dollar with their prayers, laboring men, preachers, and men in colleges, generally small colleges, who thought there was a moral issue involved and that Bryan was a preacher of righteousness.

As the campaign progressed Governor Haskell found it necessary to stay at home most of the time; so he put in his place a capable Oklahoma citizen who handled the business of treasurer in an excellent way. In the latter part of the summer my wife's hunch came true. The Hearst papers opened up on Haskell and printed page after page of his early transactions in railroad matters in Ohio. It charged him with sharp practices and dishonest dealings and also charged that he was connected with the Standard Oil Company, etc., etc. There was no ignoring these publications because not only did the Hearst papers denounce Haskell as an agent of the Standard Oil Company but Roosevelt took the matter up and denounced Haskell as corrupt and unworthy. Bryan wired Roosevelt demanding proof of his charges that Governor Haskell was ever connected with the Standard Oil Company. Roosevelt replied, vigorously reasserting the charge and quoting testimony that the Hearst papers had offered. It was in true Rooseveltian vein. In quite as vigorous a way Haskell replied to Roosevelt, denying the charges. Thus, suddenly, the big issues of the campaign veered away from the platforms and speeches of Bryan and turned to whether the treasurer of the Democratic Committee had been corrupt in his early railroad dealings and had been an agent of the Standard Oil Company.

It was very clear to me and to some others that the campaign could not be won with that issue to the front and that, whatever good things Haskell had done in Oklahoma, there was enough suspicion of his record as to make it impossible to continue him as one of the party leaders. Chairman Mack was in New York. I hurried to that city to confer with him and other Democratic committeemen. I told them the first thing to do was to get rid of the Treasurer, who should resign; that nobody was talking about anything but Haskell and if he continued as treasurer we might just as well close up headquarters. Mack agreed with me that Haskell ought to get out, but he asked me who would bell the cat and what Bryan thought about it. I suggested that I go to see Bryan.

I left New York and met Bryan by appointment and talked with him about it. I told him Mack, and others of New York headquarters, Judge Wade, and most of the others at Chicago headquarters, agreed with me that Haskell ought to relieve the party by resigning; that he need not admit his guilt but could say that his duties as Governor of Oklahoma were such that he could not give personal attention to the duties of treasurer and resign. Bryan regretfully agreed. Haskell had been an ardent friend of Bryan, who had accepted the Oklahoma plan of guaranteeing bank deposits and was paramounting it in his speeches. He saw the embarrassment of Haskell's withdrawal, but he also realized the greater embarrassment of his remaining. After we talked the matter over he was firm in his belief that Haskell would withdraw in the interest of the party. Byran always thought every man would do the right thing and would sacrifice himself for the party if necessary, but he didn't know Haskell.

He authorized me to see Haskell and say that in his judgment it was his duty to resign. I also got in touch with Kern, candidate for Vice-President. He was strongly of the opinion that Haskell should resign and so was John Lamb of Indiana, the best politician at head-quarters. While all of them thought that Haskell ought to get out, the question always came back to, "Who will bell the cat?" and they all agreed that I was the man to do it. This was unanimous and I voted for it. However, after agreeing to undertake the job, I wished very much that I could have put it on somebody else's shoulders. I returned to Chicago and, after a meeting, we telegraphed to Haskell that it was imperative that I see him within the next few days. Word came back that Haskell was not in Oklahoma but had left on a certain train for Chicago. We didn't want Haskell to come to Chicago before he resigned, for we knew that the Republican press would make a sensation. It was decided that I take the train from Chicago and meet Haskell about one hundred miles from the city and ride back with him and, en route, communicate to him that we wanted him to resign.

I met and boarded Haskell's train en route to Chicago and went into the car where he was reading a paper. He evidently knew what he was expected to do and that I was the executioner. He greeted me with the courteous remark of "What in the hell are you doing here?" I told him I had come to meet him and talk to him about a very important mater. He said, "I know what you want. I suppose you have had a meeting in Chicago and you have tried me and convicted me and executed me without a hearing." I assured him such was not the case; that we had not passed upon any of the charges against him, but we knew his great devotion to the party and loyal friendship for Mr. Bryan and we felt sure, inasmuch as the charges against him were injuring the party, he was the last man in the world who would wish to embarrass the cause or the candidate.

My attempt at diplomacy was a failure. He said, "You want me to resign, do you?" I replied in the affirmative. "I will be damned if I do. You may tell the whole crowd in Chicago and New York to go to hell. When a man's party friends convict him and ask him to admit his guilt, they are his enemies and not his friends." He turned back to his reading. The conversation seemed over. Outside the car the weather was very warm, but inside it was very cold indeed. After reading a few minutes, he turned to me and said, "Does Bryan want me to resign?" I told him he did. "Does he think I am guilty?" I told him he had never said so; that, on the contrary, he had the warmest regard for him and he wished his resignation only in the spirit of serving the party and in the warmest friendship for him. "Well, that is a damn poor way of showing friendship after all I have done for Bryan," he said, and then began reading again as if I were a million miles away. After a while, he said, "Does Kern want me to resign?" I said, "He does." "And Norman Mack?" "Yes." "The whole damn outfit, I suppose, want my head." I ventured, in a mild way, to tell him that the whole outfit had a very warm regard for him and I had come on a very painful duty, but that the charges had become an issue in the campaign and as long as he was treasurer the opposition press would talk about nothing else. The milder I talked to him the madder he got. Not long before we reached Chicago he said, "Tell the whole damn crowd they can go to hell. I will never resign." He also asked, "Do the newspaper men know you have come to meet me?" I said that I hadn't told anybody except Judge Wade and Mack. Whereupon he left the car and, upon arrival of the train in Chicago, about fifty reporters were at the depot. They had got the scent of the news and they were like dogs on the trail of a fox. They almost barked at me and surrounded me, asking, "Where is Haskell?" I said, "Haskell? He isn't in this car," and he wasn't. "Well, didn't you go in to see him and ride with him?" I said, "I don't see him," and they left me and ran back and forth through the cars looking for Haskell.

When Mr Haskell left me he had gone into the baggage car, and when the train stopped at Chicago he had gotten off, eluding the reporters. Nobody could find a trace of him. It was the most baffled crowd of reporters I ever confronted. I told them the truth when I said I didn't know where Haskell was. I went to my hotel and from my room telephoned Judge Wade. He came over and I reported to him the results of my diplomatic mission and of how Haskell had taken it. We talked, about half an hour, while we were eating a bite, and then the telephone rang. When I answered it the voice said, "Is this you, Daniels? Do you know where Judge Wade is?" "Yes," I replied, "he is in my room now." "Well, this is Haskell. I wish you and Judge Wade would come to my room at nine o'clock. I wish to see you on a matter of importance." His voice was chirpy, pleasant, and agreeable, and so friendly that you would have thought he was inviting us to take dinner with him.

At nine o'clock we went to Haskell's suite of rooms and found him sitting at a desk in the center of the room, surrounded by scores of reporters. He nodded to Wade and myself as we went in and said, "Take seats, gentlemen," with the most formal politeness and then he said: "I asked you gentlemen over because I am going to make a statement to the press and I haven't had time to confer with you before making it, or with anybody else on the committee. I have just returned from Oklahoma. I found, upon returning after the Convention, that my duties as Governor of that State were so onerous and engrossing that it is impossible for me to give the attention to the office of treasurer of the national committee which it demands; therefore, I have just written a letter, which I will read to you, announcing my resignation." Whereupon, he read his letter, acting as if he was doing something he loved to do and was laying down a very hard job. And then the reporters fired him with questions. Had he been asked to resign? He said he had not. Had Mr. Bryan requested it? He said he had not seen Mr. Bryan nor communicated with him. Had Mr. Mack requested it? He said that he had not seen Mr. Mack; that he was doing this purely voluntarily, and he parried the reporters for half an hour. When they left, he said," Goodnight, gentlemen," and retired to his bedroom. Wade and I went out, impressed with the fact that he was a fine actor and that he had pulled off a hard job as well as it could be done. Then the question was up as to who would be elected treasurer. We all agreed upon Herman Ridder, the patriotic and able editor of the *Staats Zeitung,* a German Catholic, who took the place and gave it his whole time and attention, raising money with fair success.

HEARST FORMS A PARTY

In the campaign that year there were four candidates for President who cut some figure in its early days, not to speak of the Socialist Party which, like the poor, was always with us. Hearst organized a party of his own. After Bryan's refusal to put him in nomination and support him for President in 1904, Hearst's papers became very bitter toward him. Hearst had also fallen out with Tammany because he felt it had ditched him when he ran for Governor. He had organized an Independence League Party, in a New York election, which had polled a large vote, and he had made it a national organization. He declared both the old parties were corrupt and in league with the big interests, but, seeing that the big interests were all against Bryan, it was difficult to make any headway by charging that the Democratic Party was in league with them. He nominated a ticket with Thomas Hisgen for President, and the editor of his paper, John Temple Graves, of Georgia, for Vice-President. He staged a big convention and it started out as if it were going to be a real party. The Populists had been the first party in the field and nominated Tom Watson, of Georgia, who started his campaign with a statement that Bryan had said he would never vote for a Confederate soldier for office. This was typically Watsonian. He expected it to have great effect in Georgia and other Southern states, but it proved a dud. The fact that Bryan had, in 1904, at the St. Louis convention, placed in nomination Senator Cockerell of Missouri and supported him, Cockerell having been a staunch and brave Confederate soldier, gave the lie to this statement. Watson and John Temple Graves, both of them being sensational and good phrase-makers, got to the front in the early part of the campaign. It troubled the Democrats. We knew that those who voted for either of the small parties were against the administration at Washington and would vote for Bryan if he was the only candidate against the party in power.

SAM GOMPERS FOR BRYAN

I went, one Sunday during the campaign, to a great meeting of the labor forces in New York. It was the first time I heard Samuel Gompers speak. His arraignment of the Republican administration as an enemy of labor was able and effective. I could then understand his mastery of assemblies. He was one of the most convincing and logical speakers I ever heard. As he spoke, and the great audience followed him with approval, I was convinced that labor would support Bryan. Only the election returns convinced me of my error. I was afterward to come in very close touch with Mr. Gompers in Washington during the World War, when he was a member of the Advisory Committee of the Council of National Defense and was the most influential private citizen in America in mobilizing all the forces behind Wilson in the World War.

BRYAN REFUSED TO BE STAMPEDED INTO PLEDGES

By October the Democrats in charge of the campaign in New York had convinced themselves that Bryan had a chance to carry the State. Murphy had reported that Tammany was almost 100 per cent for him. Judge Morgan J. O'Brian and other leaders of the party in New York, who were in close touch with business and professional life, reported that the only thing that stood between Bryan and election was the fear on the part of business that Mr. Bryan, if elected, might appoint to the Supreme Court bench men who would not be as great a bulwark in the protection of property rights as they felt was necessary. They talked much about this around headquarters and convinced some members of the committee that if Bryan could set this fear at rest he would carry New York. It was therefore arranged that the next time Bryan came to New York this suggestion should be presented to him.

Herman Ridder, who thought the idea a grand one, arranged to give Byran a dinner when the proposition was to be put up to him to make a public pledge of the kind of men he would appoint on the

Supreme Court bench. The company gathered at Mr. Ridder's included Chairman Mack and other members of the committee, Judge O'Brian, Charley Murphy, Big Chief of Tammany, Homer Cummings, Senator Culberson, and a dozen others. Nobody had said anything to Bryan officially about the matter which was to be presented at the dinner.

After several courses had been served—Mr. Ridder liked good champagne and it was not scarce—the subject matter of the gathering was broached. Mr. Ridder, Judge O'Brian, and others, pointed out that Bryan was headed for the White House; that New York was certain to go for him if the business interests of that city could be assured that he would do nothing to disturb business. Some of these interests had been apprehensive, they said, about the kind of men Mr. Bryan would put on the Supreme Court bench. They, therefore, believed that if he would say publicly that in case of election he would fill the vacancies by naming men such as George Gray, of Delaware, it would give such confidence that the business people of the country would rally to his support and elect him. The proposition was presented in a very persuasive way. I was sitting nearly opposite Bryan at the table and, as they talked, I saw his jaws set and a look come into his eyes which indicated that they were making no headway. Several pressed the suggestion and all who spoke thought it was the key to success and that it was a thing he should be willing and glad to do. When they had finished Bryan rose and expressed his appreciation of the gathering and of his chance to meet these distinguished Democrats, as well as of their deep interest in the success of the party—an interest which, he said, he knew was not second to his own. He was very courteous and very polite. Then he went on to say that he did not doubt their sincerity and did not doubt their friendliness but that he could not conceive that any citizen would vote for a man for President whom he could not trust to name judges of the courts without a pledge. He added that he thought, if such a pledge were made, instead of bringing success it would have the opposite effect; that it would be heralded as indicating that people didn't trust their candidate for President but had to bind him with pledges. He added that to make a statement of that kind, pointing out a certain man, for instance, Judge Gray, who had bolted the party in 1896, a distinguished gentleman of high character, would be equivalent to saying to all the other able Democrats in the country that they would be discriminated against and would have no opportunity even for consideration. He closed by saying that, under no circumstances, not even for the presidency, would he humiliate himself by making such a pledge.

This declaration almost floored Herman Ridder, who had originated the idea and who believed it was the open sesame to victory. Nobody said anything for several minutes after Bryan sat down, and then Charley Murphy turned to Bryan and said, "Mr. Bryan, you are quite right. After hearing you, I am sure you ought not to make such a pledge and nobody ought to ask you to make it." So the dinner broke up, and the next day Herman Ridder confided to me that Bryan had defeated himself.

Bryan and the committee had stressed the trust issue that year. Early in October I issued from Chicago headquarters, a statement in an open letter to Attorney General Bonaparte, which was widely published at the time and called forth a reply from Bonaparte. For a week the Bonaparte-Daniels letters got the first page in most of the newspapers. My inquiry began by asking "How many trusts have you proceeded against?" I received very many letters and telegrams of approval for drawing Bonaparte into the open and making it clear that the Republicans had done nothing against the trusts and had no program. From then on the publicity department, of which I was head, kept up the attack on the Republicans and we thought we were making great headway. Senator Charles A. Culberson joined me in the controversy with Bonaparte and wrote an able letter confounding Bonaparte in the controversy.

Hearst's paper, which got its first circulation boost by supporting Bryan in 1896 and proclaiming it was pro-labor and militantly progressive, was most vicious against Bryan in 1908. This was partly in revenge for Bryan's refusal to nominate Hearst for the Democratic presidential nomination at St. Louis, and partly because Bryan staged his campaign against colonialism and imperialism which had intrigued Hearst. The Hearst twin, Arthur Brisbane, dipped his pen in vitriol. This is a sample:

"If you want to get into trouble elect Bryan. He doesn't understand how to conduct any kind of business. I have to run a newspaper and Bryan could not be office boy on my paper. Byran is an ignorant man. You need in the White House a good brain, and you don't need a mouth. Bryan is a mouth."

The Democratic Committee was much elated one day when John Bigelow, distinguished diplomat and writer, intimate friend of Tilden and author of the *Life of Tilden,* who had been retired some years, sent word to the chairman of the committee that he wished to confer with him about the best way he could assist in electing Bryan. At once Mack and I went up to see the great man. He was then quite old, over ninety, very interesting and reminiscent. He pointed out that, although he had not supported Bryan in 1896, he wished to lend every influence he could to secure his election that year and he wrote an able letter which I sent all over the country. It had wide circulation. It was John Bigelow who, as Minister to France at the conclusion of the Civil War, paid an official visit to Louis Napoleon and told him in diplomatic language to end his support of Maximilian, who had been made Emperor of Mexico by Napoleon. Bigelow said that while the North and the South were engaged in war his government was in no position to consider other matters, but when the brotherly war ended the Washington administration would enforce the Monroe Doctrine. In the celebrated talking picture "Juarez," presented in 1939, this scene was depicted.

One of the most distinguished engineers in America, who knew more about the Panama Canal than anybody except Colonel Goethals, came to me armed with documents which had the appearance of verity, and said the Democrats could blow the Republicans to smithereens if they would expose the rotten deals that preceded the construction of the Panama Canal. He said he had evidence to prove that the money supposed to have been paid for French concessions, worth very little, and for other alleged expenditures, were honeycombed with graft reaching up to the higher-ups and to lawyers of eminence. The whole Panama Canal acquisition dishonored the country. I examined his statement. It seemed to convict big Republican officials of conduct that was corrupt. But—I was no expert, and I knew any charge reflecting upon the higher-ups would be a boomerang unless the evidence was more than conclusive. I had no doubt as to the engineer's charges as to wasteful and corrupt expenditures, but his evidence did not irrefutably trace the money into the hands of the highest public officials. I told him that the committee could not inject the matter as an issue in the campaign under those conditions. But he convinced me that all was not open and above board. He felt that the Democratic Committee was losing a good opportunity to expose corruption and in this way win the election—was he right?

There were attempts in the Taft campaign of 1908 to raise a religious question, and this found an echo in some statements in Greensboro. I had a request from Chicago, written by a preacher, for an article urging people to vote against Taft because he was a Unitarian and saying that men who denied the divinity of Christ ought not to be elected President of the United States. I declined to forward any such articles or, in any way whatsoever, to say anything or have anything to do with an attempt to introduce a religious question into the campaign.

A few days before the election John D. Rockefeller made an announcement from the Standard Oil offices that he would support Taft. That was not news, but it was played up by the Democrats as a proof of what Mr. Bryan had been saying all during the campaign, that the Republican Party was the haven of the trusts. It was accepted also by them as a guarantee that the Republicans would have plenty of money. Toward the end of the campaign the Democrats said the election would hinge upon whether the trusts could buy the election. As I look back upon it, it seems singular that the Democrats could have been so confident in view of the big majority in the electoral college and the popular vote secured for Taft. The only consolation the Democrats got out of it was that, whereas Parker had been defeated by more than two million votes, Taft won over Bryan by less than one million. Bryan carried no Northern state except Colorado, and had a total of 174 votes in the electoral college to Taft's 309.

Bryan received 6,409,106 votes to Taft's 7,679,006. In 1896 Bryan's popular vote as recorded was 6,467,946 whereas McKinley was given 7,035,638. In 1900 Bryan's vote was less than in 1896 whereas McKinley received more votes. The total in 1900 was: McKinley 7,219,530, Bryan 6,358,071. McKinley, who had been pushed into the Spanish-American war, benefited by it, whereas Bryan, who had enlisted and served as a soldier, received no benefit. In politics it often happens that way.

The *News and Observer* said: "The election Tuesday was a thing of government and graft, Roosevelt prostituting the government to party and the Republicans pouring out their ill-gotten money to defeat the right of the people to say who should be their President." It also said that Mr. Bryan was greatly disappointed and added: "The reforms of which Bryan has been the foremost leader will be tri-

umphant and as editor and private citizen Mr. Bryan will continue
the great work to which he has consecrated his life and genius, but
it is improbable that his name will ever again be presented for the
chief magistracy."

There is no doubt that Bryan's speech, when he returned from
his trip around the world, paramounting government ownership of
railroads, cost him support and materially contributed to check the
tide which seemed to be running in his direction at that time. There
was a strong belief in New York that Tammany had knifed Bryan,
but Murphy said, in view of his defeat elsewhere, it was silly to
accuse Tammany. *The News and Observer* prophecy came true.
Many of the reforms which Bryan had advocated and made possible
were afterward enacted in the administrations of Woodrow Wilson
and Franklin Rooosevelt, but he was never again a candidate for the
presidency.

CLEVELAND REFUSED TO SUPPORT BRYAN

I sincerely hoped that since Bryan was running on a platform
against imperialism, and demanding that the Filipinos be given their
independence—a policy to which Cleveland had strongly committed
himself—the chasm between the two great Democrats would be
bridged. Nearly all the members of the Cleveland cabinet who had
bolted Bryan in 1896, led by Olney and Harmon, urged Cleveland
to join with them in cementing a reunited party, so as to win a
victory over the imperialism, the "robber tariff," and the monopoly
which dominated the McKinley administration.

"I am importuned and *ordered* to the point of unhappiness to
publicly announce myself as favorable to Bryan's election," he told
Charles S. Hamlin. Henry Watterson, who had been severe in
criticism of Bryan in 1896 and had thereby divided the Kentucky
Democracy, was back in the fold, active at National Democratic
headquarters, urging Democratic solidarity to destroy Hanna-ism and
High Protection. In a conversation with "Marse Henry" late one
night at Chicago, in the 1900 campaign, he said to me:

"Josephus, if I had known your friend Bryan as well as you
did, I would have supported him as strongly as I opposed his
election in 1896. I thought he was little more than a 'Boy Orator'
advocating a remedy for the pain that was worse than the disease.
I mistook his quality then, or he has grown greatly in the four

years. His speech against the danger of imperialism was a masterpiece of logic, eloquence and fundamental Americanism."

Shortly after the New York Democratic headquarters were opened in 1908, Chairman Mack called in counsel many of the old-time Cleveland men, and in every possible way they quietly undertook to persuade Cleveland to throw the weight of his influence against the un-American Philippine policy in the only way that could be effective, by supporting the National Democratic ticket. It was believed that these appeals would be effective, but, though saying nothing until late in the campaign, Cleveland could not forget the fight on him in 1893-96, and in September he wrote to Hamlin:

> "My political thoughts are of the saddest description. I would be so glad to help the situation if I could only see the way; but I feel that I am bound 'hand and foot.' Bryanism and McKinleyism! What a choice for an American!"

Even more strongly he expressed the long-pent-up exasperation at the repudiation of his leadership in 1896, a repudiation which was galling then and which still festered. In fact, it never left him, embittering his after years to some degree and making impossible further influence in politics—an influence which was needed and without which the division in the Democratic Party continued. To his close friend Wilson S. Bissell he unbosomed himself thus:

> "I cannot write or speak favorably of Bryanism. I do not regard it as Democracy.... I have some idea the party may before long be purged of Bryanism, and that the rank and file, surprised at their wanderings and enraged at their false leaders, will be anxious to return to their old faith; and in their desire to reorganize under their old banners will welcome the counsel of those who have never yielded to disastrous heresy."

Meaning *himself*. It is undeniable that Cleveland hoped and expected, until his health failed, to be called back when the people were ready to "welcome the counsel of those who have never yielded to disastrous heresy." And he hoped, when that time came, again to move into the White House for another four years. Bryan was the lion in his path, and he could never forgive him. In addition to the old grudge, he severely criticized Bryan for urging Democratic senators to vote for the treaty annexing the Philippines. To Harmon he

Left, Herman Ridder, Treasurer of the National Democratic Committee, 1908. *Right*, Norman E. Mack, Chairman of the National Democratic Committee, 1908.

A private dinner in the Cleveland home of Mark A. Hanna. At the table are, left to right in the foreground, Hanna, Mrs. Hanna, Mrs. McKinley, President McKinley, and Ruth Hanna (Mrs. McCormick). The picture was taken about 1898 (Underwood and Underwood).

wrote: "How certain can you be that Bryan will save you from imperialism? What did he do toward that end when the treaty of peace was before the Senate?"

In all his career, Bryan never made so great a mistake as in advocating the ratification of that treaty, which bought the Filipinos at so much a head, and started the United States on an indefensible colonial policy. Bryan told me he took that course to bring an end to the war, believing that the people would later undo the evil. Instead, he fathered a wrong that he never lived to see righted, strive he ever so honestly to repudiate the effects of that action. His best friends could not persuade him that locking the stable after the horse is out does no good.

In the 1908 campaign I busied myself particularly in sending out statements from leading Democrats who had not supported Bryan in 1896, but who were back in camp, and we hoped that this trend would elect Bryan. However, large government purchases and the turning loose of much money in the Spanish-American war had made for better times, and Mark Hanna's slogans, "The Full Dinner Pail," and "Keep on Letting Well Enough Alone," carried the election for McKinley.

TAFT REJECTS REPUBLICANS

Judge Purnell had died toward the end of 1908 and the question of his successor created much interest. It rent the Republican Party in twain. Every Republican lawyer in Eastern North Carolina was a candidate. Taft was Chief Executive. He had himself been a judge. His whole temperament was judicial. As the friends of each candidate would go to Washington to see the President, each would regale him with the unfitness or bad character or both of the other candidates. The contest among the Republican candidates became so bitter and Taft became so disgusted with the criminations and recriminations that he decided it was his duty to go outside of his party and select a man purely on his record as an able and upright judge. Herbert F. Seawell, who had been a Populist in 1894, and a very violent one, had been appointed by Roosevelt before he went out of office, but the Senate had not confirmed his appointment and it expired with the coming in of the new President.

The News and Observer gave the history of Seawell and paramounted his Populist views and his vicious attacks upon both Democrats and Republicans when he was a Populist, and pointed out that he had been so vindictive that the people of Cleveland County had resented his denunciations and had given him a dose of rotten eggs. Seawell, however, had much support among the Democrats because he was personally a clean man and, though not a great lawyer, was so much better a lawyer than Purnell that his appointment would have been an improvement over past conditions. Among the Democrats who went to Washington in Seawell's behalf was Cameron Morrison, afterward Governor. He seemed to take charge of the Seawell campaign and came to Raleigh to see me and urge me to let up on Seawell. He said if I would cease to oppose him, Simmons and Overman would vote for him. My answer to him was to print, on the next day, the vile speech Seawell had made on the Wilmington revolution and to declare that the people of North Carolina would not tolerate it if Simmons and Overman voted for his confirmation. Not long after, a Washington correspondent wrote that, as a matter of fact, Roosevelt never expected Seawell to be confirmed but had simply appointed him as a complimentary gesture in payment for his support.

E. W. Timberlake, of Franklin, Harry Skinner, of Greenville, T. T. Hicks, of Vance, W. S. O'B. Robinson, of Wayne, and other lesser lights among the Republican lawyers, and their friends, kept the road hot between North Carolina and Washington, urging their appointment. Each time it looked as if any Republican was to be the favorite man, *The News and Observer* would open up on his record. If he had been an old-time Republican, it would tell of his sins. If he was a Populist, it would go back and discuss his Fusionist record. Taft had no patience with the Populist doctrines. That put Seawell out of favor with him. So many things were alleged against the others that finally Taft made up his mind to do what he had often done in the South, that is, to go outside his party for his judicial appointments.

After Republican aspirants had spent all the money they had or could borrow, going to and from Washington, Taft turned them all down. When he let it be known he was disgusted with the skulduggery of the advocates of the various aspirants of the Republicans for judge, someone suggested to him that it would be wise if he would tender the appointment to Henry Groves Connor, Associate Justice of the Supreme Court. The first intimation he had of his appointment was when *The News and Observer* said, "The new judge will be H. G. Connor or Harry Skinner." As soon as Skinner's name was brought to the attention of the President, some of the Republican opponents presented to Mr. Taft Skinner's favorite argument for the sub-treasury, which Taft regarded as heresy. That put Skinner out. It had been suggested by Simmons and Overman that Taft could appoint Connor better than any of the Democrats and give less offense to the Republicans, because in the Legislature, when the Republican judges were on trial for impeachment for which most of the Democratic leaders and members voted, Judge Connor, as a member of the House, had strongly opposed their impeachment. This pleased Taft and he became convinced that Judge Connor was the type of man who would rise above party considerations, and as he himself was keen to have a judiciary free from narrow partisanship (as shown by his appointment of Chief Justice White, Judge Sanborn, and a half dozen other eminent Democrats to the bench), he conferred with one or two Republicans in North Carolina, who agreed that the appointment of Judge Connor would be more agreeable to them than that of any other Democrat. On May 10 President Taft made the appointment of Judge Connor, on which confirmation soon followed.

Years afterward Taft told me the story of Connor's selection, which gave him, and everybody else, satisfaction—of course, except the Republican candidates who were rejected and their supporters. They never forgave Taft.

XLV

IN GOVERNOR KITCHIN'S ADMINISTRATION

GOVERNOR KITCHIN came into office in January, 1909, fresh from Congress, where he had made a splendid record. His inaugural address was excellent and his administration began with every good wish on the part of the people of the State. He was young, handsome, honest, ambitous.

The Legislature organized with Judge Augustus W. Graham, of Granville, as Speaker of the House. He was the youngest son of the Honorable William A. Graham, who had been Judge, Governor, Senator, Secretary of the Navy, and candidate for Vice-president, and who was probably the ablest all-around public man of his day in North Carolina. The Speaker had ability but little talent in debate. Though he did not possess his father's greatness, in devotion to the public good, deep interest in public affairs, and regard for the weal of the under-privileged, as well as in social and popular qualities, he led all the Grahams. We had long been very good friends and our minds ran together along most public policies. He had been an earnest advocate of Kitchin's nomination.

During the administration of Elias Carr there was a vacancy in the Superior Court judgeship in the Orange-Granville district. Most of the bar urged the appointment of Major John W. Graham, brother of the Speaker, who was an able lawyer but possessed a reserve which held him aloof. He lacked the popular touch. Moreover, in the issues that had been uppermost, leading to Governor Carr's nomination, Major Graham had sympathized with the element in the party with which Governor Carr did not then train, whereas, Augustus W. Graham, called "Gus," had been a leader in the Bryan movement. Governor Carr asked me to come to the executive office to discuss the vacancy. He told me he would not appoint Major John Graham; that he had made up his mind; and that, while he respected him, John Graham's attitude of mind was so opposed to the dominant thought of the State that nothing would induce Carr to appoint him. "I am thinking," he said, "of appointing Gus Graham," and he asked me what I thought about it. I told him the appointment of either would be excellent, of course. John Graham was probably the abler lawyer but Gus was able and, I thought would make the better judge. But, being the younger brother, Gus Graham felt he could not take the position, since he was giving his support to his brother. It was only when Governor Carr gave his ultimatum that he would not appoint the older brother that the younger one agreed to accept. Some of the friends of the older brother felt that Gus Graham should have refused peremptorily, but they did not know the inside situation.

In the Legislature Speaker Graham sought to advance causes which would serve the common good and was ever the staunch supporter of movements that would control the predatory and reactionary interests. Afterward he held a position of dignity and responsibility in the administration of Woodrow Wilson.

The Legislature reëlected Senator Overman without opposition. *The News and Observer* called upon it to amend the feeble anti-trust law of the previous session and to pass a measure with teeth in it. It pointed out that the Democratic Party in the State and nation had pledged itself to effect anti-trust legislation. A hearing was held on the Lockhart Anti-trust bill and strong arguments were made for it by Charles O. McMichael, of Rockingham, and J. O. W. Gravely, of Nash. Very shortly, as usual, the trust advocates began to cry out that *The News and Observer* was trying to drive the Legislature. Defending the paper from that charge, I said, "Its only purpose is to bring to their daily attention the duty of the legislators to stand by their platform and their pledges."

Governor Kitchin sent to the Legislature a message against monopolies which was disappointing to his friends. After Lockhart introduced his Anti-trust bill with teeth, he and other staunch Kitchin men were greatly troubled because James. S. Manning, who had been Kitchin's manager in his campaign for Governor, had introduced an amendment to the Anti-trust bill, said to embody Kitchin's idea, which Lockhart and Justice believed would exempt the American Tobacco Company. In his message to the Legislature on trusts, Governor Kitchin said the plank to destroy monopoly was deliberately inserted in the platform of the party and recommended that the old law be perfected.

Shortly after this message and Judge Manning's substitute for Subsection A, Senator Lockhart and a half dozen other members of the

Legislature, all of whom had supported Kitchin for Governor, and largely on the ground that he was bitter in denunciation of trusts, came to my office. They said they had just been to see the Governor to ask him to take the leading part in defeating the attempts to amend the Lockhart bill. They had told him the amendments offered would cut the heart out of it. They told me that, instead of speaking strongly, as he had done on the stump, against the trusts, Governor Kitchin had said the people were not so much interested in such drastic legislation as Lockhart and others supposed. Whereupon, Lockhart said, he told the Governor, "You were more drastic than I was when you were a candidate for nomination for Governor and you received support in the State in belief that you would go far enough to put an end to monopoly in North Carolina."

They were distressed to find that the Governor had lost his interest in effective legislation and they came to my office, not in a critical mood, but hurt and disturbed, because the man they had expected to blow the trumpet was, as they said, soft-pedaling. They didn't understand it. We decided our duty was to go ahead and make the fight. I asked them if they had not misunderstood the Governor, but they said they had asked him again and, instead of talking vigorously against the trust, he pointed out the difficulties in the way of reaching them and he seemed to think these difficulties were so great that they could not be overcome.

It soon developed that the difficulties in the way of passing an effective anti-trust law were very great and this because Democrats from the counties where the tobacco interests were important were determined that no bill should contain teeth that would reach the Tobacco Trust. Therefore, what was known as the Manning-Bassett-Blow bill was enacted. Just before the teeth were withdrawn from the Lockhart bill, *The News and Observer* had a long editorial headed, "Shall the Pledge Be Kept?" and quoted, at length, from Woodrow Wilson on the necessity of putting an end to monopoly, and from the vigorous anti-trust pledges Governor Kitchin made in his race for the nomination.

There was continued controversy between *The News and Observer* and Governor Kitchin on his attitude on the trust question. Editorially, it said that Governor Kitchin had disappointed his supporters because he had been elected as one who would "wage vigorous warfare on the trust." In his campaign he went over the State saying the

American Tobacco Company was fighting his nomination. He even said it was not fighting either of his opponents because "the trust felt if either of them were elected it would not be vigorously prosecuted." He was nominated by genuine anti-trust men like Senator Reuben Reid, Representative Justice, and Senator Lockhart. My paper later said: "Governor Kitchin in the contest in the Legislature failed to stand with the men who stood, after the election, where they had all stood before the election." The paper added, "The failure of Governor Kitchin to fight the trusts as earnestly after the election as his denunciation of them, particularly the Tobacco Company, when he was seeking the nomination, was as great a surprise as it was a disappointment to his supporters and to all others who had heard his speeches." In another editorial headed, "Asleep At The Switch," the paper said when Governor Kitchin was a representative in Congress he had declared that, if elected, "the human beings back of the trusts will be made to know that it is better to obey the law than to violate it and that, if they hold the law in contempt and break it at all they will be put behind prison bars." The paper went on to say that it was that promise that gave Mr. Kitchin the governorship and added: "The record tells of WORDS by the governor against the trusts but there is not a DEED in the record from the day he was inaugurated down to this hour."

During the rather warm controversy Kitchin, criticizing my paper for supporting Wilson as President, said, "and yet the Governor of New Jersey has not driven the American Tobacco Company—one of its chartered institutions—from its borders." Kitchin declared that the paper's criticism of him and of Simmons was for the benefit of the candidacies of Clark and Aycock, both of whom, he said, I had urged to get into the race for the senatorship. Two of his strongest supporters for the nomination, Senator Lockhart and Senator Glidewell, replied to Kitchin and said he had been "asleep at the switch and hadn't advocated effective anti-trust legislation although he had promised to do so." I denied Kitchin's statement that I had tried to induce Clark to enter the race. Judge James S. Manning (who as Kitchin's campaign manager and as State Senator had secured the passage of a namby-pamby so-called anti-trust act which was guaranteed not to reach the Tobacco Trust), entered the discussion and made a vigorous reply to Glidewell, and for a time the controversy waxed warm. As a matter of fact, I had never spoken to Judge Clark about entering the race for the United States Senate, but I did urge Aycock to become a candidate and tendered my earnest personal support.

Governor Kitchin, in an address before the Wake County Farmers Union defended what I called "the pink tea anti-trust law" and wrote a letter to *The News and Observer* saying he had never fought Subsection A and that no one desired an end of monopoly more than he. My paper replied by saying that Senator Lockhart was right in calling Section F "a subterfuge," and Speaker E. J. Justice wrote a letter which, indirectly, replied to Kitchin, headed "Anti-trust Law Without Form and Void and Darkness on the Face of It," and saying "I believe that immunity of all trusts from prosecution is due to The American Tobacco more than to any other one company."

Some of Governor Kitchin's best friends believed he would have won the senatorial toga if after election he had fought vigorously for an effective anti-trust act and had repudiated the pink tea substitute (Justice called it subterfuge) offered by Senator Manning, of Durham (home of the Tobacco Trust), who was his campaign manager and close political friend.

Before the campaign for the senatorship got warm, I poked some fun at the candidates for the Senate who had not yet gotten their gait, with the following paragraph in my paper:

"Senator Simmons is to speak at Mocksville on good roads. Governor Aycock has already spoken there on education and masonry. Governor Kitchin will later speak on farming and how to make home happy. Chief Justice Clark will speak on the deeds of the Confederate Soldier. Politics—Senatorial campaign—perish the thought."

Governor Kitchin put a quietus on the attempt of the Southern Railway to reopen the rate question. The railroads, early in the session, sought to repudiate the legislation which had made for harmony and progress. They came to Raleigh to confer with Governor Kitchin— a big party of railroad executives—and tried to get the rate question reopened. The Governor told them the people were not expecting such agitation and the question ought not to be reopened. For this reason the Legislature of 1909 was free of any fight on the rate question.

Kitchin's administration witnessed the calling of clean and capable men into the public service and was marked by efficiency in every department. His last message was a progressive one, with a review of the steady, if not tremendously important, measures which had characterized the administration. He reported that the penitentiary had been carried on with good business judgment and with humane management and had shown a profit of $152,000 for the last two years. He was an upright official, and people, whether agreeing or disagreeing, respected his ability and integrity.

Governor Kitchin retired from office a disappointed man. He had fully believed he would be elected to the Senate and staked everything upon it, even his health. He had never been physically very strong. When he was a boy his father had sent him to Texas for some years, fearing he had lung trouble. Although he always seemed robust and left the executive office to take up the practice of law in Raleigh in co-partnership with Judge James S. Manning and commanded a large practice, it was not long before it was evident that the malady, which shortened the lives of other brilliant Kitchin men, had laid its hand upon him. Failing health soon compelled his retirement and his return to his old home in Scotland Neck, where, with weakening powers, he lived a number of years, followed by the affection of thousands of friends who witnessed his decline with deep distress.

It was in the spring of 1909 the first real political difference came between Simmons and *The News and Observer*. It was never personal. Taft had been inaugurated and the Republicans had begun to write a new tariff bill which was to cause Senator Dolliver, of Iowa, so to excoriate the Taft administration as to be the beginning of its crushing defeat. Senator Simmons expressed views on the tariff which *The News and Observer* said were not in accord with the Democratic doctrine and were contrary to the able and vigorous advocacy of a tariff for revenue only, which had been so well expounded by Senator Vance and endorsed by the people of North Carolina. Senator Simmons urged a high tariff on lumber, defended the old Dingley rate, which was twice the rate fixed by the House in the Payne bill. He also urged that the free list be contracted, and he advocated a duty on cotton-seed oil. In fact, his advocacy was in keeping with the dictum of General Hancock, when he was a candidate for President, to wit: "Tariff is a local issue." Simmons stood for low tariff on everything except where it was necessary for him to make concessions in order to procure special favors to North

Carolina producers. The lumber companies in North Carolina were rich, influential, and powerful; and they demanded keeping on the old Dingley rate although the Republican House had cut it down one half. Simmons stood for the higher rate and for pretty much every other tariff rate desired by any considerable number of North Carolina beneficiaries.

My paper said North Carolina would be more benefited by a low tariff on everything than by the exorbitant high tariff which the Taft administration was writing; and that, if we asked for concessions on our lumber and cotton-seed oil, our people would have to pay millions in taxes on everything else in order that the lumber manufacturers, who were making plenty of money now, might become rich. The next month, *The News and Observer* reported, Simmons made a vigorous speech urging a reduction of the duty on window glass. North Carolina made no window glass but bought much from other States and Simmons' speech was approved in that connection, but he was inconsistent because he wanted low tariff on things not produced in North Carolina and a high tariff to benefit a few producers in his own State. After criticizing Senator Simmons for voting for high protection, contrary to the platform of the party, state and national, it quoted Mr. Bryan on the lumber tariff. He had pointed out that the Democratic Party was clearly committed to its repeal. Pence, our Washington correspondent, went into details as to Simmons' attitude and criticized him severely for taking the Republican position. A quotation from Bryan angered Simmons and he replied by saying, "Bryan always led to defeat. I always led to victory." With feeling, which showed that he was trying to bolster up his position, he declared, "I am satisfied with my vote," and added, "More than once we have had to repudiate Bryan's teachings and preachments to save the party from disaster and ruin." In its issue of June 13, *The News and Observer* devoted a whole page to showing that the position of Simmons was directly opposite to the whole record of Vance in the Senate. For a score of years Vance, along with Vest and Beck, were leaders of the tariff reform in the Senate in the fight against the Republican doctrine. It pointed out that Senator Simmons was voting against all Vance policies and principles, and taking his place with Aldrich and Republican leaders who used the tariff as an agency for enrichment of their favorites. It compared Simmons' remarks on Bryan on June 7, 1909, with what he had said about him in

October, 1908, when he had compared him with Jefferson, Vance, Washington, and Webster, and called him "the foremost private citizen of the world." It recalled that Simmons, in all his public utterances and actions, had been a strong supporter of free coinage of silver at sixteen to one, and had publicly stood with all Bryan's policies, except that Bryan did not favor subsidies, for which Simmons had voted, and declared, in connection with Simmons' reference to Bryan, "It is an unworthy fling at a gentleman with whom he has always declared he was in agreement on silver, tariff and other chief issues." The paper went on to prove, by their utterances, that Mr. Bryan, Mr. Tilden, Mr. Cleveland, and Mr. Parker all stood together as to tariff reform, whereas Mr. Simmons, in the particular schedules mentioned, stood with Dingley, Aldrich, and Penrose, and added, "If the Democratic position is right, Mr. Simmons is wrong; if the Republican position is right, Mr. Simmons is right."

My paper criticized those Democrats in the Senate who voted for tariff on iron as assisting the steel trust and praised Senator Overman because he voted as Vance had voted, against high tariff. Commenting on an interview with Simmons, *The News and Observer* said, "It seems to be lese majesty for an editor to express his disapproval of a Senator's repudiation of a party platform or to, by his own utterances, show up his inconsistency." Senator Simmons had said that Daniels knew well he was not referring to silver but to Bryan's letters to many North Carolina Democrats in 1898 urging a coalition of Democrats and Populists, in which Simmons had said, "If I had then yielded to Mr. Bryan, supplemented by the earnest entreaties of Mr. Daniels, and had accepted Butler's proposition of fusion, despite his record of having put the Negroes into office, there would have been no attack made upon that outrageous record; there could have been no white supremacy campaign, no constitutional amendment, and none of the other great measures which the amendment has made possible for those ambitious for the welfare and glory of North Carolina."

Senator Simmons, in that statement, also made known, for the first time, a great secret which had never before been disclosed to anybody in the State when he said, "The people of North Carolina know I did not favor Bryan's nomination in 1908." The North Carolina convention instructed its delegates to vote for Bryan and if Mr. Simmons was not in accord with it he managed to keep that secret within his own breast. Replying to Senator Simmons, *The News and Observer* said,

"Mr. Daniels remembers the contest in the convention as to whether or not it should extend the olive branch to Democrats who had gone out of the Party and joined the Populist Party, many of whom were disgusted with their new alliances and desired to return to the old roof, but he remembers very well that Simmons took absolutely no part in it, not even being present at the State Convention when the issue was brought out and decided. As a matter of fact, Simmons and Manly, who had long been law partners and intimates in politics, had favored fusion with the Populists in 1896 but Simmons was not on hand when the question was debated in 1898. Mr. Daniels recalled then the contest in the platform committee and the line-up. Those favoring tendering the olive branch to the Democrats who had joined the Populists were Governor W. W. Kitchin, Rufus A. Doughton, and Josephus Daniels. Those opposing it were Governor Jarvis, Claude Kitchin, Rudolph Duffy, J. A. Lockhart, Sr., Lee S. Overman and J. C. Martin."

I said Simmons was like the man who, after his wife had killed the bear, came out and said, "Old woman, aren't we brave?" I pointed out also that Simmons was the only North Carolina Congressman who voted for a tariff on iron ore. All the rest of the Democrats in Congress stood upon the Democratic platform and the time-honored Democratic principle and declared that Simmons' vote on the tariff issues made him and Penrose look alike.

When the Payne-Aldrich tariff bill became a law, Pence, the Washington correspondent of *The News and Observer,* pointed out that it was a sectional measure, which filled the coffers of New England at the expense of the rest of the country, and the paper called it "an iniquitous measure." That tariff bill, as my paper figured out, would increase the cost of cotton bagging $625,000 annually to farmers for the benefit of the bagging trust.

A little later Senator Simmons was referred to again under the heading, "Never Trust the Greeks," and reference was made to a speech of his vigorously accusing the Republican senators of breaking faith with the Democrats in the matter of tariff on cotton bagging and it pointed out that the Republicans got the turkey and all that the Democrats, like Simmons, got was the "turkey buzzard."

About that time H. E. C. Bryant, a Washington correspondent of the Charlotte *Observer,* anent the criticism I had made of Senator Simmons for his vote for high protective tariff, suggested that the editor of *The News and Observer* have a seat in the United States Senate. Whereupon *The News and Observer* said, "It is a great office, worthy of any man's ambition who desires high official station, but as the editor of *The News and Observer* has a higher and more useful place where he can better serve the public, he declines with thanks. Political ambition and journalistic usefulness are rarely combined. *The News and Observer,* however, is deep in politics and so is its editor."

When it celebrated its eighty-eighth volume, *The News and Observer* announced that it had twice as many subscribers as any other daily in North Carolina and contained an editorial on the duty of a party paper in which it said:

"A party paper that is run by the office-holders is contemptible. *The News and Observer* has criticized Aycock, Glenn, and when Governor Kitchin recommended to the Legislature a mere amendment to the anti-trust law instead of a vigorous and sweeping anti-trust law modelled after the Texas anti-trust act, this paper declared that he had made a mistake; when Senator Simmons voted with Roosevelt to approve the unconstitutional and lawless grabbing of Panama and again, when he voted for the ship subsidy, this paper did not hesitate to declare that he was taking the wrong course. When Representative Pou, whom this paper had before and since earnestly supported for Congress, voted for the subsidy of the Southern Railroad, this paper vigorously antagonized the improper use of public funds. When the last legislature, instead of passing a proper anti-trust law, passed some pink tea amendments to the innocuous act of 1907, this paper did not hesitate to criticize this failure to carry out the platform pledge to 'destroy private monopoly.' "

THE COUNTRY LIFE COMMISSION

In 1908 President Roosevelt appointed what was known as the Roosevelt Commission on Country Life, with the purpose of studying conditions in the United States as they affected country life. This commission—Walter H. Page was a member—came to Raleigh in November and, ignoring fundamental questions touching upon country life, as, for instance, a bad tenant system, the tremendous burden imposed upon the farmers by the credit system, the lack of health facilities and schools, and the employment of children in factories, telegraphed out to the country that the Commission had found out what was the trouble in North Carolina—the children had not enough red blood corpuscles and were suffering from hookworms. *The News and Observer* said this would deter immigrants from coming to the State and that the Commission ought to stay in North Carolina long enough to learn the true conditions and not to broadcast preconceived notions, if real and permanent good was to be accomplished. Governor Glenn, Secretary of Agriculture Graham, and Captain Samuel A. Ashe came out in a statement, saying that they hoped this Commission would make a real study of country life in North Carolina but that it had merely accepted the statements of those who believed that hookworm was the only trouble and paramounted it. The *Charlotte News* said the Commission was a body of fanatics. *The News and Observer* said, "North Carolina people are tired of being patronized and the Country Life Commission has left a distinctly bad taste in the mouths of our people." It also ridiculed the hop, skip, and jump method of investigation and denied that hookworm was the only thing the matter with country life in North Carolina. By criticism and ridicule the paper was too severe, partly prompted by a feeling of resentment at the undue stress laid on hookworm.

Although the paper at first unwisely ridiculed the Commission and said hookworm was not nearly so serious as reported, I afterwards had close touch with Dr. Charles W. Stiles, the hookworm expert, and learned from him the seriousness of the disease and coöperated with him and health officers in securing the legislation to lessen the ravages of it.

I GOT OFF ON THE WRONG FOOT

In November, 1909, commenting on a large gift by Rockefeller to fight hookworm and pellagra, Bishop Candler, of Georgia, said, "The southern people will not be taken in by Mr. Rockefeller's vermifuge fund and hookworm commission." He called Carnegie's and Rockefeller's gifts a bribe to control education. *The News and Observer* declared that Bishop Candler voiced the sentiment of many of the best men in the South and added, "Many of us in the South are getting tired of being exploited by advertisements that exaggerate conditions. They are most harmful." It said that, after widespread report that pellagra epidemic was destroying North Carolina, the Board of Health could find only six cases. "As to hookworm, this paper has accepted the statement of the wide-spread prevalence of that disease with many grains of allowance." It also said that Dr. Lewis and Dr. Rankin were probably right but it was suggested that the report of the Rockefeller Commission, to the effect that one person in twelve in the South was affected with hookworm, was a wild guess. "Let us not," my paper said, "canonize Standard Oil Rockefeller by putting laurels on his head because he seeks to buy the appreciation of the people whom he has been robbing for a quarter of a century."

Following these critical comments, *The News and Observer* expressed the need and urged a fight on hookworm, calling for a campaign for health. On July 28 *The News and Observer* devoted four columns to an illustrated story about hookworm and said that there had been some scepticism about this disease which was not justified, and investigation showed that it was so prevalent that every effort should be made to stamp it out. In October, when Rockefeller gave a million dollars to fight the hookworm, *The News and Observer* expressed its appreciation and rejoiced that the money was to be used under the direction of health officers to stamp out this disease.

When the tobacco season was opened that year *The News and Observer* pointed out that, unless a fire was built under it, the trust was determined to take the crop for nothing, and also showed how the trust was robbing the farmers and had reduced the price, since its formation, quoting prices from the Danville market, as follows:

BEFORE THE TRUST		AFTER FORMATION OF TRUST	
Crop for the year	Value	Crop for the year	Value
1869	$11.00	1893	$6.46
1874	20.45	1894	7.96
1879	11.39	1895	7.79
1884	13.54	1896	6.46
1888	13.22	1897	7.81
		1898	6.64
		1899	6.74
		1900	7.38

A Commission had been authorized by the Legislature of 1909 to construct a municipal building and auditorium for Raleigh. It purchased the lot fronting on Fayetteville, Davie, and Wilmington streets for $25,000. The commissioners had had in mind several places and had hesitated between placing it on that lot and on the one on which the Sir Walter Hotel was later built, which brought $100,000 when as president of the Sir Walter Hotel Company I purchased it a few years later. They preferred the lot purchased but never supposed the Grimes estate would sell it for a reasonable price, and when Mr. Grimes offered it for $25,000 the Commission was astounded and immediately closed the trade for fear the offer would be withdrawn. The building cost $96,000.

Upper left, Richard H. Battle, distinguished lawyer and legislator; Chairman of the Democratic State Committee in the Scales campaign. *Upper right,* Senator E. W. Sikes, scholar in politics and President of Clemson College. *Lower left,* Judge William R. Allen, member of the North Carolina Supreme Court. *Lower right,* William M. Russ, Mayor of Raleigh and Clerk of Wake County.

Upper left, J. Stanhope Wynne, pioneer industrial leader and reform Mayor of Raleigh. *Upper right,* Alexander Stronach, Police Justice of Raleigh, who set a high standard for law enforcement: later appointed as Judge of Court of Samoa. *Lower,* The Raleigh Auditorium, the dedication of which, in 1910, was considered "an epoch-making event."

XLVI

RING RULE DEFEATED

I N 1910 *The News and Observer* was in the hardest local political battle and victory in its history. The city of Raleigh had, for a long time, been in the control of a small clique of politicians, some of them allied with the saloons and other similar interests. The same was true of Wake County.

The city had a Chief of Police who was unfit, a Mayor, Iredell Johnson, of a prominent family, who was supported by the Raleigh Tammany. He made a personal appeal to a large number of good people because, outside of the policies of the Raleigh ring, he loved the city so much that he did many excellent things and had strong friends who felt that he was honest and patriotic in spite of some undesirable political associates. Johnson, who held the office for many years, was a druggist. In that hot campaign James H. Pou, in a speech scoring the Mayor, made a remark that set the whole city to laughing. He said, "Mr. Johnson's place does not even smell like a drug store."

Mayor Johnson was an official in Christ Church and many of his fellow church members gave him their support. However, his most vocal support came from what my paper called "the ring," in which J. Sherwood Upchurch was an effective member, popular in spite of his support of a "wide-open town," maybe because of it. During the hot campaign, witty Dr. Hubert Royster coined a saying widely quoted, "It will not be easy to defeat Johnson, seeing he has the support of Christ Church and Sherwood Up-Church." Some church members didn't like it.

At that time Wake County paid its officials by fees. There was no requirement for accounting of these fees. *The News and Observer,* two years before, had sought to secure legislation putting Wake County officials on salaries and requiring all fees to go into the county treasury. It had declared for this and other reforms but the particular reform was to take the Democratic politics of the county out of the hands of the ring, which, it declared, was unworthy and inefficient.

It had harbored at times some dishonest men and some of its members had been charged with election wrongs.

While the men who were opposed to the ring and its corrupt methods were planning to put an end to this regime in Wake County, *The News and Observer* leading the fight, the candidacy of my brother, Frank A. Daniels, of Goldsboro, for Superior Court Judge of the District, was announced in the Goldsboro papers. His lifelong friend and former partner, Governor Aycock, who was then living in Raleigh, and I had talked together about it and had advised him to become a candidate for this position. He was born with a judicial mind and his later long experience on the bench proved that he was ideally qualified to wear the ermine. He had served in the State Legislature which framed the constitutional suffrage amendment. The counties of Johnston and Wayne were insisting that he be a candidate for Judge. So was the majority of the bar of Wake County. All of his friends, particularly those in Goldsboro, when they saw that I was leading a movement in Wake County to try to turn the ring out of power, felt that I ought not to do so because it would jeopardize my brother's candidacy for the judgeship. They pointed out that the leaders of the ring had told them, if I would keep quiet in the county campaign, Wake County would be unanimous for my brother's nomination. Later, when the fight in Raleigh became very hot and my activity in trying to clean up the Wake County situation was solidifying the Wake ring against my brother, I made a statement about it in *The News and Observer* in its issue of May 12, in which I said I was waited upon at several separate times by a half dozen men close to the Wake County ring and told if I would take no part in the fight in Wake County politics, my brother, Frank, would get the full support of the county. To each and every such suggestion I replied that my brother ought not to be nominated unless he was the fittest man for the place and I could not discuss his candidacy for judge with anybody in connection with my duty as to Wake County matters—that I must do my duty as I saw it, independently of every other matter—and added, "Everybody knows that I could have had the support of the ring for my brother if I had played hands-off."

Before the Wake County fight started, a prominent Wake County ring politician said to a friend, *"The News and Observer* is bottled up now that we have only one primary." (Over my protest and the protest of the reform element, the county executive committee had combined the nomination of the county officers in the same primary with state officials.) "Josephus Daniels' brother is candidate for judge and he cannot take any part in Wake politics." Commenting on that, I said in *The News and Observer,* "They judge me by their own methods of trading and trafficking in public offices. So far as I know, no man of my family, from the time of Adam to the present generation, ever held public office." (I was mistaken about this for my mother's forbear, Sheriff Seabrook of Hyde County, held office, and maybe some others.) "They have lived without it. They will continue to live without it if I must stand in with the Wake ring as it is now constituted."

The way the opponents of the ring in the city administration in Raleigh had won a victory was by holding a mass meeting and nominating candidates who were not self-seekers but were willing to hold position for the good of the community. *The News and Observer* pointed out that the county could be redeemed only in the same way. We were out to defeat the ring, all in office, both the good and the bad. A mass meeting was called in Raleigh and every Democrat who wanted a change in county conditions was invited. *The News and Observer* pointed out that, under the ring rule in Wake County, the Democratic majority had been reduced from 2,500 to less than half of that; that the ring had made a trade with the Republican organization to have Republicans take part in Democratic primaries; and that it had been guilty of other election wrongs. Josiah W. Bailey, one of the signers for the mass meeting, whose fight in that campaign was one of the most magnificent and brilliant ever waged in the county, issued a ringing statement urging the Democrats to come to the meeting on April 30. "The Democratic Party," said he, "is all right. The machine is rotten." My paper pointed out how Wake County lost $32,000 by the fee system and called upon the county officers to make a statement showing how much they had received in fees each year they had held office. This infuriated the county officers, who declined to make any accounting.

On the day the mass meeting was to be held, the claquers and ward-heelers and tools of the ring, led by ring leaders, filled the court house, determined to break up the meeting. When an attempt was made to call the meeting to order, with J. W. Bailey on the judge's stand in the court house, as chairman, Armistead Jones, chairman of the Wake County Committee and head of the Wake ring, tried to take the chair from Bailey and preside over the meeting himself, after I had presented Bailey as chairman. He called Bailey a "God-damn scoundrel" and a "God-damn liar," and the ringsters kept up such a demonstration for the space of a half hour that there was bedlam in the court house.

After a while Armistead Jones sought to quiet his crowd, but part of them had been liquored up and could not be silenced. After vainly trying to get the crowd quiet enough to be heard, Bailey tried to induce them to be still so that Dr. R. H. Lewis could be called upon to take the chair and an orderly meeting held. The rioting continued. When it became clear that riot and bloodshed was imminent, Bailey and I called upon all the men who were against the Wake County ring to leave the court house and gather out in front where we could hold a meeting. We left the court house with the ring leaders cursing and threatening Bailey and me. We refused to lose our tempers. If either he or I had paid any attention to the insults flung at us, there would have been bloodshed.

We now decided to call upon all those people who were demanding defeat of the ring, which had now added to its crime against government, the crime of anarchy, to leave the court house and come under God's sunshine and hold a meeting in the open. A more enthusiastic and determined crowd I never saw, as I stood upon a stone in front of the court house and spoke to the people. I told them that the Barons of Runnymede, when battling for liberty, had nowhere to meet except under God Almighty's sky, but they extorted the Magna Charta from an autocrat. I declared that their descendants in Wake County, denied a quiet meeting in the temple of justice, would, in the open, write a new declaration of independence on the exact spot where Josiah Turner had hurled his anathemas at Kirk and his crowd when he returned from prison, where he had been sent for fighting against denial of the rights of the people. I was followed by Josiah Bailey, who made a speech that fired his hearers with the determination to win the victory.

When the forces against the Wake ring left the court house, the ring leader vainly undertook to hold a rump meeting. He ordered his henchmen in the court house to "come down in front and holler like Hell," and they obeyed and created an inferno. But it availed nothing. The men who had left the court house were courageous and militant. They passed resolutions against ring rule and called for a future meeting.

The ring crowd undertook to hold a meeting of their own. W. B. Jones nominated J. W. Bunn for chairman, but Bunn could not be found; so he named Rufus Dunn of St. Matthews Township. Armistead Jones then spoke, saying that Bailey had attempted to stifle the will of the people, that he had held office under Russell, and that *The News and Observer* had accused him of being a Republican. "I judge," said Jones, "that Mr. Bailey, manager of Locke Craig for Governor, paid money right here for votes." Speeches were made by Sherwood Upchurch, who said Bailey was a liar, and Daniel Hugh McLean, of Harnett County, addressed the meeting and urged the Democrats of Wake County to support Armistead Jones. J. N. Holding urged a primary, instead of a mass meeting or convention, and declared that Bailey wanted to form a ring of his own. Vigorous speeches were made by Bart M. Gatling and W. B. Jones along the same line, but it was recognized as a rump meeting and very few men from the county took part in it. Next day *The News and Observer* had three-column headlines as follows:

"Whom The Gods Would Destroy They First Make Mad. Tirade of Abuse Heaped Upon The Men Fighting To Give Wake Democracy An Opportunity For A Full, Free And Fair Primary and A Square Deal. Trick Resolution to Fight Salary Plan.

"In the rump convention the machine raves and rants against Bailey and Daniels, personal abuse being the strong card while there is a sop thrown to the voters in a resolution passed which requires the executive committee to arrange for a vote on the question of salaries or no salary for county officers."

Next Bailey replied to the attack upon him and declared the henchmen of the machine would curse anybody; that it was a rule-or-ruin machine. *The News and Observer* quoted Nick DeBoy, a prominent ring politician, as saying, "Yes, I will buy votes and steal them too. I will buy all I can get and what I can't get I will steal." Some days afterward Nick admitted he said this but said he was joking. That meeting, which came near being a riot and ended out of doors, called for a mass meeting on May 14 to nominate candidates, and its motto was, "Crush the machine; purify the Democratic Party, and guarantee economical government." My paper denounced the hiring of men to break up the mass meeting in Raleigh and said it was not only an outrage but a crime that should be punished. This mass meeting to nominate a ticket was composed of the most determined men I ever saw. The ticket was headed by E. W. Sikes, a Wake Forest college professor, for Senator, E. R. Pace and Richard Battle, of Raleigh, and John T. Judd, of Buckhorn, for House of Representatives. The whole ticket was composed of men of high standing and character. I called the meeting to order and ex-Senator Fabius Whitaker was made temporary chairman. Resolutions, indicting the Wake County ring for lording it over the people and for their bad government and for rough-shod methods, and calling for a salary system to replace the fee system, and no reëlection except for two terms were adopted.

Later the ring faction men nominated their ticket, which was headed by W. B. Jones for the Senate and J. H. Keith, John W. Hinsdale, and George Mitchener for the House. The ring thought to strengthen themselves by approving the salary system and announced: "All the above-named candidates favor putting the county officers on salaries and they favor local self-government." The reformers had compelled them to advocate salaries for the county officers but it fooled nobody.

A tower of strength for the ticket was obtained when the Honorable Richard H. Battle accepted the nomination for the House. He was dean of the Raleigh bar, a man of the purest personal character, who had won the confidence of the people of the county and State by his forthright honesty and clean life. He was then growing old but his righteous wrath at seeing the county in the hands of an underworld machine caused him to enter the campaign with the enthusiasm of a youth.

The anti-ring people reached high-water mark in a great mass meeting in Raleigh on June 7 in the Wake County court house. It was presided over by ex-Mayor Alf. A. Thompson, and speeches were made by Dr. E. W. Sikes, the Honorable Richard H. Battle, and Edward R. Pace, candidates for the Legislature. Mr. Battle's speech was moderate in tone but shot through with an appeal for his county to be redeemed from the control of men who had brought its administration into disrepute. The speech by Dr. E. W. Sikes aroused the militant Democracy. It had great sincerity, boldness, and ability. He had never taken active part in politics and responded to the draft to run only because he felt that in a crisis of this kind no man could decline to try to clean up the rottenness in politics. His nomination was a stroke of genius for the anti-ring people, and Otho and W. W. Holding, of Wake Forest, were responsible for it. Wake Forest Township had long been a stronghold of the ring crowd and Sikes, and others in the faculty, had felt that it was a reflection on the college that their township should side with the rotten Raleigh ring, which was always for saloons and for whiskey and never did anything to close up the houses of ill fame. Wherever Dr. Sikes spoke in the campaign, the people became enthusiastic. He had no scholastic aloofness, but delivered blows with good humor. The court house was jammed when he captured the people with his indictment of the Wake County ring. I recall that he said the only parallel to the situation in Wake County which he had found in all his reading was in some lines that certain religionists were said to have adopted in an early century, which ran like this:

> "We are the sweet selected few.
> May all the rest be damned!
> There's room enough in hell for you,
> We won't have Heaven crammed."

These lines were applied so fittingly to show how the leaders of the ring, who took all the offices for themselves or their henchmen and denied participation in government to people who would not bow down to them, that it was a palpable hit. They constituted the campaign rallying slogan.

Every day new slanders were started. The ringsters even spread the report that Dr. Sikes would not support the Democratic State ticket if nominated and declared that he was trying to turn every man out of the Baptist Church who would not vote for prohibition. *The News and Observer* quoted a statement made by James H. Pou in the election when the ring was defeated in Raleigh, to the effect that "It is no longer a question of who will be elected, but who is going to the penitentiary."

A few days before the election the paper said to the people fighting the ring in the county, "You have won the victory against the ring. First, do not let Republicans vote. Second, see that the election is honest and the count fair," and added, "This is not hearsay. It is known that certain of the ring and certain Republican bosses are conspiring to steal the fruits of victory." Toward the end of the campaign W. C. Monroe, a leading member of the Goldsboro bar, called on W. B. Jones to apologize for his reflections on Frank A. Daniels, candidate for Superior Court Judge, as printed in the Raleigh *Times*. Captain Nathan O'Berry also protested against Jones' attack in which Jones had said:

"The only real issue is whether Frank Daniels should be judge of this district. Mr. Daniels (Josephus) is willing to sacrifice the Democratic Party in the county and in the state to elect his brother. Some months ago, when Mr. Frank Daniels first announced his candidacy for the judgeship, several of us said we did not want him because we did not want to place the judiciary in the hands of *The News and Observer*."

O'Berry said everybody knew that Judge Daniels, as a Judge, would not follow the directions of anybody and *The News and Observer* would have no influence whatever with him, if it should attempt it, when it came to presiding on the bench. *The News and Observer* carried a political advertisement advocating the nomination of Frank A. Daniels for judge and signed by twenty-nine lawyers, including most of the leading members of the bar at Raleigh, some of whom were supporting the ring local ticket.

During the campaign the Wake ring issued a newspaper called *The State Democrat* and also had the support of the Raleigh *Times,* but that paper did not put as much bitterness into the denunciation as the ring desired, and so they printed their own paper. At that time *The News and Observer* printed in red ink most of its political news and appeals to turn out the ring. This was something new. The paper was distributed all over the county and the use of red ink emphasized the issues. Throughout the county, when the ring ticket would hold their meetings, their chief denunciation was of "that poke-berry sheet called *The News and Observer*."

The election was closely contested. The ring ticket had the majority in Raleigh but lost in every township in Wake except three. Sykes, the candidate for the Senate, received a majority of nearly 400 over W. B. Jones. The smallest majority was for Millard Mial over W. M. Russ, Clerk of the Court. Russ had been Mayor of Raleigh and was a very efficient clerk of the court. He was the best story-teller in Wake County and had great popularity. Most of the people had predicted he would win, but the determination of the people to have a clean-sweep was so great that nobody could stand against it. In the county executive committee the anti-ring people elected 22 and the ring 14 and the anti-ring had 100 out of 160 delegates to the county convention. The vote in the primary was the largest that had ever been cast and, on the morning after the election, *The News and Observer,* in flaming headlines of red ink across the page said, "The Embattled Farmers Saved the Day." Raleigh had given the majority to the ring ticket but the country people had risen up and asserted their power.

In the contest for Superior Court Judge, J. C. Clifford of Harnett County was a candidate against my brother, Frank A. Daniels. The vote in Wake County was: for Daniels, 2,551; for Clifford, 2,153. Mr. Clifford, as a young man, had taught school in eastern Wake and was very highly esteemed; he was a lawyer of ability and character and if he had not been endorsed by the Wake County ring he would have carried a larger vote in that section of the county. As a matter of fact, the vote in the county for Judge was, except for two or three hundred people who voted on personal grounds, a vote in which Daniels got all the anti-ring vote and Clifford the ring vote. Clifford carried his home county of Harnett and nearly half of Wake, but as Daniels carried more than half of Wake and all of Johnston and Wayne, when the convention met to nominate a judge, Mr. Clifford directed his friends to withdraw his name and Daniels was nominated unanimously.

Next to the interest in the Wake County contest and in the Superior Court judgeship, there was a very close contest between Associate Justice J. S. Manning for renomination and William R. Allen for nomination as Associate Justice. Mr. Manning had been the manager of Governor Kitchin, when he was nominated for Governor in 1908 and he entered the campaign with the natural expectation of receiving the nomination. But William R. Allen, of Wayne, had made a fine reputation as Superior Court Judge and he entered the contest for the position against Manning. Both of them had won high place at the bar, both had been Superior Court Judges and Manning's career on the bench had been entirely honorable and acceptable. In this contest Judge Manning had the active and very effective and influential support of Governor Kitchin and the State administration, whereas Judge Allen had the hearty and active support of Senator Simmons and what was known as the Simmons machine and of

Governor Aycock and his friends. I supported Judge Allen. We had been friends from boyhood and had such intimate relations that I could not do otherwise, although my relations with Judge Manning and my great friendship for his distinguished father made me enter the contest with reluctance. The vote in Wake County was so close that Manning received its votes in the State convention in the ratio of 14,378 and Allen 13,622. Bailey and I were elected delegates to the State convention and were the leaders of the anti-ring crowd. It had been a battle royal in Wake County. I never saw anything in all politics, during my life, which approached the bitterness of that contest.

The old-time habit of electing strong and independent men as aldermen in the city of Raleigh had fallen into disuse under ring rule and the men chosen had, most often, been elected on tickets gotten up by city officials and politicians with an axe to grind, and the Mayor was too often not really a leader, but had followed. In fact, if he had not followed, he could not have been elected. The city administration ordered a snap registration and *The News and Observer* said it was "pull, pie and snap." As a result of these efforts by the city administration a big indignation meeting was held in Raleigh. A discrepancy of $1,700 was found in the city official records, the books were mutilated, and *The News and Observer* compelled the authorities to offer a reward to discover who had perpetrated this mutilation. While the indignation of the people was aroused, Chief of Police Mullins was suspended and it was said this was an attempt to make him the goat and bamboozle the people. Raleigh has rarely been so stirred.

J. Stanhope Wynne, a practical business man, who had been the organizer of the first cotton mill in Raleigh, and the first savings bank, and who belonged to a large family of influential connections, was nominated for Mayor on the reform ticket and defeated James I. Johnson, then Mayor, by a vote of 1,303 to 693. This election was followed by a great jubilee meeting of the people.

The election of a new city government, with Wynne as Mayor and Alexander Stranach as Police Justice, was followed by the election of J. P. Stell as Chief of Police and a vigorous determination to clean up what *The News and Observer* called "the hell holes" of Raleigh. Under the preceding administration the red light district of Raleigh ran wide open. Instead of policemen obeying the law, a few of them were really the go-betweens of the houses of ill-fame and their patrons. When an honest policeman would do his duty and pull those in disorderly houses, the keepers never suffered any real penalty. An insignificant fine or an order to leave town was usually the penalty, and the order to leave town was not enforced—the scarlet women who left one night were usually back on the following night. That system of licensing houses of ill-fame was drastically changed. *The News and Observer* said of a denizen of East Raleigh, "She was a brunette in Raleigh. She is now a peroxide blonde." She was given eighteen months for operating a bawdy house. That shocked the underworld. A surprised resident of East Raleigh came up to police court and said to Judge Alexander Stronach, "Shore thing, this administration ain't no friend of East Raleigh." And it wasn't. It proved, by means of an honest, able, and diligent Police Justice and by policemen who really wanted to enforce the law, that the red light district could be cleaned up. And it was cleaned up, but it was not a very popular move for the underworld, and the politicians who make money by exploiting vice used every possible means to injure the city administration. As often happens, some people who had put the reform administration in office wanted special favors, and when they were not granted the favor-seekers turned upon the honest officials, and the day came when the reform administration went out of office. It went out demonstrating what could be done with a courageous Police Justice and a first class Chief of Police and his assistants who made raids on East Raleigh arresting both white and colored prostitutes and, backed by *The News and Observer,* declared that raids should not stop until Raleigh was cleaned up, as it was. Alexander Stronach was a member of a prominent and public-spirited Raleigh family, the first Stronach having come to North Carolina to help build the new State Capitol. His mother was a member of the distinguished Washington family which gave America its first President.

Later, when I was in Washington as Secretary of the Navy, and appointed, as Federal Judge in Samoa, Alexander Stronach, who, as Police Justice, had given heavy sentences against underworld denizens, one of the Raleigh politicians who had fattened on alliances with crime, sent me word that he and his crowd in Raleigh were very grateful to me for making the appointment; that they understood Samoa was three hundred thousand miles from Raleigh and they hoped it was three million miles so that Stronach could not return.

IMMORAL PLAY BANNED

One of the big sensations in Raleigh in 1910 was the action of Mayor Wynne in preventing the showing of the "Girl From Rector's." In its issue of February 15 *The News and Observer* quoted from newspapers in other States that its immoral atmosphere was such that respectable people ought not to see it, though it was said to be artistically and mechanically good. Mayor Wynne declared that it was a grossly immoral play and would not be permitted to show in Raleigh. The managers of the show and their partisans determined they would present it anyhow. Mayor Wynne ordered the police to stop it. The managers attempted to get an order restraining the Mayor from carrying into effect his order that the performance should not take place in Raleigh. At the time fixed for the performance, the street in front of the Academy of Music was crowded with people ready to go in. It seemed that the denunciation of the show, the proof that it was an immoral performance, made people all the more anxious to see it. Certainly they were there in great crowds. Some of the employees, who refused to turn over the keys of the Academy, were arrested and the performance did not take place. The crowd, bent on seeing the performance, jeered at the police, but the Mayor stood firm. The next day the show was advertised to play in Durham and arrangements were made for a special train to take the Raleigh people to see it, but the Durham authorities, having taken note of what had happened in Raleigh, demanded a rehearsal to determine whether the show was immoral and when they had seen it they refused permission for its appearance and no special train went to Durham. The aftermath is a sad commentary upon what happens to a public man who does his duty. Mayor Wynne was a man of large means. He had acted in response to the demands of many good people in Raleigh, and to the publication in *The News and Observer* of the indecency of the show and its appeal to the Mayor not to permit Raleigh to be debauched by its performance. But suit was brought against him personally, and he was compelled to employ attorneys and to fight it out in the courts. It ran a long time and gave him great trouble, but the experience of the Mayor, carrying out what he thought was his duty, was so disheartening that rotten shows have performed in Raleigh very often since, and no Mayor, even if he desired to do so, wished to invite the persecution, litigation and expense which fell to the lot of Mayor Wynne. The city ought to have defended the suit and paid the expenses.

OPENING THE CITY AUDITORIUM

In October *The News and Observer* devoted a section, headed by an eight-column red ink spread, to the week of celebration of the opening of the Raleigh Auditorium, which was the great local achievement of the decade. It contained pictures of the members of the commission which built it and would seat 3,000 people. The paper called the dedication of the auditorium "an epoch-making event," as indeed it was. The genesis of the building of the auditorium is rather interesting. The lack of a hall in Raleigh large enough to accommodate large gatherings had caused the Democratic State Conventions to be held in Greensboro and Charlotte, and the Senate passed a bill, on its second reading, to move the capital to Greensboro. It was never pressed further than the second reading, but it terrorized Raleigh, which was the purpose of the introducer. Having lost the conventions which Raleigh regarded itself as being exclusively entitled to, the suggestion of moving the capital awakened the citizens, who had been quite content to let Raleigh move along slowly and had been unwilling to act until their primacy as a political and convention city was threatened. A hurried meeting was held by prominent citizens and city officials, and it was agreed that they would ask the Legislature to pass an act authorizing the city government to build a city hall with an auditorium annex. As a matter of fact, there was no particular desire or interest for a city hall, but the lawyers held that bonds could not be issued for any city purpose except for a necessary purpose. The city hall, of course, would come under this heading, whereas an auditorium would not. The bill was drafted to meet this legal situation. Ordinarily, a bill to issue bonds in Raleigh would have caused a riotous mass meeting, but the people were too fearful that Raleigh would shrink into a small town, since it had not kept pace with other cities industrially, to offer any obstacles. Before selling the bonds, the matter was presented to the Supreme Court on a case agreed, and the Court held that the bonds were legal. When Raleigh secured the legislation, which should have been called an "Act to Ease the Mind of Raleigh as to the Location of the State

Capital," they naturally celebrated its consummation with a whole week of enthusiasm.

BUTLER, BOOZE, BOODLE, AND BONDS

During the campaign of 1910 Marion Butler came to the front as the leading speaker and the virtual manager of the Republican Party. His reappearance was the signal for *The News and Observer* to raise the issue that, in view of his leadership and dominance, a Republican victory would be followed by an attempt to compel the State of North Carolina to pay the fraudulent Reconstruction bonds. Day after day it printed the story of how the suit against North Carolina by South Dakota began, how it was hatched up in the office of Governor Russell and how Butler's intimacy with Senator Pettigrew gave him the opportunity to induce Pettigrew to have the Legislature of South Dakota accept some of these bonds and bring suit against North Carolina. The paper said that any public officer who would, for profit or otherwise, contrive to secure the bringing of a suit against the State, was guilty of moral treason. It declared that when State Treasurer Worth carried the bonds to Russell, the Governor's duty was to serve the State and the taxpayers. Instead of doing so, Russell conspired with Butler to use the bonds coming into the hands of the State Treasurer and others as the basis of a suit which might cost the State millions of dollars. It charged that the purpose of Butler and Russell in bringing this South Dakota suit was to pave the way to compel the payment of all the repudiated bonds; that this was but the entering wedge. It copied advertisements in the New York papers which, it claimed, showed that this was their purpose. It daily charged them with moral treason.

From mountain to sea, wherever Butler went, or wherever Russell sought to send a message, or any other Republican undertook to speak, they had to be on the defensive about the repudiated bonds. Indeed the issue was pressed to the front so strongly by my paper that the Republican candidates had to spend much of their time denying that they had any connection with these bonds. Butler foamed at the mouth and denied that he had any connection with the repudiated bonds; he and Russell said they appeared only in the South Dakota suit, and Russell did not appear in the case until after his term of Governor expired. All the same *The News and Observer* and Democratic speakers charged that the thing was hatched while Russell was

Governor and Butler was Senator; that they betrayed the State while they were in its employ; and that men who would be guilty of such breach of faith toward the taxpayers showed they were guilty of treachery. Butler had started out in the campaign with quite a flourish and seemed to be coming back, but his connection with Pettigrew and the bonds not only destroyed him in that campaign but showed the Republicans that any leading part he should play in politics would prevent discussion of any issue, because Butler and bonds were so connected in the popular mind that any speech from him brought back the live discussion of the heated period of Reconstruction and also the evil days of the Russell administration. It is no wonder that, though Butler had hated *The News and Observer* before, from that campaign on, whenever he spoke of it in any public utterance he showed his virulence and bitterness, and the paper was not less vigorous in denunciation of the Sampson ex-Senator. It said, repeatedly, that the Republican slogan in North Carolina was four Bs— Butler, Booze, Boodle, and Bonds. A perusal of the files of *The News and Observer* would show that this slogan and denunciation were not only in the editorial columns but also in the poke-berry—that is, in red ink on the first page. Between the excoriation of Butler and the Wake County ring, the paper was red-headed all during that summer and fall. On one occasion the paper stated, "Marion Butler is a Judas Iscariot, who betrayed his State for thirty pieces of silver and then did not have the decency to go out and hang himself." It also said, near the close of that campaign, "North Carolinians are not apt to forget that it was Butlerism that gave to the State Negro school committeemen with the authority to pass on the claims of young white women as school teachers. If Butlerism should, by any misfortune, prevail in the State again, this would come to pass as one of the evils to be met."

The News and Observer printed a copy of an advertisement in The New York *Evening Post* of April 1, 1905, asking owners to deposit all repudiated bonds with them for collection and claiming credit for having won the South Dakota suit against North Carolina. The advertisement was signed, "W. N. Coler and Company, R. F. Pettigrew, D. L. Russell, and Marion Butler." This was printed in refutation of Butler's statement denying any connection with these bonds. *The News and Observer* compared Butler with Albion Tourgee, who was the brains of the Republican Reconstruction era.

After he learned that he was trying to make brick without straw in North Carolina, Tourgee left the State and, as he left, he delivered this defi, "I go, but the day will come when North Carolina will be forced to pay the bonds that are now being repudiated." Comparing Butler with Tourgee, the paper said, "Tourgee was a carpet-bagger with brains, who made no concealment of his views; Butler is a home-born product who has, step by step, dug his own grave and has put himself beyond the pale—all the time with satanic hypocrisy, denying what he knew he had been doing."

In addition to the advertisement of the New York *Evening Post,* Thomas Pence, the Washington correspondent of my paper, sent a story that Butler and his crowd carried big advertisements in three New York newspapers in October, 1905, asking for repudiated bonds, using the New York *Sun* and the *Times,* as well as the *Post,* and said the Butler crowd used printer's ink liberally to get ahead of a rival syndicate. He went on to prove that not only had Butler and Pettigrew been interested in trying to make North Carolina pay the fraudulent bonds but that they were in partnership in one of the biggest Indian cases before the Court of Claims, involving lands valued tentatively at a half million dollars and for that reason no credence would be given to Pettigrew's attempt to secure an alibi for Butler in the bond case.

At Christmas of 1910 the North Carolina Democrats gave me a silver service in appreciation of the course taken by *The News and Observer* in the campaign. It was presented by Charles B. Aycock in behalf of the donors, in an address expressing the State's high appreciation of the leadership of *The News and Observer* and its editor in championing Democratic principles and in giving leadership in winning Democratic victories. This inscription was engraved on the service:

JOSEPHUS DANIELS

FROM

FRIENDS AND FELLOW DEMOCRATS

OF NORTH CAROLINA

IN RECOGNITION OF HIS LOYAL,

COURAGEOUS AND EMINENT SERVICES TO

HIS PARTY AND HIS STATE

DECEMBER 25TH, 1910

Upper left, W. W. Fuller, Chief Counsel of the American Tobacco Company and able lawyer. *Upper right,* R. J. Reynolds, merchant prince, who made a great success in manufacturing Camel cigarettes. *Lower left,* T. W. Bickett, Attorney General from 1909 to 1916; author of the Bickett Bill, providing for the care of the State's unfortunate: later, North Carolina's war Governor. *Lower right,* Dr. George M. Cooper, Assistant State Superintendent of Public Health, who wrote a winning essay on *The News and Observer.*

Left, Rt. Rev. Joseph Blount Cheshire, Episcopal Bishop who led the fight against loose divorce laws. *Right,* Rt. Rev. Robert Strange, Bishop of the Diocese of Eastern North Carolina, who was elected largely through the support of Democratic laymen.

XLVII

CONSERVATIVE LEGISLATION AND SIMMONS
ON THE TARIFF

THE LEGISLATURE of 1911 was organized with Mecklenburg County in the saddle. H. N. Pharr, of Mecklenburg, was elected president pro tem of the Senate, and W. C. Dowd was chosen Speaker of the House. Senator Pharr had served several terms in the Senate and was a lawyer of ability and of fine legislative knowledge. If he had not been an ultra-conservative, both from instinct and from nature, to such an extent that pleas for progressive legislation made little impress with him, he would have been nominated the next year as Lieutenant Governor. He was the best type of true North Carolina conservative—honorable, clean, high-minded—who had about him no "divine dissatisfaction," which is the essential for leadership. Carey Dowd, who was elected Speaker, had been a candidate for that office at the previous session. He had long been one of my closest friends. As editor of the Charlotte *News* he had led the fight in Mecklenburg County for prohibition, for a legalized primary, and for Bryan, and we had been real yoke-fellows in many a contest. However, in 1909, when the supreme issue was the matter of regulation of freight and passenger railroad rates, Mr. Dowd was not in harmony with the prevailing view and it was a matter of personal distress that my convictions compelled me, at that time, to support Edward J. Justice for Speaker of the House, and he defeated Dowd. Personally, Dowd and I were intimate. My intimacy with Justice was born of common convictions along the line of progressive Democracy and war upon privilege to corporations. Like Pharr, Dowd was a high type man and early had much of the crusading spirit. It was a great delight to me to see his ambition realized when, this year, he became Speaker. He believed then, as did all his friends, that it was a stepping-stone to his going to Congress from the Mecklenburg district. Under the leadership of these two fine conservatives—Dowd was not then a militant progressive—the Legislature moved along without any such hard fights as were witnessed under the leadership of Justice in a previous session.

In the previous Legislature Governor Kitchin had disappointed his most ardent friends in not taking the lead for an anti-trust bill with teeth in it and an attempt was made in this Legislature to secure the passage of such an act. An act to put an end to trust rule in North Carolina was introduced by Mr. Turlington, of Iredell, and was warmly supported. Attorney General Bickett said that no man in good conscience could oppose the Turlington bill. In his message to the General Assembly Governor Kitchin advocated anti-trust legislation but he had lost his chance to be the anti-trust leader when he failed to become, as his supporters had expected him to do, the militant champion of such a bill in the previous General Assembly.

When E. J. Justice came to Raleigh to urge a stronger law in 1911, he declared that the "present anti-trust law is a game of bunco." He said it was enacted to do nothing, and that the Tobacco Trust exerted too much influence in North Carolina to get the proper kind of legislation. He was right. An excellent anti-trust bill was strongly supported, but the Senate, as usual, was unwilling to take the burden for outright killing it and adopted a substitute which *The News and Observer* said, "Coincides with the wishes of the trust." However, the first bill passed the House by a vote of 95 to 6, every Democrat in the House voting for it. *The News and Observer* said, "The anti-trust bill was killed by the influence of the American Tobacco Company" and added, "The substitute passed would not be known even by its own daddy. The Turlington Anti-Trust Act is reduced to a spineless, boneless, gelatinous, viscous affair by the Senate Judiciary Committee."

Another attempt was made to secure fair legislation to put an end to the long hours for women in industry and the employment of young children in the cotton mills, which *The News and Observer* had long advocated. This legislation brought to Raleigh a big lobby of mill men. The bill, introduced by Representative Richard H. Battle, of Wake, reduced the hours from 66 to 60 a week and forbade the employment of children in cotton mills. At one time a number of the prominent cotton mill men expressed their willingness to accept this very mild measure and I talked with them and with Mr. Battle, as well as with the opponents of the measure, and we thought the bill would go through without any trouble. In this we were very much mistaken. The mill men, then, as in former days, after certain leaders had agreed to the bill, mobilized to defeat it, those who had agreed to it failing to come to Raleigh and its opponents coming in full force. "In this twentieth century," said *The News and Observer,* "no factory should keep people steadily at work more than sixty hours a week." Think of it! In 1911 a 60-hour-a-week law was regarded as progress and of course the 60-hour-a-week reduction and elimination of the labor of young children was a progressive step, but even so, most of the cotton mill men opposed that vigorously, one of the outstanding incidents of the session being, however, that General Julian S. Carr who, with his sons, was among the biggest employers of labor in the cotton mills, made the best speech of the session in favor of child labor laws and declared that the State could not defend working people sixty-six hours in the mills.

I coöperated in an earnest attempt to secure the passage of an honest, legalized primary law. It passed the Senate but, when it got over to the House, the machine politicians, who feared it would take away their power, mobilized to defeat it. As if ashamed of its fine record in passing a good anti-trust law, the House proceeded to kill the State-wide primary law. The fine Italian hand of what was called the "Simmons machine," led by A. D. Watts, of Iredell, was responsible for its defeat.

In the defeat of the primary law, the Republicans lined up solidly against it, doing practically the same with the anti-trust law. They had an opportunity, if they had not been under the domination of the trusts, as were so many Democrats, to make a record that would have done something to decrease the contempt which the people had for that party in North Carolina. Every time the Democrats did wrong, the Republicans joined hands with them, and every time the Democrats did right, the Republicans were sure to take the opposite side; and yet, there were always a few Republicans in the House who had the vision to see that there was no chance for their party in North Carolina except by getting on the people's side. When the primary law was defeated, *The News and Observer* said, "The reform is only deferred. The man, in this day of progressive measures, who opposes the election of Senators by vote of the people and a legalized state and county primary might as well fight against the stars in their course."

Summing up the session, my paper said that it was the soberest body ever seen in Raleigh but that sobriety did not insure progressive legislation. It also pointed out that it had defeated the Torrens system, the state primary, the Boyden-Sikes Road Law, child labor bills, care of forestry and mines, amendments to the State constitution, reform in criminal cases in our courts, improvements in court systems, putting public service corporations under the Corporation Commission, effective measures ending monopoly and insurance reforms. This was a pretty damning list of failures of that Legislature and a severe indictment of the "sleeping sickness" or acquiescence in ancient wrongs by the powers that be. Governor Kitchin, Speaker Dowd, and Senator Pharr had lost their opportunity. If these three men had shown the same spirit of fight and progress which Kitchin had always shown in Congress and which had characterized Dowd's paper in the old prohibition and Bryan contests, a different chapter might have been written. On the other hand, *The News and Observer* congratulated the General Assembly that much progressive local legislation had been enacted; that it had added $175,000 to the school fund; had substantially increased the appropriations to the State institutions of learning and eleemosynary institutions. The spirit to do very much more for education was present, but the legislators always held back because of the lack of revenue. They had not yet understood that it was always possible to strike the rock of income tax so that revenues would gush forth to meet these needs; and, although it was proposed by *The News and Observer* and Legislator Justice, the control of the Legislature by the mill men and those who were perfectly content to see things move along as they were, prevented any real action. After the Legislature adjourned, my paper printed this editorial in the form of an advertisement:

"WANTED, More Scholars in Politics Like Governor Wilson and Dr. Sikes (Senator from Wake) and less of the politicians whose only thought is to keep themselves and their supporters in office."

The Honorable Richard H. Battle, who had been elected in Wake County on a platform calling for a change from the fee system to a salary system for county officers, secured the passage of his measure but only after the old ring politicians of Wake County had secured considerable following in the legislature, and it looked, at one time, as if he and his associates would fail. Some of the more disreputable of the Wake County ring crowd would have stopped at nothing and did not stop at theft. On March 1, shortly before the session ended, friends of the ring having secured postponement of the bill, Mr. Battle, being unable to cope with them, suddenly found, when he wished to call the bill up, that it could not be found. Somebody had stolen it. *The News and Observer,* on the following day, had a three column front page box:

"Yesterday the Wake County Salary Bill disappeared from the House. The thief who sneaked it from the files and made way with it evidently thought such act would destroy the bill and prevent the redemption of the pledges made to the people by Wake's Senator and Representatives to put the county officers on salaries.

"One hundred dollars reward will be paid for information that will lead to the conviction of the person committing the crime."

The news story said:

"The mysterious disappearance of the Wake Salary Bill would have caused trouble in preparing a new one, but the Senate Bill reached the House in time and the measure has passed all readings, thus thwarting the plan to defeat it."

SIMMONS, LORIMER, AND THE LUMBER TRUST

About the time Woodrow Wilson was making his great fight for political righteousness by dethroning the bosses in New Jersey, there was being waged in the United States Senate a fight to unseat Lorimer, the Republican Senator from Illinois, who was charged with having obtained his seat by purchase. Certainly very much money had been spent for him and by him to secure his election to the Senate; and the Progressive Republicans of the West, who were to leave the Republican Party the next year, and the bulk of the Democrats, were determined to unseat Lorimer and make an example of the corrupt purchase of senatorial seats. It was a hard-fought battle. When the vote was taken, to the astonishment of North Carolina, Senator Simmons voted for the seating of Lorimer. Overman voted against it. During the contest *The News and Observer* declared that Lorimer should be driven out of the Senate in disgrace.

"Senator Simmons," said my paper, "votes with the Lorimer people. Overman lines up with those who will vote to put Lorimer out of the Senate." Later it said, "Overman vote kicks him out. Simmons says he will vote for Lorimer, whether it affects his political support or not. 'I intend,' he said, 'to try to preserve my integrity of conscience'." Lorimer held his seat, the vote being 46 to 40, two anti-Lorimer men being absent. *The News and Observer* said "The Senator who voted to put a white mark on Lorimer at the same time put a black mark on himself." This offended Senator Simmons. The matter was discussed throughout the country, and the allegation was made that the lumber trusts in the country were behind Lorimer and that Senator Simmons had been voting with the lumber people for a high tariff on lumber against the Democratic program for low tariff. Some of the Northern people charged that the influence of the lumber trust had played an important part in securing the vote of Senator Simmons for Lorimer. The resentment of the seating of Lorimer was great all over the country. Soon Senator Simmons felt the condemnation of his vote at home, for *The News and Observer* and other papers did not hesitate to voice their severe criticism. When the matter came up later in the Senate, Senator Simmons reversed himself and voted against Lorimer. I had criticized his vote for Lorimer and commended his getting on the right side. He claimed that he changed his vote because the issue was different. I contested his statement and believed the severe criticism of his Lorimer vote caused the shift.

During the debate on the Fordney Tariff act there was controversy over Senator Simmons' vote on the schedules of the Payne-Aldrich Tariff bill. It began with a fiery speech on the tariff by the Honorable Claude Kitchin, later to be chairman of the Ways and Means Committee.

In July *The News and Observer* had an article, based on Tom Pence's correspondence, headed,

"Simmons Gets Hot Grilling In Senate. His Colleagues Declare His Attitude on Tariff Is Not Democratic. Warm Colloquy Was Feature of Speech Against Reciprocity. Simmons Says Claude Kitchin's Recent Speech In The House Against Him Was Made To Further The Candidacy of Simmons' Competitors."

In the controversy in the Senate, Senators Kern, Reed, Stone and John Sharpe Williams were severe in criticism of Simmons' speech and his votes. Two days after the publication Simmons, in a letter to the paper, claimed Pence's story of the colloquy was not fair. Pence replied, saying, "Simmons sent out a full story of his speech, full of praise of himself but I could not conscientiously use it." Defending his position, Simmons said State Chairman Eller had sent out a statement making a pledge to the North Carolina lumber men which qualified the national Democratic platform declaration. Eller replied that if such circular was sent out it was without his authority; that it was Simmons and A. J. Maxwell (who was in the lumber business), who prepared and issued the circular to lumber men. *The News and Observer* said that no circulars, no chairman, or no senators could change the pledge in the national platform. With reference to Mr. Eller's statement the paper said, editorially,

"Mr. Eller's statement does not leave a peg upon which Senator Simmons can stand in his contention that the Democratic Chairman of North Carolina was untrue to the Democratic pledge.

"Senator Simmons not only voted wrong, but made a protection speech in favor of the tariff on lumber as bad a protection speech as Quay made for iron when the Wilson Bill was under consideration. During the consideration of the Payne-Aldrich Tariff Bill, Mr. Simmons voted so often with Mr. Aldrich for protection schedules that northern Democrats and independent papers referred to him as a protectionist.

"The great sin Mr. Simmons has committed against Democratic doctrine has been his support of the ship subsidy steal, the most un-Democratic measure that ever crossed the threshhold of the Senate."

"MUST TAKE IT BUT HATE IT LIKE THE DEVIL"

It is probably true that at no time in its history was *The News and Observer* more influential than when it reached national recognition in 1911. In that year *Collier's,* then edited by Norman Hapgood, offered forty-eight prizes of fifty dollars each for the best article written about a newspaper in each State. It printed all these letters. The letter that won the prize about a North Carolina newspaper was written by Dr. G. M. Cooper, a country doctor, of Sampson County, and was published in *Collier's* Prize Winning Contest in its issue of November 18, 1911, and was as follows:

"Read It Because They Have To"
The News and Observer Is An Institution, Read by Something Like 75,000 People, Two-Fifths of Whom Hate It Like the Devil.

"I read the daily 'News and Observer' of Raleigh, N. C. That paper is an institution. It is read by something like seventy-five thousand people, two fifths of whom hate it like the devil, but read it just the same. Why? Because they have to. Its policies make and unmake Governors, Senators, judges and lights of lesser magnitude. Politically it is mightier than all the politicians and bosses in the State, for the simple reason that it is backed by public opinion.

"Ask any of the enemies why they read *The News and Observer* and the answer is always the same: 'It publishes the news.' That is literally the truth; nothing of real interest is suppressed. By 'news' I do not mean the sickening stories of crime and domestic infelicity that fill the columns of most daily papers. I mean news of political importance or of significance to society in general. In other words, its news matter is clean and healthy. In its editorials it reflects the best thought of the soundest thinkers in the country and especially of the South.

"Another good reason for the influence wielded by this paper is its direct personal appeal. No one knows or cares who owns its stock, but every line it publishes is universally regarded as the honest, sincere convictions of the editor. To illustrate this point: It is Democratic in politics, and whenever a Republican speaker or paper alludes to an editorial in the *News and Observer* they always refer to 'Josephus' (its editor is Josephus Daniels). That is 'personal journalism' which might make even a Nelson or a Watterson take notice. No mortal man can measure the influence which this one paper exerts. It has fought and won many battles for better conditions in North Carolina. Its voice has been remarkably clear for the people against special privileges in national affairs.

"Much more might be said in commendation of this paper, which for many a year to come bids fair to continue master of the newspaper field in this section of the South. But what I have said is sufficient to illustrate its power for good.

"On the other hand, what criticism have I to offer? Very little. First, and chief, it is not at all times and in all things consistent. For instance, it carries no whiskey advertisements, but thousands of its friends are frequently forced to blush with shame at some of its glaring patent medicine announcements.

"Second, and in conclusion, as a friend of the principles for which this paper stands; as one who loves the glorious history of this great country, and who hopes for its future, I would beseech its editor to beware lest in its zeal for the cause he brings to me, perhaps unconsciously, just a little more of the spirit of partisanship than of the spirit of Democracy.

"Clinton, N. C.   G. M. Cooper."

I copied that letter in *The News and Observer* often and regarded it as the best tribute ever paid to the paper, agreeing with the criticism that in "its zeal for the cause" the editor was sometimes influenced by "the spirit of partisanship." I asked Dr. Cooper, long Assistant and Acting State Health Officer, to tell me why he was moved to write that prize-winning letter. He related:

"One day I was called in the country to a labor case. We travelled in horse and buggy those days, there were no trained nurses, no good roads, and no automobiles to make quick trips. I had to stay until the baby was delivered. There were many hours of waiting. I had nothing to read except a copy of *Collier's* I had gotten as I was leaving town. My attention was focused on the page advertisement offering fifty-dollars prizes for the best letter in each State describing the newspaper situation in the writer's area. As I was sitting on the porch on a sunshiny day, it occurred to me that I'd employ the time to compete as a mental exercise. The only paper I could locate was a piece of brown wrapping paper. I smoothed it out, laid it on the floor and went at it. I forgot all about it until the next copy of *Collier's* came. I got my copy out, put it in type—I did not have a typewriter— and went into the office of Congressman Fowler. His door was left open next to ours. He seldom stayed in his office, devoting most of his time to farming. I brushed off the dust, picked out the words a letter at a time. I mailed and forgot it. Three months later I received a check for $50.00 with the notification that my letter had won the North Carolina prize."

MARRIED WOMEN EMANCIPATED

One of the judicial opinions of the year 1911 was that rendered by Chief Justice Walter Clark, hailed by *The News and Observer* as "Married Women are Emancipated." The decision gave women absolute control over their property, as before marriage. The case of *Rea* vs. *Rea,* written by Chief Justice Clark, was widely commented on and highly commended all over the country. It was hailed as insuring a broader and more enlightened policy.

CHAMP CLARK SPEAKS IN RALEIGH

About the last of November, 1911, Champ Clark, then Speaker of the House of Representatives, spoke in Raleigh on "The True American and Genuine Democrat." He was, at that time, a candidate for nomination for President. I had known him well and we had been good friends. He had expected, because of his friendship with the North Carolina members of Congress, particularly Claude Kitchin, to carry North Carolina. His coming to the State at that time was in furtherance of his presidential aspirations. His general political line-up had been in accord with North Carolina's Democratic spirit, more so than that of Woodrow Wilson in the days of the nineties when Bryan was the leader. I liked Clark, and always had, but I had an instinctive feeling that Wilson was a better candidate and would make the better President. Clark had accepted an invitation of the Teachers' Assembly to come to Raleigh but had failed to let the officer know on what train he was to arrive. As he was to speak at night, the officials of the Assembly supposed he would leave Washington that morning and arrive at Raleigh at six o'clock. Instead, he left the night before, coming via Greensboro, arriving at half past ten in the morning. Nobody expected him, and there was nobody at the depot to meet him. Shortly after the arrival of the train, a gentleman dropped into my office and told me Clark was at the depot. "He says he came here on the invitation to make an address but that nobody seems to want him and so he is buying a ticket to go back to Washington on the twelve o'clock train and is in a bad state of mind." I had our first automobile and the chauffeur could not be found. He had been teaching my son Worth, who was about thirteen years old, to drive. I told Worth to get the machine and we would go to the depot. It is strange that I was not nervous at Worth's driving and he took us down all right, and when I reached the depot I found Clark very much overwrought. I greeted him cordially and said "We are glad to have you in Raleigh." He said "It doesn't look like it. I never went to speak in a place before in my life where nobody met me at the depot, and I am going back on the twelve o'clock train to Washington. Perhaps I can go where I am appreciated." It required all the cordiality I could command or borrow to change his determination to return without speaking. I told him that most people who came from Washington to speak arrived on the evening train, arriving at six o'clock, and that if he had come on that train he would have been met and received with all the honors due him. I finally mollified him enough to induce him to get into my car but I noticed, when he saw that my son, a tiny boy, was driving, he was very nervous and asked how much experience the boy had had and how old he was. I assured him that he was an expert driver and he need not fear to risk his life with that youngster. I think he was very much relieved when the car stopped at the hotel, but he was not in a very amiable mood. I don't think he quite got over it, but he made a fine speech on "The True American and Genuine Democrat," and I think the warm praise *The News and Observer* gave his speech gratified him.

XLVIII

THE DISSOLUTION OF THE TOBACCO TRUST

I N 1898 there had been organized what was known as the Continental Tobacco Company. It was widely published that this company had been created to bring into one corporation the biggest tobacco companies outside the trust; that the big New York capitalists had seen that, ultimately, all the tobacco manufacturers would be driven out of business or forced to sell out unless they were able to compete with the Tobacco Trust by putting bigness against bigness. For a long time Mr. Buck Duke had had his avid eyes on the Blackwell Durham Bull Tobacco Company. That company, for a time, was the biggest tobacco company in Durham and the biggest smoking tobacco company in the world, manufacturing the famous Durham Bull. It was born in Durham immediately after the War Between the States, in order to manufacture tobacco to meet the demands of the soldiers, who, after camping long near Durham, had scattered all over the country. It developed more rapidly than the Duke business in the same town. Until the cigarette machine, soon controlled by the trust, came into use, Blackwell Durham Bull was the premier. With the advent of the cigarette machine the trust came into sole possession of the patents. With its monopoly, most of the big cigarette companies were combined into one concern. Still, there were important independent tobacco companies, as in St. Louis, and the Bull Durham, and a few in Winston-Salem. They knew that the sword of Damocles hung over their heads. They sold out or entered a new corporation, the Continental Tobacco Company, heralded as an organization to fight the trust. It turned out that it either was a trust dummy, or that the trust soon owned it, and strengthened its monopoly.

Toward the close of the session of the Legislature of 1899 a bill had been introduced authorizing the Reynolds Tobacco Company to increase its capital stock. Shortly after the session of the Legislature, an announcement came from Winston-Salem which was a most astonishing one to those who thought that Reynolds was more than a match for Duke, that the capital stock of the R. J. Reynolds Company had been increased to five million dollars and the incorporators were R. J. Reynolds, W. N. Reynolds, J. B. Duke, George Gales, D. K. Faucette, and D. A. Keller. At the same time, it was announced that this company would be associated with the Continental Tobacco Company.

Not long after that I saw Dick Reynolds. We had long been very good friends and I expressed to him my great regret and disappointment that he had sold out to the Tobacco Trust. He said: "Don't you believe it. Sometimes you have to join hands with a fellow to keep him from ruining you and to get the under hold yourself." Then he narrated how the Dukes had gobbled up the Blackwells and the Hanes Company and said, "I don't intend to be swallowed. Buck Duke will find out he has met his equal, but I am fighting him now from the inside. You will never see the day when Dick Reynolds will eat out of Buck Duke's hands. If you will keep your eyes open, you will find that if any swallowing is done Dick Reynolds will do the swallowing. If Buck tries to swallow me he will have the belly-ache the balance of his life."

When Wickersham agreed that the Tobacco Trust should be divided into five parts, Dick Reynolds got back his company with full control, and he demonstrated that he was a merchant prince by creating such a demand for Camels that they soon sold more than any other brand of cigarettes. The World War created an abnormal demand for cigarettes, and soon all the companies were making millions on millions. One day Reynolds made me an attractive proposition, saying: "I'll make you rich if you'll come to Winston-Salem with me." I wasn't interested. He did make not a few rich who listened to him.

The suit of the Federal Government against the Tobacco Trust was docketed as *The United States* vs. *American Tobacco Company* and had been brought in the Circuit Court for the Southern District of New York, November 7, 1908—in the closing months of Theodore Roosevelt's term. The lawyers for the government were J. C. McReynolds and Edwin P. Grosvenor. The American Tobacco Company, when the case reached the Supreme Court, was represented by W. W. Fuller, John G. Johnson, William J. Wallace, DeLancey Nicoll, and Junius Parker. Three North Carolina lawyers, Cyrus B. Watson, J. T. Morehead, and A. J. Burton appeared for the R. P. Richardson, Jr.,

Company. The suit was brought under the Act of July 2, 1890, which declared illegal "every contract, combination in the form of trust or otherwise, or conspiracy in restraint of trade or commerce among the several states or foreign nations." The facts, stated by Circuit Court Judge Coxe, were as follows:

"The 'Tobacco Trust,' so called, consists of over 60 corporations, which, since January, 1890, have been united into a gigantic combination which controls a greatly preponderating proportion of the tobacco business in the United States in each and all of its branches; in some branches the volume being as high as 95 per cent. Prior to their absorption, many of these corporations had been in active competition in interstate and foreign commerce. They competed in purchasing 'raw materials,' in manufacturing, in jobbing and in selling to the consumer. Today those plants which have not been closed are, with one or two exceptions, under absolute dominion of the supreme central authority. Everything directly or indirectly connected with the manufacture and sale of tobacco products, including the ingredients, the packages, the bags and boxes, are largely controlled by it. Should a party with moderate capital desire to enter the field it would be difficult to do so against the opposition of this combination. That many of the associated corporations were not coerced into joining the combination but entered of their own volition is quite true, but in many other instances it is evident that if not actually compelled to join, they preferred to do so rather than face an unequal trade war in which the odds were all against them and in which success could only be achieved by a serious expenditure of time and money."

In delivering the opinion of the court, May 29, 1911 (there were arguments twice in 1910 and again in 1911), Chief Justice White held that the combination was in restraint of trade and an attempt to monopolize the business of tobacco in interstate commerce within the provisions of the law; the relief against the unlawful combination should be complete and efficacious, and result should be accomplished with as little injury as possible to the interests of the general public and with a proper regard for the vested property interests innocently acquired. It was held that the combination in and of itself, and also all of its constitutional elements, were illegal, and the lower courts were directed to enter a decree in conformity with the opinion. Justice Harlan was of the opinion that a decree of dissolution should be entered in the Supreme Court rather than to remand the case with directions.

After the case was remanded to the Circuit Court of the United States for the Southern District of New York, a decree was entered substantially as follows:

"The American Tobacco Company so far as its domestic business is concerned is to be divided into four companies, no one of which shall have a controlling interest in the tobacco business. The four companies are the American Tobacco Company (the then present company); Liggett & Myers Tobacco Company, to be organized; P. Lorillard Company, to be organized; and the R. J. Reynolds Tobacco Company, a then existing corporation. When the disintegration was accomplished, the volume and value of the business in the several branches of tobacco manufacture was to be divided between the four companies, as follows:

American Tobacco Company	37.11%
Liggett & Myers Company	27.82%
P. Lorillard Company	15.27%
and all other corporations	19.80%"

The decree went into details as to percentages of the different kinds of tobacco products to be distributed to each of the companies. *The News and Observer* was severe in its denunciation of Attorney General Wickersham for letting the Tobacco Trust divide itself into three companies and carry on, declaring it recalled the famous words of Caesar: "All Gaul is Divided In Three Parts," and added,

"If the American Tobacco Company can divide itself as the hand divides into fingers and nothing else and continues its monopoly, then the courts that construe the law in such a way as to make it worse than a farce are a sham, and the dissenting opinion of Justice Harlan was more than dissenting opinion— was an inspiration, the voice of a prophet and the last words of a great judge."

The paper quoted Woodrow Wilson saying that "crime is personal," and demanded that the officers of the Standard Oil Company (the same would apply to the Tobacco Trust) should be indicted and said that, while the Supreme Court had properly declared the trust illegal, the trust could not have crushed competition unless individuals had directed its policy and the individuals ought not to escape punishment. The paper added, that while crime is personal, that idea seems never to have permeated into the precincts of the department of justice at Washington.

The News and Observer, as quoted above, called Mr. Wickersham a *sham* and said if Mr. Taft approved the policy of dividing the trust into three parts, it showed that he was not genuinely in favor of destroying the trusts. The Honorable James C. McReynolds (afterward Attorney-General in Wilson's Cabinet and Associate Justice of the Supreme Court of the United States) won the case in the lower and appellate court. Justice McReynolds years later said to me, "Concerning the plan for effective dissolution, Mr. Wickersham and I disagreed. The plan which he accepted seemed to be inadequate and I asked to be relieved from further responsibility with respect to the matter." In his Washington letter, prior to the decision, in reporting the hearing before the Supreme Court, Tom Pence, the very efficient Washington correspondent, had told how "McReynolds flayed the octopus." James B. Duke, propped up in bed, gave testimony that he had never purchased any competing company in order to destroy competition, but purely as an investment. Robert Richardson, Jr., president of a tobacco manufacturing concern, testified that Duke told him, "It was not the policy of the trust to buy the business of their competitors on the basis of what the business was worth to the owners, but on the basis of what it would cost to drive them out of business." This was termed the nuisance value.

I talked much with Attorney-General Bickett, of North Carolina, during the trial and afterwards. He denounced the proposed reorganization plan and applauded McReynolds for refusing to go along with Wickersham on the dissolution. *The News and Observer* said:

> "In effect, the Supreme Court says to the American Tobacco Company, 'You are a robbing pirate. You have committed crimes, but if you will arrange to do these things inside of the law, we will forgive you for the past and bid you speed on your way to get the same result'."

Bickett had gone to Washington to hear the argument and I have always been sorry I couldn't go. I kept up with it, however, and *The News and Observer* followed this up by editorials on the crime of the Tobacco Trust, pointing out how it had used its autocratic power to put down the price of tobacco and how it had violated the Sherman

Anti-Trust Act, as well as the common law, and printing a synopsis of the brief filed by the Department of Justice. Bickett's attendance at the hearing was construed as raising the question as to whether he did not intend himself to start a suit against it in North Carolina; but since the United States Supreme Court's original decision had held the combination, "in itself and also all of its constitutional elements were illegal," and since it was expected that the parties found guilty would be punished, making the punishment fit the crime, no action under North Carolina's ineffective statute was thought to be necessary.

The day after the decision was made, the American Tobacco Company declared an extra dividend of 2½ per cent, making quarterly dividends of 10 per cent and total dividends for the year of 32½ per cent.

At the end of the litigation, Tom Pence wrote a story to the paper saying that two resolutions had been introduced in Congress by Byrnes, of Tennessee, and Fields of Kentucky, calling upon the Attorney General to inform the House whether criminal prosecution had been taken or contemplated by the government. This letter said that the seven North Carolinians who were involved and might be prosecuted were J. B. Duke, B. N. Duke, George W. Watts, Rufus L. Patterson, John B. Cobb, George G. Allen, and W. W. Fuller. *The News and Observer* strongly indorsed these resolutions and said every person who had been guilty of any part of the violation of the anti-trust law ought to be prosecuted. It also said it did not believe the administration would permit any criminal prosecution. Attorney General Wickersham told the House Committee that the Department of Justice had not decided as to what should be done. That was in accordance with the usual rule of not deciding and doing nothing in a criminal way against big law violators.

The Supreme Court of the United States rendered its famous decision that the Standard Oil Company, which had swept competition in its path, was an illegal combination in restraint of trade and ordered its dissolution in a case brought in the State of Missouri. Attorney General Wickersham was quoted as saying, "It is the most important decision ever rendered in this country." My paper, quoting this, said the oil and tobacco trusts were similar, that one victory would settle both cases, and that the Tobacco Trust case, which was pending, would undoubtedly be decided the same way. In the issue of December 23, it quoted from the briefs of Wickersham and McReynolds in the Tobacco Trust Case in the Supreme Court, in which the great evils of the Tobacco Trust were cited and the power of trusts to oppress, and declared that they had fixed purposes of destroying competition. Growing out of the proceedings of the Standard Oil Company, John D. Rockefeller, Jr., brought a suit against Hearst on a criminal libel charge, and John D. Rockefeller, Sr., testified that Flagler and Todd built up the trust. That company was found guilty of violating the Sherman Act and was ordered divided, Attorney General Wickersham thus in part defeating the decree of the Supreme Court.

The chief counsel for the American Tobacco Company was my very good friend, W. W. Fuller, who had been the attorney of the Dukes at Durham and had shepherded all the legal steps of the Dukes from the early eighties. He was one of the ablest lawyers in America and one of the most charming gentlemen. I owed his early friendship to his high regard for my wife, who was an intimate girl friend of his sisters and who was affectionately esteemed by his mother. He never permitted our opposing views about the Tobacco Trust to affect a long friendship and it continued unbroken until his death.

He told me this story, illustrative of the life of his friend and client James B. Duke:

"When Mr. Duke was intent upon acquiring tobacco companies which had popular brands, he asked me to accompany him to see a young man whose brand he very much desired to acquire. We went and the conversation proceeded half an hour when the telephone rang. The young man answered and said: 'Certainly, I'll come right away.' Turning to us, he excused himself, saying: 'Some college friends have arranged a theatre party and I must join them.' He made an engagement to meet us another night. When it arrived, the same thing happened, and it broke up five meetings held to carry on negotiations. On the fifth night as the young man hurried away with friends to a festive party, he fixed a future date to complete the negotiations. As Mr. Duke and I emerged from the hotel, Duke asked me, 'Fuller, did you ever see a man who had so many friends?' I answered in the negative. Then Duke said with a note of yearning, half serious and half otherwise: 'Fuller, I sometimes think I will take time off and buy me some friends'."

When Fuller moved to New York as Chief Attorney and adviser of the big tobacco company, Judge Robert Winston became the resident attorney of the trust at Durham. We were good enough friends for him to say to me one day, "Joe, I wish when you refer to the American Tobacco Company in *The News and Observer,* you would not always call it 'The Tobacco Trust.' Such designation offends."

"All right, Bob," I replied, "I will cease calling it the 'Tobacco Trust' when it ceases to be a trust and permits competition in the purchase of tobacco from the farmers and in the sale of cigarettes to the consumers."

My reply was not to his liking and he asked, "Are not you and Will Fuller, chief counsel of the American Tobacco Company, good friends?"

"The best of friends for many years," I answered.

"Didn't Fuller ever speak to you about this matter and ask you to cease labelling the company 'The Tobacco Trust'?" he asked. I replied in the negative. Winston said he was surprised and asked, "Why do you suppose Fuller never proffered the request I have made?"

"Because," I answered, "Fuller had too much respect for me to make such a request."

With the dissolution of the American Tobacco Trust, there came a new type of executive into the direction of its plants in North Carolina, on which *The News and Observer* commented editorially:

IS IT EVOLUTION?

"C. W. Toms, teacher, becomes manager of the American Tobacco Company's Durham factory. He now becomes head officer at Durham of Liggett-Myers Company. Also W. W. Flowers, who succeeded Toms as head of the Durham City schools and was given high position in the American Tobacco Company, now becomes head of Blackwell's Tobacco Company in Durham, and now comes the news that W. D. Carmichael, who succeeded Flowers in the Durham Public Schools, has accepted a position with the American Tobacco Company. Mr. Green succeeds Carmichael. The question is, will he become a big tobacco man?"

The answer was that Mr. Toms, Mr. Flowers, and Mr. Carmichael showed that scholastic training was a good foundation for successful careers in Big Business and advanced to executive positions of the highest rank in the tobacco companies with which they were connected.

In August, of that year, a suit was brought by the Ware-Kramer Tobacco Company of Wilson for $2,400,000 against the American Tobacco Company for illegal competition and practice. It was alleged by this company that the trust officials had said, "We will crush hell out of Ware-Kramer." It was also alleged that the trust had despoiled the tobacco growers in North Carolina and destroyed the small manufacturers. The attorneys in this case were my brothers, Judge Frank A. Daniels and Charles C. Daniels, and Frank S. Spruill. The American Tobacco Company was represented by its chief counsel, Junius Parker of New York, ex-governor Aycock, and James H. Pou. The case was tried before Judge Connor and consumed several weeks. It was hotly contested. The Ware-Kramer Company won the suit, but were not able to convince the jury that they had suffered the damages alleged and recovered only a comparatively small amount, something less than $100,000, as I recall.

The News and Observer printed a story from the New York *World* to the effect that Mr. Duke was aiming at a water power trust, and included an interview about Duke and water power with Dr. Gil Wylie. It had been said that Duke owned the Charlotte *Observer* but Wylie denied this. Seeing that hydroelectric power companies were forming, *The News and Observer* urged that all light and power companies be put under the Corporation Commission with power to fix their rates, but this failed in the Legislature, the Duke interests opposing it. It was passed, however, the next year. In advocating this, the paper had an editorial headed "The Coming Of the Water Power Trust."

XLIX

SIMMONS WINS IN RACE FOR THE SENATE

Early in the North Carolina Senatorial campaign of 1912, Senator Simmons wrote an open letter to the other candidates proposing that all join to limit the amount to be spent in the campaign, saying, "Personally, on account of my limited means and the embarrassed condition of my finances, even if I felt disposed to do so, I would be unable to invest in this campaign more than is absolutely necessary to defray the admittedly legitimate expenses thereof."

Aycock and other candidates received that statement with a guffaw. It was believed that the Southern Railway and the American Tobacco Company, the two big rich corporations in the State not averse to taking a hand politically, and rich tariff beneficiaries, were supporting Simmons. Friends of Clark, Aycock, and Kitchin believed that the chief trouble they would have in the campaign would be because the big corporations, including the big lumber concerns, having urged Simmons to vote for a high tariff on lumber, would spend more money for Simmons than all the rest of them combined could raise, as they did. Later, when he announced his candidacy for the Senate, Governor Aycock, without making specific references to Simmons' statement against the use of money, said:

"I am in favor of the election of the United States' senators by the people and when I say by the people, I *mean* by the people and not by money, not by organization, not by machinery. In a recent issue of the Charlotte *Observer,* the editor declared that in the coming senatorial contest, while my fitness for the place was recognized, I could not be elected for the reason that I am without money, without organization, and without machinery. This predication, when it first appeared, startled and frightened many of my friends. I would not wish to be elected to the United States Senate by money, by machinery, by organization—if I were elected by these means, I should glorify and honor the means which elected me. My father told me that the rungs of the ladder on which I rise should be honored by me. If I rise on the rungs of money, organization, and machinery, I know myself well enough to recognize that I should count my obligation in the Senate to these things, but if I go to the Senate as the untrammelled choice of the people of North Carolina, to them I shall owe the honor and to them shall be dedicated all the service of my heart and mind and body under God to the perfection of our government and to the betterment of the conditions of mankind."

After discussing the menace of money in politics and declaring that he believed the people in North Carolina would not dishonor themselves by suffering an election to turn upon false and corrupting things, he added, "It will be an evil day for this good State of ours when the prediction of the Charlotte *Observer* shall have become the history of the State." He went on to say, "Yes, I am without power, and without wealth, without organization and without machinery, but I am not poor and I am not helpless. I am rich in the love of North Carolinians and strong in their belief that it is my purpose now, as it has even been in the past, to serve them as a whole without being under obligation to any special man or set of men." He added that he did not wish to insinuate that any other candidate differed with him in this respect. Still, his friends and the public generally accepted his statement about machine and organization, not as an attack, but as a statement that he and Clark and Kitchin knew that Senator Simmons had kept his hands so perfectly on the Democratic machine that it would be used for him in his candidacy and that they must appeal over it to the people if they won. The result of the election proved that they were right.

Before the campaign got warmed up and while the candidates were getting under way, this incident happened:

"When Farmer Blalock, of Ashe County, who had been appointed on the Board of Agriculture by Governor Kitchin, reached Raleigh, some of the Governor's active managers sought to enlist him into active work to elect Kitchin to the Senate. No success. 'I have great admiration and regard for Governor Kitchin,' he said, 'but years ago I told Governor Aycock I hoped he would run for the Senate and pledged my support to him.' He was reminded that Governor Kitchin had appointed him to an office and it would be ungrateful not to support the man who had given him honor, and was asked, 'How do you suppose it will affect Kitchin's prospects for the Senate if his own appointees refuse to support him?' They pressed Blalock to come out for Kitchin until he lost his patience and said, 'I want you gentlemen to know that I do not wear any man's collar, not even my own.' He was one of the best farmers and cattle raisers and influential citizens of his section, but he never wore a collar. His reply to persuasion to support Kitchin became widely known and caused many a laugh. His admiration for Aycock knew no bounds, but when Aycock died before the campaign got started he gave his support to the Governor whom he esteemed more highly than any man except Aycock."

The sudden death of Aycock, while making an educational speech at Birmingham, Alabama, on April 4, before he had delivered the speech which he had prepared announcing his candidacy, changed the setting of the senatorial campaign. He had launched his campaign on a platform of, "I am in favor of tariff for revenue only," and had said he agreed with Woodrow Wilson when he said, "The tariff is the one central issue of the coming campaign. It is at the head of every other economic question we have to deal with and, until we have adjusted that properly, we can settle nothing in a way that will be lasting and satisfactory." Personally, Aycock was friendly to Senator Simmons, but that very friendliness and his statement against control by organizations and his standing upon the old Democratic doctrine of a tariff for revenue only made it certain that the tariff record of Senator Simmons would loom up as the great issue. Aycock, with Kitchin, who in Congress had made a great record for the same tariff reform and who had opposed the votes of Simmons for high tariff on lumber, etc., and against his opposition to the reciprocity treaty, brought opposing views, creating a clear-cut issue. Chief Justice Clark also held like views, but would have stressed the trust and corporation issue. After Aycock died, Kitchin raised the tariff issue, and he and his distinguished brother, Claude Kitchin, the ablest debater in the House of Representatives, pressed it with great earnestness and vigor.

Chief Justice Walter Clark was, in some respects, a better qualified man, if North Carolina wanted to have a truly national progressive, than either Kitchin or Simmons. He never got very far in his campaign. He had really no organization. Most of the active politicians were for either Simmons or Kitchin. Clark had to depend upon the unorganized people who favored his very progressive and sometimes radical views. He wrote with force and power, but on the stump had neither eloquence nor driving power. In fact he either read his speeches or spoke them as if he were making a declamation. Able and versatile as he was, he was never able to make any impression by his addresses. He, unfortunately, lived in a day before radio. If the campaign that year had been conducted over that medium, Clark would have had the same advantage over his opponents that Hoover had years after.

This was the first campaign in which political advertising was used to any large extent. *The News and Observer* sometimes had several pages of such advertising, and there was a debate kept up for some weeks between the Kitchin and Simmons cohorts in the advertising columns. The Kitchin men charged Simmons with having voted with Penrose oftener on the tariff than with John Sharpe Williams, the Democratic leader on the tariff. They declared that he was not a Democrat in the real sense of the word and pointed out how Vance, who was the idol of the people of North Carolina, had prevented his confirmation as collector of internal revenue. They said that he was a Sam Randall Democrat, that his opposition to reciprocity, being one of only three Democrats in the Senate to oppose it, and his many votes cast for high protection made him unfit to represent the Democratic Party of North Carolina in the Senate. They quoted from his speeches, as *The News and Observer* had done editorially, when he made them.

Governor Kitchin, in his opening speech in Raleigh, charged Simmons with "wandering from true Democracy" and declared that he had been gradually changing his views until he had "reached the Republican side," with the complete repudiation of both his party's and the Senator's own declarations. He declared that "every change of view on the part of Simmons had been against the interest of all the people and in favor of special classes; and so thorough has been his change that, contrary to what must have been his original inclination, he has felt compelled by speech and vote to combat the plainest teachings of Democracy." He was very severe in criticizing the Senator for his vote to seat Lorimer, for his stand on the mail subsidy (declaring that Simmons had voted for it while Vance and Ransom had voted against it), and for his votes on lumber tariff. He declared that, on forty-three roll calls, Simmons had voted nineteen times against the majority of his party. Kitchin also said that the report that Simmons would be chairman of the Finance Committee, if reëlected, had no foundation; that, if it were circulated in the North and the West that a Democrat who had voted so many times for Republican protective measures was to be chairman of that important committee, the Democratic Party would lose support.

He closed this speech with a challenge to Senator Simmons for a joint debate, knowing that Simmons would not accept because he was not impressive as a public speaker, whereas Kitchin had every gift to entertain and arouse his hearers. But, if he could not speak as well as Kitchin, it was true that Simmons could write as well or better, and he came back with a hot reply. Captain Samuel A. Ashe, of Raleigh, also made a vigorous and very extended reply, reviewing Simmons' record, saying that he had voted against Aldrich one hundred times on tariff schedules. Simmons said that if his votes were wrong in the Senate, the other Tar Heels in Congress voted as he did, except Claude Kitchin. In defense of his alleged votes with the Republicans, he said he voted only eleven times with the Republicans and against them thirty-two times, and added, "I voted fewer times with the Republican majority during that session than any other Democratic Senator, except three." He said he voted fewer times than Overman. Upon the reciprocity treaty he said he voted with the insurgent Republicans and against the Republican stand-patters.

Kitchin replied in kind to Simmons, denying his statements and declaring that he could not successfully refute the original statements Kitchin had made; that, if he thought he could, the way to show it was to accept the challenge for the joint debate. Simmons came back, in written statement, but would not agree to a joint debate. While these preliminary discussions and accusations and retorts were going on, I was in the hospital, ill and unable to attend the meeting of the Democratic State Committee, which took place in Raleigh in March. The committee passed resolutions of sympathy for my illness and expressed their wish for a speedy recovery and an "early return to the fight for Democracy and the people."

The committee directed that the party organization make plans for a senatorial primary to be held on the general election day. Friends of all the candidates favored this, or said they did. *The News and Observer,* from the moment that there was evidence that there would be several candidates, had urged it, and, after the Legislature failed to pass an act for a legalized primary, had declared that the Democratic

Party must itself hold a primary so that every candidate would have an equal chance. Even with a primary, the Kitchin-Clark men felt they would be at a disadvantage because, in the majority of the counties, the old Simmons organization controlled. The State committee directed that, in selecting the men to hold the Senatorial primary, a representative of every candidate, named by the candidate, should be appointed. This gave to each candidate an equal chance. All candidates coöperated, but an interesting story came out later. In fact, it was a story told by the late A. D. Watts, the most active and influential Simmons manager. He loved to boast of his political achievements, even when they were not such as did him credit. Explaining why it was that Clark had received a very small vote in a certain Western county, Watts told some of his friends that he had arranged it by the following means: Early in the campaign, he directed one of the most ardent Simmons men in the county to come out for Clark. This gentleman then wrote Clark, telling him of his earnest support and saying that, while he had then very few advocates in that county, he felt sure, with proper organization and the sinews of war, he would receive a large vote. Clark was very much delighted at this. He had not expected much from that county, and at the suggestion of his friends named this man as county manager. Whereupon, according to Watts, the Simmons man, masquerading as a Clark man, named as Clark's representatives at all the polling places, men who were doing the bidding of the Simmons managers. Watts' boast of this piece of political chicanery, of course, was whispered only in political circles and each side shrugged its shoulders and, with winks, indicated it was not the only place where such things were carried on. However, whatever may have been the effect of Simmons' control of the Democratic organization, which gave him the advantage, the result of the election showed that he was the choice of a great majority of the Democratic voters, and his victory and subsequent championship of the Wilson policies in the Senate assured him successive reëlections during and following the Wilson administration.

In September *The News and Observer* printed an advertisement by Frank R. McNinch, manager of the Kitchin campaign, quoting Bryan's *Commoner* of August 30, 1912, as follows:

"The Commoner does not take part in a contest between Democrats except where a principle is involved. In North Caro-

lina, where Senator Simmons is one of the candidates for re-
election, a principle is involved. He is not a progressive and it is
a mystery to the outside world how a state like North Carolina
has tolerated him so long."

On September 12 the Kitchin people printed another advertisement,
quoting from the Cincinnati *Enquirer,* a paper advocating Wilson's
nomination, saying:

"Under ordinary conditions, with Bailey [of Texas] no longer
in the Senate, Simmons would fall heir to the chairmanship
of the Committee on Finance, which carries with it leadership of
the Senate, but the Democratic Progressives will have none of the
North Carolina man if they can prevent it. They characterized him as a reactionary and as the tariff would be attacked in a
Democratic Senate, they do not want to trust the fate of a Democratic tariff measure in his hands. The fight is already becoming
very strenuous and as the Democratic Progressives are now in the
majority, the indications are that if they get the opportunity they
will dump the senator from the Tar Heel state by an action which
will split senatorial custom and practice wide open."

The next day, in a political advertisement, S. L. Rogers, manager
for Simmons, said: "Senator Simmons was at the Woodrow Wilson
campaign headquarters by invitation to give them the benefit of his
advice in the conduct of the campaign to elect Wilson." McNinch
quoted Savoyard, the nom de plume used by Norman A. Newman,
Washington correspondent for several newspapers, as saying, "Aldrich, Penrose, Smoot, and Company would be delighted with a
Democratic side made up of Martins and Simmonses." McNinch also
quoted the Chattanooga *News,* a Wilson paper, as saying the Progressive Democrats were not going to let Simmons be Finance Chairman and Senate leader. McNinch also quoted La Follette to the effect
that Simmons was a Dr. Jekyll and Mr. Hyde on tariff and that he
was justified in printing what La Follette had said because Rogers had
first introduced La Follette as witness for Simmons. The answer that
Rogers made next day was that the quotation from La Follette was
from his magazine of more than three years back.

The Kitchin forces also printed an advertisement representing
Mark Sullivan as calling Simmons "an undesirable Senator" and
quoting the *Columbia State* as against Simmons, said he was "too
intimate with the Aldrich and Penrose machine." This sort of political

advertising went on during the whole campaign. In September Governor Kitchin and Claude Kitchin made the statement that North Carolina should not elect Simmons because he stood with Penrose too often on the tariff question. They were making much headway with this until Simmons countered on September 13, when he made a speech at Charlotte. He declared there was no foundation for the publication of the Kitchin advertisements which said that there was opposition among the Democrats in the Senate to his promotion to the chairmanship of the Finance Committee if the Democrats could control that body, and he declared, with boldness which stirred his supporters and which took part of the wind out of the sails of the opposition, that "if and when the Senate is organized by the Democrats" and he was not promoted to the position of Chairman of the Finance Committee, to which his seniority entitled him, he would resign his seat in the Senate and come back to North Carolina.

That declaration was one of the most sensational of the campaign, and its very boldness and defiance made the prediction that he would not be elected less effective against him, although the anti-Simmons forces continued to use it during the campaign. They sincerely believed that a progressive Democratic Senate would refuse to elect Simmons because of his votes with the Republicans on a number of the high tariff schedules. Simmons' speech was printed as a political advertisement in *The News and Observer* and made two whole pages.

The publication of *Collier's* severe criticism of Simmons called forth a reply by S. L. Rogers, Simmons' manager, who impeached *Collier's* as a witness against the Senator. Rogers said that the way *Collier's Weekly* supported Woodrow Wilson was in accordance with the following paragraph from that paper: "We hope the third (Roosevelt) Party will run a close second and we shall be likewise happy if he wins." Rogers urged that no Democrat should be influenced by a paper which would be satisfied with Roosevelt's election.

The Charlotte *Observer* and Greensboro *News* both came out in October in support of Simmons, and the newspaper support was pretty well divided in the State, but Simmons had the best of it. *The News and Observer* did not take sides. As head of the Literary Bureau of the National Democratic Committee, I spent the summer and fall in New York at Democratic headquarters, helping direct the campaign for Wilson's election.

An attempt was made to draw Wilson into the senatorial fight, but Tumulty wired that Wilson was "hands off." I had explained to Wilson the situation in North Carolina and suggested that he remain detached.

There was a contest in the Democratic Committee as to who could vote in the senatorial primary held without law and by the Democratic Committee. After much discussion and several different definitions made during the campaign, the Committee decided that a voter might scratch a ticket and still vote in the senatorial primary if he regarded himself a Democrat and was so regarded.

The sworn statements, up to October 25, showed that Simmons spent $5,788.12; Kitchin, $5,450.23; and Clark, $1,420.22, of which sum *The News and Observer* received, in political advertising, $1,572.04 from the Simmons management; $826 from the Kitchin forces; and $112, from Clark, a total of $2,510.04. In the closing days Kitchin spent $1,355.25, of which *The News and Observer* received $109.20. Senator Simmons' supplementary expense was $1,452.60, of which my paper received $246.60. This was the most money ever paid for political advertising in North Carolina. In that campaign *The News and Observer* raised $14,087.68 for the Wilson campaign fund and North Carolina's contribution, including this fund, was $29,940.43.

During the last days before the election, Judge Clark's forces broadcast a statement from headquarters charging that the Southern Railway's attorneys were trying to defeat him, and the Simmons management printed a full page advertisement, quoting Archibald Johnson, editor of *Charity And Children,* as saying "Governor Kitchin should be buried under an avalanche of votes." The vote in the senatorial campaign stood: Simmons, 84,687; Kitchin, 47,010; Clark, 16,418. Simmons' majority was over 21,259.

Roosevelt carried a much larger vote in North Carolina than Taft and *The News and Observer,* predicting the end of the Republican Party, said that "The North Carolina law bars from recognition in the administration of election laws any political organization which did not poll 50,000 votes in a previous election." *The News and Observer* therefore, called the Republican Party in North Carolina officially dead. The North Carolina vote was: Wilson, 125,749; Taft, 23,660; and Roosevelt, 55,368.

L

CRAIG IS INAUGURATED

THE STATE CAMPAIGN in 1912 was rather tame. It was a foregone conclusion that Craig was to be nominated for Governor. He had been a close competitor of Governor Kitchin in 1908 and had been loyal and true, and almost by acclamation the people of the State felt that he deserved the honor. Permitting the nomination of Craig by acclamation—it could not have been prevented—was an admission of weakness by the Kitchin people. They thought they were stronger to make no fight for the Governor and to center their fight for Senator. The Kitchin people opposed the platform because it was regarded as approving Simmons' candidacy in that it endorsed the record of our Senators and Democrats in Congress; and, when the platform was presented by Cameron Morrison, then thick-and-thin Simmons man, who said Simmons was "the grandest statesman that North Carolina had produced in half a century," Judge J. S. Manning, leader of the Kitchin forces, opposed the platform and presented a minority report, the gist of which was to prevent what was regarded as a Simmons endorsement. Upon a test vote, which was really a vote as to the preference of the delegates for Simmons or Kitchin, Manning's substitute was defeated by 578 to 393. This vote indicated about the strength of Simmons and Kitchin for the Senate; and the endorsement of Simmons' record in Congress, along with his colleagues, made it difficult for Governor Kitchin to make a hit in his denunciation of Simmons' tariff record. If the Manning substitute had been adopted, it would have given a severe blow to Senator Simmons' candidacy. The vote was largely personal, and the partisanship was so deep on both sides that many of the Simmons men voted as they did, not because they endorsed Simmons' vote on the tariff, but because they were for Simmons, had been a part of the Democratic organization under his leadership in the hot fight of 1898 and 1900, and felt they were in the boat together. Governor Kitchin was very much perturbed by this and denounced the endorsement, saying that it was secured by steam-roller methods. Simmons, having carried the primary in the race for the United States Senate, on January 18, by a joint resolution of the caucus, was reëlected for a six-year term. This was the last election of a Senator with which the legislature had anything to do.

The Republican candidate, Thomas Settle, was a brilliant campaigner who had been elected to Congress several times in the Fifth District and who had led the fight to make the Republican Party an anti-prohibition party in North Carolina. Craig was a life-long prohibitionist. The Pritchard element in North Carolina never liked Settle, who had really lost out in the State and lacked the fire of early days. His campaign therefore did not arouse much enthusiasm. In a political advertisement announcing his position, Settle declared he stood upon the same liquor plank as Woodrow Wilson and quoted Mr. Wilson as having said, "I am in favor of local option. I am a thorough believer in local self-government and believe every self-governing community which constitutes a social unit, should have the right to control the matter of regulating or withholding license." In that campaign the Republicans were denouncing the Watts and Ward Act and were seeking to bolster up their claims by saying Settle stood with Wilson. Wilson's statement was made in response to a letter from Texas as to his attitude. At that time a man who stood for local option in a state like New Jersey was acting contrary to the majority of his party because New Jersey permitted no local option.

Early in the campaign Settle challenged Craig for a joint debate. He thought to make such a spectacular contest as his father had made in 1876 with Vance, which was by all odds the most stirring political debate between two candidates for Governor the State had known. Although it had been the general policy in North Carolina, before and after the Civil War, for the candidates for Governor to debate the questions on the stump, the Democrats were not keen for the joint debate. Craig had had a joint debate with Pritchard, when he was a candidate for the senatorial nomination and had given evidence of the fact that he was not at his best as a debater. Settle had proved himself the equal or superior of any Democrat who ran against him in the Fifth District until W. W. Kitchin was his competitor and defeated him both in debating and in getting votes, but they were well matched. In his prime Settle was unsurpassed, but though he was not old in years he had lost his snap. Craig wanted a joint debate, but the Democrats sensed that it would give Settle an advantage he could not otherwise obtain and put their foot down on it. Craig paramounted the national issues. The people were thinking more about the senatorial contest than about the gubernatorial race. Usually, the Democratic candidate for Governor in North Carolina received a larger vote by something like 10,000 than is cast for the candidate for President but, in this campaign, it was reversed and Wilson received a larger vote than was cast for Craig. This did not mean any lack of Craig's popularity, but was evidence that the chief interest was centered around the senatorship and the presidency. The only question about the gubernatorial race was the size of Craig's majority.

It was the middle of January when Locke Craig was inaugurated as Governor. *The News and Observer,* in eight-column streamers in red ink, said Governor Craig's inauguration was the most brilliant in the State's history. It was during his administration that the greatest fight was made against discrimination in freight rates, which worked injuriously to North Carolina manufacturers and industry. Governor Craig threw himself into this fight with zeal and retained counsel who were able to bring some measure of relief to the people of the State.

The Legislature of 1913 organized by electing George W. Connor, of Wilson, as Speaker of the House, and Neill Pharr, of Mecklenburg, as President pro tem of the Senate. I was much gratified at the election of Connor. At a previous session I had been largely instrumental in securing the election of his father as Speaker and had aided George in his natural ambition to follow his father in that office.

One of the first bills introduced in the Legislature was that of Representative Justice, of Guilford, which *The News and Observer* called an anti-trust bill "with handcuffs." The previous Legislature had adopted a pink tea anti-trust bill. Justice also introduced a bill to amend the constitution so as to secure for the people the initiative and referendum, and he introduced a resolution, which passed the House, inviting Wilson, Bryan, and La Follette to address the General Assembly.

Justice was a Progressive of Progressives, and the Senate killed most of his measures. The senators were not willing to have too much progressive legislation. They knew that what Justice wanted was to get Wilson, Bryan, and La Follette to come to Raleigh and advocate the initiative and referendum and strong anti-trust laws. They thought that if such distinguished men came it would be pouring water on Justice's wheels. When it was up for discussion in the House, Frank Ray, of Macon, one of the most interesting men of his day, was quoted by *The News and Observer* as having characterized Progressives as "boys who have become smarter than their daddies." He declared that everybody knew Bryan's and La Follette's views, but he didn't know that anybody knew Mr. Wilson's views on the initiative and referendum. *The News and Observer* supported the Justice resolution but the Senate tabled it. The paper also quoted Wilson's statement favoring the initiative and referendum.

The biggest measure before the General Assembly of 1913 was the passage of a bill giving a six-months school to every district in the State. There was much opposition to it outside the Legislature because of the increased taxes, but it passed both houses by an overwhelming majority. It was hailed by *The News and Observer* in big red-ink streamers as the great red-headed event of the year.

In the years between 1893 and 1913 the General Assembly was *the* center of North Carolina in government and taxation and the shaping of policies. The judiciary abstained from political affairs, but there were a few departures. No judge made political speeches or took active part in politics, though some did on the sidelines. The Governor had no veto. There were no executive budgets. His council was elected by the people, and he had little power beyond his ability to impress his views on legislators. The office of Governor in North Carolina has always been esteemed as the most exalted station, greater than that of Chief Justice or Senator. The legislature was *the* dynamo and legislators probably were less influenced by the executive than in any other period or under any other parliamentary government. It gladly heard and considered the recommendations of the executive but Governors did not control. Because the legislative branch determined the policies of state, levied taxes and controlled the purse strings, and was the highest forum in the commonwealth, its proceedings dwarfed all else in the two months of its biennial sessions. I made it a rule rarely to let a day pass without attending, occupying a seat at the reporters' desk even when a special member of the staff was covering the detailed proceedings. Often I would write a story during the debate and jot down comments. When important measures in which I was interested came up I attended the meetings of committees, sometimes in advocacy of or opposition to certain bills, but usually I was only an interested attendant taking notes and printing them.

Even more valuable in all these years I personally knew every one of the one hundred and seventy legislators, calling many by their first names. Sometimes I took a hand in the composition of committees by suggestions to the presiding officers, and in a few instances I had a part in influencing the election of the Speaker of the House, but these were exceptions, and only when I thought such action contributed to progressive legislation. I was often called a lobbyist and, if personally urging day and night to support policies my paper was seeking to advance, I may have deserved that title. I was sometimes invited and attended caucuses of legislative blocs organized to promote some measure my paper was advocating. I never received a dollar from any source for my earnest advocacy of any measure or my opposition to bills I deemed not in the public interest.

CABINET APPOINTMENT

On the twenty-third of February, 1913, President-elect Woodrow Wilson in a cordial letter tendered to me the portfolio of Secretary of the Navy in the Cabinet, saying, "I know of no one I trust more entirely or affectionately; and I am sure you will trust and believe me when I assure you that you will, in my judgment, best serve the party and its new leader by accepting this post. I cannot spare you from my council table."

Having written my acceptance, I made preparations for a return to public service in Washington, which I had laid down after nearly two years as Chief Clerk of the Department of the Interior in the second term of Grover Cleveland. It was a real wrench to tear myself away from the sanctum, for the paper was my life, my joy, and my pride. But my admiration for Woodrow Wilson and my faith that he would bring about the New Freedom to which he was consecrated, and my ambition to have a part in governmental regeneration, took me back to Washington with high resolve and a confident faith that the mantle of Thomas Jefferson in learning and statesmanship, and of Andrew Jackson in courage and democracy, had fallen upon the Republic's new leader. I had been an enthusiastic advocate of Wilson's nomination and a member of the Democratic Executive

Mrs. Josephus Daniels and her four sons: Josephus, Jr. (the tallest), Worth Bagley, Jonathan Worth, and Frank Arthur. Taken in 1912.

Sophie Liggon, Negro nurse of the four Daniels boys, with the youngest, Frank A. Daniels.

Committee which conducted the successful campaign of 1912. But I never for a moment thought of separating myself from my paper. I entrusted its conduct to faithful associates whose principles and aims were in consonance with my own.

On February 28 a banquet was given at the Yarborough House by the Democrats of the State in honor of the newly elected Governor, Locke Craig, and Senator Simmons, who had just been reëlected to the Senate, and myself. It had not been officially announced that I was to be in the Cabinet, but unofficially, it was generally known. Five hundred people attended the banquet, which was the notable event of that month. Simmons did not attend and McLean, later Governor, spoke for him. The program was for some speaker to give the outlines of the public career and pay some tribute to each of the three guests of honor. A. H. Eller, who had been Democratic Chairman in the Kitchin campaign made a speech about me which was commendatory and friendly, and I was grateful. Mr. Eller was a star graduate of the University of North Carolina, winning the Mangum medal for oratory. He gave up a promising career at the bar and in public life to become Trust Officer of the Wachovia Banking and Trust Company at Winston-Salem.

On March 2, in company with my good friend the new Secretary of State, Honorable William Jennings Bryan, who had stopped in Raleigh to make us a visit on his way to Washington and to speak on Peace, my wife and I and our four sons set out for an eight-year official residence in the national capital. It was not easy to break home ties, and the wrench was made harder when the faithful colored nurse, "Aunt Sophie Liggon," we all called her "Aunt," decided that advancing years would not permit her to accompany us. She had nursed all four of the boys since their birth and was held in real affection by the whole family. Some years before, when my wife was telling a friend of the relation between "Aunt Sophie" and the family, the friend asked: "Aren't you afraid to let her know how you depend on her? What would you do if she left your home?" My wife smilingly answered: "I would go, too." Perhaps the best proof of the relationship between "Aunt Sophie" and our boys is what our son Jonathan said when told that she could not go with us to Washington. Teary about the eyes as he bade her goodbye, the eleven-year-old cried out, "Doggone Governor Wilson." He blamed the President-elect for the grief of separation.

"Yes'um," this good and faithful nurse, whose religion had shaped her life, had said to a visitor, "The Daniels boys is pretty good boys. Me and Miss Addie are goin' to raise 'em to be good Christians." She did her part, carrying them often to St. Paul's African Methodist Church, in which she was a pillar, and, after humming them to sleep, she would emotionally raise her tuneful voice in the songs of Zion.

LI

LOOKING BACKWARD AND FORWARD

I WAS FIFTY YEARS old. I do not know how it is with other men, but it seemed to me that I had come there very swiftly, even if also, across very crowded years. I was suddenly, it seemed to me, aware of change in both myself and the State. The first thirty-one years of my life from infancy to the time when I went to Washington to serve in the second Cleveland administration seemed to have sped by. And the twenty years between 1893 and 1913 had been torn by contest between forces of progress and of reaction. What was a fight every day was also, although we hardly knew it, a political revolution that deeply stirred passions and prejudices. I threw myself with all the zeal of my convictions and strength into the issues and contests of the period. I imbibed the spirit of the times when political campaigns in North Carolina were more like pitched battles than discussion of issues and when strongly entrenched privilege fought to hold and extend its domain. With all the weapons which God and nature threw into my hands, I fought for democracy, both with a big "D" and a little "d," and against monopoly in any and every form.

It was a period of personal journalism and I practiced it to the nth degree. Quarter was neither given nor taken. I made enemies and garnered friends, and my vehemence of denunciation of opponents was not always tempered with charity. In all those days when Passion was dominant and Prejudice was not absent, I can look back and truly say that no personal ambition or enmity of individuals guided my action, and when the contests ended I bore no resentment toward any with whom I had differed. But I look back, also, amazed at my own editorial violence at times, even when I understand the circumstances which surrounded it.

Times were changing and at fifty I did not regret it. I do not regret it now. The poverty of the South, the poverty of my State, and resentment at the policies of Reconstruction, bred a violence in insecurity which reduced to pure bitterness the contest between men and groups and races. No quiet voice could have been heard in those times, but from the noisy, head-knocking fighting there did begin a less noisy advance under Aycock to make progress in a justice which considered all men and all races. I think the intensity, or some of it, was necessary. We should not have escaped without it. But without regret that I participated in it, even proud of the licks I gave in exchange for those I received, at fifty I realized that not only was I growing older but that also in terms of an increasing serenity, in a greater security, the same was true of the State. Except for my quadrennial excursions into national presidential contests and my brief service in the Cleveland administration, I was almost wholly State-minded and deemed my highest mission was to advance every good cause that would contribute to the well being of the State of my birth and of my supreme devotion.

The first fifty years had been good. At the end of them I faced the future with an appetite for more.

LEE COUNTY LIBRARY
SANFORD, N. C.

INDEX

INDEX